Core Py

Programming

Second Edition

Covers Fundamentals to Advanced topics like OOPS, Exceptions, Data Structures, Files, Threads, Networking, GUI, DB Connectivity and Data Science

Authored by:

Dr. R. Nageswara Rao

Published by:

dreamtech PRESS

ISBN: 978-93-86052-30-8

Edition: 2020

Printed at: Nisha Enterprises.

This book is dedicated to the lotus feet of
my favorite God and Divine Guide, Sri Sai Baba of Shirdi.

Acknowledgements

A year ago, the Sales Head at Wiley publications foresaw huge potentiality for Python in the coming days and asked me to write a book on Python and later Dreamtech Press gave green signal for this project. I sincerely thank both of them without whose initiation, I would not have got into writing this book.

Also, my deep gratitude goes to Mr. Apurva Gupta, my publisher, whose time-to-time encouragement has made this book possible. I was rather amused by his patience and optimism throughout the project.

My special thanks to my friend Mr. Mansoor Baig. Also sincere thanks to Prof. Prasad, Prof. S. Veerabadraiah, Mr. Sriram, Mrs. Kalyani, Mr. Nalam VSS Krishna and Mr. R. Nihhaar Chandra who have provided positive feedback about this book.

Testimonials

The emerging information technology is demanding new languages where Python will play a vital role.

The gap between supply and demand in this global market, especially India, will surely be minimized with the help of this book with coverage of 400+ realistic programs. No surprise, if this book is seen in the personal collection of every IT Professionals soon.

-Mr. Sriram, Principal Consultant, Genpact, USA.

I have gone through this book and found that it is an excellent book on Python that is immensely useful to students as well as software developers. Dr. R. Nageswara Rao's clear cut explanation augmented with hundreds of programming examples is a boon to all who want to learn Python.

-Mrs. Kalyani, Asst Consultant, TCS, Hyderabad, India.

The book 'Core Python' by Dr. Nageswara Rao is a great attempt to satisfy the need of millions of people interested in learning Python. It starts from very basic elements of programming and extended to all aspects of applications. It is very much learner friendly due to the simple language, elaborative explanation and exhaustive examples.

-Prof. Prasad, Secretary and Dean, VITAM, Berhampur, Orissa.

First of all, congratulations on producing this worthy book with 24 chapters highly useful to graduates, post graduates and trainee software engineers from basic level to data connectivity in Python.

-Prof. S.Veerabadraiah, Principal Mentor, MSIT-Learning Center, JNTUK, Kakinada.

This book is complete for learning Python language. The chapters are organized well and it's also good for quick review of the language. The concepts are explained with enormous examples making them understand easier.

-Nalam V S S Krishna Chaitanya, student, IV B.Tech CSE, IITM, Chennai.

Dr.R. Nageswara Rao is a teaching wizard who can transform toughest of the subject to best understandable and enjoyable content. Great teachings come from great experience and this book is not an exception.

-R. Nihhaar Chandra, student, II year B.Tech CSE, IITB, Mumbai.

About the Author

Dr. R. NageswaraRao, author of the best seller 'Core Java – An Integrated Approach' and 'Core C' comes out with his remarkable new book 'Core Python Programming'. His aim in writing this book is not only to teach Python to the college students but also to provide a reference to the professionals. Dr. R. NageswaraRao is associated with teaching Computer Science since 1993. He has worked in various colleges as Head of the Department, Dept. of Computers and as a freelance developer for some time for a couple of organizations. He taught C and C++ till 2004 and since then involved in teaching Java. At present, he is teaching Java and Python in Hyderabad, Telangana, India. Since 1998, Mr. Rao was on the editorial board of Computer Vignanam, a widely circulated monthly magazine published in Telugu. He wrote several articles on C, C++ and Java including articles on virtual reality, mobile applications, Bluetooth technology and global positioning systems. His dedication in teaching continues to attract thousands of students from various Indian Universities in addition to students from foreign countries.

Table of Contents

Preface

In the last few years, Python has been the choice of many computer students and programmers. Its importance as a language for learning and creating programs is ever growing. According to *US News,* in USA,8 of the top 10 Computer Science departments teach Python in introductory computer courses. Almost all the universities in USA and Europe are teaching Python in their course curriculum. In India, Python has already been introduced into IITs, IIITs, NITs and in a couple of universities. Soon it will spread to all the universities in India. Thus, Python is chosen as the best introductory programming language and going to replace C completely.

According *to blog.codeeval.com,* Python has been ranked as number 1 among the most popular coding languages for the last 4 years continuously. *The PYPL Popularity of Programming Language Index* gives 2nd rank for Python as most widely searched and learned language on Internet. According to *sitepoint.com,* Python is in the top place in terms of programmers who draw highest salary in the software development industry.

During the year 2017, *IEEE Spectrum* has given 1st rank for Python in terms of increasing popularity. The same organization gave 4th rank for Python during 2016. According to *TIOBE,* a Netherlands company that checks the software code and analyses the market trends, Python takes 4th position in the most popular programming languages during 2016.

At present, Java occupies number 1 rank as the most used programming language since almost all the projects are developed in Java. Python is already occupying 2nd to 4th position and will be the most demanded language after Java in near future. Python is used with other programming languages on Internet as well as for developing standalone applications. Python programmers are paid high salaries in the software development industry. Hence, it is time for beginners as well as existing programmers to focus their attention on Python.

At the student level, learning Python is compulsory if it is introduced as a subject of study in their college or university. Even if the student does not learn Python in their graduation or P.G., he or she should learn it sooner or later, because most of the software companies are expecting students to have knowledge in Python. Learning Python will help students to be successful in interviews. It will help professionals to occupy better positions with higher salaries.

It is surprising that all the existing books on Python are written by foreign authors. Moreover, these books are making the subject more complicated. Hence, there is a need of writing a book specifically for Indian students. The present book is an effort in that direction. This book covers all core concepts in a methodical way. The depth of each topic is decided and discussed based on its importance level. All concepts are explained in a lucid manner with hundreds of programming examples.

What this book contains

This book has 25 chapters in all, arranged in increasing order of complexity. Hence, it is advised that the readers start reading this book from the beginning unless they have some previous knowledge of the subject. The first 6 chapters will help bring readers from the novice stage to a stage where they will have gained a proper understanding of the fundamentals. These chapters cover the concepts of Python and PVM along with the basic elements of writing a Python program. These 6 chapters are very important for all beginners.

Chapter 7 covers the concept of arrays that are useful to handle groups of elements. This chapter covers various ways of creating arrays and working with arrays. The chapter also discusses how to work with multidimensional arrays using the numpy package.

Chapter 8 introduces strings and characters, performing various operations on strings, retrieving sub strings and formatting stirrings.

Chapter 9 is on functions. This chapter explains the differences between a function and method, creating and using functions and recursive functions. It also discusses different types of arguments like formal arguments, actual arguments, positional arguments and default arguments. 'lambdas' is another important topic discussed in this chapter.

Chapter 10 gives information on lists and tuples. A list is useful to store several elements, either of the same type or different types. It is possible to access and modify the elements of a list. A tuple is similar to a list. In case of a tuple, we can access or view the elements but we cannot modify them.

Chapter 11 is about dictionaries, which store the data in the form of key and value pairs. Converting strings and lists into dictionaries is also discussed in this chapter.

Chapter 12 gives overview of OOPS and discusses the concepts like class, object, encapsulation, abstraction, inheritance and polymorphism and how to implement these concepts in Python. These concepts become the platform for all Object Oriented programming languages.

Chapter 13 specifically shows how to deal with classes and objects. The reader will be able to create classes and objects along with understanding constructors and methods in this chapter.

Chapter 14 covers two most important topics of OOPS: inheritance and polymorphism. It covers concepts like method overloading and method overriding in Python.

Chapter 15 is about abstract classes and interfaces. Readers can understand the usage and differences between the abstract classes and interfaces after reading this chapter.

Chapter 16 is on exceptions which are nothing but errors which occur in Python programs and how to handle these errors. This chapter also shows how the programmer can create his or her own exceptions.

Chapter 17 is on files. This chapter discusses various types of files, pickle concept and random accessing of file contents.

Chapter 18 is written on regular expressions which are important but difficult to understand and use. These expressions are useful to retrieve data based on an expression.

Chapter 19 is about data structures like stacks, linked lists and queues.

Chapter 20 is devoted to date and time, formatting them, comparing them and sorting them. Calendar module is also introduced in this chapter.

Chapter 21 is for discussing threads which are individual processes created inside PVM. Creating threads and performing single tasking and multitasking are shown in this chapter. Also, advanced topics like thread synchronization and deadlocks are discussed.

Chapter 22 is for developing programs in GUI. Here, we discuss about how to create colors, fonts, drawing using various shapes and creating widgets like push buttons, labels, message boxes, scrollbars etc.

Chapter 23 is on networking. This chapter deals with networking fundamentals, protocols and working with TCP/IP and UDP protocols in Python programs.

Chapter 24 discusses how to connect to a database like Oracle or MySQL and retrieve data from the database and utilize the data in the Python programs.

Chapter 25 deals with the most demanded technology called data science. This is related to data analysis and visualization in order to guide a business company.

Wherever possible, the installations of the softwares are also discussed with screenshots. For example, installation of numpy, Oracle, MySQL, their drivers etc. are shown in the book.

Every chapter is concluded with 'Points to Remember' section where important points of that chapter are presented one by one to the reader. These points provide a quick review and enable the reader to easily migrate to the subsequent chapters. Remembering these points will help readers to answer the questions asked in the interviews on Python.

Version used in this book

Currently, *python.org* maintains two versions of Python. They are 2.x and 3.x. "Python 2.x is legacy, Python 3.x is the present and future of the language." – this is what Python people said in their website. So, it is better to go for Python's 3.x version. The most stable version of Python is 3.3, which was released in the year 2012. The version used in this book is 3.6.4, which is the latest one by the time the present edition of this book is released. However, all programs in this book will run in all the versions starting from 3.3 onwards.

CHAPTER 1

INTRODUCTION TO PYTHON

Programming languages like C, Pascal or FORTRAN concentrate more on the functional aspects of programming. In these languages, there will be more focus on writing the code using functions. For example, we can imagine a C program as a combination of several functions. Computer scientists thought that programming will become easy for human beings to understand if it is based on real life examples. Hence, they developed Object Oriented Programming languages like Java and .NET where programming is done through classes and objects. Programmers started migrating from C to Java and Java soon became the most popular language in the software community.

In Java, a programmer should express his logic through classes and objects only. It is not possible to write a program without writing at least one class! This makes programming lengthy. For example, a simple program to add two numbers in Java looks like this:

```
//Java program to add two numbers
class Add  //create a class
{
    public static void main(String args[])  //start execution
    {
        int a, b;  //take two variables
        a = b = 10;  //store 10 in to a, b
        System.out.println("Sum= "+ (a+b));  //display their sum
    }
}
```

Programmers understood that in certain cases where there is no need to go for classes or objects, this type of coding is consuming more time. In such cases, they do not want to create classes or objects; rather they want to write C style coding. The same program to add two numbers can be written in C as:

```
/* C program to add two numbers */
#include<stdio.h>  /* include standard header file */
void main()  /* start execution */
{
     int a, b;  /* take two variables */
     a = b = 10;   /* store 10 in to a, b */
```

```
        printf("Sum= %d", (a+b));  /* display their sum */
    }
```

Of course, the preceding program is almost same as that of Java. There is no improvement in the length of the code. Another problem is that if the programmers go for C language, they will miss the object orientation which is lacking in C. Object orientation becomes an advantage when they want to deal with heavy projects.

Nowadays, programmers want C style coding as well as the Java style object orientation. When they want to develop functional aspects like calculations or processing, they want to use C style coding and when they are in need of going for classes and objects, they will use Java style coding. The only answer for their requirement is Python!

Python

Python is a programming language that combines the features of C and Java. It offers elegant style of developing programs like C. When the programmers want to go for object orientation, Python offers classes and objects like Java. In Python, the program to add two numbers will be as follows:

```
    # Python program to add two numbers
    a = b = 10  # take two variables and store 10 in to them
    print("Sum= ", (a+b))  # display their sum
```

The preceding code is easy to understand and develop. Hence, Python is gaining popularity among the programming folks. Of course, there are several other features of Python which we will discuss in future which make it the preferred choice of most programmers.

Coming to a bit of history, Python was developed by *Guido Van Rossum* in the year 1991 at the Center for Mathematics and Computer Science managed by the Dutch Government. Van Rossum was working on a project to develop system utilities in C where he had to interact with the Bourne shell available in UNIX. He felt the necessity of developing a language that would fill the gap between C and the shell. This has led to the creation of Python.

Van Rossum picked the name *Python* for the new language from the TV show, *Monty Python's Flying Circus*. Python's first working version was ready by early 1990 and Van Rossum released it for the public on February 20, 1991. The logo of Python shows two intertwined snakes as shown in Figure 1.1:

Figure 1.1: Python Official Logo

Python is open source software, which means anybody can freely download it from *www.python.org* and use it to develop programs. Its source code can be accessed and modified as required in the projects.

Features of Python

There are various reasons why Python is gaining good popularity in the programming community. The following are some of the important features of Python:

- **Simple:** Python is a simple programming language. When we read a Python program, we feel like reading English sentences. It means more clarity and less stress on understanding the syntax of the language. Hence, developing and understanding programs will become easy.
- **Easy to learn:** Python uses very few keywords. Its programs use very simple structure. So, developing programs in Python become easy. Also, Python resembles C language. Most of the language constructs in C are also available in Python. Hence, migrating from C to Python is easy for programmers.
- **Open source:** There is no need to pay for Python software. Python can be freely downloaded from www.python.org website. Its source code can be read, modified and can be used in programs as desired by the programmers.
- **High level language:** Programming languages are of two types: low level and high level. A low level language uses machine code instructions to develop programs. These instructions directly interact with the CPU. Machine language and assembly language are called low level languages.

  High level languages use English words to develop programs. These are easy to learn and use. Like COBOL, PHP or Java, Python also uses English words in its programs and hence it is called high level programming language.
- **Dynamically typed:** In Python, we need not declare anything. An assignment statement binds a name to an object, and the object can be of any type. If a name is assigned to an object of one type, it may later be assigned to an object of a different type. This is the meaning of the saying that Python is a dynamically typed language. Languages like C and Java are statically typed. In these languages, the variable names and datatypes should be mentioned properly. Attempting to assign an object of the wrong type to a variable name triggers error or exception.
- **Platform independent:** When a Python program is compiled using a Python compiler, it generates byte code. Python's byte code represents a fixed set of instructions that run on all operating systems and hardware. Using a Python Virtual Machine (PVM), anybody can run these byte code instructions on any computer system. Hence, Python programs are not dependent on any specific operating system. We can use Python on almost all operating systems like UNIX, Linux, Windows,

Macintosh, Solaris, OS/2, Amiga, AROS, AS/400, etc. This makes Python an ideal programming language for any network or Internet.

- **Portable:** When a program yields the same result on any computer in the world, then it is called a portable program. Python programs will give the same result since they are platform independent. Once a Python program is written, it can run on any computer system using PVM. However, Python also contains some system dependent modules (or code), which are specific to operating system. Programmers should be careful about such code while developing the software if they want it to be completely portable.
- **Procedure and object oriented:** Python is a procedure oriented as well as an object oriented programming language. In procedure oriented programming languages (e.g. C and Pascal), the programs are built using functions and procedures. But in object oriented languages (e.g. C++ and Java), the programs use classes and objects.

Let's get some idea on objects and classes. An object is anything that exists physically in the real world. Almost everything comes in this definition. Let's take a dog with the name Snoopy. We can say *Snoopy* is an object since it physically exists in our house. Objects will have behavior represented by their attributes (or properties) and actions. For example, Snoopy has attributes like height, weight, age and color. These attributes are represented by variables in programming. Similarly, Snoopy can perform actions like barking, biting, eating, running, etc. These actions are represented by methods (functions) in programming. Hence, an object contains variables and methods.

A class, on the other hand, does not exist physically. A class is only an abstract idea which represents common behavior of several objects. For example, *dog* is a class. When we talk about dog, we will have a picture in our mind where we imagine a head, body, legs, tail, etc. This imaginary picture is called a class. When we take Snoopy, she has all the features that we have in our mind but she exists physically and hence she becomes the object of dog class. Similarly all the other dogs like Tommy, Charlie, Sophie, etc. exhibit same behavior like Snoopy. Hence, they are all objects of the same class, i.e. dog class. We should understand the point that the object Snoopy exists physically but the class dog does not exist physically. It is only a picture in our mind with some attributes and actions at abstract level. When we take Snoopy, Tommy, Charlie and Sophie, they have these attributes and actions and hence they are all objects of the *dog* class.

As we described in the preceding paragraph, a class indicates common behavior of objects. This common behavior is represented by attributes and actions. Attributes are represented by variables and actions are performed by methods (functions). So, a class also contains variables and methods just like an object does. Figure 1.2 shows relationship between a class and its object:

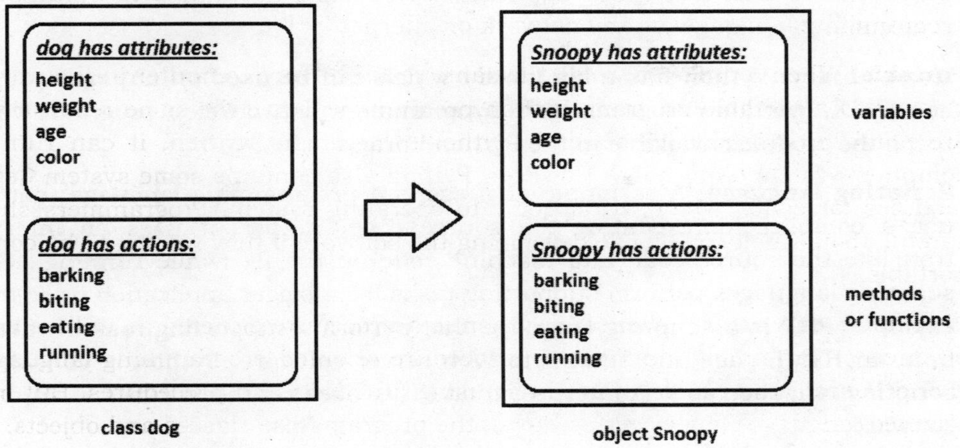

Figure 1.2: A Class and its object

Similarly, parrot, sparrow, pigeon and crow are objects of the *bird* class. We should understand that bird (class) is only an idea that defines some attributes and actions. A parrot and sparrow have the same attributes and actions but they exist physically. Hence, they are objects of the bird class.

Object oriented languages like Python, Java and .NET use the concepts of classes and objects in their programs. Since class does not exist physically, there will not be any memory allocated when the class is created. But, object exists physically and hence, a separate block of memory is allocated when an object is created. In Python language, everything like variables, lists, functions, arrays etc. are treated as objects.

- **Interpreted:** A program code is called *source code*. After writing a Python program, we should compile the source code using Python compiler. Python compiler translates the Python program into an intermediate code called *byte code*. This byte code is then executed by PVM. Inside the PVM, an interpreter converts the byte code instructions into machine code so that the processor will understand and run that machine code to produce results.
- **Extensible:** The programs or pieces of code written in C or C++ can be integrated into Python and executed using PVM. This is what we see in standard Python that is downloaded from *www.python.org*. There are other flavors of Python where programs from other languages can be integrated into Python. For example, Jython is useful to integrate Java code into Python programs and run on JVM (Java Virtual Machine). Similarly, Iron Python is useful to integrate .NET programs and libraries into Python programs and run on CLR (Common Language Runtime).
- **Embeddable:** We can insert Python programs into a C or C++ program. Several applications are already developed in Python which can be integrated into other programming languages like C, C++, Delphi, PHP, Java and .NET. It means

programmers can use these applications for their advantage in various software projects.

- **Huge library:** Python has a big library which can be used on any operating system like UNIX, Windows or Macintosh. Programmers can develop programs very easily using the modules available in the Python library.
- **Scripting language:** A scripting language is a programming language that does not use a compiler for executing the source code. Rather, it uses an interpreter to translate the source code into machine code on the fly (while running). Generally, scripting languages perform supporting tasks for a bigger application or software. For example, PHP is a scripting language that performs supporting task of taking input from an HTML page and send it to Web server software. Python is considered as a scripting language as it is interpreted and it is used on the Internet to support other software.
- **Database connectivity:** A database represents software that stores and manipulates data. For example, Oracle is a popular database using which we can store data in the form of tables and manipulate the data. Python provides interfaces to connect its programs to all major databases like Oracle, Sybase or MySql.
- **Scalable:** A program would be scalable if it could be moved to another operating system or hardware and take full advantage of the new environment in terms of performance. Python programs are scalable since they can run on any platform and use the features of the new platform effectively.
- **Batteries included:** The huge library of Python contains several small applications (or small packages) which are already developed and immediately available to programmers. These small packages can be used and maintained easily. Thus the programmers need not download separate packages or applications in many cases. This will give them a head start in many projects. These libraries are called 'batteries included'. Some interesting batteries or packages are given here:
    - *argparse* is a package that represents command-line parsing library
    - *boto*is Amazon web services library
    - *CherryPy* is anobject-oriented HTTP framework
    - *cryptography* offers cryptographic techniques for the programmers
    - *Fiona* reads and writes big data files
    - *jellyfish* is a library for doing approximate and phonetic matching of strings
    - *mysql-connector-python*is a driver written in Python to connect to MySQL database
    - *numpy* is a package for processing arrays of single or multidimensional type

- *pandas* is a package for powerful data structures for data analysis, time series and statistics
- *matplotlib* is a package for drawing electronic circuits and 2D graphs.
- *Pillow* is a Python imaging library
- *pyquery* represents jquery-like library for Python
- *scipy* is the scientific library to do scientific and engineering calculations
- *Sphinx* is the Python documentation generator
- *sympy* is a package for Computer algebra system (CAS) in Python
- *w3lib* is a library of web related functions
- *whoosh* contains fast and pure Python full text indexing, search and spell checking library

To know the entire list of packages included in Python, one can visit: https://www.pythonanywhere.com/batteries_included/

Execution of a Python Program

Let's assume that we write a Python program with the name x.py. Here, x is the program name and the .py is the extension name. Every Python program is typed with an extension name .py. After typing the program, the next step is to compile the program using Python compiler. The compiler converts the Python program into another code called byte code.

Byte code represents a fixed set of instructions that represents all operations like arithmetic operations, comparison operations, memory related operations, etc., which run on any operating system and hardware. It means the byte instructions are system independent or platform independent. The size of each byte code instruction is 1 byte and hence they are called with the name *byte code*. These byte code instructions are contained in the file x.pyc. Here, the x.pyc file represents a python compiled file.

The next step is to run the program. If we directly give the byte code to the computer, it cannot execute them. Any computer can execute only binary code which comprises 1s and 0s. Since the binary code is understandable to the machine (computer), it is also called machine code. It is therefore necessary to convert the byte code into machine code so that our computer can understand and execute it. For this purpose, we should use PVM (Python Virtual Machine).

PVM uses an interpreter which understands the byte code and converts it into machine code. PVM first understands the processor and operating system in our computer. Then it converts the byte code into machine code understandable to that processor and into that format understandable to that operating system. These machine code instructions are then executed by the processor and results are displayed.

An interpreter translates the program source code line by line. Hence, it is slow. The interpreter that is found inside the PVM runs the Python program slowly. To rectify this problem, in some flavors of Python, a compiler is added to the PVM. This compiler also converts the byte code into machine code but faster than the interpreter. This compiler is called JIT (Just In Time) compiler. The advantage of JIT compiler is to improve speed of execution of a Python program and thus improving the performance.

We should remember that JIT compiler is not available in all Python environments. For example, the standard Python software is called CPython which is created using C language that does not include a JIT compiler. But, PyPy, which is created in Python language itself uses a JIT compiler in addition to an interpreter in the PVM. So, the PyPy flavor of Python definitely offers faster execution of the Python programs than CPython. Figure 1.3 shows the steps for executing a Python program:

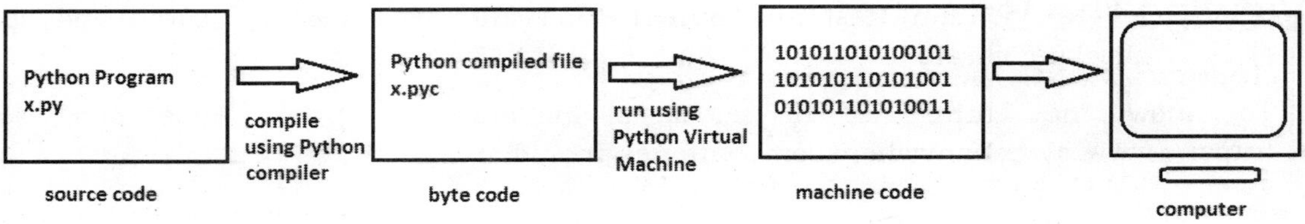

Figure 1.3: Steps of Execution of a Python Program

Normally, when we compile a Python program, we cannot see the .pyc file produced by the Python compiler and the machine code generated by the PVM. This is done internally in the memory and the output is finally visible. For example, if our Python program name is x.py, we can use Python compiler to compile it as:

```
C:\>python x.py
```

In the preceding statement, *python* is the command for calling the Python compiler. The compiler should convert the x.py file into its byte code equivalent file, x.pyc. Instead of doing this, the compiler directly displays the output or result.

If we observe, we cannot find any files in the directory with the extension .pyc. The reason is that all the steps in the sequence: **source code →byte code → machine code → output** are internally completed and then the final result is displayed. Hence, after execution, we cannot find any .pyc file in the directory.

To separately create .pyc file from the source code, we can use the following command:

```
C:\>python -m py_compile x.py
```

In the preceding command, we are calling the Python compiler with *–m* option. *-m* represents module and the module name is *py_compile*. This module generates the .pyc file for the specified .py file. The compiler creates a separate directory in the current directory by the name *__pycache__* where it stores the .pyc file. The .pyc file name may be something like: x.cpython-34.pyc. The word *cpython* here indicates that we are using the Python compiler that was created using C. This is of course, the standard Python compiler.

So the question is 'What is the use of the .pycfiles'? We know that the .pyc files contain byte code. We get these files after the compilation is completed. Hence, the first step is over. The next step is to interpret them using PVM. This can be done by calling the Python compiler as:

```
C:\>python x.cpython-34.pyc
```

In this case, we are supplying .pyc file to the Python compiler. Now, Python compiler will skip the first step where it has to convert the source code into byte code as already it sees the byte code inside this .pyc file. This file is executed directly by the PVM to produce the output. Hence, the program takes less time to run and the performance will be improved. This is the reason that after the completion of the project, the .pyc files are distributed to the user who can directly run these files using PVM and view the output.

Viewing the Byte Code

Let's consider the following Python program:

```
# Python program to add two numbers
a = b = 10  # take two variables and store 10 in to them
print("Sum= ", (a+b))  # display their sum
```

We can type this program in a text editor like Notepad and then save it as 'first.py'. It means, the first.py file contains the source code.

Now, let's compile the program using Python compiler as:

```
C:\>python  first.py
```

It will display the result as:

```
Sum= 20
```

That is ok. But we do not want the output of the program. We want to see the byte code instructions that were created internally by the Python compiler before they are executed by the PVM. For this purpose, we should specify the *dis* module while using python command as:

```
C:\>python  -m  dis  first.py
```

It will produce the following output:

```
  2          0 LOAD_CONST               0 (10)
             3 DUP_TOP
             4 STORE_NAME               0 (a)
             7 STORE_NAME               1 (b)
  3          10 LOAD_NAME               2 (print)
             13 LOAD_CONST              1 ('Sum= ')
             16 LOAD_NAME               0 (a)
             19 LOAD_NAME               1 (b)
             22 BINARY_ADD
             23 CALL_FUNCTION           2 (2 positional, 0 keyword pair)
             26 POP_TOP
             27 LOAD_CONST              2 (None)
             30 RETURN_VALUE
```

The preceding byte code is displayed by the dis module, which is also known as 'disassembler' that displays the byte code in the human understandable format. If we observe the preceding code, we can find 5 columns. The left-most or first column represents the line number in our source program (first.py). The second column represents the offset position of the byte code. The third column shows the name of the byte code instruction. The 4th column represents instruction's argument and the last column represents constants or names as specified by 4th column. For example, see the following instructions:

```
10 LOAD_NAME                2 (print)
13 LOAD_CONST               1 ('Sum= ')
16 LOAD_NAME                0 (a)
19 LOAD_NAME                1 (b)
22 BINARY_ADD
```

The LOAD_NAME specifies that this byte code instruction has 2 arguments. The name that has 2 arguments is (print) function. Since there are 2 arguments, the next byte code instructions will represent those 2 arguments as LOAD_CONST represents the string constant name ('Sum= ') and (a) and (b) as names involved in the second argument for the print function. Then BINARY_ADD instruction adds the previous (i.e. a and b) values.

Flavors of Python

Flavors of Python refer to the different types of Python compilers. These flavors are useful to integrate various programming languages into Python. The following are some of them:

- **CPython**: This is the standard Python compiler implemented in C language. This is the Python software being downloaded and used by programmers directly from *https://www.python.org/downloads/*. In this, any Python program is internally converted into byte code using C language functions. This byte code is run on the interpreter available in Python Virtual Machine (PVM) created in C language. The advantage is that it is possible to execute C and C++ functions and programs in CPython.
- **Jython**: This is earlier known as JPython. This is the implementation of Python programming language which is designed to run on Java platform. Jython compiler first compiles the Python program into Java byte code. This byte code is executed by Java Virtual Machine (JVM) to produce the output. Jython contains libraries which are useful for both Python and Java programmers. This can be downloaded from *http://www.jython.org/*.
- **IronPython**: This is another implementation of Python language for .NET framework. This is written in C# (C Sharp) language. The Python program when compiled gives an intermediate language (IL) which runs on Common Language Runtime (CLR) to produce the output. This flavor of Python gives flexibility of using both the .NET and Python libraries. IronPython can be downloaded from *http://ironpython.net/*.

- **PyPy**: This is Python implementation using Python language. Actually, PyPy is written in a language called RPython which was created in Python language. RPython is suitable for creating language interpreters. PyPy programs run very fast since there is a JIT (Just In Time) compiler added to the PVM. PyPy can be downloaded by visiting the page: *http://pypy.org/download.html.*

  Since the original Python uses only an interpreter in the Python Virtual Machine (PVM), the Python programs run slowly. To improve the speed of execution, a compiler called JIT (Just In Time) is introduced into the PVM of PyPy. Hence, PyPy programs run faster than those of Python. We can download PyPy from *http://pypy.org/download.html.*

- **RubyPython**: This is a bridge between the Ruby and Python interpreters. It encloses a Python interpreter inside Ruby applications. This flavor of Python can be downloaded from *https://rubygems.org/gems/rubypython/versions/0.6.3.*

- **StacklessPython**: Small tasks which should run individually are called tasklets. Tasklets run independently on CPU and can communicate with others via channels. A channel is a manager that takes care of scheduling the tasklets, controlling them and suspending them. A thread is a process which runs hundreds of such tasklets. We can create threads and tasklets in StacklessPython which is reimplementation of original Python language. This can be downloaded from *https://pypi.python.org/pypi/stackless-python/10.0.*

- **Pythonxy**: This is pronounced as Python xy and written as Python(X,Y). This is the Python implementation that we get after adding scientific and engineering related packages. We can download Pythonxy from *https://python-xy.github.io/downloads.html.*

- **AnacondaPython**: When Python is redeveloped for handling large-scale data processing, predictive analytics and scientific computing, it is called Anaconda Python. This implementation mainly focuses on large scale of data. This can be downloaded from *https://www.continuum.io/downloads.*

Python Virtual Machine (PVM)

We know that computers understand only machine code that comprises 1s and 0s. Since computer understands only machine code, it is imperative that we should convert any program into machine code before it is submitted to the computer for execution. For this purpose, we should take the help of a compiler. A compiler normally converts the program source code into machine code.

A Python compiler does the same task but in a slightly different manner. It converts the program source code into another code, called byte code. Each Python program statement is converted into a group of byte code instructions. Then what is byte code? Byte code represents the fixed set of instructions created by Python developers representing all types of operations. The size of each byte code instruction is 1 byte (or 8 bits) and hence these are called byte code instructions. Python organization says that there may be newer instructions added to the existing byte code instructions from time to time. We can find byte code instructions in the .pyc file. Figure 1.4 shows the role of virtual machine in converting byte code instructions into machine code:

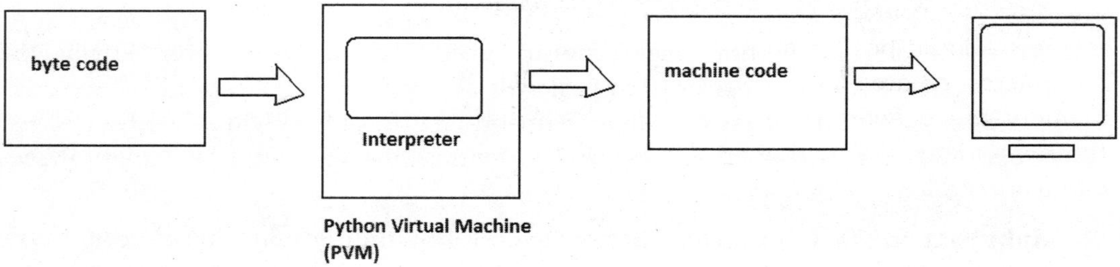

Figure 1.4: The Python Virtual Machine

The role of Python Virtual Machine (PVM) is to convert the byte code instructions into machine code so that the computer can execute those machine code instructions and display the final output. To carry out this conversion, PVM is equipped with an interpreter. The interpreter converts the byte code into machine code and sends that machine code to the computer processor for execution. Since interpreter is playing the main role, often the Python Virtual Machine is also called an interpreter.

Frozen Binaries

When a software is developed in Python, there are two ways to provide the software to the end user. The first way is to provide the .pyc files to the user. The user will install PVM in his computer and run the byte code instructions of the .pyc files.

The other way is to provide the .pyc files, PVM along with necessary Python library. In this method, all the .pyc files, related Python library and PVM will be converted into a single executable file (generally with .exe extension) so that the user can directly execute that file by double clicking on it. In this way, converting the Python programs into true executables is called *frozen binaries*. But frozen binaries will have more size than that of simple .pyc files since they contain PVM and library files also.

For creating frozen binaries, we need to use other party software. For example, py2exe is a software that produces frozen binaries for Windows operating system. We can use pyinstaller for UNIX or LINUX. Freeze is another program from Python organization to generate frozen binaries for UNIX.

Memory Management in Python

In C or C++, the programmer should allocate and deallocate (or free) memory dynamically, during runtime. For example, to allocate memory, the programmer may use malloc() function and to deallocate the memory, he may use the free() function. But in

Python, memory allocation and deallocation are done during runtime automatically. The programmer need not allocate memory while creating objects or deallocate memory when deleting the objects. Python's PVM will take care of such issues.

Everything is considered as an object in Python. For example, strings are objects. Lists are objects. Functions are objects. Even modules are also objects. For every object, memory should be allocated. Memory manager inside the PVM allocates memory required for objects created in a Python program. All these objects are stored on a separate memory called *heap*. Heap is the memory which is allocated during runtime. The size of the heap memory depends on the Random Access Memory (RAM) of our computer and it can increase or decrease its size depending on the requirement of the program.

We know that the actual memory (RAM) for any program is allocated by the underlying Operating system. On the top of the Operating system, a raw memory allocator oversees whether enough memory is available to it for storing objects. On the top of the raw memory allocator, there are several object-specific allocators operate on the same heap. These memory allocators will implement different types of memory management policies depending on the type of the objects. For example, an integer number should be stored in memory in one way and a string should be stored in a different way. Similarly, when we deal with tuples and dictionaries, they should be stored differently. These issues are taken care of by object-specific memory allocators. Figure 1.5 shows the allocation of memory by Python's Virtual Machine:

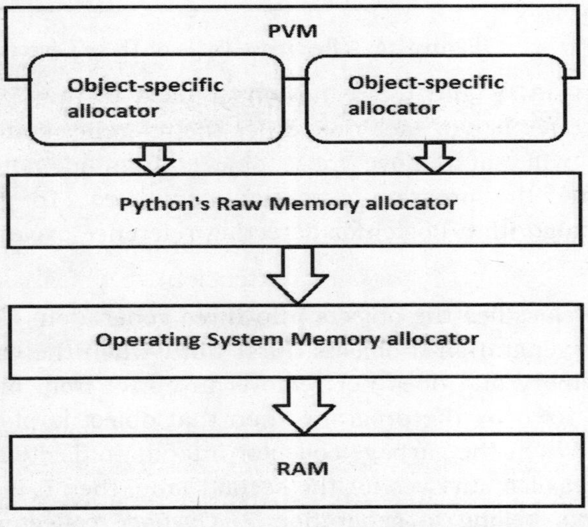

Figure 1.5: Allocation of memory by Python's Virtual Machine (PVM)

Garbage Collection in Python

A module represents Python code that performs a specific task. Garbage collector is a module in Python that is useful to delete objects from memory which are not used in the program. The module that represents the garbage collector is named as *gc*. Garbage collector in the simplest way to maintain a count for each object regarding how many times that object is referenced (or used). When an object is referenced twice, its reference count will be 2. When an object has some count, it is being used in the program and hence garbage collector will not remove it from memory. When an object is found with a reference count 0, garbage collector will understand that the object is not used by the program and hence it can be deleted from memory. Hence, the memory allocated for that object is deallocated or freed.

Garbage collector can detect reference cycles. A reference cycle is a cycle of references pointing to the first object from last object. For example, take three objects A, B and C. The object A refers to the object B whereas the object B holds a reference to the object C. Now if the object C refers to the first object A, it will form a reference cycle. Figure 1.6 shows the reference cycle of three objects:

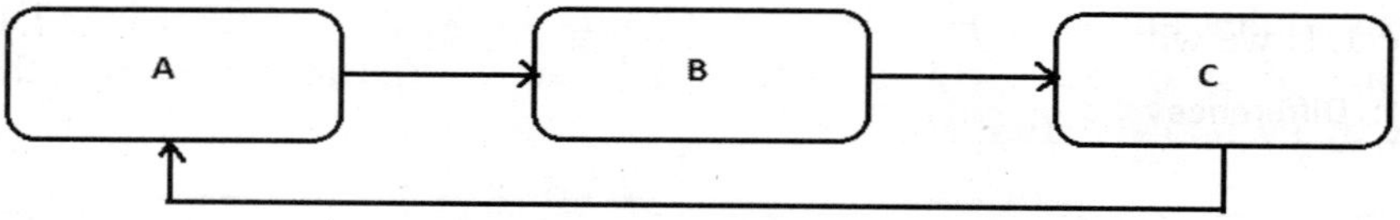

Figure1.6: A Reference Cycle of Three Objects

Even if the objects A, B and C are no longer used in the Python program, still these objects contain 1 reference to each one. Since the reference count for each object is 1, the garbage collector will not remove these objects from memory. These objects stay in memory even after the program execution completes. To get around this, garbage collector uses an algorithm (logic) for detecting reference cycles and removing objects in the cycle.

Garbage collector classifies the objects into three generations. The newly created objects are considered as generation 0 objects. First time, when the garbage collector examines the objects in memory and does not remove an object from memory due to the reason that the object is used by the program, then that object is placed into next generation, say generation 1. When the garbage collector intends to delete the objects for the second time and the object also survives for the second time, then it is placed into generation 2. Thus, older objects belong to generation 2. Garbage collector tries to delete younger objects which are not referenced in the program rather than the old objects.

Garbage collector runs automatically. Python schedules garbage collector depending upon a number called *threshold*. This number represents the frequency of how many times the garbage collector removed (or collected) the objects. When the number of allocations minus the number of de-allocations is greater than the *threshold* number, the garbage collector will run automatically. One can know the threshold number by using the method *get_threshold()* of *gc* module.

When more and more objects are created and if the system runs out of memory, then the automatic garbage collector will not run. Instead, the Python program will throw exception (runtime error). When the programmer is sure that his program does not contain any reference cycles, then automatic garbage collector is best suitable.

In some cases, where reference cycles are found in the program, it is better to run the garbage collector manually. For this purpose, *collect()* method of *gc* module can be used. Manual garbage collection can be done in two ways: time-based and event-based. If the garbage collector is called in certain intervals of time, it is called time-based garbage collection. If the garbage collector is called on the basis of an event, for example, when the user disconnects from an application, it is called event-based garbage collection. However, running the garbage collector too frequently will slow down the program execution.

Comparisons between C and Python

In Table 1.1, we will compare some of the important features of C and Python languages:

Table 1.1: Differences between C and Python

C	Python
C is procedure-oriented programming language. It does not contain the features like classes, objects, inheritance, polymorphism, etc.	Python is object-oriented oriented language. It contains features like classes, objects, inheritance, polymorphism, etc.
C programs execute faster.	Python programs are slower compared to C. PyPy flavor or Python programs run a bit faster but still slower than C.
It is compulsory to declare the datatypes of variables, arrays etc. in C.	Type declaration is not required in Python.
C language type discipline is static and weak.	Python type discipline is dynamic and strong.
Pointers concept is available in C.	Python does not use pointers.
C does not have exception handling facility and hence C programs are weak.	Python handles exceptions and hence Python programs are robust.
C has do… while, while and for loops.	Python has while and for loops.
C has switch statement.	Python does not have switch statement.
The variable in for loop does not increment automatically.	The variable in for loop increments automatically.

C	Python
The programmer should allocate and deallocate memory using malloc(), calloc(), realloc() or free() functions.	Memory allocation and deallocation is done automatically by PVM.
C does not contain a garbage collector.	Automatic garbage collector is available in Python.
C supports single and multi-dimensional arrays.	Python supports only single dimensional arrays. To work with multi-dimensional arrays, we should use third party applications like numpy.
The array index should be positive integer.	Array index can be positive or negative integer number. Negative index represents locations from the end of the array.
Checking the location outside the allocation of an array is not supported in C.	Python performs checking outside an array for all iterations while looping.
Indentation of statements is not necessary in C.	Indentation is required to represent a block of statements.
A semicolon is used to terminate the statements in C and comma is used to separate expressions.	New line indicates end of the statements and semicolon is used as an expression separator.
C supports in-line assignments.	Python does not support in-line assignments.

Comparisons between Java and Python

In Table 1.2, we will compare some of the important features of Java and Python languages:

Table 1.2: Differences between Java and Python

Java	Python
Java is object-oriented programming language. Functional programming features are introduced into Java 8.0 through lambda expressions.	Python blends the functional programming with object-oriented programming features. Lambdas are already available in Python.
Java programs are verbose. It means they contain more number of lines.	Python programs are concise and compact. A big program can be written using very less number of lines.
It is compulsory to declare the datatypes of variables, arrays etc. in Java.	Type declaration is not required in Python.
Java language type discipline is static and weak.	Python type discipline is dynamic and strong.

Java	Python
Java has do... while, while, for and for each loops.	Python has while and for loops.
Java has switch statement.	Python does not have switch statement.
The variable in for loop does not increment automatically. But in for each loop, it will increment automatically.	The variable in the for loop increments automatically.
Memory allocation and deal location is done automatically by JVM (Java Virtual Machine).	Memory allocation and deal location is done automatically by PVM (Python Virtual Machine).
Java supports single and multi-dimensional arrays.	Python supports only single dimensional arrays. To work with multi-dimensional arrays, we should use third party applications like numpy.
The array index should be a positive integer.	Array index can be positive or negative integer number. Negative index represents locations from the end of the array.
Checking the location outside the allocation of an array is not supported in Java.	Python performs checking outside an array for all iterations while looping.
Indentation of statements is not necessary in Java.	Indentation is required to represent a block of statements.
A semicolon is used to terminate the statements and comma is used to separate expressions.	New line indicates end of the statements and semicolon is used as an expression separator.
In Java, the collection objects like Stack, LinkedList or Vector store only objects but not primitive datatypes like integer numbers.	Python collection objects like lists and dictionaries can store objects of any type, including numbers and lists.

Points to Remember

- Python was developed by Guido Van Rossum in the year 1991.
- Python is a high level programming language that contains features of functional programming language like C and object oriented programming language like Java.
- In object oriented terminology, an object represents a physical entity that contains behavior. The behavior of an object is represented by attributes (or properties) and actions. The attributes are represented by variables and actions are performed by functions or methods.
- In object oriented terminology, a class is an abstract idea which represents common behavior of several objects. Class represents behavior and does not exist physically.

Behavior is represented by attributes (variables) and actions (functions). So, a class also contains variables and functions.

- A group of objects having same behavior comes under the same class.
- The standard Python compiler is written in C language and hence called CPython.
- There are other flavors of Python, namely Jython, IronPython and PyPy.
- A Python program contains source code that is first compiled by Python compiler to produce byte code. This byte code is given to Python Virtual Machine (PVM) which converts the byte code to machine code so that the processor will execute it and display the results.
- Python's byte code is a set of instructions created by the Python development team to represent all type of operations. Each byte code occupies 1 byte of memory and hence the name byte code.
- Python Virtual Machine (PVM) is the software containing an interpreter that converts the byte code into machine code depending on the operating system and hardware of the computer system where the Python program runs.
- The standard PVM contains only an interpreter and hence Python is called an interpreted language.
- PVM is most often called Python interpreter.
- The PVM of PyPy contains a compiler in addition to the interpreter. This compiler is called Just In Time (JIT) compiler which is useful to speed up the execution of the Python program.
- The programmer need not allocate or deallocate memory in Python. It is the duty of the PVM to allocate or deallocate memory for Python programs.
- Memory manager is a module (or sub program) in PVM which will allocate memory for objects. Garbage collector is another module in PVM that will deallocate (or free) memory for the unused objects.
- The programmer need not call the garbage collector. It will execute automatically when the Python program is running in memory. In addition, the programmer can also call the garbage collector whenever needed.
- The files that contain Python programs along with Python compiler and libraries that can be executed directly are called frozen binaries.
- The 'py_compile' module converts a Python source file into a .pyc file that contains byte code instructions. Generally, the .pyc files are provided to the end user.
- When the Python source file is given, the 'dis' module displays the equivalent byte code instructions in human readable format.

WRITING OUR FIRST PYTHON PROGRAM

CHAPTER 2

In this chapter, we will learn to write a simple Python program and execute it using Python software. For this purpose, it is necessary to first install the Python software in our computer system. So, we will first learn how to install Python on Windows Operating system and then we will see how to execute a Python program using Python compiler and PVM.

Installing Python for Windows

The latest version of Python (at the beginning of 2018) is Python 3.6.4. This version has again got two variations, a 32-bit version and a 64-bit version. Depending upon our operating system, we can choose a version. Nowadays most people use 64-bit operating system and hence we can use the 64-bit version of Python by visiting the following link:

```
https://www.python.org/downloads/release/python-364/
```

At the bottom of this page, click the 'Windows x86-64 executable installer' link. The file by the name *'python-3.6.4-amd64.exe'* will be downloaded in our computer. By double clicking and following the instructions, we can easily install the Python software latest version in our system.

Let's perform the following steps to install Python:

1. Double click the *'python-3.6.4-amd64.exe'* file. The Setup dialog box appears (Figure 2.1).
2. Select the Install launcher for all users and Add Python 3.6 to PATH checkboxes.

3. Click the 'Install Now' link, as shown in Figure 2.1:

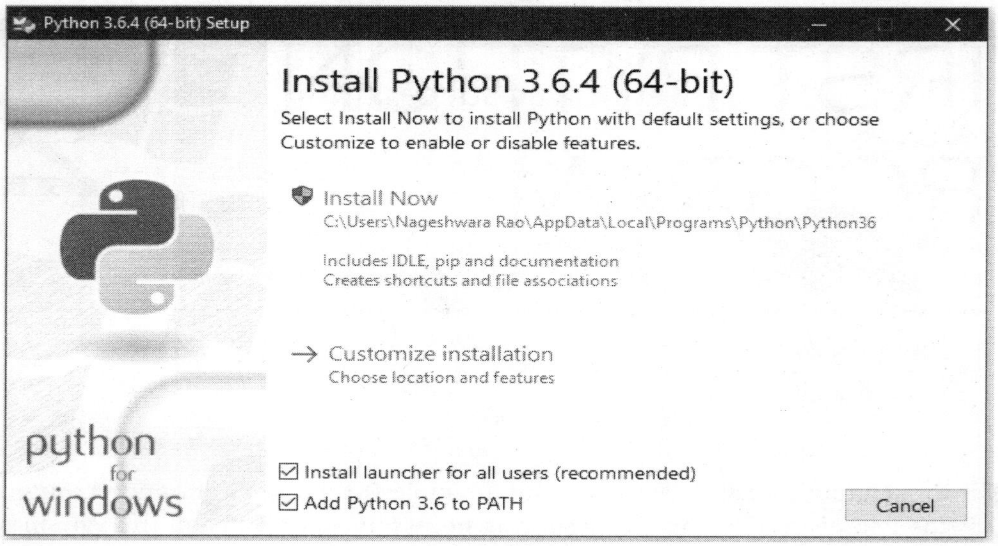

Figure 2.1: Running the Python Setup file

The Setup Progress bar will appear as shown in Figure 2.2:

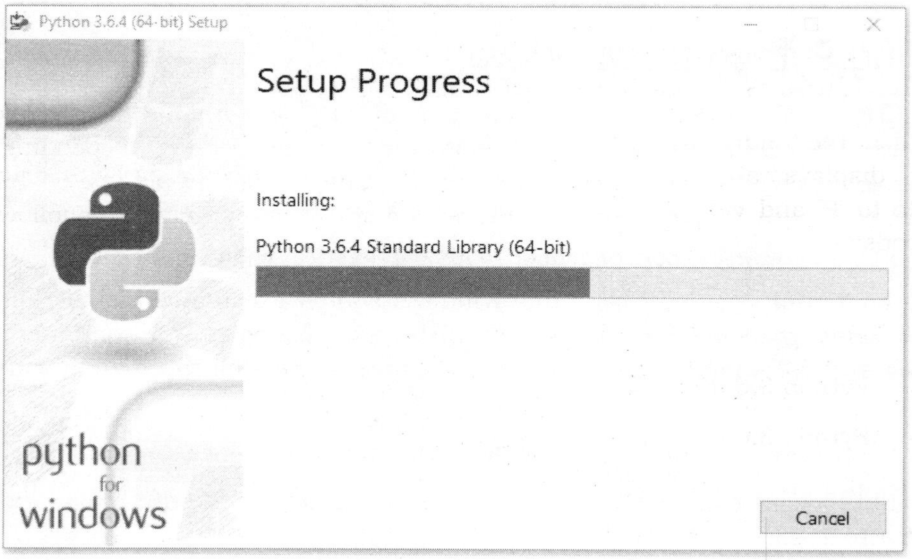

Figure 2.2: Python installation progress

When Python installation is complete, we can see 'Setup was successful' message, as shown in Figure 2.3.

4. Click the 'Close' button, as shown in Figure 2.3:

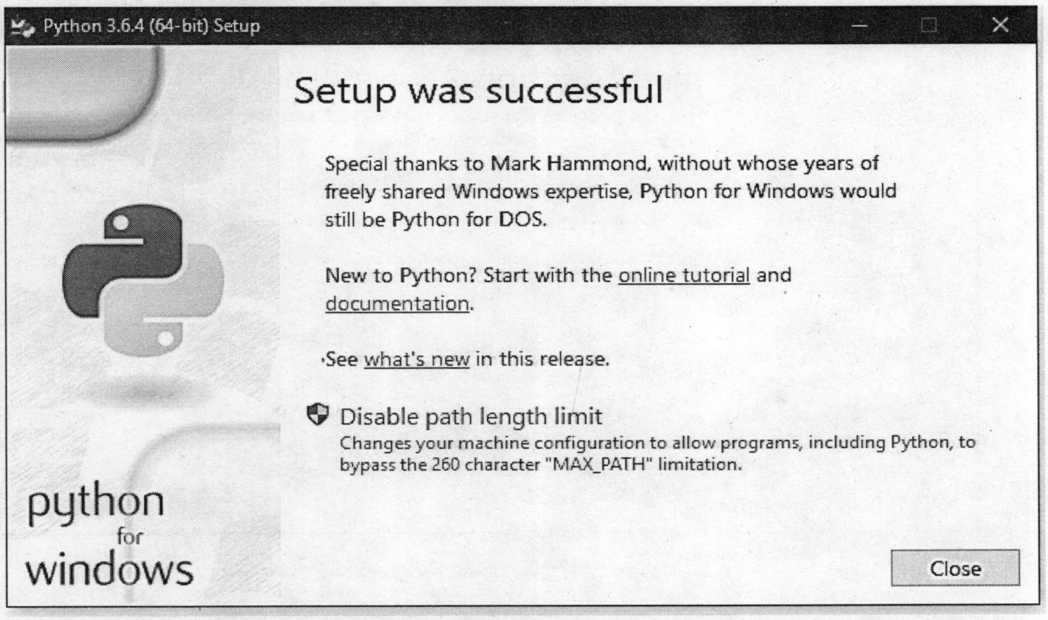

Figure 2.3: Python installation complete window

Testing the Installation in Windows 10

1. Click the 'Start' button on the task bar of the Windows 10 operation system. It displays all applications available in your system in alphabetical order. Go to 'P' and view the 'Python 3.6' folder. In this folder, you can see the following icons:
   - IDLE (Python 3.6 64-bit)
   - Python 3.6 (64-bit)
   - Python 3.6 anuals (64-bit)
   - Python 3.6 Module Docs (64-bit)

   This is shown in Figure 2.4:

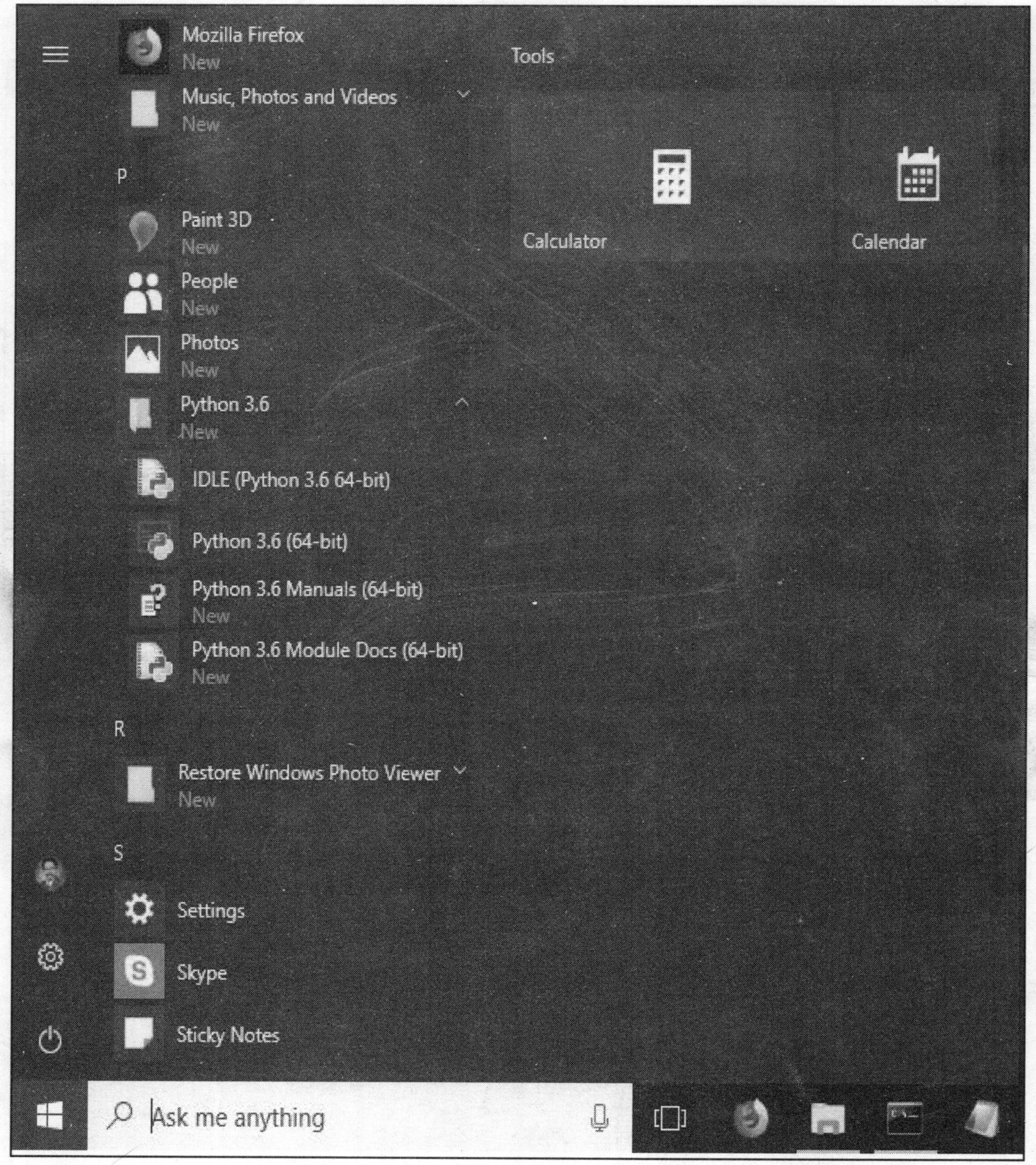

Figure 2.4: Windows start button displaying Python installation

2. Click the 'IDLE (Python 3.6 64-bit)' option. The Python's IDLE (Integrated Development Environment)'s Graphical user interface window opens (Figure 2.5).

   At the bottom of the screen, we can see a white icon displayed on the taskbar.

3. Right click on the icon and click the 'Pin to taskbar' option. Clicking on this taskbar icon will be sufficient to open Python IDLE whenever we want, as shown in Figure 2.5:

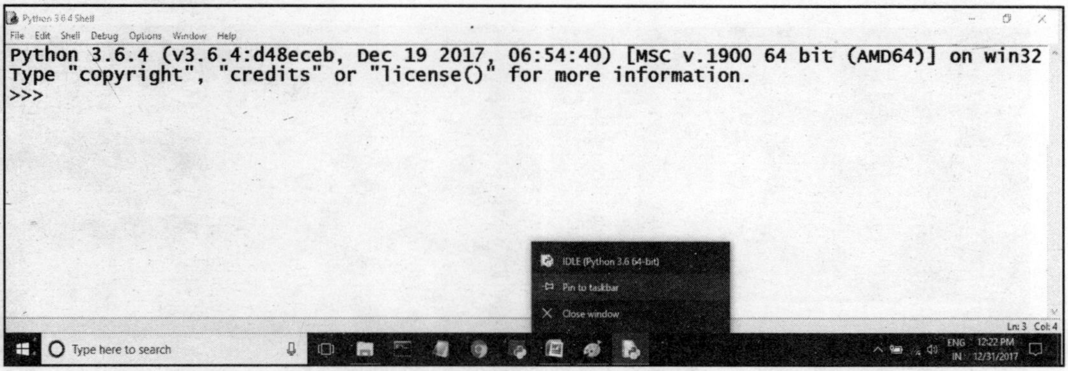

Figure 2.5: The Python IDLE Window

4. Click the Python prompt, i.e., triple greater than symbol and type quit() to close the Python window (Figure 2.6). A prompt asking 'Do you want to kill it?' appears.

5. Click the 'OK' button to quit from the IDLE window, as shown in Figure 2.6:

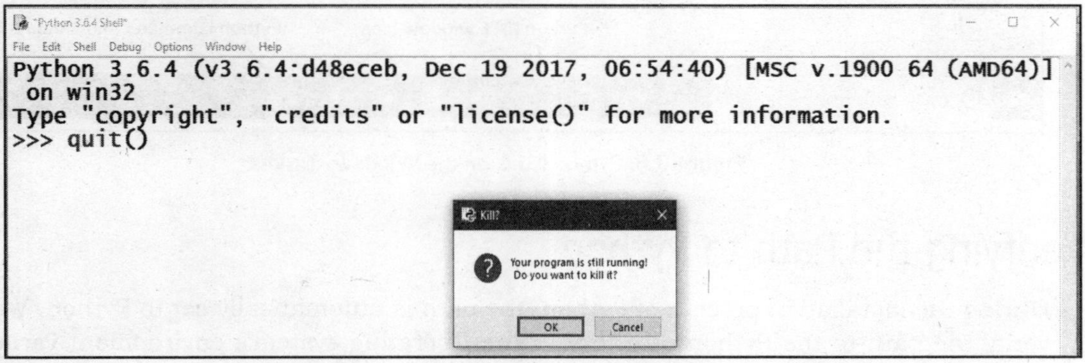

Figure 2.6: Closing the Python IDLE Window

6. Click the windows 'Start' button and then click 'Python 3.6 (64 - bit)' to open the 'Python command line window' which displays a black screen (Figure 2.7).

The Python command line window is also useful in the same manner as the Python's IDLE window to type the Python code and run it. Right click the Python command line window icon displayed on the taskbar at the bottom of the monitor and pin it to the taskbar so that we can simply click on this icon to open Python command line window at any time.

To quit from this command line window, we can simply type quit() at the Python prompt (the triple greater than symbol), as shown in Figure 2.7:

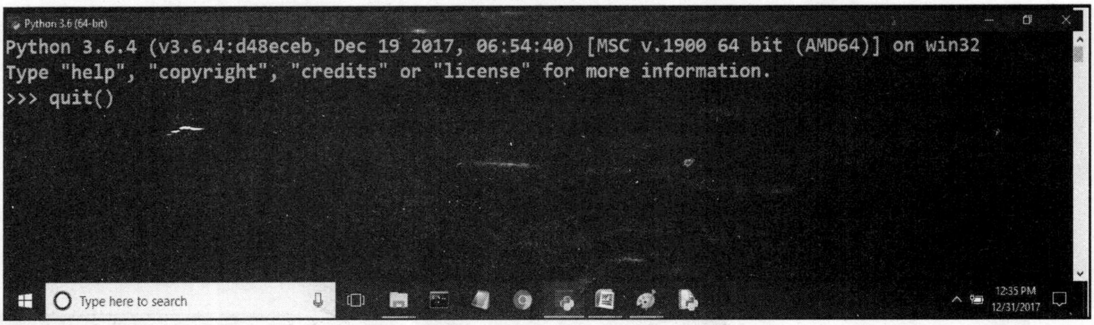

Figure 2.7: Python command line window

7. As discussed in the previous steps, we would have two icons added to our windows taskbar. They are: the Python IDLE window icon (white in color) and the Python command line window icon (black in color). We can click any of these icons to open these windows, type Python programs and run them in these windows. Figure 2.8 shows the Python icons:

Figure 2.8: Python Icons on the Windows Taskbar

Verifying the Path to Python

During the installation process of Python, the path is automatically set to Python. We can verify the path to the Python directory in the Operating system's environment variables. Let's perform the following steps to view the path to the Python directory:

1. Right click the 'This PC' icon in Windows 10. Then click the 'Properties' option as shown in Figure 2.9:

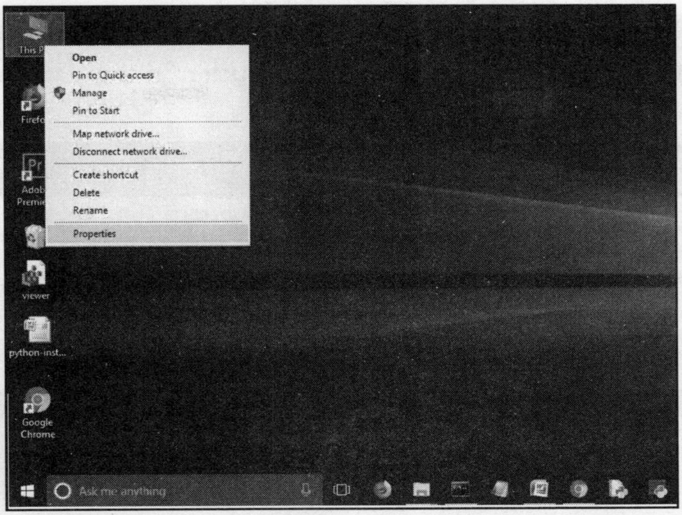

Figure 2.9: Going to properties of Computer system

It will display a page where we should click the 'Advanced system settings' option. It will display a System Properties dialog box.

2. Click the 'Environment Variables' button, as shown in Figure 2.10:

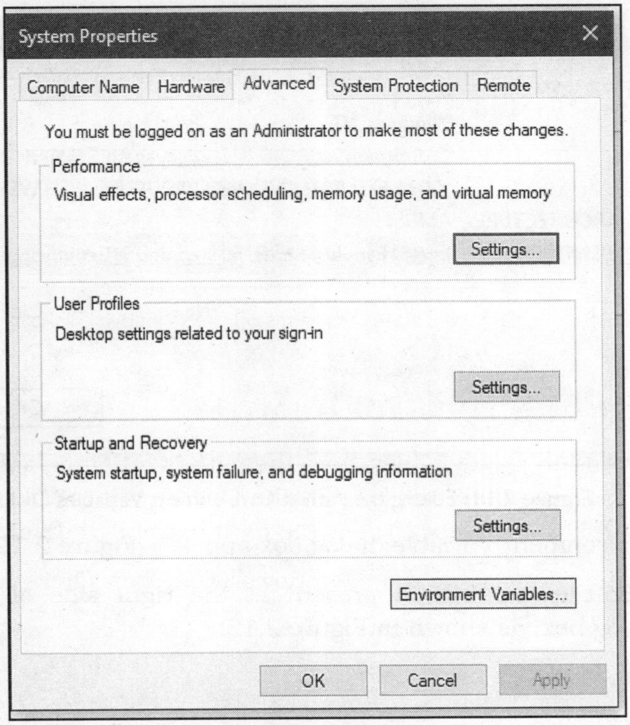

Figure 2.10: Going to Environment Variables in Advanced System Settings

It will display User variables and System variables (Figure 2.11).

3. Select 'Path' variable and click the 'Edit...' button in the User variables, as shown in Figure 2.11:

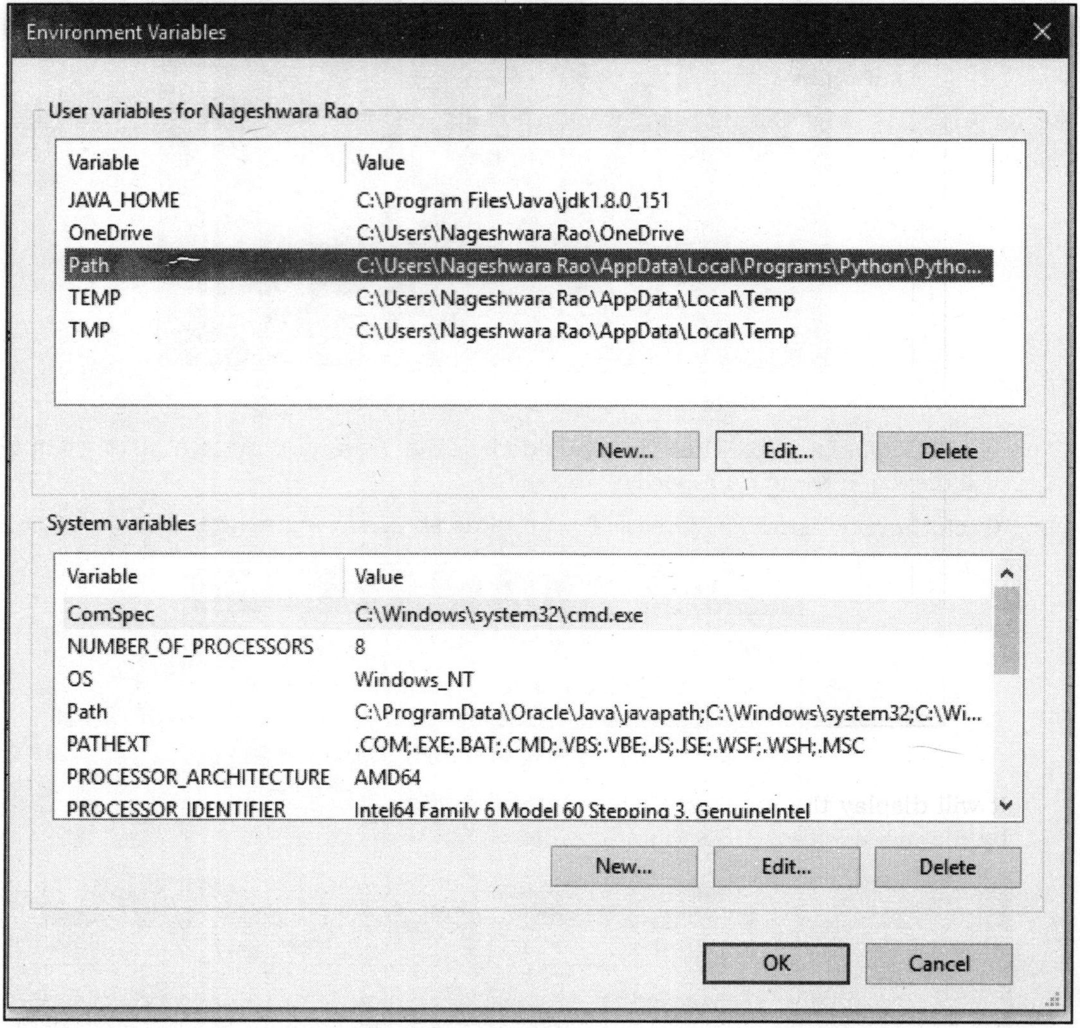

Figure 2.11: Editing the Path in Environment Variables Dialog Box

The Edit Environment Variable dialog box appears (Figure 2.12).

4. Click the 'Edit text...' button present at the right side of the Edit Environment Variable dialog box, as shown in Figure 2.12:

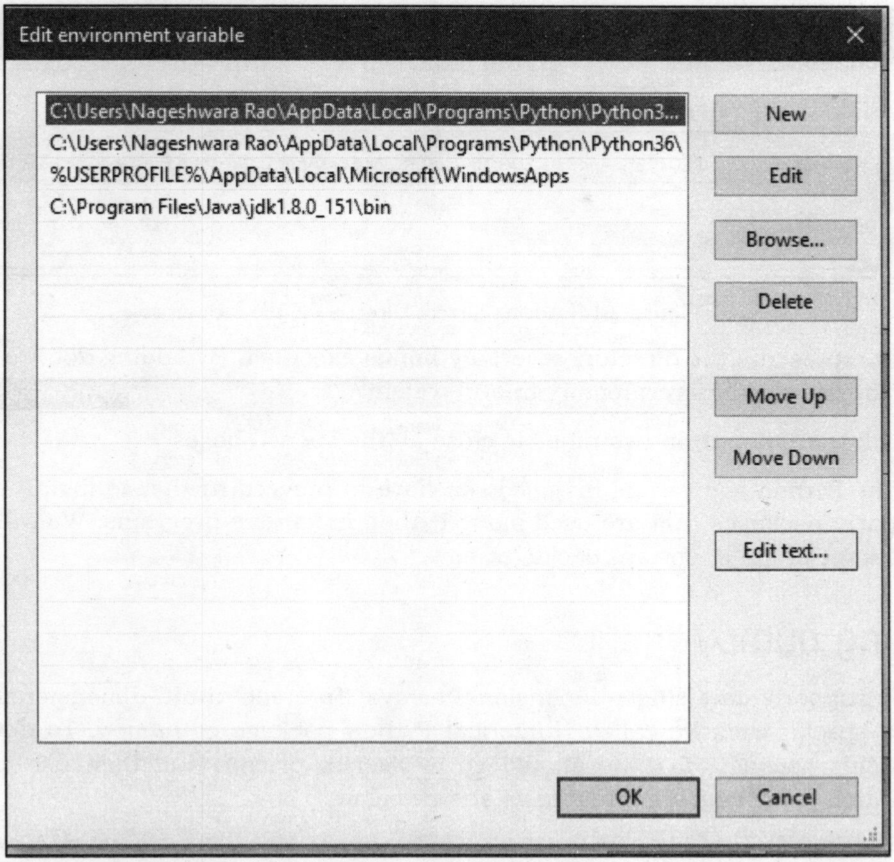

Figure 2.12: Viewing Python Directory in the Path variable

It will display the directories involved in the Path. We can observe that the directory by the name Python36\Scripts is added to the Path, as shown in Figure 2.13:

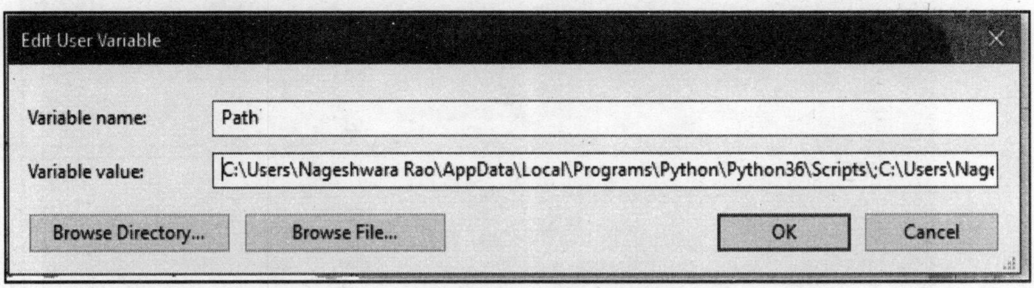

Figure 2.13: Viewing Python Directory in the Path variable

5. Add a dot (.) at the end of that path and click the 'OK' button, as shown in Figure 2.14:

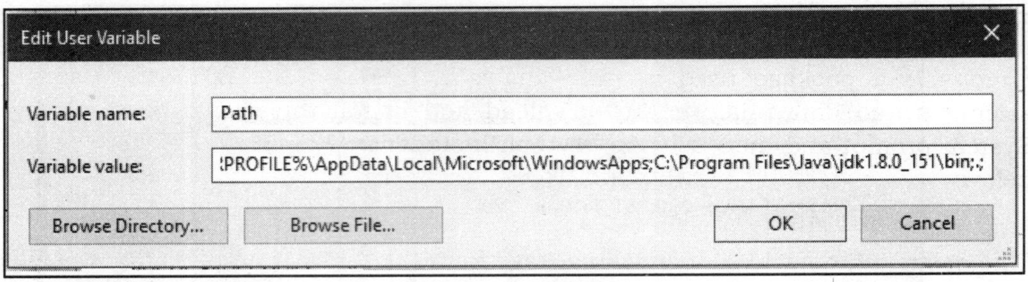

Figure 2.14: Adding current Directory in the Path variable

Dot represents the directory where Python is executed. By adding dot, we are making Python to run in any directory in our system.

6. Click the 'OK' button two times to close all the opened boxes.

Once the Python software is installed, we have to proceed further to install other useful third party packages that are used along Python in various programs. We will see how to install some of the important packages now.

Installing numpy

Python supports only single dimensional arrays. To create multi-dimensional arrays, we need a special package called Numerical Python package or *numpy*. To download and install this package, first we should go to System prompt and then use 'pip' (Python Installation of Packages) command as shown below:

```
C:\> pip install numpy
```

'pip' program comes with Python software by default. When this command is given, it searches the latest version of the numpy package on the Internet, downloads it and installs it, as shown in Figure 2.15:

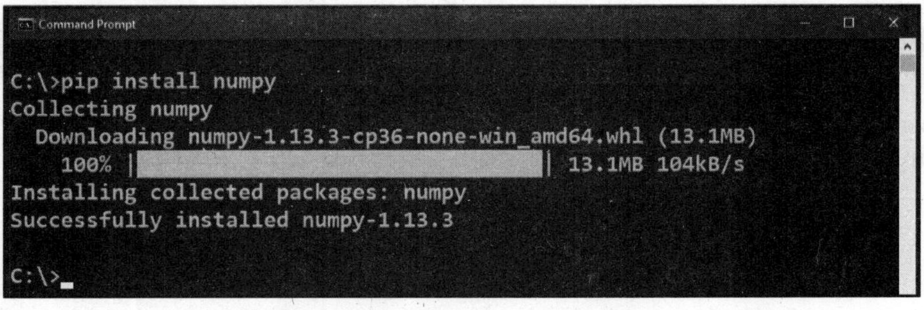

Figure 2.15: Installation of numpy package

Of course, our computer would have connected to the Internet while using this command.

Installing pandas

pandas is a package used in data analysis. This package is mostly used by data scientists and data analysts. To download and install this package, we should go to System prompt and then use 'pip' (Python Installation of Packages) command as shown below:

```
C:\> pip install pandas
```

This command downloads pandas package from the Internet and installs it, as shown in Figure 2.16:

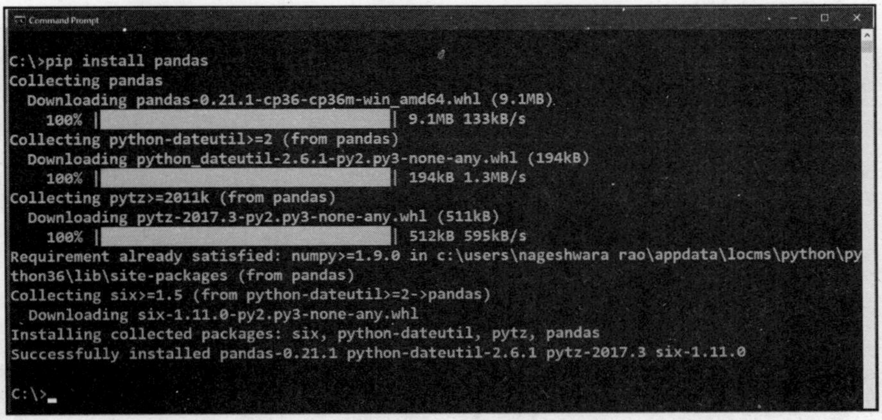

Figure 2.16: Installation of pandas package

Installing xlrd

xlrd is a package that is useful to retrieve data from Microsoft Excel spreadsheet files. Hence, it is useful in data analysis. To download and install this package, we should go to System prompt and then use 'pip' (Python Installation of Packages) command as shown below:

```
C:\> pip install xlrd
```

This command downloads xlrd package from the Internet and installs it, as shown in Figure 2.17:

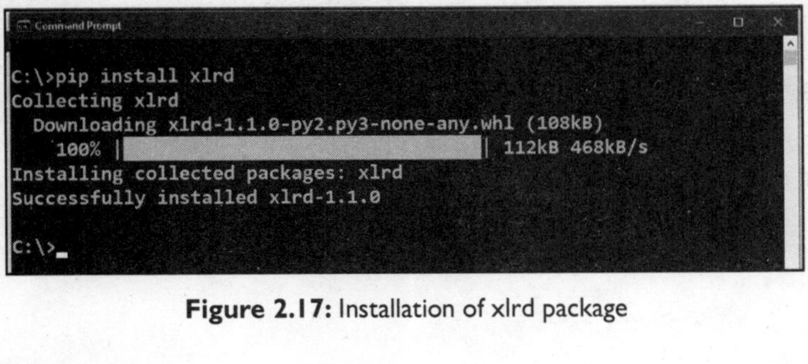

Figure 2.17: Installation of xlrd package

Installing matplotlib

matplotlib is another important package in Python that is useful to produce good quality 2D graphics. It is mostly used for the purpose of showing data in the form of graphs and also for designing electronic circuits, machinery parts, etc. To download and install this package, we should go to System prompt and then use 'pip' (Python Installation of Packages) command as shown below:

```
C:\> pip install matplotlib
```

This command downloads the matplotlib package from the Internet and installs it as shown in Figure 2.18:

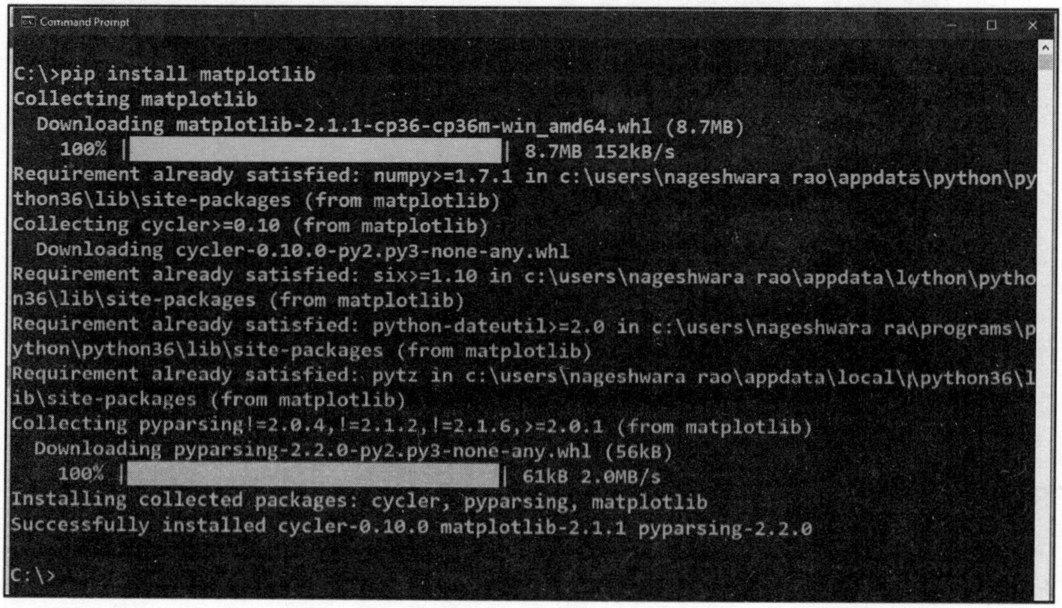

Figure 2.18: Installation of matplotlib package

Verifying Installed Packages

We can verify whether the installed packages are added to our Python software properly or not by going into Python and typing the following command at Python prompt (triple greater than symbol) as:

```
>>> help('modules')
```

For this purpose, first click the Python IDLE Window pinned at the taskbar and then type the preceding command as shown in Figure 2.19:

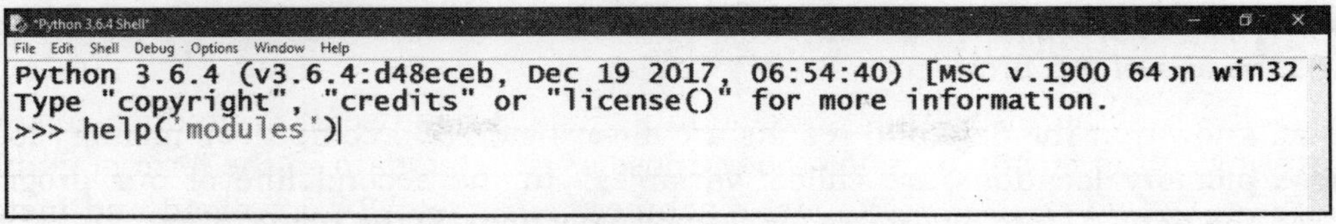

Figure 2.19: To view the modules available in Python

It will display all the module names currently available in your Python software as shown in Figure 2.20:

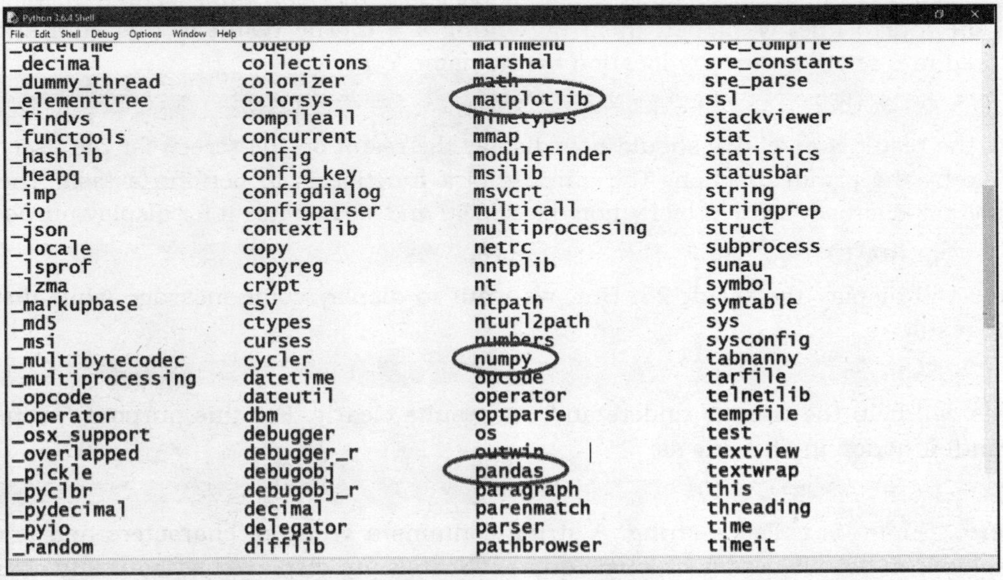

Figure 2.20: To verify installed packages in Python

You can verify that your Python software now has the packages like: numpy, xlrd, pandas, and matplotlib available as modules.

Writing Our First Python Program

We want to write our first Python program and execute it. This will also help us to test whether our installation is correct or not. Let's write our first program to add two numbers. First have a look at the Python program code given here:

```
# first program to add two numbers - line 1
a = 10  # store 10 into variable a - line 2
b = 15  # store 15 into variable b - line 3
c = a + b  # add 10 and 15 and store into variable c - line 4
print("Sum= ", c)  # display the sum - line 5
```

The hash symbol '#' represents the comment line in Python. A comment is useful to describe the elements of a program. Comments are not executed by the Python compiler or PVM. Hence, it is not compulsory to write comments; however, comments improve understanding of a program. We started the above program with a comment line that gives the aim of our program.

We all know that the data and results are always stored in computer's memory locations. These memory locations are called 'variables'. In the second line of our program, we stored the data 10 into a variable (or memory location) by the name 'a' as:

```
a = 10
```

Similarly, in the third line, we stored data 15 into another variable 'b' as:

```
b = 15
```

In the fourth line, we added them by writing a + b. The result of this sum should be stored into another memory location by the name 'c' as:

```
c= a +b
```

So, the result is in 'c'. We should now display the result on the screen for the user. This is done by the print() function. The purpose of a function is to perform a task. The print() function is already written by Python developers and we can use it for display purpose as:

```
print(c)
```

This will display the result 25. But, we want to display some message while displaying the result as:

```
Sum= 25
```

This will help the user to understand the results clearly. For this purpose, we used the print() function in fifth line as:

```
print("Sum= ", c)
```

Here, "Sum= "is called a string. A string contains a group of characters and is usually enclosed in double quotes or single quotes. Strings are displayed without any change, as they are. After this string, we put a comma and then wrote 'c'. This will display the result as:

```
Sum= 25
```

Executing a Python Program

There are three ways of executing a Python program.

- Using Python's command line window
- Using Python's IDLE graphics window
- Directly from System prompt

The first two are called *interactive modes* where we can type the program one line at a time and the PVM executes it immediately. The last one is called *non-interactive mode* where we ask the PVM to execute our program after typing the entire program.

Using Python's Command Line Window

Click the Python's command line icon which is already added to our taskbar present at the bottom of the desktop as shown in Figure 2.8.

This will open Python's command line window. We can see >>> symbol which is called Python prompt. Type our first Python program at the >>> prompt, as shown in Figure 2.21:

```
Python 3.6 (64-bit)
Python 3.6.4 (v3.6.4:d48eceb, Dec 19 2017, 06:54:40) [MSC v.1900 64 bit (AMD64)] on win32
Type "help", "copyright", "credits" or "license" for more information.
>>> # first program to add two numbers
... a = 10
>>> b = 20
>>> c = a + b
>>> print("Sum = ", c)
Sum =  30
>>> exit()_
```

Figure 2.21: The Python Command Line Window

After typing the last line and pressing the Enter button, we can see the result of our program. After that, type exit() or quit() at the Python prompt. This will terminate the PVM and close the window. Note that it is possible to select / modify the font style and font size in the command line window by right clicking on the top title bar and then selecting 'Properties' option.

Using Python's IDLE Graphics Window

It is possible to execute a Python program by going to Integrated Development Environment (IDLE) which provides graphical interface to the user. Click the Python's IDLE icon (Figure 2.8). This will open the Python's IDLE window. Type the program. After entering the last line, we can see the result, as shown in Figure 2.22:

```
*Python 3.6.4 Shell*
File Edit Shell Debug Options Window Help
Python 3.6.4 (v3.6.4:d48eceb, Dec 19 2017, 06:54:40) [MSC v.1900 64 bit (AMD64)] on win32
Type "copyright", "credits" or "license()" for more information.
>>> # first program to add two numbers
>>> a = 10
>>> b = 20
>>> c = a + b
>>> print("Sum= ", c)
Sum=  30
>>> exit()|
```

Figure 2.22: Python's IDLE Shell Window

To terminate the IDLE window, type exit() or quit() at the Python prompt. It will display a message as to kill the program or not, as shown in Figure 2.23:

Figure 2.23: Closing IDLE window

Click the 'OK' button. The Python compiler will terminate and the window will close.

Note that we can select a particular font and also increase or decrease the font size in the IDLE window by choosing the 'Options' menu → Configure IDLE... option.

Running the Python programs as discussed in the preceding sections may not be convenient as we can type only one statement at a time. When the programmer wants to type a big program, then the best way is to use the File → New File option in the IDLE window. Then it opens a new window where we can type the entire program, as shown in Figure 2.24:

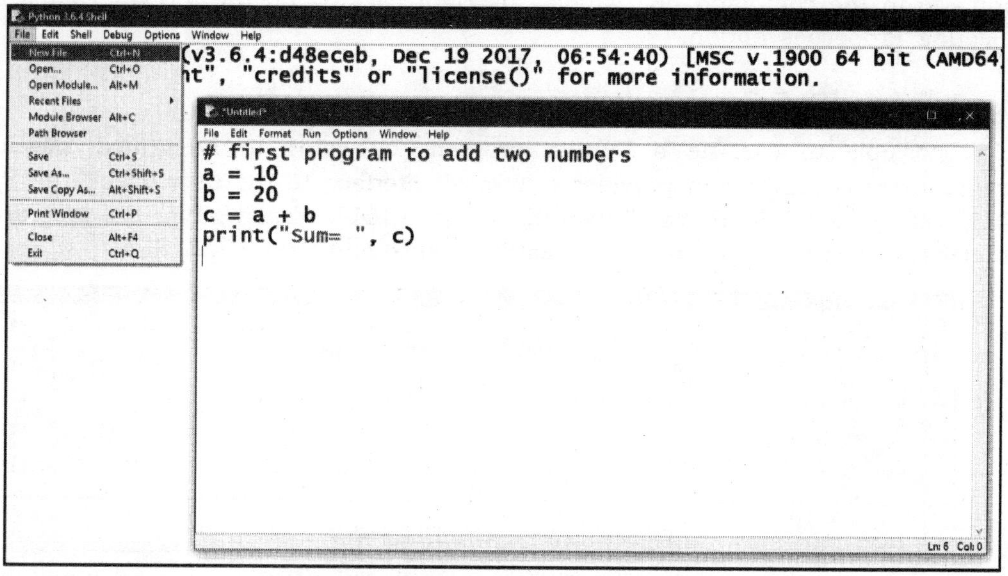

Figure 2.24: Typing a big Program in IDLE window

After typing the program, save it by clicking File → Save in the program window and then type a file name and .py as extension name in a directory. This is shown in Figure 2.25:

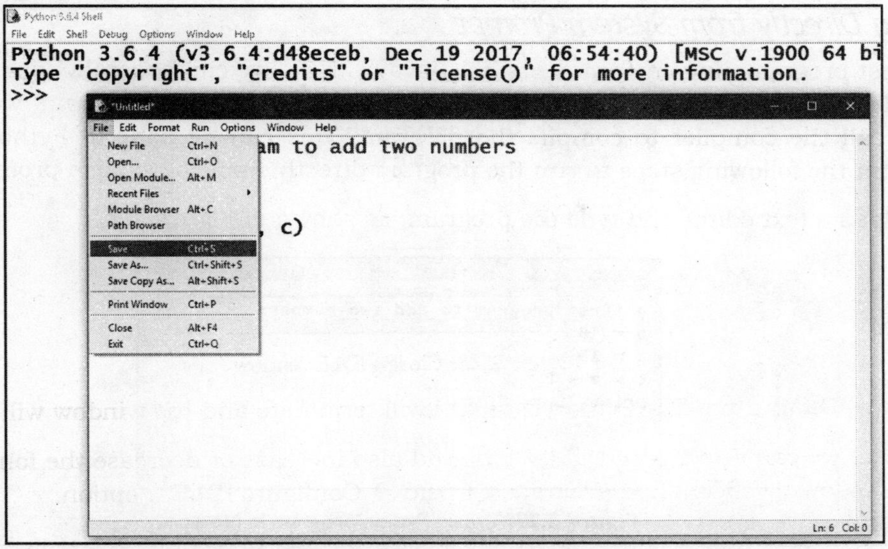

Figure 2.25: Saving a Program in IDLE window

We can compile and run the program by using the options File Run → Run Module or by simply pressing the F5 button on the keyboard. A new window will open where the results are displayed, as shown in Figure 2.26:

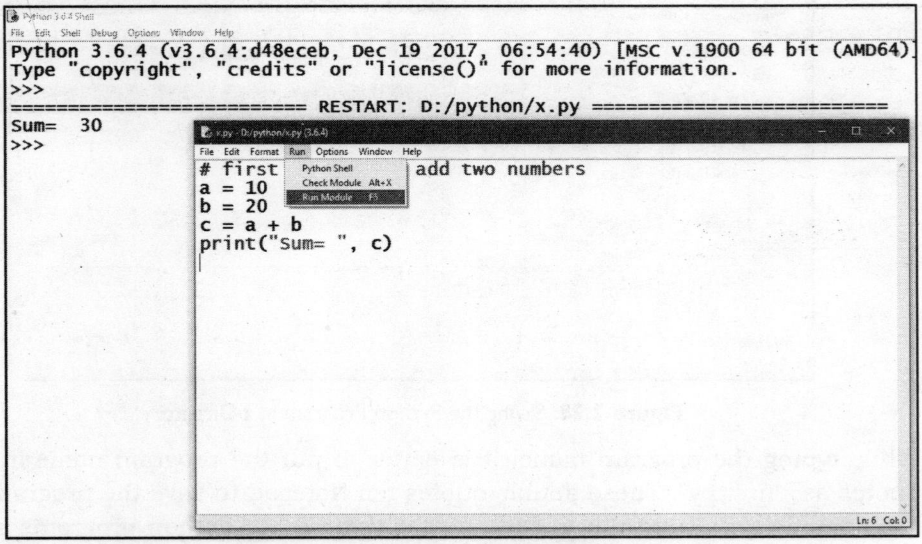

Figure 2.26: Running a Program in IDLE window

To reopen a Python program that is already saved in the Python IDLE window, we can use File → Open option and then go to the directory where the file is saved and click the filename.

Running Directly from System Prompt

In most programming environments like Java or .NET, we can generally type the program in a Text editor like Notepad or EditPlus. After typing the entire program, we save it and then call the compiler to compile the program. This can be done in Python also. Let's perform the following steps to run the program directly from the system prompt:

1. Open a text editor and type the program, as shown in Figure 2.27:

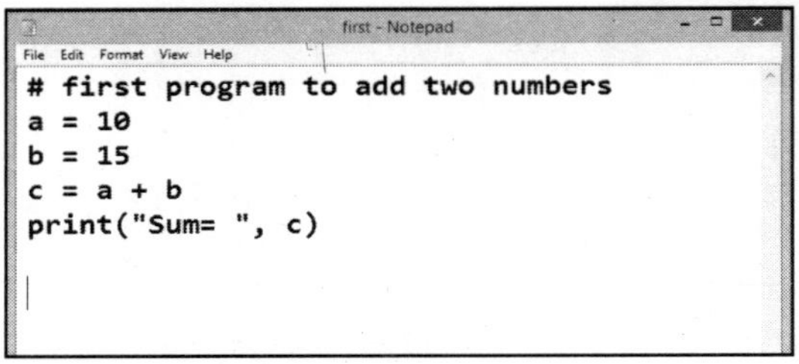

Figure 2.27: Typing Python program in Notepad

2. Save the program by clicking File → Save As. Type the program name as "first.py", as shown in Figure 2.28:

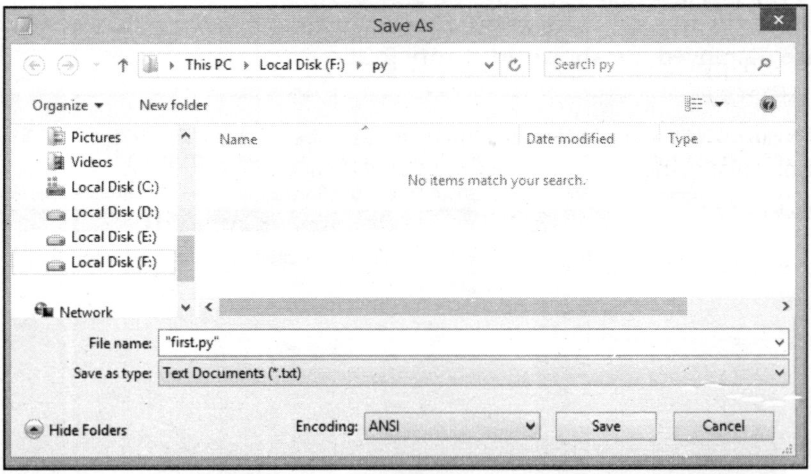

Figure 2.28: Saving the Python Program in a Directory

While typing the program name, it is better to put the program name inside double quotes as: "first.py". These double quotes tell Notepad to save the program exactly as the name is typed and not to save it as a text file. All Python programs should have .py as the file name extension.

3. Open the command prompt (or DOS prompt) window and go to that directory where the program is saved. This can be done by typing COMMAND or CMD commands at Start → Run.

4. In Windows 10 operating system, we should first right click on the 'Start' button and then click 'Run' to see the Run dialog box where we should type 'command', as shown in Figure 2.29:

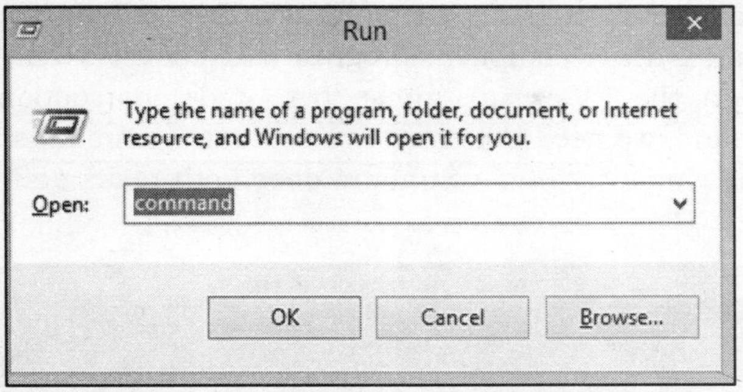

Figure 2.29: Going to DOS prompt

5. Click the 'OK' button. This opens the command prompt window.
6. Go to that directory where our Python program is saved. Suppose, we have saved our program in 'F:' drive and in the 'py' directory. Now, change the directory to F:\py using the CD (Change Directory to) command as:

```
C:\>f:
F:\>cd py
F:\PY>
```

To see the directory contents and verify whether our first.py program is already available in that directory or not, we can display the directory contents as:

```
F:\PY>dir
```

The above DOS command will display the contents of the directory, as shown in Figure 2.30:

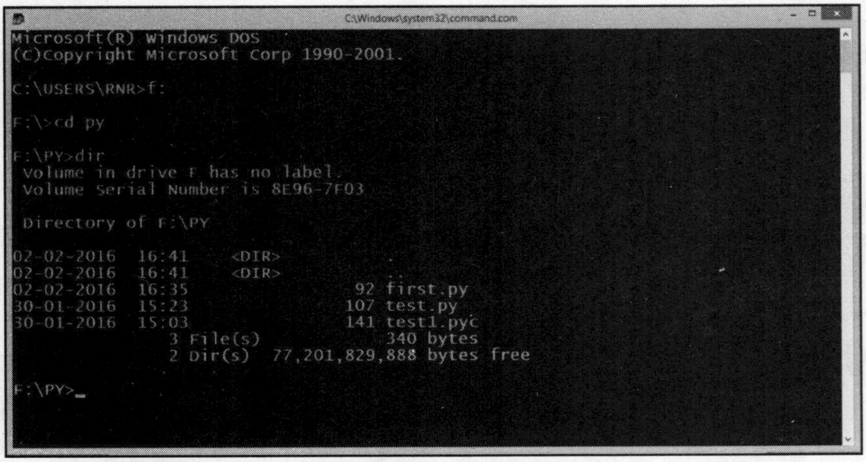

Figure 2.30: Entering the Directory where Python Programs are Saved

Let's now execute the first.py program by calling the python command. For this purpose, type python along with the file name at the command prompt window as:

```
F:\PY>python first.py
```

Here, the command 'python' is a program that contains Python compiler as well as PVM. Hence, first of all, Python compiler compiles and converts our program into byte code instructions. Then the PVM runs those byte code instructions to produce the final results. That means, we need not enter two separate commands to compile and then run our program. The single 'python' command does both tasks and gives the final result, as shown in Figure 2.31:

Figure 2.31: Running the Python Program at System Prompt

We should understand that the Python compiler along with PVM is loaded into memory only when we type 'python' at the command prompt window. When the program execution is completed and the results are displayed, the Python compiler and the PVM will be terminated from memory. When we execute another program, then again the Python compiler is loaded into memory along with PVM. To close the command prompt window, we can type exit as:

```
F:\PY>exit
```

Note

All the programs in this book are executed from the command prompt window; however, readers can run these programs in any of the three modes discussed in the previous sections.

Getting Help in Python

When a programmer faces some doubt about how to use a particular feature of the Python language, he can view the help. To get help, one can enter help mode by typing help() at Python prompt (i.e. >>> prompt). We can see the help utility appearing as shown in Figure 2.32:

```
*Python 3.6.4 Shell*
File Edit Shell Debug Options Window Help
Python 3.6.4 (v3.6.4:d48eceb, Dec 19 2017, 06:54:40) [MSC v.1900 64 bit (AMD64)] on win32
Type "copyright", "credits" or "license()" for more information.
>>> help()

Welcome to Python 3.6's help utility!

If this is your first time using Python, you should definitely check out
the tutorial on the Internet at http://docs.python.org/3.6/tutorial/.

Enter the name of any module, keyword, or topic to get help on writing
Python programs and using Python modules.  To quit this help utility and
return to the interpreter, just type "quit".

To get a list of available modules, keywords, symbols, or topics, type
"modules", "keywords", "symbols", or "topics".  Each module also comes
with a one-line summary of what it does; to list the modules whose name
or summary contain a given string such as "spam", type "modules spam".

help> |
```

Figure 2.32: Entering Help Mode in Python

Now, we can type 'modules' to see which modules are available in Python. We can type 'topics' to know about topics in Python. Let's enter topics at the help prompt, as shown in Figure 2.33:

```
*Python 3.6.4 Shell*
File Edit Shell Debug Options Window Help
help> topics

Here is a list of available topics.  Enter any topic name to get more help.

ASSERTION           DELETION            LOOPING             SHIFTING
ASSIGNMENT          DICTIONARIES        MAPPINGMETHODS      SLICINGS
ATTRIBUTEMETHODS    DICTIONARYLITERALS  MAPPINGS            SPECIALATTRIBUTES
ATTRIBUTES          DYNAMICFEATURES     METHODS             SPECIALIDENTIFIERS
AUGMENTEDASSIGNMENT ELLIPSIS            MODULES             SPECIALMETHODS
BASICMETHODS        EXCEPTIONS          NAMESPACES          STRINGMETHODS
BINARY              EXECUTION           NONE                STRINGS
BITWISE             EXPRESSIONS         NUMBERMETHODS       SUBSCRIPTS
BOOLEAN             FLOAT               NUMBERS             TRACEBACKS
CALLABLEMETHODS     FORMATTING          OBJECTS             TRUTHVALUE
CALLS               FRAMEOBJECTS        OPERATORS           TUPLELITERALS
CLASSES             FRAMES              PACKAGES            TUPLES
CODEOBJECTS         FUNCTIONS           POWER               TYPEOBJECTS
COMPARISON          IDENTIFIERS         PRECEDENCE          TYPES
COMPLEX             IMPORTING           PRIVATENAMES        UNARY
CONDITIONAL         INTEGER             RETURNING           UNICODE
CONTEXTMANAGERS     LISTLITERALS        SCOPING
CONVERSIONS         LISTS               SEQUENCEMETHODS
DEBUGGING           LITERALS            SEQUENCES


help> |
```

Figure 2.33: Getting Help on Topics

Among the topics, suppose we want to know about functions, we should enter 'FUNCTIONS' in capital letters since the FUNCTIONS topic is shown in capital letters in the help window, as shown in Figure 2.34:

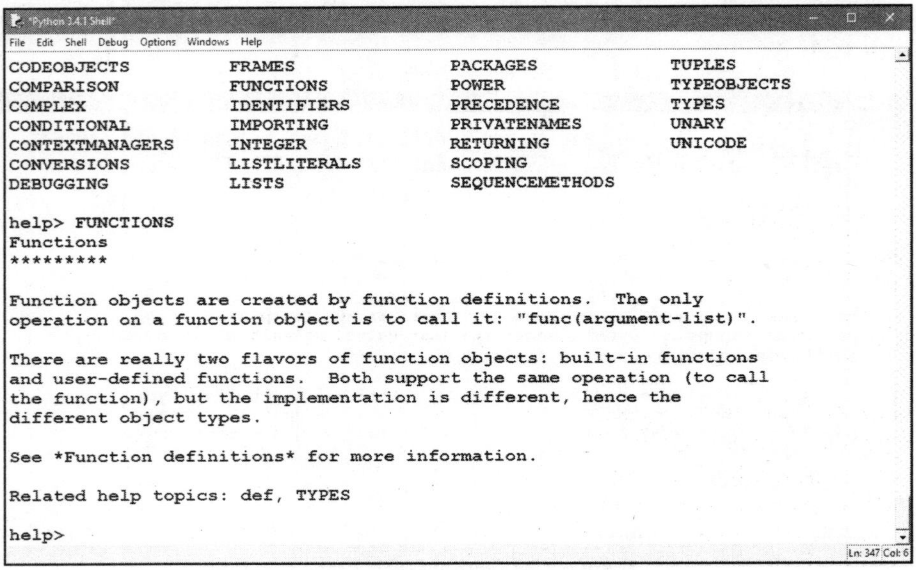

```
*Python 3.4.1 Shell*
File Edit Shell Debug Options Windows Help
CODEOBJECTS         FRAMES              PACKAGES            TUPLES
COMPARISON          FUNCTIONS           POWER               TYPEOBJECTS
COMPLEX             IDENTIFIERS         PRECEDENCE          TYPES
CONDITIONAL         IMPORTING           PRIVATENAMES        UNARY
CONTEXTMANAGERS     INTEGER             RETURNING           UNICODE
CONVERSIONS         LISTLITERALS        SCOPING
DEBUGGING           LISTS               SEQUENCEMETHODS

help> FUNCTIONS
Functions
*********

Function objects are created by function definitions.  The only
operation on a function object is to call it: "func(argument-list)".

There are really two flavors of function objects: built-in functions
and user-defined functions.  Both support the same operation (to call
the function), but the implementation is different, hence the
different object types.

See *Function definitions* for more information.

Related help topics: def, TYPES

help>
Ln: 347 Col: 6
```

Figure 2.34: Getting Help on Functions

To get help on the print function, we can type 'print' at the help prompt, as shown in Figure 2.35:

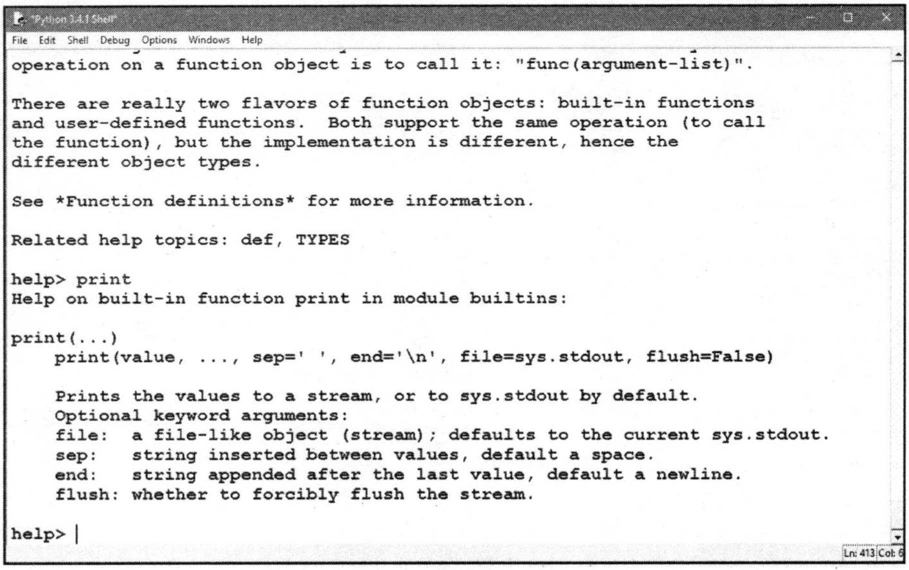

```
*Python 3.4.1 Shell*
File Edit Shell Debug Options Windows Help
operation on a function object is to call it: "func(argument-list)".

There are really two flavors of function objects: built-in functions
and user-defined functions.  Both support the same operation (to call
the function), but the implementation is different, hence the
different object types.

See *Function definitions* for more information.

Related help topics: def, TYPES

help> print
Help on built-in function print in module builtins:

print(...)
    print(value, ..., sep=' ', end='\n', file=sys.stdout, flush=False)

    Prints the values to a stream, or to sys.stdout by default.
    Optional keyword arguments:
    file:  a file-like object (stream); defaults to the current sys.stdout.
    sep:   string inserted between values, default a space.
    end:   string appended after the last value, default a newline.
    flush: whether to forcibly flush the stream.

help> |
Ln: 413 Col: 6
```

Figure 2.35: Getting Help on Print Function

To quit from the help mode, we should simply press the Enter button once again without typing anything. A message appears that we are leaving the help mode and then we arrive at the Python prompt, i.e. >>>. To exit the Python interpreter (or PVM), we should type either exit() or quit(), as shown in Figure 2.36:

```
See *Function definitions* for more information.

Related help topics: def, TYPES

help> print
Help on built-in function print in module builtins:

print(...)
    print(value, ..., sep=' ', end='\n', file=sys.stdout, flush=False)

    Prints the values to a stream, or to sys.stdout by default.
    Optional keyword arguments:
    file:  a file-like object (stream); defaults to the current sys.stdout.
    sep:   string inserted between values, default a space.
    end:   string appended after the last value, default a newline.
    flush: whether to forcibly flush the stream.

help>

You are now leaving help and returning to the Python interpreter.
If you want to ask for help on a particular object directly from the
interpreter, you can type "help(object)".  Executing "help('string')"
has the same effect as typing a particular string at the help> prompt.
>>> exit()
```

Figure 2.36: Exiting the Python IDLE Window

We can also view help without entering the help mode. Viewing help is possible at the Python prompt. We can use the help() command and inside the parentheses, type the item name in single quotes. For example, to get help on topics, we can type help ('topics') and to get help on the print function, we can type help('print'), as shown in Figure 2.37:

```
Python 3.6.4 (v3.6.4:d48eceb, Dec 19 2017, 06:54:40) [MSC v.1900 64 bit (AMD64)] on win32
Type "copyright", "credits" or "license()" for more information.
>>> help('print')
Help on built-in function print in module builtins:

print(...)
    print(value, ..., sep=' ', end='\n', file=sys.stdout, flush=False)

    Prints the values to a stream, or to sys.stdout by default.
    Optional keyword arguments:
    file:  a file-like object (stream); defaults to the current sys.stdout.
    sep:   string inserted between values, default a space.
    end:   string appended after the last value, default a newline.
    flush: whether to forcibly flush the stream.

>>> |
```

Figure 2.37: Using the help() function

Getting Python Documentation Help

Python developers have provided extensive description of all Python features in a document that is called 'Python documents'. This provides a great help for beginners and for professional programmers to understand all the features of Python. To see Python documentation help, we should open the IDLE window. Then select Help → Python Docs, as shown in Figure 2.38:

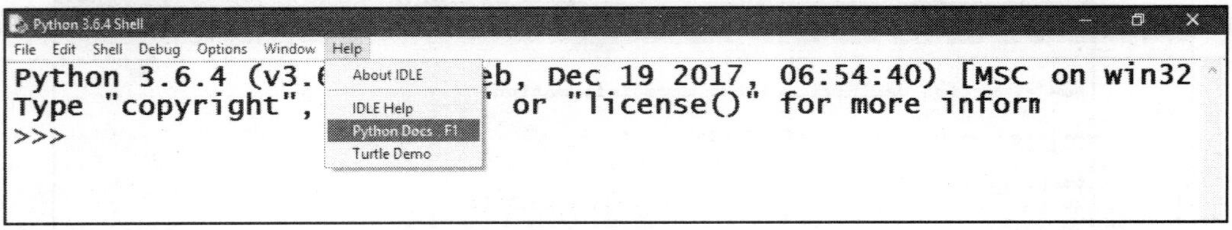

Figure 2.38: Getting Help from Python Documentation

It will display the Python 3.6.4 documentation help with all available features so that one can select any feature by clicking on it, as shown in Figure 2.39:

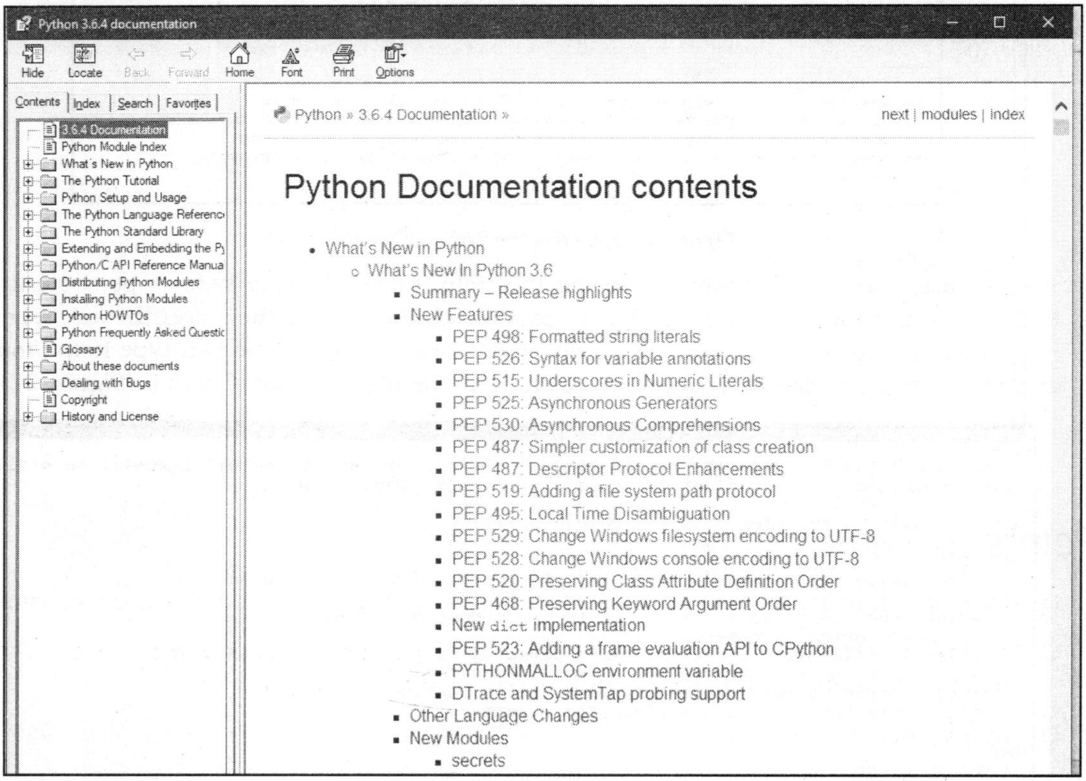

Figure 2.39: The Python documentation window

At the left side frame, we see contents out of which the following are very useful for us:

- The Python Tutorial
- The Python Language Reference
- The Python Standard Library

For example, click 'The Python Standard Library' to see the topic-wise comprehensive help on Python Standard Library. We can click on the close button (X) to close this help window, as shown in Figure 2.40:

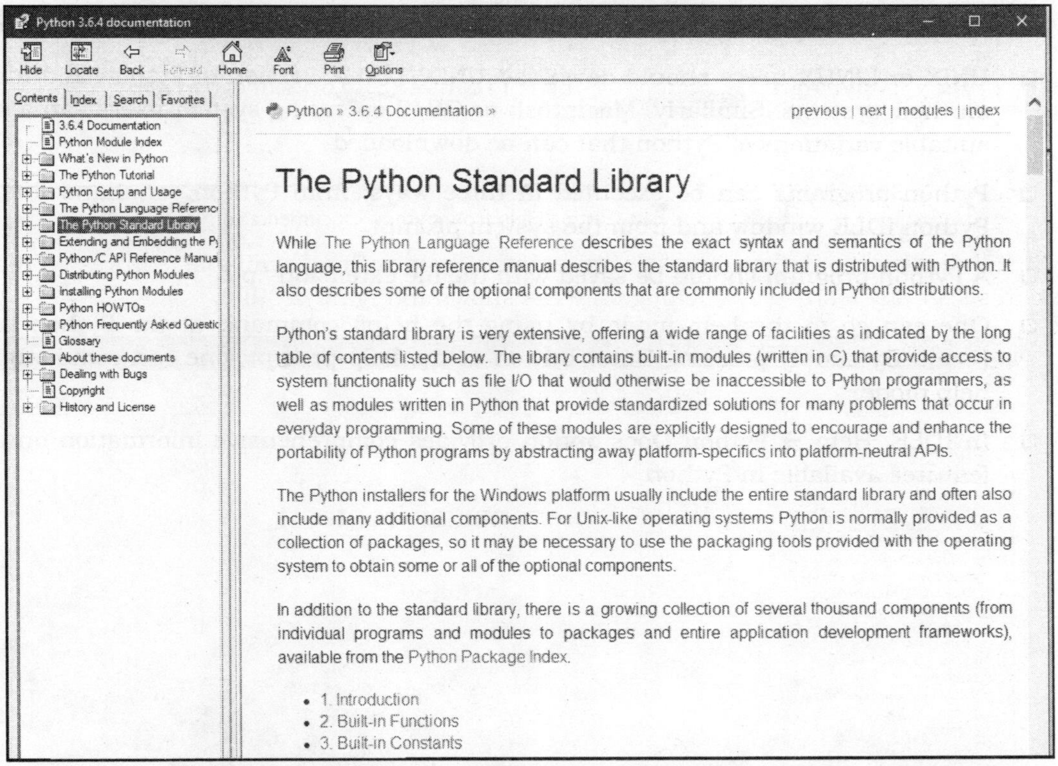

Figure 2.40: Going to Python Standard Library

Points to Remember

- Python is free software and can be downloaded freely from the python.org website.
- It is also possible to see the source code of Python developed by Python development team and modify and use it as per our requirements in our projects.
- In python.org, once we click on the Downloads tab, we can see all the available versions. We can select any version of Python and download it depending upon our operating system.
- We should select Python 32-bit version or 64-bit version depending whether our operating system is 32-bit or 64-bit.
- We should install Python 3.6.4 version along with the packages like numpy, pandas, xlrd and matplotlib.
- numpy is a package used to handle multidimensional arrays in Python.
- pandas is a package that is useful to analyze the data.
- xlrd is a package that is useful to extract data from Excel spreadsheet files.

- matplotlib is a package useful to represent data in the form of graphs and diagrams.
- UNIX or LINUX users should download UNIX/LINUX version of Python and install it on their systems. Similarly, Macintosh or OS/2 operating system users can also find suitable variations of Python that can be downloaded.
- Python programs can be executed in three ways: from Python command line, from Python IDLE window and from the system prompt.
- A Python program should be saved with the file extension '.py'.
- One can go to the help mode by using the help() command at the Python prompt (>>>). By simply pressing Enter button at the help prompt, one can come out of the help mode.
- In IDLE, Help → Python Docs option provides comprehensive information on all the features available in Python.

DATATYPES IN PYTHON

CHAPTER 3

We have already written a Python program to add two numbers and executed it. Let's now view the program once again here:

```
# First Python program to add two numbers
a = 10
b = 15
c = a + b
print("Sum= ", c)
```

When we compile this program using Python compiler, it converts the program source code into byte code instructions. This byte code is then converted into machine code by the interpreter inside the Python Virtual Machine (PVM). Finally, the machine code is executed by the processor in our computer and the result is produced as:

```
F:\PY>python first.py
Sum= 25
```

Observe the first line in the program. It starts with the # symbol. This is called the comment line. A comment is used to describe the features of a program. When we write a program, we may write some statements or create functions or classes, etc. in our program. All these things should be described using comments. When comments are written, not only our selves but also any programmer can easily understand our program. It means comments increase readability (understandability) of our programs. This is highly needed when we are working on a project. We should remember that project development is not a single man's task. It is a collective work from a team of professionals. Since a project is handled by several people, everyone in the project should be able to understand each and every program. This makes possible modifying and reusing of the programs. Hence, writing comments will make our programs clear to others.

Comments in Python

There are two types of comments in Python: single line comments and multi line comments.

Single line comments

These comments start with a hash symbol (#) and are useful to mention that the entire line till the end should be treated as comment. For example,

```
# To find sum of two numbers
a = 10  # store 10 into variable a
```

Here, the first line is starting with a # and hence the entire line is treated as a comment. In the second line, a = 10 is a statement. After this statement, # symbol starts the comment describing that the value 10 is stored into variable 'a'. The part of this line starting from # symbol to the end is treated as a comment.

Comments are non-executable statements. It means neither the Python compiler nor the PVM will execute them. Comments are for the purpose of understanding human beings and not for the compiler or PVM. Hence, they are called non-executable statements.

Multi line comments

When we want to mark several lines as comment, then writing # symbol in the beginning of every line will be a tedious job. For example,

```
# This is a program to find net salary of an employee
# based on the basic salary, provident fund, house rent allowance,
# dearness allowance and income tax.
```

Instead of starting every line with # symbol, we can write the previous block of code inside """ (triple double quotes) or ''' (triple single quotes) in the beginning and ending of the block as:

```
"""
This is a program to find net salary of an employee
based on the basic salary, provident fund, house rent allowance,
dearness allowance and income tax.
"""
```

Or,

```
'''
This is a program to find net salary of an employee
based on the basic salary, provident fund, house rent allowance,
dearness allowance and income tax.
'''
```

The triple double quotes (""") or triple single quotes (''') are called 'multi line comments' or 'block comments'. They are used to enclose a block of lines as comments.

Docstrings

In fact, Python supports only single line comments. Multi line comments are not available in Python. The triple double quotes or triple single quotes are actually not multi line comments but they are regular strings with the exception that they can span multiple lines. That means memory will be allocated to these strings internally. If these strings are not assigned to any variable, then they are removed from memory by the garbage collector and hence these can be used as comments.

So, using """ are ''' or not recommended for comments by Python people since they internally occupy memory and would waste time of the interpreter since the interpreter has to check them.

If we write strings inside """ or ''' and if these strings are written as first statements in a module, function, class or a method, then these strings are called *documentation strings* or *docstrings*. These docstrings are useful to create an API documentation file from a Python program. An API (Application Programming Interface) documentation file is a text file or html file that contains description of all the features of software, language or a product. When a new software is created, it is the duty of the developers to describe all the classes, modules, functions, etc. which are written in that software so that the user will be able to understand the software and use it in a proper way. These descriptions are provided in a separate file either as a text file or an html file. So, we can understand that the API documentation file is like a help file for the end user.

Let's take an example to understand how to create an API documentation file. The following Python program contains two simple functions. The first function is add() function that takes two numbers and displays their sum. The second one is message() function that displays a message "Welcome to Python". A function contains a group of statements and intends to perform a specific task. In Python, a function should start with the 'def' keyword. After that, we should write the function name along with parentheses as def add(). We will learn about functions fully in a later chapter.

Observe that the add(x,y) function calls a print() function that displays the sum of x and y. But it also contains documentation strings inside a pair of """. Similarly, the message() function which is the second function calls a print() function that displays the message "Welcome to Python". This function also contains documentation strings written inside a pair of '''. At the end of this program, we are calling these two functions. While calling the first function, we are passing two values 10 and 25 and calling it as add(10, 25). While calling the second function, we are not passing any value. We are calling it as message() only. Now, consider the following program:

```
# program with two functions
def add(x, y):
    """
    This function takes two numbers and finds their sum.
    It displays the sum as result.
    """
    print("Sum= ", (x+y))
```

```
def message():
    '''
    This function displays a message.
    This is a welcome message to the user.
    '''
    print("Welcome to Python")

# now call the functions
add(10, 25)
message()
```

After typing this program, save it as ex.py and then execute it as:

```
F:\PY>python ex.py
Sum= 35
Welcome to Python
```

This is the general way of executing any Python program. Now, we will execute this program once again to create API documentation file. For this purpose, we need a module *pydoc*. In the following command, we are using –m to represent a module and pydoc is the module name that is used by the python interpreter. After that –w indicates that an html file is to be created. The last word 'ex' represents the source file name.

```
F:\PY>python  -m  pydoc  -w  ex
Sum= 35
Welcome to Python
Wrote to ex.html
```

As understandable from the above lines, the output of the program is displayed and also the ex.html file is created. Open the ex.html file in any Web browser, as shown in Figure 3.1:

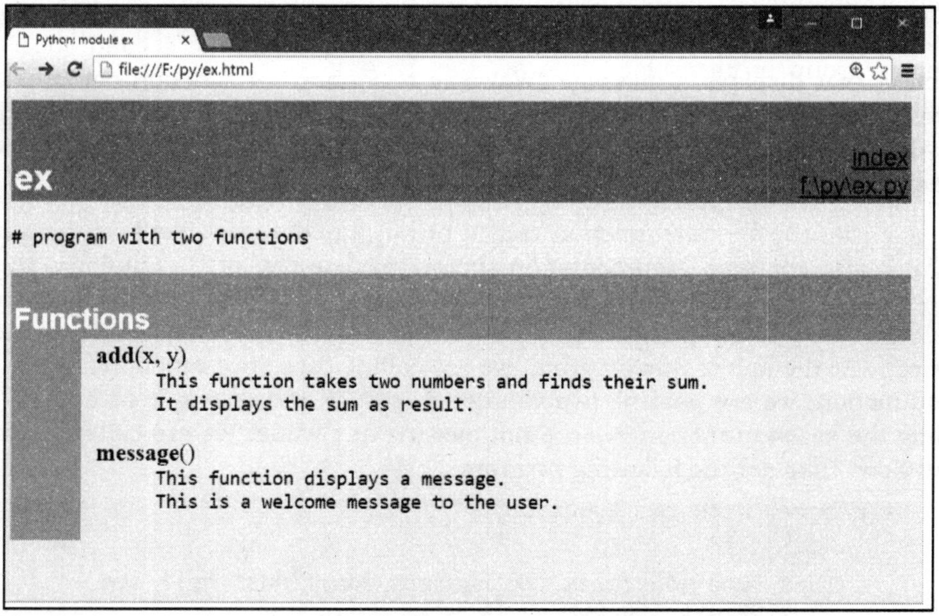

Figure 3.1: API Documentation File

After seeing Figure 3.1, we can understand that the API documentation file contains nothing but the names and the descriptions of the two functions written in our program. In this way, the API documentation file contains complete help on all the features including functions, classes, modules, etc.

After discussing about comments in Python, let's go through the following statements:

```
a = 10
b = 15
```

In the first statement, the value 10 is stored into the left side variable 'a'. Storage is done by the symbol '=' which is called *assignment operator*. In the second statement, the value 15 is stored into another variable 'b'. A variable can be imagined like a memory location where we can store data. The name given to a variable is called *identifier*. Identifiers represent names of variables, functions, objects or any such thing.

Depending upon the type of data stored into a variable, Python interpreter understands how much memory is to be allocated for that variable. Hence, we need not declare the datatype of the variable explicitly like we do in case of C or Java. For example, in C or Java we declare a variable as 'int' type as:

```
int a;     //declare a as int type variable
a = 10;  //store 10 into a
```

But, in Python we can simply write as:

```
a = 10
```

This creates a variable by the name 'a' and stores the value 10. Since we are storing 10 which is an integer, Python will understand that 'a' is of integer type variable and allocates memory required to store an integer value. On the other hand, if we store a string (a group of characters) into 'a', then Python will understand 'a' as string type variable and then allocates memory required to store the string.

How Python Sees Variables

In programming languages like C, Java and many other languages, the concept of variable is connected to memory location. In all languages, a variable is imagined as a storage box which can store some value. Suppose, we write a statement as:

```
a = 1;
```

Some memory is allocated with the name 'a' and there the value '1' is stored. Here, we can imagine the memory as a box or container that stores the value, as shown in Figure 3.2:

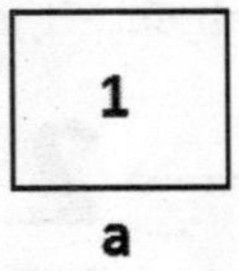

Figure 3.2: The effect of a = 1

In this way, for every variable we create, there will be a new box created with the variable name to store the value. If we change the value of the variable, then the box will be updated with the new value. For example, if we write:

```
a = 2;
```

then the new value '2' is stored into the same box, as shown in Figure 3.3:

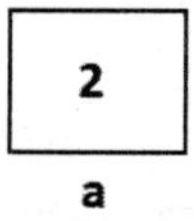

Figure 3.3: The effect of a = 2

When we assign one variable to another variable as:

```
int b = a;
```

A new memory box is created by the name 'b' and the value of the variable 'a' is copied into that box as shown in Figure 3.4:

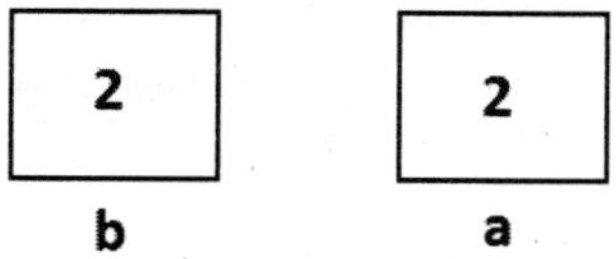

Figure 3.4: The effect of b = a;

This is how variables are visualized in other languages. However in Python, a variable is seen as a tag (or name) that is tied to some value. For example, the statement:

```
a = 1
```

means the value '1' is created first in memory and then a tag by the name 'a' is created to show that value as shown in Figure 3.5:

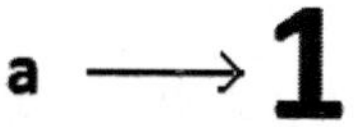

Figure 3.5: The effect of a = 1

Python considers the values (i.e. 1 or 2 etc.) as 'objects'. If we change the value of 'a' to a new value as:

```
a = 2
```

then the tag is simply changed to the new value (or object), as shown in Figure 3.6. Since the value '1' becomes unreferenced object, it is removed by garbage collector.

Figure 3.6: The effect of a = 2

Assigning one variable to another variable makes a new tag bound to the same value. For example,

```
b = a
```

Here, we are storing 'a' value into 'b'. A new tag 'b' will be created that refers to '2' as shown in Figure 3.7:

Figure 3.7: The effect of b = a

Let's understand that while other languages have variables, Python has 'tags' (or names) to represent the values. Compare Figure 3.4 and Figure 3.7. In Figure 3.4, there are two memory locations created to store two values. But in Figure 3.7, there is only one memory referenced by two names. It means Python is using memory efficiently. This is the actual way of understanding Python variables.

Datatypes in Python

A datatype represents the type of data stored into a variable or memory. The datatypes which are already available in Python language are called *Built-in* datatypes. The datatypes which can be created by the programmers are called *User-defined* datatypes.

Built-in datatypes

The built-in datatypes are of five types:

- None Type
- Numeric types
- Sequences
- Sets
- Mappings

The None Type

In Python, the 'None' datatype represents an object that does not contain any value. In languages like Java, it is called 'null' object. But in Python, it is called 'None' object.

In a Python program, maximum of only one 'None' object is provided. One of the uses of 'None' is that it is used inside a function as a default value of the arguments. When calling the function, if no value is passed, then the default value will be taken as 'None'. If some value is passed to the function, then that value is used by the function. In Boolean expressions, 'None' datatype represents 'False'.

Numeric Types

The numeric types represent numbers. There are three sub types:

- int
- float
- complex

int Datatype

The int datatype represents an integer number. An integer number is a number without any decimal point or fraction part. For example, 200, -50, 0, 9888998700, etc. are treated as integer numbers. Now, let's store an integer number -57 into a variable 'a'.

```
a = -57
```

Here, 'a' is called int type variable since it is storing -57 which is an integer value. In Python, there is no limit for the size of an int datatype. It can store very large integer numbers conveniently.

float Datatype

The float datatype represents floating point numbers. A floating point number is a number that contains a decimal point. For example, 0.5, -3.4567, 290.08, 0.001 etc. are called floating point numbers. Let's store a float number into a variable 'num' as:

```
num = 55.67998
```

Here num is called float type variable since it is storing floating point value. Floating point numbers can also be written in scientific notation where we use 'e' or 'E' to represent the power of 10. Here 'e' or 'E' represents 'exponentiation'. For example, the number 2.5×10^4 is written as 2.5E4. Such numbers are also treated as floating point numbers. For example,

```
x = 22.55e3
```

Here, the float value 22.55×10^3 is stored into the variable 'x'. The type of the variable 'x' will be internally taken as float type. The convenience in scientific notation is that it is possible to represent very big numbers using less memory.

Complex Datatype

A complex number is a number that is written in the form of a + bj or a + bJ. Here, 'a' represents the real part of the number and 'b' represents the imaginary part of the number. The suffix 'j' or 'J' after 'b' indicates the square root value of -1. The parts 'a' and 'b' may contain integers or floats. For example, 3+5j, -1-5.5J, 0.2+10.5J are all complex numbers. See the following statement:

```
c1 = -1-5.5J
```

Here, the complex number -1-5.5J is assigned to the variable ‘c1’. Hence, Python interpreter takes the datatype of the variable ‘c1’ as complex type.

We will write a Python program (Program 1) that adds two complex numbers and displays their sum. In this program, we store a complex number in a variable ‘c1’ and another complex number in another variable ‘c2’ and then add them. The result of addition is stored into ‘c3’ which is another complex type variable and then the value of ‘c3’ is displayed by the print() function.

Program

Program 1: A Python program to display the sum of two complex numbers.

```
# python program to add two complex numbers
c1 = 2.5+2.5J
c2 = 3.0-0.5J
c3 = c1 + c2
print("Sum= ", c3)
```

Output:

```
C:\>python add.py
Sum= (5.5+2j)
```

Representing Binary, Octal and Hexadecimal Numbers

A binary number should be written by prefixing 0b (zero and b) or 0B (zero and B) before the value. For example, 0b110110, 0B101010011 are treated as binary numbers. Hexadecimal numbers are written by prefixing 0x (zero and x) or 0X (zero and big X) before the value, as 0xA180 or 0X11fb91 etc. Similarly, octal numbers are indicated by prefixing 0o (zero and small o) or 0O (zero and then O) before the actual value. For example, 0O145 or 0o773 are octal values.

Converting the Datatypes Explicitly

Depending on the type of data, Python internally assumes the datatype for the variable. But sometimes, the programmer wants to convert one datatype into another type on his own. This is called *type conversion* or *coercion*. This is possible by mentioning the datatype with parentheses. For example, to convert a number into integer type, we can write int(num).

- int(x) is used to convert the number x into int type. See the example:

```
x = 15.56
int(x) # will display 15
```

- float(x) is used to convert x into float type. For example,

```
num = 15
float(num) # will display 15.0
```

- complex(x) is used to convert x into a complex number with real part x and imaginary part zero. For example,

```
n = 10
complex(n) # will display (10+0j)
```

- complex(x, y) is used to convert x and y into a complex number such that x will be the real part and y will be the imaginary part. For example,

```
a = 10
b = -5
complex(a, b) # will display (10-5j)
```

From the previous discussion, we can understand that int(x) is converting the datatype of x into int type and producing decimal integer number. So, we can use int(x) to convert a value from other number systems into our decimal number system. This is what we are trying to do in Program 2. In this program, we are going to convert binary, octal and hexadecimal numbers into decimal integers using type conversion.

Program

Program 2: A program to convert numbers from octal, binary and hexadecimal systems into decimal number system.

```
#  python program to convert into decimal number system
n1 = 0O17
n2 = 0B1110010
n3 = 0X1c2

n = int(n1)
print('Octal 17 = ', n)
n = int(n2)
print('Binary 1110010 = ', n)
n = int(n3)
print('Hexadecimal 1c2 = ', n)
```

Output:

```
C:\>python convert.py
Octal 17 =  15
Binary 1110010 =  114
Hexadecimal 1c2 =  450
```

There is a function in the form of int (string, base) that is useful to convert a string into a decimal integer. 'string' represents the string format of the number. It should contain integer number in string format. 'base' represents the base of the number system to be used for the string. For example, base 2 indicates binary number and base 16 indicates hexadecimal number. For example,

```
str = "1c2"   #  string str contains a hexadecimal number
n = int(str, 16)   # hence base is 16. Convert str into int
print(n)  # this will display 450
```

Program

Program 3: In this program, we are going to rewrite Program 2 using int() function to convert numbers from different number systems into decimal number system.

```
# python program to convert into decimal number system - v2.0
s1 = "17"
s2 = "1110010"
s3 = "1c2"

n = int(s1, 8)
print('Octal 17 = ', n)
n = int(s2, 2)
print('Binary 1110010 = ', n)
n = int(s3, 16)
print('Hexadecimal 1c2 = ', n)
```

Output:

```
C:\>python convert.py
Octal 17 =  15
Binary 1110010 =  114
Hexadecimal 1c2 =  450
```

We can also use functions bin() for converting a number into binary number system. The function oct() will convert a number into octal number system and the function hex() will convert a number into hexadecimal number system. See the following examples:

```
a = 10
b = bin(a)
print(b) # displays 0b1010

b = oct(a)
print(b) # displays 0o12

b = hex(a)
print(b) # displays 0xa
```

bool Datatype

The bool datatype in Python represents boolean values. There are only two boolean values True or False that can be represented by this datatype. Python internally represents True as 1 and False as 0. A blank string like "" is also represented as False. Conditions will be evaluated internally to either True or False. For example,

```
a = 10
b = 20
if(a<b): print("Hello") # displays Hello.
```

In the previous code, the condition a<b which is written after if - is evaluated to True and hence it will execute print("Hello").

```
a = 10>5  # here ‘a’ is treated as bool type variable
print(a) # displays True

a = 5>10
print(a) # displays False
```

```
True+True will display 2  # True is 1 and false is 0

True-False will display 1
```

Sequences in Python

Generally, a sequence represents a group of elements or items. For example, a group of integer numbers will form a sequence. There are six types of sequences in Python:

- str
- bytes
- bytearray
- list
- tuple
- range

str Datatype

In Python, str represents string datatype. A string is represented by a group of characters. Strings are enclosed in single quotes or double quotes. Both are valid.

```
str = “Welcome”  # here str is name of string type variable
str = ‘Welcome’  # here str is name of string type variable
```

We can also write strings inside """ (triple double quotes) or ''' (triple single quotes) to span a group of lines including spaces.

```
str1 = """This is a book on Python which
discusses all the topics of Core Python
in a very lucid manner."""

str2 = '''This is a book on Python which
discusses all the topics of Core Python
in a very lucid manner.'''
```

The triple double quotes or triple single quotes are useful to embed a string inside another string as shown below:

```
str = """This is 'Core Python' book."""
print(str) # will display: This is 'Core Python' book.

str = '''This is "Core Python" book.'''
print(str) # will display: This is "Core Python" book.
```

The slice operator represents square brackets [and] to retrieve pieces of a string. For example, the characters in a string are counted from 0 onwards. Hence, str[0] indicates the 0th character or beginning character in the string. See the examples below:

```
s = 'Welcome to Core Python'  # this is the original string
print(s)
Welcome to Core Python
```

```
print(s[0])  # display 0th character from s
W

print(s[3:7])  # display from 3rd to 6th characters
come

print(s[11:])  # display from 11th characters onwards till end
Core Python

print(s[-1])  # display first character from the end
n
```

The repetition operator is denoted by '*' symbol and useful to repeat the string for several times. For example s * n repeats the string for n times. See the example:

```
print(s*2)
Welcome to Core PythonWelcome to Core Python
```

bytes Datatype

The bytes datatype represents a group of byte numbers just like an array does. A byte number is any positive integer from 0 to 255 (inclusive). bytes array can store numbers in the range from 0 to 255 and it cannot even store negative numbers. For example,

```
elements = [10, 20, 0, 40, 15]  # this is a list of byte numbers
x = bytes(elements)  # convert the list into bytes array
print(x[0])   # display 0th element, i.e 10
```

We cannot modify or edit any element in the bytes type array. For example, x[0] = 55 gives an error. Here we are trying to replace 0th element (i.e. 10) by 55 which is not allowed.

Now, let's write a Python program (Program 4) to create a bytes type array with a group of elements and then display the elements using a for loop. In this program, we are using a for loop as:

```
for i in x: print(i)
```

It means, if 'i' is found in the array 'x' then display i value using print() function. Remember, we need not declare the datatypes of variables in Python. Hence, we need not tell which type of variable 'i' is. In the above loop, 'i' stores each element of the array 'x' and with every element, print(i) will be executed once. Hence, print(i) displays all elements of the array 'x'. We will discuss for loop in detail in the next chapter.

Program

Program 4: A Python program to create a byte type array, read and display the elements of the array.

```
# program to understand bytes type array
# create a list of byte numbers
elements = [10, 20, 0, 40, 15]

# convert the list into bytes type array
x = bytes(elements)
```

```
# retrieve elements from x using for loop and display
for i in x: print(i)
```

Output:

```
C:\>python bytes.py
10
20
0
40
15
```

bytearray Datatype

The bytearray datatype is similar to bytes datatype. The difference is that the bytes type array cannot be modified but the bytearray type array can be modified. It means any element or all the elements of the bytearray type can be modified. To create a bytearray type array, we can use the function bytearray as:

```
elements = [10, 20, 0, 40, 15]  # this is a list of byte numbers
x = bytearray(elements)  # convert the list into bytearray type array
print(x[0])   # display 0th element, i.e 10
```

We can modify or edit the elements of the bytearray. For example, we can write:

```
x[0] = 88  # replace 0th element by 88
x[1] = 99  # replace 1st element by 99
```

We will write program to create a bytearray type array and then modify the first two elements. Then we will display all the elements using a for loop. This can be seen in Program 5.

Program

Program 5: A Python program to create a bytearray type array and retrieve elements

```
# program to understand bytearray type array
# create a list of byte numbers
elements = [10, 20, 0, 40, 15]

# convert the list into bytearray type array
x = bytearray(elements)

# modify the first two elements of x
x[0] = 88
x[1] = 99

# retrieve elements from x using for loop and display
for i in x: print(i)
```

Output:

```
C:\>python bytearray.py
88
99
0
40
15
```

list Datatype

Lists in Python are similar to arrays in C or Java. A list represents a group of elements. The main difference between a list and an array is that a list can store different types of elements but an array can store only one type of elements. Also, lists can grow dynamically in memory. But the size of arrays is fixed and they cannot grow at runtime. Lists are represented using square brackets [ ] and the elements are written in [ ], separated by commas. For example,

```
list = [10, -20, 15.5, 'Vijay', "Mary"]
```

will create a list with different types of elements. The slicing operation like [0: 3] represents elements from 0th to 2nd positions, i.e. 10, 20, 15.5. Have a look at some of the operations on a list in the following IDLE window, as shown in Figure 3.8:

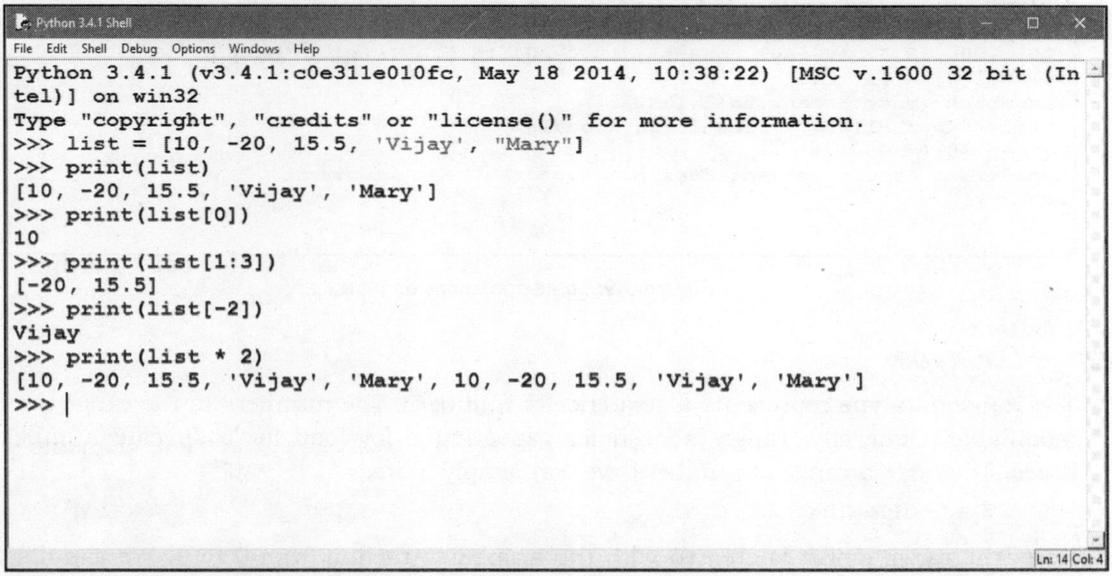

Figure 3.8: Some Operations on Lists

tuple Datatype

A tuple is similar to a list. A tuple contains a group of elements which can be of different types. The elements in the tuple are separated by commas and enclosed in parentheses ( ). Whereas the list elements can be modified, it is not possible to modify the tuple elements. That means a tuple can be treated as a read-only list. Let's create a tuple as:

```
tpl = (10, -20, 15.5, 'Vijay', "Mary")
```

The individual elements of the tuple can be referenced using square braces as tpl[0], tpl[1], tpl[2], ... Now, if we try to modify the 0th element as:

```
tpl[0] = 99
```

This will result in error. The slicing operations which can be done on lists are also valid in tuples. See the general operations on the tuple in Figure 3.9:

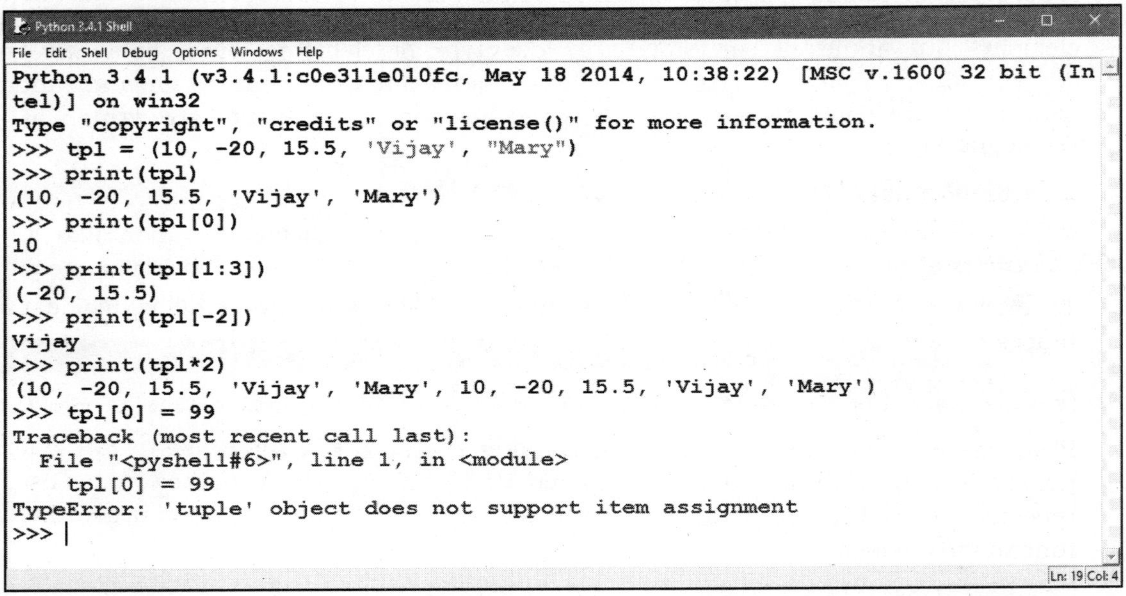


```
Python 3.4.1 (v3.4.1:c0e311e010fc, May 18 2014, 10:38:22) [MSC v.1600 32 bit (In
tel)] on win32
Type "copyright", "credits" or "license()" for more information.
>>> tpl = (10, -20, 15.5, 'Vijay', "Mary")
>>> print(tpl)
(10, -20, 15.5, 'Vijay', 'Mary')
>>> print(tpl[0])
10
>>> print(tpl[1:3])
(-20, 15.5)
>>> print(tpl[-2])
Vijay
>>> print(tpl*2)
(10, -20, 15.5, 'Vijay', 'Mary', 10, -20, 15.5, 'Vijay', 'Mary')
>>> tpl[0] = 99
Traceback (most recent call last):
  File "<pyshell#6>", line 1, in <module>
    tpl[0] = 99
TypeError: 'tuple' object does not support item assignment
>>> |
```

Figure 3.9: Some operations on tuples

range Datatype

The range datatype represents a sequence of numbers. The numbers in the range are not modifiable. Generally, range is used for repeating a for loop for a specific number of times. To create a range of numbers, we can simply write:

```
r = range(10)
```

Here, the range object is created with the numbers starting from 0 to 9. We can display these numbers using a for loop as:

```
for i in r: print(i)
```

The above statement will display numbers from 0 to 9. We can use a starting number, an ending number and a step value in the range object as:

```
r = range(30, 40, 2)
```

This will create a range object with a starting number 30 and an ending number 39. The step size is 2. It means the numbers in the range will increase by 2 every time. So, the for loop

```
for i in r: print(i)
```

will display numbers: 30, 32, 34, 36, 38. Let's create a list with a range of numbers from 0 to 9 as:

```
lst = list(range(10))
print(lst) # will display: [0, 1, 2, 3, 4, 5, 6, 7, 8, 9]
```

Sets

A set is an unordered collection of elements much like a set in Mathematics. The order of elements is not maintained in the sets. It means the elements may not appear in the same order as they are entered into the set. Moreover, a set does not accept duplicate elements. There are two sub types in sets:

- set datatype
- frozenset datatype

set Datatype

To create a set, we should enter the elements separated by commas inside curly braces {}.

```
s = {10, 20, 30, 20, 50}
print(s) # may display {50, 10, 20, 30}
```

Please observe that the set 's' is not maintaining the order of the elements. We entered the elements in the order 10, 20, 30, 20 and 50. But it is showing another order. Also, we repeated the element 20 in the set, but it has stored only one 20. We can use the set() function to create a set as:

```
ch = set("Hello")
print(ch) # may display {'H', 'e', 'l', 'o'}
```

Here, a set 'ch' is created with the characters H,e,l,o. Since a set does not store duplicate elements, it will not store the second 'l'. We can convert a list into a set using the set() function as:

```
lst = [1,2,5,4,3]
s = set(lst)
print(s) # may display {1, 2, 3, 4, 5}
```

Since sets are unordered, we cannot retrieve the elements using indexing or slicing operations. For example, the following statements will give error messages:

```
print(s[0])   # indexing, display 0th element
print(s[0:2])  # slicing, display from 0 to 1st elements
```

The update() method is used to add elements to a set as:

```
s.update([50,60])
print(s) # may display {1, 2, 3, 4, 5, 50, 60}
```

On the other hand, the remove() method is used to remove any particular element from a set as:

```
s.remove(50)
print(s) # may display {1, 2, 3, 4, 5, 60}
```

frozenset Datatype

The frozenset datatype is same as the set datatype. The main difference is that the elements in the set datatype can be modified; whereas, the elements of frozenset cannot be modified. We can create a frozenset by passing a set to frozenset() function as:

```
s = {50,60,70,80,90}
print(s) # may display {80, 90, 50, 60, 70}

fs = frozenset(s)  # create frozenset fs
print(fs) # may display frozenset({80, 90, 50, 60, 70})
```

Another way of creating a frozenset is by passing a string (a group of characters) to the frozenset() function as:

```
fs = frozenset("abcdefg")
print(fs) # may display frozenset({'e', 'g', 'f', 'd', 'a', 'c', 'b'})
```

However, update() and remove() methods will not work on frozensets since they cannot be modified or updated.

Mapping Types

A map represents a group of elements in the form of key value pairs so that when the key is given, we can retrieve the value associated with it. The *dict* datatype is an example for a map. The 'dict' represents a 'dictionary' that contains pairs of elements such that the first element represents the key and the next one becomes its value. The key and its value should be separated by a colon (:) and every pair should be separated by a comma. All the elements should be enclosed inside curly brackets { }.

We can create a dictionary by typing the roll numbers and names of students. Here, roll numbers are keys and names will become values. We write these key value pairs inside curly braces as:

```
d = {10: 'Kamal', 11: 'Pranav', 12:  'Hasini', 13: 'Anup', 14:
'Reethu'}
```

Here, d is the name of the dictionary. 10 is the key and its associated value is 'Kamal'. The next key is 11 and its value is 'Pranav'. Similarly 12 is the key and 'Hasini' is it value. 13 is the key and 'Anup' is the value and 14 is the key and 'Reethu' is the value.

We can create an empty dictionary without any elements as:

```
d = {}
```

Later, we can store the key and values into d as:

```
d[10] = 'Kamal'
d[11] = 'Pranav'
```

In the preceding statements, 10 represents the key and 'Kamal' is its value. Similarly, 11 represents the key and its value is 'Pranav'. Now, if we write

```
print(d)
```

It will display the dictionary as:

```
{10: 'Kamal', 11: 'Pranav'}
```

We can perform various operations on dictionaries. To retrieve value upon giving the key, we can simply mention d[key]. To retrieve only keys from the dictionary, we can use the method keys() and to get only values, we can use the method values().

We can update the value of a key, as: d[key] = newvalue. We can delete a key and corresponding value, using del module. For example del d[11] will delete a key with 11 and its value. Figure 3.10 demonstrates these operations:

```
Python 3.4.1 (v3.4.1:c0e311e010fc, May 18 2014, 10:38:22) [MSC v.1600 32 bit (In
tel)] on win32
Type "copyright", "credits" or "license()" for more information.
>>> d = {10:'Kamal', 11:'Pranav', 12: 'Hasini', 13:'Anup', 14:'Reethu'}
>>> print(d)
{10: 'Kamal', 11: 'Pranav', 12: 'Hasini', 13: 'Anup', 14: 'Reethu'}
>>> print(d[11])
Pranav
>>> print(d.keys())
dict_keys([10, 11, 12, 13, 14])
>>> print(d.values())
dict_values(['Kamal', 'Pranav', 'Hasini', 'Anup', 'Reethu'])
>>> d[10] = 'Hareesh'
>>> print(d)
{10: 'Hareesh', 11: 'Pranav', 12: 'Hasini', 13: 'Anup', 14: 'Reethu'}
>>> del d[11]
>>> print(d)
{10: 'Hareesh', 12: 'Hasini', 13: 'Anup', 14: 'Reethu'}
>>>
```

Figure 3.10: Some Operations on Dictionaries

Literals in Python

A *literal* is a constant value that is stored into a variable in a program. Observe the following statement:

```
a = 15
```

Here, 'a' is the variable into which the constant value '15' is stored. Hence, the value 15 is called 'literal'. Since 15 indicates integer value, it is called 'integer literal'. The following are different types of literals in Python:

- Numeric literals
- Boolean literals
- String literals

Numeric Literals

These literals represent numbers. Please observe the different types of numeric literals available in Python, as shown in Table 3.1:

Table 3.1: Numeric Literals

Examples	Literal name
450, -15	Integer literal
3.14286, -10.6, 1.25E4	Float literal
0x5A1C	Hexadecimal literal
0557	Octal literal
0B110101	Binary literal
18+3J	Complex literal

Boolean Literals

Boolean literals are the True or False values stored into a bool type variable.

String Literals

A group of characters is called a string literal. These string literals are enclosed in single quotes (') or double quotes (") or triple quotes (''' or """). In Python, there is no difference between single quoted strings and double quoted strings. Single or double quoted strings should end in the same line as:

```
s1 = 'This is first Indian book'
s2 = "Core Python"
```

When a string literal extends beyond a single line, we should go for triple quotes as:

```
s1 = '''This is first Indian book on
     Core Python exploring all important
     and useful features'''

s2 = """This is first Indian book on
     Core Python exploring all important
     and useful features"""
```

In the preceding examples, the strings have taken up to 3 lines. Hence, we inserted them inside triple single quotes (''') or triple double quotes ("""). When a string spans more than one line adding backslash (\ ) will join the next string to it. For example,

```
str = "This is first line and \
this will be continued with the first line"
print(str)
This is first line and this will be continued with the first line
```

We can use escape characters like \n inside a string literal. For example,

```
str = "This is \nPython"
print(str)
This is
Python
```

Escape characters escape the normal meaning and are useful to perform a different task. When a \n is written, it will throw the cursor to the new line. Table 3.2 gives some important escape characters:

Table 3.2: Important Escape Characters in Strings

Escape character	Meaning
\	New line continuation
\\	Display a single \
\’	Display a single quote
\”	Display a double quote
\b	backspace
\r	Enter
\t	Horizontal tab space
\v	Vertical tab
\n	New line

Determining the Datatype of a Variable

To know the datatype of a variable or object, we can use the type() function. For example, type(a) displays the datatype of the variable ‘a’.

```
a = 15
print(type(a))
<class 'int'>
```

Since we are storing an integer number 15 into variable ‘a’, the type of ‘a’ is assumed by the Python interpreter as ‘int’. Observe the last line. It shows class ‘int’. It means the variable ‘a’ is an object of the class ‘int’. It means ‘int’ is treated as a class. Every datatype is treated as an object internally by Python. In fact, every datatype, function, method, class, module, lists, sets, etc. are all objects in Python, as shown in Figure 3.11:

```
Python 3.4.1 (v3.4.1:c0e311e010fc, May 18 2014, 10:38:22) [MSC v.1600 32 bit (In
tel)] on win32
Type "copyright", "credits" or "license()" for more information.
>>> a = 15
>>> print(type(a))
<class 'int'>
>>> a = 15.5
>>> print(type(a))
<class 'float'>
>>> s = 'Hello'
>>> print(type(s))
<class 'str'>
>>> print(type("Hai"))
<class 'str'>
>>> lst = [1, 2, 3, 4]
>>> print(type(lst))
<class 'list'>
>>> t = (1, 2, 3, 4)
>>> print(type(t))
<class 'tuple'>
>>> s = {1, 2, 3, 4}
>>> print(type(s))
<class 'set'>
>>>
```

Figure 3.11: All datatypes are class objects in Python

What about Characters

Languages like C and Java contain char datatype that represents a single character. Python does not have a char datatype to represent individual characters. It has str datatype which represents strings. We know a string is composed of several characters. Hence, when we think of a character, we should think of it as an element in a string. In the following statements, we are assigning a single character 'A' to a variable 'ch'. Then we find out the type of the 'ch' variable using the type() function.

```
ch = 'A'
print(type(ch))
<class 'str'>
```

See that the type of 'ch' is displayed as 'str' type. So, there is no concept like char datatype in Python. To work with strings, we have to access the individual characters of a string using index or position number. Suppose there is a string str where we stored a string literal 'Bharat' as:

```
str = 'Bharat'
print(str[0])
B
```

In the preceding example, the str[0] represents the 0th character, i.e. 'B'. Similarly, str[1] represents 'h' and str[2] represents 'a' and so on. To retrieve all the characters using a for loop, we can write:

```
for i in str: print(i)
```

and it will display the characters as:

```
B
h
a
r
a
t
```

However, some of the useful methods in case of strings can also be used for characters. For example, isupper() is a method that tests whether a string is uppercase or lowercase. It returns True if the string is uppercase otherwise False. This method can be used on a character to know whether it is uppercase letter or not. Let's check the case of first two letters in 'Bharat' as:

```
str[0].isupper()   # checking if 'B' is capital letter or not
True

str[1].isupper()  # checking if 'h' is capital letter or not
False
```

User-defined Datatypes

The datatypes which are created by the programmers are called 'user-defined' datatypes. For example, an array, a class, or a module is user-defined datatypes. We will discuss about these datatypes in the later chapters.

Constants in Python

A constant is similar to a variable but its value cannot be modified or changed in the course of the program execution. We know that the variable value can be changed whenever required. But that is not possible for a constant. Once defined, a constant cannot allow changing its value. For example, in Mathematics, 'pi' value is 22/7 which never changes and hence it is a constant. In languages like C and Java, defining constants is possible. But in Python, that is not possible. A programmer can indicate a variable as constant by writing its name in all capital letters. For example, MAX_VALUE is a constant. But its value can be changed.

Identifiers and Reserved words

An identifier is a *name* that is given to a variable or function or class etc. Identifiers can include letters, numbers, and the underscore character (_). They should always start with a nonnumeric character. Special symbols such as ?, #, $, %, and @ are not allowed in identifiers. Some examples for identifiers are salary, name11, gross_income, etc.

We should also remember that Python is a case sensitive programming language. It means capital letters and small letters are identified separately by Python. For example, the names 'num' and 'Num' are treated as different names and hence represent different variables. Figure 3.12 shows examples of a variable, an operator and a literal:

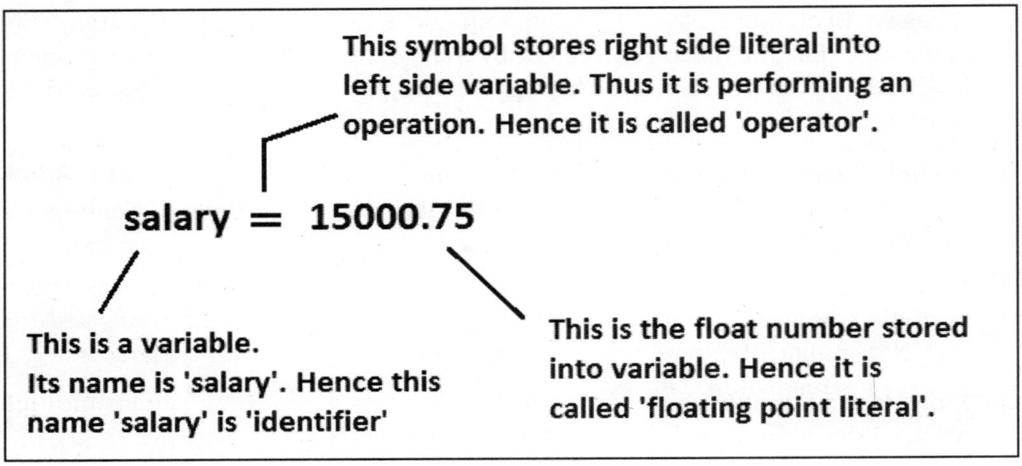

Figure 3.12: Variable, Operator and Literal

Reserved words are the words that are already reserved for some particular purpose in the Python language. The names of these reserved words should not be used as identifiers. The following are the reserved words available in Python:

and	del	from	nonlocal	try
as	elif	global	not	while
assert	else	if	or	with
break	except	import	pass	yield
class	exec	in	print	False
continue	finally	is	raise	True
def	for	lambda	return	

Naming Conventions in Python

Python developers made some suggestions to the programmers regarding how to write names in the programs. The rules related to writing names of packages, modules, classes, variables, etc. are called *naming conventions.* The following naming conventions should be followed:

- **Packages:** Package names should be written in all lower case letters. When multiple words are used for a name, we should separate them using an underscore (_).

- **Modules:** Modules names should be written in all lower case letters. When multiple words are used for a name, we should separate them using an underscore (_).
- **Classes:** Each word of a class name should start with a capital letter. This rule is applicable for the classes created by us. Python's built-in class names use all lowercase words. When a class represents exception, then its name should end with a word 'Error'.
- **Global variables or Module-level variables:** Global variables names should be all lower case letters. When multiple words are used for a name, we should separate them using an underscore (_).
- **Instance variables:** Instance variables names should be all lower case letters. When multiple words are used for a name, we should separate them using an underscore (_). Non-public instance variable name should begin with an underscore.
- **Functions:** Function names should be all lower case letters. When multiple words are used for a name, we should separate them using an underscore (_).
- **Methods:** Method names should be all lower case letters. When multiple words are used for a name, we should separate them using an underscore (_).
- **Method arguments:** In case of instance methods, their first argument name should be 'self'. In case of class methods, their first argument name should be 'cls'.
- **Constants:** Constants names should be written in all capital letters. If a constant has several words, then each word should be separated by an underscore (_).
- **Non accessible entities**: Some variables, functions and methods are not accessible outside and they should be used as they are in the program. Such entities names are written with two double quotes before and two double quotes after. For example, __init__(self) is a function used in a class to initialize variables.

Points to Remember

- A variable represents a memory location where some data can be stored.
- Python has only single line comments starting with a hash symbol (#).
- Triple single quotes (''') or triple doubles quotes (""") can be used to create multi line comments.
- Docstrings are the strings written inside triple single quotes or triple double quotes and as first statements in a function, class or a method. These docstrings are useful to create API documentation file that contains the description of all features of a program or software.
- A datatype represents the type of data stored into a variable. The data stored into the variable is called literal.

- There are four built-in datatypes in Python. They are numeric types, sequences, sets and mappings.
- A binary literal is represented using 0b or 0B in the beginning of a number.
- An octal literal is represented using 0o or 0O in the beginning of a number.
- If a number starts with 0x or 0X, then it is considered as a hexadecimal number.
- The 'bool' datatype represents either True or False. True is represented by 1 and False is represented by 0.
- A string literal can be enclosed in single quotes or double quotes. When a string spans more than single line, then we need to enclose it inside triple single quotes (''') or triple double quotes (""").
- A list is a dynamically growing array that can store different types of elements. Lists are written using square brackets [ ].
- A tuple is similar to a list but its elements cannot be modified. A tuple uses parentheses ( ) to enclose its elements.
- The 'range' datatype represents sequence of numbers and is generally used to repeat a for loop.
- A set is an unordered collection of elements. A set uses curly braces { } to enclose its elements.
- A frozenset is similar to a set but its elements cannot be modified.
- A 'dict' datatype represents a group of elements written in the form of several key-value pairs such that when the key is given, its corresponding value can be obtained.
- We can use the type() function to determine the datatype of a variable.
- Python does not have a datatype to represent single character.
- A constant represents a fixed value that cannot be changed. Defining constants is not possible in Python.
- An identifier is a name that is given to a variable, function, class, etc.
- The rules related to writing names for packages, modules, classes, functions, variables, etc., are called naming conventions.

CHAPTER 4

OPERATORS IN PYTHON

The general purpose of a program is to accept data and perform some operations on the data. The data in the program is stored in variables. The next question is how to perform operations on the data. For example, when a programmer wants to add two numbers, he can simply type ' + ' symbol. This symbol performs the addition operation. Such symbols are called *operators*. Let's now learn more about these types of operators.

Operator

An operator is a symbol that performs an operation. An operator acts on some variables called *operands*. For example, if we write a + b, the operator ' + ' is acting on two operands 'a' and 'b'. If an operator acts on a single variable, it is called *unary* operator. If an operator acts on two variables, it is called *binary* operator. If an operator acts on three variables, then it is called *ternary* operator. This is one type of classification. We can classify the operators depending upon their nature, as shown below:

- Arithmetic operators
- Assignment operators
- Unary minus operator
- Relational operators
- Logical operators
- Boolean operators
- Bitwise operators

- Membership operators
- Identity operators

Arithmetic Operators

These operators are used to perform basic arithmetic operations like addition, subtraction, division, etc.

There are seven arithmetic operators available in Python. Since these operators act on two operands, they are called 'binary operators' also. Let's assume a = 13 and b = 5 and see the effect of various arithmetic operators in the Table 4.1:

Table 4.1: Arithmetic Operators in Python

Operator	Meaning	Example	Result
+	Addition operator. Adds two values.	a+b	18
-	Subtraction operator. Subtracts one value from another.	a-b	8
*	Multiplication operator. Multiplies values on either side of the operator.	a*b	65
/	Division operator. Divides left operand by the right operand.	a/b	2.6
%	Modulus operator. Gives remainder of division.	a%b	3
**	Exponent operator. Calculates exponential power value. a ** b gives the value of a to the power of b.	a**b	371293
//	Integer division. This is also called Floor division. Performs division and gives only integer quotient.	a//b	2

When there is an expression that contains several arithmetic operators, we should know which operation is done first and which operation is done next. In such cases, the following order of evaluation is used:

1. First parentheses are evaluated.
2. Exponentiation is done next.
3. Multiplication, division, modulus and floor divisions are at equal priority.
4. Addition and subtraction are done afterwards.
5. Finally, assignment operation is performed.

Let's take a sample expression: d = (x+y)*z**a//b+c. Assume the values of variables as: x=1; y=2; z=3; a=2; b=2; c=3. Then, the given expression d = (1+2)*3**2//2+3 will evaluate as:

1. First parentheses are evaluated. d = 3*3**2//2+3.
2. Exponentiation is done next. d = 3*9//2+3.

3. Multiplication, division, modulus and floor divisions are at equal priority. d = 27//2+3 and then d = 13+3.
4. Addition and subtraction are done afterwards. d = 16.
5. Finally, assignment is performed. The value 16 is now stored into 'd'.

Hence, the total value of the expression becomes 16 which is stored in the variable 'd'.

Using Python Interpreter as Calculator

It is interesting to know that we can use Python interpreter as a simple calculator that can perform basic arithmetic calculations. Open Python IDLE graphics window and type some arithmetic operations, as shown in Figure 4.1:

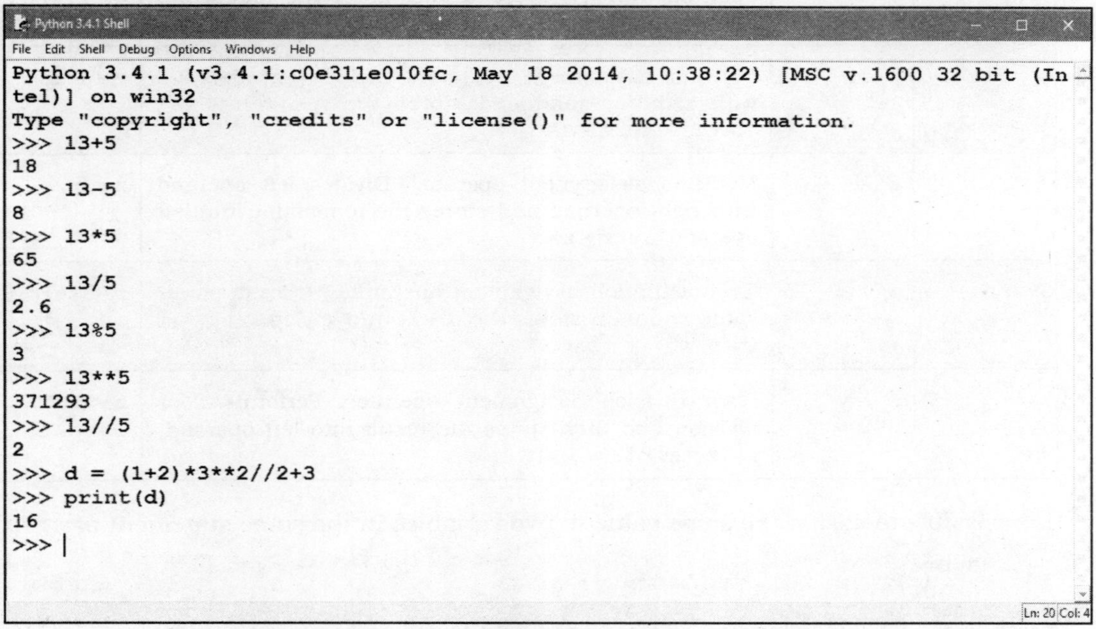

Figure 4.1: Python Interpreter as Calculator

Assignment Operators

These operators are useful to store the right side value into a left side variable. They can also be used to perform simple arithmetic operations like addition, subtraction, etc., and then store the result into a variable. These operators are shown in Table 4.2. In Table 4.2, let's assume the values x = 20, y = 10 and z = 5:

Table 4.2: Assignment Operators

Operator	Example	Meaning	Result
=	z = x+y	Assignment operator. Stores right side value into left side variable, i.e. x+y is stored into z.	z = 30
+=	z+=x	Addition assignment operator. Adds right operand to the left operand and stores the result into left operand, i.e. z = z+x.	z = 25
-=	z-=x	Subtraction assignment operator. Subtracts right operand from left operand and stores the result into left operand, i.e. z = z-x.	z = -15
*=	z*=x	Multiplication assignment operator. Multiplies right operand with left operand and stores the result into left operand, i.e. z = z *x.	z = 100
/=	z/=x	Division assignment operator. Divides left operand with right operand and stores the result into left operand, i.e. z = z/x.	z = 0.25
%=	z%=x	Modulus assignment operator. Divides left operand with right operand and stores the remainder into left operand, i.e. z = z%x.	z = 5
**=	z**=y	Exponentiation assignment operator. Performs power value and then stores the result into left operand, i.e. z = z**y.	z= 9765625
//=	z//=y	Floor division assignment operator. Performs floor division and then stores the result into left operand, i.e. z = z// y.	z = 0

It is possible to assign the same value to two variables in the same statement as:

```
a=b=1
print(a, b) # will display 1 1
```

Another example is where we can assign different values to two variables as:

```
a=1; b=2
print(a, b) # will display 1 2
```

The same can be done using the following statement:

```
a, b = 1, 2
print(a, b) # will display 1 2
```

A word of caution: Python does not have increment operator (++) and decrement operator (--) that are available in C and Java.

Unary Minus Operator

The unary minus operator is denoted by the symbol minus (-). When this operator is used before a variable, its value is negated. That means if the variable value is positive, it will be converted into negative and vice versa. For example, consider the following statements:

```
n = 10
print(-n) # displays -10

num = -10
num = - num
print(num) # displays 10
```

Relational Operators

Relational operators are used to compare two quantities. We can understand whether two values are same or which one is bigger or which one is lesser, etc. using these operators. These operators will result in True or False depending on the values compared, as shown in Table 4.3. In this table, we are assuming a =1 and b = 2.

Table 4.3: Relational Operators

Operator	Example	Meaning	Result
>	a>b	Greater than operator. If the value of left operand is greater than the value of right operand, it gives True else it gives False.	False
>=	a>=b	Greater than or equal operator. If the value of left operand is greater or equal than that of right operand, it gives True else False.	False
<	a<b	Less than operator. If the value of left operand is less than the value of right operand, it gives True else it gives False.	True
<=	a<=b	Less than or equal operator. If the value of left operand is lesser or equal than that of right operand, it gives True else False.	True
==	a==b	Equals operator. If the value of left operand is equal to the value of right operand, it gives True else False.	False
!=	a != b	Not equals operator. If the value of the left operand is not equal to the value of right operand, it returns True else it returns False.	True

Relational operators are generally used to construct conditions in if statements. For example,

```
a=1; b=2
if (a>b):
    print("Yes")
else:
    print("No")
```

will display 'No'. Observe the expression (a>b) written after if. This is called a 'condition'. When this condition becomes True, if statement will display 'Yes' and if it becomes False, then it will display 'No'. In this case, (1>2) is False and hence 'No' will be displayed.

Relational operators can be chained. It means, a single expression can hold more than one relational operator. For example,

```
x=15
10<x<20  # displays True
```

Here, 10 is less than 15 is True, and then 15 is less than 20 is True. Since both the conditions are evaluated to True, the result will be True.

```
10>=x<20 # displays False
```

Here, 10 is greater than or equal to 15 is False. But 15 is less than 20 is True. Since we get False and True, the result will be False.

```
10<x>20 # displays False
```

Here, 10 is less than 15 is True. But 15 is greater than 20 is False. Since we are getting True and False, the total result will be False. So, the point is this: in the chain of relational operators, if we get all True, then only the final result will be True. If any comparison yields False, then we get False as the final result. Thus,

```
1<2<3<4 # will give True

1<2>3<4 # will give False

4>2>=2>1 # will give True
```

Logical Operators

Logical operators are useful to construct compound conditions. A compound condition is a combination of more than one simple condition. Each of the simple condition is evaluated to True or False and then the decision is taken to know whether the total condition is True or False. We should keep in mind that in case of logical operators, False indicates 0 and True indicates any other number. There are 3 logical operators as shown in Table 4.4. Let's take x = 1 and y=2 in this table.

Table 4.4: Logical Operators

Operator	Example	Meaning	Result
And	x and y	And operator. If x is False, it returns x, otherwise it returns y.	2
Or	x or y	Or operator. If x is False, it returns y, otherwise it returns x.	1
Not	not x	Not operator. If x is False, it returns True, otherwise True.	False

Let's take some statements to understand the effect of logical operators.

```
x = 100
y = 200
print(x and y)  # will display 200

print(x or y)  # will display 100

print (not x) # will display False

x=1;  y=2; z=3
if(x<y and y<z): print('Yes')
else: print('No')
```

In the above statement, observe the compound condition after if. That is x <y and y<z. This is a combination of two simple conditions, x<y and y<z. When 'and' is used, the total condition will become True only if both the conditions are True. Since both the conditions became True, we will get 'Yes' as output. Observe another statement below:

```
if(x>y or y<z): print('Yes')
else: print('No')
```

Here, x>y is False but y<z is True. When using 'or' if any one condition is True, it will take the total compound condition as 'True' and hence it will display 'Yes'.

Boolean Operators

We know that there are two 'bool' type literals. They are True and False. Boolean operators act upon 'bool' type literals and they provide 'bool' type output. It means the result provided by Boolean operators will be again either True or False. There are three Boolean operators as mentioned in Table 4.5. Let's take x = True and y = False in Table 4.5:

Table 4.5: Boolean Operators

Operator	Example	Meaning	Result
and	x and y	Boolean and operator. If both x and y are True, then it returns True, otherwise False.	False
or	x or y	Boolean or operator. If either x or y is True, then it returns True, else False.	True
not	not x	Boolean not operator. If x is True, it returns False, else True.	False

In Figure 4.2, we can observe the effect of Boolean operators:

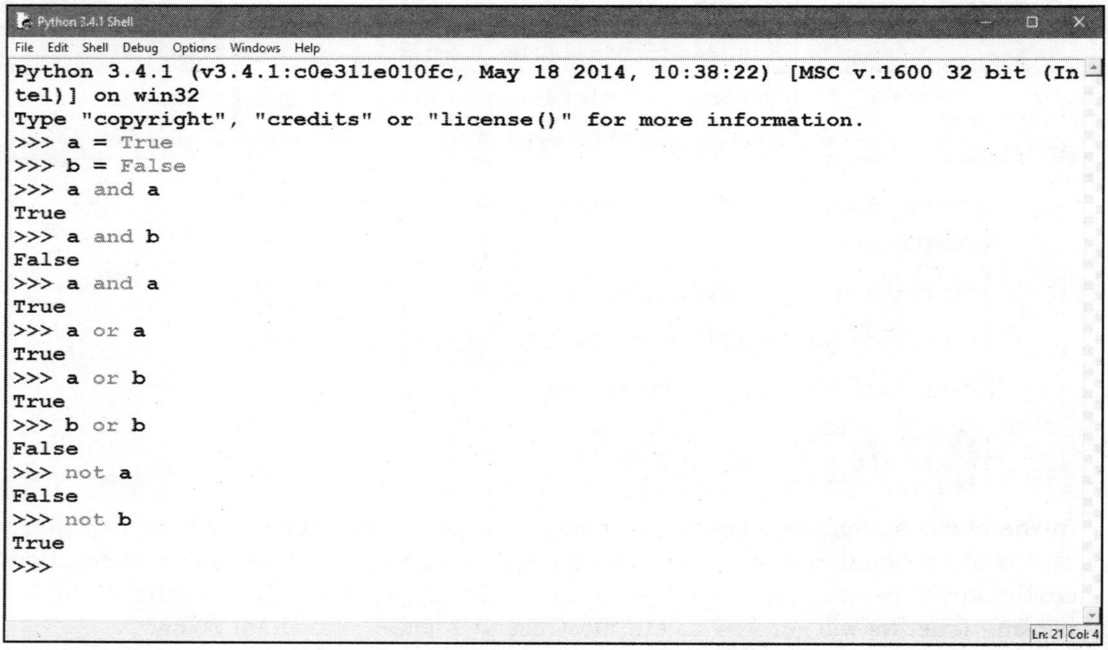

Figure 4.2: Boolean Operators and Their Usage

Bitwise Operators

These operators act on individual bits (0 and 1) of the operands. We can use bitwise operators directly on binary numbers or on integers also. When we use these operators on integers, these numbers are converted into bits (binary number system) and then bitwise operators act upon those bits. The results given by these operators are always in the form of integers.

We use decimal number system in our daily life. This number system consists of 10 digits from 0 to 9. We count all numbers using these 10 digits only. But in case of binary number system that is used by computers internally, there are only 2 digits, i.e. 0 and 1 which are called *bits* (binary digits). All values are represented only using these two bits. It is possible to convert a decimal number into binary number and vice versa.

Example 1: Converting 45 into binary number system.

Rule: Divide the number successively by 2 and take the remainders from bottom to top, as shown in Figure 4.3. The decimal number 45 is represented as 101101 in binary. If we use 8 bit representation, we can write it as: 0010 1101.

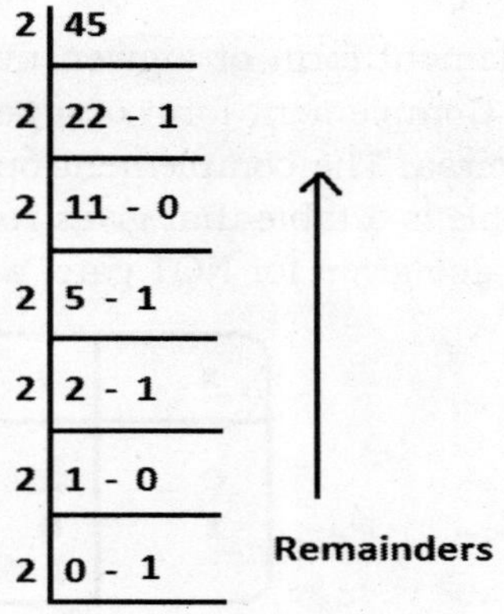

Figure 4.3: Converting into Binary

Example 2: Converting binary number 0010 1101 into decimal number.

Rule: Multiply the individual bits by the powers of 2 and take the sum of the products, as shown in Figure 4.4. Here, the sum is coming to 45. So 0010 1101 in binary is equal to 45 in decimal number system.

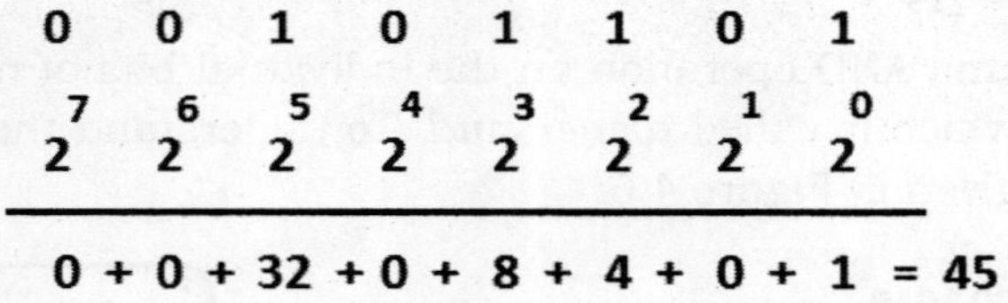

Figure 4.4: Converting from Binary to Decimal

There are 6 types of bitwise operators as shown below:

- Bitwise Complement operator (~)
- Bitwise AND operator (&)
- Bitwise OR operator (|)
- Bitwise XOR operator (^)
- Bitwise Left shift operator (<<)
- Bitwise Right shift operator (>>)

We will discuss each of these operators one by one.

Bitwise Complement Operator (~)

This operator gives the complement form of a given number. This operator symbol is ~, which is pronounced as *tilde*. Complement form of a positive number can be obtained by changing 0's as 1's and vice versa. The complement operation is performed by NOT gate circuit in electronics. Truth table is a table that gives relationship between the inputs and the output. The truth table is also given for NOT gate, as shown in Figure 4.5:

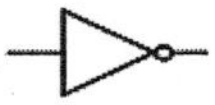

NOT gate

x	y
0	1
1	0

truth table for NOT gate

Figure 4.5: NOT gate that Performs Complement of Bits

```
If x = 10, find the ~x value.
x = 10 = 0000 1010.
```

By changing 0's as 1's and vice versa, we get 1111 0101. This is nothing but -11(in decimal). So, ~x = -11.

Bitwise AND Operator (&)

This operator performs AND operation on the individual bits of numbers. The symbol for this operator is &, which is called *ampersand*. To understand the bitwise AND operation, see the truth table given in Figure 4.6:

x = 10 = 0000 1010
y = 11 = 0000 1011

x & y = 0000 1010

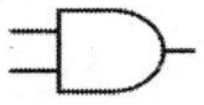

AND gate

x	y	x & y
0	0	0
0	1	0
1	0	0
1	1	1

truth table for AND gate

Figure 4.6: AND Operation

From the truth table, we can conclude that by multiplying the input bits, we can get the output bit. The AND gate circuit present in the computer chip will perform the AND operation.

```
If x = 10, y = 11. Find the value of x&y.
x = 10 = 0000 1010.
y = 11 = 0000 1011.
```

From the truth table, by multiplying the bits, we can get x&y = 0000 1010. This is nothing but 10 (in decimal).

Bitwise OR Operator (|)

This operator performs OR operation on the bits of the numbers. The symbol of bitwise OR operator is |, which is called *pipe* symbol. To understand this operation, see the truth table given in Figure 4.7. From the table, we can conclude that by adding the input bits, we can get the output bit. The OR gate circuit, which is present in the computer chip will perform the OR operation.

x = 10 = 0000 1010
y = 11 = 0000 1011

---

x | y = 0000 1011

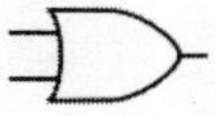

OR gate

x	y	x | y
0	0	0
0	1	1
1	0	1
1	1	1

truth table for OR gate

Figure 4.7: OR Operation

```
If x = 10, y = 11, find the value of x|y.
x = 10 = 0000 1010.
y = 11 = 0000 1011.
```

The truth table shows that by adding the bits, we can get x|y = 0000 1011. This is nothing but 11 (in decimal).

Bitwise XOR Operator (^)

This operator performs *exclusive or (XOR)* operation on the bits of numbers. The symbol is ^, which is called *cap, carat,* or *circumflex* symbol. To understand the *XOR* operation, see the truth table given in Figure 4.8. From the table, we can conclude that when we have odd number of 1's in the input bits, we can get the output bit as 1. The *XOR* gate circuit of the computer chip will perform this operation.

x = 10 = 0000 1010
y = 11 = 0000 1011

x ^ y = 0000 0001

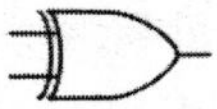

XOR gate

x	y	x ^ y
0	0	0
0	1	1
1	0	1
1	1	0

truth table for XOR gate

Figure 4.8: XOR Operation

```
If x = 10, y = 11, find the value of x^y.
x = 10 = 0000 1010.
y = 11 = 0000 1011.
```

From the truth table, when odd number of 1's are there, we can get a 1 in the output. Thus, x^y = 0000 0001 is nothing but 1 (in decimal).

Bitwise Left Shift Operator (<<)

This operator shifts the bits of the number towards left a specified number of positions. The symbol for this operator is <<, read as *double less than.* If we write x<<n, the meaning is to shift the bits of x towards left n positions.

```
If x = 10, calculate x value if we write x<<2.
```

Shifting the value of x towards left 2 positions will make the leftmost 2 bits to be lost. The value of x is 10 = 0000 1010. Now, x<<2 will be 0010 1000 = 40 (in decimal). The procedure to do this is explained, as shown in Figure 4.9:

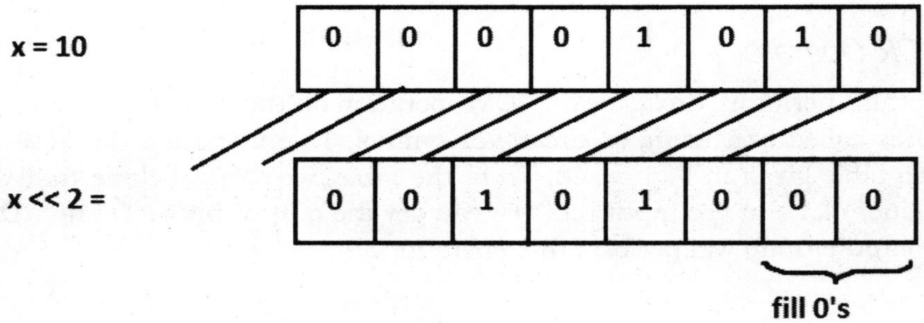

Figure 4.9: Shifting bits towards left 2 times

Bitwise Right Shift Operator (>>)

This operator shifts the bits of the number towards right a specified number of positions. The symbol for this operator is >>, read as *double greater than.* If we write x>>n, the meaning is to shift the bits of x towards right n positions.

>> shifts the bits towards right and also preserves the sign bit, which is the leftmost bit. Sign bit represents the sign of the number. Sign bit 0 represents a positive number and 1 represents a negative number. So, after performing >> operation on a positive number, we get a positive value in the result also. If right shifting is done on a negative number, again we get a negative value only.

`If x = 10, then calculate x>>2 value.`

Shifting the value of x towards right 2 positions will make the rightmost 2 bits to be lost. x value is 10 = 0000 1010. Now x>>2 will be: 0000 0010 = 2 (in decimal) (Figure 4.10).

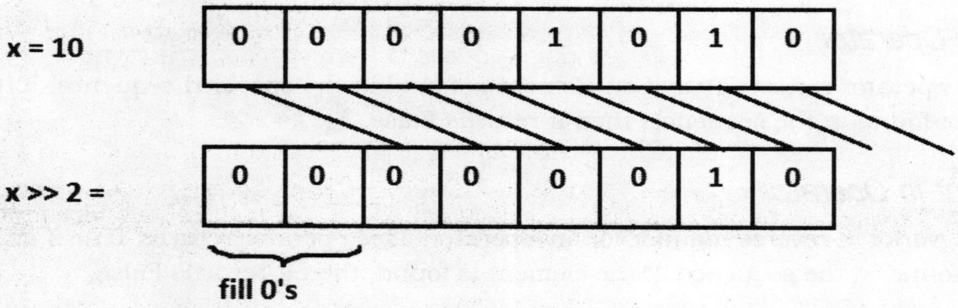

Figure 4.10: Shifting bits towards right 2 times

Let's check the effects of various bitwise operators so far discussed. We will use IDLE window and type the Python statements and confirm the results, as shown in Figure 4.11:

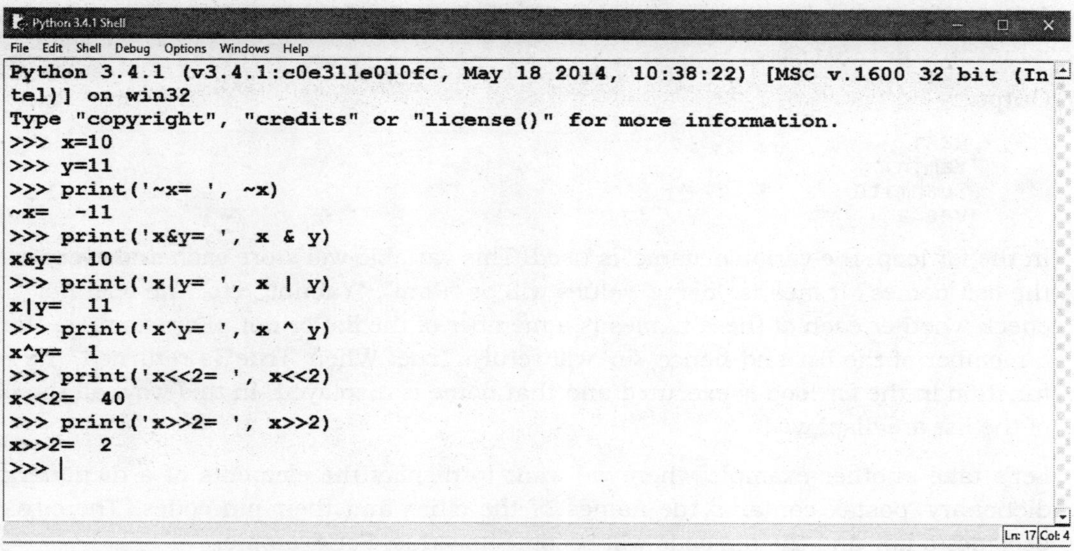

Figure 4.11: Using the Python Bitwise Operators

Membership Operators

The membership operators are useful to test for membership in a sequence such as strings, lists, tuples or dictionaries. For example, if an element is found in the sequence or not can be asserted using these operators. There are two membership operators as shown here:

- in
- not in

The in Operator

This operator returns True if an element is found in the specified sequence. If the element is not found in the sequence, then it returns False.

The not in Operator

This works in reverse manner for 'in' operator. This operator returns True if an element is not found in the sequence. If the element is found, then it returns False.

Let's take a group of strings in a list. We want to display the members of the list using a for loop where the 'in' operator is used. The list of names is given below:

```
    names = ["Rani", "Yamini", "Sushmita", "Veena"]
```

Here the list name is 'names'. It contains a group of names. Suppose, we want to retrieve all the names from this list, we can use a for loop as:

```
    for name in names:
        print (name)
```

Output:

```
    Rani
    Yamini
    Sushmita
    Veena
```

In the for loop, the variable 'name' is used. This variable will store each and every value of the list 'names'. It means, 'name' values will be "Rani", "Yamini", etc. The operator 'in' will check whether each of these names is a member of the list or not. For example, "Rani" is a member of the list and hence, 'in' will return True. When 'True' is returned, the print() function in the for loop is executed and that name is displayed. In this way, all the names of the list are displayed.

Let's take another example where we want to display the elements of a dictionary. The dictionary 'postal' contains the names of the cities and their pin codes. The city name becomes a key and the pin code will become its value. For example,

```
    postal = {'Delhi': 110001, 'Chennai': 600001, 'Kolkata': 700001,
'Bangalore':560001}
```

Now, we want to retrieve each key and its corresponding value. For this purpose, we take a variable 'city' in for loop. Every time in the for loop, 'city' will get the name of the city. To get the corresponding value, we can use postal[city]. So, the following for loop will display the cities and their pin codes from 'postal' dictionary:

```
for city in postal:
    print(city, postal[city])
```

Output:

```
Kolkata 700001
Bangalore 560001
Delhi 110001
Chennai 600001
```

Identity Operators

These operators compare the memory locations of two objects. Hence, it is possible to know whether the two objects are same or not. The memory location of an object can be seen using the id() function. This function returns an integer number, called the *identity number* that internally represents the memory location of the object. For example, id(a) gives the identity number of the object referred by the name 'a'. See the following statements:

```
a = 25
b = 25
```

In the first statement, we are assigning the name (or identifier) 'a' to the object 25. In the second statement, we are assigning another name 'b' to the same object 25. In Python, everything is considered as an object. Here, 25 is the object for which two names are given. If we display an identity number of these two variables, we will get same numbers as they refer to the same object.

```
id(a)
1670954952
id(b)
1670954952
```

There are two identity operators:

- is
- is not

The is Operator

The 'is' operator is useful to compare whether two objects are same or not. It will internally compare the identity number of the objects. If the identity numbers of the objects are same, it will return True; otherwise, it returns False.

The is not Operator

This is not operator returns True, if the identity numbers of two objects being compared are not same. If they are same, then it will return False.

The 'is' and 'is not' operators do not compare the values of the objects. They compare the identity numbers or memory locations of the objects. If we want to compare the value of the objects, we should use equality operator (==).

```
a = 25
b = 25
if(a is b):
    print("a and b have same identity")
else:
    print("a and b do not have same identity")
```

Output:

```
a and b have same identity
```

As another example, we will take two lists with 4 elements each as:

```
one = [1,2,3,4]
two = [1,2,3,4]
if(one is two):
    print("one and two are same")
else:
    print("one and two are not same")
```

Output:

```
one and two are not same
```

In the preceding example, the lists one and two are having same elements or values. But the output is "one and two are not same". The reason is this: 'is' operator does not compare the values. It compares the identity numbers of the lists. Let's see the identity numbers of these two lists by using the id() function:

```
id(one)
51792432
id(two)
51607192
```

Since both the lists are created at different memory locations, we have their identity numbers different. So, 'is' operator will take the lists 'one' and 'two' as two different lists even though their values are same. It means, 'is' is not comparing their values. We can use equality (==) operator to compare their values as:

```
if(one == two):
    print("one and two are same")
else:
    print("one and two are not same")
```

Output:

```
one and two are same
```

Operator Precedence and Associativity

An expression or formula may contain several operators. In such a case, the programmer should know which operator is executed first and which one is executed next. The sequence of execution of the operators is called *operator precedence*. The following table summarizes the operators according to their precedence. The table shows precedence in descending order. It means the operators which are having highest precedence are listed at the top of the table, shown in Table 4.6:

Table 4.6: Precedence of Operators in Python

Operator	Name
( )	Parenthesis
**	Exponentiation
-, ~	Unary minus, Bitwise complement
*, / , // , %	Multiplication, Division, Floor division, Modulus
+ , -	Addition, Subtraction
<< , >>	Bitwise left shift, Bitwise right shift
&	Bitwise AND
^	Bitwise XOR
|	Bitwise OR
>, >=, <, <= , == , !=	Relational (comparison) operators
= , %= , /= , //= , -= , += , *= , **=	Assignment operators
is , is not	Identity operators
in , not in	Membership operators
not	Logical not
or	Logical or
and	Logical and

Precedence represents the priority level of the operator. The operators with higher precedence will be executed first than of lower precedence.

Suppose an expression contains operators having same precedence, then which operator is executed first is another question. It means knowing whether the execution is from left to right or right to left. This is called *associativity*. 'Associativity' is the order in which an expression is evaluated that has multiple operators of the same precedence. Almost all the operators have left-to-right associativity in Python. Let's take an expression value = 3/2*4+3+(10/4)**3-2 to understand how these precedence rules can be applied. The final value of this expression will be 22.625, as shown in Table 4.7:

Table 4.7: Evaluation of an Expression

Expression	Explanation
value = 3/2*4+3+(10/4)**3-2	
value = 3/2*4+3+2.5**3-2	The expression in ( ) is evaluated first.
value = 3/2*4+3+15.625-2	Exponentiation ** is next.
value = 1.5*4+3+15.625-2 value = 6.0+3+15.625-2	* and / have equal precedence. They are evaluated from left to right (associativity). So, first / and then *.
value = 9.0+15.625-2 value = 24.625-2 value = 22.625	+ and – have equal precedence. They are evaluated from left to right (associativity). So, first + and then -.

Mathematical Functions

While operators are very handy when dealing with fundamental operations in a program, we can use built-in functions given in Python to perform various advanced operations. For example, to calculate square root value of a number, we need not develop any logic. We can simply use the sqrt() function that is already given in the 'math' module. For example, to calculate square root of 16, we can call the function as: sqrt(16). This function returns the positive square root value of 16, i.e. 4.0.

In Python, a module is a file that contains a group of useful objects like functions, classes or variables. 'math' is a module that contains several functions to perform mathematical operations. If we want to use any module in our Python program, first we should import that module into our program by writing 'import' statement. For example, to import 'math' module, we can write:

```
import math
```

Once this is done, we can use any of the functions available in math module. Now, we can refer to sqrt() function from math module by writing module name before the function as: math.sqrt().

```
x = math.sqrt(16)
```

Here, 'x' value will become 4.0.

We can also use import statement as:

```
import math as m
```

In this case, we are importing 'math' module and naming it as 'm' in our program. Hence, hereafter, 'm' represents 'math'. So to calculate square root of 16, we can write as:

```
x = m.sqrt(16)
```

Import math statement is useful to import all the functions from math module. On the other hand, if the programmer wants to import only one or two functions from math module, he can write as:

```
from math import sqrt
```

This will make only sqrt() function available to our program. The programmer can use only that function from the math module but not other functions in his program. Similarly, to import more than one function, one can write:

```
from math import factorial, sqrt
```

Here, the programmer is importing two functions by the names factorial() and sqrt(). The programmer can use these functions without using module name before them, as:

```
x = sqrt(16)
y = factorial(5)
```

Here, 'x' value will be 4.0 and 'y' value will be 120. The following table (Table 4.8) summarizes important mathematical functions from math module. Please note that these functions cannot be used with complex numbers. To use these functions with complex numbers, a separate module by the name 'cmath' is available in Python. Also, Table 4.9 gives the available constants in math module.

Table 4.8: Important Math Functions

Function	Description
ceil(x)	Raises x value to the next higher integer. If x is integer, then same value is returned. Ex: ceil(4.5) gives 5
floor(x)	Decreases x value to the previous integer value. If x integer, then same value is returned. Ex: floor(4.5) gives 4
degrees(x)	Converts angle value x from radians into degrees. Ex: degrees(3.14159) gives 179.9998479605043
radians(x)	Converts x value from degrees into radians. Ex: radians(180) gives 3.141592653589793
sin(x)	Gives sine value of x. Here x value is given in radians. Ex: sin(0.5) gives 0.479425538604203

Function	Description
cos(x)	Gives cosine value of x. Here x value is given in radians. Ex: cos(0.5) gives 0.8775825618903728
tan(x)	Returns tangent value of x, given x value in radians. Ex: tan(0.5) gives 0.5463024898437905
exp(x)	Returns exponentiation of x. This is same as e **x. Ex: exp(0.5) returns 1.6487212707001282
fabs(x)	Gives the absolute value (or positive quantity) of x. Ex: fabs(-4.56) gives 4.56
factorial(x)	Returns factorial value of x. Raises 'ValueError' if x is not integer or is negative. Ex: factorial(4) gives 24
fmod(x, y)	Returns remainder of division of x and y. fmod() is preferred to calculate modulus for float values than '%' operator. '%' operator works well for integer values. Ex: fmod(14.5, 3) gives 2.5
fsum(values)	Returns accurate sum of floating point values. Ex: fsum([1.5, 2.4, -3.3]) returns 0.6000000000000001
modf(x)	Returns float and integral parts of x. Ex: modf(2.56) gives (0.56, 2.0)
log10(x)	Returns base-10 logarithm of x. Ex: log10(5.2345) gives 0.7188752041406328
log(x, [, base])	Returns the natural logarithm of x of specified base. Ex: log(5.5, 2) gives 2.4594316186372973
sqrt(x)	Returns positive square root value of x. Ex: sqrt(49) gives 7.0
pow(x, y)	Raises x value to the power of y. Ex: pow(5, 3) returns 125.0

Function	Description
gcd(x, y)	Gives greatest common divisor of x and y. Available from Python 3.5 onwards. Ex: gcd(25, 30) gives 5
trunc(x)	The real value of x is truncated to integer value and returned. Ex: trunc(15.5676) gives 15
isinf(x)	Returns True if x is a positive or negative infinity, and False otherwise. Ex: num = float('Inf') # num is a float number that indicates infinity. Isinf(num) gives True
isnan(x)	Returns True if x is a NaN (not a number), and False otherwise. Ex: num = float('NaN') # convert NaN into a float representation. isnan(num) gives True

Table 4.9: Constants in Math Module

Constant	Description
pi	The mathematical constant π = 3.141592..., with high precision.
e	The mathematical constant e = 2.718281..., with high precision.
inf	A floating-point positive infinity. (For negative infinity, use -math.inf.) Equivalent to the output of float('inf')
nan	A floating-point "not a number" (NaN) value. Equivalent to the output of float('nan').

Let's write a Python program to calculate the area of a circle. We know that the formula to calculate the area of a circle is pi * r *r. This logic is used in our program. Of course, to refer to the 'pi' value, we can use the constant in 'math' module. Hence, we should import 'math' module.

This program is executed in all the three environments: using IDLE window, using command line window and from system prompt. Let's see how to execute the program in these three environments.

Using IDLE Window

Click on 'Python IDLE window' icon available at task bar. This will open the Python Shell window where we should type the program. When last statement is typed and Enter is pressed, the result will be displayed, as shown in Figure 4.12:

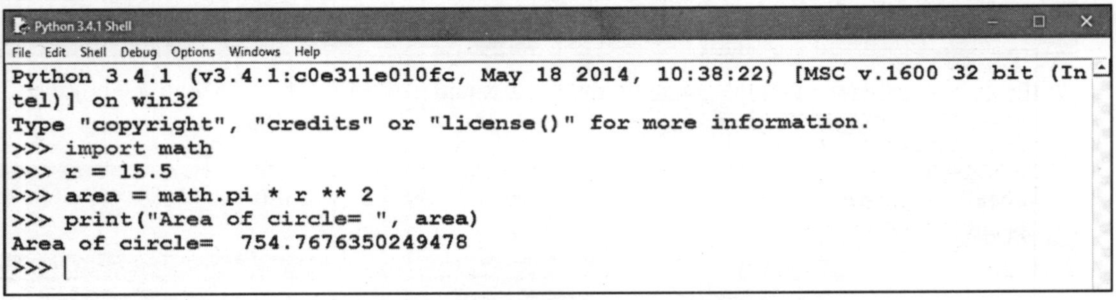

Figure 4.12: Executing the Program in IDLE Window

Using Command Line Window

Click on 'Python command line window' icon available at task bar. This will open the Python command line window where we should type the program. When last statement is typed and Enter is pressed, the result will be displayed, as shown in Figure 4.13:

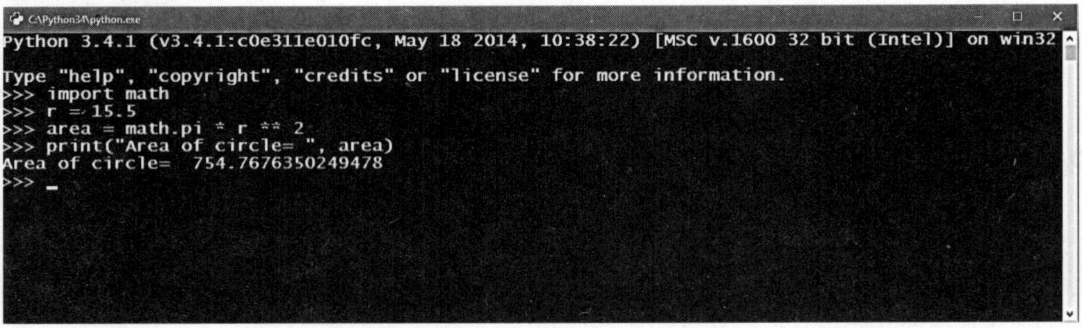

Figure 4.13: Executing the Program in Command Line Window

Executing at System Prompt

Open a text editor like Notepad or Edit Plus and then type the program. Save the program as "circle.py" in a directory. Open command prompt window and go to that directory where the program is stored. Then invoke python interpreter by typing:

```
F:\PY>python area.py
```

Then the result is displayed, as shown in Figure 4.14:

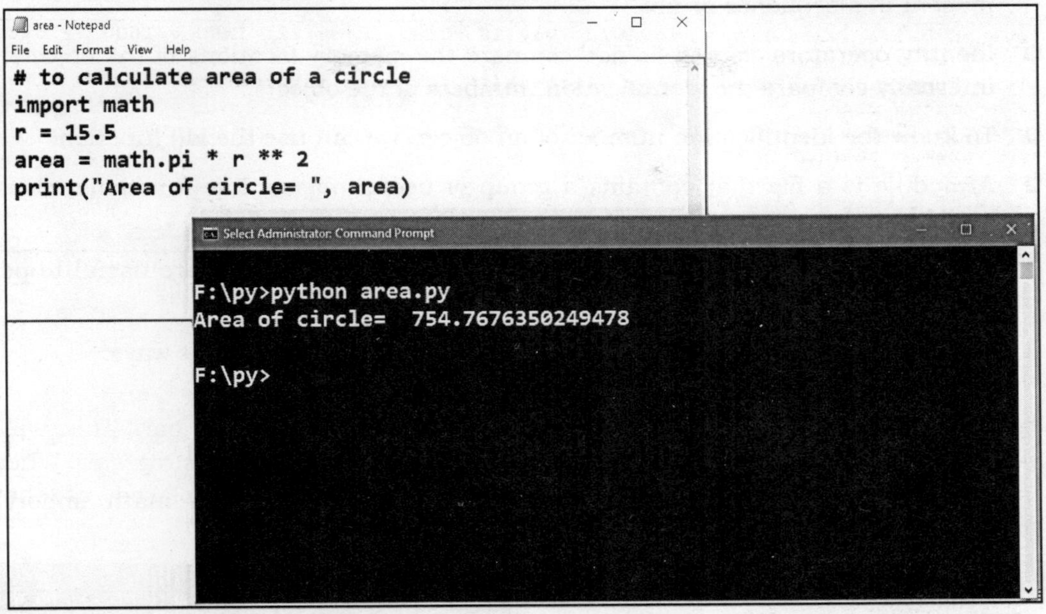

Figure 4.14: Executing Python Program at Command Prompt

Points to Remember

- An operator is a symbol that performs an operation.
- An operator acts on variables which are called operands.
- It is possible to use Python interpreter as a calculator.
- Arithmetic operators perform addition, subtraction, multiplication, division, floor division, modulus, and exponentiation operations.
- Assignment operators are useful to assign a value to the left side variable.
- Unary minus operator is useful to negate a value.
- Relational operators are useful to compare two quantities. They are used to create simple conditions which may evaluate to True or False.
- Logical operators are useful to create compound conditions. A compound condition is a combination of more than one simple condition.
- Boolean operators act on 'bool' type literals. They give again 'bool' type result.
- Bitwise operators act on individual bits (1 and 0) of the numbers.

- Membership operators 'in' and 'not in' are useful to test whether an element is present in a sequence or not.
- Identity operators 'is' and 'is not' compare the memory locations of the objects. They internally compare the identification numbers of the objects.
- To know the identification number of an object, we can use the id() function.
- A module is a file that contains a group of useful objects like functions, classes or variables.
- The 'math' module in Python contains several functions which are useful to perform various mathematical calculations.
- To import a module into a Python program, we can use 3 different ways:
  - import modulename (Ex: import math)
  - import modulename as anothername (Ex: import math as m)
  - from modulename import object1, object2, ... (Ex: from math import sqrt, factorial)

CHAPTER 5

INPUT AND OUTPUT

The purpose of a computer is to process data and return results. It means that first of all, we should provide data to the computer. The data given to the computer is called *input*. The results returned by the computer are called *output*. So, we can say that a computer takes input, processes that input and produces the output, as shown in Figure 5.1:

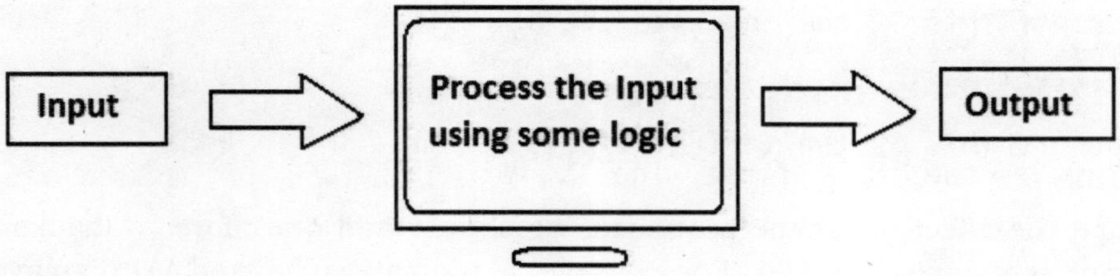

Figure 5.1: Processing Input by the Computer

To provide input to a computer, Python provides some statements which are called Input statements. Similarly, to display the output, there are Output statements available in Python. We should use some logic to convert the input into output. This logic is implemented in the form of several topics in subsequent chapters. We will discuss the input and output statements in this chapter, but in the following order:

- Output statements
- Input statements

Output statements

To display output or results, Python provides the print() function. This function can be used in different formats which are discussed hereunder.

The print() Statement

When the print() function is called simply, it will throw the cursor to the next line. It means that a blank line will be displayed.

The print("string") Statement

A string represents a group of characters. When a string is passed to the print() function, the string is displayed as it is. See the example:

```
print("Hello")
Hello
```

Please remember that in case of strings, double quotes and single quotes have the same meaning and hence can be used interchangeably.

```
print('Hello')
Hello
```

We can use escape sequence characters inside the print() function. An escape sequence is a character that contains a special meaning. For example, '\n' indicates new line. '\t' represents tab space.

```
print("This is the \nfirst line")
This is the
first line

print("This is the \tfirst line")
This is the        first line
```

To escape the effect of escape sequence, we should add one more '\' (backslash) before the escape sequence character. For example, \\n displays '\n' and \\t displays '\t'.

```
print("this is the \\nfirst line")
this is the \nfirst line
```

We can use repetition operator (*) to repeat the strings in the output as:

```
print(3*'Hai')
HaiHaiHai
```

The operator '+' when used on numbers will perform addition operation. The same '+' will not do addition operation on strings as it is not possible to perform arithmetic operations on strings. When we use '+' on strings, it will join one string with another string. Hence '+' is called concatenation (joining) operator when used on strings.

```
print("City name="+"Hyderabad")
City name=Hyderabad
```

The '+' operator in the preceding statement joined the two strings without any space in between. We can also write the preceding statement by separating the strings using ', ' as:

```
print("City name=","Hyderabad")
City name= Hyderabad
```

In this case, a space is used by the print() function after each string. In the output, observe the single space after the string 'City name='. When the print() function sees a comma, it will assume that the values are different and hence a space should be used between them for clarity.

The print(variables list) Statement

We can also display the values of variables using the print() function. A list of variables can be supplied to the print() function as:

```
a, b = 2, 4
print(a)
2

print(a, b)
2 4
```

Observe that the values in the output are separated by a space by default. To separate the output with a comma, we should use 'sep' attribute as shown below. 'sep' represents separator. The format is sep="characters" which are used to separate the values in the output.

```
print(a, b, sep=",")
2,4

print(a, b, sep=':')
2:4

print(a, b, sep='----')
2----4
```

When several print() functions are used to display output, each print() function will display the output in a separate line as shown below:

```
print("Hello")
print("Dear")
print('How are U?')
```

Output:

```
Hello
Dear
How are U?
```

Each print() function throws the cursor into the next line after displaying the output. This is the reason we got the output in 3 lines. We can ask the print() function not to throw the cursor into the next line but display the output in the same line. This is done using 'end' attribute. The way one can use it is end="characters" which indicates the ending characters for the line. Suppose, we write end=", then the ending character for each line will be " (nothing) and hence it will display the next output in the same line. See the example:

```
print("Hello", end='')
print("Dear", end='')
print('How are U?', end='')
```

Output:

```
HelloDearHow are U?
```

If we use end='\t' then the output will be displayed in the same line but tab space will separate them as:

```
print("Hello", end='\t')
print("Dear", end='\t')
print('How are U?', end='\t')
```

Output:

```
Hello       Dear    How are U?
```

If we use end='\n' then the output is displayed in a separate line. So, '\n' is the default value for 'end' attribute.

The print(object) Statement

We can pass objects like lists, tuples or dictionaries to the print() function to display the elements of those objects. For example,

```
lst = [10, 'A', 'Hai']
print(lst)
[10, 'A', 'Hai']

d = {'Idly':30.00, 'Roti':45.00, 'Chappati':55.50}
print(d)
{'Idly': 30.0, 'Roti': 45.0, 'Chappati': 55.5}
```

The print("string", variables list) Statement

The most common use of the print() function is to use strings along with variables inside the print() function.

```
a=2
print(a, "is even number")
2 is even number

print('You typed ', a, 'as input')
You typed  2 as input
```

The print(formatted string) Statement

The output displayed by the print() function can be formatted as we like. The special operator '%' (percent) can be used for this purpose. It joins a string with a variable or value in the following format:

```
print("formatted string" % (variables list))
```

In the "formatted string", we can use %i or %d to represent decimal integer numbers. We can use %f to represent float values. Similarly, we can use %s to represent strings. See the example below:

```
x=10
print('value= %i' %  x)
value= 10
```

As seen above, to display a single variable (i.e. 'x') , we need not wrap it inside parentheses. When more than one variable is to be displayed, then parentheses are needed as:

```
x, y = 10, 15
print('x= %i y= %d' % (x, y))
x= 10 y= 15
```

To display a string, we can use %s in the formatted string. When we use %20s, it will allot 20 spaces and the string is displayed right aligned in those spaces. To align the string towards left side in the spaces, we can use %-20s. Consider the following examples:

```
name='Linda'
print('Hai %s' % name)
Hai Linda

print('Hai (%20s)' % name)
Hai (               Linda)

print('Hai (%-20s)' % name)
Hai (Linda               )
```

We can use %c to display a single character as shown below:

```
name='Linda'
print('Hai %c, %c' % (name[0], name[1]))
Hai L, i
```

The above example displayed 0th and 1st characters from name variable. We can use slicing operator on a string to display required characters from the string. For example, name[0:2] gives 0th to 1st characters from name as:

```
print('Hai %s' %(name[0:2]))
Hai Li
```

To display floating point values, we can use %f in the formatted string. If we use %8.2f, then the float value is displayed in 8 spaces and within these spaces, a decimal point and next 2 fraction digits.

When we use %.3f, then the float value is displayed with 3 fraction digits after the decimal point. However, the digits before decimal point will be displayed as they are. Consider the following examples:

```
num=123.456789
print('The value is: %f' % num)
The value is: 123.456789

print('The value is: %8.2f' %num)
```

```
The value is:   123.46   # observe 2 spaces before the value
print('The value is: %.2f' %num)
The value is: 123.46
```

Inside the formatted string, we can use replacement field which is denoted by a pair of curly braces { }. We can mention names or indexes in these replacement fields. These names or indexes represent the order of the values. After the formatted string, we should write member operator and then format() method where we should mention the values to be displayed. Consider the general format given below:

```
print('format string with replacement fields'.format(values))
```

To display a single value using index in the replacement field, we can write as:

```
n1, n2, n3 = 1, 2, 3
print('number1={0}'.format(n1))
number1=1
```

In the above statement, observe {0} which was replaced by the value of n1. To display all the three numbers, we can use:

```
print('number1={0}, number2={1}, number3={2}'.format(n1, n2, n3))
number1=1, number2=2, number3=3
```

In the above statement, {0}, {1}, {2} represent the values of n1, n2 and n3, respectively. Hence, if we change the order of these fields, we will have order of the values to be changed in the output as:

```
print('number1={1}, number2={0}, number3={2}'.format(n1, n2, n3))
number1=2, number2=1, number3=3
```

As an alternate, we can also use names in the replacement fields. But the values for these names should be provided in the format() method. Consider the following example:

```
print('number1={two}, number2={one}, number3={three}'.format(one=n1,
      two=n2, three=n3))
number1=2, number2=1, number3=3
```

We can also use the curly braces without mentioning indexes or names. In this case, those braces will assume the sequence of values as they are given. Consider the following statements:

```
print('number1={}, number2={}, number3={}'. format(n1, n2, n3))
number1=1, number2=2, number3=3
```

All the four examples given below will display the same output:

```
name, salary = 'Ravi', 12500.75
print('Hello {0}, your salary is {1}'.format(name, salary))
Hello Ravi, your salary is 12500.75

print('Hello {n}, your salary is {s}'.format(n=name, s=salary))
Hello Ravi, your salary is 12500.75

print('Hello {:s}, your salary is {:.2f}'.format(name, salary))
Hello Ravi, your salary is 12500.75

print('Hello %s, your salary is %.2f' % (name, salary))
Hello Ravi, your salary is 12500.75
```

Input Statements

To accept input from keyboard, Python provides the input() function. This function takes a value from the keyboard and returns it as a string. For example,

```
str = input()   # this will wait till we enter a string
Raj kumar  # enter this string

print(str)
Raj kumar
```

It is a better idea to display a message to the user so that the user understands what to enter. This can be done by writing a message inside the input() function as:

```
str = input('Enter your name: ')
Enter your name: Raj kumar

print(str)
Raj kumar
```

Once the value comes into the variable 'str', it can be converted into 'int' or 'float' etc. This is useful to accept numbers as:

```
str = input('Enter a number: ')
Enter a number: 125
x =  int(str)  # str is converted into int
print(x)
125
```

We can use the int() function before the input() function to accept an integer from the keyboard as:

```
x = int(input('Enter a number: '))
Enter a number: 125
print(x)
125
```

Similarly, to accept a float value from the keyboard, we can use the float() function along with the input() function as:

```
x = float(input('Enter a number: '))
Enter a number: 12.345
print(x)
12.345
```

We will understand these concepts with the help of a Python program. Let's write a program to accept a string and display it, as shown in Program 1.

Program

Program 1: A Python program to accept a string from keyboard and display it.

```
# accepting a string from keyboard
str = input("Enter a string: ")
print('U entered: ', str)  #display entire string
```

Output:

```
C:\>python Input.py
Enter a string: Hello
U entered: Hello
```

The way we accept a character from the keyboard is also same as accepting a string. This is shown in Program 2.

Program

Program 2: A Python program to accept a character as a string.

```
# accepting a single character or string from keyboard
ch = input("Enter a char: ")
print("U entered: "+ch)
```

Output:

```
C:\>python Input.py
Enter a char: A
U entered: A

C:\>python Input.py
Enter a char: abcd
U entered: abcd
```

From the output of the above program, we can understand that the input() function is accepting the character as a string only. If we need only a character, then we should use the index, as: ch[0]. Here 0th character is taken from the string. This is shown in Program 3.

Program

Program 3: A Python program to accept a single character from keyboard.

```
# accepting a single character from keyboard
ch = input("Enter a char: ")
print("U entered: "+ch[0])
```

Output:

```
C:\>python Input.py
Enter a char: abcd
U entered: a
```

Now, let's plan a program to accept an integer number from the keyboard. Since, the input() function accepts only a string, it will accept the integer number also as a string. Hence, we should convert that string into integer number using the int() function. This is shown in Program 4.

Program

Program 4: A Python program to accept an integer number from keyboard.

```
# accepting integer from keyboard
str = input('Enter a number: ')
```

```
x = int(str)  #convert string into int
print('U entered: ', x);  #display the int number
```

Output:

```
C:\>python Input.py
Enter a number: 88778
U entered: 88778
```

The same program can be rewritten by combining the first two statements, as shown in Program 5.

Program

Program 5: A Python program to accept an integer number from keyboard – version 2.

```
# accepting integer number from keyboard - v2.0
x = int(input('Enter a number: '))
print('U entered: ', x);  #display the int number
```

Output:

```
C:\>python Input.py
Enter a number: 98798798423422
U entered: 98798798423422
```

The same procedure can be adopted to accept a floating point number from the keyboard. While the input() function accepts a float value as a string, it should be converted into float number using the float() function. This is shown in Program 6.

Program

Program 6: A Python program to accept a float number from keyboard.

```
# accepting float number from keyboard
x = float(input('Enter a number: '))
print('U entered: ', x);  #display the float number
```

Output:

```
C:\>python Input.py
Enter a number: 9.123456789123456789
U entered: 9.123456789123457
```

From the above output, we can understand that the float values are displayed to an accuracy of 15 digits after decimal point. In the next program, we will accept two integer numbers and display them.

Program

Program 7: A Python program to accept two integer numbers from keyboard.

```
# accepting two numbers from keyboard
x = int(input('Enter first number: '))
y = int(input('Enter second number: '))
print('U entered: ', x, y) #display both the numbers separating with a space
```

Output:

```
C:\>python Input.py
Enter first number: 12
Enter second number: 45
U entered: 12 45
```

The two numbers in the output are displayed using a space. Suppose we want to display these numbers using a comma as separator, then we can use sep=',' in the print() function as:

```
print('U entered: ', x, y, sep=',');
```

In this case, the output will be:

```
U entered: ,12,45
```

Observe the commas after 'U entered:' and after 12. A better way to display these numbers separating them using commas is this:

```
print('U entered: %d, %d' %(x, y))
```

Let's write a Python program to accept two numbers from keyboard and find their sum. This is shown in Program 8.

Program

Program 8: A Python program to accept two numbers and find their sum.

```
# find sum of two numbers
x = int(input('Enter first number: '))
y = int(input('Enter second number: '))
print('The sum of ',x, ' and ', y,' is ', x+y)  #display sum
print('The sum of {} and {} is {}'.format(x,y, x+y))  #display again
```

Output:

```
C:\>python Input.py
Enter first number: 88
Enter second number: 98
The sum of  88  and  98  is  186
The sum of 88 and 98 is 186
```

Let's find the product of two given numbers. The previous program is improved to find product of the numbers as shown in Program 9.

Program

Program 9: A Python program to find sum and product of two numbers.

```
# find sum and product of two numbers
x = int(input('Enter first number: '))
y = int(input('Enter second number: '))

#display sum
print('The sum of {0} and {1} is {2}'.format(x,y, x+y))
#display product
print('The product of {0} and {1} is {2}'.format(x,y, x*y))
#display both sum and product
```

```
print('The sum of {0} and {1} is {2} and product of {0} and {1} is
        {3}'.format(x,y, x+y, x*y))
```

Output:

```
C:\>python Input.py
Enter first number: 45
Enter second number: 65
The sum of 45 and 65 is 110
The product of 45 and 65 is 2925
The sum of 45 and 65 is 110 and product of 45 and 65 is 2925
```

In Program 10, we accept numbers in hexadecimal, octal and binary systems and display their equivalent decimal numbers.

Program

Program 10:A Python program to convert numbers from other systems into decimal number system.

```
# input from other number systems
str = input('Enter hexadecimal number: ')  # accept input as string
n = int(str, 16)  # inform the number is base 16
print('Hexadecimal to Decimal= ', n);

str = input('Enter octal number: ')
n = int(str, 8)  # inform the number is base 8
print('Octal to Decimal= ', n);

str = input('Enter binary number: ')
n = int(str, 2)  # inform the number is base 2
print('Binary to Decimal= ', n);
```

Output:

```
C:\>python convert.py
Enter hexadecimal number: a
Hexadecimal to Decimal= 10
Enter octal number: 10
Octal to Decimal= 8
Enter binary number: 1101
Binary to Decimal= 13
```

To accept more than one input in the same line, we can use a for loop along with the input() function in the following format:

```
a, b = [int(x) for x in input("Enter two numbers: ").split()]
```

In the previous statement, the input() function will display the message 'Enter two numbers: ' to the user. When the user enters two values, they are accepted as strings. These strings are divided wherever a space is found by split() method. So, we get two strings as elements of a list. These strings are read by for loop and converted into integers by the int() function. These integers are finally stored into a and b.

The spilt() method by default splits the values where a space is found. Hence, while entering the numbers, the user should separate them using a space. The square brackets [ ] around the total expression indicates that the input is accepted as elements of a list. Program 11 shows how to accept 3 integer numbers from in the same line. While entering the numbers, the user should separate them with at least one space.

Program

Program 11: A Python program to accept 3 integers in the same line and display their sum.

```
# accepting 3 numbers separated by space
var1, var2, var3 = [int(x) for x in input("Enter three numbers: ").split()]
print('Sum = ', var1+var2+var3)
```

Output:

```
C:\>python Input.py
Enter three numbers: 10 20 30
Sum = 60
```

Suppose the user wants to separate the input with commas while entering them, we can specify a comma for the split() method as shown in Program 12.

Program

Program 12: A Python program to accept 3 integers separated by commas and display their sum.

```
# accepting 3 numbers separated by comma.
var1, var2, var3 = [int(x) for x in input("Enter three numbers:").
                    split(',')]
print('Sum = ', var1+var2+var3)
```

Output:

```
C:\>python Input.py
Enter three numbers: 10, 20, 30
Sum = 60
```

Now we will see how to accept a group of strings from the keyboard and display them again. We should remember that the input() function reads given data in the form of strings. Hence the variable 'x' in Program 13 takes the strings one by one from the input() function.

Program

Program 13: A Python program to accept a group of strings separated by commas and display them again.

```
# accepting a group of strings from keyboard.
lst = [x for x in input('Enter strings: ').split(',')]
print('You entered:\n', lst)
```

Output:

```
C:\>python Input.py
Enter strings: Anil, Vijay Kumar, Priya
You entered:
['Anil', 'Vijay Kumar', 'Priya']
```

The eval() function takes a string and evaluates the result of the string by taking it as a Python expression. For example, let's take a string: "a+b-4" where a = 5 and b = 10. If we pass the string to the eval() function, it will evaluate the string and returns the result. Consider the following example:

```
a, b = 5, 10
result = eval("a+b-4")
print(result)
11
```

We can use the eval() function along with input() function. Since the input() function accepts a value in the form of a string, the eval() function receives that string and evaluates it. In Program 14, we can enter an expression that is evaluated by the eval() function and result is displayed.

Program

Program 14: Evaluating an expression entered from keyboard.

```
# using eval() along with input() function
x = eval(input("Enter an expression: "))
print("Result= %d " % x)
```

Output:

```
C:\>python Input.py
Enter an expression: 10 + 5 - 4
Result= 11
```

We can use the combination of eval() and input() functions to accept objects like lists or tuples. When the user types the list using square braces [ ], eval() will understand that it is a list, as shown in Program 15:

Program

Program 15: A Python program to accept a list and display it.

```
# accepting a list from keyboard
lst = eval(input("Enter a list: "))
print("List= ", lst)
```

Output:

```
C:\>python Input.py
Enter a list: ["Ajay", "Preethi", "Sashank", "Vishnu"]
List = ['Ajay', 'Preethi', "Sashank', 'Vishnu']

C:\>python Input.py
Enter a list: [10, 20, 30]
List = [10, 20, 30]
```

Similarly, when the user types a tuple using parentheses ( ), eval() will understand that it is a tuple, as shown in Program 16.

Program

Program 16: A Python program to accept a tuple and display it.

```
# accepting a tuple from keyboard
tpl = eval(input("Enter a tuple: "))
print("Tuple= ", tpl)
```

Output:

```
C:\>python Input.py
Enter a tuple: (10, 20, 30, 40)
Tuple= (10, 20, 30, 40)
```

Command Line Arguments

We can design our programs in such a way that we can pass inputs to the program when we give run command. For example, we write a program by the name 'add.py' that takes two numbers and adds them. We can supply the two numbers as input to the program at the time of running the program at command prompt as:

```
C:\>python add.py  10  22
Sum = 22
```

Here, add.py is our Python program name. While running this program, we are passing two arguments 10 and 22 to the program, which are called *command line arguments*. So, command line arguments are the values passed to a Python program at command prompt (or system prompt). Command line arguments are passed to the program from outside the program. All the arguments should be entered from the keyboard separating them by a space. These arguments are stored by default in the form of strings in a list with the name 'argv' which is available in *sys* module. Since argv is a list that contains all the values passed to the program, argv[0] represents the name of the program, argv[1] represents the first value, argv[2] represents the second value and so on, as shown in Figure 5.2:

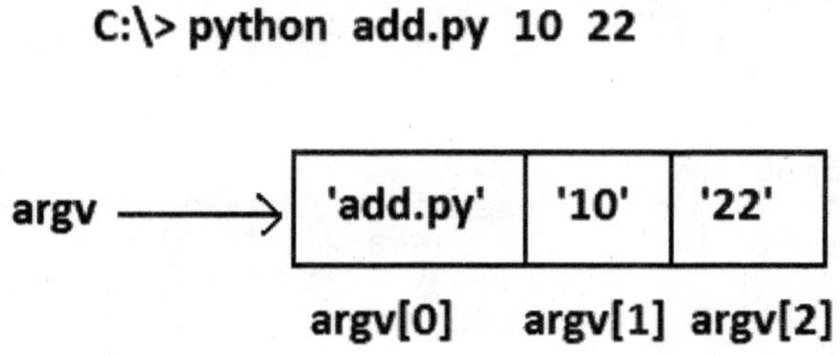

Figure 5.2: Command line args are stored as strings in argv list

If we want to find the number of command line arguments, we can use the len() function as: len(argv). The following program reads the command line arguments entered at command prompt and displays them.

Program

Program 17: A Python program to display command line arguments.

```
# to display command line args. Save this as cmd.py.
import sys

n = len(sys.argv)   # n is the number of arguments
args = sys.argv   # args list contains arguments
print('No. of command line args= ', n)
print('The args are: ', args)
print('The args one by one: ')
for a in args:
    print(a)
```

Output:

```
C:\>python cmd.py 10 Aishwarya Rai 22500.75
No. of command line args=  5
The args are:  ['cmd.py', '10', 'Aishwarya', 'Rai', '22500.75']
The args one by one:
cmd.py
10
Aishwarya
Rai
22500.75
```

Observe the output of the Program 17. Actually, we are passing 3 arguments: 10, Aishwarya Rai and 22500.75. But they are stored as 4 arguments as we can see in the output. The reason is the string 'Aishwarya Rai' has two words and hence it is taken as two arguments instead of one. So, how to make 'Aishwarya Rai' as a single argument? For this purpose, we should enclose this string within quotation marks in either of the two ways shown below:

```
'"Aishwarya Rai"'    # double quotes inside single quotes
"'Aishwarya Rai'"    # single quotes inside double quotes
```

Let's run the Program 17 again and see the output.

```
C:\>python cmd.py 10 "'Aishwarya Rai'" 22500.75
No. of command line args=  4
The args are:  ['cmd.py', '10', "'Aishwarya Rai'", '22500.75']
The args one by one:
cmd.py
10
'Aishwarya Rai'
22500.75
```

In Program 18, we are accepting two numbers from command line and finding their sum. The logic is straight forward. We know that all the command line arguments are stored by default in argv. So, argv[0] represents our program name. argv[1] represents the first number and argv[2] represents the second number entered at command prompt. Since by default, all command line arguments are stored in the form of strings, we can convert them into numeric format using int() or float() functions as:

```
int(sys.argv[1])   # converts argv[1] into int type
float(sys.argv[2])   # converts argv[2] into float type
```

Once the arguments are available as numbers, we can perform any arithmetic operations on them.

Program

Program 18: A Python program to find sum of two numbers using command line arguments.

```
# to add two numbers. Save this as add.py
import sys

# convert args into integers and add them
sum = int(sys.argv[1])+int(sys.argv[2])
print('Sum= ', sum)
```

Output:

```
C:\>python add.py  10 22
Sum= 22
```

We will write another program where we enter some numbers and find the sum of even numbers. This is shown in Program 19.

Program

Program 19: A Python program to find the sum of even numbers using command line arguments.

```
# to find sum of even numbers
import sys

# read command line arguments except the program name
args = sys.argv[1:]
print(args)

sum=0
# find sum of even arguments
for a in args:
    x = int(a)
    if x%2==0:
        sum+=x

print('Sum of evens= ', sum)
```

Output:

```
C:\>python cmd.py 6 8 9 10 11
['6', '8', '9', '10', '11']
Sum of evens= 24
```

Parsing Command Line Arguments

The *argparse* module in Python is useful to develop user-friendly programs using command line arguments. The argparse module automatically generates help and usage messages when user gives the program invalid arguments. It may also display appropriate error messages to the users. To work with argparse module, first we should import it as:

```
import argparse
```

Then we should create an object of ArgumentParser class object with description of the program as:

```
parser = argparse.ArgumentParser(description='This program displays the
          square value of given number')
```

If the programmer does not want to display the help on his program, he can skip this description and create the object as:

```
parser = argparse.ArgumentParser()
```

The next step is adding arguments to the parser using add_argument() method. A program may have one or more arguments that are to be inputted by the user at the time of running the program.

```
parser.add_argument("num", type=int, help="Please input integer type
                    number.")
```

In the preceding statement, "num" represents the variable where the argument is stored. type=int represents that the user should enter only integer as argument. If this type=int is omitted, then the user can enter any type of argument. help="Please input integer type number." This represents the help text that is displayed to the user when the user asks for help. The parser will parse (or go through) the arguments provided by the user. These arguments are received by parse_args() method as:

```
args = parser.parse_args()
```

Here, 'args' represents an object of 'Namespace' class of argparse module. The actual argument is available in this object with the name "num" and hence it can be referred as: args.num. Now, it is possible to perform any operation on this args.num value. In Program 19, we are showing all these steps where we want to accept a number and display its square value.

Program

Program 20: Using argument parser to find the square of a given number.

```
# to find square of a given number. Save this as args.py
import argparse

# create ArgumentParser class object
parser = argparse.ArgumentParser(description='This program displays the
square value of given number')

# add one argument with the name num and type as integer
parser.add_argument("num", type=int, help="Please input integer type
number.")

# retrieve the arguments passed to the program
args = parser.parse_args()
```

```
    # find the square of the argument passed
    result = args.num**2
    print("Square value= ", result)
```

Output:

```
C:\>python args.py 5
Square value= 25
```

Please observe the output. We have passed an argument '5' at the time of running this program. This is stored with the name 'num' in the args object. Hence, args.num**2 would calculate its square value. So, this program is running nice. Now, it is possible that the user may provide wrong inputs to this program while running this program. Then what would be the response from argument parser?

Suppose, the user enters a float number as argument, the argument parser will display error message and indicates that it is expecting an 'int' type value. This is because we already added that the user should enter only 'int' type value in the parser.add_argument() method.

```
C:\>python args.py 5.5
usage: args.py [-h] num
args.py: error: argument num: invalid int value: '5.5'
```

Suppose, the user enters two numbers as arguments, then the argument parser will display error message where it says the other argument is not recognized.

```
C:\>python args.py 5 15
usage: args.py [-h] num
args.py: error: unrecognized arguments: 15
```

Suppose, the user does not enter any arguments, then the argument parser will display error message and shows that it is expecting an argument by the name 'num'.

```
C:\>python args.py
usage: args.py [-h] num
args.py: error: the following arguments are required: num
```

Suppose, the user got confused regarding how to use this program and he wants to have some help, then, he can type '-h'. The argument parser helps him by displaying help as shown below:

```
C:\>python args.py  -h
usage: args1.py [-h] num
This program displays the square value of given number
positional arguments:
num          Please input integer type number.
optional arguments:
  -h, --help  show this help message and exit
```

In this way, argument parser provides help and tells the user how to use the program through command line. Now, we will write another program that accepts two arguments from the user and displays their sum (Program 21).

Program

Program 21: A Python program to add two numbers using argument parser.

```
# to find sum of two given numbers. Save this as args.py
import argparse

# create ArgumentParser class object
parser = argparse.ArgumentParser(description= "This program calculates
        sum of two given numbers")

# add two arguments with the names n1 and n2 and type as float
parser.add_argument("n1", type=float, help="Input first number")
parser.add_argument("n2", type=float, help="Input second number")

# retrieve the arguments passed to the program
args = parser.parse_args()

# convert the n1 and n2 values into float type then add them
result = float(args.n1)+float(args.n2)
print("Sum of two= ", result)
```

Output:

```
C:\>python args.py
usage: args.py [-h] n1 n2
args.py: error: the following arguments are required: n1, n2
```

Output:

```
C:\>python args.py 10.5 15
Sum of two= 25.5
```

We can specify the number of arguments in the add_argument() method using 'nargs' attribute as:

```
parser.add_argument('nums', nargs=2)
```

Now, the parser will accept only 2 arguments. Since type is not specified, they can be of any type. These arguments are referred by the name 'nums'. The parse_args() method retrieves them into args object as:

```
args = parser.parse_args()
```

Now, args.nums is a list object that contains the arguments as its elements. So, args.nums[0] represents the first argument and args.nums[1] represents the second argument. This is shown in Program 22.

Program

Program 22: A Python program to find the power value of a number when it is raised to a particular power.

```
# to find power value of a number. Save this as args.py
import argparse

# call the ArgumentParser()
parser = argparse.ArgumentParser()
```

```
# add the arguments to the parser
parser.add_argument('nums', nargs=2)

# retrieve the arguments into args object
args = parser.parse_args()
# find the power value
# args.nums represents a list
print('Number= ', args.nums[0])
print('Its power= ', args.nums[1])

# convert the arguments into float and then find power
result = float(args.nums[0])** float(args.nums[1])
print('Result= ', result)
```

Output:

```
C:\>python args.py 10.5 3
Number= 10.5
Its power= 3
Result= 1157.625
```

The add_argument() method can be called with nargs='*' to accept all the arguments passed by the user as:

```
parser.add_argument('nums', nargs='*')
```

On the other hand, if we use nargs='+', it accepts 1 or more arguments as:

```
parser.add_argument('nums', nargs='+')
```

Program

Program 23: To accept 1 or more arguments and display them as list elements.

```
# to find power value of a number. Save this as args.py
import argparse

# call the ArgumentParser()
parser = argparse.ArgumentParser()

# add the arguments to the parser
parser.add_argument('nums', nargs='+')

# retrieve the arguments into args object
args = parser.parse_args()

# display the arguments from the list: args.nums
for x in args.nums:
    print(x)
```

Output:

```
C:\>python args.py 10 Prasad 78.5
10
Prasad
78.5
```

Python programs using command line arguments should be executed only at the command prompt as shown in the previous sections. They cannot be executed in Python IDLE, as it does not support passing the arguments at runtime.

Points to Remember

- Python provides the print() function to display output or results. We can use the print() function with variables, strings and objects like lists, tuples and dictionaries.
- The print() function with replacement fields and the format() method can be used as:

  print('number1={}, number2={}, number3={}'. format(n1, n2, n3))

- Another important format of the print() function is to use with format strings like %d, %c, %s as:

  print('Hello %s, your salary is %.2f % (name, salary))

- Python provides the input() function that accepts data or input from the keyboard.
- The general format of input() function is this:

  str = input('Enter a string: ')

- The input() function accepts every value as a string. We can use int() or float() functions to convert this string into integer value or float value as:
  - x = int(input('Enter a number: '))
  - x = float(input('Enter a number: '))
- To accept more than one value in the same line, we can use input() function along with split() method as:

  a, b = [int(x) for x in input("Enter two numbers: ").split('separator')]

- Command line arguments are the values passed to a Python program at command prompt (or system prompt).
- Command line arguments are stored by default in argv[] as a list.
- argv[0] represents the program name, argv[1] represents the first command line argument, argv[2] represents the second command line argument, and so on.
- len(argv) gives the number of command line arguments.

- To read all command line arguments except 0th argument (i.e. the program name), we can use:

  args = sys.argv[1:]

- The argparse module is useful to create user-friendly command line arguments programs. The parser in the argparse module automatically generates help and usage messages and error messages when user gives invalid arguments to the program.

CHAPTER

CONTROL STATEMENTS

6

When we write a program, the statements in the program are normally executed one by one. This type of execution is called 'sequential execution'. Let's write a program to understand about the concept of sequential execution. In Program 1, we are calculating the area of a circle. We know that the formula used to calculate the area of circle is pi * r * r. Since 'pi' is a constant in 'math' module, we can refer to it as math.pi. Also, to find the square of r, we can use exponentiation operator (**) as r **2. So the area of a circle is given by math.pi * r**2. Since we are using the constant 'pi' from the math module, we are supposed to import that module in our program. Consider Program 1 in which a constant 'pi' is imported from the math module and used to calculate the area of a circle.

Program

Program 1: A Python program to calculate the area of a circle.

```
# to find area of a circle
import math  # here math module is imported
r = float(input('Enter radius: '))
area = math.pi * r**2  # pi is a constant in math module
print('Area of circle= ', area)
print('Area of circle= {:0.2f}'.format(area))
```

Output:

```
C:\>python area.py
Enter radius: 15.5
Area of circle= 754.7676350249478
Area of circle= 754.77
```

If we consider the output of the preceding program, we can understand that the statements written in Program 1 are executed one by one by the Python interpreter. This is called sequential execution. This type of execution is suitable only for developing simple programs. It is not suitable for developing critical programs where complex logic is needed.

To develop critical programs, the programmer should be able to change the flow of execution as needed by him. For example, the programmer may wish to repeat a group of statements several times or he may want to directly jump from one statement to another statement in the program. For this purpose, we need control statements. In this chapter, you will learn more about control statements.

Control Statements

Control statements are statements which control or change the flow of execution. The following are the control statements available in Python:

- if statement
- if ... else statement
- if ... elif ... else statement
- while loop
- for loop
- else suite
- break statement
- continue statement
- pass statement
- assert statement
- return statement

Please note that the switch statement found in many languages like C and Java is not available in Python.

The if Statement

This statement is used to execute one or more statement depending on whether a condition is True or not. The syntax or correct format of if statement is given below:

```
if condition:
    statements
```

First, the condition is tested. If the condition is True, then the statements given after colon (:) are executed. We can write one or more statements after colon (:). If the condition is False, then the statements mentioned after colon are not executed.

To understand the simple if statement, let's write a Python program to display a digit in words.

Program

Program 2: A Python program to express a digit in a word.

```
# understanding if statement
num=1
if num==1:
    print("One")
```

Output:

```
C:\>python Demo.py
One
```

We can also write a group of statements after colon. The group of statements in Python is called a *suite*. While writing a group of statements, we should write them all with proper indentation. Indentation represents the spaces left before the statements. The default indentation used in Python is 4 spaces. Let's write a program to display a group of messages using if statement.

Program

Program 3: A Python program to display a group of messages when the condition is true.

```
# understanding if statement
str = 'Yes'
if str == 'Yes':
    print("Yes")
    print("This is what you said")
    print("Your response is good")
```

Output:

```
C:\>python Demo.py
Yes
This is what you said
Your response is good
```

Observe that every print() function mentioned after colon is starting after 4 spaces only. When we write the statements with same indentation, then those statements are considered as a suite (or belonging to same group). In Program 3, the three print statements written after the colon form a suite.

A Word on Indentation

Understanding indentation is very important in Python. Indentation refers to spaces that are used in the beginning of a statement. The statements with same indentation belong to same group called a *suite*. By default, Python uses 4 spaces but it can be increased or decreased by the programmers. Consider the statements given in Figure 6.1:

```
if x==1:
—print('a')
—print('b')
—if y==2:
——print('c')
——print('d')
print('end')
```

Figure 6.1: Indentation in if... Statements

In Figure 6.1, the statements:

```
if x==1:
print('end')
```

belong to same group as they do not have any spaces before them. So, after executing the if statement, Python interpreter goes to the next statement, i.e. print('end'). Even if the statement 'if x==1' is not executed, interpreter will execute print('end') statement as it is the next executable statement in our program.

In the next level, the following statements are typed with 4 spaces before them and hence they are at the same level (same suite).

```
print('a')
print('b')
if y==2:
```

These statements are inside 'if x==1' statement. Hence if the condition is True (i.e. x==1 is satisfied), then the above 3 statements are executed. Thus, the third statement 'if y==2' is executed only if x==1 is True. At the next level, we can find the following statements:

```
print('c')
print('d')
```

These two statements are typed with 8 spaces before them and hence they belong to the same group (or suite). Since they are inside 'if y==2' statement, they are executed only if condition y==2 is True. Table 6.1 shows the outputs that we obtain when the statements given in Figure 6.1 are executed with different value of x and y:

Table 6.1: The Effect of Indentation

Output when x=1, y=0	Output when x=1, y=2	Output when x=0, y=2
a b end	a b c d end	end

The if ... else Statement

The if ... else statement executes a group of statements when a condition is True; otherwise, it will execute another group of statements. The syntax of if ... else statement is given below:

```
if condition:
    statements1
else:
    statements2
```

If the condition is True, then it will execute statements1 and if the condition is False, then it will execute statements2. It is advised to use 4 spaces as indentation before statements1 and statements2. In Program 4, we are trying to display whether a given number is even or odd. The logic is simple. If the number is divisible by 2, then it is an even number; otherwise, it is an odd number. To know whether a number is divisible by 2 or not, we can use modulus operator (%). This operator gives remainder of division. If the remainder is 0, then the number is divisible, otherwise not.

Program

Program 4: A Python program to test whether a number is even or odd.

```
# to know if a given number is even or odd
x=10
if x % 2 == 0:
    print(x, " is even number")
else:
    print(x, " is odd number")
```

Output:

```
C:\>python Demo.py
10 is even number
```

The same program can be rewritten to accept input from keyboard. In Program 5, we are accepting an integer number from keyboard and testing whether it is even or odd.

Program

Program 5: A Python program to accept a number from the keyboard and test whether it is even or odd.

```
# to know if a given number is even or odd - v2.0
x = int(input("Enter a number: "))
if x % 2 == 0:
    print(x, " is even number")
else:
    print(x, " is odd number")
```

Output:

```
C:\>python Demo.py
Enter a number: 11
11  is odd number
```

We will write another program where we accept a number from the user and test whether that number is in between 1 and 10 (inclusive) or not. If the entered number is x, then the condition x>=1 and x<=10 checks whether the number is in between 1 and 10.

Program

Program 6: A Python program to test whether a given number is in between 1 and 10.

```
# using ‘and’ in if ... else statement
x = int(input('Enter a number: '))
if x>=1 and x<=10:
    print("You typed", x, "which is between 1 and 10")
else:
    print("You typed", x, "which is below 1 or above 10")
```

Output:

```
C:\>python Demo.py
Enter a number: 9
You typed 9 which is between 1 and 10
```

Observe the condition after ‘if’. We used ‘and’ to combine two conditions x>=1 and x<=10. Such a condition is called compound condition.

The if ... elif ... else Statement

Sometimes, the programmer has to test multiple conditions and execute statements depending on those conditions. if ... elif ... else statement is useful in such situations. Consider the following syntax of if ... elif ... else statement:

```
if condition1:
    statements1
elif condition2:
    statements2
elif condition3:
    statements3
else:
    statements4
```

When condition1 is True, the statements1 will be executed. If condition1 is False, then condition2 is evaluated. When condition2 is True, the statements2 will be executed. When condition2 is False, the condition3 is tested. If condition3 is True, then statements3 will be executed. When condition3 is False, the statements4 will be executed. It means statements4 will be executed only if none of the conditions are True.

Observe colon (:) after each condition. The statements1, statements2, ... represent one statement or a suite. The final ‘else’ part is not compulsory. It means, it is possible to write if ... elif statement, without ‘else’ and statements4. Let’s write a program to understand the usage of if ... elif ... else statement. In Program 7, we are checking whether a number is positive or negative. A number becomes positive when it is greater than 0. A number becomes negative when it is lesser than 0. Apart from positive and negative, a number can also become zero (neither +ve nor –ve). All these 3 combinations are checked in the program.

Program

Program 7: A Python program to know if a given number is zero, positive or negative.

```
# to know if a given number is zero or +ve or -ve
num=-5
if num==0:
    print(num, "is zero")
elif num>0:
    print(num, "is positive")
else:
    print(num, "is negative")
```

Output:

```
C:\>python Demo.py
-5 is negative
```

In the previous program, observe the indentation. There are 4 spaces before every statement after colon. Now, we write another program that accepts a numeric digit from keyboard and prints it in words. In this program, we will use several elif conditions. After colon, we are leaving only one space before every print() statement. While this is not recommended way of using indentation, this program will run properly since every statement has equal number of spaces (1 space) as indentation. Consider Program 8.

Program

Program 8: A program to accept a numeric digit from keyboard and display in words.

```
# to display a numeric digit in words
x = int(input('Enter a digit: '))
if x==0: print("ZERO")
elif x==1: print("ONE")
elif x==2: print("TWO")
elif x==3: print("THREE")
elif x==4: print("FOUR")
elif x==5: print("FIVE")
elif x==6: print("SIX")
elif x==7: print("SEVEN")
elif x==8: print("EIGHT")
elif x==9: print("NINE")  # else part not compulsory
```

Output:

```
C:\>python Demo.py
Enter a digit: 5
FIVE
```

In the above program, if we enter a digit '15', then the program does not display any output. On the other hand, if we want to display a message like 'Please enter digit between 0 and 9', we can add 'else' statement at the end of the program, as:

```
else: print('Please enter digit between 0 and 9')
```

The while Loop

A statement is executed only once from top to bottom. For example, 'if' is a statement that is executed by Python interpreter only once. But a loop is useful to execute repeatedly. For example, while and for are loops in Python. They are useful to execute a group of statements repeatedly several times.

The while loop is useful to execute a group of statements several times repeatedly depending on whether a condition is True or False. The syntax or format of while loop is:

```
while condition:
    statements
```

Here, 'statements' represents one statement or a suite of statements. Python interpreter first checks the condition. If the condition is True, then it will execute the statements written after colon (:). After executing the statements, it will go back and check the condition again. If the condition is again found to be True, then it will again execute the statements. Then it will go back to check the condition once again. In this way, as long as the condition is True, Python interpreter executes the statements again and again. Once the condition is found to be False, then it will come out of the while loop.

In Program 9, we are using while loop to display numbers from 1 to 10. Since, we should start from 1, we will store '1' into a variable 'x'. Then we will write a while loop as:

```
while x<=10:
```

Observe the condition. It means, as long as x value is less than or equal to 10, continue the while loop. Since we want to display 1,2,3, ... up to 10, we need this condition. To display x value, we can use:

```
print(x)
```

Once this is done, we have to increment x value by 1, by writing x+=1 or x = x+1. Now, consider Program 9 in which while loop is used to display numbers.

Program

Program 9: A Python program to display numbers from 1 to 10 using while loop.

```
# to display numbers from 1 to 10
x=1
while x<=10:
    print(x)
    x+=1
print("End")
```

Output:

```
C:\>python Demo.py
1
2
3
4
5
6
```

```
7
8
9
10
End
```

In the previous program, observe that the first two statements are written using same indentation. They are:

```
print(x)
x+=1
```

That means, these two statements will come under one group. Hence, both these statements are executed when the condition is True. The last statement,

```
print("End")
```

is having same indentation as the while. Hence this statement will not come under same group like the previous two statements. This will come under a separate statement having same level as while loop. So, Python interpreter executes it after coming out of while loop. Suppose, we write the print("End")statement with the same indentation as the other two statements as:

```
while x<=10:
    print(x)
    x+=1
    print("End")
```

Then the output will be as shown below:

```
1
End
2
End
3
End
4
End
5
End
6
End
7
End
8
End
9
End
10
End
```

In Program 10, we will use while loop to display even numbers between 100 and 200. We will take x value as 100 since it is the first even number. Every time we will add 2 to the value of x to get the next even number. We will repeat the while loop as long as x>=100 and x<=200.

Program

Program 10: A Python program to display even numbers between 100 and 200.

```
# to display even numbers between 100 and 200
x=100
while x>=100 and x<=200:
    print(x)
    x+=2
```

Output:

```
C:\>python Demo.py
100
102
104
:
:
200
```

We can improve the Program 10 so that the user can enter his choice regarding from where to where he wants to display even numbers. In this program 'm' and 'n' represent the minimum and maximum range of even numbers to be displayed.

Program

Program 11: A Python program to display even numbers between m and n.

```
# to display even numbers between m and n
m, n = [int(i) for i in input("Enter minimum and maximum range:
      ").split(',')]
x=m  # start from m onwards
if x % 2 !=0 :   # if x is not even, start from next number
    x=x+1

while x>=m and x<=n:
    print(x)
    x+=2
```

Output:

```
C:\>python Demo.py
Enter minimum and maximum range: 11,20
12
14
16
18
20
```

The for Loop

The for loop is useful to iterate over the elements of a sequence. It means, the for loop can be used to execute a group of statements repeatedly depending upon the number of elements in the sequence. The for loop can work with sequence like string, list, tuple, range etc. The syntax of the for loop is given below:

```
for var in sequence:
    statements
```

The first element of the sequence is assigned to the variable written after 'for' and then the statements are executed. Next, the second element of the sequence is assigned to the variable and then the statements are executed second time. In this way, for each element of the sequence, the statements are executed once. So, the for loop is executed as many times as there are number of elements in the sequence.

We will write a Python program to retrieve the letters of a string using for loop. Now, consider Program 12.

Program

Program 12: A Python program to display characters of a string using for loop.

```
# to display each character from a string
str='Hello'
for ch in str:
    print(ch)
```

Output:

```
C:\>python Demo.py
H
e
l
l
o
```

In the above program, the string 'str' contains 'Hello'. There are 6 characters in the string. The for loop has a variable 'ch'. First of all, the first character of the string, i.e. 'H' is stored into ch and the statement, i.e. print(ch) is executed. As a result, it will display 'H'. Next, the second character of the string, i.e. 'e' is stored into ch. Then print(ch) is once again executed and 'e' will be displayed. In the third iteration, the third character 'l' will be displayed. In this way the for loop is executed for 6 times and all the 6 characters are displayed in the output.

In Program 13, we are using the for loop to display the elements of the string using 'index'. An index represents the position number of element in the string or sequence. For example, str[0] represents the 0th character, i.e. 'H' and str[1] represents the first character, i.e. 'e', and so on. Hence we can take an index 'i' that may change from 0 to n-1 where 'n' represents the total number of elements. We can use range(n) object that generates numbers from 0 to n-1. Now, consider Program 13.

Program

Program 13: A Python program to display each character from a string using sequence index.

```
# to display each character from a string - v2.0
str='Hello'
n = len(str)  # find no. of chars in str
```

```
for i in range(n):
    print(str[i])
```

The output of the above program will be the same as that of Program 12. Here, 'n' value will be 6 as the length of the string is 6. We used range(n) that gives the numbers from 0 to n-1. Hence for loop repeats from 0 to 5 and print() function displays str[0], str[1], ... str[5]. It means H,e,l,l,o will be displayed. Please note that the *len()* function gives the total number of elements in a sequence like string, list or tuple.

The range() object is also known as range() function in Python is useful to provide a sequence of numbers. range(n) gives numbers from 0 to n-1. For example, if we write range(10), it will return numbers from 0 to 9. We can also mention the starting number, ending number, as: range(5, 10). In this case, it will give numbers from 5 to 9. We can also specify the step size. The step size represents the increment in the value of the variable at each step. For example, range(1, 10, 2) will give numbers from 1 to 9 in steps of 2. That means, we should add 2 to each number to get the next number. Thus, it will give the numbers: 1, 3, 5, 7 and 9. This can be verified through Program 14.

Program

Program 14: A Python program to display odd numbers from 1 to 10 using range() object.

```
# to display odd numbers between 1 and 10
for i in range(1, 10, 2):
    print(i)
```

Output:

```
C:\>python Demo.py
1
3
5
7
9
```

Let's write another program to display numbers from 10 to 1 in descending order using the range() object. In this case, we use range(10, 0, -1). Here, the starting number is 10 and the ending number is one before 0. The step size is -1. It means we should decrement 1 every time. Thus we will get 10, 9, 8, up to 1. Observe that it will not return 0 as the last number. It will stop at 1 that is one number before 0. Now, consider Program 15.

Program

Program 15: A program to display numbers from 10 to 1 in descending order.

```
# to display numbers in descending order
for x in range (10, 0, -1):
    print(x)
```

Output:

```
C:\>python Demo.py
10
```

```
9
8
7
6
5
4
3
2
1
```

We will use for loop to access the elements of a list. As we know, a list is a sequence that contains a group of elements. It is like an array. But the difference is that an array stores only one type of elements; whereas, a list can store different types of elements. Let's write a program to create a list and retrieve elements from the list using for loop.

Program

Program 16: A program to display the elements of a list using for loop.

```
# take a list of elements
list = [10,20.5,'A','America']

# display each element from the list
for element in list:
    print(element)
```

Output:

```
C:\>python Demo.py
10
20.5
A
America
```

In Program 16, each element of the list is stored into the variable 'element'. It means, in the first iteration, element stores 10. In the second iteration, it stores 20.5. In the third iteration, it stores 'A'. In the fourth iteration, it stores 'America'. Hence, print(element) displays all the elements of the list.

In Program 17, we are going to take a list of integer numbers. We will use a for loop to find the sum of all those numbers.

Program

Program 17: A Python program to display and find the sum of a list of numbers using for loop.

```
# to find sum of list of numbers using for.
# take a list of numbers
list = [10,20,30,40,50]
sum=0  #initially sum is zero
for i in list:
    print(i)  #display the element from list
    sum+=i    #add each element to sum
print('Sum= ', sum)
```

Output:

```
C:\> python Demo.py
10
20
30
40
50
Sum= 150
```

Observe that there are only two statements in the for loop. They are:

```
print(i)
sum+=i
```

These two statements form a group (or suite) as they are typed with the same indentation, i.e. 4 spaces before each statement. The last print() function does not come into this group as it is typed at the same level as that of for loop. Hence, print() is considered as a next statement after for loop. So, it is executed only after completion of for loop.

If we want to write the same program using while loop, we have to put a few extra statements as seen in Program 18.

Program

Program 18: A Python program to display and sum of a list of numbers using while loop.

```
# to find sum of a list of numbers using while - v2.0
# take a list of numbers
list = [10,20,30,40,50]
sum=0  #initially sum is zero
i=0    #take a variable
while i <len(list):
    print(list[i])  #display the element from list
    sum+=list[i]    #add each element to sum
    i+=1
print('Sum= ', sum)
```

Output:

```
Same as that of previous program.
```

Infinite Loops

Please see the following loop:

```
i=1
while i<=10:
    print(i)
    i+=1
```

Here, 'i' value starts at 1. print(i) will display 1. Then the value of 'i' is incremented by 1 so that it will become 2. In this way, 'i' values 1, 2, 3, ... up to 10 are displayed. When 'i' value is 11, the condition, i.e. i<=10 becomes 'False' and hence the loop terminates.

In the previous while loop, what happens if we forget to write the last statement, i.e. 'i+=1' ? The initial 'i' value 1 is displayed first, but it is never incremented to reach 10. Hence this loop will always display 1 and never terminates. Such a loop is called 'infinite loop'. An infinite loop is a loop that executes forever. So, the following is an example for an infinite loop:

```
i=1
while i<=10:
    print(i)
```

It will display the value 1 forever. To stop the program, we have press Control+C at system prompt. Another way of creating an infinite loop is to write 'True' in the condition part of the while loop so that the Python interpreter thinks that the condition is True always and hence executes it forever. See the example:

```
while(True):
    print("Hai")
```

This loop will always display 'Hai' without stopping since the condition is read as 'True' always.

Infinite loops are drawbacks in a program because when the user is caught in an infinite loop, he cannot understand how to come out of the loop. So, it is always recommended to avoid infinite loops in any program.

Nested Loops

It is possible to write one loop inside another loop. For example, we can write a for loop inside a while loop or a for loop inside another for loop. Such loops are called 'nested loops'. Take the following for loops:

```
for i in range(3):  # i values are from 0 to 2
    for j in range(4):  # j values are from 0 to 3
        print('i=', i, '\t', 'j=',j)  # display i and j values
```

The outer for loop repeats for 3 times by changing i values from 0 to 2. The inner for loop repeats for 4 times by changing j values from 0 to 3. Observe the indentation (4 spaces) before the inner for loop. The indentation represents that the inner for loop is inside the outer for loop. Similarly, print() function is inside the inner for loop.

When outer for loop is executed once, the inner for loop is executed for 4 times. It means, when i value is 0, j values will change from 0 to 3. So, print() function will display the following output:

```
i= 0 j= 0
i= 0 j= 1
i= 0 j= 2
i= 0 j= 3
```

Once the inner for loop execution is completed (j reached 3), then Python interpreter will go back to outer for loop to repeat the execution for second time. This time, i value will be

1. Again, the inner for loop is executed for 4 times. Hence the print() function will display the following output:

```
i= 1 j= 0
i= 1 j= 1
i= 1 j= 2
i= 1 j= 3
```

Since the inner for loop execution is completed, again the interpreter will go back to outer for loop. This time i value will be 2 and the output will be:

```
i= 2 j= 0
i= 2 j= 1
i= 2 j= 2
i= 2 j= 3
```

In this way, the print() function in the inner for loop is executed for 12 times. If we observe the output given above, we can understand that the outer for loop is executed for 3 times and the inner for loop is executed for 4 times. Therefore the print() function in the inner for loop is executed for 3 X 4 = 12 times.

We will write a Python program to display stars (*s) in a right angled triangular form. The expected output in our program is given below:

```
*
* *
* * *
* * * *
* * * * *
* * * * * *
* * * * * * *
* * * * * * * *
* * * * * * * * *
* * * * * * * * * *
```

In the first row, there is only one star. In the second row, there are two stars. In the third row, there are three stars. It means,

```
Row number = number of stars in that row.
```

Since there are 10 rows, we can write an outer for loop that repeats for 10 times from 1 to 10 as:

```
for i in range(1, 11):  # to display 10 rows
```

To represent the columns (or stars) in each row, we can write an inner for loop. This for loop should repeat as many times as the row number indicated by the outer for loop. Suppose row number is 'i' then the inner for loop should repeat for 1 to i times. Hence the inner for loop can be written as:

```
for j in range(1, i+1):  # repeat for 1 to i times.
```

This logic is given in Program 19.

Program

Program 19: A Python program that displays stars in right angled triangular form using nested loops.

```
# to display stars in right angled triangular form
for i in range(1, 11):  # to display 10 rows
    for j in range(1, i+1):  # no. of stars = row number
        print('* ', end='')
    print()
```

Output:

```
C:\>python Demo.py

*
* *
* * *
* * * *
* * * * *
* * * * * *
* * * * * * *
* * * * * * * *
* * * * * * * * *
* * * * * * * * * *
```

In the above program, observe the following print() statement:

```
print('* ', end='')
```

This will display the star symbol. The end='' represents that it should not throw the cursor to the next line after displaying each star. So, all the stars are displayed in the same line. But we need to throw the cursor into the next line when there is a new row starting, i.e. when i value changes. This can be achieved by another print() statement in the outer for loop that does not display anything but simply throws the cursor into the next line.

In Program 19, we have used two for loops; one inside another. These are called nested for loops. We can also rewrite the same program with a single for loop. Now, consider Program 20.

Program

Program 20: A Python program that displays stars in right angled triangular form using a single loop.

```
# to display stars in right angled triangular form - v2.0
for i in range(1, 11):
    print ('* '*(i))  # repeat star for i times
```

The code in Program 20 is an example for elegant (simple and beautiful) style of writing a program in Python.

Program 20 can be improved to display stars in equilateral triangular form. For this purpose, we have to start displaying the stars slightly at the center of the screen or monitor. For this purpose, we should release some spaces and then display the star. This can be done using the following statements:

```
print(' '*n, end='')  # repeat space for n times in the same line.
print ('* ')) # then display the star and throw cursor to next line.
```

Every time, we need to reduce the number of spaces so that the stars will form the equilateral triangle. For this purpose, we write:

```
n-=1   # reduce the spaces by 1 in every row.
```

Program

Program 21: A Python program to display the stars in an equilateral triangular form using a single for loop.

```
# to display stars in equilateral triangular form
n=40
for i in range(1, 11):
    print(' '*n, end='')  # repeat space for n times
    print ('* '*(i))  # repeat star for i times
    n-=1
```

Output:

```
C:\>python Demo.py
                                        * 
                                       * * 
                                      * * * 
                                     * * * * 
                                    * * * * * 
                                   * * * * * * 
                                  * * * * * * * 
                                 * * * * * * * * 
                                * * * * * * * * * 
                               * * * * * * * * * * 
```

Program 21 can also be rewritten using the elegant style of Python as:

```
n=40
for i in range(1, 11):
    print(' '*(n-i) + '* '*(i))
```

Finally, we will write another program using nested loops to display numbers from 1 to 100 in 10 rows and 10 columns. To display numbers the following loops are sufficient:

```
for x in range(1, 11):
    for y in range(1, 11):
        print(x*y, end='')  # print product of x and y
    print()
```

But this code gives the following output that looks awkward:

```
12345678910
2468101214161820
36912151821242730
481216202428323640
```

```
5101520253035404550
6121824303642485460
7142128354249566370
8162432404856647280
9182736455463728190
102030405060708090100
```

We need to display each number in a column with fixed size so that the output will look nice. For this purpose, we can specify column size using replacement field {} and format() method as:

```
print('{:8}'.format(x*y), end='')
```

Here, {:8} represents that the produce value (x*y) should be displayed in the field size of 8. Now, see the Program 22. The output is displayed in Figure 6.2.

Program

Program 22: A Python program to display numbers from 1 to 100 in a proper format.

```
# Displaying numbers from 1 to 100 in 10 rows and 10 cols.
for x in range(1, 11):
    for y in range(1, 11):
        print('{:8}'.format(x*y), end='')  # each column size is 8
    print()
```

Output:

```
Administrator: Command Prompt

F:\py>python Demo.py
       1       2       3       4       5       6       7       8       9      10
       2       4       6       8      10      12      14      16      18      20
       3       6       9      12      15      18      21      24      27      30
       4       8      12      16      20      24      28      32      36      40
       5      10      15      20      25      30      35      40      45      50
       6      12      18      24      30      36      42      48      54      60
       7      14      21      28      35      42      49      56      63      70
       8      16      24      32      40      48      56      64      72      80
       9      18      27      36      45      54      63      72      81      90
      10      20      30      40      50      60      70      80      90     100

F:\py>_
```

Figure 6.2: Output of the Program 22

The else Suite

In Python, it is possible to use 'else' statement along with for loop or while loop in the form shown in Table 6.2:

Table 6.2: Else suite with loops

for with else	**while with else**

for(var in sequence) :
statements
else:
statements
	while(condition):
	statements
	else:
	statements

The statements written after 'else' are called suite. The else suite will be always executed irrespective of the statements in the loop are executed or not. For example,

```
for i in range(5):
    print("Yes")
else:
    print("No")
```

this will display the following output:

```
Yes
Yes
Yes
Yes
Yes
No
```

It means, the for loop statement is executed and also the else suite is executed. Suppose, we write:

```
for i in range(0):
    print("Yes")
else:
    print("No")
```

This will display the following output:

```
No
```

Here, the statement in the for loop is not even executed once, but the else suite is executed as usual. So, the point is this: the else suite is always executed. But then where is this else suite useful?

Sometimes, we write programs where searching for an element is done in the sequence. When the element is not found, we can indicate that in the else suite easily. In this case, else with for loop or while loop - is very convenient. Let's now write a program where we take a list of elements and using for loop we will search for a particular element in the list. If the element is found in the list, we will display that is found in the group; else we will display a message that the element is not found in the list. This is displayed using else suite.

Program

Program 23: A Python program to search for an element in the list of elements.

```
# searching for an element in a list
group1 = [1,2,3,4,5]    #take a list of elements
search = int(input('Enter element to search: '))
for element in group1:
    if search == element:
        print('Element found in group1')
        break  # come out of for loop
else:
    print('Element not found in group1')   # this is else suite
```

Output:

```
C:\>python Demo.py
Enter element to search: 4
Element found in group1

C:\>python Demo.py
Enter element to search: 6
Element not found in group1
```

The break Statement

The break statement can be used inside a for loop or while loop to come out of the loop. When 'break' is executed, the Python interpreter jumps out of the loop to process the next statement in the program.

We have already used break inside for loop in Program 23. When the element is found, it would break the for loop and comes out. We can also use break inside a while loop. Suppose, we want to display numbers from 10 to 1 in descending order using while loop. For this purpose, we can write a simple while loop as:

```
x = 10
while x>=1:
    print ('x= ', x)
    x-=1
print("Out of loop")
```

The above loop will display the following output:

```
x=  10
x=  9
x=  8
x=  7
x=  6
x=  5
x=  4
x=  3
x=  2
x=  1
Out of loop
```

Now, suppose we want to display x values up to 6 and if it is 5 then we want to come out of the loop, we can introduce a statement like this:

```
if x==5:  # if x is 5 then come out from while loop
    break
```

This is what is done in Program 24. A break statement is breaking the while loop when a condition is met.

Program

Program 24: A Python program to display numbers from 10 to 6 and break the loop when the number about to display is 5.

```
# Using break to come out of while loop
x = 10
while x>=1:
    print ('x= ', x)
    x-=1
    if x==5:  # if x is 5 then come out from while loop
        break
print("Out of loop")
```

Output:

```
x= 10
x= 9
x= 8
x= 7
x= 6
Out of loop
```

The continue Statement

The continue statement is used in a loop to go back to the beginning of the loop. It means, when continue is executed, the next repetition will start. When continue is executed, the subsequent statements in the loop are not executed.

In Program 25, the while loop repeats for 10 times from 0 to 9. Every time, 'x' value is displayed by the loop. When x value is greater than 5, 'continue' is executed that makes the Python interpreter to go back to the beginning of the loop. Thus the next statements in the loop are not executed. As a result, the numbers up to 5 are only displayed.

Program

Program 25: A Python program to display numbers from 1 to 5 using continue statement.

```
# Using continue to execute next iteration of while loop
x = 0
while x<10:
    x+=1
    if x>5:  # if x > 5 then continue next iteration
```

```
            continue
        print ('x= ', x)
    print("Out of loop")
```

Output:

```
C:\>python Demo.py
x= 1
x= 2
x= 3
x= 4
x= 5
Out of loop
```

The pass Statement

The pass statement does not do anything. It is used with 'if' statement or inside a loop to represent no operation. We use pass statement when we need a statement syntactically but we do not want to do any operation.

The 'continue' statement in Program 25 redirected the flow of execution to the beginning of the loop. If we use 'pass' in the place of 'continue', the numbers from 1 to 10 are displayed as if there is no effect of 'pass'.

Program

Program 26: A program to know that pass does nothing.

```
# Using pass to do nothing
x = 0
while x<10:
    x+=1
    if x>5:  # if x > 5 then continue next iteration
        pass
    print ('x= ', x)
print("Out of loop")
```

Output:

```
C:\>python Demo.py
x= 1
x= 2
x= 3
x= 4
x= 5
x= 6
x= 7
x= 8
x= 9
x= 10
Out of loop
```

A more meaningful usage of the 'pass' statement is to inform the Python interpreter not to do anything when we are not interested in the result. This can be seen in Program 27.

Program

Program 27: A Python program to retrieve only negative numbers from a list of numbers.

```
# Retrieving only negative numbers from a list.
num = [1,2,3,-4,-5,-6,-7, 8, 9]
for i in num:
    if(i>0):
        pass  # we are not interested
    else:
        print(i)  # this is what we need
```

Output:

```
C:\>python Demo.py
-4
-5
-6
-7
```

The assert Statement

The assert statement is useful to check if a particular condition is fulfilled or not. The syntax is as follows:

```
assert expression, message
```

In the above syntax, the 'message' is not compulsory. Let's take an example. If we want to assure that the user should enter only a number greater than 0, we can use assert statement as:

```
assert x>0, "Wrong input entered"
```

In this case, the Python interpreter checks if x>0 is True or not. If it is True, then the next statements will execute, else it will display AssertionError along with the message "Wrong input entered". This can be easily understood from Program 28.

Program

Program 28: A program to assert that the user enters a number greater than zero.

```
# understanding assert statement
x = int(input('Enter a number greater than 0: '))
assert x>0, "Wrong input entered"
print('U entered: ',x)
```

Output:

```
C:\>python Demo.py
Enter a number greater than 0: 5
U entered: 5
C:\> python Demo.py
Enter a number greater than 0: -2
Traceback (most recent call last):
    File "Demo.py", line 3, in <module>
        assert x>0, "Wrong input entered"
AssertionError: Wrong input entered
```

The 'AssertionError' shown in the above output is called an exception. An exception is an error that occurs during runtime. To avoid such type of exceptions, we can handle them using 'try ... except' statement. After 'try', we use 'assert' and after 'except', we write the exception name to be handled. In the except block, we write the statements that are executed in case of exception. Consider Program 29.

Program

Program 29: A Python program to handle the AssertionError exception that is given by assert statement.

```
# to handle AssertionError raised by assert
x = int(input('Enter a number greater than 0: '))
try:
    assert(x>0)  # exception may occur here
    print('U entered: ',x)
except AssertionError:
    print("Wrong input entered")  # this is executed in case of
    # exception
```

Output:

```
C:\>python Demo.py
Enter a number greater than 0:  -5
Wrong input entered
```

We will discuss exceptions clearly in a later chapter.

The return Statement

A function represents a group of statements to perform a task. The purpose of a function is to perform some task and in many cases a function returns the result. A function starts with the keyword *def*that represents the definition of the function. After 'def', the function should be written. Then we should write variables in the parentheses. For example,

```
def sum(a, b):
    function body
```

After the function name, we should use a colon (:) to separate the name with the body. The body of the statements contains logic to perform the task. For example, to find sum of two numbers, we can write:

```
def sum(a, b):
    print(a+b)
```

A function is executed only when it is called. At the time of calling the sum() function, we should pass values to variables a and b. So, we can call this function as:

```
sum(5, 10)
```

Now, the values 5 and 10 are passed to a and b respectively and the sum() function displays their sum. In Program 30, we will now write a simple function to perform sum of two numbers.

Program

Program 30: A function to find the sum of two numbers.

```
# a function to find sum of two numbers
def sum(a, b):
    print('Sum= ', a+b)

sum(5, 10)  # call sum() and pass 5 and 10
sum(1.5, 2.5)  # call sum() and pass 1.5 and 2.5
```

Output:

```
C:\>python Demo.py
Sum= 15
Sum= 4.0
```

In the above program, the sum() function is not returning the computed result. It is simply displaying the result using print() statement. In some cases, it is highly useful to write the function as if it is returning the result. This is done using 'return' statement. return statement is used inside a function to return some value to the calling place. The syntax of using the return statement is:

```
return expression
```

We will rewrite Program 30 such that the sum() function returns the result with the help of return statement.

Program

Program 31: A Python program to write a function that returns the result of sum of two numbers.

```
# a function to return sum of two numbers
def sum(a, b):
    return a+b  # result is returned from here

# call sum() and pass 5 and 10
# get the returned result into res
res = sum(5, 10)
print('The result is ', res)
```

Output:

```
C:\>python Demo.py
The result is 15
```

When a function does not return anything, then we need not write 'return' statement inside the function.

Once we understand control statements, we would be ready to develop better programs. In the next program, we want to display prime numbers. The general logic for checking whether a number 'n' is prime or not is to divide 'n' with every number starting from 2 to n-1. If 'n' is not divisible by all numbers from 2 to n-1, then it is prime and should be displayed. On the other hand, if 'n' is divisible by any number from 2 to n-1, then we can say it is not prime and hence it should be left. This logic is used in Program 32.

Program

Program 32: Write a Python program to display prime number series.

```
# program to print prime numbers upto a given number
# accept upto what number the user wants
max = int(input("Upto what number? "))

for num in range(2, max+1):    # generate from 2 onwards till max
    for i in range(2,num):  # i represents numbers from 2 to num-1
        if (num % i) == 0:  # if num is divisible by i
            break  # then it is not prime, hence go back and check next
            # number
    else:
            print(num)  # otherwise it is prime and hence display
```

Output:

```
C:\>python primes.py
Upto what number? 30
2
3
5
7
11
13
17
19
23
29
```

In the previous program, observe the following statements:

```
if (num % i) == 0:  # if num is divisible by i
    break
```

If the number 'num' is not prime then 'break' is executed. This 'break' statement will break the inner for loop and Python interpreter goes back to outer for loop where the next number comes into 'num'. The reader is urged to understand the indentation of the statements in the program without confusion.

Let's write a program to display Fibonacci numbers. The Fibonacci number series are given as: 0, 1, 1, 2, 3, 5, 8, 13, 21, 34, etc. If we take the first two Fibonacci numbers as:

```
f1 = 0
f2 = 1
```

Then the third Fibonacci f can be obtained by adding the two previous Fibonacci numbers as:

```
f = f1+ f2
```

Now, the two recent Fibonacci numbers are f2 and f. So, to get the next Fibonacci number, we should add them by taking them as f1 and f2. It means,

```
f1 = f2  # take f2 as f1
f2 = f  # take f as f2
f = f1+ f2  # get next Fibonacci number
```

The above logic is represented in Figure 6.3. To repeatedly generate the Fibonacci numbers, we can use the above logic in a loop as:

```
while c<n:
        f = f1+f2
        print(f)
        f1=f2
        f2=f
        c+=1    # increment count
```

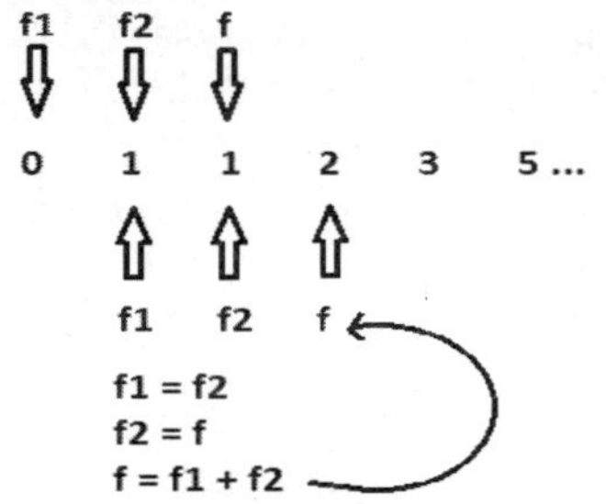

Figure 6.3: Logic to generate Fibonacci numbers

Program

Program 33: Write a Python program to generate Fibonacci number series.

```
# program to display Fibonacci series
n = int(input('How many Fibonaccis ? '))
f1=0  # this is first Fibonacci no
f2=1  # this is the second one
c=2   # counts the no of Fibonaccis
if n==1:
    print(f1)
elif n==2:
    print(f1, '\n', f2, sep='')
else:
    print(f1, '\n', f2, sep='')
    while c<n:
        f = f1+f2 # add two Fibonaccis to get the new one
        print(f)
        f1, f2 = f2, f   # this is same as f1=f2, f2=f
        c+=1   # increment counter
```

Output:

```
C:\>python fibo.py
How many Fibonaccis ? 10
0
1
1
2
3
5
8
13
21
34
```

Let's write a Python program to find Sine value of a given angle using Sine series. Sine series is represented by the following formula:

$$\sin x = x - \frac{x^3}{3!} + \frac{x^5}{5!} - \frac{x^7}{7!} + \cdots$$

In the above formula, 'x' value is assumed to be in radians. If the user inputs the angle value in radians, then it can be used in the above formula directly. But if the user inputs the angle value in degrees, then it should be converted into radians. To convert into radians, we should multiply degrees value by 3.14159/180 as:

```
r = x *3.14159/180
```

This becomes the first term. So, let's take it as 't'.

```
t = r
```

Now, we want to find out the second term. Please observe that the second term contains the first term. So, the second term can be written as:

$$\frac{x^3}{3!} = x * \frac{x^2}{2*3} = t * \frac{r^2}{i*(i+1)}$$

where 't' represents the previous term and i value is taken as 2. Similarly, the third term contains the second term.

$$\frac{x}{5!} = \frac{x^3}{3!} * \frac{x^2}{4*5} = t * \frac{r^2}{i*(i+1)}$$

where 't' represents the previous term. Here 'i' value will be 4. So, each new term in the series can be obtained by the following expression:

```
t= (-1) * t * r * r/( i * (i + 1))
```

The -1 in the beginning of the preceding expression represents alternate positive and negative terms in the formula. This expression is used in the Program 34. This program accepts the angle value in degrees from the user and finds the Sine of that angle value. This program also accepts the number of iterations from the user. If the number of iterations is limited like 3 or 4, then the accuracy may not be good. Hence the user should give 10 to 15 iterations so that accurate result can be obtained.

Program

Program 34: Write a Python program to calculate the Sine value of a given angle in degrees by evaluating Sine series.

```
# program to evaluate sine series.
# accept user input
x, n = [int(i) for i in input("Enter angle value, no. of iterations:
      ").split(',')]
```

```
# convert the angle from degrees into radians
r=(x*3.14159)/180

# this becomes the first term
t=r

# till now, find the sum
sum=r
# display the iteration number and sum
print('Iteration= %d\tSum= %f' % (1, sum))

# denominator for the second term
i=2

# repeat for 2nd to nth terms

for j in range(2, n+1):
    t=(-1)*t*r*r/(i*(i+1))  # find the next term
    sum=sum+t;  # add it to sum
    print('Iteration= %d\tSum= %f' % (j, sum))
    i +=2  # increase i value by 2 for denominator for next term
```

Output:

```
C:\>python sine.py
Enter angle value, no. of iterations: 60, 10
Iteration= 1        Sum= 1.047197
Iteration= 2        Sum= 1.855800
Iteration= 3        Sum= 1.866295
Iteration= 4        Sum= 1.866021
Iteration= 5        Sum= 1.866025
Iteration= 6        Sum= 1.866025
Iteration= 7        Sum= 1.866025
Iteration= 8        Sum= 1.866025
Iteration= 9        Sum= 1.866025
Iteration= 10       Sum= 1.866025
```

If we observe the output, from 5th iteration onwards, the sum value has been stabilized. This value should be taken as the Sine of 60 degrees. So, sin(60) = 1.866025.

Similarly, we can write another program for finding the value of Cosine series. The formula for Cosine series is:

$$\cos x = 1 - \frac{x^2}{2!} + \frac{x^4}{4!} - \frac{x^6}{6!} + \cdots$$

To find the value of cosine series, we take the first term as 1 and the sum value as 1 as:

```
t = 1
sum = 1
```

We can imagine the second term as:

$$\frac{x^2}{2!} = 1 * \frac{x^2}{1 * (2)} = t * \frac{r^2}{i * (i+1)}$$

where 't' represents the previous term, i.e. 1 and i value is 1. In the same manner, the third term can be:

$$\frac{x^4}{4!} = \frac{x^2}{2!} * \frac{x^2}{3 * (4)} = t * \frac{r^2}{i * (i+1)}$$

where 't' represents the previous terms and I value is 3. In this way we can find the terms in the series and add them to 'sum' which is initially '1'. So, each term in the series can be obtained using the following expression:

```
t=(-1)*t*r**2/(i*(i+1))
```

The beginning (-1) helps to generate the positive and negative terms alternately. This logic is shown in Program 35.

Program

Program 35: Write a Python program to find Cosine value of a given angle in degrees by evaluating the Cosine series.

```
# program to evaluate Cosine series.
# accept user input
x, n = [int(i) for i in input("Enter angle value, no. of iterations:
      ").split(',')]

# convert the angle from degrees into radians
r=(x*3.14159)/180

# this becomes the first term
t=1

# till now, sum is 1 only
sum=1

# display the iteration number and sum
print('Iteration= %d\tSum= %f' % (1, sum))

# denominator for the second term
i=1

# repeat for 2nd to nth terms

for j in range(2, n+1):
    t=(-1)*t*r**2/(i*(i+1))  # find the next term
    sum=sum+t;  # add it to sum
    print('Iteration= %d\tSum= %f' % (j, sum))
    i +=2  # increase i value by 2 for denominator for next term
```

Output:

```
C:\>python cos.py
Enter angle value, no. of iterations: 60, 10
Iteration= 1        Sum= 1.000000
Iteration= 2        Sum= 0.451690
Iteration= 3        Sum= 0.501797
Iteration= 4        Sum= 0.499965
```

```
Iteration= 5        Sum= 0.500001
Iteration= 6        Sum= 0.500001
Iteration= 7        Sum= 0.500001
Iteration= 8        Sum= 0.500001
Iteration= 9        Sum= 0.500001
Iteration= 10       Sum= 0.500001
```

Observe the output of the previous program. From 5th iteration onwards, the result has stabilized. Hence we can say cos(60) = 0.500001.

Similarly, we can construct logic for finding the value of Exponential series, which is represented by the following formula:

$$e^x = 1 + \frac{x}{1!} + \frac{x^2}{2!} + \frac{x^3}{3!} + \cdots$$

To find the value of Exponential series, we take the first term as 1 and the sum value as 1 as:

```
t = 1
sum = 1
```

We can imagine the second term, as:

$$\frac{x}{1!} = 1 * \frac{x}{1 * 1} = t * \frac{x}{j}$$

where 'j' value is '1'. Now the third term can be written as:

$$\frac{x^2}{2!} = \frac{x}{1!} * \frac{x}{2} = t * \frac{x}{j}$$

where t represent the previous terms and j value will be '2'. Thus 'j' values are incremented by '1' for each new term. This logic is shown in Program 36.

Program

Program 36: Write a Python program to evaluate exponential series.

```
# program to evaluate Exponential series.
# accept user input
x, n = [int(i) for i in input("Enter power of e, no. of iterations:
       ").split(',')]

# this becomes the first term
t=1

# till now, sum is 1 only
sum=t

# display the iteration number and sum
print('Iteration= %d\tSum= %f' % (1, sum))

# repeat for 1st to n-1th terms
```

```
    for j in range(1, n):
        t= t * x/j  # find the next term
        sum=sum+t;  # add it to sum
        print('Iteration= %d\tSum= %f' % (j+1, sum))
```

Output:

```
C:\>python eval.py
Enter power of e, no. of iterations: 2, 15
Iteration= 1        Sum= 1.000000
Iteration= 2        Sum= 3.000000
Iteration= 3        Sum= 5.000000
Iteration= 4        Sum= 6.333333
Iteration= 5        Sum= 7.000000
Iteration= 6        Sum= 7.266667
Iteration= 7        Sum= 7.355556
Iteration= 8        Sum= 7.380952
Iteration= 9        Sum= 7.387302
Iteration= 10       Sum= 7.388713
Iteration= 11       Sum= 7.388995
Iteration= 12       Sum= 7.389046
Iteration= 13       Sum= 7.389055
Iteration= 14       Sum= 7.389056
Iteration= 15       Sum= 7.389056
```

Points to Remember

- Control statements are statements that control the flow of execution of statements so that they can be executed repeatedly and randomly.
- The if statement executes a group of statements depending upon whether a condition is True or False.
- The difference between a statement and loop is that the statement is executed only once but a loop can be executed repeatedly. Python offers for and while loops for repeated execution.
- Indentation represents the spaces before a statement that identifies the statement as belonging to a block. The default indentation in Python is 4 spaces.
- The for loop is generally used to iterate over the elements of a sequence like a string, a list or tuple.
- It is possible to use 'else suite' along with loops.
- It is possible to write one loop inside another loop. Such loops are called 'nested loops'.
- An infinite loop is a loop that is executed forever. Using infinite loops in a program is not advisable.
- The break statement is useful to come out of a loop.

- The continue statement is useful to continue with the next repetition of a loop.
- The pass statement does nothing and hence used to send execution to the next statement.
- The assert statement is useful to check if a particular condition is fulfilled or not. If the condition is not fulfilled then it will raise AssertionError. Its general format is: assert expression, 'message'
- The return statement is used in a function to return some value from the function.

CHAPTER

ARRAYS IN PYTHON

7

Suppose there is a group of students whose marks are to be listed. The first student's marks are stored in a variable m1, the second student's marks are stored in m2, the third student's marks in m3, and so on and the 100th student's marks are stored in m100. It means, we are supposed to create 100 variables to store 100 students' marks. Thus, we are supposed to write 100 statements like this:

```
1=65
m2=61
m3=70
:
m100=67
```

Now, if we want to display these marks, we need to write another 100 statements. It means, a simple program will contain hundreds of statements and this becomes difficult for the programmer. On the other hand, just imagine there is only one variable that stores 100 students' marks. That variable will be very much useful to us since we have to write only 1 statement instead of writing 100 statements. For example, we can declare 'm' variable as an array and store all the marks there. This reduces the program size considerably and the programmer's task will become easy. Let's now learn more about array.

Array

So, what is an array? An array is an object that stores a group of elements (or values) of same datatype. The main advantage of any array is to store and process a group of elements easily. There are two points we should remember in case of arrays in Python.

- Arrays can store only one type of data. It means, we can store only integer type elements or only float type elements into an array. But we cannot store one integer, one float and one character type element into the same array.

- Arrays can increase or decrease their size dynamically. It means, we need not declare the size of the array. When the elements are added, it will increase its size and when the elements are removed, it will automatically decrease its size in memory.

In Python, there is a standard module by the name 'array' that helps us to create and use arrays. To get help on 'array' module, we can type help() at Python prompt to get the help prompt as:

```
>>>help()
help>
```

Then we should type simply 'array' at the help prompt to see all information about the array module as shown in Figure 7.1:

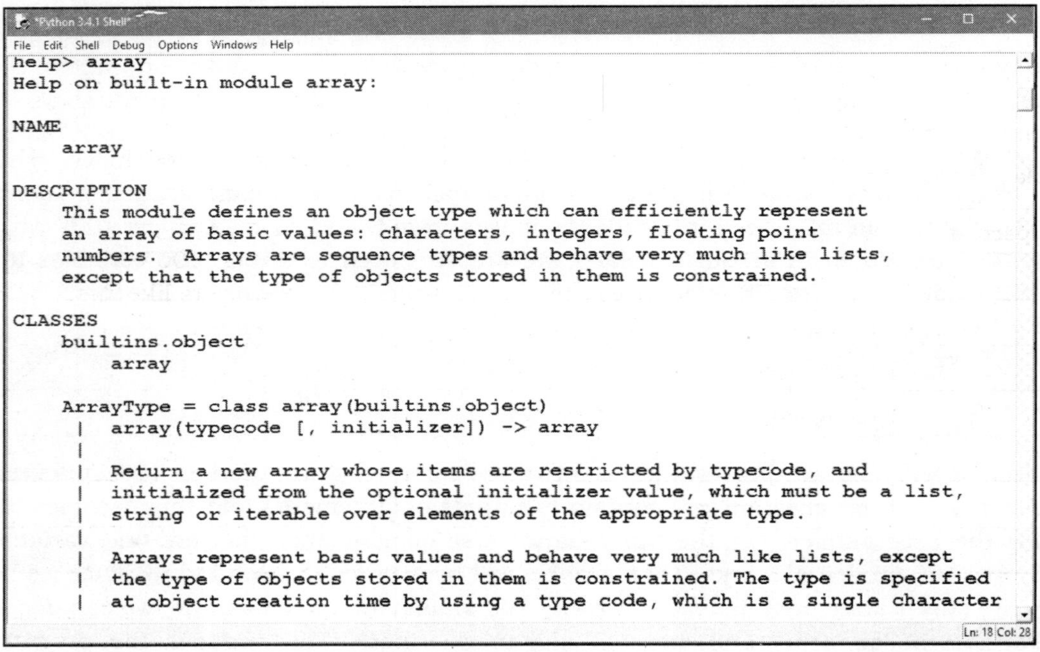

Figure 7.1: Getting Help on Array Module

Advantages of Arrays

The following are some advantages of arrays:

- Arrays are similar to lists. The main difference is that arrays can store only one type of elements; whereas, lists can store different types of elements. When dealing with a huge number of elements, arrays use less memory than lists and they offer faster execution than lists.

- The size of the array is not fixed in Python. Hence, we need not specify how many elements we are going to store into an array in the beginning.

- Arrays can grow or shrink in memory dynamically (during runtime).
- Arrays are useful to handle a collection of elements like a group of numbers or characters.
- Methods that are useful to process the elements of any array are available in 'array' module.

Creating an Array

We have already discussed that arrays can hold data of same type. The type should be specified by using a type code at the time of creating the array object as:

```
arrayname = array(type code, [elements])
```

The type code 'i', represents integer type array where we can store integer numbers. If the type code is 'f' then it represents float type array where we can store numbers with decimal point. The important type codes are given in Table 7.1:

Table 7.1: The Type Codes to Create Arrays

Typecode	C Type	Minimum size in bytes
'b'	signed integer	1
'B'	unsigned integer	1
'i'	signed integer	2
'I'	unsigned integer	2
'l'	signed integer	4
'L'	unsigned integer	4
'f'	floating point	4
'd'	double precision floating point	8
'u'	unicode character	2

We will take an example to understand how to create an integer type array. We should first write the module name 'array' and then the type code we can use is 'i' for integer type array. After that the elements should be written inside the square braces [ ] as,

```
a = array('i', [4, 6, 2, 9])
```

This is creating an array whose name is 'a' with integer type elements 4, 6, 2 and 9.

Similarly, to create a float type array, we can write:

```
arr = array('d', [1.5, -2.2, 3, 5.75])
```

This will create an array by the name 'arr' with float type elements 1.5, -2.2, 3.0 and 5.75. The type code is 'd' which represents double type elements each taking 8 bytes memory.

Of course, in the previous statements we are using 'array' module to create arrays. To use this module, we have to first import 'array' module into our program.

Importing the Array Module

There are three ways to import the array module into our program. The first way is to import the entire array module using import statement as,

```
import array
```

When we import the array module, we are able to get the 'array' class of that module that helps us to create an array. See the following example:

```
a=array.array('i',[4,6,2,9])
```

Here, the first 'array' represents the module name and the next 'array' represents the class name for which the object is created. We should understand that we are creating our array as an object of array class.

The second way of importing the array module is to give it an alias name, as:

```
import array as ar
```

Here, the array is imported with an alternate name 'ar'. Hence we can refer to the array class of 'ar' module as:

```
a=ar.array('i', [4,6,2,9])
```

The third way of importing the array module is to write:

```
from array import *
```

Observe the '*' symbol that represents 'all'. The meaning of this statement is this: import all (classes, objects, variables etc) from the array module into our program. That means we are specifically importing the 'array' class (because of * symbol) of 'array' module. So, there is no need to mention the module name before our array name while creating it. We can create the array as:

```
a=array('i',[4,6,2,9])
```

Here, the name 'array' represents the class name that is available from the 'array' module. Let's write a Python program to create an integer type array with some integer elements. Program 1 shows how to create an integer type array.

Program

Program 1: A Python program to create an integer type array.

```
# creating an array
import array
a = array.array('i', [5, 6, -7, 8])

print('The array elements are: ')
for element in a:
    print(element)
```

Output:

```
C:\>python arr.py
5
6
-7
8
```

Observe the for loop in the previous program. The variable 'element' assumes each element value from the array 'a' and hence print(element) will display all the elements of the array. The same program can be rewritten using a different type of import statement as shown in Program 2.

Program

Program 2: A Python program to create an integer type array.

```
# creating an array - v 2.0
from array import *
a = array('i', [5, 6, -7, 8])

print('The array elements are: ')
for element in a:
    print(element)
```

Output:

```
C:\>python arr.py
5
6
-7
8
```

Let's write another program to see how to create an array with a group of characters and display the elements of the array. This is shown in Program 3.

Program

Program 3: A Python program to create an array with a group of characters.

```
# creating an array with characters
from array import *
arr = array('u', ['a','b','c','d','e'])

print('The array elements are: ')
for ch in arr:
    print(ch)
```

Output:

```
C:\>python arr.py
a
b
c
d
e
```

It is possible to create an array from another array. For example, there is an array 'arr1' as:

```
arr1 = array('d', [1.5, 2.5, -3.5, 4])
```

This is a float type array with 4 elements. We want to create another array with the name 'arr2' from arr1. It means, 'arr2' should have same type code and same elements as that of 'arr1'. For this purpose, we can write:

```
arr2 = array(arr1.typecode, (a for a in arr1))
```

Here, 'arr1.typecode' gives the type code character of the array 'arr1'. This type code is used for 'arr2' array also. Observe the expression:

```
a for a in arr1
```

The first 'a' represents that its value is stored as elements in the array 'arr2'. This 'a' value is got from 'a' (each element) in arr1. So, all the elements in arr1 will be stored into arr2. Suppose, we write the expression,

```
arr2 = array(arr1.typecode, (a*3 for a in arr1))
```

In this case, the value of 'a' obtained from arr1, is multiplied by 3 and then stored as element into arr2. So, arr2 will get the elements: 4.5, 7.5, -10.5, and 12.0. This can be verified from Program 4.

Program

Program 4: A Python program to create one array from another array.

```
# creating one array from another array
from array import *
arr1 = array('d', [1.5, 2.5, -3.5, 4])

# use same type code and multiply each element of arr1 with 3
arr2 = array(arr1.typecode, (a*3 for a in arr1))
print('The arr2 elements are: ')
for i in arr2:
    print(i)
```

Output:

```
C:\>python arr.py
The arr2 elements are:
4.5
7.5
-10.5
12.0
```

Indexing and Slicing on Arrays

An *index* represents the position number of an element in an array. For example, when we create the following integer type array:

```
x = array('i', [10, 20, 30, 40, 50])
```

Python interpreter allocates 5 blocks of memory, each of 2 bytes size and stores the elements 10, 20, 30, 40 and 50 in these blocks. Figure 7.2 shows the arrangement of elements the array 'x':

10	20	30	40	50
x[0]	x[1]	x[2]	x[3]	x[4]

Figure 7.2: Arrangement of Elements in an Array

When we observe Figure 7.2, we can understand that the 0th element of the array is represented by x[0], the 1st element is represented by x[1] and so on. Here, 0, 1, 2, etc, are representing the position numbers of the elements. So, in general we can use i to represent the position of any element. This 'i' is called 'index' of the array. Using 'index, we can refer to any element of the array as x[i] where 'i' values will change from 0 to n-1. Here n represents the total number of elements in the array.

To find out the number of elements in an array we can use the len() function as:

```
n = len(x)
```

The len(x) function returns the number of elements in the array 'x' into 'n'. In Program 5, we are showing how to access the elements of an array using index.

Program

Program 5: A Python program to retrieve the elements of an array using array index.

```
# accessing elements of an array using index
from array import *
x = array('i', [10, 20, 30, 40, 50])

# find number of elements in the array
n = len(x)

# display array elements using indexing
for i in range(n):   # repeat from 0 to n-1
    print(x[i], end=' ')
```

Output:

```
C:\>python arr.py
10 20 30 40 50
```

It is also possible to access the elements of an array using while loop. The same program can be rewritten using while loop as Program 6.

Program

Program 6: A Python program to retrieve elements of an array using while loop.

```
# accessing elements of an array using index - v 2.0
from array import *
x = array('i', [10, 20, 30, 40, 50])
```

```
# find number of elements in the array
n = len(x)

# display array elements using indexing
i=0
while i<n:
    print(x[i], end=' ')
    i+=1
```

Output:

```
C:\>python arr.py
10 20 30 40 50
```

A *slice* represents a piece of the array. When we perform 'slicing' operations on any array, we can retrieve a piece of the array that contains a group of elements. Whereas indexing is useful to retrieve element by element from the array, slicing is useful to retrieve a range of elements. The general format of a slice is:

```
arrayname[start:stop:stride]
```

We can eliminate any one or any two in the items: 'start', 'stop' or 'stride' from the above syntax. For example,

```
arr[1:4]
```

The above slice gives elements starting from 1st to 3rd from the array 'arr'. Counting of the elements starts from 0. All the items 'start', 'stop' and 'stride' represent integer numbers either positive or negative. The item 'stride' represents step size excluding the starting element.

To understand how one can perform slicing operations on an array, we will write a Python program where we take an array 'x' and do slicing on the elements of the array 'x'. The result of slicing operations will be a new array 'y'. Please go through Program 7.

Program

Program7: A Python program that helps to know the effects of slicing operations on an array.

```
# create array y with elements from 1st to 3rd from x
y = x[1:4]
print(y)

# create array y with elements from 0th till the last element in x
y = x[0:]
print(y)

# create array y with elements from 0th to 3rd from x
y = x[:4]
print(y)

# create array y with last 4 elements from x
y = x[-4:]
print(y)

# create y with last 4th element and with 3 [-4-(-1)= -3]elements
# towards right.
```

```
y = x[-4: -1]
print(y)

# create y with 0th to 7th elements from x.
# stride 2 means, after 0th element, retrieve every 2nd element from x
y = x[0:7:2]
print(y)
```

Output:

```
C:\>python arr.py
array('i', [20, 30, 40])
array('i', [10, 20, 30, 40, 50, 60, 70])
array('i', [10, 20, 30, 40])
array('i', [40, 50, 60, 70])
array('i', [40, 50, 60])
array('i', [10, 30, 50, 70])
```

From Program 7, we can understand that slicing can be used to create new arrays from existing arrays. For example, when we write:

```
y = x[-4:]
```

we are creating a new array 'y' with the last 4 elements of 'x' that we obtained through slicing. Slicing can also be used to update an array. For example, to replace the 1st and 2nd elements of 'x' array with the elements [5, 7] of another array, we can write:

```
x[1:3] = array('i',[5, 7])
```

The elements 5, 7 are stored in the positions 1 and 2 in the array 'x'. The remaining element of the array will not be changed.

Just like indexing, slicing can also be used to retrieve elements from an array. In Program 8, we are displaying only a range of elements from the array 'x'.

Program

Program 8: A Python program to retrieve and display only a range of elements from an array using slicing.

```
# using slicing to display elements of an array.
from array import *
x = array('i', [10, 20, 30, 40, 50, 60, 70])

# display elements from 2nd to 4th only
for i in x[2:5]:
    print(i)
```

Output:

```
C:\>python arr.py
30
40
50
```

Processing the Arrays

The arrays class of arrays module in Python offers methods to process the arrays easily. The programmers can easily perform certain operations by using these methods. We should understand that a method is similar to a function that performs a specific task. But methods are written inside a class whereas a function can be written inside or outside the class. Methods are generally called as: objectname.method(). Please see Table 7.2 for methods that can be used on arrays:

Table 7.2: Array Methods

Method	Description
a.append(x)	Adds an element x at the end of the existing array a.
a.count(x)	Returns the numbers of occurrences of x in the array a.
a.extend(x)	Appends x at the end of the array a. 'x' can be another array or an iterable object.
a.fromfile(f, n)	Reads n items (in binary format) from the file object f and appends to the end of the array a. 'f' must be a file object. Raises 'EOFError' if fewer than n items are read.
a.fromlist(lst)	Appends items from the lst to the end of the array. 'lst' can be any list or iterable object.
a.fromstring(s)	Appends items from string s to the end of the array a.
a.index(x)	Returns the position number of the first occurrence of x in the array. Raises 'ValueError' if not found.
a.insert(i, x)	Inserts x in the position i in the array.
a.pop(x)	Removes the item x from the array a and returns it.
a.pop()	Remove last item from the array a.
a.remove(x)	Removes the first occurrence of x in the array a. Raises 'ValueError' if not found.
a.reverse()	Reverses the order of elements in the array a.
a.tofile(f)	Writes all elements to the file f.
a.tolist()	Converts the array 'a' into a list.
a.tostring()	Converts the array into a string.

Apart from the methods shown in Table 7.2, we can also use the following variables of Array class as shown in Table 7.3:

Table 7.3: Variables of Array Class

Variable	Description
a.typecode	Represents the type code character used to create the array a
a.itemsize	Represents the size of items stored in the array (in bytes)

Most of these methods are used in Program 9 so that there will be better clarity regarding their results.

Program

Program 9: A Python program to understand various methods of arrays class.

```
# operations on arrays
from array import*

# create an array with int values
arr = array('i', [10,20,30,40,50])
print('Original array: ', arr)

# append 30 to the array arr
arr.append(30)
arr.append(60)
print('After appending 30 and 60: ', arr)

# insert 99 at position number 1 in arr
arr.insert(1, 99)
print('After inserting 99 in 1st position: ', arr)

# remove an element from arr
arr.remove(20)
print('After removing 20: ', arr)

# remove last element using pop() method
n = arr.pop()
print('Array after using pop(): ', arr)
print('Popped element: ', n)

# finding position of element using index() method
n = arr.index(30)
print('First occurrence of element 30 is at: ', n)

# convert an array into a list using tolist() method
lst = arr.tolist()
print('List: ', lst)
print('Array: ', arr)
```

Output:

```
C:\>python arr.py
Original array:  array('i', [10, 20, 30, 40, 50])
After appending 30 and 60:  array('i', [10, 20, 30, 40, 50, 30, 60])
After inserting 99 in 1st position:  array('i', [10, 99, 20, 30, 40,
   50, 30, 60])
After removing 20:  array('i', [10, 99, 30, 40, 50, 30, 60])
Array after using pop():  array('i', [10, 99, 30, 40, 50, 30])
Popped element:  60
First occurrence of element 30 is at:  2
List:  [10, 99, 30, 40, 50, 30]
Array:  array('i', [10, 99, 30, 40, 50, 30])
```

Let's write a program to accept marks of a student and find the total marks and percentage of marks. This is done in Program 10. In this program, we first use input() function to accept marks into a string 'str' as:

```
str = input('Enter marks: ').split(' ')
```

When this statement is executed, the user should type marks separating them by a space as indicated by split(' ') method. These marks are stored into the string 'str'. Then we should convert this string into an array as:

```
marks = [int(num) for num in str]
```

Here, 'marks' is the name of the array. Observe the for loop at right hand side. It takes each number from 'str' and stores it into 'num'. The 'num' value is converted into 'int' using int(num). This integer number is then stored into 'marks' array. To represent that 'marks' is an array, we used square brackets for the expression at right side. These brackets store the numbers as a list into 'marks' array.

To find total marks, we can use another for loop as:

```
for x in marks:
    print(x)
    sum+=x
```

This for loop is doing two things. It is printing 'x' value that represents each element of the 'marks' array and then adding that 'x' value to sum. So, finally, 'sum' represents the total marks of the student.

To find percentage, we divide the 'sum' using number of element as:

```
percent =  sum/n
```

Here, 'n' represents the number of elements in the 'marks' array which can be obtained by calling the len() function as len(marks).

Program

Program 10: A Python program to storing student's marks into an array and finding total marks and percentage of marks.

```
from array import *
# accept marks as a string
str = input('Enter marks: ').split(' ')
```

```
# store the marks into 'marks' array
marks = [int(num) for num in str]

# display the marks and find total
sum=0
for x in marks:
    print(x)
    sum+=x
print('Total marks: ', sum)

# display percentage
n = len(marks)   # n = no. of elements in marks array
percent =  sum/n
print('Percentage: ', percent)
```

Output:

```
C:\>python arr.py
Enter marks: 50 56 75 67 45
50
56
75
67
45
Total marks: 293
Percentage: 58.6
```

We are going to develop a program to sort the elements of an array into ascending order. For this purpose, we are going to use bubble sort technique in Program 11. In this technique, all the 'n' elements from 0 to n are taken and the first element of the array x[j] is compared with the immediate element x[j+1]. If x[j] is bigger than x[j+1], then they are swapped (or interchanged) since in ascending order, we expect the smaller elements to be in the first place. When two elements are interchanged, the number of elements to be sorted becomes lesser by 1. When there are no more swaps found, the 'flag' will become 'False' and we can abort sorting. Suppose, we give the following elements for sorting:

```
Original array: 1, 5, 4, 3, 2
Compare 1 with other elements. 1 is smallest hence no swaps.
We get: 1, 5, 4, 3, 2
Compare 5 with other elements. Swap 5 with 4, 5 with 3, 5 with 2.
We get: 1, 4, 3, 2, 5
Compare 4 with other elements. Swap 4 with 3, 4 with 2.
We get: 1, 3, 2, 4, 5
Compare 3 with other elements. Swap 3 with 2.
We get: 1, 2, 3, 4, 5
```

Swapping means interchanging the values of two variables. If 'a' and 'b' are variables, we are supposed to store 'a' value into 'b' and vice versa. Swapping the values of 'a' and 'b' can be done using a temporary variable 't' as:

```
Store a value into t. i.e. t= a
Store b value into a. i.e. a = b
Store t value into b. i.e. b= t
```

These steps are shown in Figure 7.3 by taking 'a' value 1 and 'b' value 2 initially. After swapping is done, 'a' value will be 2 and 'b' value will be 1.

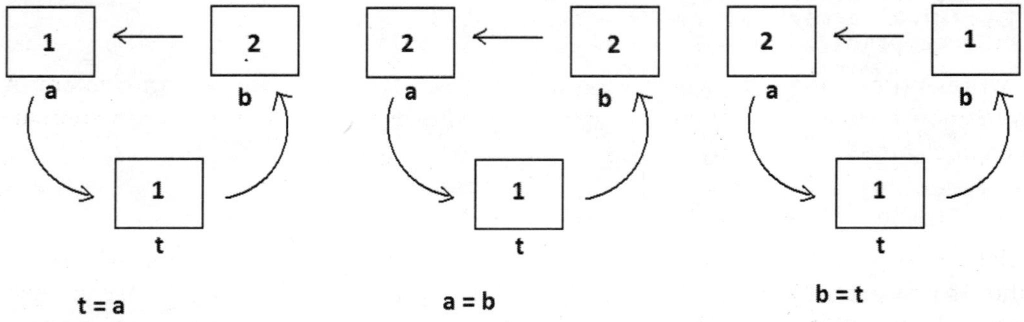

Figure 7.3: Swapping a and b Values using a Temporary Variable t

Program

Program 11: A Python program to sort the array elements using bubble sort technique.

```
# sorting an array using Bubble sort technique
from array import*
# create an empty array to store integers
x = array('i', [])

# store elements into the array x
print('How many elements? ', end='')
n = int(input()) # accept input into n

for i in range(n):  # repeat for n times
    print('Enter element: ', end='')
    x.append(int(input()))  # add the element to the array x

print('Original array: ', x)

# bubble sort
flag = False  # when swapping is done, flag becomes True
for i in range(n-1):  # i is from 0 to n-1
    for j in range(n-1-i):  # j is from 0 to one element lesser than i
        if x[j] > x[j+1]:  # if 1st element is bigger than the 2nd one
            t = x[j]  # swap j  and j+1  elements
            x[j] = x[j+1]
            x[j+1] = t
            flag = True  # swapping done, hence flag is True
    if flag==False:  # no swapping means array is in sorted order
        break  # come out of inner for loop
    else:
        flag = False  # assign initial value to flag

print('Sorted array= ', x)
```

Output:

```
C:\>python arr.py
How many elements? 5
```

```
Enter element: 1
Enter element: 5
Enter element: 4
Enter element: 3
Enter element: 2
Original array:  array('i', [1, 5, 4, 3, 2])
Sorted array:  array('i', [1, 2, 3, 4, 5])
```

Let's write another program, where we want to search for the position of an element in an array. Suppose we want to know the position of 's' in the array 'x', we have to compare 's' with each element of the array x[i] as:

```
if s == x[i]:
    print('Found at Position= ', i+1)
```

The element position is given by the index 'i'. Since array elements start from 0th position, we should add 1 to this position and display the position as i+1. Since we are comparing 's' with all elements of the array linearly, this is called 'linear search' or 'sequential search'. This logic is shown in Figure 7.4:

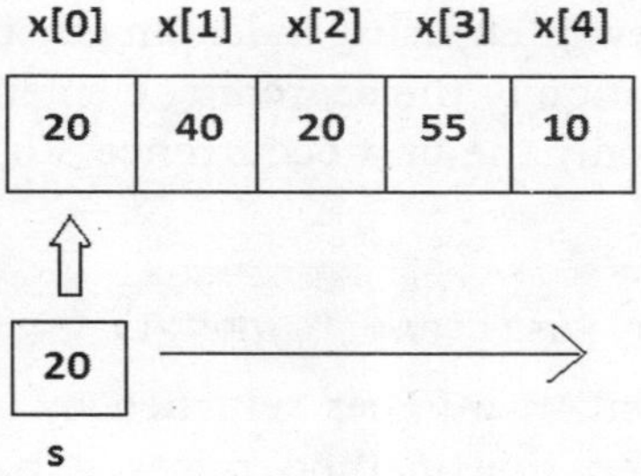

Figure 7.4: Searching for an Element in an Array using Sequential Search

Program

Program 12: A Python program to search for the position of an element in an array using sequential search.

```
# Searching an array for an element.
from array import*
# create an empty array to store integers
x = array('i', [])

# store elements into the array x
print('How many elements? ', end='')
n = int(input()) # accept input into n

for i in range(n):  # repeat for n times
    print('Enter element: ', end='')
    x.append(int(input()))  # add the element to the array x

print('Original array: ', x)

print('Enter element to search: ', end='')
s = int(input())  # accept element to be searched

# linear search or sequential search
```

```
    flag=False  # this becomes True if element is found

    for i in range(len(x)):  # repeat i from 0 to no. of elements
        if s == x[i]:
            print('Found at Position= ', i+1)
            flag=True
    if flag==False:
        print('Not found in the array')
```

Output:

```
C:\>python arr.py
How many elements? 5
Enter element: 20
Enter element: 40
Enter element: 20
Enter element: 55
Enter element: 10
Original array: array('i', [20, 40, 20, 55, 10])
Enter element to search: 20
Found at Position= 1
Found at Position= 3
```

The same program can be rewritten using index() method provided for arrays. The index() method returns the first position of the searching element. If the element is found several times, this method returns only the first occurrence. To search for 's' in the array 'x', we can write:

```
pos = x.index(s)
    print('Found at Position= ', pos+1)
```

Here, 'pos' indicates the position number returned by index() method. If the element is not found in the array, then this method raises a runtime error called 'ValueError'. Hence, it is recommended to handle this error using try and except blocks, as:

```
try:
    statements to execute
except ValueError:
    display a message if this error raises
```

When there is a runtime error inside the try block, the control of execution jumps into except block and displays the message written there. We will discuss about runtime errors (or exceptions) in a later chapter.

Program

Program 13: A Python program to search for the position of an element in an array using index() method.

```
# searching an array for an element - v2.0
from array import*
# create an empty array to store integers
x = array('i', [])

# store elements into the array x
print('How many elements? ', end='')
n = int(input()) # accept input into n

for i in range(n):  # repeat for n times
```

```
    print('Enter element: ', end='')
    x.append(int(input()))  # add the element to the array x

print('Original array: ', x)

print('Enter element to search: ', end='')
s = int(input())  # accept element to be searched

# index() method gives the location of the element in the array
try:
    pos = x.index(s)
    print('Found at Position= ', pos+1)

except ValueError:  # if element not found then ValueError will rise
    print('Not found in the array')
```

Output:

```
C:\>python arr.py
How many elements? 5
Enter element: 20
Enter element: 40
Enter element: 20
Enter element: 55
Enter element: 10
Original array: array('i', [20, 40, 20, 55, 10])
Enter element to search: 20
Found at Position= 1
```

Types of Arrays

Till now, we got good idea on arrays in Python. When talking about arrays, any programming language like C or Java offers two types of arrays. They are:

- **Single dimensional arrays:** These arrays represent only one row or one column of elements. For example, marks obtained by a student in 5 subjects can be written as 'marks' array, as:

```
marks = array('i', [50, 60, 70, 66, 72])
```

The above array contains only one row of elements. Hence it is called single dimensional array or one dimensional array.

- **Multi-dimensional arrays:** These arrays represent more than one row and more than one column of elements. For example, marks obtained by 3 students each one in 5 subjects can be written as 'marks' array as:

```
marks = array([[50, 60, 70, 66, 72],
               [60, 62, 71, 56, 70],
               [55, 59, 80, 68, 65]])
```

The first student's marks are written in first row. The second student's marks are in second row and the third student's marks are in third row. In each row, the marks in 5 subjects are mentioned. Thus this array contains 3 rows and 5 columns and hence it is called multi-dimensional array.

Each row of the above array can be again represented as a single dimensional array. Thus the above array contains 3 single dimensional arrays. Hence, it is called a two dimensional array. A two dimensional array is a combination of several single dimensional arrays. Similarly, a three dimensional array is a combination of several two dimensional arrays.

In Python, we can create and work with single dimensional arrays only. So far, the examples and methods discussed by us are applicable to single dimensional arrays. Python does not support multi-dimensional arrays. But that is not a bad news. We can construct multidimensional arrays using third party packages like *numpy* (numerical python). The following sections are devoted for a discussion on 'numpy' which is very important for Python programmers.

Working with Arrays using numpy

numpy is a package that contains several classes, functions, variables etc. to deal with scientific calculations in Python. numpy is useful to create and also process single and multi-dimensional arrays. In addition, numpy contains a large library of mathematical functions like linear algebra functions and Fourier transforms. To get complete help on numpy, the reader can refer to the following link at scipy.org: http://docs.scipy.org/doc/numpy/reference/

The arrays which are created using numpy are called n dimensional arrays where n can be any integer. If n=1, it represents a one dimensional array. If n=2, it is a two dimensional array. Similarly, if n=3, it is a three dimensional array. The arrays created in numpy can accept only one type of elements. We cannot store different datatypes into same array.

To work with numpy, we should first import numpy module into our Python programs as:

```
import numpy
```

This will import numpy module into our program so that we can use any of the objects from that package. But, to refer to an object we should use the format: numpy.object. See the Program 14 to know how to create an array in numpy.

Program

Program 14: A Python program to create a simple array using numpy.

```
# creating single dimensional array using numpy
import numpy
arr = numpy.array([10, 20, 30, 40, 50])  # create array
print(arr) # display array
```

Output:

```
C:\>python arr.py
[10, 20, 30, 40, 50]
```

In Program 14, we used array() function to create an array with 5 elements. Please observe that we called this function as: numpy.array(). In this way, adding the word 'numpy' before every object or function would be difficult for the programmer. Hence, there is another way to write import statement, as:

```
import numpy as np
```

Here, we are using 'np' to refer to the word 'numpy'. Hence, wherever we need to type 'numpy', we simply type 'np'. This makes typing easy for the programmer as shown in Program 15.

Program

Program 15: Another version of Program 14 to create an array.

```
# creating single dimensional array using numpy - v2.0
import numpy as np
arr = np.array([10, 20, 30, 40, 50])  # create array
print(arr) # display array
```

Can't we eliminate writing even 'np' to refer to the objects or functions in our program? Yes, that is possible by writing import statement as:

```
from numpy import *
```

This will import everything (* means all) specifically from numpy package. Now, we need not use any name to refer the objects or functions in our program. See Program 16 which is another variation for the previous two programs.

Program

Program 16: Another version of Program 15 to create an array.

```
# creating single dimensional array using numpy - v3.0
from numpy import *
arr = array([10, 20, 30, 40, 50])  # create array
print(arr) # display array
```

In Program 16, we are straight away calling the function as array() and there is no need of using any word before the function.

We will see how to create arrays using numpy. We already know that an array is similar to lists except that every element of an array should be of the same datatype. Creating arrays in numpy can be done in several ways. Some of the important ways are:

- Using array() function
- Using linspace() function
- Using logspace() function
- Using arange() function
- Using zeros() and ones() functions

Creating Arrays using array()

We can call array() function of numpy module to create an array. When we create an array, we can specify the datatype of the elements either as 'int' or 'float'. We can create an integer type array as:

```
arr = array([10, 20, 30, 40, 50], int)
```

We can also eliminate 'int' in the above statement since Python can assess the datatypes of elements.

To create an array with float type elements, we should specify 'float' as:

```
arr = array([1.5, 2.5, 3, 4, -5.1], float)
```

The same statement can be rewritten by eliminating 'float' as Python can judge the datatypes of the elements. In the array, if Python interpreter finds one element belonging to 'float type', then it will convert all the other elements also into float type by adding a decimal point after the element as:

```
arr = array([10, 20, 30.1, 40])
```

If we display this array using print() function, we can see the array as:

```
[10., 20., 30.1, 40.]
```

To create an array with character type elements, we need not specify the datatype. We can simply write:

```
arr = array(['a', 'b', 'c', 'd'])
```

Program

Program 17: A Python program to create a character type array with a group of characters.

```
# creating an array with characters
from numpy import *
arr = array(['a','b','c','d'])  # create array
print(arr) # display array
```

Output:

```
C:\>python arr.py
['a' 'b' 'c' 'd']
```

To create a string type array where can store a group of strings, we should use additional attribute 'dtype = str' in the array() function as:

```
arr = array(['Delhi', 'Hyderabad', 'Mumbai', 'Ahmedabad'], dtype=str)
```

Alternately, we can omit the 'dtype=str' in the above statement and write it as:

```
arr = array(['Delhi', 'Hyderabad', 'Mumbai', 'Ahmedabad'])
```

Program

Program 18: A Python program to create a string type array using numpy.

```
# creating an array with characters
from numpy import *
# create array
arr = array(['Delhi', 'Hyderabad', 'Mumbai', 'Ahmedabad'], dtype=str)
print(arr) # display array
```

It is possible to create an array from other arrays, as shown in Program 19.

Program

Program 19: A Python program to create an array from another array.

```
# creating an array from another array
from numpy import *
a = array([1,2,3,4,5])  # original array
b = array(a)  # create b from a using array() function
c = a  # create c by assigning a to c

# display the arrays
print("a = ", a)
print("b = ", b)
print("c = ", c)
```

Output:

```
C:\>python arr.py
a = [1 2 3 4 5]
b = [1 2 3 4 5]
c = [1 2 3 4 5]
```

Creating Arrays using linspace

The linspace() function is used to create an array with evenly spaced points between a starting point and ending point. The form of the linspace() function is:

```
linspace(start, stop, n)
```

'start' represents the starting element and 'stop' represents the ending element. 'n' is an integer that represents the number of parts the elements should be divided. If 'n' is omitted, then it is taken as 50. Let's take one example to understand this.

```
a = linspace(0, 10, 5)
```

In the above statement, we are creating an array 'a' with starting element 0 and ending element 10. This range is divided into 5 equal parts and hence the points will be 0, 2.5, 5, 7.5 and 10. These elements are stored into 'a'. Please remember the staring and elements 0 and 10 are included. Program 20 shows how to create an array with 5 equal points using the linspace() function.

Program

Program 20: A Python program to creating an array with 5 equal points using linspace().

```
# creating an array using linspace()
from numpy import *

# divide 0 to 10 into 5 parts and take those points in the array
a = linspace(0, 10, 5)
print('a = ', a)
```

Output:

```
C:\>python arr.py
a = [ 0.   2.5   5.   7.5   10. ]
```

Creating Arrays using logspace

The logspace() function is similar to linspace(). The linspace() function produces the evenly spaced points. Similarly, logspace() produces evenly spaced points on a logarithmically spaced scale. The logspace() function is used in the following format:

```
logspace(start, stop, n)
```

The logspace() function starts at a value which is 10 to the power of 'start' and ends at a value which is 10 to the power of 'stop' . If 'n' is not specified, then its value is taken as 50. For example, if we write:

```
a = logspace(1, 4, 5)
```

This function represents values starting from 10^1 to 10^4. These values are divided into 5 equal points and those points are stored into the array 'a'. This can be seen in sample Program 21.

Program

Program 21: A Python program to create an array using logspace().

```
# creating an array using logspace()
from numpy import *

# divide the range: 10 power 1 to 10 power 4 into 5 equal parts
# and take those points in the array
a = logspace(1, 4, 5)

# find no. of elements in a
n = len(a)

# repeat from 0 to n-1 times
for i in range(n):
    print('%.1f' % a[i], end=' ') # display 1 digit after decimal point
```

Output:

```
C:\>python arr.py
10.0  56.2  316.2  1778.3  10000.0
```

Creating Arrays using arange() Function

The arange() function in numpy is same as range() function in Python. The arange() function is used in the following format:

```
arange(start, stop, stepsize)
```

This creates an array with a group of elements from 'start' to one element prior to 'stop' in steps of 'stepsize'. If the 'stepsize' is omitted, then it is taken as 1. If the 'start' is omitted, then it is taken as 0. For example,

```
arange(10)
```

will produce an array with elements 0 to 9.

```
arange(5, 10)
```

will produce an array with elements from 5 to 9.

```
arange(1, 10, 3)
```

will create an array with the elements starting from 1 to 9. So, the first element will be 1. Since the stepsize is 3, we should 3 to get the subsequent elements. Thus, the second element can be obtained as 1+3 = 4 and the third element can be obtained as 4+3 = 7 and so on. Hence, the array will contain the following elements: [1 4 7]

```
arange(10, 1, -1)
```

Since the stepsize is -1, it represents the elements in descending order from 10 to 2, as: [10 9 8 7 6 5 4 3 2].

The following example creates a float type array with stepsize 1.5:

```
arange(0, 10, 1.5)
```

In this case, the array elements will be: [0. 1.5 3. 4.5 6. 7.5 9.]. We will now write a Python program to create an array with even numbers up to 10. In this program, we will use the arange() function as:

```
a = arange(2, 11, 2)
```

the starting even number is 2 and everytime we are adding 2 (stepsize) to get the next even number. This will continue till 10 (one element prior to 11).

Program

Program 22: A Python program to create an array with even number up to 10.

```
# creating an array with even numbers up to 10
from numpy import *

# create an array using arange() function
a = arange(2, 11, 2)
print(a)
```

Output:

```
C:\>python arr.py
[ 2  4  6  8  10]
```

Creating Arrays using zeros() and ones() Functions

We can use the zeros() function to create an array with all zeros. The ones() function is useful to create an array with all 1s. They are written in the following format:

```
zeros(n, datatype)
ones(n, datatype)
```

where 'n' represents the number of elements. we can eliminate the 'datatype' argument. If we do not specify the 'datatype', then the default datatype used by numpy is 'float'. See the examples:

```
zeros(5)
```

This will create an array with 5 elements all are zeros, as: [0. 0. 0. 0. 0.]. If we want this array in integer format, we can use 'int' as datatype, as:

```
zeros(5, int)
```

this will create an array as: [0 0 0 0 0].

If we use ones() function, it will create an array with all elements 1. For example,

```
ones(5, float)
```

will create an array with 5 integer elements all are 1s as: [1. 1. 1. 1. 1.]. Program 23 shows how to create arrays using zeros() and ones().

Program

Program 23: A Python program to create arrays using zeros() and ones().

```
# creating arrays using zeros() and ones()
from numpy import *

a = zeros(5, int)
print(a)

b = ones(5)  # default datatype is float
print(b)
```

Output:

```
C:\>python arr.py
[0  0  0  0  0]
[1.  1.  1.  1.  1.]
```

Mathematical Operations on Arrays

It is possible to perform various mathematical operations like addition, subtraction, division, etc. on the elements of an array. Also, the functions of 'math' module can be applied to the elements of the array. For example, to add the value 5 to every element of an array, we can write:

```
arr = array([10, 20, 30.5, -40])   # create an array
arr = arr+5  # add 5 to the array
```

This will store the following elements into the array: [15.   25.   35.5   -35.] . In the same way, we can perform addition, subtraction, multiplication, division etc. operations on two different arrays as:

```
arr1 = array([10, 20, 30.5, -40])
arr2 = array([1, 2, 3, 4])
arr3 = arr1 - arr2   # subtract arr2 from arr1
```

The resultant array 'arr3' contains the following elements: [9.   18.   27.5   -44.]. So, to add two arrays 'a' and 'b', we can simply write a+b. Similarly, to divide one array 'a' with another array 'b', we can write a/b. These kinds of operations are called *vectorized* operations since the entire array (or vector) is processed just like a variable. Vectorized operations are important because of two reasons:

- Vectorized operations are faster. Adding two arrays in the form of a+b is much faster than taking the corresponding elements of both the arrays and then adding them.
- Vectorized operations are syntactically clearer. To add two arrays, we can simply write a+b. This is clearer than using loops and iterating through all the elements of the arrays while adding them.
- Vectorized operations provide compact code.

We can apply mathematical functions like sin(), cos(), sqrt(), exp(), abs(), etc. on the elements of the array. All these functions are re-defined in numpy module. In Table 7.4, we can see the list of functions that can be used on numpy arrays:

Table 7.4: Useful Mathematical Functions in numpy

Function	Meaning
sin(arr)	Calculates sine value of each element in the array 'arr'.
cos(arr)	Calculates cosine value of each element in the array 'arr'.
tan(arr)	Calculates tangent value of each element in the array 'arr'.
arcsin(arr)	Calculates sine inverse value of each element in the array 'arr'.
arcos(arr)	Calculates cosine inverse value of each element in the array 'arr'.
arctan(arr)	Calculates tangent inverse value of each element in the array 'arr'.
log(arr)	Calculates natural logarithmic value of each element in the array 'arr'.
abs(arr)	Calculates absolute value of each element in the array 'arr'.
sqrt(arr)	Calculates square root value of each element in the array 'arr'.
power(arr, n)	Returns power value of each element in the array 'arr' when raised to the power of 'n'.
exp(arr)	Calculates exponentiation value of each element in the array 'arr'.
sum(arr)	Returns sum of all the elements in the array 'arr'.
prod(arr)	Returns product of all the elements in the array 'arr'.
min(arr)	Returns smallest element in the array 'arr'.
max(arr)	Returns biggest element in the array 'arr'.

Function	Meaning
mean(arr)	Returns mean value (average) of all elements in the array 'arr'.
median(arr)	Returns median value of all elements in the array 'arr'.
var(arr)	Returns variance of all elements in the array 'arr'.
cov(arr)	Returns covariance of all elements in the array 'arr'.
std(arr)	Gives standard deviation of elements in the array 'arr'.
argmin(arr)	Gives index of the smallest element in the array. Counting starts from 0.
argmax(arr)	Gives index of the biggest element in the array. Counting starts from 0.
unique(arr)	Gives an array that contains unique elements of the array 'arr'.
sort(arr)	Gives an array with sorted elements of the array 'arr' in ascending order.
concatenate([a,b])	Returns an array after joining a, b arrays. The arrays a, b should be entered as elements of a list.

Now, let's take an example to understand how to calculate sine value for each element of an array.

```
arr = array([10, 20, 30.5, -40])   # create an array
arr = sin(arr)  # apply sin() function to the array
```

The output of the previous operation will be: [-0.54402111 0.91294525 -0.79312724 -0.74511316]. Observe that the sin() function has worked on each element of the array and displayed the sine values by taking them as angles in radians. So, the first value in the output -0.54402111 is nothing but the value of sin(10) where 10 is taken as angle value in radians. Program 24 shows how to perform various mathematical operations on arrays.

Program

Program 24: A Python program to perform some mathematical operations on a numpy array.

```
# mathematical operations on arrays
# import all from numpy module
from numpy import *

# create a numpy array using array() function
arr = array([10, 20, 30.5, -40])
print("Original array: ", arr)

# do arithmetic operations on the elements of the array
print("After adding 5: ", arr+5)
print("After subtracting 5: ", arr-5)
print("After multiplying with 5: ", arr*5)
print("After dividing with 5: ", arr/5)
print("After modulus with 5: ", arr%5)

# we can use the arrays in expressions also
print("Expression value: ", (arr+5)**2-10)
```

```
# do some math functions
print("Sin values: ", sin(arr))
print("Cos values: ", cos(arr))
print("Tan values: ", tan(arr))
print("Biggest element: ", max(arr))
print("Smallest element: ", min(arr))
print("Sum of all elements: ", sum(arr))
print("Average of all elements: ", mean(arr))
```

Output:

```
C:\>python arr.py
Original array:  [ 10.   20.   30.5  -40. ]
After adding 5:  [ 15.   25.   35.5  -35. ]
After subtracting 5:  [  5.   15.   25.5  -45. ]
After multiplying with 5:  [  50.   100.   152.5  -200. ]
After dividing with 5:  [ 2.   4.   6.1  -8. ]
After modulus with 5:  [ 0.   0.   0.5  -0. ]
Expression value:  [  215.     615.     1250.25  1215.  ]
Sin values:  [-0.54402111  0.91294525  -0.79312724  -0.74511316]
Cos values:  [-0.83907153  0.40808206  0.60905598  -0.66693806]
Tan values:  [ 0.64836083  2.23716094  -1.30222389  1.11721493]
Biggest element:  30.5
Smallest element:  -40.0
Sum of all elements:  20.5
Average of all elements:  5.125
```

Comparing Arrays

We can use the relational operators >, >=, <, <=, == and != to compare the arrays of same size. These operators compare the corresponding elements of the arrays and return another array with Boolean type values. It means the resultant array contains elements which are True or False. Observe the Program 25.

Program

Program 25: A Python program to compare two arrays and display the resultant Boolean type array.

```
# to know the result of comparing two arrays
from numpy import *
a = array([1,2,3,0])
b = array([0,2,3,1])

c = a == b
print('Result of a==b: ', c)
c = a > b
print('Result of a>b: ', c)
c = a <= b
print('Result of a<=b: ', c)
```

Output:

```
C:\>python arr.py
Result of a==b: [False True True False]
Result of a>b: [True False False False]
Result of a<=b: [False True TrueTrue]
```

The any() function can be used to determine if any one element of the array is True. The all() function can be used to determine whether all the elements in the array are True. The any() and all() functions return either True or False. This is shown in Program 26.

Program

Program 26: A Python program to know the effects of any() and all() functions.

```
# using any() and all() functions
from numpy import *
a = array([1,2,3,0])
b = array([0,2,3,1])

c = a > b
print('Result of a>b: ', c)

print('Check if any one element is true: ', any(c))
print('Check if all elements are true: ', all(c))

if(any(a>b)):
    print('a contains atleast one element greater than those of b')
```

Output:

```
C:\>python arr.py
Result of a>b:  [ True False False False]
Check if any one element is true:  True
Check if all elements are true:  False
a contains atleast one element greater than those of b
```

The functions logical_and(), logical_or() and logical_not() are useful to get the Boolean array as a result of comparing the compound condition. We already knew that any compound condition is a combination of more than one simple condition. For example,

```
c = logical_and(a>0, a<4)
```

In the above statement, the logical_and() function applies the compound condition a>0 and a<4 on every element of the array 'a' and returns another array 'c' that contains True or False values. We should understand that Python represents 0 as False and any other number as True. See Program 27 for further understanding of these functions.

Program

Program 27: A Python program to understand the use of logical functions on arrays.

```
# using logical_and(), logical_or(), logical_not()
from numpy import *
a = array([1,2,3], int)
b = array([0,2,3], int)

c = logical_and(a>0, a<4)
print(c)

c = logical_or(b>=0, b==1)
print(c)

c = logical_not(b)
print(c)
```

Output:

```
C:\>python arr.py
[ True True  True]
[ True True  True]
[ True False False]
```

The where() function can be used to create a new array based on whether a given condition is True or False. The syntax of the where() function is:

```
array = where(condition, expression1, expression2)
```

If the 'condition' is true, 'expression1' is executed and the result is stored into the array, else 'expression2' is executed and its result is stored into the array. For example,

```
a = array([10, 21, 30, 41, 50], int)
c = where(a%2==0, a, 0)
```

The new array 'c' contains elements from 'a' based on the condition a%2==0. This condition is applied to each element of the array 'a' and if it is True, the element of 'a' is stored into 'c' else '0' is stored into c. Hence the array 'c' looks like this: [10 0 30 0 50]. We can understand the where() function from the Program 28 in a better manner.

Program

Program 28: A Python program to compare the corresponding elements of two arrays and retrieve the biggest elements.

```
# using where() function.
from numpy import *
a = array([10, 20, 30, 40, 50], int)
b = array([1, 21, 3, 40, 51], int)
# if a>b then take element from a else from b
c = where(a>b, a, b)
print(c)
```

Output:

```
C:\>python arr.py
[10  21  30  40  51]
```

The nonzero() function is useful to know the positions of elements which are non zero. This function returns an array that contains the indexes of the elements of the array which are not equal to zero. For example,

```
a = array([1, 2, 0, -1, 0, 6], int)
```

In the preceding array, the elements which are non zero are: 1, 2, -1 and 6. Their positions or indexes are: 0, 1, 3, 5. These indexes can be retrieved into another array 'c' as:

```
c = nonzero(a)
```

Program

Program 29: A Python program to retrieve non zero elements from an array.

```
# using nonzero() function.
from numpy import *
a = array([1, 2, 0, -1, 0, 6], int)
```

```
# retrieve indexes of non zero elements from a
c = nonzero(a)

# display indexes
for i in c:
    print(i)

# display the elements
print(a[c])
```

Output:

```
C:\>python arr.py
[0  1  3  5]
[ 1   2   -1   6]
```

Aliasing the Arrays

If 'a' is an array, we can assign it to 'b', as:

```
b = a
```

This is a simple assignment that does not make any new copy of the array 'a'. It means, 'b' is not a new array and memory is not allocated to 'b'. Also, elements from 'a' are not copied into 'b' since there is no memory for 'b'. Then how to understand this assignment statement? We should understand that we are giving a new name 'b' to the same array referred by 'a'. It means the names 'a' and 'b' are referencing same array. This is called 'aliasing'. Figure 7.5 shows the aliasing of array a as b:

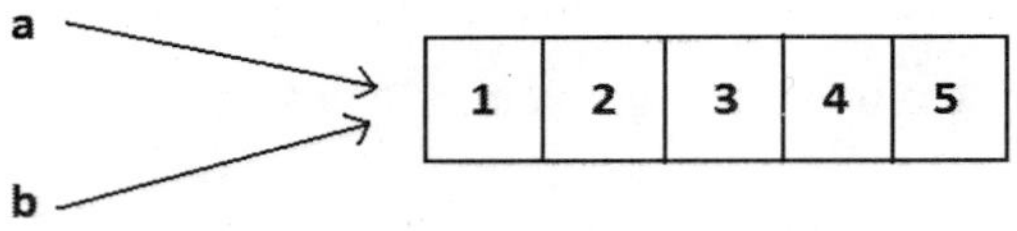

Figure 7.5: Aliasing the Array a as b

'Aliasing' is not 'copying'. Aliasing means giving another name to the existing object. Hence, any modifications to the alias object will reflect in the existing object and vice versa. To know about this, please refer to Program 30.

Program

Program 30: A Python program to alias an array and understand the affect of aliasing.

```
# aliasing an array.
from numpy import *

a = arange(1, 6)  # create a with elements 1 to 5.
b = a  # give another name b to a

print('Original array: ', a)
print('Alias array: ', b)

b[0]=99  # modify 0th element of b
```

```
print('After modification: ')
print('Original array: ', a)
print('Alias array: ', b)
```

Output:

```
C:\>python arr.py
Original array:  [1 2 3 4 5]
Alias array:  [1 2 3 4 5]
After modification:
Original array:  [99  2  3  4  5]
Alias array:  [99  2  3  4  5]
```

Viewing and Copying Arrays

We can create another array that is same as an existing array. This is done by the view() method. This method creates a copy of an existing array such that the new array will also contain the same elements found in the existing array. The original array and the newly created arrays will share different memory locations. If the newly created array is modified, the original array will also be modified since the elements in both the arrays will be like mirror images. Figure 7.6 explains how to create a view of an array:

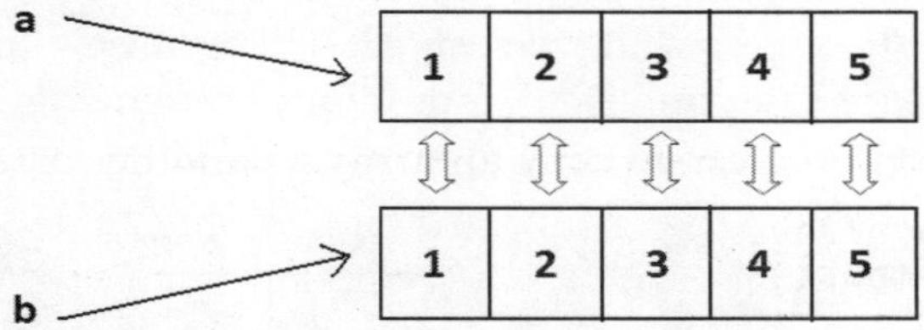

Figure 7.6: Creating a View of an Array

Program

Program 31: A Python program to create a view of an existing array.

```
# creating view for an array
from numpy import *

a = arange(1, 6)  # create a with elements 1 to 5.
b = a.view()  # create a view of a and call it b
print('Original array: ', a)
print('New array: ', b)

b[0]=99  # modify 0th element of b

print('After modification: ')
print('Original array: ', a)
print('New array: ', b)
```

Output:

```
C:\>python arr.py
Original array:  [1 2 3 4 5]
New array:  [1 2 3 4 5]
```

```
After modification:
Original array:  [99  2  3  4  5]
New array:  [99  2  3  4  5]
```

Viewing is nothing but copying only. It is called 'shallow copying' as the elements in the view when modified will also modify the elements in the original array. So, both the arrays will act as one and the same. Suppose we want both the arrays to be independent and modifying one array should not affect another array, we should go for 'deep copying'. This is done with the help of copy() method. This method makes a complete copy of an existing array and its elements. When the newly created array is modified, it will not affect the existing array or vice versa. There will not be any connection between the elements of the two arrays. Figure 7.7 shows copying an array as another array:

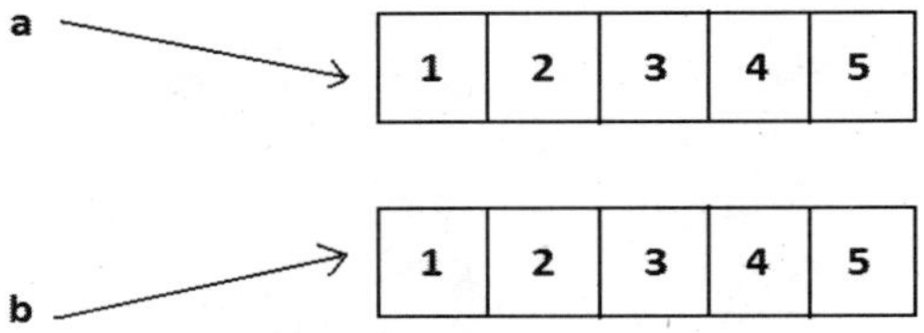

Figure 7.7: Copying an Array as another Array

Program

Program 32: A Python program to copy an array as another array.

```
# copying an array.
from numpy import *

a = arange(1, 6)  # create a with elements 1 to 5.
b = a.copy()  # create a copy of a and call it b

print('Original array: ', a)
print('New array: ', b)

b[0]=99  # modify 0th element of b

print('After modification: ')
print('Original array: ', a)
print('New array: ', b)
```

Output:

```
C:\>python arr.py
Original array:  [1 2 3 4 5]
New array:  [1 2 3 4 5]
After modification:
Original array:  [1 2 3 4 5]
New array:  [99  2  3  4  5]
```

Slicing and Indexing in numpyArrays

Slicing refers to extracting a range of elements from the array. The format of slicing operation is given here:

```
arrayname[start:stop:stepsize]
```

The default value for 'start' is 0, for 'stop' is n (n is number of elements) and for 'stepsize' is 1. Counting starts from 0th position. For example, if we write:

```
a = [10, 11, 12, 13, 14, 15]
a[1:6:2]
```

Here, 'start' is 1. So, it will extract from 1st element, i.e. from 11. Since 'stop' is 6, it will stop at one element prior to 6. That means it will stop at 15. Since 'stepsize' is 2, we should add 2 to the starting index to get the next element index, as: 1+2 = 3rd element and then 3+2= 5th element. So, the following elements will be extracted: [11, 13, 15]. Figure 7.8 shows an example of slicing:

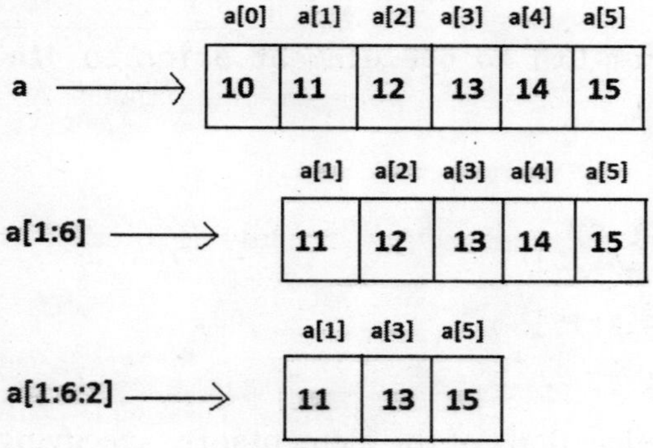

Figure 7.8: Slicing Example

Suppose, we write a[:] or a[::] without specifying anything for start, stop and stepsize, it will extract from 0th element till the end of the array. So, all elements are extracted.

Suppose, we write a[2:], it starts at 2nd element and ends at last element. So, the extracted array will be:

```
[12, 13, 14, 15]
```

When negative number 'i' is used for 'start', it should be taken as n+i. When negative number 'j' is used for 'stop', it should be taken as n+j. When negative number is used for 'stepsize', the stepping goes towards smaller indexes. Thus, if we write:

```
a[-1:-4:-1]
```

Since there are totally 6 elements in the array 'a', we have 'start' as 6-1 = 5, 'stop' is 6-4=2, and 'stepsize' is -1, i.e. going towards least index. Hence, it will retrieve elements starting from 5th element till one element prior to 2nd element going backwards. So, the retrieved array will be: [15, 14, 13]. These things can be easily understood by Program 33.

Program

Program 33: A Python program to understand slicing operations on arrays.

```
# slicing an array
from numpy import *
# create array a with elements 10 to 15.
a = arange(10, 16)
print(a)

# retrieve from 1st to one element prior to 6th element in steps of 2
b = a[1:6:2]
print(b)

# retrieve all elements from a
b = a[::]
print(b)

# retrieve from 6-2= 4th to one element prior to 2nd element in
# decreasing step size.
b = a[-2:2:-1]
print(b)

# retrieve from 0th to one element prior to 4th element (6-2= 4th)
b = a[:-2:]
print(b)
```

Output:

```
C:\>python arr.py
[10 11 12 13 14 15]
[11 13 15]
[10 11 12 13 14 15]
[14 13]
[10 11 12 13]
```

Indexing refers to the locations of the elements. By specifying the location numbers from 0 onwards till n-1, we can refer to all elements as a[0], a[1], ... a[n-1]. So, in general we can refer to the elements of an array as a[i] where i can change from 0 to n-1. In Program 34, we are showing how to display the elements of an array using indexing.

Program

Program 34: A Python program to retrieve and display elements of a numpy array using indexing.

```
# indexing an array
from numpy import *
# create array a with elements 10 to 15.
a = arange(10, 16)
print(a)
# retrieve from 1st to one element prior to 6th element in steps of 2
a = a[1:6:2]
print(a)

# display elements using indexing
i=0
while(i<len(a)):
```

```
        print(a[i])
        i+=1
```

Output:

```
C:\>python arr.py
[10 11 12 13 14 15]
[11 13 15]
11
13
15
```

Dimensions of Arrays

The dimension of an array represents the arrangement of elements in the array. If the elements are arranged horizontally, it is called a row and if the elements are arranged vertically, then it is called a column. When an array contains only 1row or only 1 column of elements, it is called Single dimensional array or one dimensional array (1D array). In the following example, 'arr1' represents a 1D array that contains 1 row and 'arr2' represents another 1D array that contains only 1 column.

```
# array with 1 row
arr1 = array([1,2,3,4,5])
print(arr1) displays [1  2  3  4  5]

# array with 1 column
arr2 = array([10,
              20,
              30,
              40])
print(arr2)
```

The preceding lines of code will display the following output:

```
[10  20  30  40]
```

If an array contains more than 1 row and 1 column, then it is called two dimensional array or 2D array. In the following example, we are creating 'arr2' as a 2D array with 2 rows and 3 columns.

```
# create a 2D array with 2 rows and 3 cols in each row
arr2 = array([[1,2,3],
              [4,5,6]])
print(arr2)
```

The preceding lines of code will display the following output:

```
[[1  2  3]
 [4  5  6]]
```

We can imagine a 2D array as a combination of several 1D arrays. In the above example, each row of 'arr2' in turn represents a 1D array. Similarly, we can imagine a 3D array as a combination of several 2D arrays. The following example creates a 3D array by the name 'arr3' that contains two 2D arrays. Each of these 2D arrays contains 2 rows and 3 columns of elements.

```
arr3 = array([[[1,2,3],[4,5,6]],
              [[1,1,1], [1,0,1]]])
```

If we display the elements of this 3D array using print(arr3), it shows the following output:

```
[[[1 2 3]
  [4 5 6]]

 [[1 1 1]
  [1 0 1]]]
```

The 2D arrays and 3D arrays are called multi-dimensional arrays in general.

Attributes of an Array

Numpy's array class is called *ndarray*. It is also known by alias name *array*. Let's remember that there is another class 'array' in Python that is different from numpy's 'array' class. This class contains the following important attributes (or variables):

The ndim Attribute

The 'ndim' attribute represents the number of dimensions or axes of the array. The number of dimensions is also referred to as 'rank'. For a single dimensional array, it is 1 and for a two dimensional array, it is 2. Consider the following code snippet:

```
arr1 = array([1,2,3,4,5])  # 1D array
print(arr1.ndim)
```

The preceding lines of code will display the following output:

```
1
```

Now, consider the following lines of code:

```
arr2 = array([[1,2,3], [4,5,6]])  # 2D array with 2 rows and 3 elements
print(arr2.ndim)
```

The preceding lines of code will display the following output:

```
2
```

The shape Attribute

The 'shape' attribute gives the shape of an array. The shape is a tuple listing the number of elements along each dimension. A dimension is called an axis. For a 1D array, shape gives the number of elements in the row. For a 2D array, it specifies the number of rows and columns in each row. We can also change the shape using 'shape' attribute. Consider the following code snippet:

```
arr1 = array([1,2,3,4,5])
print(arr1.shape)
```

The preceding lines of code will display the following output:

```
(5,)   # no. of elements
```

Now, consider the following lines of code:

```
arr2 = array([[1,2,3], [4,5,6]])
print(arr2.shape)
```

It will display the following output:

```
(2, 3)  # 2 rows and 3 cols
```

Also, consider the following lines of code:

```
arr2.shape = (3, 2)  # change shape of arr2 to 3 rows and 2 cols
print(arr2)
```

The preceding lines of code will display the following output:

```
[[1  2]
 [3  4]
 [5  5]]
```

The size Attribute

The 'size' attribute gives the total number of elements in the array. For example, consider the following code snippet:

```
arr1 = array([1,2,3,4,5])
print(arr1.size)
```

The preceding lines of code will display the following output:

```
5
```

Now, consider the following lines of code:

```
arr2 = array([[1,2,3], [4,5,6]])
print(arr2.size)
```

It will display the following output:

```
6
```

The itemsize Attribute

The 'itemsize' attribute gives the memory size of the array element in bytes. As we know, 1 byte is equal to 8 bits. For example consider the following code snippet:

```
arr1 = array([1,2,3,4,5])
print(arr1.itemsize)
```

The preceding lines of code will display the following output:

```
4
```

Now, consider the following lines of code:

```
arr2 = array([1.1,2.1,3.5,4,5.0])
print(arr2.itemsize)
```

The preceding lines of code will display the following output:

```
8
```

The dtype Attribute

The 'dtype'attribute gives the datatype of the elements in the array. For example, consider the following code snippet:

```
arr1 = array([1,2,3,4,5])  # integer type array
print(arr1.dtype)
```

The preceding lines of code will display the following output:

```
int32
```

Now, consider the following lines of code:

```
arr2 = array([1.1,2.1,3.5,4,5.0])  # float type array
print(arr2.dtype)
```

It will display the following output:

```
float64
```

The nbytes Attribute

The 'nbytes' attributegives the total number of bytes occupied by an array. The total number of bytes = size of the array * item size of each element in the array. For example,

```
arr2 = array([[1,2,3], [4,5,6]])
print(arr2.nbytes)
```

The preceding lines of code will display the following output:

```
24
```

Apart from the attributes discussed in the preceding sections, we can use reshape() and flatten() methods which are useful to convert the 1D array into a 2D array and vice versa.

The reshape() Method

The 'reshape()' method is useful to change the shape of an array. The new array should have the same number of elements as in the original array. For example,

```
arr1 = arange(10)  # 1D array with 10 elements
print(arr1)
```

The preceding lines of code will display the following output:

```
[0 1 2 3 4 5 6 7 8 9]
```

Now, consider the following code snippet:

```
arr1 = arr1.reshape(2, 5)  # change the shape as 2 rows, 5 cols
print(arr1)
```

It will display the following output:

```
[[0 1 2 3 4]
 [5 6 7 8 9]]
```

Also, consider the following code snippet:

```
arr1 = arr1.reshape(5, 2) # change the shape as 5 rows, 2 cols
print(arr1)
```

The preceding lines of code will display the following output:

```
[[0 1]
 [2 3]
 [4 5]
 [6 7]
 [8 9]]
```

The flatten() Method

The flatten() method is useful to return a copy of the array collapsed into one dimension. For example, let's take a 2D array as:

```
arr1 = array([[1,2,3],[4,5,6]])
print(arr1)
```

The preceding lines of code will display the following output:

```
[[1 2 3]
 [4 5 6]]
```

By using the flatten() method, we can convert this array into 1D array as:

```
arr1 = arr1.flatten()
print(arr1)
```

It will display the following output:

```
[1 2 3 4 5 6]
```

Working with Multi-dimensional Arrays

The 2D arrays, 3D arrays etc. are called multi-dimensional arrays. A 2D array contains more than 1 row and 1 column and it can be treated as a combination of several 1D arrays. A 2D array is also considered as a *matrix*. For example, a 2D array with 'm' rows and 'n' columns is called m x n matrix. As we know in Mathematics, a matrix contains elements arranged in several rows and columns. Hence, we can take a matrix as a 2D array and vice versa.

We can create multi-dimensional arrays in the following ways:

- Using array() function
- Using ones() and zeroes() functions
- Using eye() function
- Using reshape() function

The array() Function

Numpy's array() function can be used to create a multidimensional array. Usually, we pass lists of elements to this function. If we pass one list of elements to this function, then it will create a 1D array. If we pass two lists of elements, then this function creates a 2D array.

```
a = array([1,2,3,4])    # this creates a 1D array with 1 row
a = array([[1,2,3,4], [5,6,7,8]])#creates a 2D array with 2 rows and 4
# cols
```

Suppose, we display the array 'a' using print() function as print(a), we see the 2D array as:

```
[[1  2  3  4]
 [5  6  7  8]]
```

Even though the elements are displayed in 2 rows and 4 columns, the internal memory allocated to all these elements would be in the form of a single row containing 8 blocks (2 x 4 = 8). The elements are stored in the contiguous memory locations as shown in Figure 7.9:

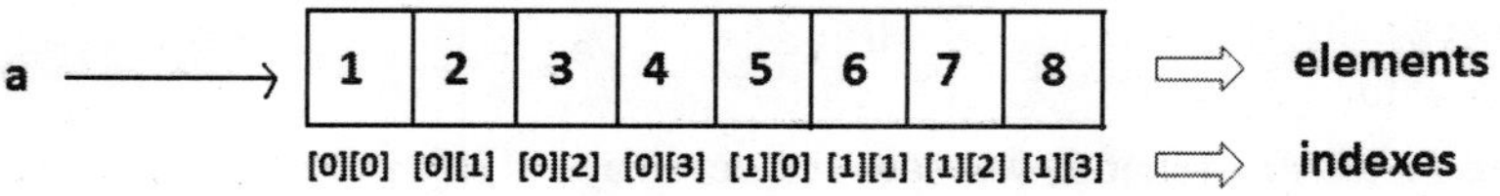

Figure 7.9: The arrangement of 2D array elements in the memory

The ones() and zeros() Functions

The ones() function is useful to create a 2D array with several rows and columns where all the elements will be taken as 1. The format of this function is:

```
ones((r, c), dtype)
```

Here, 'r' represents the number of rows and 'c' represents the number of columns. 'dtype' represents the datatype of the elements in the array. For example,

```
a = ones((3, 4), float)
```

will create a 2D array with 3 rows and 4 columns and the datatype is taken as float. If 'dtype' is omitted, then the default datatype taken will be 'float'. Now, if we display 'a', we can see the array as:

```
[[1. 1. 1. 1.]
 [1. 1. 1. 1.]
 [1. 1. 1. 1.]]
```

The decimal point after each element represents that the elements are float type.

Just like the ones() function, we can also use the zeros() function to create a 2D array with elements filled with zeros. Suppose, we write:

```
b = zeros((3,4), int)
```

Then a 2D array with 2 rows and 4 columns will be created where all elements will be 0s, as shown below:

```
[[0  0  0  0]
 [0  0  0  0]
 [0  0  0  0]]
```

The eye() Function

The eye() function creates a 2D array and fills the elements in the diagonal with 1s. The general format of using this function is:

```
eye(n, dtype=datatype)
```

This will create an array with 'n' rows and 'n' columns. The default datatype is 'float'. For example, eye(3) will create a 3x3 array and fills the diagonal elements with 1s as shown below:

```
a = eye(3)
[[1.  0.  0.]
 [0.  1.  0.]
 [0.  0.  1.]]
```

The reshape() Function

The reshape() function has been already discussed in the previous section. We will have an elaborate discussion about this function now. This function is useful to convert a 1D array into a multidimensional (2D or 3D) array. The syntax of writing this function is:

```
reshape(arrayname, (n, r, c))
```

Here, 'arrayname' represents the name of the array whose elements to be converted. 'n' indicates the number of arrays in the resultant array. 'r' , 'c' indicates the number of rows and columns, respectively. For example, we take a 1D array 'a' with 6 elements as:

```
a = array([1, 2, 3, 4, 5, 6])
```

To convert 'a' into a 2D array using the reshape() function, we can write:

```
b = reshape(a, (2, 3))
```

We are converting the elements of the array 'a' into a 2D array with 2 rows and 3 columns, and the resultant array is 'b'. So, the 2D array 'b' looks like this:

```
[[1  2  3]
 [4  5  6]]
```

Observe the starting two pairs of square brackets which indicate that it is a 2D array. Suppose, we write:

```
b = reshape(a, (3, 2))
```

This will convert 'a' into a 2D array with 3 rows and 2 columns that looks like this:

```
[[1  2]
 [3  4]
 [5  6]]
```

It is possible to use the reshape() function to convert a 1D array into a 3D array. Let's take a 1D array 'a' with 12 elements as:

```
a = arange(12)
```

Here, we are creating the array 'a' with 12 elements starting from 0 to 11 as:

```
[0  1  2  3  4  5  6  7  8  9  10  11]
```

Now, to convert this 1D array into a 3D array, we can use the reshape() function as:

```
b = reshape(a, (2, 3, 2))
```

Here, 'a' represents the arrayname that is being converted. In the reshape() function, after 'a', observe the figures (2, 3, 2). They represent that we want 2 arrays each with 3 rows and 2 columns. So, the resultant 3D array 'b' looks like this:

```
[[[ 0  1]
  [ 2  3]
  [ 4  5]]

 [[ 6  7]
  [ 8  9]
  [10 11]]]
```

So, 'b' is a 3D array of size 2x3x2. Suppose, we write:

```
b = reshape(a, (3, 2, 2))
```

Then we can expect a 3D array with 3 inner arrays each one having 2 rows and 2 columns of elements. It means the size of 'b' will be 3x2x2 and can be displayed as:

```
[[[ 0  1]
  [ 2  3]]

 [[ 4  5]
  [ 6  7]]

 [[ 8  9]
  [10 11]]]
```

Indexing in Multi-dimensional Arrays

Index represents the location number. The individual elements of a 2D array can be accessed by specifying the location number of the row and column of the element in the array as:

```
a[0][0]  # represents 0th row and 0th column element in the array 'a'
b[1][3]  # represents 1st row and 3rd column element in the array 'b'
```

Let's see how to retrieve elements from a 2D array. Suppose 'a' is the array name. len(a) function will give the number of rows in the array. a[0] represents the 0th row, a[1] represents the 1st row, etc. So, in general, a[i] represents the ith row elements. Hence, to display only rows of the 2D array, we can write:

```
for i in range(len(a)):
    print(a[i])
```

Each row may contain some columns which represent the elements. To know, how many elements are there in a row, we can use len(a[i]). Here, if i = 0, then len(a[0]) represents the number of columns in 0th row. Similarly if i=1, then len(a[1]) represents the number of columns in 1st row and so on. In this way, len(a[i]) represents the number of columns in i^{th} row. So, the following loops will access all elements from the 2D array:

```
for i in range(len(a)):
    for j in range(len(a[i])):
        print(a[i][j], end=' ')
```

In the preceding code, the outer for loop represents the rows and the inner for loop represents the columns in each row. The individual elements can be retrieved as a[i][j]. Figure 7.10 shows how to access the elements of a 2D array with 3 rows and 3 cols:

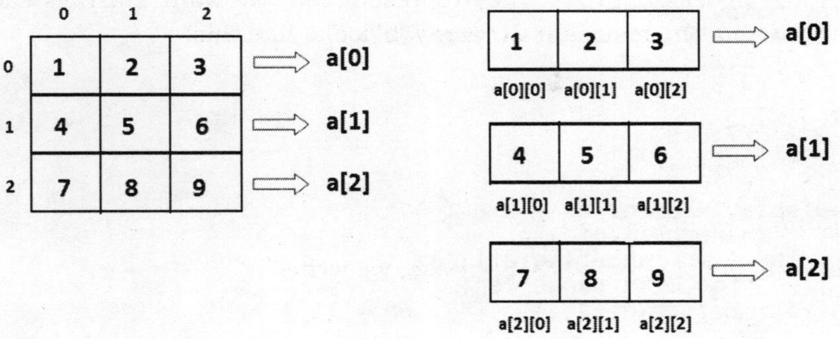

Figure 7.10: Accessing the Elements of a 2D Array with 3 Rows and 3 Cols

Program

Program 35: A Python program to retrieve the elements from a 2D array and display them using for loops.

```
# retrieving the elements from a 2D array using indexing
from numpy import *

# create a 2D array with 3 rows and 3 cols
a = [[1,2,3], [4,5,6], [7,8,9]]

# display only rows
for i in range(len(a)):
    print(a[i])

# display element by element
for i in range(len(a)):
    for j in range(len(a[i])):
        print(a[i][j], end=' ')
```

Output:

```
C:\>python arr.py
[1, 2, 3]
[4, 5, 6]
[7, 8, 9]
1 2 3 4 5 6 7 8 9
```

In the previous program, we used 2 for loops to retrieve elements from a 2D array. In the same way, 3 for loops can be used to retrieve elements from a 3D array. In Program 36, we have created a 3D array that contains two 2D array of each 2 rows and 3 columns. So, the size of this 3D array is 2x2x3. Then we have displayed all the elements of the array using 3 for loops.

Program

Program 36: A Python program to retrieve the elements from a 3D array.

```
# retrieving the elements from a 3D array using indexing
from numpy import *
# create a 3D array with size 2x2x3
a = [[[1,2,3],
      [4,5,6]],

      [[7,8,9],
      [10,11,12]]]

# display element by element
for i in range(len(a)):
    for j in range(len(a[i])):
        for k in range(len(a[i][j])):
            print(a[i][j][k], end='\t')
        print()
    print()
```

Output:

```
C:\>python arr.py
1      2       3
4      5       6
7      8       9
10     11      12
```

Slicing the Multi-dimensional Arrays

A slice represents a part or piece of the array. In the previous sections, we already discussed about slicing in case of single dimensional arrays. Now, we will see how to do slicing in case of multi-dimensional arrays, especially in 2D arrays. We take a 2D array with 3 rows and 3 columns as:

```
a = [[1, 2, 3], [4, 5, 6], [7, 8, 9]]
```

We can reshape this array such that it will show elements in 3 rows and 3 columns, as:

```
a = reshape(a, (3,3))
```

Now, print(a) will display the 2D array as:

```
[[1 2 3]
 [4 5 6]
 [7 8 9]]
```

The format of slice operator is:

```
arrayname[start:stop:stepsize]
```

The default value for 'start' is 0, for 'stop' is n (n is number of elements) and for 'stepsize' is 1. Counting starts from 0th position. So, if we do not mention these values, then starting from 0th element till the last element, the entire array will be displayed. For example, if we write:

```
a[: , :]
```

```
a[:]
a[: :]
```

Any of the above will display the entire 2D array as:

```
[[1 2 3]
 [4 5 6]
 [7 8 9]]
```

Suppose, we want to display the 0th row from the array, we can write:

```
a[0, :]
```

Observe the 0 in the place of the 'row'. It will refer to 0th row. In the place of 'column', we simply used ':' that refers to all columns (or elements) in that row. As a result it will display: [1 2 3]. Similarly, a[1, :] refers to 1st row and a[2, :] refers to 2nd row.

Suppose, we want to display 0th column of the array, we can write:

```
a[:, 0]
```

This will refer to the 0th column, i.e. [1 4 7]. Similarly, a[:, 1] refers to 1st column and a[:, 2] refers to 2nd column.

If we want to retrieve only a particular element, then we have to provide both the row and column positions. For example, to retrieve 0th row and 0th column element, we can write:

```
a[0:1, 0:1]
```

This will refer to the element 1 in the array. Similarly, to access the 1st row and 2nd column element, we can write:

```
a[1:2, 1:2]
```

This will refer to the element 5. Similarly, to access the 2nd row and 2nd column element, we can write:

```
a[2:3, 1:2]
```

This will refer to 8.

For the same of better understanding, let's create a 2D array with 5 rows and 5 columns with elements from 11 to 35. This can be done as:

```
a = reshape(arange(11, 36, 1), (5,5))
print(a)
```

The preceding lines of code will display the following output:

```
[[11 12 13 14 15]
 [16 17 18 19 20]
 [21 22 23 24 25]
 [26 27 28 29 30]
 [31 32 33 34 35]]
```

Suppose, we want to display the left top 2 rows and 3 columns, we can write as:

```
print(a[0:2, 0:3])
```

The preceding lines of code will display the following output:

```
[[11 12 13]
 [16 17 18]]
```

This can be understood better from the diagram in Figure 7.11:

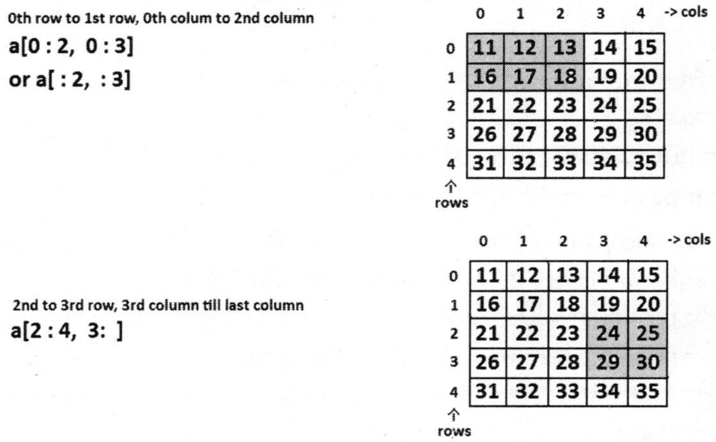

Figure 7.11: Understanding Slicing in 2D numpy Arrays

In the same way, we can access the right top 2 rows and 3 columns as:

```
print(a[0:2, 2:])
```

The preceding line of code will display the following output:

```
[[13 14 15]
 [18 19 20]]
```

To access the lower right 3 rows and 2 columns, we can write:

```
print(a[2:, 3:])
```

The preceding line of code will display the following output:

```
[[24 25]
 [29 30]
 [34 35]]
```

Matrices in numpy

In Mathematics, a matrix represents a rectangular array of elements arranged in rows and columns. It means elements are available in a matrix in the form of several rows and columns. If a matrix has only 1 row, it is called a 'row matrix'. If a matrix has only 1 column, then it is called a 'column matrix'. We can understand that the row matrix and column matrices are nothing but 1D arrays.

When a matrix has more than 1 row and more than 1 column, it is called m x n matrix where m represents the rows and n represents the columns. Thus, a 2 x 3 matrix contains 2 rows and 3 columns. We can show these matrices using numpy 2D arrays. To work with matrices, numpy provides a special object called *matrix*. In numpy, a matrix is a specialized 2D array that retains its 2D nature through operations.

We can create numpy matrices using the following syntax:

```
matrix-name = matrix(2D array or string)
```

It means, the matrix object receives a 2D array or a string that contains elements which can be converted into a matrix. For example, we are taking a 2D array with 2 rows and 3 columns as:

```
arr = [[1, 2, 3], [4, 5, 6]]
```

This array can be converted into a matrix 'a' as:

```
a = matrix(arr)
```

If we display the matrix 'a', we can see the following format:

```
[[1 2 3]
 [4 5 6]]
```

Alternately, we can also pass the 2D array directly to matrix object as:

```
a = matrix([[1,2,3],[4,5,6]])
```

Another way of creating a matrix is by passing a string with elements to matrix object as:

```
str = '1  2; 3  4; 5  6' # observe the semicolons after each row of
                         # elements
b = matrix(str)
```

If we display the matrix 'b', we can see a 3 x 2 matrix as:

```
[[1 2]
 [3 4]
 [5 6]]
```

We can also pass the string directly to matrix object as:

```
b = matrix("1 2; 3 4; 5 6")
```

which will also create the matrix 'b' as indicated above.

Getting Diagonal Elements of a Matrix

To retrieve the diagonal elements of a matrix, we can use diagonal() function as:

```
a = diagonal(matrix)
```

The diagonal() function returns a 1D array that contains diagonal elements of the original matrix. To understand this function, we can take an example.

```
a = matrix('1 2 3; 4 5 6; 7 8 9')  # create a 3 x 3 matrix
print(a)
```

The preceding lines of code will display the following output:

```
[[1 2 3]
 [4 5 6]
 [7 8 9]]
```

Consider the following code:

```
d = diagonal(a)  # find diagonal of a
print(d)
```

The preceding lines of code will display the following output:

```
[1 5 9]  # this is the diagonal
```

Finding Maximum and Minimum Elements

To know the maximum element, we can use max() method and to know the minimum element, we can use min() methods. These methods should be called using the matrix name. See the following examples:

```
big = a.max()
print(big)
9

small = a.min()
print(small)
1
```

Finding Sum and Average of Elements

To find sum of all the elements in the matrix, we can use sum() method and to find average, we can use mean() method. These methods should be called using the matrix name. See the following examples:

```
a.sum()
45

a.mean()
5.0
```

Products of Elements

It is possible to know the products of elements in a matrix. For this purpose, numpy provides prod() method. For example, prod(0) returns a matrix that contains the products of elements in each column of the original matrix. prod(1) returns a matrix that contains products of elements in each row. These methods should be called using the matrix name.

As an example, we are creating a matrix from a 3 x 4 array as:

```
m = matrix(arange(12).reshape(3,4))
```

This will create a matrix 'm' with elements from 0 to 11 in the form of 3 rows and 4 columns as:

```
 [[ 0  1  2  3]
  [ 4  5  6  7]
  [ 8  9 10 11]]
```

To find the products of elements column-wise, we can call prod() method as:

```
a = m.prod(0)
```

The array 'a' looks like this: [[0 45 120 231]]. Each of these values represents products of elements present in 0th column, 1st element, and so on up to 3rd column. Now, to find the products of elements row-wise, we can call prod() method as:

```
b = m.prod(1)
```

The array 'b' would be:

```
[[   0]
 [ 840]
 [7920]]
```

Each of these values represents products of elements in 0th row, 1st row and 2nd row.

Sorting the Matrix

numpy provides sort() function that sorts the matrix elements into ascending order. See the syntax of this function:

```
sort(matrixname, axis)
```

If we use, axis=1, it sorts the elements in each row into ascending order. If we use, axis=0, then it sorts the elements in each column into ascending order. The default value of axis is 1. It means, if we do not mention 'axis', then its value will be taken as 1. In the following example, we are taking a matrix 'm' with 2 rows and 3 columns as:

```
m = matrix([[5, 4, 1], [2, 7, 0]])
print(m)
```

The preceding lines of code will display the following output:

```
[[5 4 1]
 [2 7 0]]
```

To sort the elements in the rows, we can use sort() function as:

```
a = sort(m)
print(a)
```

The preceding lines of code will display the following output:

```
[[1 4 5]
 [0 2 7]]
```

Observe the sorted matrix 'a' contains the elements in each row arranged in ascending order. To sort the elements vertically, i.e. column-wise, we can use sort() function with axis=0 attribute as:

```
b = sort(m, axis=0)
print(b)
```

The preceding lines of code will display the following output:

```
[[2 4 0]
 [5 7 1]]
```

Transpose of a Matrix

Rewriting matrix rows into columns and vice versa is called 'transpose'. Thus, the rows in the original matrix will become columns in the transpose matrix and the columns in the original matrix will become rows in the transpose matrix. It means if the original matrix has m x n size, the transpose matrix will have n x m size. To find the transpose, we can use transpose() and getT() methods in numpy. These methods should be called using matrix name. Consider the following code snippet:

```
m = matrix('1 2 3; 4 5 6; 7 8 9')  # create a matrix of 3 x 3 size
print(m)  # display the original matrix, i.e., m
```

The preceding lines of code will display the following output:

```
[[1 2 3]
 [4 5 6]
 [7 8 9]]
```

Now, consider the following code snippet:

```
t = m.transpose()  # find the transpose matrix
print(t)  # display the transpose matrix, i.e. t
```

The preceding lines of code will display the following output:

```
[[1 4 7]
 [2 5 8]
 [3 6 9]]
```

Also, consider the following code snippet:

```
t1 = m.getT()  # find transpose using getT().
print(t1)  # display the transpose matrix, i.e., t1
```

The preceding lines of code will display the following output:

```
[[1 4 7]
 [2 5 8]
 [3 6 9]]
```

Program

Program 37: A Python program to accept a matrix from the keyboard and display its transpose matrix.

```
# transpose of a matrix
from numpy import*

# accept number of rows and cols into r, c
r, c = [int(a) for a in input("Enter rows, cols: ").split()]

# accept matrix elements as a string into str
str = input('Enter matrix elements:\n ')

# convert the string into a matrix with size rxc
x = reshape(matrix(str), (r, c))
print('The original matrix: ')
print(x)

print('The transpose matrix: ')
```

```
y = x.transpose()
print(y)
```

Output:

```
C:\>python arr.py
Enter rows, cols: 2 3
Enter matrix elements:
1 2 3 4 5 6
The original matrix:
[[1 2 3]
 [4 5 6]]
The transpose matrix:
[[1 4]
 [2 5]
 [3 6]]
```

Matrix Addition and Multiplication

We can use arithmetic operators like +, - and / to perform addition, subtraction and division operations on 2 matrices. Consider the following code snippet:

```
a = matrix('1 2 3; 4 5 6')    # create matrix a with size 2 x 3
b = matrix('2 2 2; 1 -1 2')   # create matrix b with size 2 x 3
print(a)  # display a
```

The preceding lines of code will display the following output:

```
[[1 2 3]
 [4 5 6]]
```

If you write,

```
print(b)  # display b
```

Then, the preceding line of code will display the following output:

```
[[ 2  2  2]
 [ 1 -1  2]]
```

Now, consider the following code snippet:

```
c = a+b   # add a and b
print(c)  # display the resultant matrix, i.e. c
```

The preceding lines of code will display the following output:

```
[[3 4 5]
 [5 4 8]]
```

Also, consider the following code snippet:

```
d=a/b  # divide a with b
print(d)  # display the resultant matrix, i.e. d
```

The preceding lines of code will display the following output:

```
[[ 0.5  1.   1.5]
 [ 4.  -5.   3. ]]
```

We can use * operator to perform matrix multiplication. Please remember this operator does not multiply the corresponding elements of the matrices to produce the new matrix with those results as in the case of + or / seen in the preceding code. The * operator performs matrix multiplication according to Mathematics. As an example, we will take two matrices 'a' and 'b' and multiply them to get a new matrix 'c'.

```
a = [[1 2 3]
     [4 5 6]]
b = [[ 1  0]
     [ 0  2]
     [ 1 -1]]
```

Please observe that the matrix 'a' contains 2 rows and 3 columns and the matrix 'b' contains 3 rows and 2 columns. To multiply these two matrices, the condition that is to be satisfied is that the number of columns in 'a' should be equal to the number of rows in 'b'. Since this is satisfied, it is possible to multiply these two matrices.

If the matrix 'a' has r1xc1 size and the matrix 'b' has r2xc2 size, then the resultant matrix after their multiplication will have r1xc2 size. In our example, 'a' is a 2x3 matrix and 'b' is a 3x2 matrix. Hence, the resultant matrix will be a 2x2 matrix.

First, take the first row of 'a' and first column of 'b'. Multiply each element in the first row of 'a' with each element in the first column of 'b' and find their sum, as: 1x1+2x0+3x1 = 4. This becomes the first row and first column element in the resultant matrix.

Next, multiply each element in the first row of 'a' with each element in the second column of 'b' and find their sum, as: 1x0+2x2+3x(-1) = 1. This becomes the first row and second column element in the resultant matrix.

Now, repeat the same steps with second row of the matrix 'a'. Multiply each element in the second row of 'a' with each element in the first column of 'b' and take their sum, as: 4x1+5x0+6x1 = 10. This becomes the second row and first column element in the new matrix.

Multiply each element in the second row of 'a' with each element in the second column of 'b' and take their sum, as: 4x0+5x2+6x(-1) = 4. This becomes the second row and second column element in the new matrix.

The next step is to write these sums in the form a matrix as:

```
[[ 4  1]
 [10  4]]
```

This is the resultant matrix of multiplication of 'a' and 'b' matrices. Observe that this is a 2x2 matrix.

However, to multiply two matrices, we can simply use * (multiplication) operator on the matrices and obtain the resultant matrix easily. This is shown in the following code snippet:

```
a = matrix([[1,2,3], [4,5,6]])  # take a 2 x 3 matrix
print(a)
```

The preceding lines of code will display the following output:

```
[[1 2 3]
 [4 5 6]]
```

Consider the following code snippet:

```
b = matrix([[1,0], [0,2], [1, -1]])  # take a 3 x 2 matrix
print(b)
```

It will display the following output:

```
[[ 1  0]
 [ 0  2]
 [ 1 -1]]
```

Also, consider the following code snippet:

```
c = a*b   # multiply a and b to get c
print(c)  # display the resultant matrix
```

The preceding lines of code will display the following output:

```
[[ 4  1]
 [10  4]]
```

In Program 38, we are taking two matrices from keyboard and finding the product matrix.

Program

Program 38: A Python program to accept two matrices and find their product.

```
# matrix multiplication
import sys
from numpy import*

# accept number of rows and cols of first matrix into r1, c1
r1, c1 = [int(a) for a in input("First matrix rows, cols: ").split()]

# accept number of rows and cols of second matrix into r2, c2
r2, c2 = [int(a) for a in input("Second matrix rows, cols: ").split()]

# test the condition if c1 != r2, then multiplication is not possible
if c1!=r2:
    print('Multiplication is not possible')
    sys.exit()  # terminate the program

# accept first matrix elements as a string into str1
str1 = input('Enter first matrix elements:\n ')

# convert str1 into a matrix with size r1xc1
x = reshape(matrix(str1), (r1, c1))

# accept second matrix elements as a string into str2
str2 = input('Enter second matrix elements:\n ')

# convert str2 into a matrix with size r2xc2
y = reshape(matrix(str2), (r2, c2))
print('The product matrix: ')
z = x * y
print(z)
```

Output:

```
C:\>python arr.py
First matrix rows, cols: 2 3
Second matrix rows, cols: 3 2
Enter first matrix elements:
1 2 3 4 5 6
Enter second matrix elements:
1 0 0 2 1 -1
The product matrix:
[[4    1]
 [10   4]]
```

Please observe that exit() is a function in the module *sys* that terminates the program execution. When using this function, we should import 'sys' module. This has been done in the beginning of the Program 38.

Random Numbers

A random number is a number that cannot be guessed by anyone. When a random number is generated, we do not know which number we are going to get. numpy has a sub module called *random* that is equipped with the rand() function that is useful to create random numbers. To call this function, we should use: random.rand() since it belongs to the 'random' sub module.

When we simply call the rand() function, it will generate a random number between 0.0 and 1.0. For example,

```
random.rand()
0.827315889219082
```

Please remember that when we call this function, every time we may have a different number. We can create a 1D array of random numbers by passing the size of the array to the rand() function as:

```
a = random.rand(5)
```

This will create a 1D array 'a' with 5 elements which are random numbers between 0.0 and 1.0 as:

```
[ 0.77936722,  0.07741308,  0.13805453,  0.90238821,  0.3422711 ]
```

We can also create a 2D array of random numbers by passing the size of the 2D array to the random() function as:

```
b = random.rand(2, 3)
print(b)
[[ 0.94777612  0.07496758  0.77621813]
 [ 0.71328036  0.13507592  0.56528705]]
```

Points to Remember

- An array represents a group of elements of same data type.
- Arrays are highly useful to store and process groups of elements easily.
- Python arrays can increase or decrease their size in memory at runtime. Hence, no need to mention the array size at the time of creating it.
- Arrays are of two types: single dimensional arrays or 1D arrays and multi-dimensional arrays, which can be 2D or 3D arrays.
- Python offers only 1D arrays. If we want to create multi-dimensional arrays, we need to use a separate package called numpy.
- Python's 'array' module is useful to create 1D arrays.
- The simple way to create a 1D array is: arrayname = array(type code, [elements]) where type code 'i' or 'I' represents integer type array and 'f' or 'd' represents float type array.
- An index represents the position number of an element in an array. Indexes are written inside square brackets. For example, x[i] represents i^{th} element of the array 'x'.
- A slice represents a piece of part of an array. To mention which part of the array we need, we can using slicing operation in the form: arrayname[start:stop:stride]. For example, x[1:5:2] represents a slice of the array 'x' starting from 1st element to 4th element in steps of 2.
- 'array' class offers several methods to process the arrays, for example: append(), insert(), index(), pop(), remove(), reverse() etc.
- 1D arrays in numpy can be created using functions like array(), linspace(), logspace(), arrange(), zeros() and ones().
- It is possible to perform mathematical operations like addition, subtraction, multiplication, division etc. on 1D arrays.
- Functions like sin(), cos(), tan(), sqrt(), pow(), sum(), prod(), min(), max(), sort() are available in numpy to process the elements of 1D arrays.
- Relational operators >, >=, <, <=, ==, != and logical functions logical_and(), logical_or(), logical_not() are used to compare the elements of two arrays.
- Aliasing an array represents giving another name to the same array. For example, b = a. Here we are giving alias name 'b' to the array 'a'. The elements of 'a' are not copied into 'b'. Also, any modifications to 'a' will also reflect in 'b' and vice versa.
- Viewing an array represents copying the elements of an array into another array. For example, b = a.view(). This will create a view for the array 'a' and the view name is 'b'.

Any modifications done to 'a' will also reflect in 'b' and vice versa even though 'a' and 'b' are two different arrays.

- Copying an array represents copying and creating an independent array. For example, b = a.copy(). This will create 'b' as a copy of the array 'a'. Any modifications done to 'a' will not modify the array 'b' and vice versa.
- The reshape() method is useful to change a 1D array into a 2D array or 3D array. For example, if 'a' is a 1D array, we can change its shape as 2D array with 3 rows and 3 columns, as: a.reshape(3,3).
- The flatten() method is useful to change the 2D array or 3D array into 1D array. For example, if 'a' is a 2D array, we can convert it into a 1D array as: a.flatten().
- The ones() function creates an array and fills the elements with all 1s.
- The zeros() function creates an array and fills the elements with all 0s.
- The eye() function creates a 2D array and fills the elements in the diagonal with 1s.
- A matrix represents a group of elements arranged in rows and columns. If a matrix has only 1 row, it is called a 'row matrix'. If a matrix has only 1 column, then it is called a 'column matrix'. Row matrix and column matrices are nothing but 1D arrays.
- When a matrix has m rows and n columns, it is called 'm x n' matrix. This is an example for 2D array.
- In numpy, a matrix is a specialized 2D array that retains its 2D nature through operations.
- To create a matrix in numpy, we can use matrix object, as: matrix-name = matrix(2D array or string).
- The prod() method is useful to find products of elements row-wise and column-wise.
- The sort() function is useful to sort the elements in the rows or columns.
- To find the transpose of a matrix, we can use transpose() and getT() methods in numpy.
- The operators +, -, / can be used on matrices to add, subtract or divide the matrices. But, the operator ' * ' performs matrix multiplication when used on two matrices.
- The rand() function of 'random' sub module in numpy can be used to generate random numbers.

CHAPTER

STRINGS AND CHARACTERS

8

A string represents a group of characters. Strings are important because most of the data that we use in daily life will be in the form of strings. For example, the names of persons, their addresses, vehicle numbers, their credit card numbers, etc. are all strings. In Python, the *str* datatype represents a string.

Since every string comprises several characters, Python handles strings and characters almost in the same manner. There is no separate datatype to represent individual characters in Python.

Creating Strings

We can create a string in Python by assigning a group of characters to a variable. The group of characters should be enclosed inside single quotes or double quotes as:

```
s1 = 'Welcome to Core Python learning'
s2 = "Welcome to Core Python learning"
```

There is no difference between the single quotes and double quotes while creating the strings. Both will work in the same manner.

Sometimes, we can use triple single quotes or triple double quotes to represent strings. These quotation marks are useful when we want to represent a string that occupies several lines as:

```
str = '''Welcome to Core Python, a book on Python
language that discusses all important concepts of Python
in a lucid and comprehensive manner.'''
```

In the preceding statement, the string 'str' is created using triple single quotes. Alternately, the above string can be created using triple double quotes as:

```
str = """Welcome to Core Python, a book on Python
language that discusses all important concepts of Python
in a lucid and comprehensive manner."""
```

Thus, triple single quotes or triple double quotes are useful to create strings which span into several lines.

It is possible to display quotation marks to mark a sub string in a string. In that case, we should use one type of quotes for outer string and another type of quotes for inner string as:

```
s1 = 'Welcome to "Core Python" learning'
print(s1)
```

The preceding lines of code will display the following output:

```
Welcome to "Core Python" learning
```

Here, the string 's1' contains two strings. The outer string is enclosed in single quotes and the inner string, i.e. "Core Python" is enclosed in double quotes. Alternately, we can use double quotes for outer string and single quotes for inner string as:

```
s1 = "Welcome to 'Core Python' learning"
print(s1)
```

The preceding lines of code will display the following output:

```
Welcome to 'Core Python' learning
```

It is possible to use escape characters like \t or \n inside the strings. The escape character \t releases tab space of 6 or 8 spaces and the escape character \n throws cursor into a new line. For example,

```
s1 = "Welcome to\tCore Python\nlearning"
print(s1)
```

The preceding lines of code will display the following output:

```
Welcome to      Core Python
learning
```

Table 8.1 summarizes the escape characters that can be used in strings:

Table 8.1: Escape Characters and their Meanings

Escape Character	Meaning
\a	Bell or alert
\b	Backspace
\n	New line
\t	Horizontal tab space
\v	Vertical tab space
\r	Enter button
\x	Character x
\\	Displays single \

To nullify the effect of escape characters, we can create the string as a 'raw' string by adding 'r' before the string as:

```
s1 = r"Welcome to\tCore Python\nlearning"
print(s1)
```

The preceding lines of code will display the following output:

```
Welcome to\tCore Python\nlearning
```

This is not showing the effect of \t or \n. It means we could not see the horizontal tab space or new line. Raw strings take escape characters, like \t, \n, etc., as ordinary characters in a string and hence display them as they are.

To create a string with Unicode characters, we should add 'u' at the beginning of the string. Unicode is a standard to include the alphabet of various human languages into programming languages like Python or Java. For example, it is possible to display the alphabet of Hindi, French, and German languages using Unicode system. Each Unicode character contains 4 digits preceded by a \u. The following statement displays 'Core Python' in Hindi using Unicode characters. There are 8 Unicode characters used for this purpose.

```
name = u'\u0915\u094b\u0930  \u092a\u0948\u0925\u0964\u0928'
print(name)
```

The preceding lines of code will display the following output:

```
कोर पैथ।न
```

Length of a String

Length of a string represents the number of characters in a string. To know the length of a string, we can use the len() function. This function gives the number of characters including spaces in the string.

```
str = 'Core Python'
n = len(str)
print(n)
```

The preceding lines of code will display the following output:

```
11
```

Indexing in Strings

Index represents the position number. Index is written using square braces []. By specifying the position number through an index, we can refer to the individual elements (or characters) of a string. For example, str[0] refers to the 0th element of the string and str[1] refers to the 1st element of the string. Thus, str[i] can be used to refer to i^{th} element of the string. Here, 'i' is called the string index because it is specifying the position number of the element in the string.

When we use index as a negative number, it refers to elements in the reverse order. Thus, str[-1] refers to the last element and str[-2] refers to second element from last. Figure 8.1 shows how the indexes refer to the individual elements in the string:

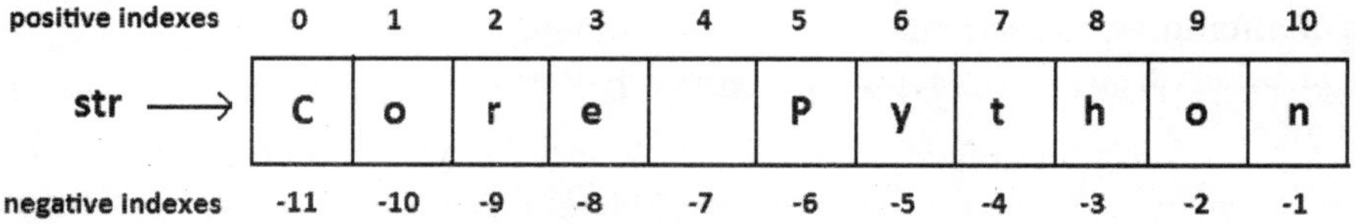

Figure 8.1: Indexing in String

In Program 1, we are showing how to access each element of a string in forward and reverse orders using the while loop.

Program

Program 1: A Python program to access each element of a string in forward and reverse orders using while loop.

```
# indexing on strings
str = 'Core Python'

# access each character using while loop
n = len(str)   # n = no. of chars in str
i=0  # i = 0,1,2,... n-1
while i<n:
    print(str[i], end=' ')
    i+=1

print()  # put cursor into next line
# access in reverse order
i=-1  # i = -1,-2,-3,... -n
while i>=-n:
    print(str[i], end=' ')
    i-=1

print()  # put cursor into next line

# access in reverse order using negative index
i=1  # i = 1,2,3,... n
n = len(str)   # n = no. of chars in str
while i<=n:
    print(str[-i], end=' ')
    i+=1
```

Output:

```
C:\>python str.py
C o r e   P y t h o n
n o h t y P   e r o C
n o h t y P   e r o C
```

We can also use the for loop to access each element (or character) of a string. The following for loop simply takes each element into a variable 'i' and displays it.

```
for i in str:
    print(i)
```

To display the string in the reverse order, we should use slicing operation on string. The format of slicing is stringname[start: stop: stepsize]. If 'start' and 'stop' are not specified, then it is taken from 0th to $n-1^{th}$ elements. If 'stepsize' is not written, then it is taken to be 1. Hence, the following loop will display all the elements of the string:

```
for i in str[: : ]:   # do not mention start, stop and stepsize
    print(i)
```

To get the elements in reverse order, we should use stepsize negative as: -1. This will display the elements from last to first in steps of 1 in reverse order. The for loop in this case looks like this:

```
for i in str[: : -1]:   # take stepsize as -1
    print(i)
```

This is what we have shown in Program 2. In this program, we used for loop to access the characters of a string in forward direction and then another for loop to access the characters in reverse order.

Program

Program 2: A Python program to access the characters of a string using for loop.

```
# accessing elements of a string using for loop
str = 'Core Python'

# access each letter using for loop
for i in str:
    print(i, end=' ')

print()  # put cursor into next line

# access in reverse order
for i in str[:: -1]:
    print(i, end=' ')
```

Output:

```
C:\>python str.py
C o r e   P y t h o n
n o h t y P   e r o C
```

Slicing the Strings

A slice represents a part or piece of a string. The format of slicing is:

```
stringname[start: stop: stepsize]
```

If 'start' and 'stop' are not specified, then slicing is done from 0th to n-1th elements. If 'stepsize' is not written, then it is taken to be 1. See the following example:

```
str = 'Core Python'
str[0:9:1]    # access string from 0th to 8th element in steps of 1
Core Pyth
```

When 'stepsize' is 2, then it will access every other character from 1st character onwards. Hence it retrieves the 0th, 2nd, 4th , 6th characters and so on.

```
str[0:9:2]
Cr yh
```

Some other examples are given below to have a better understanding on slicing. Consider the following code snippet:

```
str = 'Core Python'
str[::]  # access string from 0th to last character
```

The preceding lines of code will display the following output:

```
Core Python
```

If you write,

```
str[2:4:1]  # access from str[2] to str[3] in steps of 1
```

Then, the following output appears:

```
re
```

If you write the following statement:

```
str[::2]  # access entire string in steps of 2
```

Then, the following output appears:

```
Cr yhn
```

Now, if you write the following statement:

```
str[2::]  # access string from str[2] to ending
```

Then, the preceding lines of code display the following output:

```
re Python
```

Suppose if you write the following statement:

```
str[:4:]  # access string from str[0] to str[3] in steps of 1
```

The following output appears:

```
Core
```

It is possible to use reverse slicing to retrieve the elements from the string in reverse order. The 'start', 'stop' can be specified as negative numbers. For example,

```
str = 'Core Python'
str[-4:-1]  # access from str[-4] to str[-2] from left to right in str.
```

The following output appears:

```
tho
```

Now, if you write the following statement:

```
str[-6::]  # access from str[-6] till the end of the string
```

The following output appears:

```
Python
```

When stepsize is negative, then the elements are counted from right to left. See the examples:

```
str[-1:-4:-1]  # retrieve from str[-1] to str[-3] from right to left
```

The output of the preceding statement is as follows:

```
'noh'
```

Now, if you write the following statement:

```
str[-1::-1]  # retrieve from str[-1] till first element from right to
left
```

The output of the preceding statement is as follows:

```
'nohtyP eroC'
```

Repeating the Strings

The repetition operator is denoted by '*' symbol and is useful to repeat the string for several times. For example, str * n repeats the string for n times. See the example:

```
str = 'Core Python'
print(str*2)
```

The preceding lines of code will display the following output:

```
Core PythonCore Python
```

Similarly, it is possible to repeat a part of the string obtained by slicing as:

```
s = str[5:7]*3   # repeat 5th 6th characters for 3 times
print(s)
```

The output of the preceding statement is as follows:

```
PyPyPy
```

Concatenation of Strings

We can use '+' on strings to attach a string at the end of another string. This operator '+' is called addition operator when used on numbers. But, when used on strings, it is called 'concatenation' operator since it joins or concatenates the strings. Similar result can be achieved using the join() method also which will be discussed a little later.

```
s1='Core'
s2="Python"
s3=s1+s2   # concatenate s1 and s2
print(s3)   # display the total string s3
```

The output of the preceding statement is as follows:

```
CorePython
```

Checking Membership

We can check if a string or character is a member of another string or not using 'in' or 'not in' operators. The 'in' operator returns True if the string or character is found in the main string. It returns False if the string or character is not found in the main string. The 'not in' operator returns False if a string or character is not found in the main string, otherwise True.

The operators 'in' and 'not in' make case sensitive comparisons. It means these operators consider the upper case and lower case letters or strings differently while comparing the strings.

In Program 3, we input a main string and a sub string from the keyboard and check whether the sub string is found in the main string or not.

Program

Program 3: A Python program to know whether a sub string exists in main string or not.

```
# to know whether sub string is in main string or not
str = input('Enter main string: ')
sub = input('Enter sub string: ')
if sub in str:
    print(sub+' is found in main string')
else:
    print(sub+' is not found in the main string')
```

Output:

```
C:\>python str.py
Enter main string: This is Core Python
Enter sub string: Core
Core is found in main string
```

Comparing Strings

We can use the relational operators like >, >=, <, <=, == or != operators to compare two strings. They return Boolean value, i.e. either True or False depending on the strings being compared.

```
s1='Box'
s2='Boy'
if(s1==s2):
    print('Both are same')
else:
    print('Not same')
```

This code returns 'Not same' as the strings are not same. While comparing the strings, Python interpreter compares them by taking them in English dictionary order. The string which comes first in the dictionary order will have a low value than the string which comes next. It means, 'A' is less than 'B' which is less than 'C' and so on. In the above example, the string 's1' comes before the string 's2' and hence s1 is less than s2. So, if we write:

```
if s1<s2:
    print('s1 less than s2')
else:
    print('s1 greater than or equal to s2')
```

Then, the preceding statements will display 's1 less than s2'.

Removing Spaces from a String

A space is also considered as a character inside a string. Sometimes, the unnecessary spaces in a string will lead to wrong results. For example, a person typed his name 'Mukesh ' (observe two spaces at the end of the string) instead of typing 'Mukesh'. If we compare these two strings using '==' operator as:

```
if 'Mukesh  '=='Mukesh':
    print('Welcome')
else:
    print('Name not found')
```

The output will be 'Name not found'. In this way, spaces may lead to wrong results. Hence such spaces should be removed from the strings before they are compared. This is possible using rstrip(), lstrip() and strip() methods. The rstrip() method removes the spaces which are at the right side of the string. The lstrip() method removes spaces which are at the left side of the string. strip() method removes spaces from both the sides of the strings. These methods do not remove spaces which are in the middle of the string. Consider the following code snippet:

```
name = '  Mukesh Deshmukh  ' #observe spaces before and after the name
print(name.rstrip()) # remove spaces at right
```

The output of the preceding statement is as follows:

```
Mukesh Deshmukh
```

Now, if you write:

```
print(name.lstrip())  # remove spaces at left
```

The output of the preceding statement is as follows:

```
Mukesh Deshmukh
```

Now, if you write:

```
print(name.strip())  # remove spaces from both sides
```

The output of the preceding statement is as follows:

```
Mukesh Deshmukh
```

Finding Sub Strings

The find(), rfind(), index() and rindex() methods are useful to locate sub strings in a string. These methods return the location of the first occurrence of the sub string in the main string. The find() and index() methods search for the sub string from the beginning of the main string. The rfind() and rindex() methods search for the sub string from right to left, i.e. in backward order.

The find() method returns -1 if the sub string is not found in the main string. The index() method returns 'ValueError' exception if the sub string is not found. The format of find() method is:

```
mainstring.find(substring, beginning, ending)
```

The same format is used for other methods also. In Program 4, we are trying to display the first occurrence of the sub string in the main string by accepting both the strings from the user. In Program 4, we are using find() method.

Program

Program 4: A Python program to find the first occurrence of sub string in a given main string.

```
# to find first occurrence of sub string in a main string
str = input('Enter main string: ')
sub = input('Enter sub string: ')

# find position of sub in str
# search from 0th to last characters in str
n = str.find(sub, 0, len(str))

# find() returns -1 if sub string is not found
if n == -1:
    print('Sub string not found')
else:
    print('Sub string found at position: ', n+1)
```

Output:

```
C:\>python str.py
Enter main string: This is a book
Enter sub string: is
Sub string is found at position:  3
```

In the above program, observe that the Sub string position is displayed to be at 'n+1'. Since find() method starts counting from 0th position and we count from 1st position, we need to add 1 to the result given by find() method to get correct position number.

The same program can be rewritten using index() method. If the sub string is not found, index() method returns 'ValueError' exception, we have to handle the exception in our program. This is what we did in Program 5.

Program

Program 5: A Python program to find the first occurrence of sub string in a given string using index() method.

```
# to find first occurrence of sub string in a main string
str = input('Enter main string: ')
sub = input('Enter sub string: ')

# find position of sub in str
# search from 0th to last characters in str
try:
    n = str.index(sub, 0, len(str))
except ValueError:
    print('Sub string not found')
else:
    print('Sub string found at position: ', n+1)
```

Output:

```
Same as in case of Program 4.
```

The find() method and index() methods return only the first occurrence of the sub string. When the sub string occurs several times in the main string, they cannot return all those occurrences. Is there any way that we can find out all the occurrences of the sub string - is the question. For this purpose, we should develop additional logic.

Initially, searching should start from 0th character in the main string 'str' up to the last character 'n' which is given by len(str). So, 'i' value will start initially at 0. When the find() method finds the position of the sub string, we should display it. Suppose the sub string is found at 2nd position, then we need not again search for the sub string up to the 2nd position. This time, we should continue searching from 3rd character onwards. Thus, 'i' value will become 3 i.e. i = pos+1. If find() method could not find the sub string, then normal incrementing of 'i' is done, i.e. i= i+1. This logic is used in Program 6.

Program

Program 6: A Python program to display all positions of a sub string in a given main string.

```
# to find all occurrences of sub string in a main string
str = input('Enter main string: ')
sub = input('Enter sub string: ')

i=0
flag=False  # becomes True if sub string is found
n = len(str)
while i<n:  # repeat from 0th to nth characters
    pos = str.find(sub, i, n)
    if pos != -1:  # if found display its position
        print('Found at position: ', pos+1)
        i=pos+1  # search from pos+1 position onwards
        flag=True
    else:
        i=i+1  # search from next character onwards
```

```
    if flag == False:
        print('Sub string not found')
```

Output:

```
C:\>python str.py
Enter main string: This is a book
Enter sub string: is
Found at position:  3
Found at position:  6
```

The above program can be simplified by taking 'pos' value initially as -1 and rewriting find() method as:

```
pos = str.find(sub, pos+1, n)
```

First time, find() method will start searching from 0th to n^{th} character since 'pos = -1'. If the sub string is found, then its position is assigned to 'pos' and hence the next time, find() method will search from 'pos+1' till the end of the string. In this way, when the sub string position is found, find() method will continue searching from its next position onwards. If the string is found not even once, then 'pos' value will continue to be -1 and hence we can break the loop as:

```
if pos == -1: break
```

This logic is used in Program 7 which gives same output as the Program 6.

Program

Program 7: A program to display all positions of a sub string in a given main string – version 2.

```
# to find all occurrences of sub string in a main string - v2.0
str = input('Enter main string: ')
sub = input('Enter sub string: ')

flag=False
pos = -1
n = len(str)
while True:  # repeat forever
    pos = str.find(sub, pos+1, n)
    if pos == -1:
        break

    print('Found at position: ', pos+1)
    flag=True

if flag==False:
    print('Not found')
```

Counting Substrings in a String

The method count() is available to count the number of occurrences of a sub string in a main string. The format of this method is:

```
stringname.count(substring)
```

This returns an integer number that represents how many times the substring is found in the main string. We can limit our search by specifying beginning and ending positions in the count() method so that the substring position is counted only in that range. Hence, the other form of count() method is:

```
stringname.count(substring, beg, end)
```

For example, we want to search for substring 'Delhi' in the main string 'New Delhi' to know how many times the substring appeared in the main string. We can use count() method as:

```
str = 'New Delhi'
n = str.count('Delhi')
print(n)
```

The output of the preceding statements is as follows:

```
1
```

Suppose, we want to know how many times 'e' is repeated in the main string in the range from 0th to 2nd characters, we can write:

```
n = str.count('e', 0, 3)
print(n)
```

The output of the preceding statements is as follows:

```
1
```

If we search for 'e' in the main string starting from 0th character to the end of the string, we can write:

```
n = str.count('e', 0, len(str))
print(n)
```

The output of the preceding statements is as follows:

```
2
```

Strings are Immutable

An *immutable* object is an object whose content cannot be changed. On the other hand, a *mutable* object is an object whose content can be changed as and when required. In Python, numbers, strings and tuples are immutable. Lists, sets, dictionaries are mutable objects.

There are two reasons why string objects are made immutable in Python.

- **Performance:** When an object is immutable, it will have fixed size in memory since it cannot be modified. Because strings are immutable, we can easily allocate memory space for them at creation time, and the storage requirements are fixed and unchanging. Hence it takes less time to allocate memory for strings and less time to access them. This increases the performance of the software.

- **Security:** Since string objects are immutable, any attempts to modify the existing string object will create a new object in memory. Thus the identity number of the new object will change that lets the programmer to understand that somebody modified the original string. This is useful to enforce security where strings can be transported from one application to another application without modifications.

In the following code, we create a string 'str' where we stored 4 characters: 'abcd'. When we display 0th character, i.e. str[0], it will display 'a'. If we try to replace the 0th character with a new character 'x', then there will be an error called 'TypeError'. This is a proof that strings are immutable.

```
str = 'abcd'
print(str[0])
a

str[0] = 'x'
Traceback (most recent call last):
    File "<pyshell#7>", line 1, in <module>
    str[0] = 'x'
TypeError: 'str' object does not support item assignment
```

We will take an ambiguous example. In this example, we are creating two strings 's1' and 's2', as:

```
s1='one'
s2='two'
```

Now, we are modifying the content of the string 's2' by storing the content of 's1' into it as:

```
s2 = s1  # store s1 into s2
```

If we display, the 's2' string, we can see the same content of 's1'.

```
print(s2)   # display s2
```

The output of the preceding statement is as follows:

```
one
```

If you write,

```
print(s1)   # display s1
```

Then, the output of the preceding statement is as follows:

```
one
```

It seems that the content of 's2' is replaced by the content of 's1' and hence 's2' became mutable. But this is wrong. When we write:

```
s2 = s1
```

The name 's2' will be adjusted to refer to the object that is referenced by 's1'. But, the original value of 's2' that is 'two' is not altered. Since 'two' is not referenced, the garbage collector deletes that object from memory. Figure 8.2 shows the immutability of string objects:

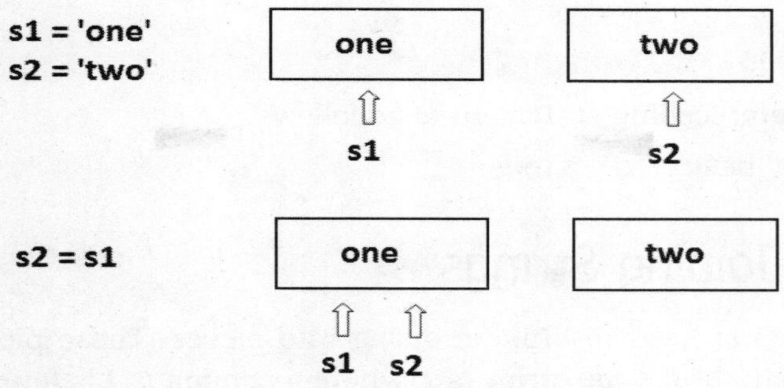

Figure 8.2: Immutability of String Objects

Identity number of an object internally refers to the memory address of the object and is given by id() function. If we display identity numbers using id() function, we can find that the identity number of 's2' and 's1' are same since they refer to one and the same object.

```
s1='one'
s2='two'
id(s1)
50848256
id(s2)
50848000
s2 = s1
id(s1)
50848256
id(s2)
50848256
```

Observe that the identity number of 's2' is changed after its modification, since it is referencing to a new object.

Replacing a String with another String

The replace() method is useful to replace a sub string in a string with another sub string. The format of using this method is:

```
stringname.replace(old, new)
```

This will replace all the occurrences of 'old' sub string with 'new' sub string in the main string. For example,

```
str = 'That is a beautiful girl'
s1 = 'girl'
s2 = 'flower'
str1 = str.replace(s1, s2)
```

If we display the contents of 'str' and 'str1', we can understand that the original string 'str' is not modified. Consider the following statement:

```
print(str)
```

The output of the preceding statement is as follows:

```
That is a beautiful girl
```

If you write,

```
print(str1)
```

The output of the preceding statement is as follows:

```
That is a beautiful flower
```

Splitting and Joining Strings

The split() method is used to brake a string into pieces. These pieces are returned as a list. For example, to brake the string 'str' where a comma (,) is found, we can write:

```
str.split(',')
```

Observe the comma inside the parentheses. It is called separator that represents where to separate or cut the string. Similarly, the separator will be a space if we want to cut the string at spaces. In the following example, we are cutting the string 'str' wherever a comma is found. The resultant string is stored in 'str1' which is a list.

```
str = 'one,two,three,four'
str1 = str.split(',')
print(str1)
```

The output of the preceding statements is as follows:

```
['one', 'two', 'three', 'four']
```

In Program 8, we are accepting a group of numbers as a string from the user. The numbers should be entered with space as separator. The numbers are stored by input() function into a string 'str' which is split into pieces where a space is found. The group of numbers are stored into a list 'lst' from where we display them using a for loop.

Program

Program 8: A Python program to accept and display a group of numbers.

```
# to accept a group of numbers and display them.
str = input('Enter numbers separated by space: ')

# cut the string where a space is found
lst = str.split(' ')

# display the numbers from the list
for i in lst:
    print(i)
```

Output:

```
C:\>python str.py
Enter numbers separated by space: 10 20 30 40
10
20
30
40
```

When a group of strings are given, it is possible to join them all and make a single string. For this purpose, we can use join() method as:

```
separator.join(str)
```

where, the 'separator' represents the character to be used between the strings in the output. 'str' represents a tuple or list of strings. In the following example, we are taking a tuple 'str' that contains 3 strings as:

```
str = ('one', 'two', 'three')
```

We want to join the three strings and form a single string. Also, we want to use hyphen (-) between the three strings in the output. The join() method can be written as:

```
str1 = "-".join(str)   # the output string is str1.
print(str1)
```

The output of the preceding statements is as follows:

```
one-two-three
```

In the following example, we are taking a list comprising 4 strings and we are joining them using a colon (:) between them.

```
str = ['apple', 'guava', 'grapes', 'mango']
sep = ':'
str1 = sep.join(str)
print(str1)
```

The output of the preceding statements is as follows:

```
apple:guava:grapes:mango
```

Changing Case of a String

Python offers 4 methods that are useful to change the case of a string. They are upper(), lower(), swapcase(), title(). The upper() method is used to convert all the characters of a string into uppercase or capital letters. The lower() method converts the string into lowercase or into small letters. The swapcase() method converts the capital letters into small letters and vice versa. The title() method converts the string such that each word in the string will start with a capital letter and remaining will be small letters. See the following examples:

```
str = 'Python is the future'
print(str.upper())
```

The output of the preceding statements is as follows:

```
PYTHON IS THE FUTURE
```

If you write,

```
print(str.lower())
```

Then, the output will be:

```
python is the future
```

If you write,

```
print(str.swapcase())
```

Then, the output will be:

```
pYTHON IS THE FUTURE
```

If you write the following statement:

```
print(str.title())
```

Then, the output will be:

```
Python Is The Future
```

Checking Starting and Ending of a String

The startswith() method is useful to know whether a string is starting with a sub string or not. The way to use this method is:

```
str.startswith(substring)
```

When the sub string is found in the main string 'str', this method returns True. If the sub string is not found, it returns False. Consider the following statements:

```
str = 'This is Python'
print(str.startswith('This'))
```

The output will be:

```
True
```

Similarly, to check the ending of a string, we can use endswith() method. It returns True if the string ends with the specified sub string, otherwise it returns False.

```
str.endswith(substring)
str = 'This is Python'
print(str.endswith('Python'))
```

The output of the preceding statements is as follows:

```
True
```

String Testing Methods

There are several methods to test the nature of characters in a string. These methods return either True or False. For example, if a string has only numeric digits, then isdigit() method returns True. These methods can also be applied to individual characters. Table 8.2 mentioned the string and character testing methods:

Table 8.2: String and Character Testing Methods

Method	Description
isalnum()	This method returns True if all characters in the string are alphanumeric (A to Z, a to z, 0 to 9) and there is at least one character; otherwise it returns False.

Method	Description
isalpha()	Returns True if the string has at least one character and all characters are alphabetic (A to Z and a to z); otherwise, it returns False.
isdigit()	Returns True if the string contains only numeric digits (0 to 9) and False otherwise.
islower()	Returns True if the string contains at least one letter and all characters are in lower case; otherwise, it returns False.
isupper()	Returns True if the string contains at least one letter and all characters are in upper case; otherwise, it returns False.
istitle()	Returns True if each word of the string starts with a capital letter and there is at least one character in the string; otherwise, it returns False.
isspace()	Returns True if the string contains only spaces; otherwise, it returns False.

To understand how to use these methods on strings, let's take an example. In this example, we take a string as:

```
str = 'Delhi999'
```

Now, we want to check if this string 'str' contains only alphabets, i.e. A to Z, a to z and not other characters like digits or spaces. We will use isalpha() method on the string as:

```
str.isalpha()
False
```

Since the string 'Delhi999' contains digits, the isalpha() method returned False. Another example:

```
str = 'Delhi'
str.isalpha()
True
```

Formatting the Strings

Formatting a string means presenting the string in a clearly understandable manner. The format() method is used to format strings. This method is used as:

```
'format string with replacement fields' . format(values)
```

We should first understand the meaning of the first attribute, i.e. 'format string with replacement fields'. The replacement fields are denoted by curly braces { } that contain names or indexes. These names or indexes represent the order of the values. For example, let's take an employee details like id number, name and salary in 3 variables 'id', 'name' and 'sal'.

```
id=10
name='Shankar'
sal=19500.75
```

We want to create a format string by the name 'str' to display these 3 values. These 3 values or variables should be mentioned inside the format() method as format(id,name,sal). The total format string can be written as:

```
str = '{},{},{}'.format(id,name,sal)
```

This string contains 3 replacement fields. The first field {} is replaced by 'id' value and the second field {} is replaced by the 'name' value and the third field {} is replaced by 'sal' value. So, if we display this string using print() method as given below:

```
print(str)
```

We can see the following output:

```
10,Shankar,19500.75
```

Suppose we do not want to display commas after each value, rather we want to display hyphens (-). In that case, the format string can be written as:

```
str = '{}-{}-{}'.format(id,name,sal)
print(str)
```

The output will be:

```
10-Shankar-19500.75
```

We can also display message strings before every value, which can be done as:

```
str = 'Id= {}\nName= {}\nSalary= {}'.format(id,name,sal)
print(str)
Id= 10
Name= Shankar
Salary= 19500.75
```

We can mention the escape characters like '\n' '\t' inside the format string as shown in the previous example. We can also mention the order numbers in the replacement fields as 0, 1, 2, etc. Consider the following example:

```
str = 'Id= {0}\tName= {1}\tSalary= {2}'.format(id,name,sal)
print(str)
```

The preceding statements will give the following output:

```
Id= 10                 Name= Shankar          Salary= 19500.75
```

By changing the numbers in the replacement fields, we can change the order of the values being displayed as:

```
str = 'Id= {2}\tName= {0}\tSalary= {1}'.format(id,name,sal)
print(str)
```

The preceding statements will give the following output:

```
Id= 19500.75           Name= 10               Salary= Shankar
```

Please observe that the replacement fields {0} represented id number, {1} represented name and {2} represented salary of the employee. These values are displayed in the following order: {2}, {0} and {1} in the preceding statement.

We can also mention names in the replacement fields to represent the values. These names should refer to the values in the format() method as:

```
str = 'Id= {one}, Name= {two}, Salary= {three}'.format(one=id,
      two=name, three=sal)
print(str)
```

The preceding statements will give the following output:

```
Id= 10, Name= Shankar, Salary= 19500.75
```

Formatting specification starts with a colon (:) and after that, we can specify the format in the curly braces. We can use 'd' or 'i' for decimal number, 'c' for character, 's' for string, 'f' or 'F' for floating point numbers. If we do not use any type specifier, then it would assume string datatype. Also, 'x' or 'X' should be used for hexadecimal number, 'b' for finery and 'o' for octal number. Consider the following example:

```
str = 'Id= {:d}, Name= {:s}, Salary= {:10.2f}'.format(id, name, sal)
print(str)
```

The preceding statements will give the following output:

```
Id= 10, Name= Shankar, Salary=   19500.75
```

Observe, the third replacement field {:10.2f}. This represents that the 'sal' value should be displayed in 10 places. Among these 10 places, a decimal point and then 2 fraction digits should be displayed. Suppose, we write {:.4f}, it means the 'sal' value should be displayed with 4 fraction digits after decimal point and before decimal point, all the available digits should be displayed.

It is possible to align the value in the replacement field. '<' represents align left, '>' represents align right, '^' (carat) represents align in the center and '=' represents justified. Any character in the replacement field represents that the field will be filled with that character. For example, we are going to display 'num' value which is 5000 right aligned in the spaces. We are going to allot 15 spaces and justify the value towards right in the spaces and remaining spaces will be filled with '*'.

```
num=5000
print('{:*>15d}'.format(num))
```

The preceding statements will give the following output:

```
***********5000
```

In the above example '>' aligns the value towards right. If we use '^', then the value is aligned in the center. Consider the following statement:

```
print('{:*^15d}'.format(num))
```

The preceding statement will give the following output:

```
*****5000******
```

Let's display a value in the form of hexadecimal number and a binary number in the next example.

```
n1=1000
print('Hexadecimal= {:.>15X}\nBinary= {:.<15b}'.format(n1, n1))
```

The preceding statements will display the following output:

```
Hexadecimal= ...........3E8
Binary= 1111101000.....
```

In the above example, the number 'n1' whose value 1000 is converted into hexadecimal and binary numbers and then displayed. Observe 'X' and 'b' in the format strings that represent the hexadecimal and binary formats. Observe the output displayed by print() function. It displayed '3E8' and '1111101000'. Suppose, we want to display these numbers by adding the appropriate prefixes 0X and 0B, we can add a hash (#) symbol in the replacement field as:

```
print('Hexadecimal= {:.>#15X}\nBinary= {:.<#15b}'.format(n1, n1))
```

The preceding statement will give the following output:

```
Hexadecimal= .........0X3E8
Binary= 0b1111101000...
```

Working with Characters

Characters are nothing but the individual elements of a string. As we know, a string may contain 1 or more characters. When the programmer is interested to work with characters, he has to accept a string and then retrieve the characters from the string using indexing or slicing. For example,

```
str = 'Hello'
```

To retrieve the 0th character, we can write str[0] and to retrieve the 1st character, we can write str[1].

```
ch = str[0]
print(ch)
```

The preceding statements will give the following output:

```
H
```

Consider the following statements:

```
ch1 = str[1]
print(ch1)
```

The preceding statements will give the following output:

```
e
```

We can also retrieve the characters from the string using slicing as:

```
ch = str[0:1]
print(ch)
```

The preceding statements will give the following output:

```
H
```

Consider the following statements:

```
ch1 = str[1:2]
print(ch1)
```

The preceding statements will give the following output:

```
e
```

We can apply the string testing methods mentioned in Table 8.2 for testing not only strings but also the individual characters. These methods are useful to test a character and know which type of character it is. For example,

```
ch.isalpha()
```

method tests whether the character 'ch' is alphabetic character (A to A, a to z) or not. It returns True if it is an alphabet; otherwise, False. In the following program, we accept a string from the user and take the first character from the string. Then we test the character to know which kind of character it is. Program 9 shows how to know the type of character entered by the user.

Program

Program 9: A Python program to know the type of character entered by the user.

```
# to know the nature of a character
str = input('Enter a character: ')
ch = str[0]   # take only the 0th character into ch

# test ch
if ch.isalnum():
    print('It is alphabet or numeric character')
    if ch.isalpha():
        print('It is an alphabet')
        if ch.isupper():
            print('It is captial letter')
        else:
            print('It is lowercase letter')
    else:
        print('It is a numeric digit')
elif ch.isspace():
        print('It is a space')
else:
    print('It may be a special character')
```

Output:

```
C:\>python str.py
Enter a character: a
It is alphabet or numeric character
It is an alphabet
It is lowercase letter

C:\>python str.py
Enter a character: &
It may be a special character
```

Sorting Strings

We can sort a group of strings into alphabetical order using sort() method and sorted() function. The sort() method is used in the following way:

```
str.sort()
```

Here, 'str' represents an array that contains a group of strings. When sort() method is used, it will sort the original array, i.e. 'str'. So, the original order of strings will be lost and we will have only one sorted array. To retain the original array even after sorting, we can use sorted() function as:

```
str1 = sorted(str)
```

Here, 'str' is the original array whose elements are to be sorted. After sorting the array, the sorted array will be referenced by 'str1'. So, the sorted strings appear in the array 'str1'. The original array 'str' is undisturbed. Program 10 shows how to sort an array of strings into alphabetical order.

Program

Program 10: A Python program to sort a group of strings into alphabetical order.

```
# sorting a group of strings
# take an empty array
str = []

# accept how many strings
n = int(input('How many strings? '))

# append strings to str array
for i in range(n):
    print('Enter string: ', end='')
    str.append(input())

# sort the array
# str.sort()
str1 = sorted(str)

# display the sorted array
print('Sorted list: ')
for i in str1:
    print(i)
```

Output:

```
C:\>python str.py
How many strings? 5
Enter string: Hyderabad
Enter string: Delhi
Enter string: Ahmedabad
Enter string: Kolkata
Enter string: Chennai
Sorted list:
Ahmedabad
Chennai
Delhi
Hyderabad
Kolkata
```

Searching in the Strings

The easiest way to search for a string in a group of 'n' strings is by using sequential search or linear search technique. This is done by comparing the searching string 's' with every string in the group. For this purpose, we can use a for loop that iterates from 0th to n-1th string in the group. By comparing the searching string 's' with every one of these strings, we can decide whether 's' is available in the group or not. The logic looks something like this:

```
for i in range(len(str)):   # repeat from 0th to n-1th  strings
    if s==str[i]:   # if s is matching with str[i] then found.
```

Program

Program 11: A Python program to search for the position of a string in a given group of strings.

```
# searching for a string in a group of strings
# take an empty array
str = []

# accept how many strings
n = int(input('How many strings? '))

# append strings to str array
for i in range(n):
    print('Enter string: ', end='')
    str.append(input())

# ask for the string to search
s = input('Enter string to search: ')

# linear search or sequential search
flag = False

for i in range(len(str)):
    if s==str[i]:
        print('Found at: ', i+1)
        flag=True

if flag==False:
    print('Not found')
```

Output:

```
C:\>python str.py
How many strings? 5
Enter string: Ramesh
Enter string: Kumar
Enter string: Sriya
Enter string: Vinod
Enter string: Ramesh
Enter string to search: Ramesh
Found at:  1
Found at:  5
```

Finding Number of Characters and Words

We have len() function that returns the number of characters in a string. Suppose we want to find the length of a string without using len() function, we can use a for loop as:

```
i=0
for s in str:
    i+=1
```

This for loop repeats once for each character of the string 'str'. So, if the string has 10 characters, the for loop repeats for 10 times. Hence, by counting the number of repetitions, we can find the number of characters. This is done by simply incrementing a counting variable 'i' inside the loop as shown in the preceding code.

Program

Program 12: A Python program to find the length of a string without using len() function.

```
# to find no. of characters in a string
str = input('Enter a string: ')

i=0
for s in str:
    print(str[i], end='')
    i+=1
print('\nNo. of characters: ', i)
```

Output:

```
C:\>python str.py
Enter a string: This is a book
This is a book
No. of characters:  14
```

To find the number of words in a string, we have to first find out the number of spaces. For example, take a string: 'R Nageswara Rao'. The number of spaces here is 2, but there are 3 words separated. Hence, we have to add 1 to the number of spaces to get the number of words.

In many cases, there is possibility of having more than 1 space between the words in a string. In that case, we should not count all the spaces. When a space is counted, the next immediate space should not be counted. For this purpose, we can take a Boolean type variable 'flag'. When a space is encountered, we will make 'flag' as True otherwise False as:

```
if str[i]==' ':
    flag=True
 else:
    flag=False
```

We will count the space only when flag is False. It means if there was no space found previously, then only the present space is counted. In this way, we can obtain the number of words correctly.

Program

Program 13: A Python program to find the number of words in a string.

```
# to find no. of words in a string
str = input('Enter a string: ')

i=c=0
flag=True  # this becomes False when no space is found
for s in str:
    # count only when there is no space previously
    if flag==False and str[i]==' ':
        c+=1
    # if a space is found take flag as True
    if str[i]==' ':
        flag=True
    else:
        flag=False
    i+=1

print('No. of words: ', c+1)
```

Output:

```
C:\>python str.py
Enter a string: R Nageswara Rao
No. of words:  3
```

Inserting Sub String into a String

Let's take a string with some characters. In the middle of the string, we want to insert a sub string. This is not possible because of immutable nature of strings. But, we can find a way for this problem. Let's assume the main string is 'str' and sub string is 'sub'. After inserting 'sub' into 'str', the total string will be 'str1'. To represent this total string, we will declare an empty list 'str1' as:

```
str1 = []
```

If n is the position where the sub string to be inserted, we will append the first n-1 characters from str into str1. Then the entire sub string will be appended to str1. In the final step, we will append the remaining characters (from n till the end) from str to str1. Thus, the total string will be available in str1 as a list. Figure 8.3 shows the insertion of a sub string in a particular position into a main string.

Since a list contains characters as individual elements, we have to convert the list into a string format so that we will have continuous flow of characters. See the difference between elements of a list and of a string:

```
['I', 't', ' ', 'i', 's', ' ', 'h', 'o', 't', 's', 'u', 'm', 'm', 'e', 'r']

It is hotsummer
```

Above, the first line represents a list and the second line represents a string. We need the result in the form of a string, hence we have to convert the list into a string. For this purpose, we can use join() method with empty string as separator as:

```
str1 = ''.join(str1)
```

Since the separator is an empty string, the elements of str1 will be joined without any gaps in between and we will have the final string into 'str1'. Another way to convert the list 'str1' into a string 'str2' is by using concatenation operator (+) as:

```
str2=''    # take an empty string
for i in str1:
    str2=str2+i    # concatenate characters from str1 to str2
```

Thus the final string will be available in 'str2'.

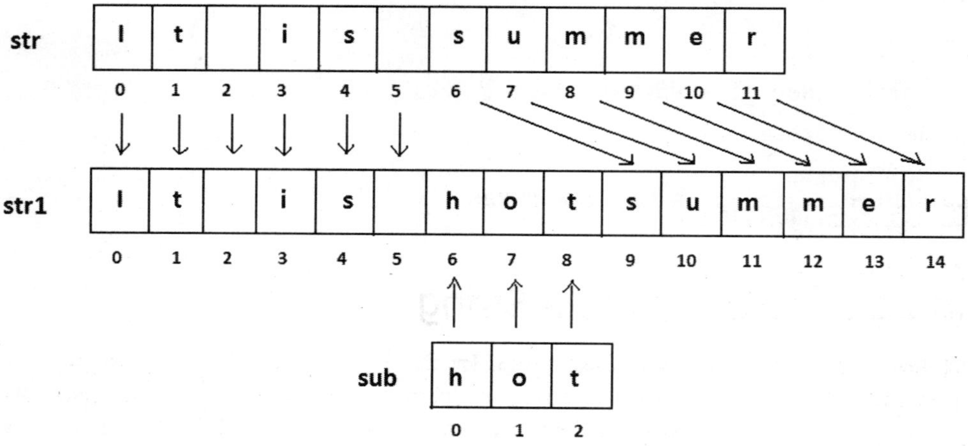

Figure 8.3: Inserting a Sub String in a Particular Position into a Main String

Program

Program 14: A Python program to insert a sub string in a string in a particular position.

```
# to insert a sub string in a string
str = input('Enter a string: ')
sub = input('Enter a sub string: ')
n = int(input('Enter position no: '))

# decrease n by 1 to insert in correct position
n-=1

# find the number of characters in str, sub
l1 = len(str)
l2 = len(sub)

# take another string as a list
str1 = []

# append 0 to n-1 characters from str to str1
for i in range(n):
```

```
        str1.append(str[i])

    # append sub string to str1
    for i in range(l2):
        str1.append(sub[i])

    # append the remaining characters from str to str1
    for i in range(n, l1):
        str1.append(str[i])

    # convert the individual characters of list into
    # a string using join() method with empty string as separator
    str1 = ''.join(str1)

    # display the total string
    print(str1)
```

Output:

```
C:\>python str.py
Enter a string: It is summer
Enter a sub string: hot
Enter position no: 7
It is hotsummer
```

Points to Remember

- A string represents a group of characters.
- We can create strings by assigning a group of characters to a variable.
- There is no difference between single quotes and double quotes while writing the strings.
- Triple double quotes or triple single quotes are useful to extend the string beyond several lines.
- The len() function gives the length or number of characters in a string.
- Indexing and slicing are the two ways to access elements or characters of a string.
- Index is an integer that represents the position number of the element in the string. It is written in the form of str[i].
- Slicing represents a part or piece of the string. It is written in the form of str[start: stop: stepsize].
- Concatenation of strings can be done using '+' operator or join() method.
- The 'in' and 'not in' operators are used to check if a sub string is found in the main string or not. They return Boolean value, i.e. either True or False.
- Relational operators like >, >=, <, <=, == or != can be used to compare two strings. They return Boolean value, i.e. either True or False.
- The rstrip(), lstrip() and strip() methods are used to remove spaces from a string.

- The find(), rfind(), index() and rindex() methods are useful to locate sub strings in a string. These methods return the location of the first occurrence of the sub string.
- The method count() is useful to count the number of occurrences of a sub string in a main string.
- Strings are immutable objects. Hence, their content cannot be modified. Any attempts to modify the content of a string will create a new string object in the memory.
- The replace() method is useful to replace a sub string in a string with another sub string.
- The split() method is useful to brake a string into pieces.
- Python offers 4 methods: upper(), lower(), swapcase(), title() that are useful to change the case of a string.
- The startswith() and endswith() methods are useful to check the beginning and ending parts of a string.
- Several string testing methods are available in Python which can be applied on characters also.

CHAPTER 9

FUNCTIONS

A function is similar to a program that consists of a group of statements that are intended to perform a specific task. The main purpose of a function is to perform a specific task or work. Thus when there are several tasks to be performed, the programmer will write several functions. There are several 'built-in' functions in Python to perform various tasks. For example, to display output, Python has print() function. Similarly, to calculate square root value, there is sqrt() function and to calculate power value, there is power() function. Similar to these functions, a programmer can also create his own functions which are called 'user-defined' functions. The following are the advantages of functions:

- Functions are important in programming because they are used to process data, make calculations or perform any task which is required in the software development.
- Once a function is written, it can be reused as and when required. So functions are also called reusable code. Because of this reusability, the programmer can avoid code redundancy. It means it is possible to avoid writing the same code again and again.
- Functions provide modularity for programming. A module represents a part of the program. Usually, a programmer divides the main task into smaller sub tasks called modules. To represent each module, the programmer will develop a separate function. Then these functions are called from a main program to accomplish the complete task. Modular programming makes programming easy.
- Code maintenance will become easy because of functions. When a new feature has to be added to the existing software, a new function can be written and integrated into the software. Similarly, when a particular feature is no more needed by the user, the corresponding function can be deleted or put into comments.

- When there is an error in the software, the corresponding function can be modified without disturbing the other functions in the software. Thus code debugging will become easy.
- The use of functions in a program will reduce the length of the program.

Difference between a Function and a Method

We discussed that a function contains a group of statements and performs a specific task. A function can be written individually in a Python program. A function is called using its name. When a function is written inside a class, it becomes a 'method'. A method is called using one of the following ways:

```
objectname.methodname()
Classname.methodname()
```

So, please remember that a function and a method are same except their placement and the way they are called. In this chapter, we will learn how to create and use our own functions. Creating a function means defining a function or writing a function. Once a function is defined, it can be used by calling the function.

Defining a Function

We can define a function using the keyword *def* followed by function name. After the function name, we should write parentheses ( ) which may contain parameters. Consider the syntax of function, as shown in Figure 9.1:

function definition

```
def functionname( para1, para2, ...) :
    """ function docstring """
    function statements
```

example

```
def sum(a, b):
    """This function finds sum of two numbers"""
    c=a+b
    print(c)
```

Figure 9.1: Understanding the Function Definition

For example, we can write a function to add two values as:

```
def sum(a, b) :
```

Here, 'def' represents the starting of function definition. 'sum' is the name of the function. After this name, parentheses ( ) are compulsory as they denote that it is a function and not a variable or something else. In the parentheses, we wrote two variables 'a' and 'b'. These variables are called 'parameters'. A parameter is a variable that receives data from outside into a function. So, this function can receive two values from outside and those values are stored in the variables 'a' and 'b'.

After parentheses, we put a colon (:) that represents the beginning of the function body. The function body contains a group of statements called 'suite'. Generally, we should write a string as the first statement in the function body. This string is called a 'docstring' that gives information about the function. Please remember a docstring is a string literal that is written as the first statement in a module, function or class. Docstrings are generally written inside triple double quotes or triple single quotes. In our sum() function, we wrote the following docstring:

```
""" This function finds sum of two numbers """
```

This docstring contains only one line. But we can write docstrings spanning several lines. However, these docstrings are optional. That means it is not compulsory to write them. When an API (Application Programming Interface) documentation file is created, the function name and docstring are stored in that file thus providing clear description about the function. Writing docstrings is a good programming habit.

After writing the docstring in the function, the next step is to write other statements which constitute the logic of the function. This reflects how to do the task. These statements should be written using proper indentation. In our example, we want to find the sum of two numbers. Hence, the logic would be:

```
c = a + b
print(c)
```

The parameters 'a' and 'b' contain the values which are added and the result is stored into 'c'. Then the result is displayed using the print() function. So, this function can accept two values and display their sum.

Calling a Function

A function cannot run on its own. It runs only when we call it. So, the next step is to call the function using its name. While calling the function, we should pass the necessary values to the function in the parentheses as:

```
sum(10, 15)
```

Here, we are calling the 'sum' function and passing two values 10 and 15 to that function. When this statement is executed, the Python interpreter jumps to the function definition and copies the values 10 and 15 into the parameters 'a' and 'b' respectively. These values are processed in the function body and result is obtained. The values passed to a function are called 'arguments'. So, 10 and 15 are arguments. In Program 1, we are showing the sum() function discussed so far.

Program

Program 1: A function that accepts two values and finds their sum.

```
# a function to add two numbers
def sum(a, b):
    """ This function finds sum of two numbers """
    c = a+b
```

```
        print('Sum= ', c)

    # call the function
    sum(10, 15)
    sum(1.5, 10.75)  # call second time
```

Output:

```
    C:\>python fun.py
    Sum= 25
    Sum= 12.25
```

In Program 1, we are calling the sum() function two times as:

```
    sum(10, 15)  # call first time and pass 10 and 15
    sum(1.5, 10.75)  # call second time and pass 1.5 and 10.75
```

The point is that once a function is written, it can be used again and again whenever required. So, functions are called reusable code. Also, observe that integer type data is passed to the function when it is called first time and float type data is passed to the same function when called second time. Observe the sum() function definition:

```
    def sum(a, b):
```

The parameters 'a' and 'b' do not know which type of values they are going to receive till the values are passed at the time of calling the function. During run time, 'a' and 'b' may assume any type of data, may be int or may be float or may be strings. This is called 'dynamic typing'. In dynamic typing, the type of data is determined only during runtime, not at compile time. Dynamic typing is one of the features of Python that is not available in languages like C or Java.

Returning Results from a Function

We can return the result or output from the function using a 'return' statement in the body of the function. For example,

```
    return c    # returns c value out of function
    return 100   # returns 100
    return lst   # return the list that contains values
    return x, y, c   # returns 3 values
```

When a function does not return any result, we need not write the return statement in the body of the function. Now, we will rewrite our sum() function such that it will return the sum value rather than displaying it. This is done in Program 2.

Program

Program 2: A Python program to find the sum of two numbers and return the result from the function.

```
    # a function to add two numbers
    def sum(a, b):
        """ This function finds sum of two numbers """
        c = a+b
        return c   # return result
```

```
# call the function
x = sum(10, 15)
print('The sum is: ', x)
y = sum(1.5, 10.75)
print('The sum is: ', y)
```

Output:

```
C:\>python fun.py
The sum is:  25
The sum is:  12.25
```

In the above program, the result is returned by the sum() function through 'c' using the statement:

```
return c
```

When we call the function as:

```
x = sum(10, 15)
```

the result returned by the function comes into the variable 'x'. Similarly, when we call the function as:

```
y = sum(1.5, 10.75)
```

The returned result will come into 'y'.

To understand the concept of functions in a better way, we will write a couple of programs. Let's write a function that accepts a number and tests whether it is even or odd. The function definition can be written as:

```
def even_odd(num):
```

Please observe that this function has only 1 parameter, i.e. 'num' whose value is to be tested to know whether it is even or odd. If 'num' is divisible by 2, then we can say it is even; otherwise it is odd. This logic can be written as:

```
if num % 2 == 0:
    print(num," is even")
```

In the preceding statement, the '%' operator is called modulus operator that gives the remainder of division. If the remainder is 0, then we can display that 'num' is even. This logic is used in even_odd() function in Program 3.

Program

Program 3: A function to test whether a number is even or odd.

```
# a function to test whether a number is even or odd
def even_odd(num):
    """ to know num is even or odd """
    if num % 2 == 0:
        print(num," is even")
    else:
        print(num," is odd")

# call the function
even_odd(12)
even_odd(13)
```

Output:

```
C:\>python fun.py
12  is even
13  is odd
```

We want to write a function that calculates factorial value of a number. Suppose, we want to calculate the factorial of 4, we can write as:

```
4! = 4 X 3 X 2 X 1
```

So, if we want to calculate factorial of 'n', then we can write:

```
n! = n X n-1 X n-2 ... 1
```

So, the number 'n' value should be decremented till it reaches the value 1 and the cumulative products of these numbers should be calculated. We can use a while loop as:

```
prod = 1   # initialize prod to 1
while n>=1:    # repeat as long as n >=1
    prod=prod*n    # multiply n with prod and store in prod
    n=n-1    # decrement n value by 1 every time
```

This logic is used in creating the fact() function that accepts 'n' as parameter and returns the 'prod' value that is nothing but the factorial value of 'n'.

Program

Program 4: A Python program to calculate factorial values of numbers.

```
# a function to calculate factorial value
def fact(n):
    """ to find factorial value """
    prod=1
    while n>=1:
        prod*=n
        n-=1

    return prod

# display factorials of first 10 numbers
# call fact() function and pass the numbers from 1 to 10
for i in range(1, 11):
    print('Factorial of {} is {}'.format(i, fact(i)))
```

Output:

```
C:\>python fun.py
Factorial of 1 is 1
Factorial of 2 is 2
Factorial of 3 is 6
Factorial of 4 is 24
Factorial of 5 is 120
Factorial of 6 is 720
Factorial of 7 is 5040
Factorial of 8 is 40320
Factorial of 9 is 362880
Factorial of 10 is 3628800
```

We will write a program that accepts a number and tests whether it is prime or not. We know a prime number is a number that is not divisible by any other number except by 1 and itself. For example, 5 is a prime number as it is not divisible by another number. But 1 and 5 divide this number as 1 divides any number and any number divides itself. So, 1 and 5 need not be counted in deciding the divisibility.

To decide whether 5 is prime or not, we have to divide this number with other numbers except 1 and 5. It means, we have to divide this number by 2, 3 and 4. If 5 is divisible by 2 or 3 or 4, then we can say it is not prime. If 5 is not divisible by any number from 2 to 4, then we can say it is prime. So, the logic to know whether 'n' is prime or not is to divide that number with all numbers from 2 to n-1. If any one number in this range divides it, then it is not prime, otherwise it is prime. This logic can be written as:

```
for i in range(2, n):    # divide n from 2 to n-1
    if n%i == 0:    # if divisible by any number it is not prime
```

When the number is divisible any number in the range from 2 to n-1, it is not prime and we store 0 into a variable 'x'. On the other hand, if it is prime, we keep 'x' as 1. Thus 'x' value indicates whether 'n' is prime or not. Consider Program 5.

Program

Program 5: A Python function to check if a given number is prime or not.

```
# a function to test whether a number is prime or not
def prime(n):
    """ to check if n is prime or not """
    x=1   # this will be 0 if not prime
    for i in range(2, n):    # divide n from 2 to n-1
        if n%i == 0:    # if divisible by any number
            x=0    # take x as 0
            break
        else:
            x=1    # else take x as 1
    return x

# test if a number is prime or not
num = int(input('Enter a number: '))

# check if num is prime or not
result = prime(num)
if result == 1:
    print(num, ' is prime')
else:
    print(num, ' is not prime')
```

Output:

```
C:\>python fun.py
Enter a number: 5
5 is prime
```

The function prime() that we developed in the previous program can be used to generate prime number series. Suppose we want to generate the first 10 prime numbers, then the numbers starting from 2, 3, 4, ... etc. are passed one by one to prime() function. This function returns 1 if the number is prime; otherwise, the function returns 0. When the function returns 1, that number is displayed and counted. When the function returns 0, we will not count it as it is not a prime number but we will pass the next number to prime(). When the required number of primes are generated, we will terminate the loop.

Program

Program 6: A Python program that generates prime numbers with the help of a function to test prime or not.

```
# a function to test whether a number is prime or not
def prime(n):
    """ to check if n is prime or not """
    x=1   # this will be 0 if not prime
    for i in range(2, n):
        if n%i == 0:
            x=0
            break
        else:
            x=1
    return x

# generate prime number series
num = int(input('How many primes do you want? '))
i=2   # start with i value 2
c=1   # this counts the no. of primes
while True:   # repeat forever
    if prime(i):   # if i is prime, display it
        print(i)
        c+=1    # increase counter
    i+=1        # generate next number to test
    if c>num:   # if count exceeds num
        break   # come out of while loop
```

Output:

```
C:\>python fun.py
How many primes do you want? 10
2
3
5
7
11
13
17
19
23
29
```

In the previous program, observe the following if statement:

```
if prime(i):   # if i is prime, display it
    print(i)
```

In this statement, we are calling the prime() function and passing 'i' value to it. If 'i' is a prime number, then the function prime() returns 1. So, this if statement looks like this:

```
if 1:
    print(i)
```

Please understand that Python treats 1 as True and 0 as False. Hence the above statement reads as:

```
if True:
    print(i)
```

Hence, the print() function is executed and 'i' value is displayed.

Returning Multiple Values from a Function

A function returns a single value in the programming languages like C or Java. But in Python, a function can return multiple values. When a function calculates multiple results and wants to return the results, we can use the return statement as:

```
return a, b, c
```

Here, three values which are in 'a', 'b', and 'c' are returned. These values are returned by the function as a tuple. Please remember a tuple is like a list that contains a group of elements. To grab these values, we can use three variables at the time of calling the function as:

```
x, y, z = function()
```

Here, the variables 'x', 'y' and 'z' are receiving the three values returned by the function. To understand this practically, we can create a function by the name sum_sub() that takes 2 values and calculates the results of addition and subtraction. These results are stored in the variables 'c' and 'd' and returned as a tuple by the function.

```
def sum_sub(a, b):
    c = a + b
    d = a - b
    return c, d
```

Since this function has two parameters, at the time of calling this function, we should pass two values, as:

```
x, y = sum_sub(10, 5)
```

Now, the result of addition which is in 'c' will be stored into 'x' and the result of subtraction which is in 'd' will be stored into 'y'. This is shown in Program 7.

Program

Program 7: A Python program to understand how a function returns two values.

```
# a function that returns two results
def sum_sub(a, b):
    """ this function returns results of
        addition and subtraction of a, b """
    c = a + b
    d = a - b
    return c, d

# get the results from the sum_sub() function
x, y = sum_sub(10, 5)
```

```
# display the results
print("Result of addition: ", x)
print("Result of subtraction: ", y)
```

Output:

```
C:\>python fun.py
Result of addition:  15
Result of subtraction:  5
```

When several results are returned, we can retrieve them from the tuple using a for loop or while loop. This is shown in Program 8. This is an extension to Program 7.

Program

Program 8: A function that returns the results of addition, subtraction, multiplication and division.

```
# a function that returns multiple results
def sum_sub_mul_div(a, b):
    """ this function returns results of addition,
        subtraction, multiplication and division of a, b """
    c = a + b
    d = a - b
    e = a * b
    f = a / b
    return c, d, e, f

# get results from sum_sub_mul_div() function and store into t
t = sum_sub_mul_div(10, 5)

# display the results using for loop
print('The results are: ')
for i in t:
    print(i, end=', ')
```

Output:

```
C:\>python fun.py
The results are:
15, 5, 50, 2.0,
```

Functions are First Class Objects

In Python, functions are considered as first class objects. It means we can use functions as perfect objects. In fact when we create a function, the Python interpreter internally creates an object. Since functions are objects, we can pass a function to another function just like we pass an object (or value) to a function. Also, it is possible to return a function from another function. This is similar to returning an object (or value) from a function. The following possibilities are noteworthy:

- It is possible to assign a function to a variable.
- It is possible to define one function inside another function.

- It is possible to pass a function as parameter to another function.
- It is possible that a function can return another function.

To understand these points, we will take a few simple programs. In Program 9, we have taken a function by the name display() that returns a string. This function is called and the returned string is assigned to a variable 'x'.

Program

Program 9: A Python program to see how to assign a function to a variable.

```
# assign a function to a variable
def display(str):
    return 'Hai '+str

# assign function to variable x
x = display("Krishna")
print(x)
```

Output:

```
C:\>python fun.py
Hai Krishna
```

In Program 10, we write message() function inside display() function. We call message() function from display() and return the result.

Program

Program 10: A Python program to know how to define a function inside another function.

```
# define a function inside another function
def display(str):
    def message():
        return 'How are U?'

    result = message()+str
    return result

# call display() function
print(display("Krishna"))
```

Output:

```
C:\>python fun.py
How are U? Krishna
```

In Program 11, we are trying to pass message() function as a parameter or argument to display() function. Since display() function has to receive another function as its parameter, it should be defined with another function 'fun' as parameter as:

```
def display(fun):
```

Program

Program 11: A Python program to know how to pass a function as parameter to another function.

```
# functions can be passed as parameters to other functions
def display(fun):
    return 'Hai '+ fun

def message():
    return 'How are U? '

# call display() function and pass message() function
print(display(message()))
```

Output:

```
C:\>python fun.py
Hai How are U?
```

In Program 12, we are writing message() function inside display() function. Inside the display() function, when we write:

```
return message
```

This will return the message() function out of display() function. The returned message() function can be referenced with a new name 'fun'.

Program

Program 12: A Python program to know how a function can return another function.

```
# functions can return other functions
def display():
    def message():
        return 'How are U?'

    return message

# call display() function and it returns message() function
# in the following code, fun refers to the name: message.
fun = display()
print(fun())
```

Output:

```
C:\>python fun.py
How are U?
```

Pass by Object Reference

In the languages like C and Java, when we pass values to a function, we think about two ways:

- Pass by value or call by value
- Pass by reference or call by reference

Pass by value represents that a copy of the variable value is passed to the function and any modifications to that value will not reflect outside the function. Pass by reference represents sending the reference or memory address of the variable to the function. The variable value is modified by the function through memory address and hence the modified value will reflect outside the function also.

Neither of these two concepts is applicable in Python. In Python, the values are sent to functions by means of object references. We know everything is considered as an object in Python. All numbers are objects, strings are objects, and the datatypes like tuples, lists, and dictionaries are also objects. If we store a value into a variable as:

```
x = 10
```

In this case, in other programming languages, a variable with a name 'x' is created and some memory is allocated to the variable. Then the value 10 is stored into the variable 'x'. We can imagine 'x' as a box where 10 is stored. This is not the case in Python. In Python, everything is an object. An object can be imagined as a memory block where we can store some value. In this case, an object with the value '10' is created in memory for which a name 'x' is attached. So, 10 is the object and 'x' is the name or tag given to that object. Also, objects are created on heap memory which is a very huge memory that depends on the RAM of our computer system. Heap memory is available during runtime of a program.

To know the location of an object in heap, we can use id() function that gives identity number of an object. For example, consider the following code snippet:

```
x = 10
id(x)
```

The preceding lines of code may display the following output:

```
1617805016
```

This number may change from computer to computer as it is computed depending on the available memory location where object '10' is stored in the computer. In general, two different objects will have different identity numbers.

When we pass values like numbers, strings, tuples or lists to a function, the references of these objects are passed to the function. To understand this concept, let's take a small program. In Program 13, we are calling modify() function and passing 'x' value, i.e. 10 to that function. Inside this function, we are modifying the value of 'x' as 15. Inside the function, we are displaying 'x' value and its identity number, as:

```
print(x, id(x))
```

In the same manner, after coming out of the function, we are again displaying these values. Now see the program and its output.

Program

Program 13: A Python program to pass an integer to a function and modify it.

```
# passing an integer to a function
def modify(x):
    """ reassign a value to the variable """
    x=15
    print(x, id(x))

# call modify() and pass x
x= 10
modify(x)
print(x, id(x))
```

Output:

```
C:\>python fun.py
15  1617805096
10  1617805016
```

From the output, we can understand that the value of 'x' in the function is 15 and that is not available outside the function. When we call the modify() function and pass 'x' as:

```
modify(x)
```

we should remember that we are passing the object reference to the modify() function. The object is 10 and its reference name is 'x'. This is being passed to the modify() function. Inside the function, we are using:

```
x = 15
```

This means another object 15 is created in memory and that object is referenced by the name 'x'. The reason why another object is created in the memory is that the integer objects are immutable (not modifiable). So in the function, when we display 'x' value, it will display 15. Once we come outside the function and display 'x' value, it will display the old object value, i.e. 10. Consider the diagram in Figure 9.2. If we display the identity numbers of 'x' inside and outside the function, we see different numbers since they are different objects.

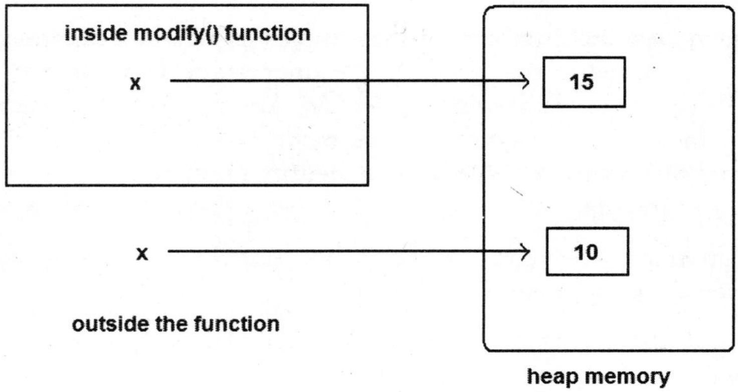

Figure 9.2: Passing Integer to a Function

In Python integers, floats, strings and tuples are immutable. That means their data cannot be modified. When we try to change their value, a new object is created with the modified value. On the other hand, lists and dictionaries are mutable. That means, when we change their data, the same object gets modified and new object is not created. In Program 14, we are passing a list of numbers to modify() function. When we append a new element to the list, the same list is modified and hence the modified list is available outside the function also.

Program

Program 14: A Python program to pass a list to a function and modify it.

```
# passing a list to a function
def modify(lst):
    """ to add a new element to list """
    lst.append(9)
    print(lst, id(lst))

# call modify() and pass lst
lst = [1,2,3,4]
modify(lst)
print(lst, id(lst))
```

Output:

```
C:\>python fun.py
[1, 2, 3, 4, 9]  37762552
[1, 2, 3, 4, 9]  37762552
```

In Program 14, the list 'lst' is the name or tag that represents the list object. Before calling the modify() function, the list contains 4 elements as:

```
lst = [1,2,3,4]
```

Please understand that the object here is [1, 2, 3, 4] and its reference name is 'lst'. When we call the function as modify(lst), we are passing the object reference 'lst' to the function. Inside the function, we are appending a new element '9' to the list. Since lists are mutable, adding a new element to the same object is possible. Hence, append() method modifies the same object. When we display 'lst' inside the function, we can see:

```
[1, 2, 3, 4, 9]
```

After coming out of the function, we can see the modified list as the same object got modified. So, when we display the list outside the function, we can see:

```
[1, 2, 3, 4, 9]
```

This is shown in the diagram in Figure 9.3. If we display the identity numbers of the list inside and outside of the function, we will get same number since they refer to same object. So, the final point is this: in Python, values are passed to functions by object references. If the object is immutable, the modified value is not available outside the function and if the object is mutable, its modified version is available outside the function.

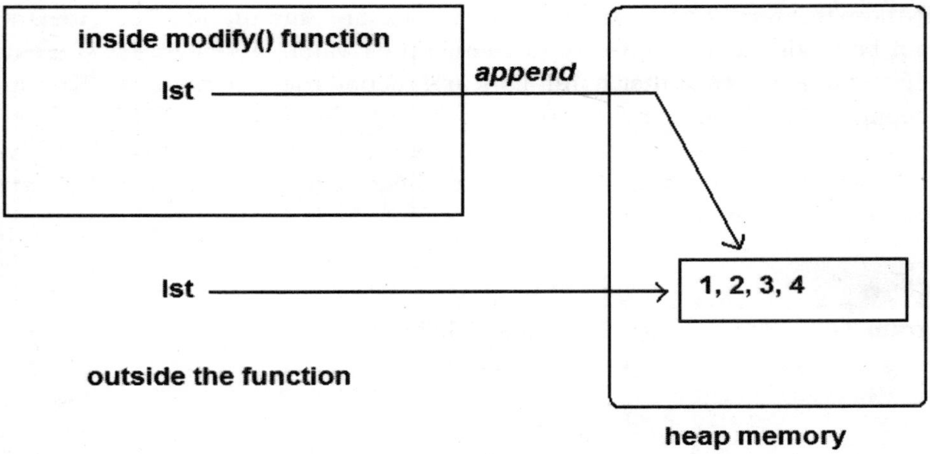

Figure 9.3: Passing a list to the function.

A caution is needed here. If we create altogether a new object inside the function, then it will not be available outside the function. To understand this, we will rewrite the Program 10 where we are passing the following list to the modify() function:

```
[1,2,3,4]
```

But, inside the function, we are creating a new list as:

```
lst = [10, 11, 12]
```

It means, a new object is created in the function and that is referenced by the name 'lst'. So, inside the function, the list is displayed as:

```
[10, 11, 12]
```

But the object that is outside the function is different. Hence it remains as it is, i.e. [1, 2, 3, 4]. This can be easily understood from the diagram in Figure 9.4.

Program

Program 15: A Python program to create a new object inside the function does not modify outside object.

```
# passing a list to a function
def modify(lst):
    """ to create a new list """
    lst = [10, 11, 12]
    print(lst, id(lst))

# call modify() and pass lst
lst = [1,2,3,4]
modify(lst)
print(lst, id(lst))
```

Output:

```
C:\>python fun.py
[10, 11, 12]  29505976
[1, 2, 3, 4]   29505016
```

Now, consider Figure 9.4:

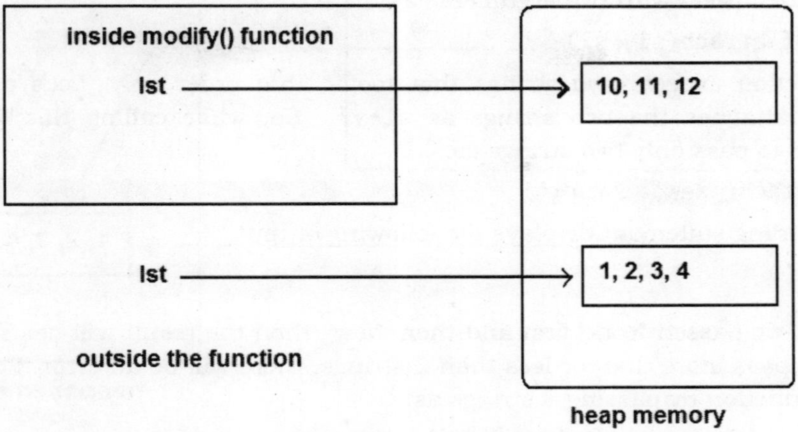

Figure 9.4: Creating new object inside a function

Formal and Actual Arguments

When a function is defined, it may have some parameters. These parameters are useful to receive values from outside of the function. They are called 'formal arguments'. When we call the function, we should pass data or values to the function. These values are called 'actual arguments'. In the following code, 'a' and 'b' are formal arguments and 'x' and 'y' are actual arguments.

```
def sum(a, b):  # a, b are formal arguments
    c = a+b
    print(c)

# call the function
x=10; y=15
sum(x, y)    # x, y are actual arguments
```

The actual arguments used in a function call are of 4 types:

- Positional arguments
- Keyword arguments
- Default arguments
- Variable length arguments

Positional Arguments

These are the arguments passed to a function in correct positional order. Here, the number of arguments and their positions in the function definition should match exactly with the number and position of the argument in the function call. For example, take a function definition with two arguments as:

```
def attach(s1, s2)
```

This function expects two strings that too in that order only. Let's assume that this function attaches the two strings as s1+s2. So, while calling this function, we are supposed to pass only two strings as:

```
attach('New', 'York')
```

The preceding statement displays the following output:

```
NewYork
```

Suppose, we passed 'York' first and then 'New', then the result will be: 'YorkNew'. Also, if we try to pass more than or less than 2 strings, there will be an error. For example, if we call the function by passing 3 strings as:

```
attach('New', 'York', City')
```

Then there will be an error displayed.

Program

Program 16: A Python program to understand the positional arguments of a function.

```
# positional arguments demo
def attach(s1, s2):
    """ to join s1 and s2 and display total string """
    s3 = s1+s2
    print('Total string: '+s3)

# call attach() and pass 2 strings
attach('New', 'York')  # positional arguments
```

Output:

```
C:\>python fun.py
Total string: NewYork
```

Keyword Arguments

Keyword arguments are arguments that identify the parameters by their names. For example, the definition of a function that displays grocery item and its price can be written as:

```
def grocery(item, price):
```

At the time of calling this function, we have to pass two values and we can mention which value is for what. For example,

```
grocery(item='Sugar', price=50.75)
```

Here, we are mentioning a keyword 'item' and its value and then another keyword 'price' and its value. Please observe these keywords are nothing but the parameter names which receive these values. We can change the order of the arguments as:

```
grocery(price=88.00, item='Oil')
```

In this way, even though we change the order of the arguments, there will not be any problem as the parameter names will guide where to store that value. Program 17 demonstrates how to use keyword arguments while calling grocery() function.

Program

Program 17: A Python program to understand the keyword arguments of a function.

```
# key word arguments demo
def grocery(item, price):
    """ to display the given arguments """
    print('Item = %s' % item)
    print('Price = %.2f' % price)

# call grocery() and pass 2 arguments
grocery(item='Sugar', price=50.75)   # keyword arguments
grocery(price=88.00, item='Oil')  # keyword arguments
```

Output:

```
C:\>python fun.py
Item = Sugar
Price = 50.75
Item = Oil
Price = 88.00
```

Default Arguments

We can mention some default value for the function parameters in the definition. Let's take the definition of grocery() function as:

```
def grocery(item, price=40.00):
```

Here, the first argument is 'item' whose default value is not mentioned. But the second argument is 'price' and its default value is mentioned to be 40.00. At the time of calling this function, if we do not pass 'price' value, then the default value of 40.00 is taken. If we mention the 'price' value, then that mentioned value is utilized. So, a default argument is an argument that assumes a default value if a value is not provided in the function call for that argument. Program 18 will clarify this.

Program

Program 18: A Python program to understand the use of default arguments in a function.

```
# default arguments demo
def grocery(item, price=40.00):
    """ to display the given arguments """
    print('Item = %s' % item)
```

```
    print('Price = %.2f' % price)

# call grocery() and pass arguments
grocery(item='Sugar', price=50.75)   # pass 2 arguments
grocery(item='Sugar')  # default value for price is used.
```

Output:

```
C:\>python fun.py
Item = Sugar
Price = 50.75
Item = Sugar
Price = 40.00
```

Variable Length Arguments

Sometimes, the programmer does not know how many values a function may receive. In that case, the programmer cannot decide how many arguments to be given in the function definition. For example, if the programmer is writing a function to add two numbers, he can write:

```
add(a, b)
```

But, the user who is using this function may want to use this function to find sum of three numbers. In that case, there is a chance that the user may provide 3 arguments to this function as:

```
add(10, 15, 20)
```

Then the add() function will fail and error will be displayed. If the programmer wants to develop a function that can accept 'n' arguments, that is also possible in Python. For this purpose, a variable length argument is used in the function definition. A variable length argument is an argument that can accept any number of values. The variable length argument is written with a ' * ' symbol before it in the function definition as:

```
def add(farg, *args):
```

Here, 'farg' is the formal argument and '*args' represents variable length argument. We can pass 1 or more values to this '*args' and it will store them all in a tuple. A tuple is like a list where a group of elements can be stored. In Program 19, we are showing how to use variable length argument.

Program

Program 19: A Python program to show variable length argument and its use.

```
# variable length argument demo
def add(farg, *args):   # *args can take 0 or more values
    """ to add given numbers """
    print('Formal argument= ', farg)

    sum=0
    for i in args:
        sum+=i
    print('Sum of all numbers= ',(farg+sum))
```

```
# call add() and pass arguments
add(5, 10)
add(5, 10, 20, 30)
```

Output:

```
C:\>python fun.py
Formal argument=  5
Sum of all numbers=  15
Formal argument=  5
Sum of all numbers=  65
```

A keyword variable length argument is an argument that can accept any number of values provided in the format of keys and values. If we want to use a keyword variable length argument, we can declare it with ' ** ' before the argument as:

```
def display(farg, **kwargs):
```

Here '**kwargs' is called keyword variable argument. This argument internally represents a dictionary object. A dictionary stores data in the form of key and value pairs. It means, when we provide values for '**kwargs', we can pass multiple pairs of values using keywords as:

```
display(5, rno=10)
```

Here, 5 is stored into 'farg' which is formal argument. 'rno' is stored as key and its value '10' is stored as value in the dictionary that is referenced by 'kwargs'. Program 20 provides better understanding of this concept.

Program

Program 20: A Python program to understand keyword variable argument.

```
# keyword variable argument demo
def display(farg, **kwargs):   # **kwarg can take 0 or more values
    """ to display given values """
    print('Formal argument= ', farg)

    for x, y in kwargs.items():   # items() will give pairs of items
        print('key = {}, value = {}'.format(x, y))

# pass 1 formal argument and 2 keyword arguments
display(5, rno=10)
print()
# pass 1 formal argument and 4 keyword arguments
display(5, rno=10, name='Prakash')
```

Output:

```
C:\>python fun.py
Formal argument=  5
key = rno, value = 10
Formal argument=  5
key = name, value = Prakash
key = rno, value = 10
```

Local and Global Variables

When we declare a variable inside a function, it becomes a local variable. A local variable is a variable whose scope is limited only to that function where it is created. That means the local variable value is available only in that function and not outside of that function. In the following example, the variable 'a' is declared inside myfunction() and hence it is available inside that function. Once we come out of the function, the variable 'a' is removed from memory and it is not available. Consider the following code:

```
# local variable in a function
def myfunction():
    a=1   # this is local var
    a+=1   # increment it
    print(a)   # displays 2

myfunction()
print(a)   # error, not available
```

See the last statement where we are displaying 'a' value outside the function. This statement raises an error with a message: name 'a' is not defined.

When a variable is declared above a function, it becomes global variable. Such variables are available to all the functions which are written after it. Consider the following code:

```
# global variable example
a=1   # this is global var
def myfunction():
    b=2   # this is local var
    print('a= ', a)   # display globalvar
    print('b= ', b)   # display localvar

myfunction()
print(a)   # available
print(b)   # error, not available
```

Whereas the scope of the local variable is limited only to the function where it is declared, the scope of the global variable is the entire program body written below it.

The Global Keyword

Sometimes, the global variable and the local variable may have the same name. In that case, the function, by default, refers to the local variable and ignores the global variable. So, the global variable is not accessible inside the function but outside of it, it is accessible. Consider Program 21.

Program

Program 21: A Python program to understand global and local variables.

```
# same name for global and local variables
a=1   # this is global var
def myfunction():
    a=2   # this is local var
    print('a= ', a)   # display local var
```

```
myfunction()
print('a= ', a)   #display global var
```

Output:

```
C:\>python fun.py
a= 2
a= 1
```

When the programmer wants to use the global variable inside a function, he can use the keyword 'global' before the variable in the beginning of the function body as:

```
global a
```

In this way, the global variable is made available to the function and the programmer can work with it as he wishes. In the following program, we are showing how to work with a global variable inside a function.

Program

Program 22: A Python program to access global variable inside a function and modify it.

```
# accessing the global variable inside a function
a=1   # this is global var
def myfunction():
    global a   # this is global var
    print('global a= ', a)   # display global var
    a=2   # modify global var value
    print('modifed a= ', a)   # display new value

myfunction()
print('global a= ', a)   # display modified value
```

Output:

```
C:\>python fun.py
global a= 1
modified a= 2
global a= 2
```

When the global variable name and local variable names are same, the programmer will face difficulty to differentiate between them inside a function. For example there is a global variable 'a' with some value declared above the function. The programmer is writing a local variable with the same name 'a' with some other value inside the function. Consider the following code:

```
a=1   # this is global var
def myfunction():
    a = 2   # a is local var
```

Now, if the programmer wants to work with global variable, how is it possible? If he uses 'global' keyword, then he can access only global variable and the local variable is no more available.

The globals() function will solve this problem. This is a built in function which returns a table of current global variables in the form of a dictionary. Hence, using this function, we can refer to the global variable 'a', as: globals()['a']. Now, this value can be assigned to another variable, say 'x' and the programmer can work with that value. This is shown in Program 23.

Program

Program 23: A Python program to get a copy of global variable into a function and work with it.

```
# same name for global and local variables
a=1   # this is global var
def myfunction():
     a = 2    # a is local var
     x = globals()['a']    # get global var into x
     print('global var a= ', x)
     print('local var a= ', a)

myfunction()
print('global var a= ', a)
```

Output:

```
C:\>python fun.py
globalvar a= 1
localvar a= 2
globalvar a= 1
```

Passing a Group of Elements to a Function

To pass a group of elements like numbers or strings, we can accept them into a list and then pass the list to the function where the required processing can be done. In Program 24, we are accepting a group of integers from the keyboard in a single line using the following statement:

```
lst = [int(x) for x in input().split()]
```

The input() function takes a group of integers as a string. This string is split into pieces where a space is found as a space is the default for split() method. These pieces are then converted into integers by the int() function and returned into the list 'lst'. We pass this list of integers to the calculate() function as:

```
x, y = calculate(lst)
```

The calculate() function returns sum and average which are stored into x and y, respectively.

Program

Program 24: A function to accept a group of numbers and find their total average.

```
# a function to find total and average
def calculate(lst):
```

```
    """ to find total and average """
    n = len(lst)
    sum=0
    for i in lst:
        sum+=i
        avg = sum/n
        return sum, avg

# take a group of integers from keyboard
print('Enter numbers separated by space: ')
lst = [int(x) for x in input().split()]

# call calculate() and pass the list
x, y = calculate(lst)
print('Total: ', x)
print('Average: ', y)
```

Output:

```
C:\>python fun.py
Enter numbers separated by space:
10 20 30 40 51
Total:  151
Average:  30.2
```

Program 25 shows how to accept a group of strings from keyboard and display them using display() function.

Program

Program 25: A function to display a group of strings.

```
# a function to display a group of strings
def display(lst):
    """ to display the strings """
    for i in lst:
        print(i)

# take a group of strings from keyboard
print('Enter strings separated by comma: ')
lst = [x for x in input().split(',')]

# call display() and pass the list
display(lst)
```

Output:

```
C:\>python fun.py
Enter strings separated by comma:
Gaurav,Vinod,Visal,Ankit
Gaurav
Vinod
Visal
Ankit
```

Recursive Functions

A function that calls itself is known as 'recursive function'. For example, we can write the factorial of 3 as:

```
factorial(3) = 3 * factorial(2)
Here, factorial(2) = 2 * factorial(1)
And, factorial(1) = 1 * factorial(0)
```

Now, if we know that the factorial(0) value is 1, all the preceding statements will evaluate and give the result as:

```
factorial(3) = 3 * factorial(2)
= 3 * 2 * factorial(1)
= 3 * 2 * 1 * factorial(0)
= 3 * 2 * 1 * 1
= 6
```

From the above statements, we can write the formula to calculate factorial of any number 'n' as:

```
factorial(n) = n * factorial(n-1)
```

When we observe this formula, we can understand that the factorial() function to calculate factorial of 'n' value will call itself to calculate factorial of 'n-1' value. So, we can implement factorial() function using recursion, as shown in Program 26.

Program

Program 26: A Python program to calculate factorial values using recursion.

```
# recursive function to calculate factorial
def factorial(n):
    """ to find factorial of n """
    if n==0:
        result=1
    else:
        result=n*factorial(n-1)
    return result

# find factorial values for first 10 numbers
for i in range(1, 11):
    print('Factorial of {} is {}'.format(i, factorial(i)))
```

Output:

```
C:\>python fun.py
Factorial of 1 is 1
Factorial of 2 is 2
Factorial of 3 is 6
Factorial of 4 is 24
Factorial of 5 is 120
Factorial of 6 is 720
Factorial of 7 is 5040
Factorial of 8 is 40320
Factorial of 9 is 362880
Factorial of 10 is 3628800
```

Let's write a program to solve the Towers of Hanoi problem through recursion. Towers of Hanoi is a famous game from ancient China. It is believed that this game helps to develop intelligence of the children who play it. In this game, there will be a group of disks on a pole 'A' such that the biggest disk will be at the bottom and the smaller disks will be on its top. One is supposed to transfer all these disks from pole 'A' to another pole, let's say 'C' in minimum number of steps. While moving these disks from 'A' to 'C', we can take the help of an intermediate pole 'B'. But, the rule is that while moving the disks from one pole to another, we should never place a bigger disk on a smaller disk.

For example, to transfer 3 disks from the pole 'A' to 'C' with the help of an intermediate pole 'B', we can use the steps shown in Figure 9.5:

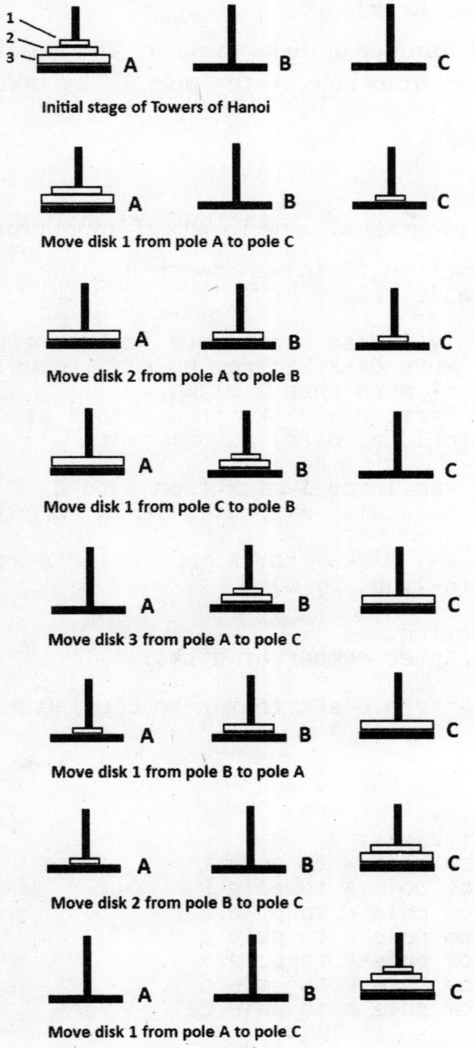

Figure 9.5: Towers of Hanoi with 3 disks

These steps can be performed easily by using recursion. Suppose the number of disks to be moved is 'n'. If n==1, move that disk from 'A' to 'C'. Otherwise, the process of moving 'n' disks will be divided into two parts: move the top n-1 disks and move the remaining 1 disk. The steps are:

1. Move top n-1 disks from 'A' to 'B', using 'C' as intermediate pole.
2. Move remaining disks, i.e. 1 disk from 'A' to 'C'.
3. Move n-1 disks from 'B' to 'C' using 'A' as intermediate pole.

This logic is presented in Program 27. This program contains towers() function which calls itself and is defined as:

```
def towers(n, a, c, b):
```

Here 'n' represents the number of disks to move. The variables a, c, b indicate that the disks need to be moved from pole 'A' to pole 'C' by taking the help of intermediate pole 'B'.

Program

Program 27: A Python program to solve Towers of Hanoi problem.

```
# recursive function to solve Towers of Hanoi
def towers(n, a, c, b):
    `if n==1:
        # if only 1 disk, then move it from A to C
        print('Move disk %i from pole %s to pole %s' %(n, a, c))
    else:   # if more than 1 disk
        # move first n-1 disks from A to B using C as intermediate pole
        towers(n-1, a, b, c)

        # move remaining 1 disk from A to C
        print('Move disk %i from pole %s to pole %s'%(n, a, c))

        # move n-1 disks from B to C using A as intermediate pole
        towers(n-1, b, c, a)

# call the function
n = int(input('Enter number of disks: '))

# we should change n disks from A to C using B as intermediate pole
towers(n, 'A', 'C', 'B')
```

Output:

```
C:\>python fun.py
Enter number of disks: 3
Move disk 1 from pole A to pole C
Move disk 2 from pole A to pole B
Move disk 1 from pole C to pole B
Move disk 3 from pole A to pole C
Move disk 1 from pole B to pole A
Move disk 2 from pole B to pole C
Move disk 1 from pole A to pole C
```

The concept of recursion helps the programmers to solve complex programs in less number of steps. Imagine if we attempt to write the Towers of Hanoi program without using recursion, it would have been a highly difficult task.

Anonymous Functions or Lambdas

A function without a name is called 'anonymous function'. So far, the functions we wrote were defined using the keyword 'def'. But anonymous functions are not defined using 'def'. They are defined using the keyword *lambda*and hence they are also called 'Lambda functions'. Let's take a normal function that returns square of a given value.

```
def square(x):
    return x*x
```

The same function can be written as anonymous function as:

```
lambda x: x*x
```

Observe the keyword 'lambda'. This represents that an anonymous function is being created. After that, we have written an argument of the function, i.e. 'x'. Then colon (:) represents the beginning of the function that contains an expression x * x. Please observe that we did not use any name for the function here. So, the format of lambda functions is:

```
lambda argument_list : expression
```

Normally, if a function returns some value, we assign that value to a variable as:

```
y = square(5)
```

But, lambda functions return a function and hence they should be assigned to a function as:

```
f = lambda x: x*x
```

Here, 'f' is the function name to which the lambda expression is assigned. Now, if we call the function f() as:

```
value = f(5)
```

Now, 'value' contains the square value of 5, i.e. 25. This is shown in Program 28.

Program

Program 28: A Python program to create a lambda function that returns a square value of a given number.

```
# a lambda function to calculate square value
f = lambda x: x*x   # write lambda function
value = f(5)   # call lambda function
print('Square of 5 = ', value)   # display result
```

Output:

```
C:\>python fun.py
Square of 5 = 25
```

Lambda functions contain only one expression and they return the result implicitly. Hence we should not write any 'return' statement in the lambda functions. Here is a lambda function that calculates sum of two numbers.

Program

Program 29: A lambda function to calculate the sum of two numbers.

```
# a lambda function to calculate sum of two numbers
f = lambda x, y: x+y  # write lambda function
result = f(1.55, 10)   # call lambda function
print('Sum = ', result)   # display result
```

Output:

```
C:\>python fun.py
Sum =  11.55
```

The following is a program that contains a lambda function to find the bigger number in two given numbers.

Program

Program 30: A lambda function to find the bigger number in two given numbers.

```
# a lambda function that returns bigger number
max = lambda x, y: x if x>y else y  # write lambda function
a, b = [int(n) for n in input("Enter two numbers: ").split(',')]
print('Bigger number = ', max(a,b))   # call lambda function
```

Output:

```
C:\>python fun.py
Enter two numbers: 10, 25
Bigger number =  25
```

Because a lambda functions is always represented by a function, we can pass a lambda function to another function. It means we are passing a function (i.e. lambda) to another function. This makes processing the data very easy. For example, lambda functions are generally used with functions like filter(), map() or reduce().

Using Lambdas with filter() Function

The filter() function is useful to filter out the elements of a sequence depending on the result of a function. We should supply a function and a sequence to the filter() function as:

```
filter(function, sequence)
```

Here, the 'function' represents a function name that may return either True or False; and 'sequence' represents a list, string or tuple. The 'function' is applied to every element of the 'sequence' and when the function returns True, the element is extracted otherwise it is ignored. Before using the filter() function, let's first write a function that tests whether a given number is even or odd.

```
def is_even(x):
    if x%2==0:
        return True
    else:
        return False
```

Now, we can use this function inside filter() to test the elements of a list 'lst' as:

```
filter(is_even, lst)
```

Now, is_even() function acts on every element of the list 'lst' and returns only those elements which are even. The resultant element can be stored into another list. This is shown in Program 31.

Program

Program 31: A Python program using filter() to filter out even numbers from a list.

```
# filter() function that returns even numbers from a list
def is_even(x):
    if x%2==0:
        return True
    else:
        return False

# let us take a list of numbers
lst = [10, 23, 45, 46, 70, 99]

# call filter() with is_even() and lst
lst1 = list(filter(is_even, lst))
print(lst1)
```

Output:

```
C:\>python fun.py
[10, 46, 70]
```

Passing lambda function to filter() function is more elegant. We will rewrite the Program 31 using lambda function.

Program

Program 32:A lambda that returns even numbers from a list.

```
# a lambda function that returns even numbers from a list
lst = [10, 23, 45, 46, 70, 99]
lst1 = list(filter(lambda x: (x%2 == 0) , lst))
print(lst1)
```

Using Lambdas with map() Function

The map() function is similar to filter() function but it acts on each element of the sequence and perhaps changes the elements. The format of map() function is:

```
map(function, sequence)
```

The 'function' performs a specified operation on all the elements of the sequence and the modified elements are returned which can be stored in another sequence. In Program 33, we are using map() function to find squares of elements of a list.

Program

Program 33: A Python program to find squares of elements in a list.

```
# map() function that gives squares
def squares(x):
    return x*x

# let us take a list of numbers
lst = [1, 2, 3, 4, 5]

# call map() with squares() and lst
lst1 = list(map(squares, lst))
print(lst1)
```

Output:

```
C:\>python fun.py
[1, 4, 9, 16, 25]
```

When the same program is rewritten using lambda function, it becomes more elegant. This is done in Program 34.

Program

Program 34: A lambda function that returns squares of elements in a list.

```
# Lambda that returns squares
lst = [1, 2, 3, 4, 5]
lst1 = list(map(lambda x: x*x, lst))
print(lst1)
```

It is possible to use map() function on more than one list if the lists are of same length. In this case, map() function takes the lists as arguments of the lambda function and does the operation. For example,

```
map(lambda x, y: x*y, lst1, lst2)
```

Here, lambda function has two arguments 'x' and 'y'. Hence, 'x' represents 'lst1' and 'y' represents 'lst2'. Since lambda is showing x*y, the respective elements from lst1 and lst2 are multiplied and the product is returned.

Program

Program 35: A Python program to find the products of elements of two different lists using lambda function.

```
# Lambda that returns products of elements of two lists
lst1 = [1, 2, 3, 4, 5]
lst2 = [10, 20, 30, 40, 50]
lst3 = list(map(lambda x, y: x*y, lst1, lst2))
print(lst3)
```

Output:

```
C:\>python fun.py
[10, 40, 90, 160, 250]
```

Using Lambdas with reduce() Function

The reduce() function reduces a sequence of elements to a single value by processing the elements according to a function supplied. The reduce() function is uses in the format:

```
reduce(function, sequence)
```

For example, we write the reduce() function with a lambda expression, as:

```
lst = [1, 2, 3, 4, 5]    # take a list of numbers
reduce(lambda x, y: x*y, lst)
```

Here, the reduce() function reduces the list to a final value as indicated by the lambda function. The lambda function is taking two arguments and returning their product. Hence, starting from the 0th element of the list 'lst', the first two elements are multiplied and the product is obtained. Then this product is multiplied with the third element and the product is obtained. Again this product is multiplied with the fourth element and so on. The final product value is returned, as shown in Figure 9.6:

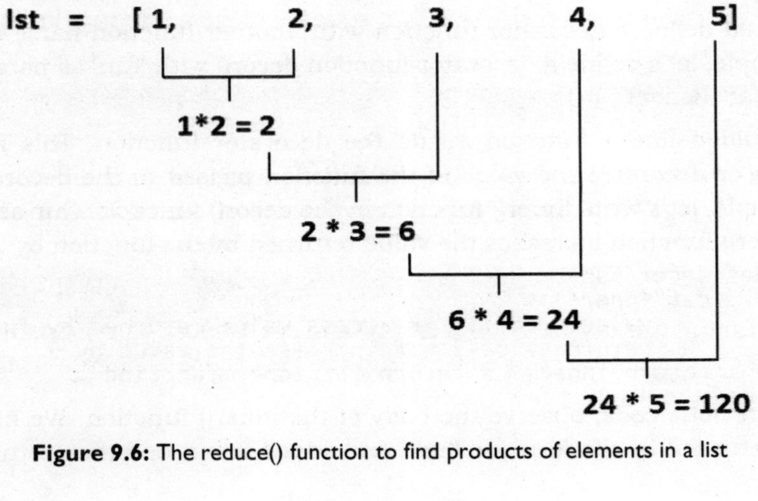

Figure 9.6: The reduce() function to find products of elements in a list

Program

Program 36: A lambda function to calculate products of elements of a list.

```
# Lambda that returns products of elements of a list
from functools import *
lst = [1, 2, 3, 4, 5]
result = reduce(lambda x, y: x*y, lst)
print(result)
```

Output:

```
C:\>python fun.py
120
```

Since reduce() function belongs to functools module in Python, we are importing all from that module using the following statement in Program 36:

```
from functools import *
```

As another example, to calculate the sum of numbers from 1 to 50, we can write reduce() function with a lambda function, as:

```
sum = reduce(lambda a, b: a+b, range(1, 51))
print(sum)
1275
```

Function Decorators

A decorator is a function that accepts a function as parameter and returns a function. A decorator takes the result of a function, modifies the result and returns it. Thus decorators are useful to perform some additional processing required by a function. Decorators concept is a bit confusing but not difficult to understand. The following steps are generally involved in creation of decorators:

1. We should define a decorator function with another function name as parameter. As an example, let's define a decorator function decor() with 'fun' as parameter.

   ```
   def decor(fun):
   ```

2. We should define a function inside the decorator function. This function actually modifies or decorates the value of the function passed to the decorator function. As an example, let's write inner() function in the decor() function. Our assumption is that this inner() function increases the value returned by the function by 2.

   ```
   def decor(fun):
       def inner():
           value = fun()   # access value returned by fun()
           return value+2   # increase the value by 2
       return inner   # return the inner function
   ```

   In the previous code, observe the body of the inner() function. We have accessed the 'value' returned by the function 'fun', and added 2 to it and then returned it.

3. Return the inner function that has processed or decorated the value. In our example, in the last statement, we were returning inner() function using return statement. With this, the decorator is completed.

   The next question is how to use the decorator. Once a decorator is created, it can be used for any function to decorate or process its result. For example, let's take num() function that returns some value, e.g. 10.

```
def num():
    return 10
```

   Now, we should call decor() function by passing num() function name as:

```
result_fun = decor(num)
```

Now the name 'num' is copied into the parameter of the decor() function. Thus, 'fun' refers to 'num'. In the inner() function, 'value' represents 10 and it is incremented by 2. The returned function 'inner' is referenced by 'result_fun'. So, 'result_fun' indicates the resultant function. Call this function and print the result as:

```
print(result_fun())
```

This will display 12. Thus the value returned by the num() function (i.e. 10) is incremented by 2 by the decor() function. Consider Program 37.

Program

Program 37: A decorator to increase the value of a function by 2.

```
# a decorator that increments the value of a function by 2
def decor(fun):   # this is decorator function
    def inner():   # this is the inner function that modifies
        value = fun()
        return value+2
    return inner   # return inner function

# take a function to which decorator should be applied
def num():
    return 10

# call decorator function and pass num
result_fun = decor(num)   # result_fun represents 'inner' function
print(result_fun())   # call result_fun and display the result
```

Output:

```
C:\>python fun.py
12
```

To apply the decorator to any function, we can use the '@' symbol and decorator name just above the function definition. For example, to apply our decor() function to the num() function, we can write @decor statement above the function definition as:

```
@decor   # apply decorator decor to the following function
def num():
    return 10
```

It means decor() function is applied to process or decorate the result of the num() function. When we apply the decorator in this way, we need not call the decorator explicitly and pass the function name. Instead, we can call our num() function naturally as:

```
print(num())
```

So, the '@' symbol is useful to call the associated decorator internally, whenever the function is called. The same program revised version using the '@' symbol is shown in Program 38.

Program

Program 38: A Python program to apply a decorator to a function using @ symbol.

```
# a decorator that increments the value of a function by 2
def decor(fun):   # this is decorator function
    def inner():   # this is the inner function that modifies
        value = fun()
        return value+2
    return inner   # return inner function

# take a function to which decorator should be applied
@decor   # apply decor to the below function
def num():
        return 10

# call num() function and display its result
print(num())
```

Output:

```
C:\>python fun.py
12
```

We will extend this program where we are going to add one more decorator by the name 'decor1()' that doubles the value of the function passed to it. That means we want to apply two decorators to the same function num() to decorate its result. Consider Program 39.

Program

Program 39: A Python program to create two decorators.

```
# a decorator that increments the value of a function by 2
def decor(fun):
    def inner():
        value = fun()
        return value+2
    return inner

# a decorator that doubles the value of a function
def decor1(fun):
    def inner():
        value = fun()
        return value*2
    return inner
```

```
# take a function to which decorator should be applied
def num():
    return 10

# callnum() function and apply decor1 and then decor
result_fun = decor(decor1(num))
print(result_fun())
```

Output:

```
C:\>python fun.py
22
```

To apply the decorators to num() function using '@' symbol, we can rewrite the above program as Program 40.

Program

Program 40: A Python program to apply two decorators to the same function using @ symbol.

```
# a decorator that increments the value of a function by 2
def decor(fun):
    def inner():
        value = fun()
        return value+2
    return inner

# a decorator that doubles the value of a function
def decor1(fun):
    def inner():
        value = fun()
        return value*2
    return inner

# take a function to which decorator should be applied
@decor
@decor1
def num():
    return 10

# call num() function and apply decor1 and then decor
print(num())
```

Output:

```
C:\>python fun.py
22
```

So, the syntax of decorators is:

```
@dec1
@dec2
def func(arg1, arg2, ...):
    pass
```

This is equivalent to:

```
def func(arg1, arg2, ...):
    pass
func = dec1(dec2(func))
```

Generators

Generators are functions that return a sequence of values. A generator function is written like an ordinary function but it uses 'yield' statement. This statement is useful to return the value. For example, let's write a generator function to return numbers from x to y.

```
def mygen(x, y):    # our generator name is 'mygen'
    while x<=y:    # this is the loop repeats from x to y
        yield x    # return x value
        x+=1   # increment x value by 1
```

When we call this function by passing 5 and 10 as:

```
g = mygen(5, 10)
```

Then the mygen() function returns a generator object that contains sequence of numbers as returned by 'yield' statement. So, 'g' refers to the generator object with the sequence of numbers from 5 to 10. We can display the numbers from 'g' using a for loop as:

```
for i in g:
    print(i, end=' ')
```

In the following program, we are creating a generator function that generates numbers from x to y and displaying those numbers.

Program

Program 41: A Python program to create a generator that returns a sequence of numbers from x to y.

```
# generator that returns sequence from x to y
def mygen(x, y):
    while x<=y:
        yield x
        x+=1
# fill generator object with 5 and 10
g = mygen(5, 10)

# display all numbers in the generator
for i in g:
    print(i, end=' ')
```

Output:

```
C:\>python fun.py
5 6 7 8 9 10
```

Once the generator object is created, we can store the elements of the generator into a list and use the list as we want. For example, to store the numbers of generator 'g' into a list 'lst' we can using list() function as:

```
lst = list(g)
```

Now, the list 'lst' contains the elements: [5, 6, 7, 8, 9, 10].

If we want to retrieve element by element from a generator object, we can use next() function as:

```
print(next(g))
```

will display first element in 'g'. When we call the above function the next time, it will display the second element in 'g'. Thus by repeatedly calling the next() function, we will be able to display all the elements of 'g'. In the following program, a simple generator is created that returns 'A', 'B', 'C'.

```
def mygen():
    yield 'A'
    yield 'B'
    yield 'C'
```

Here, mygen() is returning 'A', 'B', 'C' using yield statements. So, yield statement returns the elements from a generator function into a generator object. So, when we call mygen() function as:

```
g = mygen()
```

The characters 'A','B','C' are contained in the generator object 'g'. Using next(g) we can refer to these elements. Consider Program 42.

Program

Program 42: A generator that returns characters from A to C.

```
# generator that returns characters from A to C.
def mygen():
    yield 'A'
    yield 'B'
    yield 'C'

# call generator function and get generator object g
g = mygen()

# display all characters in the generator
print(next(g))    # display 'A'
print(next(g))    # display 'B'
print(next(g))    # display 'C'
print(next(g))    # error
```

Output:

```
C:\>python fun.py
A
B
C
Traceback (most recent call last):
    File "fun.py", line 14, in <module>
        print(next(g))    # error
StopIteration
```

Structured Programming

The purpose of programming is to solve problems related to various areas. Starting from simple problems like adding two numbers to very complex problems like designing the engine of an aircraft, any problem can be solved through programming. When there is a simple problem, the programmer can solve it by writing a simple program. But when there is a complex problem, he may have to develop a lengthy code.

Solving a complex problem is a challenging task for the programmer. For this purpose, structured programming is the strategy used by programmers in general. In structured programming, the main task is divided into several parts called sub tasks and each of these sub tasks is represented by one or more functions. By using these functions, the programmer can accomplish the main task. To understand this concept, let's take an example where we are supposed to calculate the net salary of an employee. Every employee will have some basic salary. The company may provide some benefits like dearness allowance (da) and house rent allowance (hra), which when added to basic salary will give the gross salary. So,

```
Gross salary = basic salary + da + hra.
```

The net salary or take home salary is calculated based on gross salary. After making deductions like provident fund and income tax from the gross salary, the remaining amount is called net salary. So,

```
Net salary = gross salary - pf - income tax.
```

Hence, in a program to calculate the net salary, we need to calculate the following: da, hra, pf and income tax. All these will come under sub tasks and to represent these sub tasks, we can write functions. Finally, using these functions we can calculate the net salary of the employee. This methodology is called structured programming or sometimes functional programming. Consider the diagram given in Figure 9.7:

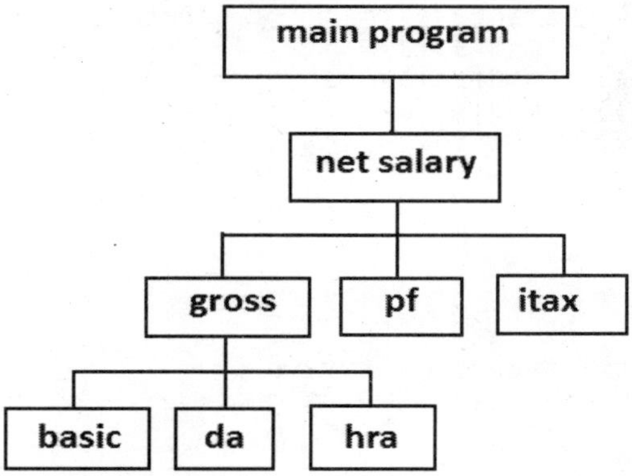

Figure 9.7: Structured Programming Methodology

We are going to calculate the net salary of an employee by developing the functions: da(), hra(), pf() and itax(). Once these functions are developed, then calculating gross salary and net salary will become very easy. Consider Program 43.

Program

Program 43: A Python program to calculate the gross salary and net salary of an employee.

```
# to calculate dearness allowance
def da(basic):
    """ da is 80% of basic salary """
    da = basic*80/100
    return da

# to calculate house rent allowance
def hra(basic):
    """ hra is 15% of basic salary """
    hra = basic*15/100
    return hra

# to calculate provident fund amount
def pf(basic):
    """ pf is 12% of basic salary """
    pf = basic*12/100
    return pf

# to calculate income tax payable by employee
def itax(gross):
    """ tax is calculated at 10% on gross """
    tax = gross*0.1
    return tax

# this is the main program
# calculate gross salary of employee by taking basic
basic = float(input('Enter basic salary: '))

# calculate gross salary
gross = basic+da(basic)+hra(basic)
print('Your gross salary: {:10.2f}'. format(gross))

# calculate net salary
net = gross - pf(basic)-itax(gross)
print('Your net salary: {:10.2f}'. format(net))
```

Output:

```
C:\>python fun.py
Enter basic salary: 20000
Your gross salary:    39000.00
Your net salary:    32700.00
```

Creating our Own Modules in Python

A module represents a group of classes, methods, functions and variables. While we are developing software, there may be several classes, methods and functions. We should first group them depending on their relationship into various modules and later use these modules in the other programs. It means, when a module is developed, it can be reused in any program that needs that module.

In Python, we have several built-in modules like sys, io, time etc. Just like these modules, we can also create our own modules and use them whenever we need them. Once a module is created, any programmer in the project team can use that module. Hence, modules will make software development easy and faster.

Now, we will create our own module by the name 'employee' and store the functions da(), hra(), pf() and itax() in that module. Please remember we can also store classes and variables etc. in the same manner in any module. So, please type the following functions and save the file as 'employee.py'.

```
# save this code as employee.py
# to calculate dearness allowance
def da(basic):
    """ da is 80% of basic salary """
    da = basic*80/100
    return da

# to calculate house rent allowance
def hra(basic):
    """ hra is 15% of basic salary """
    hra = basic*15/100
    return hra

# to calculate provident fund amount
def pf(basic):
    """ pf is 12% of basic salary """
    pf = basic*12/100
    return pf

# to calculate income tax payable by employee
def itax(gross):
    """ tax is calculated at 10% on gross """
    tax = gross*0.1
    return tax
```

Now, we have our own module by the name 'employee.py'. This module contains 4 functions which can be used in any program by importing this module. To import the module, we can write:

```
import employee
```

In this case, we have to refer to the functions by adding the module name as: employee.da(), employee.hra(), employee.pf(), employee.itax(). This is a bit cumbersome and hence we can use another type of import statement as:

```
from employee import *
```

In this case, all the functions of the employee module is referenced and hence, we can refer to them without using the module name, simply as: da(), hra(), pf() and itax(). Now see the following program, where we are using the 'employee' module and calculating the gross and net salaries of an employee.

Program

Program 44: A Python program that uses the functions of employee module and calculates the gross and net salaries of an employee.

```
# using employee module to calculate gross and net salaries of an employee
from employee import *

# calculate gross salary of employee by taking basic
basic = float(input('Enter basic salary: '))

# calculate gross salary
gross = basic+da(basic)+hra(basic)
print('Your gross salary: {:10.2f}'. format(gross))

# calculate net salary
net = gross - pf(basic)-itax(gross)
print('Your net salary: {:10.2f}'. format(net))
```

Output:

```
C:\>python fun.py
Enter basic salary: 15000
Your gross salary:     29250.00
Your net salary:     24525.00
```

The Special Variable __name__

When a program is executed in Python, there is a special variable internally created by the name '__name__'. This variable stores information regarding whether the program is executed as an individual program or as a module. When the program is executed directly, the Python interpreter stores the value '__main__' into this variable. When the program is imported as a module into another program, then Python interpreter stores the module name into this variable. Thus, by observing the value of the variable '__name__', we can understand how the program is executed.

Let's assume that we have written a program. When this program is run, Python interpreter stores the value '__main__' into the special variable '__name__'. Hence, we can check if this program is run directly as a program or not as:

```
if __name__ == '__main__' :
print('This code is run as a program')
```

Suppose, if '__name__' variable does not contain the value '__main__', it represents that this code is run as a module from another external program. To understand this concept, first we will write a program with a display() function that displays some message as 'Hello Python!'. This code is shown in Program 45.

Program

Program 45: A Python program using the special __name__ variable.

```
# python program to display a message. save this as one.py
def display():
```

```
    print('Hello Python!')

if __name__ == '__main__':
    display()   # call display function
    print('This code is run as a program')
else:
    print('This code is run as a module')
```

Output:

```
C:\>python one.py
Hello Python!
This code is run as a program
```

So, the code in the Program 45 is run directly by the Python interpreter and hence it is saying that 'this code is run as a program'.

Now, we will write another program (Program 46) where we want to import 'one.py' program as a module and call the display() function.

Program

Program 46: A Python program that import the previous Python program as a module.

```
# in this program one.py is imported as a module. save this as two.py
import one
one.display()   # call module one's display() function
```

Output:

```
C:\>python two.py
This code is run as a module
Hello Python!
```

In Program 46, when the first statement: 'import one' is executed by the Python interpreter, it will set the value of the special variable __name__ as 'one' (i.e. the module name) in one.py program and hence we got the output as: 'This code is run as a module'.

Points to Remember

- A function is similar to a program that consists of a group of statements which performs a task.
- Functions represent reusable code. Once a function is written, it can be used again and again.
- A function is defined in the form of: def functionname(para1, para2, ...).
- A function is executed only when it is called using its name.
- The 'return' statement is used inside the function body to return values out of the function. A function can return one or more values.
- In Python, functions are called using 'pass by object reference' where the object reference is sent to the function while calling the function.

- The parameters in the function definition are called formal argument. The values passed to the function at the time of calling the function are called actual arguments.
- The arguments passed to a function in the correct position and number are called positional arguments.
- The keyword arguments are arguments that identify the parameters by their names which are mentioned in the functional call.
- A default argument is an argument that assumes a default value if a value is not provided in the function call for that argument.
- A variable length argument is an argument that can accept any number of values. The variable length argument is declared with a ' * ' symbol before it in the function definition.
- A keyword variable length argument is an argument that can accept any number of values provided in the format of keys and values. The keyword variable length argument is declared with a ' ** ' symbol before it in the function definition.
- A local variable is a variable declared inside a function and whose scope is limited only to that function where it is declared.
- When a variable is declared above a function, it becomes global variable. Global variables are available to all the functions which are written after it.
- A function that calls itself is known as 'recursive function'. Recursion is useful to solve complex programs in fewer steps.
- A function without a name is called 'anonymous function' or 'lambda function'.
- The lambda functions are generally used with filter(), map() and reduce() functions.
- The filter() function is useful to extract elements from a sequence depending on the result of a function.
- The map() function is useful to perform some operation on each element of a sequence depending on a function.
- The reduce() function reduces a sequence of elements to a single value by processing the elements according to a function supplied.
- A module represents a group of classes, methods, functions and variables. There are several built-in modules in Python. Similar to those modules, we can also create and use our own modules.
- A decorator is a function that accepts a function as parameter and returns a function. Decorators are useful to perform some additional processing required by a function.
- Decorators can be applied to a function using @ symbol above the function definition.

- A generator is a function that returns a sequence of values or elements. To return elements from a generator, we have to use yield statement.
- The value of the special variable '__name__' indicates whether the program is run as an individual program or as a module. If the value of the variable '__name__' is '__main__' then the program is run directly as a program or script; otherwise, it is run as a module from another program.

CHAPTER 10

LISTS AND TUPLES

A sequence is a datatype that represents a group of elements. The purpose of any sequence is to store and process a group of elements. In Python, strings, lists, tuples and dictionaries are very important sequence datatypes. All sequences allow some common operations like indexing and slicing. In this chapter, you will learn about lists, tuples and their operations in Python.

List

A list is similar to an array that consists of a group of elements or items. Just like an array, a list can store elements. But, there is one major difference between an array and a list. An array can store only one type of elements whereas a list can store different types of elements. Hence lists are more versatile and useful than an array. Perhaps lists are the most used datatype in Python programs.

In our daily life, we do not have elements of the same type. For example, we take marks of a student in 5 subjects:

```
50, 55, 62, 74, 66
```

These are all belonging to the same type, i.e. integer type. Hence, we can represent such elements as an array. But, we need other information about the student, like his roll number, name, gender along with his marks. So, the information looks like this:

```
10, Venu gopal, M, 50, 55, 62, 74, 66
```

Here, we have different types of data. Roll number (10) is an integer. Name ('Venu gopal') is a string. Gender ('M') is a character and the marks (50, 55, 62, 74, 66) are again integers. In daily life, generally we have this type of information that is to be stored and processed. This type of information cannot be stored in an array because an array can store only one type of elements. In this case, we need to go for list datatype. A list can store different types of elements. To store the student's information discussed so far, we can create a list as:

```
student = [10, 'Venu gopal', 'M', 50, 55, 62, 74, 66]
```

Please observe that the elements of the 'student' list are stored in square braces []. We can create an empty list without any elements by simply writing empty square braces as:

```
e_lst = []   # this an empty list
```

Thus we can create a list by embedding the elements inside a pair of square braces []. The elements in the list should be separated by a comma (,). To view the elements of a list as a whole, we can simply pass the list name to the print() function as:

```
print(student)
```

The list appears as given below:

```
[10, 'Venu gopal', 'M', 50, 55, 62, 74, 66]
```

Indexing and slicing operations are commonly done on lists. Indexing represents accessing elements by their position numbers in the list. The position numbers start from 0 onwards and are written inside square braces as: student[0], student[1], etc... It means, student[0] represents 0th element, student[1] represents 1st element and so forth. For example, to print the student's name, we can write:

```
print(student[1])
```

The name of student appears as given below:

```
Venu gopal
```

Slicing represents extracting a piece of the list by mentioning starting and ending position numbers. The general format of slicing is: [start: stop: stepsize]. By default, 'start' will be 0, 'stop' will be the last element and 'stepsize' will be 1. For example, student[0:3:1] represents a piece of the list containing 0th to 2nd elements.

```
print(student[0:3:1])
```

The elements are given below:

```
[10, 'Venu gopal', 'M']
```

We can also write the above statement as:

```
print(student[:3:])
```

The same elements appears as shown following:

```
[10, 'Venu gopal', 'M']
```

Here, since we did not mention the starting element position, it will start at 0 and stepsize will be taken as 1. Suppose, we do not mention anything in slicing, then the total list will be extracted as:

```
print(student[::])
```

It displays the output as:

```
[10, 'Venu gopal', 'M', 50, 55, 62, 74, 66]
```

Apart from indexing and slicing, the 5 basic operations: finding length, concatenation, repetition, membership and iteration operations can be performed on lists and other sequences like strings, tuples or dictionaries.

In the following program, we are creating lists with different types of elements and also displaying the list elements.

Program

Program 1: A Python program to create lists with different types of elements.

```
# a general way to create lists
# create a list with integer numbers
num = [10, 20, 30, 40, 50]
print('Total list= ', num)  # display total list
print('First= %d, Last= %d' % (num[0], num[4]))  # display first and
    # last elements

# create a list with strings
names = ["Raju", "Vani", "Gopal", "Laxmi"]
print('Total list= ', names)  # display entire list
print('First= %s, Last= %s' % (names[0], names[3]))  # display first
    # and last elements

# create a list with different elements
x = [10, 20, 10.5, 2.55, "Ganesh", 'Vishnu']
print('Total list= ', x)  # display entire list
print('First= %d, Last= %s' % (x[0], x[5]))  # display first and last
    # elements
```

Output:

```
C:\>python lists.py
Total list=  [10, 20, 30, 40, 50]
First= 10, Last= 50
Total list=  ['Raju', 'Vani', 'Gopal', 'Laxmi']
First= Raju, Last= Laxmi
Total list=  [10, 20, 10.5, 2.55, 'Ganesh', 'Vishnu']
First= 10, Last= Vishnu
```

Creating Lists using range() Function

We can use range() function to generate a sequence of integers which can be stored in a list. The format of the range() function is:

```
range(start, stop, stepsize)
```

If we do not mention the 'start', it is assumed to be 0 and the 'stepsize' is taken as 1. The range of numbers stops one element prior to 'stop'. For example,

```
range(0, 10, 1)
```

This will generate numbers from 0 to 9, as: [0, 1, 2, 3, 4, 5, 6, 7, 8, 9]. Consider another example:

```
range(4,9,2)
```

The preceding statement will generate numbers from 4th to 8th in steps of 2, i.e. [4, 6, 8].

In fact, the range() function does not return list of numbers. It returns only range class object that stores the data about 'start', 'stop' and 'stepsize'. For example, if we write:

```
print(range(4,9,2))
```

The preceding statement will display:

```
range(4, 9, 2)   # this is the object given by range()
```

This range object should be used in for loop to get the range of numbers desired by the programmer. For example:

```
for i in range(4,9,2):
    print(i)
```

The preceding statement will display 4, 6, 8. Hence, we say range object is 'iterable', that is, suitable as a target for functions and loops that expect something from which they can obtain successive items. For example, range object can be used in for loops to display the numbers, or with list() function to create a list. In the following example, the range() function is used in the list() function to create a list:

```
lst = list(range(4, 9, 2))
print(lst)
```

The list is shown below:

```
[4, 6, 8]
```

If we are not using the list() function and using range() alone to create a list, then we will have only range class object returned by the range() function. For example,

```
lst = range(4, 9, 2)
print(lst)
```

The preceding statements will give the following output:

```
range(4, 9, 2)   # this is not a list, it is range object
```

In this case, using a loop like for or while is necessary to view the elements of the list. For example,

```
for i in lst:
    print (i)
```

will display 4, 6, 8. In Program 2, we are showing examples of how to create lists using the range() function. In this program, we are not using the list() function.

Program

Program 2: A Python program to create lists using range() function.

```
# creating lists using range() function
# create a list with 0 to 9 consecutive integer numbers
```

```
list1 = range(10)
for i in list1:  # display element by element
    print(i, ', ', end='')
print()  # throw cursor to next line

#create list with integers from 5 to 9
list2 = range(5, 10)
for i in list2:
    print(i, ', ', end='')
print()

# create a list with odd numbers from 5 to 9
list3 = range(5, 10, 2)  # step size is 2
for i in list3:
    print(i, ', ', end='')
```

Output:

```
C:\>python lists.py
0 , 1 , 2 , 3 , 4 , 5 , 6 , 7 , 8 , 9 ,
5 , 6 , 7 , 8 , 9 ,
5 , 7 , 9 ,
```

We can use while loop or for loop to access elements from a list. The len() function is useful to know the number of elements in the list. For example, len(list) gives total number of elements in the list. The following while loop retrieves starting from 0th to the last element of the list:

```
i=0
while i<len(list):  # repeat from 0 to length of list
    print(list[i])
    i=i+1
```

Observe the len(list) function in the while condition as: while i<len(list). This will return the total number of elements in the list. If the total number of elements is 'n', then the condition will become: while(i<n). It means i values are changing from 0 to n-1. Thus this loop will display all elements of the list from 0 to n-1.

Another way to display elements of a list is by using a for loop, as:

```
for i in list:  # repeat for all elements
    print(i)
```

Here, 'i' will assume one element at a time from the list and hence if we display 'i' value, it will display the elements one by one. In Program 3, we are showing how to access the elements of a list using a while loop and a for loop.

Program

Program 3: A Python program to access list elements using loops.

```
# displaying list elements using while and for loops
list = [10,20,30,40,50]

print('Using while loop')
i=0
while i<len(list):  # repeat from 0 to length of list
    print(list[i])
    i=i+1
```

```
print('Using for loop')
for i in list:  # repeat for all elements
    print(i)
```

Output:

```
C:\>python lists.py
Using while loop
10
20
30
40
50
Using for loop
10
20
30
40
50
```

Updating the Elements of a List

Lists are *mutable*. It means we can modify the contents of a list. We can append, update or delete the elements of a list depending upon our requirements.

Appending an element means adding an element at the end of the list. To append a new element to the list, we should use the append() method. In the following example, we are creating a list with elements from 1 to 4 and then appending a new element 9.

```
lst = list(range(1,5))    # create a list using list() and range()
print(lst)
```

The preceding statements will give the following output:

```
[1, 2, 3, 4]
```

Now, consider the following statements:

```
lst.append(9)    # append a new element to lst
print(lst)
```

The preceding statements will give the following output:

```
[1, 2, 3, 4, 9]
```

Updating an element means changing the value of the element in the list. This can be done by accessing the specific element using indexing or slicing and assigning a new value. Consider the following statements:

```
lst[1]= 8    # update 1st element of lst
print(lst)
```

The preceding statements will give:

```
[1, 8, 3, 4, 9]
```

Consider the following statements:

```
lst[1:3] = 10, 11   #update 1st and 2nd elements of lst
print(lst)
```

The preceding statements will give:

```
[1, 10, 11, 4, 9]
```

Deleting an element from the list can be done using 'del' statement. The del statement takes the position number of the element to be deleted.

```
del lst[1]   # delete 1st element from lst
print(lst)
```

Now, the list appears as:

```
[1, 11, 4, 9]
```

We can also delete an element using the remove() method. In this method, we should pass the element to be deleted.

```
lst.remove(11)   # delete 11 from lst
print(lst)
```

Now, the list appears as:

```
[1, 4, 9]
```

Let's write a program to retrieve the elements of a list in reverse order. This can be done easily by using the reverse() method, as:

```
list.reverse()
```

This will reverse the order of elements in the list and the reversed elements are available in the list. Suppose, we do not have the reverse() method, then how can we develop logic to display the elements in reverse order? This can be done using while loop and accessing the elements in reverse order. For example, let's assume a list with 5 elements. The positions of these elements can be specified using indexing, as: list[0] to list[4]. To display in reverse order, we should follow the order: list[4] to list[0]. The following while loop can be used to display the list in reverse order:

```
while i>=0:   # i represents initially 4.
    print(list[i])  # display from 4th to 0th elements
    i-=1   # decrease the position every time.
```

In the previous code, 'i' starts with a value 'n-1' where 'n' represents the number of elements of the list. Thus if the list has 5 elements, i would start from 4th element onwards till 0th element.

Another way to access elements in reverse order is by using negative indexing. When we write list[-1], it represents the last element. List[-2] represents 2nd element from the end. Hence, we should display from list[-1] to list[-5] so that the list will be displayed in reverse order.

```
i=-1  # last element
while i>=-5:  # display from -1th to -5th elements
    print(days[i])
    i-=1   # decrease the position every time.
```

This logic is shown in Program 4 where we are displaying the elements of a list in reverse order using while loop in two different ways.

Program

Program 4: A Python program to display the elements of a list in reverse order.

```
# displaying list elements in reverse order
days = ['Sunday', 'Monday', 'Tuesday', 'Wednesday', 'Thursday']

print('\nIn reverse order: ')
i=len(days)-1  # i will be 4
while i>=0:
    print(days[i])  # display from 4th to 0th elements
    i-=1

print('\nIn reverse order: ')
i=-1  # days[-1] represents last element
while i>=-len(days):  # display from -1th to -5th elements
    print(days[i])
    i-=1
```

Output:

```
C:\>python lists.py
In reverse order:
Thursday
Wednesday
Tuesday
Monday
Sunday

In reverse order:
Thursday
Wednesday
Tuesday
Monday
Sunday
```

Concatenation of Two Lists

We can simply use '+' operator on two lists to join them. For example, 'x' and 'y' are two lists. If we write x+y, the list 'y' is joined at the end of the list 'x'.

```
x = [10,20,30,40,50]
y = [100,110,120]
print(x+y)   # concatenate x and y
```

The concatenated list appears:

```
[10, 20, 30, 40, 50, 100, 110, 120]
```

Repetition of Lists

We can repeat the elements of a list 'n' number of times using '*' operator. For example, if we write x*n, the list 'x' will be repeated for n times as:

```
print(x*2)   # repeat the list x for 2 times
```

Now, the list appears as:

```
[10, 20, 30, 40, 50, 10, 20, 30, 40, 50]
```

Membership in Lists

We can check if an element is a member of a list or not by using 'in' and 'not in' operator. If the element is a member of the list, then 'in' operator returns True else False. If the element is not in the list, then 'not in' operator returns True else False. See the examples below:

```
x = [10,20,30,40,50]
a = 20
print(a in x)   # check if a is member of x
```

The preceding statements will give:

```
True
```

If you write,

```
print(a not in x)   # check if a is not a member of x
```

Then, it will give

```
False
```

Aliasing and Cloning Lists

Giving a new name to an existing list is called 'aliasing'. The new name is called 'alias name'. For example, take a list 'x' with 5 elements as

```
x = [10,20,30,40,50]
```

To provide a new name to this list, we can simply use assignment operator as:

```
y = x
```

In this case, we are having only one list of elements but with two different names 'x' and 'y'. Here, 'x' is the original name and 'y' is the alias name for the same list. Hence, any modifications done to 'x' will also modify 'y' and vice versa. Observe the following statements where an element x[1] is modified with a new value. This is shown in Figure 10.1.

```
x = [10,20,30,40,50]
y = x   # x is aliased as y
print(x)  will display [10,20,30,40,50]
print(y) will display [10,20,30,40,50]
```

```
x[1] = 99    # modify 1st element in x
print(x)  will display [10,99,30,40,50]
print(y) will display [10,99,30,40,50]
```

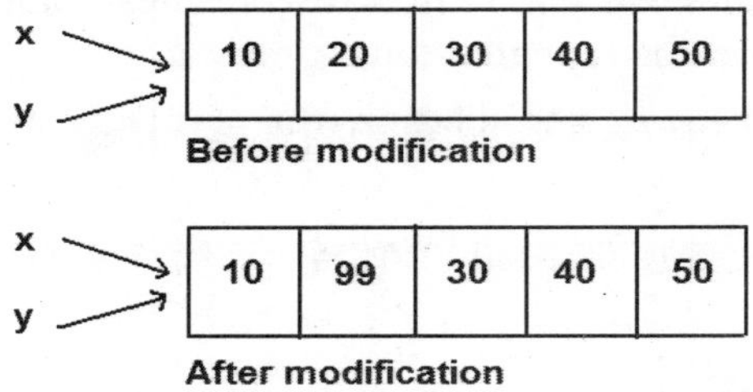

Figure 10.1: Effect of modifications in aliasing

Hence, if the programmer wants two independent lists, he should not go for aliasing. On the other hand, he should use cloning or copying.

Obtaining exact copy of an existing object (or list) is called 'cloning'. To clone a list, we can take help of the slicing operation as:

```
y = x[:]    # x is cloned as y
```

When we clone a list like this, a separate copy of all the elements is stored into 'y'. The lists 'x' and 'y' are independent lists. Hence, any modifications to 'x' will not affect 'y' and vice versa. Consider the following statements:

```
x = [10,20,30,40,50]
y = x[:]    # x is cloned as y
print(x)  will display [10,20,30,40,50]
print(y) will display [10,20,30,40,50]

x[1] = 99    # modify 1st element in x
print(x)  will display [10,99,30,40,50]
print(y) will display [10,20,30,40,50]
```

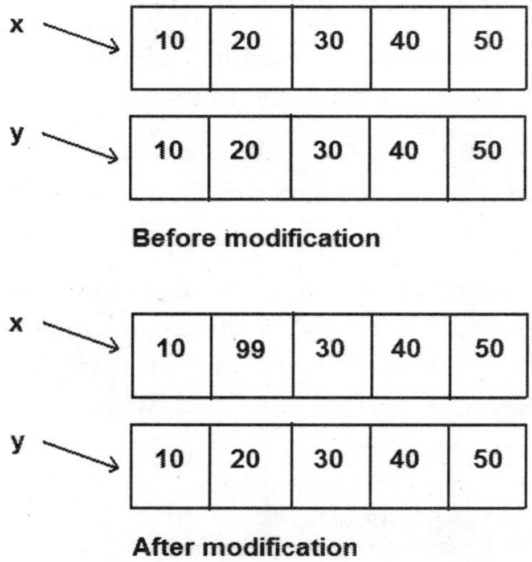

Figure 10.2: Effect of modifications in cloning or copying

We can observe that in cloning, modifications to a list are confined only to that list. The same can be achieved by copying the elements of one list to another using copy() method. For example, consider the following statement:

```
y = x.copy()   # x is copied as y
```

When we copy a list like this, a separate copy of all the elements is stored into 'y'. The lists 'x' and 'y' are independent. Hence, any modifications to 'x' will not affect 'y' and vice versa. Figure 2 depicts the concept of cloning and copying.

Methods to Process Lists

The function len() is useful to find the number of elements in a list. We can use this function as:

```
n = len(list)
```

Here, 'n' indicates the number of elements of the list. Similar to len() function, we have max() function that returns biggest element in the list. Also, the min() function returns the smallest element in the list. Other than these function, there are various other methods provided by Python to perform various operations on lists. These methods are shown in Table 10.1:

Table 10.1: The List methods and their Description

Method	Example	Description
sum()	list.sum()	Returns sum of all elements in the list.
index()	list.index(x)	Returns the first occurrence of x in the list
append()	list.append(x)	Appends x at the end of the list
insert()	list.insert(i, x)	Inserts x in to the list in the position specified by i
copy()	list.copy()	Copies all the list elements into a new list and returns it
extend()	list.extend(list1)	Appends list1 to list
count()	list.count(x)	Returns number of occurrences of x in the list
remove()	list.remove(x)	Removes x from the list
pop()	list.pop()	Removes the ending element from the list
sort()	list.sort()	Sorts the elements of the list into ascending order
reverse()	list.reverse()	Reverses the sequence of elements in the list
clear()	list.clear()	Deletes all elements from the list

We have used these methods in Program 5 to understand how these methods can be used on an example list.

Program

Program 5: A Python program to understand list processing methods.

```
# Python's list methods
num = [10,20,30,40,50]

n = len(num)
print('No. of elements in num: ', n)

num.append(60)
print('num after appending 60: ', num)

num.insert(0,5)
print('num after inserting 5 at 0th position: ', num)

num1 = num.copy()
print('Newly created list num1: ', num1)

num.extend(num1)
print('num after appending num1: ', num)

n = num.count(50)
print('No. of times 50 found in the list num: ', n)

num.remove(50)
print('num after removing 50: ', num)

num.pop()
print('num after removing ending element: ', num)

num.sort()
print('num after sorting: ', num)

num.reverse()
print('num after reversing: ', num)

num.clear()
print('num after removing all elements: ', num)
```

Output:

```
C:\>python lists.py
No. of elements in num:  5
num after appending 60:  [10, 20, 30, 40, 50, 60]
num after inserting 5 at 0th position:  [5, 10, 20, 30, 40, 50, 60]
Newly created list num1:  [5, 10, 20, 30, 40, 50, 60]
num after appending num1:  [5, 10, 20, 30, 40, 50, 60, 5, 10, 20, 30,
    40, 50, 60]
No. of times 50 found in the list num:  2
num after removing 50:  [5, 10, 20, 30, 40, 60, 5, 10, 20, 30, 40, 50, 60]
num after removing ending element:  [5, 10, 20, 30, 40, 60, 5, 10, 20,
    30, 40, 50]
num after sorting:  [5, 5, 10, 10, 20, 20, 30, 30, 40, 40, 50, 60]
num after reversing:  [60, 50, 40, 40, 30, 30, 20, 20, 10, 10, 5, 5]
num after removing all elements:  []
```

Finding Biggest and Smallest Elements in a List

Python provides two functions, max() and min(), which return the biggest and smallest elements from a list. For example, if the list is 'x', then:

```
n1 = max(x)    # n1 gives the biggest element
n2=  min(x)    # n2 gives the smallest element
```

If we do not want to use these functions, but want to find the biggest and smallest elements in the list, how is it possible? For this purpose, we should develop our own logic.

First of all, we will store the elements in a list. Let's take the example list as:

```
x = [20, 10, 5, 20, 15]
```

The list elements here are represented as x[0], x[1], ... x[4]. That means the elements in the list are in general represented as x[i]. We will take the first element as the biggest and also as the smallest one as:

```
big=x[0]
small=x[0]
```

We will compare 'big' and 'small' elements with other elements in the list. If the other element is > big, then it should be taken as 'big'. That means,

```
if x[i]>big: big= x[i]
```

Similarly, if the other element is < 'small', we should take that other element as 'small' as:

```
if x[i]<small: small = x[i]
```

Since the comparison starts from 1st element onwards, 'i' value will change from 1 till the end of the list. This logic is used in Program 6.

Program

Program 6: A Python program to find maximum and minimum elements in a list of elements.

```
# finding biggest and smallest numbers in a list of numbers
x = []  # take an empty list

print('How many elements? ', end='')
n = int(input()) # accept input into n

for i in range(n):  # repeat for n times
    print('Enter element: ', end='')
    x.append(int(input()))  # add the element to the list x

print('The list is: ', x)  # display the list

big=x[0]  # initially 0th element becomes maximum and minimum
small=x[0]

for i in range(1, n):  # repeat from 1 to n-1 elements
    if x[i]>big: big= x[i]  # if any other element is > big, take it as
     # big
```

```
        if x[i]<small: small = x[i]  # if any other element is < small,
         # take it as small

    print('Maximum is: ', big)  # display max and min elements
    print('Minimum is: ', small)
```

Output:

```
    C:\>python lists.py
    How many elements? 5
    Enter element: 20
    Enter element: 10
    Enter element: 5
    Enter element: 20
    Enter element: 15
    The list is: [20, 10, 5, 20, 15]
    Maximum is: 20
    Minimum is: 5
```

Sorting the List Elements

Python provides the sort() method to sort the elements of a list. This method can be used as:

```
    x.sort()
```

This will sort the list 'x' into ascending order. If we want to sort the elements of the list into descending order, then we can mention 'reverse=True' in the sort() method as:

```
    x.sort(reverse=True)
```

This will sort the list 'x' into descending order.

Suppose, we want to sort a list without using sort() method, we have to develop our own logic like bubble sort technique. In this technique, all the 'n' elements from 0 to n are taken and the first element of the list x[j] is compared with the immediate element x[j+1]. If x[j] is bigger than x[j+1], then they are swapped (or interchanged) since in ascending order we expect the smaller elements to be in the first place. When two elements are interchanged, the number of elements to be sorted becomes lesser by 1. When there are no more swaps found, the 'flag' will become 'False' and we can abort sorting. Suppose, we give the following elements for sorting:

```
    Original list: 1, 5, 4, 3, 2
    Compare 1 with other elements. 1 is smallest hence no swaps.  We get:
        1, 5, 4, 3, 2
    Compare 5 with other elements. Swap 5 with 4, 5 with 3, 5 with 2. We
        get: 1, 4, 3, 2, 5
    Compare 4 with other elements. Swap 4 with 3, 4 with 2. We get: 1, 3,
        2, 4, 5
    Compare 3 with other elements. Swap 3 with 2. We get: 1, 2, 3, 4, 5
```

Swapping means interchanging the values of two variables. If 'a' and 'b' are variables, we are supposed to store 'a' value into 'b' and vice versa. Swapping the values of 'a' and 'b' can be done using a temporary variable 't' as:

```
Store a value into t. i.e. t= a
Store b value into a. i.e. a = b
Store t value into b. i.e. b= t
```

These steps are shown in Figure10.3 by taking 'a' value 1 and 'b' value 2 initially. After swapping is done, 'a' value will be 2 and 'b' value will be 1.

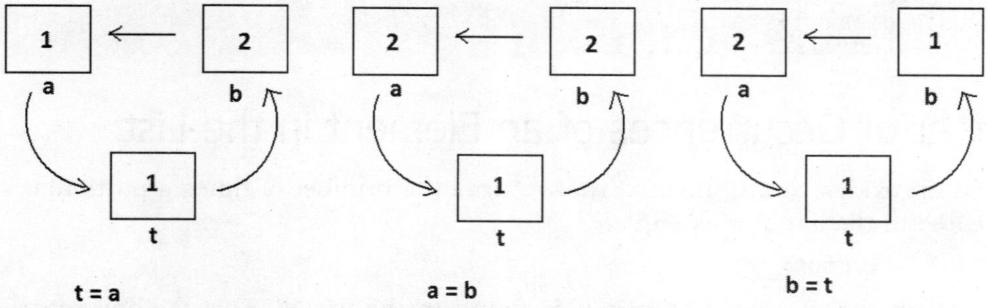

Figure 10.3: Swapping a and b values using a temporary variable t.

Program 7 shows how to sort the elements of a list using bubble sort technique.

Program

Program 7: A Python program to sort the list elements using bubble sort technique.

```
# sorting a list using bubble sort technique
# create an empty list to store integers
x = []

# store elements into the list x
print('How many elements? ', end='')
n = int(input()) # accept input into n

for i in range(n):  # repeat for n times
    print('Enter element: ', end='')
    x.append(int(input()))  # add the element to the list x

print('Original list: ', x)

# bubble sort
flag = False  # when swapping is done, flag becomes True
for i in range(n-1):  # i is from 0 to n-1
    for j in range(n-1-i):  # j is from 0 to one element lesser than i
        if x[j] > x[j+1]:  # if 1st element is bigger than the 2nd one
            t = x[j]  # swap j  and j+1  elements
            x[j] = x[j+1]
            x[j+1] = t
            flag = True  # swapping done, hence flag is True
    if flag==False:  # no swapping means list is in sorted order
        break  # come out of inner for loop
```

```
    else:
        flag = False  # assign initial value to flag

print('Sorted list: ', x)
```

Output:

```
C:\>python arr.py
How many elements? 5
Enter element: 1
Enter element: 5
Enter element: 4
Enter element: 3
Enter element: 2
Original list:  [1, 5, 4, 3, 2]
Sorted list:  [1, 2, 3, 4, 5]
```

Number of Occurrences of an Element in the List

Python provides count() method that returns the number of times a particular element is repeated in the list. For example,

```
n = x.count(y)
```

will return the number of times 'y' is found in the list 'x'. This method returns 0 if the element is not found in the list.

It is possible to develop our own logic for the count() method. Let's take 'y' as the element to be found in the list 'x'. We will use a counter 'c' that counts how many times the element 'y' is found in the list 'x'. Initially 'c' value will be 0. When 'y' is found in the list, 'c' will increment by 1. We need a for loop that iterates over all the elements of the list as:

```
for i in x:
```

This for loop stores each element from the list 'x' into 'i'. So, if 'y == i' we found the element and hence we should increment i value by 1. This is shown by the following code snippet:

```
c=0
for i in x:
    if(y==i): c+=1
print('{} is found {} times.'.format(y, c))
```

The above code represents our own logic to find the number of occurrences of 'y' in the list 'x'. The same is shown in Program 8.

Program

Program 8: A Python program to know how many times an element occurred in the list.

```
# counting how many times an element occurred in the list
x = []  # take an empty list

n = int(input('How many elements? ')) # accept input into n

for i in range(n):  # repeat for n times
    print('Enter element: ', end='')
```

```
    x.append(int(input()))  # add the element to the list x

print('The list is: ', x)  # display the list

y = int(input('Enter element to count: '))
c=0
for i in x:
    if(y==i): c+=1
print('{} is found {} times.'.format(y, c))
```

Output:

```
C:\>python lists.py
How many elements? 5
Enter element: 40
Enter element: 20
Enter element: 30
Enter element: 40
Enter element: 50
The list is: [40, 20, 30, 40, 50]
Enter element to count: 40
40 is found 2 times.
```

Finding Common Elements in Two Lists

Sometimes, it is useful to know which elements are repeated in two lists. For example, there is a scholarship for which a group of students enrolled in a college. There is another scholarship for which another group of students got enrolled. Now, we want to know the names of the students who enrolled for both the scholarships so that we can restrict them to take only one scholarship. That means, we are supposed to find out the common students (or elements) in both the lists.

Let's take the two groups of students as two lists. First of all, we should convert the lists into sets, using set() function, as: set(list). Then we should find the common elements in the two sets using intersection() method as:

```
set1.intersection(set2)
```

This method returns a set that contains common or repeated elements in the two sets. This gives us the names of the students who are found in both the sets. This logic is presented in Program 9.

Program

Program 9: A Python program to find common elements in two lists.

```
# finding common elements in two lists

# take two lists
scholar1 = ['Vinay', 'Krishna', 'Saraswathi', 'Govind']
scholar2 = ['Rosy', 'Govind', 'Tanushri', 'Vinay', 'Vishal']

# convert them into sets
s1 = set(scholar1)
s2 = set(scholar2)
```

```
# find intersection of two sets
s3 = s1.intersection(s2)

# convert the resultant set into a list
common = list(s3)
# display the list
print(common)
```

Output:

```
C:\>python lists.py
['Vinay', 'Govind']
```

Storing Different Types of Data in a List

The beauty of lists is that they can store different types of elements. For example, we can store an integer, a string a float type number etc. in the same string. It is also possible to retrieve the elements from the list. This has advantage for lists over arrays. We can create list 'emp' as an empty list as:

```
emp = []
```

Then we can store employee data like id number, name and salary details into the 'emp' list using the append() method. After that, it is possible to retrieve employee details depending on id number of the employee. This is shown in Program 10.

Program

Program 10: A Python program to create a list with employee data and then retrieve a particular employee details.

```
# retrieving employee details from a list
emp = []  # take an empty list

n = int(input('How many employees? ')) # accept input into n

for i in range(n):  # repeat for n times
    print('Enter id: ', end='')
    emp.append(int(input()))
    print('Enter name: ', end='')
    emp.append(input())
    print('Enter salary: ', end='')
    emp.append(float(input()))

print('The list is created with employee data.')

id = int(input('Enter employee id: '))

# display employee details upon taking id.
for i in range(len(emp)):
    if id==emp[i]:
        print('Id= {:d}, Name= {:s}, Salary= {:.2f}'.format(emp[i],
     emp[i+1], emp[i+2]))
        break
```

Output:

```
C:\>python lists.py
How many employees? 4
Enter id: 10
Enter name: Vijaya lakshmi
Enter salary: 7000.50
Enter id: 11
Enter name: Gouri shankar
Enter salary: 9500.50
Enter id: 12
Enter name: Anil kumar
Enter salary: 8000
Enter id: 13
Enter name: Hema chandra
Enter salary: 8500.75
The list is created with employee data.
Enter employee id: 12
Id= 12, Name= Anil kumar, Salary= 8000.00
```

Nested Lists

A list within another list is called a *nested* list. We know that a list contains several elements. When we take a list as an element in another list, then that list is called a nested list. For example, we have two lists 'a' and 'b' as:

```
a = [80, 90]
b = [10, 20, 30, a]
```

Observe that the list 'a' is inserted as an element in the list 'b' and hence 'a' is called a nested list. Let's display the elements of 'b', by writing the following statement:

```
print(b)
```

The elements of b appears:

```
[10, 20, 30, [80, 90]]
```

The last element [80, 90] represents a nested list. So, 'b' has 4 elements and they are:

```
b[0] = 10
b[1] = 20
b[2] = 30
b[3] = [80, 90]
```

So, b[3] represents the nested list and if we want to display its elements separately, we can use a for loop as:

```
for x in b[3]:
    print(x)
```

Program

Program 11: A Python program to create a nested list and display its elements.

```
# To create a list with another list as element
list = [10, 20, 30, [80, 90]]
print('Total list= ', list)  # display entire list
print('First element= ', list[0])  # display first element
```

```
print('Last element is nested list= ', list[3])  # display nested list
for x in list[3]:  # display all elements in nested list
    print(x)
```

Output:

```
C:\>python lists.py
Total list=  [10, 20, 30, [80, 90]]
First element=  10
Last element is nested list=  [80, 90]
80
90
```

In Program 11, we used a for loop to display the nested list. We can refer to the individual elements of the nested list, as:

```
list[3][0]    # represents 80
list[3][1]    # represents 90
```

One of the main uses of nested lists is that they can be used to represent matrices. A matrix represents a group of elements arranged in several rows and columns. If a matrix contains 'm' rows and 'n' columns, then it is called m x n matrix. In Python, matrices are created as 2D arrays or using matrix object in numpy. We can also create a matrix using nested lists.

Nested Lists as Matrices

Suppose we want to create a matrix with 3 rows and 3 columns, we should create a list with 3 other lists as:

```
mat = [[1,2,3], [4,5,6], [7,8,9]]
```

Here, 'mat' is a list that contains 3 lists which are rows of the 'mat' list. Each row contains again 3 elements as:

```
[[1,2,3],    # first row
 [4,5,6],    # second row
 [7,8,9]]    # third row
```

If we use a for loop to retrieve the elements from 'mat', it will retrieve row by row, as:

```
for r in mat:
    print(r)   # display row by row
```

But we want to retrieve columns (or elements) in each row; hence we need another for loop inside the previous loop, as:

```
for r in mat:
    for c in r:   # display columns in each row
        print(c, end=' ')
    print()
```

Another way to display the elements of a matrix is using indexing. For example, mat[i][j] represents the ith row and j^{th} column element. Suppose the matrix has 'm' rows and 'n' columns, we can retrieve the elements as:

```
for i in range(len(mat)):   # i values change from 0 to m-1
    for j in range(len(mat[i])):   # j values change from 0 to n-1
```

```
            print('%d ' %mat[i][j], end=' ')
        print()
```

Program 12 shows various ways of displaying the elements of matrix. Please pay attention to this program.

Program

Program 12: A Python program to retrieve elements from a matrix and display them.

```
# displaying nested list as a matrix
# take a nested list
mat = [[1,2,3], [4,5,6], [7,8,9]]

print('Display the list as it is: ')
print(mat)

print('Display row by row: ')
for r in mat:
    print(r)

print('Display each column in row 0: ')
for c in mat[0]:
    print('%d ' %c, end='')
print()

print('Display each column in row 1: ')
for c in mat[1]:
    print('%d ' %c, end='')
print()

print('Display each column in row 2: ')
for c in mat[2]:
    print('%d ' %c, end='')
print()

print('Display all elements using for: ')
for r in mat:
    for c in r:   # display columns in each row
        print(c, end=' ')
    print()

print('Display all elements using for: ')
for i in range(len(mat)):
    for j in range(len(mat[i])):
        print('%d ' %mat[i][j], end='')
    print()
```

Output:

```
C:\>python lists.py
Display the list as it is:
[[1, 2, 3], [4, 5, 6], [7, 8, 9]]
Display row by row:
[1, 2, 3]
[4, 5, 6]
[7, 8, 9]
Display each column in row 0:
1 2 3
Display each column in row 1:
```

```
4 5 6
Display each column in row 2:
7 8 9
Display all elements using for:
1 2 3
4 5 6
7 8 9
Display all elements using for:
1 2 3
4 5 6
7 8 9
```

We can create two matrices using nested lists and find their sum matrix. This is shown in Program 13. In this program, m1 and m2 represent matrix of 3 rows and 4 columns each. To add them we need a simple logic where the elements in corresponding positions in the two matrices are added, as:

```
m3[i][j]= m1[i][j]+m2[i][j]
```

Program

Program 13: A Python program to add two matrices and display the sum matrix using lists.

```
# nested lists - matrix addition
# take matrix one with 3 rows and 4 cols
m1 = [ [1, 2, 3, 0],
       [4, 5, 6, 0],
       [7, 8, 9, 0] ]

# take matrix two with 3 rows and 4 cols
m2 = [ [1, 2, 3, 4],
       [1, 0, 1, 0],
       [2, -1, -2, 1] ]

# take matrix three with 3 rows and 4 cols and initialize with all 0s
m3= [ 4*[0] for i in range(3) ]  # repeat four 0s for 3 times

# add the corresponding elements of m1 and m2 and store into m3
for i in range(3):
    for j in range(4):
        m3[i][j]= m1[i][j]+m2[i][j]

# display the third matrix using for loop
for i in range(3):
    for j in range(4):
        print('%d ' %m3[i][j], end='')
    print()
```

Output:

```
C:\>python lists.py
2 4 6 4
5 5 7 0
9 7 7 1
```

List Comprehensions

List comprehensions represent creation of new lists from an iterable object (like a list, set, tuple, dictionary or range) that satisfy a given condition. List comprehensions contain very compact code usually a single statement that performs the task.

Example 1: We want to create a list with squares of integers from 1 to 10. We can write code as:

```
squares = []    # create empty list
for x in range(1, 11):   # repeat x values from 1 to 10
    squares.append(x**2)   # add squares of x to the list
```

The preceding code will create 'squares' list with the elements as shown below:

```
[1, 4, 9, 16, 25, 36, 49, 64, 81, 100]
```

The previous code can be rewritten in a compact way as:

```
squares = [x**2 for x in range(1, 11)]
```

This is called list comprehension. From this, we can understand that a list comprehension consists of square braces containing an expression (i.e. x**2). After the expression, a for loop and then zero or more if statements can be written. Consider the following syntax:

```
[ expression for item1 in iterable1 if statement1
for item2 in iterable2 if statement2
for item3 in iterable3 if statement3 ... ]
```

Here, 'iterable' represents a list, set, tuple, dictionary or range object. The result of a list comprehension is a new list that contains elements as a result of executing the expression according to the for loops and if statements. So, we can store the result of a list comprehension in a new list.

Example 2: Suppose, we want to get squares of integers from 1 to 10 and take only the even numbers from the result, we can write a list comprehension as:

```
even_squares = [x**2 for x in range(1, 11) if x % 2==0]
```

If we display the list 'even_squares', it will display the following list:

```
[4, 16, 36, 64, 100]
```

The same list comprehension can be written without using the if statement as:

```
even_squares = [x**2 for x in range(2, 11, 2)]
```

Example 3: If we have two lists 'x' and 'y' and we want to add each element of 'x' with each element of 'y', we can write for loops as:

```
x = [10, 20, 30]
y = [1, 2, 3, 4]
lst=[]
for i in x:
    for j in y:
        lst.append(i+j)
```

Here, the resultant list 'lst' contains the following elements:

```
[11, 12, 13, 14, 21, 22, 23, 24, 31, 32, 33, 34]
```

The same result can be achieved by using list comprehension as:

```
lst = [i+j for i in x for j in y]
```

or we can directly mention the lists in the list comprehension as:

```
lst = [i+j for i in [10, 20, 30] for j in [1,2,3,4]]
```

The previous list comprehension can be written using strings as:

```
lst = [ i+j for i in 'ABC' for j in 'DE']
```

In this case, the output will be:

```
['AD', 'AE', 'BD', 'BE', 'CD', 'CE']
```

Example 4: Let's take a list 'words' that contains a group of words or strings as:

```
words = ['Apple', 'Grapes', 'Banana', 'Orange']
```

We want to retrieve only the first letter of each word from the above list and store those first letters into another list 'lst'. We can write code as:

```
lst = []
for w in words:
    lst.append(w[0])
```

Now, lst contains the following letters:

```
['A', 'G', 'B', 'O']
```

This task can be achieved through list comprehension as:

```
lst = [w[0] for w in words]
```

Example 5: Let's take two lists 'num1' and 'num2' with some numbers as:

```
num1 = [1,2,3,4,5]
num2 = [10,11,1,2]
```

We want to create another list 'num3' with numbers present in 'num1' but not in 'num2'. We can develop the logic like this:

```
num3=[]
for i in num1:
    if i not in num2:
        num3.append(i)
```

If we display 'num3' we can see the following elements:

```
[3, 4, 5]
```

The same can be achieved using list comprehension as:

```
num3 = [i for i in num1 if i not in num2]
```

Example 6: Like list comprehensions, it is also possible to create set comprehensions and dictionary comprehensions in the same manner as discussed in the previous examples. Let's see how to create a dictionary comprehension. A dictionary contains key and value pairs separated by colons. A dictionary uses curly braced {} to embed the elements. We take a dictionary with hall ticket number and student name as:

```
dict = {1001: 'Pratap', 1002: 'Mohan', 1003: 'Ankita'}
```

Here, 1001 is hall ticket number of the student and 'Pratap' is the name of the student. The hall ticket number is called key and the name is called its value. We can create dictionary comprehension to convert keys as values and vice versa as:

```
dict1 = {value: key for key,value in dict.items()}
```

Here, dict.items() represents all items in the dictionary in the form of key value pairs. In the above expression, we are writing value: key which is the reverse order for writing key and value pairs. If we display 'dict1', it will show:

```
{'Pratap': 1001, 'Ankita': 1003, 'Mohan': 1002}
```

Tuples

A tuple is a Python sequence which stores a group of elements or items. Tuples are similar to lists but the main difference is tuples are immutable whereas lists are mutable. Since tuples are immutable, once we create a tuple we cannot modify its elements. Hence we cannot perform operations like append(), extend(), insert(), remove(), pop() and clear() on tuples. Tuples are generally used to store data which should not be modified and retrieve that data on demand.

Creating Tuples

We can create a tuple by writing elements separated by commas inside parentheses (). The elements can be of same datatype or different types. For example, to create an empty tuple, we can simply write empty parenthesis, as:

```
tup1 = ()  # empty touple
```

If we want to create a tuple with only one element, we can mention that element in parentheses and after that a comma is needed, as:

```
tup2 = (10,)  # tuple with one element. Observe comma after the element.
```

Here is a tuple with different types of elements:

```
tup3 = (10, 20, -30.1, 40.5, 'Hyderabad', 'New Delhi')
```

We can create a tuple with only one of type of elements also, like the following:

```
tup4 = (10, 20, 30)  # tuple with integers
```

If we do not mention any brackets and write the elements separating them by commas, then they are taken by default as a tuple. See the following example:

```
tup5 = 1, 2, 3, 4  #no braces
```

The point to remember is that if do not use any brackets, it will become a tuple and not a list or any other datatype.

It is also possible to create a tuple from a list. This is done by converting a list into a tuple using the tuple() function. Consider the following example:

```
list = [1, 2, 3]   # take a list
tpl = tuple(list)   # convert list into tuple
print(tpl)   # display tuple
```

The tuple is shown below:

```
(1, 2, 3)
```

Another way to create a tuple is by using range() function that returns a sequence. To create a tuple 'tpl' that contains numbers from 4 to 8 in steps of 2, we can use the range() function along with tuple() function, as:

```
tpl= tuple(range(4, 9, 2)) # numbers from 4 to 8 in steps of 2
print(tpl)
```

The preceding statements will give:

```
(4, 6, 8)
```

Accessing the Tuple Elements

Accessing the elements from a tuple can be done using indexing or slicing. This is same as that of a list. For example, let's take a tuple by the name 'tup' as:

```
tup = (50,60,70,80,90,100)
```

Indexing represents the position number of the element in the tuple. Now, tup[0] represents the 0th element, tup[1] represents the 1st element and so on.

```
print(tup[0])
```

The preceding will give:

```
50
```

Now, if you write:

```
print(tup [5])
```

Then the following element appears:

```
100
```

Similarly, negative indexing is also possible. For example, tup[-1] indicates the last element and tup[-2] indicates the second element from the end and so on. Consider the following statement:

```
print(tup[-1])
```

The preceding statement will give:

```
100
```

If you write,

```
print(tup[-6])
```

Then the following output appears:

```
50
```

Slicing represents extracting a piece or part of the tuple. Slicing is done in the format: [start: stop: stepsize]. Here, 'start' represents the position of the starting element and 'stop' represents the position of the ending element and the 'stepsize' indicates the incrementation. If the tuple contains 'n' elements, the default values will be 0 for 'start' and n-1 for 'stop' and 1 for 'stepsize'. For example, to extract all the elements from the tuple, we can write:

```
print(tup[:])
```

The elements of tuple appear:

```
(50, 60, 70, 80, 90, 100)
```

For example, to extract the elements from 1st to 4th, we can write:

```
print(tup[1:4])
```

The elements of tuple appear:

```
(60, 70, 80)
```

Similarly, to extract every other element, i.e. alternate elements, we can write:

```
print(tup[::2])    # here, start and stop assume default values.
```

The following output appears:

```
(50, 70, 90)
```

Negative values can be given in the slicing. If the 'step size' is negative, the elements are extracted in reverse order as:

```
print(tup[::-2])
```

The elements appear in the reverse order:

```
(100, 80, 60)
```

When the step size is not negative, the elements are extracted from left to right. In the following example, starting position -4 indicates the 4th element from the last. Ending position -1 indicates the last element. Hence, the elements from 4th to one element before the ending element (left to right) will be extracted.

```
print(tup[-4:-1])    # here, step size is 1
```

The following elements appear:

```
(70, 80, 90)
```

In most of the cases, the extracted elements from the tuple should be stored in separate variables for further use. In the following example, we are extracting the first two elements from the 'student' tuple and storing them into two variables.

```
student = (10, 'Vinay kumar', 50,60,65,61,70)
rno, name = student[0:2]
```

Now, the variable 'rno' represents 10 and 'name' represents Vinaykumar. Consider the following statement:

```
print(rno)
```

The preceding statement will give:

```
10
```

Now, if you write:

```
print(name)
```

The preceding statement will provide the name of the student:

```
Vinay kumar
```

If we want to retrieve the marks of the student from 'student' tuple, we can do it as:

```
marks = student[2:7] # store the elements from 2nd to 6th into 'marks'
# tuple
for i in marks:
    print(i)
```

The preceding statements will give the following output:

```
50
60
65
61
70
```

Basic Operations on Tuples

The 5 basic operations: finding length, concatenation, repetition, membership and iteration operations can be performed on any sequence may be it is a string, list, tuple or a dictionary.

To find length of a tuple, we can use len() function. This returns the number of elements in the tuple.

Consider the following example:

```
student = (10, 'Vinaykumar', 50,60,65,61,70)
len(student)
```

The preceding statement will give the following output:

```
7
```

We can concatenate or join two tuples and store the result in a new tuple. For example, the student paid a fees of Rs. 25,000.00 every year for 4 terms, then we can create a 'fees' tuple as:

```
fees = (25000.00,)*4   # repeat the tuple elements for 4 times.
print(fees)
```

The preceding statement will give the following output:

```
(25000.0, 25000.0, 25000.0, 25000.0)
```

Now, we can concatenate the 'student' and 'fees' tuples together to form a new tuple 'student1' as:

```
student1 = student+fees
print(student1)
```

The preceding statement will give:

```
(10, 'Vinay kumar', 50, 60, 65, 61, 70, 25000.0, 25000.0, 25000.0,
    25000.0)
```

Searching whether an element is a member of the tuple or not can be done using 'in' and 'not in' operators. The 'in' operator returns True if the element is a member. The 'not in' operator returns True if the element is not a member. Consider the following statements:

```
name='Vinay kumar'    # to know if this is member of student1 or not
name in student1
```

The preceding statements will give:

```
True
```

Suppose if you write:

```
name not in student1
```

Then the following output will appear:

```
False
```

The repetition operator repeats the tuple elements. For example, we take a tuple 'tpl' and repeat its elements for 4 times as:

```
tpl = (10, 11, 12)
tpl1 = tpl*3    # repeat for 3 times and store in tpl1
print(tpl1)
```

The preceding statements will give the following output:

```
(10, 11, 12, 10, 11, 12, 10, 11, 12)
```

Functions to Process Tuples

There are a few functions provided in Python to perform some important operations on tuples. These functions are mentioned in Table 10.2. Any function is called directly with its name. In this table, count() and index() are not functions. They are methods. Hence, they are called in the format: object.method().

Table 10.2: The functions available to process tuples

Function	Example	Description
len()	len(tpl)	Returns the number of elements in the tuple.
min()	min(tpl)	Returns the smallest element in the tuple.
max()	max(tpl)	Returns the biggest element in the tuple.

Function	Example	Description
count()	tpl.count(x)	Returns how many times the element 'x' is found in tpl.
index()	tpl.index(x)	Returns the first occurrence of the element 'x' in tpl. Raises ValueError if 'x' is not found in the tuple.
sorted()	sorted(tpl)	Sorts the elements of the tuple into ascending order. sorted(tpl, reverse=True) will sort in reverse order.

We will write a program to accept elements of a tuple from the keyboard and find their sum and average. In this program, we are using the following statement to accept elements from the keyboard directly in the format of a tuple (i.e. inside parentheses).

```
num = eval(input("Enter elements in (): "))
```

The eval() function is useful to evaluate whether the typed elements are a list or a tuple depending upon the format of brackets given while typing the elements. If we type the elements inside the square braces as: [1,2,3,4,5] then they are considered as elements of a list. If we enter the elements inside parentheses as: (1,2,3,4,5), then they are considered as elements of a tuple. Even if do not type any brackets, then by default they are taken as elements of tuple.

Program

Program 14: A Python program to accept elements in the form of a tuple and display their sum and average.

```
# program to find sum and average of elements in a tuple
num = eval(input("Enter elements in (): "))
sum=0
n=len(num) # n is no. of elements in the tuple
for i in range(n):  # repeat i from 0 to n-1
    sum+=num[i]  # add each element to sum
print('Sum of numbers: ', sum)  # display sum
print('Average of numbers: ', sum/n)  #display average
```

Output:

```
C:\>python tuples.py
Enter elements in (): (1,2,3,4,5,6)
Sum of numbers: 21
Average of numbers: 3.5
```

When the above program asks the user for entering the elements, the user can type the elements inside the parentheses as: (1,2,3,4,5,6) or without any parentheses as: 1,2,3,4,5,6. When a group of elements are entered with commas (,), then they are by default taken as a tuple in Python.

In Program 15, first we enter the elements separated by commas. These elements are stored into a string 'str' as:

```
str = input('Enter elements separated by commas: ').split(',')
```

Then each element of this string is converted into integer and stored into a list 'lst' as:

```
lst = [int(num) for num in str]
```

This list can be converted into a tuple using tuple() function as:

```
tup = tuple(lst)
```

Later, index() method is used to find the first occurrence of the element 'ele' as:

```
pos = tup.index(ele)    # returns first occurrence of element
```

If the 'ele' is not found in the tuple, then there will be an error by the name 'ValueError' which should be handled using try and except blocks which is shown in the program.

Program

Program 15: A Python program to find the first occurrence of an element in a tuple.

```
# inserting elements from keyboard into the tuple and finding element
    # position
# accept elements from keyboard as strings separated by commas
str = input('Enter elements separated by commas: ').split(',')

lst = [int(num) for num in str]   # convert strings into integers and
# store into a list
tup = tuple(lst)   # convert list into tuple

print('The tuple is: ', tup)  # display the tuple

ele = int(input('Enter an element to search: '))
try:
    pos = tup.index(ele)   # returns first occurrence of element
    print('Element position no: ', pos+1)

exceptValueError:  # if element not found, ValueError will rise
    print('Element not found in tuple')
```

Output:

```
C:\>python tuples.py
Enter elements separated by commas: 10,20,30,20,40
The tuple is: (10, 20, 30, 20, 40)
Enter an element to search: 20
Element position no: 2
```

Nested Tuples

A tuple inserted inside another tuple is called nested tuple. For example,

```
tup = (50,60,70,80,90, (200, 201))  # tuple with 6 elements
```

Observe the last parentheses in the tuple 'tup', i.e. (200, 201). These parentheses represent that it is a tuple with 2 elements inserted into the tuple 'tup'. The tuple (200, 201) is called nested tuple as it is inside another tuple.

The nested tuple with the elements (200, 201) is treated as an element along with other elements in the tuple 'tup'. To retrieve the nested tuple, we can access it as an ordinary element as tup[5] as its index is 5. Now, consider the following statement:

```
print('Nested tuple= ', tup[6])
```

The preceding statement will give the following output:

```
Nested tuple=  (200, 201)
```

Every nested tuple can represent a specific data record. For example, to store 4 employees data in 'emp' tuple, we can write:

```
emp = ((10, "Vijay", 9000.90), (20, "Nihaar", 5500.75), (30,
    "Vanaja",8900.00), (40, "Kapoor", 5000.50))
```

Here, 'emp' is the tuple name. It contains 4 nested tuples each of which represents the data of an employee. Every employee's identification number, name and salary are stored as a nested tuples.

Sorting Nested Tuples

To sort a tuple, we can use sorted() function. This function sorts by default into ascending order. For example,

```
print(sorted(emp))
```

will sort the tuple 'emp' in ascending order of the 0th element in the nested tuples, i.e. identificaton number. If we want to sort the tuple based on employee name, which is the 1st element in the nested tuples, we can use a lambda expression as:

```
print(sorted(emp, key=lambda x: x[1]))  # sort on name
```

Here, key indicates the key for the sorted() function that tells on which element sorting should be done. The lambda function: lambda x: x[1] indicates that x[1] should be taken as the key that is nothing but 1st element. If we want to sort the tuple based on salary, we can use the lambda function as: lambda x: x[2]. Consider Program 16.

Program

Program 16: A Python program to sort a tuple with nested tuples.

```
# sorting a tuple that contains tuples as elements
# take employee tuple with id number, name and salary
emp = ((10, "Vijay", 9000.90), (20, "Nihaar", 5500.75), (30,
    "Vanaja",8900.00), (40, "Kapoor", 5000.50))

print(sorted(emp))  # sorts by default on id
print(sorted(emp, reverse=True))  # reverses on id
print(sorted(emp, key=lambda x: x[1]))  # sort on name
print(sorted(emp, key=lambda x: x[2]))  # sort on salary
```

Output:

```
C:\>python tuples.py
[(10, 'Vijay', 9000.9), (20, 'Nihaar', 5500.75), (30, 'Vanaja',
     8900.0), (40, 'Kapoor', 5000.5)]
[(40, 'Kapoor', 5000.5), (30, 'Vanaja', 8900.0), (20, 'Nihaar',
     5500.75), (10, 'Vijay', 9000.9)]
[(40, 'Kapoor', 5000.5), (20, 'Nihaar', 5500.75), (30, 'Vanaja',
     8900.0), (10, 'Vijay', 9000.9)]
[(40, 'Kapoor', 5000.5), (20, 'Nihaar', 5500.75), (30, 'Vanaja',
     8900.0), (10, 'Vijay', 9000.9)]
```

Inserting Elements in a Tuple

Since tuples are immutable, we cannot modify the elements of the tuple once it is created. Now, let's see how to insert a new element into an existing tuple. Let'stake 'x' as an existing tuple. Since 'x' cannot be modified, we have to create a new tuple 'y' with the newly inserted element. The following logic can be used:

1. First of all, copy the elements of 'x' from 0th position to pos-2 position into 'y' as:

```
y = x[0:pos-1]
```

2. Concatenate the new element to the new tuple 'y'.

```
y = y+new
```

3. Concatenate the remaining elements (from pos-1 till end) of x to the new tuple 'y'. The total tuple can be stored again with the old name 'x'.

```
x = y+x[pos-1:]
```

This logic is depicted in Figure 10.4 and shown in Program 17:

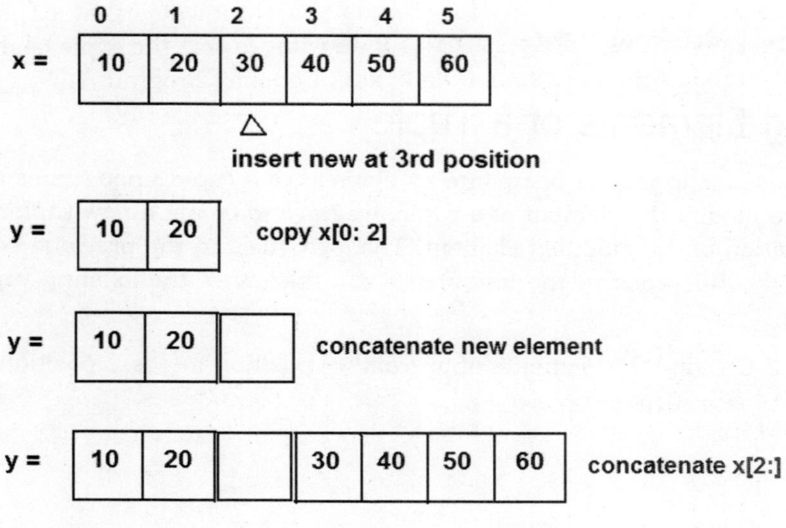

Figure 10.4: To insert a new element into a tuple

Program

Program 17: A Python program to insert a new element into a tuple of elements at a specified position.

```
# inserting a new element into a tuple
names = ('Visnu', 'Anupama', 'Lakshmi', 'Bheeshma')
print(names)

# accept new name and position number
lst= [input('Enter a new name: ')]
new = tuple(lst)
pos = int(input('Enter position no: '))

# copy from 0th to pos-2 into another tuple names1
names1 = names[0:pos-1]

# concatenate new element at pos-1
names1 = names1+new

# concatenate the remaining elements of names from pos-1 till end
names = names1+names[pos-1:]
print(names)
```

Output:

```
C:\>python tuples.py
('Vishnu', 'Anupama', 'Lakshmi', 'Bheeshma')
Enter a new name: Ganesh
Enter position no: 2
('Vishnu','Ganesh', 'Anupama', 'Lakshmi', 'Bheeshma')
```

This program works well with strings. Of course the same program can be used with integers also, if we change the input statement that accepts an integer number as:

```
lst= [int(input('Enter a new integer: '))]
```

Modifying Elements of a Tuple

It is not possible to modify or update an element of a tuple since tuples are immutable. If we want to modify the element of a tuple, we have to create a new tuple with a new value in the position of the modified element. The logic used in the previous section holds good with a slight difference in the last step. Let's take 'x' is the existing tuple and 'y' is the new tuple.

1. First of all, copy the elements of 'x' from 0th position to pos-2 position into 'y' as:

```
y = x[0:pos-1]
```

2. Concatenate the new element to the new tuple 'y'. Thus the new element is stored in the position of the element being modified.

```
y = y+new
```

3. Now concatenate the remaining elements from 'x' by eliminating the element which is at 'pos-1'. It means we should concatenate elements from 'pos' till the end. The total tuple can be assigned again to the old name 'x'.

```
x = y+x[pos:]
```

This logic is depicted in Figure 10.5 and shown in Program 18:

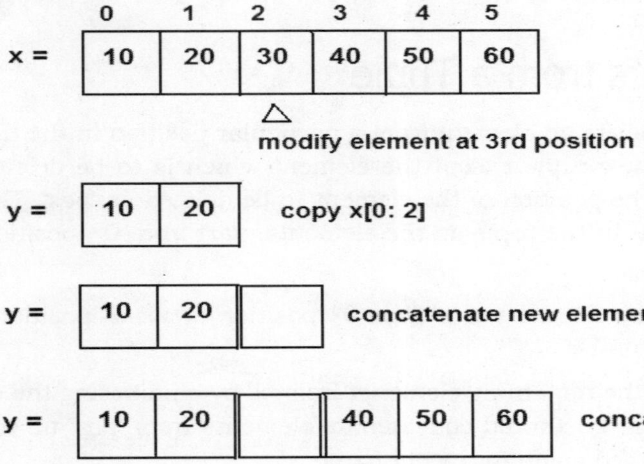

Figure 10.5: To modify a particular element in a tuple

Program

Program 18: A Python program to modify or replace an existing element of a tuple with a new element.

```
# modifying an existing element of a tuple
num = (10, 20, 30, 40, 50)
print(num)

# accept new element and position number
lst= [int(input('Enter a new element: '))]
new = tuple(lst)
pos = int(input('Enter position no: '))

# copy from 0th to pos-2 into another tuple num1
num1 = num[0:pos-1]
```

```
    # concatenate new element at pos-1
    num1 = num1+new

    # concatenate the remaining elements of num from pos till end
    num = num1+num[pos:]
    print(num)
```

Output:

```
C:\>python tuples.py
(10, 20, 30, 40, 50)
Enter a new element: 88
Enter position no: 3
(10, 20, 88, 40, 50)
```

Deleting Elements from a Tuple

The simplest way to delete an element from a particular position in the tuple is to copy all the elements into a new tuple except the element which is to be deleted. Let's assume that the user enters the position of the element to be deleted as 'pos'. The corresponding position will be 'pos-1' in the tuple as the elements start from 0th position. Now the logic will be:

1. First of all, copy the elements of 'x' from 0th position to pos-2 position into 'y' as:

```
y = x[0:pos-1]
```

2. Now concatenate the remaining elements from 'x' by eliminating the element which is at 'pos-1'. It means we should concatenate elements from 'pos' till the end. The total tuple can be assigned again to the old name 'x'.

```
x = y+x[pos:]
```

Program

Program 19: A program to delete an element from a particular position in the tuple.

```
# deleting an element of a tuple
num = (10, 20, 30, 40, 50)
print(num)
# accept position number of the element to delete
pos = int(input('Enter position no: '))

# copy from 0th to pos-2 into another tuple num1
num1 = num[0:pos-1]

# concatenate the remaining elements of num from pos till end
num = num1+num[pos:]
print(num)
```

Output:

```
C:\>python tuples.py
(10, 20, 30, 40, 50)
Enter position no: 3
(10, 20, 40, 50)
```

Points to Remember

- A sequence is a datatype that represents a group of elements. In Python, strings, lists, tuples and dictionaries are very important sequence datatypes.
- A list is similar to an array but a list can store different types of elements; whereas, an array can store only one type of elements.
- The elements of a list are written inside square braces [].
- It is possible to create a list using range() function. This returns an iterable object whose elements form a sequence. Another function to create a list is list() function.
- Any sequence (strings, lists, tuples, dictionaries) follow some operations like slicing, indexing, finding length using len() function, concatenation, repetition, membership and iteration operations.
- Lists are mutable. That means it is possible to modify or change the elements of a list.
- Aliasing a list represents giving a new name to the same list. Hence, if we change the aliased list, the changes will affect the original list and vice versa.
- Cloning a list can be done using slice operation. In cloning, if the cloned list is modified, the original list will not be modified as both will represent different copies of lists. The same effect can be seen if we copy the list using copy() method.
- The intersection() method of sets is useful to filter the common elements from two sets.
- A list within another list is called nested list. Nested lists are useful to create matrices.
- List comprehensions represent creation of new lists from an iterable object (like a list, set, tuple, dictionary or range) that satisfies a given condition.
- Tuples are similar to lists with the difference that tuples are immutable, whereas lists are mutable. Since tuples are immutable, once we create a tuple, we cannot modify its elements.

- We can create a tuple by writing elements separated by commas inside parentheses ().
- We can convert a list into a tuple using tuple() function.
- The eval() function is useful to evaluate whether the typed elements are a list or a tuple depending upon the format of brackets given while typing the elements.
- If we want to delete, modify or insert elements of a tuple, since tuples are immutable, we have to create a new tuple and store the updated elements.

CHAPTER 11

DICTIONARIES

A dictionary represents a group of elements arranged in the form of key-value pairs. In the dictionary, the first element is considered as 'key' and the immediate next element is taken as its 'value'. The key and its value are separated by a colon (:). All the key-value pairs in a dictionary are inserted in curly braces { }. Let's take a dictionary by the name 'dict' that contains employee details:

```
dict = {'Name': 'Chandra', 'Id': 200, 'Salary': 9080.50}
```

Here, the name of the dictionary is 'dict'. The first element in the dictionary is a string 'Name'. So, this is called 'key'. The second element is 'Chandra' which is taken as its 'value'. Observe that the key and its value are separated by a colon. Similarly, the next element is 'Id' which becomes 'key' and the next element '200' becomes its value. Finally, 'Salary' becomes key and '9080.50' becomes its value. So, we have 3 pairs of keys and values in this dictionary. This is shown in Figure 11.1:

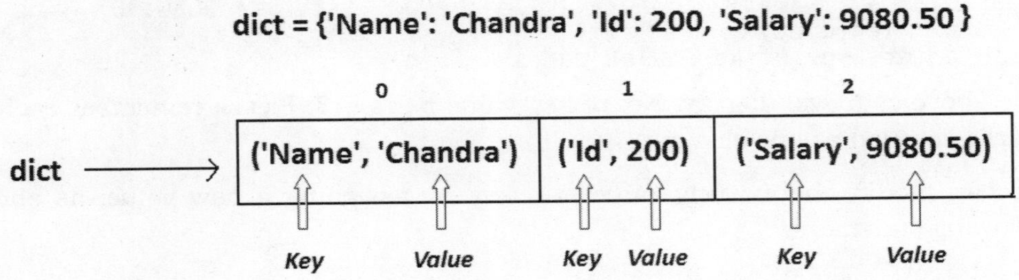

Figure 11.1: A Dictionary with 3 Key-Value Pairs

When the 'key' is provided, we can get back its 'value'. This is how we search for the values in a dictionary. For example, 'Name' is the key. To get its value, i.e. 'Chandra', we should mention the key as an index to the dictionary, as: dict['Name']. This will return the value 'Chandra'. Similarly, dict['Id'] returns its value, i.e. 200. See Program 1.

Program

Program 1: A Python program to create a dictionary with employee details and retrieve the values upon giving the keys.

```
# creating dictionary with key- value pairs
"""
Create a dictionary with employee details.
Here 'Name' is key and 'Chandra' is its value.
'Id' is key and 200 is its value.
'Salary' is key and 9080.50 is its value.
"""

dict = {'Name': 'Chandra', 'Id': 200, 'Salary': 9080.50}

# access value by giving key
print('Name of employee= ', dict['Name'])
print('Id number= ', dict['Id'])
print('Salary= ', dict['Salary'])
```

Output:

```
C:\>python dict.py
Name of employee= Chandra
Id number= 200
Salary= 9080.5
```

Operations on Dictionaries

To access the elements of a dictionary, we should not use indexing or slicing. For example, dict[0] or dict[1:3] etc. expressions will give error. To access the value associated with a key, we can mention the key name inside the square braces, as: dict['Name']. This will return the value associated with 'Name'. This is nothing but 'Chandra'.

If we want to know how many key-value pairs are there in a dictionary, we can use the len() function, as shown in the following statements:

```
dict = {'Name': 'Chandra', 'Id': 200, 'Salary': 9080.50}
n = len(dict)
print('No. of key-value pairs = ', n)
```

The above code will display: No. of key-value pairs = 3. Please remember each key-value pair is counted as one element.

We can modify the existing value of a key by assigning a new value, as shown in the following statement:

```
dict['Salary'] = 10500.00
```

Here, the 'Salary' value is modified as '10500.00'. The previous value of 'Salary', i.e. 9080.50 is replaced by the new value, i.e. 10500.00.

We can also insert a new key-value pair into an existing dictionary. This is done by mentioning the key and assigning a value to it, as shown in the following statement:

```
dict['Dept'] = 'Finance'
```

Here, we are giving a new key 'Dept' and its value 'Finance'. This pair is stored into the dictionary 'dict'. Now, if we display the dictionary using print(dict), it will display:

```
{'Name': 'Chandra', 'Dept': 'Finance', 'Id': 200, 'Salary': 10500.0}
```

Observe the new pair 'Dept': 'Finance' is added to the dictionary. Also, observe that this pair is not added at the end of existing pairs. It may be added at any place in the dictionary.

Suppose, we want to delete a key-value pair from the dictionary, we can use del statement as:

```
del dict['Id']
```

This will delete the key 'Id' and its corresponding value from the dictionary. Now, the dictionary looks like this:

```
{'Name': 'Chandra', 'Dept': 'Finance', 'Salary': 10500.0}
```

To test whether a 'key' is available in a dictionary or not, we can use 'in' and 'not in' operators. These operators return either True or False. Consider the following statement:

```
'Dept' in dict   # check if 'Dept is a key in dict
```

The preceding statement will give:

```
True
```

Now, consider the following statement:

```
'Gender' in dict   # check if 'Gender' is a key in dict
```

The preceding statement will give:

```
False
```

Now, if you write:

```
'Gender' not in dict   # check if 'Gender' is not a key in dict
```

Then the following output appears:

```
True
```

We can use any datatypes for values. For example, a value can be a number, string, list, tuple or another dictionary. But keys should obey the following rules:

- Keys should be unique. It means, duplicate keys are not allowed. If we enter same key again, the old key will be overwritten and only the new key will be available. Consider the following example:

  ```
  emp = {'Nag':10, 'Vishnu':20, 'Nag':30}   # Key 'Nag' entered twice
  print(emp)
  ```

  The output appears as:

  ```
  {'Nag': 30, 'Vishnu': 20} # first 'Nag' is replaced by new key and its
  # value
  ```

- Keys should be immutable type. For example, we can use a number, string or tuples as keys since they are immutable. We cannot use lists or dictionaries as keys. If they are used as keys, we will get 'TypeError'. Consider the following example:

```
emp = {['Nag']:10, 'Vishnu':20, 'Raj':30}   # ['Nag'] is a list element
      - so error
Traceback (most recent call last):
  File "<pyshell#12>", line 1, in <module>
    emp = {['Nag']:10, 'Vishnu':20, 'Raj':30}
TypeError: unhashable type: 'list'
```

Dictionary Methods

Various methods are provided to process the elements of a dictionary. These methods generally retrieve or manipulate the contents of a dictionary. They are summarized in Table 11.1:

Table 11.1: Methods to Process Dictionaries

Method	Example	Description
clear()	d.clear()	Removes all key-value pairs from dictionary 'd'.
copy()	d1= d.copy()	Copies all elements from 'd' into a new dictionary 'd1'.
fromkeys()	d.fromkeys(s [,v])	Create a new dictionary with keys from sequence 's' and values all set to 'v'.
get()	d.get(k [,v])	Returns the value associated with key 'k'. If key is not found, it returns 'v'.
items()	d.items()	Returns an object that contains key-value pairs of 'd'. The pairs are stored as tuples in the object.
keys()	d.keys()	Returns a sequence of keys from the dictionary 'd'.
values()	d.values()	Returns a sequence of values from the dictionary 'd'.
update()	d.update(x)	Adds all elements from dictionary 'x' to 'd'.
pop()	d.pop(k [,v])	Removes the key 'k' and its value from 'd' and returns the value. If key is not found, then the value 'v' is returned. If key is not found and 'v' is not mentioned then 'KeyError' is raised.
setdefault()	d.setdefault(k [,v])	If key 'k' is found, its value is returned. If key is not found, then the k, v pair is stored into the dictionary 'd'.

In Program 2, we are going to retrieve keys from a dictionary using the keys() method. The keys() method returns dict_keys object that contains only keys. We will also retrieve values from the dictionary using values() method. This method returns all values in the form of dict_values object. Similarly, the items() method can be used to retrieve all key-value pairs into dict_items object.

Program

Program 2: A Python program to retrieve keys, values and key-value pairs from a dictionary.

```
# dictionary methods
# create a dictionary with employee details.
dict = {'Name': 'Chandra', 'Id': 200, 'Salary': 9080.50}

# print entire dictionary
print(dict)

# display only keys
print('Keys in dict= ', dict.keys())

# display only values
print('Values in dict= ', dict.values())

# display both key and value pairs as tuples
print('Items in dict= ', dict.items())
```

Output:

```
C:\>python dict.py
{'Name': 'Chandra', 'Id': 200, 'Salary': 9080.5}
Keys in dict=  dict_keys(['Name', 'Id', 'Salary'])
Values in dict=  dict_values(['Chandra', 200, 9080.5])
Items in dict=  dict_items([('Name', 'Chandra'), ('Id', 200),
     ('Salary', 9080.5)])
```

In Program 3, we are going to create a dictionary by entering the elements from the keyboard. When we enter the elements from the keyboard inside curly braces, then they are treated as key – value pairs of a dictionary by eval() function. Once the elements are entered, we want to find sum of the values using sum() function on the values of the dictionary.

Program

Program 3: A Python program to create a dictionary and find the sum of values.

```
# program to find sum of values in a dictionary
# enter the dictionary entries from keyboard
dict = eval(input("Enter elements in { }: "))

# find the sum of values
s = sum(dict.values())
print('Sum of values in the dictionary: ', s)  # display sum
```

Output:

```
C:\>python dict.py
Enter elements in { }: {'A':10, 'B':20, 'C':35, 'Anil': 50}
Sum of values in the dictionary: 115
```

In Program 4, first we create an empty dictionary 'x'. We enter the key into 'k' and value into 'v' and then using the update() method, we will store these key-value pairs into the dictionary 'x', as shown in the following statement:

```
x.update({k:v})
```

Here, the update() method stores the 'k' and 'v' pair into the dictionary 'x'.

Program

Program 4: A Python program to create a dictionary from keyboard and display the elements.

```
# creating a dictionary from the keyboard
x = {}  # take an empty dictionary

print('How many elements? ', end='')
n = int(input()) # n indicates no. of key-value pairs

for i in range(n):  # repeat for n times
    print('Enter key: ', end='')
    k = input()  #  key is string
    print('Enter its value: ', end='')
    v = int(input())  # value is integer
    x.update({k:v})  # store the key-value pair in dictionary x

# display the dictionary
print('The dictionary is: ', x)
```

Output:

```
C:\>python dict.py
How many elements? 3
Enter key: Raju
Enter its value: 10
Enter key: Laxmi
Enter its value: 22
Enter key: Salman
Enter its value: 33
The dictionary is: {'Laxmi': 22, 'Raju': 10, 'Salman': 33}
```

Please observe the output of Program 4. The key-value pairs which are entered by us from the keyboard are not displayed in the same order. Dictionaries will not maintain orderliness of pairs.

In Program 5, we are creating a dictionary with cricket players' names and scores. That means, player name becomes key and the score becomes its value. Once the dictionary 'x' is created, we can display the players' names by displaying the keys as:

```
for pname in x.keys():  # keys() will give players names
    print(pname)
```

To find the score of a player, we can use get() method, as:

```
runs = x.get(name, -1)
```

In the get() method, we should provide the key, i.e. player name. If the key is found in the dictionary, this method returns his 'runs'. If the player is not found in the dictionary, then it returns -1.

Program

Program 5: A Python program to create a dictionary with cricket players names and scores in a match. Also we are retrieving runs by entering the player's name.

```
# creating a dictionary with cricket players names and scores
x = {}  # take an empty dictionary

print('How many players? ', end='')
n = int(input()) # n indicates no. of key-value pairs

for i in range(n):  # repeat for n times
    print('Enter player name: ', end='')
    k = input()  #  key is string
    print('Enter runs: ', end='')
    v = int(input())  # value is integer
    x.update({k:v})  # store the key-value pair in dictionary x

# display only players names
print('\nPlayers in this match: ')
for pname in x.keys():  # keys() will give only keys
    print(pname)

# accept a player name from keyboard
print('Enter player name: ', end='')
name = input()

# find the runs done by the player
runs = x.get(name, -1)
if(runs == -1):
    print('Player not found')
else:
    print('{} made runs {}.'.format(name, runs))
```

Output:

```
C:\>python dict.py
How many players? 3
Enter player name: Sachin
Enter runs: 77
Enter player name: Kohli
Enter runs: 40
Enter player name: Sehwag
Enter runs: 89
Players in this match:
Kohli
Sachin
Sehwag
Enter player name: Kohli
Kohli made runs 40.
```

Using for Loop with Dictionaries

For loop is very convenient to retrieve the elements of a dictionary. Let's take a simple dictionary that contains color code and its name as:

```
colors = {'r': "Red", 'g': "Green", 'b': "Blue", 'w': "White"}
```

Here, 'r', 'g', 'w' represent keys and "Red", "Green", "White" indicate values. Suppose, we want to retrieve only keys from 'colors' dictionary, we can use a for loop as:

```
for k in colors:
    print (k)
```

In the above loop, 'k' stores each element of the colors dictionary. Here, 'k' assumes only keys and hence this loop displays only keys. Suppose, we want to retrieve values, then we can obtain them by passing the key to colors dictionary, as: colors[k]. The following for loop retrieves all the values from the colors dictionary:

```
for k in colors:
    print (colors[k])
```

Since values are associated with keys, we can retrieve them only when we mention the keys. Suppose, we want to retrieve both the keys and values, we can use the items() method in for loop as:

```
for k, v in colors.items():
    print('Key= {} Value= {}'. format(k, v))
```

In the preceding code, the colors.items() method returns an object by the name 'dict_items' that contains key and value pairs. Each of these pairs is stored into 'k', 'v' and then displayed. Consider Program 6.

Program

Program 6: A Python program to show the usage of for loop to retrieve elements of dictionaries.

```
# Using for loop with dictionaries
# take a dictionary
colors = {'r': "Red", 'g': "Green", 'b': "Blue", 'w': "White"}

# display only keys
for k in colors:
    print (k)

# pass keys to dictionary and display the values
for k in colors:
    print (colors[k])

# items() method returns key and value pair into k, v
for k, v in colors.items():
    print('Key= {} Value= {}'. format(k, v))
```

Output:

```
C:\>python dict.py
b
w
r
g
Blue
White
Red
Green
Key= b Value= Blue
```

```
Key= w Value= White
Key= r Value= Red
Key= g Value= Green
```

We will write another program to count the number of times each letter has occurred in a string. For example, "Book" is the string and we are supposed to find the number of occurrences of each letter in this string. It means the letter 'B' has occurred for 1 time, the letter 'o' occurred for 2 times and the letter 'k' occurred for 1 time. In this program, we use get() method very effectively. Please recollect that the get() method is used on a dictionary to retrieve the value by giving the key. If the key is not found in the dictionary, then it returns some default value. The format of the get() method is:

```
dict.get(x, 0)
```

This statement says that if the key 'x' is found in the dictionary 'dict', then return its 'value' from the dictionary, else return 0. Now, consider the following code:

```
dict = {}    # initially dict is empty
str = "Book"    # str indicates "Book"
for x in str:    # x indicates each letter of "Book"
    dict[x] = dict.get(x, 0) + 1
```

In the preceding code, the last statement is very important.

```
dict[x] = dict.get(x, 0) + 1
```

Observe the right hand side expression with get() method. It says if 'x' (this is the letter of the string) is found in the dictionary 'dict', then return its value, else return 0. But we added '1' to the value returned by get() method and hence, if 'x' is not found, it returns 1. If 'x' is found then it returns the value of 'x' plus 1.

Observe the left side expression, i.e. dict[x]. This represents 'x' is stored as key in the dictionary. Whatever the value returned by the right side expression will be stored into that dictionary as value for the key 'x'. That means:

```
dict[x] = value returned by get() + 1
```

Let's take the first letter of the string, i.e. 'B'. Since the dictionary is initially empty, there are no elements in it and hence 'B' is not found in the dictionary. So, dict.get(x, 0) + 1 returns 1. At the left side, we are having dict[x]. It represents dict['B']. Here, 'B' is taken as key. So, the statement becomes:

```
dict['B'] = 1
```

It means 'B' is stored as key and 1 is stored as its value into the dictionary 'dict'. So the dictionary contains a pair of elements as: {'B': 1}. In the next step, 'o' is the letter for which the get() method searches in the dictionary. It is not found in the 'dict' and hence 1 is returned. So,

```
dict['o'] = 1
```

This will store the new key – value pair, i.e. 'o' and 1 into the 'dict' and hence the dictionary contains:

```
{'B': 1, 'o': 1}.
```

In the next repetition of for loop, we get 'o' into 'x'. Since it is already available in the 'dict', its value 1 is returned by get() method for which 1 will be added. So, we get:

```
dict['o'] = 2
```

It means, the old value of 'o' is now updated to 2 in the dictionary and 'dict' contains the elements: {'B': 1, 'o': 2}. In this way, 'dict' stores each letter as key and its number of occurrences as value. Table 11.2 summarizes the steps for the string "Book". Each letter of this string is represented by 'x'.

Table 11.2: Finding the Occurrences of Each Letter of a String using a Dictionary

x	Found in dict	dict.get(x, 0) + 1	dict[x] = dict.get(x, 0) + 1	dict
B	No	1	dict['B'] = 1	{'B':1}
o	No	1	dict['o'] = 1	{'B':1, 'o':1}
o	Yes	2	dict['o'] = 2	{'B':1, 'o':2}
k	No	1	dict['k'] = 1	{'B':1, 'o':2, 'k':1}

Program

Program 7: A Python program to find the number of occurrences of each letter in a string using dictionary.

```
# Finding how many times each letter is repeated in a string.
# take a string with some letters
str = "Book"

# take an empty dictionary
dict = {}

# store into dict each letter as key and its
# number of occurrences as value
for x in str:
    dict[x] = dict.get(x, 0) + 1

# display key and value pairs of dict
for k, v in dict.items():
    print('Key = {}\t Its occurrences= {}'.format(k, v))
```

Output:

```
C:\>python dict.py
Key = k        Its occurrences= 1
Key = o        Its occurrences= 2
Key = B        Its occurrences= 1
```

The output of the above program may not show the letter occurrences in an orderly manner. This is because the dictionary does not store the elements in the same order as they were entered.

Sorting the Elements of a Dictionary using Lambdas

A lambda is a function that does not have a name. Lambda functions are written using a single statement and hence look like expressions. Lambda functions are written without using 'def' keyword. They are useful to perform some calculations or processing easily. For example,

```
f = lambda x, y: x+y
```

The above expression is a lambda function with 2 arguments, x and y. After colon (:), we wrote the body, i.e. x+y. this is the value returned by the lambda function. At the time of calling this function, we are supposed to pass 2 values for x and y as: f(10, 15). This will return 25 as result. For understanding lambdas, kindly refer to the chapter on 'Functions'.

Let's take an example dictionary as:

```
colors = {10: "Red", 35: "Green", 15: "Blue", 25: "White"}
```

Here, color code and its name are given as key-value pairs. Suppose we want to sort this dictionary into ascending order of keys, i.e. on color codes, we can use sorted() function in the following format:

```
sorted(elements, key = color code)
```

Here, elements of the dictionary can be accessed using the colors.items() method. A key can be prescribed using a lambda function as:

```
key = lambda t: t[0]
```

Here, 't' is the argument for the lambda function and t[0] is the value returned by the function. Since we are supposed to sort the dictionary, we should pass the entire dictionary to lambda function. So, 't' represents the dictionary that is passed to the function and t[0] represents the 0th element in the dictionary, i.e. color code. So, the sorted() function can be written as:

```
sorted(colors.items(), key = lambda t: t[0])
```

This will sort all the elements of the dictionary by taking color code (indicated by t[0]) as the key. If we want to sort the dictionary based on color name, then we can write:

```
sorted(colors.items(), key = lambda t: t[1])
```

This will sort the elements of the dictionary by taking color name (indicated by t[1]) as the key. Consider Program 8 to understand how to sort the elements of a dictionary.

Program

Program 8: A Python program to sort the elements of a dictionary based on a key or value.

```
# Sorting a dictionary by key or value
# take a dictionary
colors = {10: "Red", 35: "Green", 15: "Blue", 25: "White"}
```

```
# sort the dictionary by keys, i.e. 0th element
c1 = sorted(colors.items(), key = lambda t: t[0])
print(c1)

# sort the dictionary by values, i.e. 1st element
c2 = sorted(colors.items(), key = lambda t: t[1])
print(c2)
```

Output:

```
C:\>python dict.py
[(10, 'Red'), (15, 'Blue'), (25, 'White'), (35, 'Green')]
[(15, 'Blue'), (35, 'Green'), (10, 'Red'), (25, 'White')]
```

Converting Lists into Dictionary

When we have two lists, it is possible to convert them into a dictionary. For example, we have two lists containing names of countries and names of their capital cities.

```
countries = ["USA", "India", "Germany", "France"]
cities = ['Washington', 'New Delhi', 'Berlin', 'Paris']
```

We want to create a dictionary out of these two lists by taking the elements of 'countries' list as keys and of 'cities' list as values. The dictionary should look something like this:

```
d = {"USA" : 'Washington', "India" : 'New Delhi' , "Germany" :
     'Berlin', "France" : 'Paris'}
```

There are two steps involved to convert the lists into a dictionary. The first step is to create a 'zip' class object by passing the two lists to zip() function as:

```
z = zip(countries, cities)
```

The zip() function is useful to convert the sequences into a zip class object. There may be 1 or more sequences that can be passed to zip() function. Of course, we passed only 2 lists to zip() function in the above statement. The resultant zip object is 'z'.

The second step is to convert the zip object into a dictionary by using dict() function.

```
d = dict(z)
```

Here, the 0th element of z is taken as 'key' and 1st element is converted into its 'value'. Similarly, 2nd element becomes 'key' and 3rd one becomes its 'value', etc. They are stored into the dictionary 'd'. If we display 'd', we can see the following dictionary:

```
{'India': 'New Delhi', 'USA': 'Washington', 'Germany': 'Berlin',
     'France': 'Paris'}
```

Program

Program 9: A Python program to convert the elements of two lists into key-value pairs of a dictionary.

```
# converting lists into a dictionary
# take two separate lists with elements
countries = ["USA", "India", "Germany", "France"]
cities = ['Washington', 'New Delhi', 'Berlin', 'Paris']
```

```
    # make a dictionary
    z = zip(countries, cities)
    d = dict(z)

    # display key - value pairs from dictionary d
    print('{:15s} -- {:15s}'.format('COUNTRY', 'CAPITAL'))
    for k in d:
        print('{:15s} -- {:15s}'.format(k, d[k]))
```

Output:

```
C:\>python dict.py
COUNTRY         -- CAPITAL
India           -- New Delhi
USA             -- Washington
Germany         -- Berlin
France          -- Paris
```

Converting Strings into Dictionary

When a string is given with key and value pairs separated by some delimiter (or separator) like a comma (,) we can convert the string into a dictionary and use it as dictionary. Let's take an example string:

```
str = "Vijay=23,Ganesh=20,Lakshmi=19,Nikhil=22"
```

This string 'str' contains names and their ages. Each pair is separated by a comma (,). Also, each name and age are separated by equals (=) symbol. To convert such a string into a dictionary, we have to follow 3 steps. First, we should split the string into pieces where a comma is found using split() method and then brake the string at equals (=) symbol. This can be done using a for loop as:

```
for x in str.split(','):
    y= x.split('=')
```

Each piece of the string is available in 'y'. The second step is to store these pieces into a list 'lst' using append() method as:

```
lst.append(y)
```

The third step is to convert the list into a dictionary 'd' using dict() function as:

```
d = dict(lst)
```

Now, this dictionary 'd' contains the elements as:

```
{'Vijay': '23', 'Ganesh': '20', 'Lakshmi': '19', 'Nikhil': '22'}
```

Please observe that this dictionary contains all elements as strings only. See first pair: 'Vijay': '23'. Here, 'Vijay' is string and his age '23' is also stored as string. If we want we can convert this '23' into an integer using int() function. Then we can store the name and age into another dictionary 'd1' as:

```
for k, v in d.items():
    d1[k] = int(v)   # store k and int(v) as key-value pair into d1.
```

Here, k represents the key and int(v) represents the converted value being stored into d1. This logic is shown in Program 10.

Program

Program 10: A Python program to convert a string into key-value pairs and store them into a dictionary.

```
# converting a string into a dictionary
# take a string
str = "Vijay=23,Ganesh=20,Lakshmi=19,Nikhil=22"

# brake the string at ',' and then at '='
# store the pieces into a list lst
lst=[]
for x in str.split(','):
    y= x.split('=')
    lst.append(y)

# convert the list into dictionary 'd'
# but this 'd' will have both name and age as strings
d = dict(lst)

# create a new dictionary 'd1' with name as string
# and age as integer
d1={}
for k, v in d.items():
    d1[k] = int(v)

# display the final dictionary
print(d1)
```

Output:

```
C:\>python dict.py
{'Ganesh': 20, 'Vijay': 23, 'Lakshmi': 19, 'Nikhil': 22}
```

Passing Dictionaries to Functions

We can pass a dictionary to a function by passing the name of the dictionary. Let's define a function that accepts a dictionary as a parameter.

```
def fun(dictionary):
    for i, j in dictionary.items():
        print(i, '--', j)
```

This function fun() is taking 'dictionary' object as parameter. Using for loop, we are displaying the key – value pairs of the dictionary. To call this function and pass a dictionary 'd', we can simply write:

```
fun(d)
```

Program

Program 11: A Python function to accept a dictionary and display its elements.

```
# A function that takes a dictionary as parameter
def fun(dictionary):
    for i, j in dictionary.items():
        print(i, '--', j)
```

```
# take a dictionary
d = {'a':'Apple', 'b': 'Book', 'c': 'Cook'}

# call the function and pass the dictionary
fun(d)
```

Output:

```
C:\>python dict.py
b -- Book
a -- Apple
c -- Cook
```

Ordered Dictionaries

We already discussed that the elements of a dictionary are not ordered. It means the elements are not stored into the same order as they were entered into the dictionary. Sometimes this becomes a problem. For example, take an employee database in a company which stores employees details depending on their seniority, i.e. senior most employee's data may be in the beginning of the database. If the employees' details are stored in a dictionary, this database will not show the employees details in the same order. When the employees' details are changed, the seniority is disturbed and the data of the employee who joined the company first may not appear in the beginning of the dictionary. In such a case, the solution is to use ordered dictionaries.

An ordered dictionary is a dictionary but it will keep the order of the elements. The elements are stored and maintained in the same order as they were entered into the ordered dictionary. We can create an ordered dictionary using the OrderedDict() method of 'collections' module. So, first we should import this method from collections module, as:

```
from collections import OrderedDict
```

Once this is done, we can create an ordered dictionary with the name 'd' as:

```
d = OrderedDict()
```

We can store the key and values into 'd', as:

```
d[10] = 'A'
d[11] = 'B'
d[12] = 'C'
d[13] = 'D'
```

Here, 10 is the key and 'A' is its value and so on. This order is not disturbed as 'd' is ordered dictionary. When we display the key – value pairs from the dictionary 'd', we can see the same order. This is shown in Program 12.

Program

Program 12: A Python program to create a dictionary that does not change the order of elements.

```
# create an ordered dictionary
from collections import OrderedDict
d = OrderedDict()   # d is ordered dictionary
```

```
    d[10] = 'A'
    d[11] = 'B'
    d[12] = 'C'
    d[13] = 'D'

    # display the ordered dictionary
    for i, j in d.items():
        print(i, j)
```

Output:

```
C:\>python dict.py
10  A
11  B
12  C
13  D
```

Points to Remember

- A dictionary represents a group of elements arranged in the form of key-value pairs. In the dictionary, the first element is considered as 'key' and the immediate next element is taken as its 'value'.
- The key and value pairs should be written inside a dictionary by separating them with a colon (:). Each pair should be separated by a comma. All the key-value pairs of the dictionary should be written inside curly braces { }.
- Indexing and slicing are not useful to access the elements of a dictionary.
- While inserting a new element or modifying the existing element, we can use the format: dict[key] = value.
- The keys of a dictionary should be unique and belong to immutable datatype. The value can be immutable or mutable.
- The get(k, v) method returns the value upon taking the key 'k'. If the key is not found in the dictionary, then it will return a default value 'v'.
- The update({k:v}) method stores the key 'k' and its value 'v' pair into an existing dictionary.
- The dict() method converts a list or tuple or zip object into a dictionary.
- The zip() method is useful to convert the sequences like lists into a zip class object.
- An ordered dictionary is a dictionary but it will keep the order of the elements.
- Ordered dictionaries are created using the OrderedDict() method of collections module.

CHAPTER 12

INTRODUCTION TO OOPS

In this chapter, we will introduce a revolutionary concept called *Object Oriented Programming System* (OOPS) based on which the languages like Smalltalk, Simula-67, C++, Java, Python, etc. are created. In this chapter, however, we are going to have a bird's eye view of the fundamental concepts of OOPS while an in depth discussion will be held only in the subsequent chapters.

The languages like C, Pascal, Fortran etc., are called Procedure Oriented Programming languages since in these languages, a programmer uses procedures or functions to perform a task. While developing software, the main task is divided into several sub tasks and each sub task is represented as a procedure or function. The main task is thus composed of several procedures and functions. This approach is called *Procedure oriented approach.* Consider Figure 12.1:

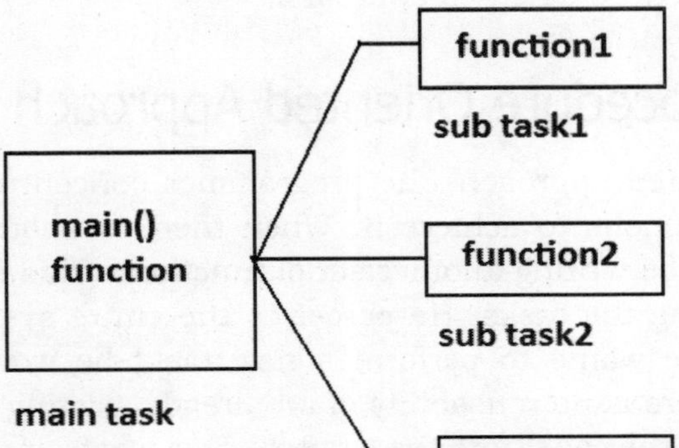

Figure 12.1: Procedure Oriented Approach

On the other hand, languages like C++, Java and Python use classes and objects in their programs and are called Object Oriented Programming languages. A class is a module which itself contains data and methods (functions) to achieve the task. The main task is divided into several sub tasks, and these are represented as classes. Each class can perform several inter-related tasks for which several methods are written in a class. This approach is called *Object Oriented approach.* Consider Figure 12.2:

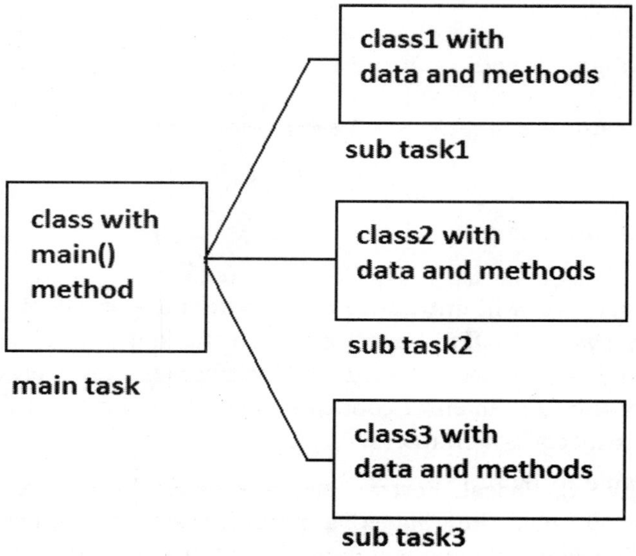

Figure 12.2: Object Oriented Approach

Programmers have followed Procedure Oriented approach for several decades, but as experience and observation teaches new lessons, programmers slowly realized several problems with Procedure Oriented approach.

Problems in Procedure Oriented Approach

In Procedure Oriented approach, the programmer concentrates on a specific task, and writes a set of functions to achieve it. When there is another task to be added to the software, he would be writing another set of functions. This means his concentration will be only on achieving the tasks. He perceives the entire system as fragments of several tasks. Whenever he wants to perform a new task, he would be writing a new set of functions. Thus there is no reusability of an already existing code. A new task every time requires developing the code from the scratch. This wastes programmer's time and effort.

In Procedure Oriented approach, every task and sub task is represented as a function and one function may depend on another function. Hence, an error in the software needs examination of all the functions. Thus debugging or removing errors will become difficult. Any updations to the software will also be difficult.

When the software is developed, naturally code size will also be increased. It has been observed in most of the software developed following the Procedure Oriented approach that when the code size exceeds 10,000 lines and before reaching 100,000 lines, suddenly at a particular point, the programmers start losing control on the code. This means, the programmers could not understand the exact behavior of the code and could neither debug it, nor extend it. This posed many problems, especially when the software was constructed to handle bigger and complex systems. For example, to create software to send satellites into the sky and control their operations from the ground stations, we may have to write millions of lines of code. In such systems, Procedure Oriented approach fails and programmers realized the need of another approach.

There is another problem with Procedure Oriented approach. Programming in this approach is not developed from human being's life. Statements, functions or procedures never reflect the human beings. So, from the human beings' point of view, they are unnatural. Unnatural activities are difficult to perform. For example, as human beings, we can walk or run. But, if we are asked to fly like birds; that would become impossible for us since flying is not natural for human beings. In the same way, if programming is developed from human beings' life, we can adapt to it easily. This idea forced computer scientists to develop a new approach that would be closer to human beings' life.

Due to the preceding reasons, computer scientists felt the need of a new approach where programming will have several modules. Each module represents a 'class' and the classes can be reusable and hence maintenance of code will become easy. When there is an error, it is possible to debug only on that class where error occurred without disturbing the other classes. This approach is suitable not only to develop bigger and complex applications but also to manage them easily. Moreover, this approach is built from a single root concept 'object', which represents anything that physically exists in this world. It means that all human beings are objects. All animals are objects. All existing things will become objects. This new approach is called 'Object Oriented Approach'. Programming in this approach is called Object Oriented Programming System (OOPS).

In OOPS, everything is an object. In real life, some objects will have similar behavior. For example, all birds have similar behavior like having two wings, two legs, etc. Also, all birds have the ability to fly in the sky. Such objects with similar behavior belong to the same class. So, a class represents common behavior of a group of objects. Since a class represents behavior, it does not exist physically. But objects exist physically. For example, bird is a class; whereas, sparrow, pigeon, crow and peacock are objects of the bird class. Similarly, human being is a class and Arjun, Krishna, Sita are objects of the human being class.

Specialty of Python Language

In OOPS, all programs involve creation of classes and objects. This makes programs lengthy. For example, we have to write all the statements of the program inside a class and then create objects to the class. Then use the features of the class through objects. This type of programming requires much code to perform a simple task like adding two numbers. Also, the program execution takes more time. So, for simple tasks, it is still better to go for procedure oriented approach which offers less code and more speed. For example, a C program executes faster than its equivalent program written in Python or Java!

Even though, Python is an object oriented programming language like Java, it does not force the programmers to write programs in complete object oriented way. Unlike Java, Python has a blend of both the object oriented and procedure oriented features. Hence, Python programmers can write programs using procedure oriented approach (like C) or object oriented approach (like Java) depending on their requirements. This is definitely an advantage for Python programmers!

Features of Object Oriented Programming System (OOPS)

There are five important features related to Object Oriented Programming System. They are:

- Classes and objects
- Encapsulation
- Abstraction
- Inheritance
- Polymorphism

Let's move further to have clear understanding of each of these features.

Classes and Objects

The entire OOPS methodology has been derived from a single root concept called 'object'. An object is anything that really exists in the world and can be distinguished from others. This definition specifies that everything in this world is an object. For example, a table, a ball, a car, a dog, a person, etc. will come under objects. Then what is not an object? If something does not really exist, then it is not an object. For example, our thoughts, imagination, plans, ideas etc. are not objects, because they do not physically exist.

Every object has some behavior. The behavior of an object is represented by attributes and actions. For example, let's take a person whose name is 'Raju'. Raju is an object because he exists physically. He has attributes like name, age, sex, etc. These attributes can be represented by variables in our programming. For example, 'name' is a string type variable, 'age' is an integer type variable.

Similarly, Raju can perform some actions like talking, walking, eating and sleeping. We may not write code for such actions in programming. But, we can consider calculations and processing of data as actions. These actions are performed by methods. We should understand that a function written inside a class is called a method. So an object contains variables and methods.

It is possible that some objects may have similar behavior. Such objects belong to same category called a 'class'. For example, not only Raju, but all the other persons have various common attributes and actions. So they are all objects of same class, 'Person'. Now observe that the 'Person' will not exist physically but only Raju, Ravi, Sita, etc. exist physically. This means, a class is a group name and does not exist physically, but objects exist physically. See Figure 12.3:

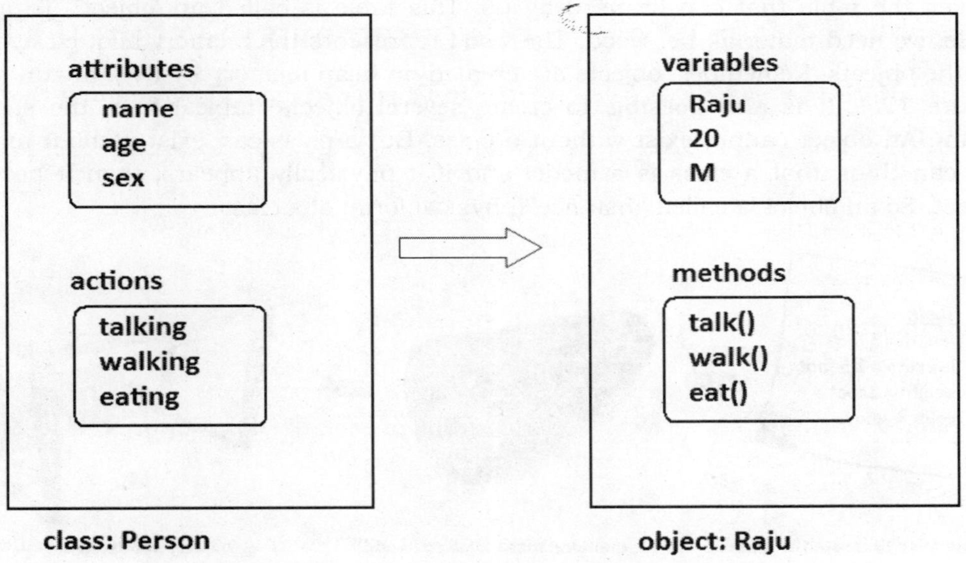

Figure 12.3: Person Class and Raju Object

To understand a class, take a pen and paper and write down all the attributes and actions of any person. The paper contains the model that depicts a person, so it is called a class. We can find a person with the name 'Raju', who got all the attributes and actions as written on the paper. So 'Raju' becomes an object of the class, Person. This gives a definition for the class. A class is a model or blueprint for creating objects. By following the class, one can create objects. So we can say, whatever is there in the class, will be seen in its objects also.

We can use a class as a model for creating objects. To write a class, we can write all the characteristics of objects which should follow the class. These characteristics will guide us to create objects. A class and its objects are almost the same with the difference that a class does not exist physically, while an object does. For example, let's say we want to construct a house. First of all, we will go to an architect who provides a plan. This plan is only an idea and exists on paper. This is called a class. However, based on this plan, if we construct the house, it is called an object since it exists physically. So, we can say that we can create objects from the class. An object does not exist without a class. But a class can exist without any objects.

Let's take another example. Flower is a class but if we take Rose, Lily, and Jasmine – they are all objects of flower class. The class flower does not exist physically but its objects, like Rose, Lily and Jasmine exist physically.

Let's take another example. We want a table made by a carpenter. First of all, the carpenter takes a paper and writes the measurements regarding length, breadth and height of the table. He may also draw a picture on the paper that works like a model for creating the original table. This plan or model is called a 'class'. Following this model, he makes the table that can be used by us. This table is called an 'object'. To make the table, we need material, i.e. wood. The wood represents the memory allotted by the PVM for the objects. Remember, objects are created on heap memory by PVM at run time. See Figure 12.4. It is also possible to create several objects (tables) from the same class (plan). An object cannot exist without a class. But a class can exist without any object. We can think that a class is a model and if it physically appears, then it becomes an object. So an object is called 'instance' (physical form) of a class.

Figure 12.4: Creation of a Class and Object

Creating Classes and Objects in Python

Let's create a class with the name Person for which Raju and Sita are objects. A class is created by using the keyword, class. A class describes the attributes and actions performed by its objects. So, we write the attributes (variables) and actions (functions) in the class as:

```
# This is a class
class Person:
```

```
        # attributes means variables
        name = 'Raju'
        age = 20

        # actions means functions
        def talk(cls):
            print(cls.name)
            print(cls.age)
```

Observe the preceding code. Person class has two variables and one function. The function that is written in the class is called method. When we want to use this class, we should create an object to the class as:

```
    p1 = Person()
```

Here, p1 is an object of Person class. Object represents memory to store the actual data. The memory needed to create p1 object is provided by PVM. Observe the function (or method) in the class:

```
    def talk(cls):
```

Here, 'cls' represents a default parameter that indicates the class. So, cls.name refers to class variable 'Raju'. We can call the talk() method to display Raju's details as:

```
    p1.talk()
```

Encapsulation

Encapsulation is a mechanism where the data (variables) and the code (methods) that act on the data will bind together. For example, if we take a class, we write the variables and methods inside the class. Thus, class is binding them together. So class is an example for encapsulation.

The variables and methods of a class are called 'members' of the class. All the members of a class are by default available outside the class. That means they are *public* by default. Public means available to other programs and classes. Python follows *Uniform Access Principle* that says that in OOPS, all the members of the class whether they are variables or methods should be accessible in a uniform manner. So, Python variables and methods are available outside alike. That means both are *public* by default. Usually, in C++ and Java languages, the variables are kept *private*, that means they are not available outside the class and the methods are kept *public* meaning that they are available to other programs. But in Python, both the variables and methods are *public* by default.

Encapsulation isolates the members of a class from the members of another class. The reason is when objects are created, each object shares different memory and hence there will not be any overwriting of data. This gives an advantage to the programmer to use same names for the members of two different classes. For example, a programmer can declare and use the variables like 'id', 'name', and 'address' in different classes like Employee, Customer, or Student classes.

Encapsulation in Python

Encapsulation is nothing but writing attributes (variables) and methods inside a class. The methods process the data available in the variables. Hence data and code are bundled up together in the class. For example, we can write a Student class with 'id' and 'name as attributes along with the display() method that displays this data. This Student class becomes an example for encapsulation.

```
# a class is an example for encapsulation
class Student:
    # to declare and initialize the variables
    def __init__(self):
        self.id = 10
        self.name = 'Raju'

    # display students details
    def display(self):
        print(self.id)
        print(self.name)
```

Observe the first method: def __init__(self). This is called a special function since its name is starting and ending with two underscores. If a variable or method name starts and ends with two underscores, they are built-in variables or methods which are defined for a specific purpose. The programmer should not create any variable or method like them. It means we should not create variables or methods with two underscores before and after their names.

The purpose of the special method def __init__(self) is to declare and initialize the instance variables of a class. Instance variables are the variables whose copy is available in the object (or instance). The first parameter for this method is 'self' that represents the object (or instance) of the present class. So, self.id refers to the variable in the object. In the Student class, we have written another method by the name display() that displays the instance variables.

Abstraction

There may be a lot of data, a class contains and the user does not need the entire data. The user requires only some part of the available data. In this case, we can hide the unnecessary data from the user and expose only that data that is of interest to the user. This is called abstraction.

A good example for abstraction is a car. Any car will have some parts like engine, radiator, battery, mechanical and electrical equipment etc. The user of the car (driver) should know how to drive the car and does not require any knowledge of these parts. For example driver is never bothered about how the engine is designed and the internal parts of the engine. This is why the car manufacturers hide these parts from the driver in a separate panel, generally at the front of the car.

The advantage of abstraction is that every user will get his own view of the data according to his requirements and will not get confused with unnecessary data. A bank clerk should see the customer details like account number, name and balance amount in the account. He should not be entitled to see the sensitive data like the staff salaries, profit or loss of the bank, interest amount paid by the bank, loans amount to be recovered, etc. Hence, such sensitive data can be abstracted from the clerk's view. The bank manager may, however, require the sensitive data and so it will be provided to the manager.

Abstraction in Python

In languages like Java, we have keywords like private, protected and public to implement various levels of abstraction. These keywords are called *access specifiers*. In Python, such words are not available. Everything written in the class will come under public. That means everything written in the class is available outside the class to other people. Suppose, we do not want to make a variable available outside the class or to other members inside the class, we can write the variable with two double scores before it as: __var. This is like a private variable in Python. In the following example, 'y' is a private variable since it is written as: __y.

```
class Myclass:
    # this is constructor.
    def __init__(self):
        self.__y = 3   # this is private variable
```

Now, it is not possible to access the variable from within the class or out of the class as:

```
m = Myclass()
print(m.y)   # error
```

The preceding print() statement displays error message as: AttributeError: 'Myclass' object has no attribute 'y'. Even though, we cannot access the private variable in this way, it is possible to access it in the format: instancename._Classname__var. That means we are using Classname differently to access the private variable. This is called *name mangling.* In name mangling, we have to use one underscore before the classname and two underscores after the classname. Like this, using the names differently to access the private variables is called name mangling. For example, to display a private variable 'y' value, we can write:

```
print(m._Myclass__y)   # display private variable y
```

The same statement can be written inside the method as: print(self._Myclass__z). When we use single underscore before a variable as _var, then that variable or object will not be imported into other files. The following code represents the public and private variables and how to access them.

```
# understanding public and private variables
class Myclass:
    # this is constructor.
    def __init__(self):
        self.x = 1   # public var
        self.__y = 2  # private var
```

```
        # instance method to access variables
        def display(self):
            print(self.x)  # x is available directly
            print(self._Myclass__y)   # name mangling required

    print('Accessing variables through method:')
    m = Myclass()
    m.display()

    print('Accessing variables through instance:')
    print(m.x)    # x is available directly
    print(m._Myclass__y)   # name mangling required
```

Output:

```
C:\>python oops.py
Accessing variables through method:
1
2
Accessing variables through instance:
1
2
```

We are planning to write Bank class with 'accno', 'name', 'balance' and 'loan' as variables. Since the clerk should not see the loan amount of the customer, we can write that variable with two underscores before the variable, as: ' __loan'. Then this variable is not available directly outside the class or inside the class to other methods.

In the Bank class, the first method is a special method with the name: __init__(self) is useful to declare variables and initialize them with some data. In the program, 'self' represents current class object. In this method, we are making loan variable as private by writing it as:

```
self. __loan = 1500000.00;
```

This variable is not available outside the class. It is not even available to other methods in the same class. Hence, it is abstracted completely from the user of the class. If the bank clerk calls the display_to_clerk(self) method, he will be able to see account number, name and balance amount only. He cannot see loan amount of the customer. That means some part of the data is hidden from the clerk. See the example code:

```
# accessing some part of data
class Bank :
    def __init__(self):
        self.accno = 10
        self.name = 'Srinu'
        self.balance = 5000.00
        self. __loan = 1500000.00

    def display_to_clerk(self):
        print(self.accno)
        print(self.name)
        print(self.balance)
```

In the preceding class, in spite of several data items, the display_to_clerk() method is able to access and display only the 'accno', 'name' and 'balance' values. It cannot access loan of the customer. This means the loan data is hidden from the view of the bank clerk. This is called abstraction. Suppose, we try to display the loan amount in the display_to_clerk() method, by writing:

```
print(self.loan)
```

This raises an error saying 'loan' is not an attribute of Bank class.

Inheritance

Creating new classes from existing classes, so that the new classes will acquire all the features of the existing classes is called Inheritance. A good example for Inheritance in nature is parents producing the children and children inheriting the qualities of the parents.

Let's take a class A with some members i.e., variables and methods. If we feel another class B wants almost same members, then we can derive or create class B from A as:

```
class B(A):
```

Now, all the features of A are available to B. If an object to B is created, it contains all the members of class A and also its own members. Thus, the programmer can access and use all the members of both the classes A and B. Thus, class B becomes more useful. This is called inheritance. The original class (A) is called the base class or super class and the derived class (B) is called the sub class or derived class.

There are three advantages of inheritance. First, we can create more useful classes needed by the application (software). Next, the process of creating the new classes is very easy, since they are built upon already existing classes. The last, but very important advantage is managing the code becomes easy, since the programmer creates several classes in a hierarchical manner, and segregates the code into several modules.

An Example for Inheritance in Python

Here, we take a class A with two variables 'a' and 'b' and a method, method1(). Since all these members are needed by another class B, we extend class B from A. We want some additional members in B, for example a variable 'c' and a method, method2(). So, these are written in B. Now remember, class B can use all the members of both A and B. This means the variables 'a','b','c 'and also the methods method1() and method2() are available to class B. That means all the members of A are inherited by B.

```
# Creating class B from class A
class A :
    a = 1
    b = 2
```

```
        def method1(cls):
            print(cls.a)
            print(cls.b)

    class B(A):
        c = 3
        def method2(cls):
            print(cls.c)
```

By creating an object to B, we can access all the members of both the classes A and B.

Polymorphism

The word 'Polymorphism' came from two Greek words 'poly' meaning 'many' and 'morphos' meaning 'forms'. Thus, polymorphism represents the ability to assume several different forms. In programming, if an object or method is exhibiting different behavior in different contexts, it is called polymorphic nature.

Polymorphism provides flexibility in writing programs in such a way that the programmer uses same method call to perform different operations depending on the requirement.

Example Code for Polymorphism in Python:

When a function can perform different tasks, we can say that it is exhibiting polymorphism. A simple example is to write a function as:

```
def add(a, b):
    print(a+b)
```

Since in Python, there the variables are not declared explicitly, we are passing two variables 'a', and 'b' to add() function where they are added. While calling this function, if we pass two integers like 5 and 15, then this function displays 15. If we pass two strings, then the same function concatenates or joins those strings. That means the same function is adding two integers or concatenating two strings. Since the function is performing two different tasks, it is said to exhibit polymorphism. Now, consider the following example:

```
# a function that exhibits polymorphism
def add(a, b):
    print(a+b)

# call add() and pass two integers
add(5, 10)  # displays 15

# call add() and pass two strings
add("Core", "Python")  # displays CorePython
```

The programming languages which follow all the five features of OOPS are called object oriented programming languages. For example, C++, Java and Python will come into this category.

Points to Remember

- Procedure oriented approach is the methodology where programming is done using procedures and functions. This is followed by languages like C, Pascal and FORTRAN.
- Object oriented approach is the methodology where programming is done using classes and objects. This is followed in the languages like C++, Java and Python.
- Python programmers can write programs using procedure oriented approach (like C) or object oriented approach (like Java) depending on their requirements.
- An object is anything that really exists in the world and can be distinguished from others.
- Every object has some behavior that is characterized by attributes and actions. Attributes are represented by variables and actions are performed by methods. So an object contains variables and methods.
- A function written inside a class is called method.
- A class is a model or blueprint for creating objects. A class also contains variables and methods.
- Objects are created from a class.
- An object does not exist without a class; however, a class can exist without any object.
- Encapsulation is a mechanism where the data (variables) and the code (methods) that act on the data will bind together.
- Class is an example for encapsulation since it contains data and code.
- Hiding unnecessary data and code from the user is called abstraction.
- To hide variables or methods, we should declare them as private members. This is done by writing two underscores before the names of the variable or method.
- Private members can be accessed using name mangling where the class name is used with single underscore before it and two underscores after it in the form of: instancename. _Classname__variable or instancename. _Classname__method().
- Creating new classes from existing classes, so that new classes will acquire all the features of the existing classes is called Inheritance.

- In inheritance, the already existing class is called base class or super class. The newly created class is called sub class or derived class.
- Polymorphism represents the ability of an object or method to assume several different forms.
- The programming languages which follow all the five features of OOPS namely, classes and objects, encapsulation, abstraction, inheritance and polymorphism are called object oriented programming languages. For example, C++, Java and Python will come into this category.

CHAPTER 13

CLASSES AND OBJECTS

We know that a class is a model or plan to create objects. This means, we write a class with the attributes and actions of objects. Attributes are represented by variables and actions are performed by methods. So, a class contains variable and methods. The same variables and methods are also available in the objects because they are created from the class. These variables are also called 'instance variables' because they are created inside the instance (i.e. object).

Please remember the difference between a function and a method. A function written inside a class is called a method. Generally, a method is called using one of the following two ways:

- classname.methodname()
- instancename.methodname()

The general format of a class is given as follows:

```
Class Classname(object):
    """ docstring describing the class """
    attributes
    def __init__(self):
    def method1():
    def method2():
```

Creating a Class

A class is created with the keyword *class* and then writing the Classname. After the Classname, 'object' is written inside the Classname. This 'object' represents the base class name from where all classes in Python are derived. Even our own classes are also derived from 'object' class. Hence, we should mention 'object' in the parentheses. Please note that writing 'object' is not compulsory since it is implied.

The docstring is a string which is written using triple double quotes or triple single quotes that gives the complete description about the class and its usage. The docstring is used to create documentation file and hence it is optional. 'attributes' are nothing but variables that contains data. __init__(self) is a special method to initialize the variables. method1() and method2(), etc. are methods that are intended to process variables.

If we take 'Student' class, we can write code in the class that specifies the attributes and actions performed by any student. For example, a student has attributes like name, age, marks, etc. These attributes should be written inside the Student class as variables. Similarly, a student can perform actions like talking, writing, reading, etc. These actions should be represented by methods in the Student class. So, the class Student contains these attributes and actions, as shown here:

```
class Student:      # another way is: class Student(object):
    # the below block defines attributes
    def __init__(self):
        self.name = 'Vishnu'
        self.age = 20
        self.marks = 900

    # the below block defines a method
    def talk(self):
        print('Hi, I am ', self.name)
        print('My age is', self.age)
        print('My marks are', self.marks)
```

Observe that the keyword *class* is used to declare a class. After this, we should write the class name. So, 'Student' is our class name. Generally, a class name should start with a capital letter, hence 'S' is capital in 'Student'. In the class, we write attributes and methods. Since in Python, we cannot declare variables, we have written the variables inside a special method, i.e. __init__(). This method is useful to initialize the variables. Hence, the name 'init'. The method name has two underscores before and after. This indicates that this method is internally defined and we cannot call this method explicitly. Observe the parameter 'self' written after the method name in the parentheses. 'self' is a variable that refers to current class instance. When we create an instance for the Student class, a separate memory block is allocated on the heap and that memory location is by default stored in 'self'. The instance contains the variables 'name', 'age', 'marks' which are called *instance variables*. To refer to instance variables, we can use the dot operator notation along with self as: 'self.name', 'self.age' and 'self.marks'.

See the method talk(). This method also takes the 'self' variable as parameter. This method displays the values of the variables by referring them using 'self'.

The methods that act on instances (or objects) of a class are called *instance methods.* Instance methods use 'self' as the first parameter that refers to the location of the instance in the memory. Since instance methods know the location of instance, they can act on the instance variables. In the previous code, the two methods __init__(self) and talk(self) are called instance methods.

In the Student class, a student is talking to us through talk() method. He is introducing himself to us, as shown here:

```
Hi, I am Vishnu
My age is 20
My marks are 900
```

This is what the talk() method displays. Writing a class like this is not sufficient. It should be used. To use a class, we should create an instance (or object) to the class. Instance creation represents allotting memory necessary to store the actual data of the variables, i.e., Vishnu, 20 and 900. To create an instance, the following syntax is used:

```
instancename  = Classname()
```

So, to create an instance (or object) to the Student class, we can write as:

```
s1 = Student()
```

Here, 's1' is nothing but the instance name. When we create an instance like this, the following steps will take place internally:

1. First of all, a block of memory is allocated on heap. How much memory is to be allocated is decided from the attributes and methods available in the Student class.
2. After allocating the memory block, the special method by the name '__init__(self)' is called internally. This method stores the initial data into the variables. Since this method is useful to construct the instance, it is called 'constructor'.
3. Finally, the allocated memory location address of the instance is returned into 's1' variable. To see this memory location in decimal number format, we can use id() function as id(s1).

Now, 's1' refers to the instance of the Student class. Hence any variables or methods in the instance can be referenced by 's1' using dot operator as:

```
s1.name    # this refers to data in name variable, i.e. Vishnu
s1.age        # this refers to data in age variable, i.e. 20
s1.marks   # this refers to data in marks variable, i.e. 900
s1.talk()   # this calls the talk() method
```

The dot operator takes the instance name at its left and the member of the instance at the right hand side. Figure 13.1 shows how 's1' instance of Student class is created in memory:

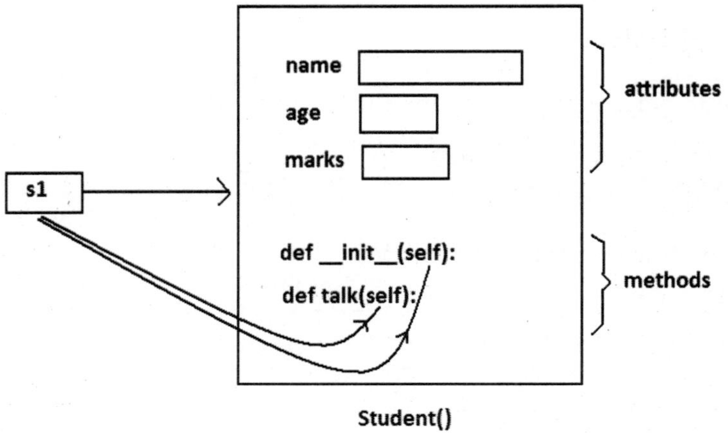

Figure 13.1: Student class instance in memory

Program

Program 1: A Python program to define Student class and create an object to it. Also, we will call the method and display the student's details.

```
# instance variables and instance method
class Student:
    # this is a special method called constructor.
    def __init__(self):
        self.name = 'Vishnu'
        self.age = 20
        self.marks = 900

# this is an instance method.
def talk(self):
    print('Hi, I am', self.name)
    print('My age is', self.age)
    print('My marks are', self.marks)

# create an instance to Student class.
s1 = Student()

# call the method using the instance.
s1.talk()
```

Output:

```
C:\>python cl.py
Hi, I am Vishnu
My age is 20
My marks are 900
```

In Program 1, we used the 'self' variable to refer to the instance of the same class. Also, we used a special method '__init__(self)' that initializes the variables of the instance. Let's have more clarity on these two concepts.

The Self Variable

'self' is a default variable that contains the memory address of the instance of the current class. So, we can use 'self' to refer to all the instance variables and instance methods.

When an instance to the class is created, the instance name contains the memory location of the instance. This memory location is internally passed to 'self'. For example, we create an instance to Student class as:

```
s1 = Student()
```

Here, 's1' contains the memory address of the instance. This memory address is internally and by default passed to 'self' variable. Since 'self' knows the memory address of the instance, it can refer to all the members of the instance. We use 'self' in two ways:

- The 'self' variable is used as first parameter in the constructor as:

```
def __init__(self):
```

  In this case, 'self' can be used to refer to the instance variables inside the constructor.

- 'self' can be used as first parameter in the instance methods as:

```
def talk(self):
```

  Here, talk() is instance method as it acts on the instance variables. If this method wants to act on the instance variables, it should know the memory location of the instance variables. That memory location is by default available to the talk() method through 'self'.

Constructor

A constructor is a special method that is used to initialize the instance variables of a class. In the constructor, we create the instance variables and initialize them with some starting values. The first parameter of the constructor will be 'self' variable that contains the memory address of the instance. For example,

```
def __init__(self):
    self.name = 'Vishnu'
    self.marks = 900
```

Here, the constructor has only one parameter, i.e. 'self'. Using 'self.name' and 'self.marks', we can access the instance variables of the class. A constructor is called at the time of creating an instance. So, the above constructor will be called when we create an instance as:

```
s1 = Student()
```

Here, 's1' is the name of the instance. Observe the empty parentheses after the class name 'Student'. These empty parentheses represent that we are not passing any values to the constructor. Suppose, we want to pass some values to the constructor, then we have to pass them in the parentheses after the class name. Let's take another example. We can write a constructor with some parameters in addition to 'self' as:

```
def __init__(self, n = '', m=0):
    self.name = n
    self.marks = m
```

Here, the formal arguments are 'n' and 'm' whose default values are given as '' (None) and 0 (zero). Hence, if we do not pass any values to constructor at the time of creating an instance, the default values of these formal arguments are stored into name and marks variables. For example,

```
s1 = Student()
```

Since we are not passing any values to the instance, None and zero are stored into name and marks. Suppose, we create an instance as:

```
s1 = Student('Lakshmi Roy', 880)
```

In this case, we are passing two actual arguments: 'Lakshmi Roy' and 880 to the Student instance. Hence these values are sent to the arguments 'n' and 'm' and from there stored into name and marks variables. We can understand this concept from Program 2.

Program

Program 2: A Python program to create Student class with a constructor having more than one parameter.

```
# instance vars and instance method - v.20
class Student:
    # this is constructor.
    def __init__(self, n = '', m=0):
        self.name = n
        self.marks = m

    # this is an instance method.
    def display(self):
        print('Hi', self.name)
        print('Your marks', self.marks)

# constructor is called without any arguments
s = Student()
s.display()
print('------------------')

# constructor is called with 2 arguments
s1 = Student('Lakshmi Roy', 880)
s1.display()
print('------------------')
```

Output:

```
C:\>python cl.py
Hi
Your marks 0
```

```
------------------
Hi Lakshmi Roy
Your marks 880
------------------
```

We should understand that a constructor does not create an instance. The duty of the constructor is to initialize or store the beginning values into the instance variables. A constructor is called only once at the time of creating an instance. Thus, if 3 instances are created for a class, the constructor will be called once per each instance, thus it is called 3 times.

Types of Variables

The variables which are written inside a class are of 2 types:

- Instance variables
- Class variables or Static variables

Instance variables are the variables whose separate copy is created in every instance (or object). For example, if 'x' is an instance variable and if we create 3 instances, there will be 3 copies of 'x' in these 3 instances. When we modify the copy of 'x' in any instance, it will not modify the other two copies. Consider Program 3.

Program

Program 3: A Python program to understand instance variables.

```
# instance vars example
class Sample:
    # this is a constructor.
    def __init__(self):
        self.x = 10

    # this is an instance method.
    def modify(self):
        self.x+=1

# create 2 instances
s1 = Sample()
s2 = Sample()
print('x in s1= ', s1.x)
print('x in s2= ', s2.x)

# modify x in s1
s1.modify()
print('x in s1= ', s1.x)
print('x in s2= ', s2.x)
```

Output:

```
C:\>python cl.py
x in s1= 10
x in s2= 10
x in s1= 11
x in s2= 10
```

Instance variables are defined and initialized using a constructor with 'self' parameter. Also, to access instance variables, we need instance methods with 'self' as first parameter. It is possible that the instance methods may have other parameters in addition to the 'self' parameter. To access the instance variables, we can use self.variable as shown in Program 3. It is also possible to access the instance variables from outside the class, as: instancename.variable, e.g. s1.x.

Unlike instance variables, class variables are the variables whose single copy is available to all the instances of the class. If we modify the copy of class variable in an instance, it will modify all the copies in the other instances. For example, if 'x' is a class variable and if we create 3 instances, the same copy of 'x' is passed to these 3 instances. When we modify the copy of 'x' in any instance using a class method, the modified copy is sent to the other two instances. This can be easily grasped from Program 4. Class variables are also called static variables.

Program

Program 4: A Python program to understand class variables or static variables.

```
# class vars or static vars example
class Sample:
    # this is a class var
    x = 10

    # this is a class method.
    @classmethod
    def modify(cls):
        cls.x+=1

# create 2 instances
s1 = Sample()
s2 = Sample()
print('x in s1= ', s1.x)
print('x in s2= ', s2.x)

# modify x in s1
s1.modify()
print('x in s1= ', s1.x)
print('x in s2= ', s2.x)
```

Output:

```
C:\>python cl.py
x in s1= 10
x in s2= 10
x in s1= 11
x in s2= 11
```

Observe Program 4. The class variable 'x' is defined in the class and initialized with value 10. A method by the name 'modify' is used to modify the value of 'x'. This method is called 'class method' since it is acting on the class variable. To mark this method as class method, we should use built-in decorator statement @classmethod. For example,

```
@classmethod    # this is a decorator
    def modify(cls):    # cls must be the first parameter
        cls.x+=1    # cls.x refers to class variable x
```

A class method contains first parameter by default as 'cls' with which we can access the class variables. For example, to refer to the class variable 'x', we can use 'cls.x'. We can also write other parameters in the class method in addition to the 'cls' parameter. The point is that the class variables are defined directly in the class. To access class variables, we need class methods with 'cls' as first parameter. We can access the class variables using the class methods as: cls.variable. If we want to access the class variables from outside the class, we can use: classname.variable, e.g. Sample.x.

Namespaces

A *namespace* represents a memory block where names are mapped (or linked) to objects. Suppose we write:

```
n = 10
```

Here, 'n' is the name given to the integer object 10. Please recollect that numbers, strings, lists etc. are all considered as objects in Python. The name 'n' is linked to 10 in the namespace. A class maintains its own namespace, called 'class namespace'. In the class namespace, the names are mapped to class variables. Similarly, every instance will have its own name space, called 'instance namespace'. In the instance namespace, the names are mapped to instance variables. In the following code, 'n' is a class variable in the Student class. So, in the class namespace, the name 'n' is mapped or linked to 10 as shown Figure 13.2. Since it is a class variable, we can access it in the class namespace, using classname.variable, as: Student.n which gives 10.

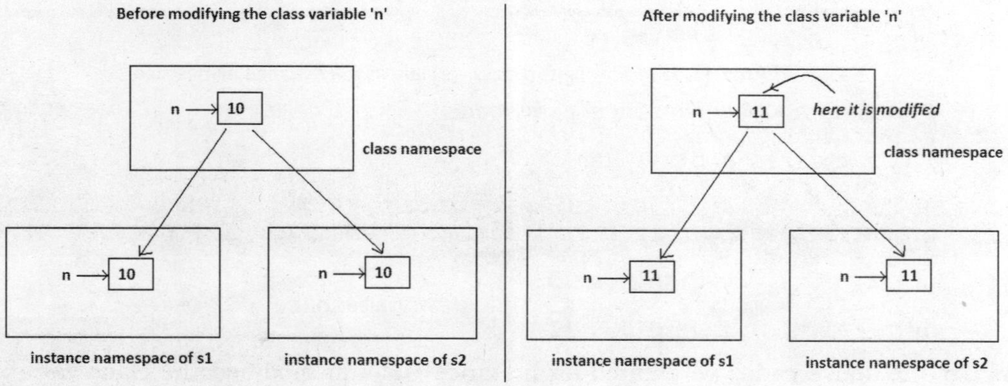

Figure 13.2: Modifying the class variable in the class namespace

```
# understanding class namespace
class Student:
    # this is a class var
    n=10

# access class var in the class namespace
print(Student.n)   # displays 10
Student.n+=1       # modify it in class namespace
print(Student.n)   # displays 11
```

We know that a single copy of class variable is shared by all the instances. So, if the class variable is modified in the class namespace, since same copy of the variable is modified, the modified copy is available to all the instances. This is shown in Figure 13.2.

```
# modified class var is seen in all instances
s1 = Student()    # create s1 instance
print(s1.n)       # displays 11
s2 = Student()    # create s2 instance
print(s2.n)       # displays 11
```

What happens when the class variable is modified in the instance namespace? Since every instance will have its own namespace, if the class variable is modified in one instance namespace, it will not affect the variables in the other instance namespaces. This is shown in Figure 13.3. To access the class variable at the instance level, we have to create instance first and then refer to the variable as instancename.variable.

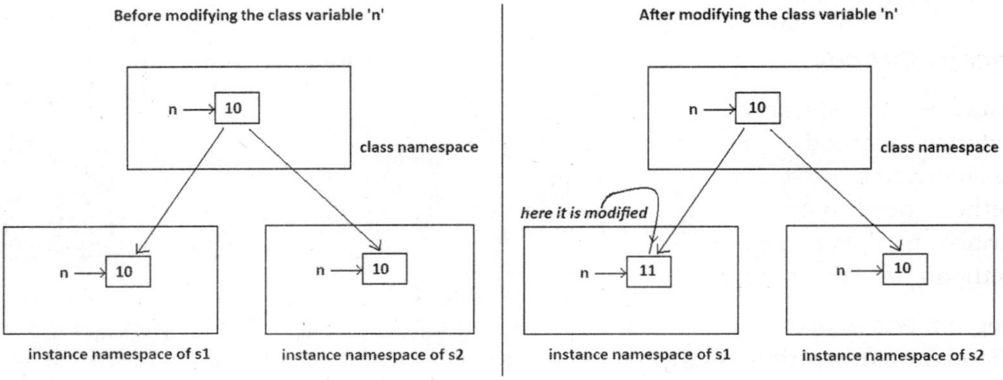

Figure 13.3: Modifying the class variable in the instance namespace

```
# understanding instance namespace
class Student:
    # this is a class var
    n=10

# access class var in the s1 instance namespace
s1 = Student()
print(s1.n)    # displays 10
s1.n+=1    # modify it in s1 instance namespace
print(s1.n)    # displays 11
```

As per the above code, we created an instance 's1' and modified the class variable 'n' in that instance. So, the modified value of 'n' can be seen only in that instance. When we create other instances like 's2', there will be still the original value of 'n' available. See the code below:

```
# modified class var is not seen in other instances
s2 = Student()    # this is another instance
print(s2.n)    # displays 10, not 11
```

Types of Methods

By this time, we got some knowledge about the methods written in a class. The purpose of a method is to process the variables provided in the class or in the method. We already know that the variables declared in the class are called class variables (or static variables) and the variables declared in the constructor are called instance variables. We can classify the methods in the following 3 types:

- Instance methods
  - (a) Accessor methods
  - (b) Mutator methods
- Class methods
- Static methods

Instance Methods

Instance methods are the methods which act upon the instance variables of the class. Instance methods are bound to instances (or objects) and hence called as: instancename.method(). Since instance variables are available in the instance, instance methods need to know the memory address of the instance. This is provided through 'self' variable by default as first parameter for the instance method. While calling the instance methods, we need not pass any value to the 'self' variable.

Program 5 is an extension to our previous Student class. In this program, we are creating a Student class with a constructor that defines 'name' and 'marks' as instance variables. An instance method display() will display the values of these variables. We added another instance methods by the name calculate() that calculates the grades of the student depending on the 'marks'.

Program

Program 5: A Python program using a student class with instance methods to process the data of several students.

```
# instance methods to process data of the objects
class Student:
    # this is a constructor.
    def __init__(self, n = '', m=0):
        self.name = n
        self.marks = m
    # this is an instance method.
    def display(self):
        print('Hi', self.name)
        print('Your marks', self.marks)

    # to calculate grades based on marks.
    def calculate(self):
        if(self.marks>=600):
            print('You got first grade')
```

```
        elif(self.marks>=500):
            print('You got second grade')
        elif(self.marks>=350):
            print('You got third grade')
        else:
            print('You are failed')

# create instances with some data from keyboard
n = int(input('How many students? '))

i=0
while(i<n):
    name = input('Enter name: ')
    marks = int(input('Enter marks: '))

    # create Student class instance and store data
    s = Student(name, marks)
    s.display()
    s.calculate()
    i+=1
    print('---------------------')
```

Output:

```
C:\>python cl.py
How many students? 3
Enter name: Vishnu Vardhan
Enter marks: 800
Hi Vishnu Vardhan
Your marks 800
You got first grade
---------------------
Enter name: Tilak Prabhu
Enter marks: 360
Hi Tilak Prabhu
Your marks 360
You got third grade
---------------------
Enter name: Gunasheela
Enter marks: 550
Hi Gunasheela
Your marks 550
You got second grade
---------------------
```

Instance methods are of two types: accessor methods and mutator methods. Accessor methods simply access or read data of the variables. They do not modify the data in the variables. Accessor methods are generally written in the form of getXXX() and hence they are also called *getter* methods. For example,

```
def getName(self):
    return self.name
```

Here, getName() is an accessor method since it is reading and returning the value of 'name' instance variable. It is not modifying the value of the name variable. On the other hand, mutator methods are the methods which not only read the data but also modify them. They are written in the form of setXXX() and hence they are also called *setter* methods. For example,

```
    def setName(self, name):
        self.name = name
```

Here, setName() is a mutator method since it is modifying the value of 'name' variable by storing new name. In the method body, 'self.name' represents the instance variable 'name' and the right hand side 'name' indicates the parameter that receives the new value from outside. In Program 6, we are redeveloping the Student class using accessor and mutator methods.

Program

Program 6: A Python program to store data into instances using mutator methods and to retrieve data from the instances using accessor methods.

```
# accessor and mutator methods
class Student:

    # mutator method
    def setName(self, name):
        self.name = name

    # accessor method
    def getName(self):
        return self.name

    # mutator method
    def setMarks(self, marks):
        self.marks = marks

    # accessor method
    def getMarks(self):
        return self.marks

# create instances with some data from keyboard
n = int(input('How many students? '))

i=0
while(i<n):
    # create Student class instance
    s = Student()
    name = input('Enter name: ')
    s.setName(name)
    marks = int(input('Enter marks: '))
    s.setMarks(marks)

    # retrieve data from Student class instance
    print('Hi', s.getName())
    print('Your marks', s.getMarks())

    i+=1
    print('-------------------')
```

Output:

```
C:\>python cl.py
How many students? 2
Enter name: Vinay Krishna
Enter marks: 890
Hi Vinay Krishna
```

```
Your marks 890
------------------
Enter name: Vimala Rao
Enter marks: 750
Hi Vimala Rao
Your marks 750
------------------
```

Since mutator methods define the instance variables and store data, we need not write the constructor in the class to initialize the instance variables. This is the reason we did not use constructor in Student class in Program 6.

Class Methods

These methods act on class level. Class methods are the methods which act on the class variables or static variables. These methods are written using @classmethod decorator above them. By default, the first parameter for class methods is 'cls' which refers to the class itself. For example, 'cls.var' is the format to refer to the class variable. These methods are generally called using the classname.method(). The processing which is commonly needed by all the instances of the class is handled by the class methods. In Program 7, we are going to develop Bird class. All birds in the Nature have only 2 wings. So, we take 'wings' as a class variable. Now a copy of this class variable is available to all the instances of Bird class. The class method fly() can be called as Bird.fly().

Program

Program 7: A Python program to use class method to handle the common feature of all the instances of Bird class.

```
# understanding class methods
class Bird:
    # this is a class var
    wings = 2

    # this is a class method
    @classmethod
    def fly(cls, name):
        print('{} flies with {} wings'.format(name, cls.wings))

# display information for 2 birds
Bird.fly('Sparrow')
Bird.fly('Pigeon')
```

Output:

```
C:\>python cl.py
Sparrow flies with 2 wings
Pigeon flies with 2 wings
```

Static Methods

We need static methods when the processing is at the class level but we need not involve the class or instances. Static methods are used when some processing is related to the class but does not need the class or its instances to perform any work. For example, setting environmental variables, counting the number of instances of the class or changing an attribute in another class, etc. are the tasks related to a class. Such tasks are handled by static methods. Also, static methods can be used to accept some values, process them and return the result. In this case the involvement of neither the class nor the objects is needed. Static methods are written with a decorator @staticmethod above them. Static methods are called in the form of classname.method(). In Program 8, we are creating a static method noObjects() that counts the number of objects or instances created to Myclass. In Myclass, we have written a constructor that increments the class variable 'n' every time an instance is created. This incremented value of 'n' is displayed by the noObjects() method.

Program

Program 8: A Python program to create a static method that counts the number of instances created for a class.

```
# understanding static methods
class Myclass:
    # this is class var or static var
    n=0

    # constructor that increments n when an instance is created
    def __init__(self):
        Myclass.n = Myclass.n+1

    # this is a static method to display the no. of instances
    @staticmethod
    def noObjects():
        print('No. of instances created: ', Myclass.n)

# create 3 instances
obj1 = Myclass()
obj2 = Myclass()
obj3 = Myclass()
Myclass.noObjects()
```

Output:

```
C:\>python cl.py
No. of instances created: 3
```

In the next program, we accept a number from the keyboard and return the result of its square root value. Here, there is no need of class or object and hence we can write a static method to perform this task.

Program

Program 9: A Python program to create a static method that calculates the square root value of a given number.

```
# a static method to find square root value
import math
class Sample:
    @staticmethod
    def calculate(x):
```

```
        result = math.sqrt(x)
        return result

# accept a number from keyboard
num = float(input('Enter a number: '))

# call the static method and pass num
res = Sample.calculate(num)
print('The square root of {} is {:.2f}'.format(num, res))
```

Output:

```
C:\>python calc.py
Enter a number: 49
The square root of 49.0 is 7.00
```

In Program 10, we are creating a Bank class. An account in the bank is characterized by name of the customer and balance amount in the account. Hence a constructor is written that defines 'name' and 'balance' attributes. If balance is not given, then it is taken as 0.0. The deposit() method is useful to handle the deposits and the withdraw() method is useful to handle the withdrawals. Bank class can be used by creating an instance 'b' to it as:

```
b = Bank(name)
```

Since the constructor expects the name of the customer, we have to pass the name in the parentheses while creating the instance of the Bank class. In the while loop, we are displaying a one line menu as:

```
print('d -Deposit, w -Withdraw, e -Exit')
```

When the user choice is 'e' or 'E', we will terminate the program by calling the exit() method of 'sys' module.

Program

Program 10: A Python program to create a Bank class where deposits and withdrawals can be handled by using instance methods.

```
# A class to handle deposits and withdrawals in a bank
import sys
class Bank(object):
    """ Bank related transactions """

    # to initialize name and balance instance vars
    def __init__(self, name, balance=0.0):
        self.name = name
        self.balance = balance

    # to add deposit amount to balance
    def deposit(self, amount):
        self.balance += amount
        return self.balance

    # to deduct withdrawal amount from balance
    def withdraw(self, amount):
        if amount >self.balance:
            print('Balance amount is less, so no withdrawal.')
        else:
```

```
                self.balance -= amount
            return self.balance

# using the Bank class
# create an account with the given name and balance 0.00
name = input('Enter name: ')
b = Bank(name)   # this is instance of Bank class

# repeat continuously till choice is 'e' or 'E'.
while(True):
    print('d -Deposit, w -Withdraw, e -Exit')
    choice = input('Your choice: ')
    if choice == 'e' or choice == 'E':
        sys.exit()
    # amount for deposit or withdraw
    amt = float(input('Enter amount: '))

    # do the transaction
    if choice == 'd' or choice == 'D':
        print('Balance after deposit: ', b.deposit(amt))
    elif choice == 'w' or choice == 'W':
        print('Balance after withdrawal: ', b.withdraw(amt))
```

Output:

```
C:\>python cl.py
Enter name: Madhuri
d -Deposit, w -Withdraw, e -Exit
Your choice: d
Enter amount: 10000
Balance after deposit: 10000.0
d -Deposit, w -Withdraw, e -Exit
Your choice: w
Enter amount: 3500
Balance after withdrawal: 6500.0
d -Deposit, w -Withdraw, e -Exit
Your choice: e
```

Passing Members of One Class to Another Class

It is possible to pass the members (i.e. attributes and methods) of a class to another class. Let's take an Emp class with a constructor that defines attributes 'id', 'name', and 'salary'. This class has an instance method display() to display these values. If we create an object (or instance) of Emp class, it contains a copy of all the attributes and methods. To pass all these members of Emp class to another class, we should pass Emp class instance to the other class. For example, let's create an instance of Emp class as:

```
e = Emp()
```

Then pass this instance 'e' to a method of other class, as:

```
Myclass.mymethod(e)
```

Here, Myclass is the other class and mymethod() is a static method that belongs to Myclass. In Myclass, the method mymethod() will be declared as a static method as it acts neither on the class variables nor instance variables of Myclass. The purpose of mymethod() is to change the attribute of Emp class. For example, mymethod() may increment the employee salary by 1000 rupees as shown below:

```
def mymethod(e):
    # increment salary in e by 1000
    e.salary+=1000;    # modify attribute of Emp class
    e.display()   # call the method of Emp class
```

So, the point is this: by passing the instance of a class, we are passing all the attributes and methods to another class. In the other class, it is possible to utilize them as needed. In our example, Myclass method, i.e. mymethod() is utilizing the salary attribute and display() methods of Emp class.

Program

Program 11: A Python program to create Emp class and make all the members of the Emp class available to another class, i.e. Myclass.

```
# this class contains employee details
class Emp:
    # this is a constructor.
    def __init__(self, id, name, salary):
        self.id = id
        self.name = name
        self.salary = salary

    # this is an instance method.
    def display(self):
        print('Id=', self.id)
        print('Name=', self.name)
        print('Salary= ', self.salary)

# this class displays employee details
class Myclass:
    # method to receive Emp class instance
    # and display employee details
    @staticmethod
    def mymethod(e):
        # increment salary of e by 1000
        e.salary+=1000;
        e.display()

# create Emp class instance e
e = Emp(10, 'Raj kumar', 15000.75)
# call static method of Myclass and pass e
Myclass.mymethod(e)
```

Output:

```
C:\>python cl.py
Id= 10
Name= Raj kumar
Salary= 16000.75
```

Let's understand that static methods are used when the class variables or instance variables are not disturbed. We have to use a static method when we want to pass some values from outside and perform some calculation in the method. Here, we are not touching the class variable or instance variables. Program 12 shows a static method that calculates the value of a number raised to a power.

Program

Program 12: A Python program to calculate power value of a number with the help of a static method.

```
# another example for static method
class Myclass:
    # method to calculate x to the power of n
    @staticmethod
    def mymethod(x, n):
        result = x**n
        print('{} to the power of {} is {}'.format(x, n, result))

# call the static method
Myclass.mymethod(5, 3)
Myclass.mymethod(5, 4)
```

Output:

```
C:\>python cl.py
5 to the power of 3 is 125
5 to the power of 4 Is 625
```

Inner Classes

Writing a class within another class is called creating an inner class or nested class. For example, if we write class B inside class A, then B is called inner class or nested class. Inner classes are useful when we want to sub group the data of a class. For example, let's take a person's data like name, age, date of birth etc. Here, name contains a single value like 'Charles', age contains a single value like '30' but the date of birth does not contain a single value. Rather, it contains three values like date, month and year. So, we need to take these three values as a sub group. Hence it is better to write date of birth as a separate class Dob inside the Person class. This Dob will contain instance variables dd, mm and yy which represent the date of birth details of the person.

Generally, the inner class object is created within the outer class. Let's take Person class as outer class and Dob as inner class. Dob class object is created in the constructor of the Person class as:

```
class Person:
    def __init__(self):
        self.name = 'Charles'
        self.db = self.Dob()   # this is Dob object
```

In the preceding code, 'db' represents the inner class object. When the outer class object is created, it contains a sub object that is inner class object. Hence, we can refer outer class and inner class members as:

```
p = Person()    # create outer class object
p.display()   # call outer class method
print(p.name)   # refer to outer class instance variable
```

```
x = p.db    # create inner class object
x.display()    # call inner class method
print(x.yy)    # refer to inner class instance variable
```

Program

Program 13: A Python program to create Dob class within Person class.

```
# inner class example
class Person:
    def __init__(self):
        self.name = 'Charles'
        self.db = self.Dob()

    def display(self):
        print('Name= ', self.name)

    # this is inner class
    class Dob:
        def __init__(self):
            self.dd = 10
            self.mm = 5
            self.yy = 1988
        def display(self):
            print('Dob= {}/{}/{}'.format(self.dd, self.mm, self.yy))

# creating Person class object
p = Person()
p.display()

# create inner class object
x = p.db
x.display()
```

Output:

```
C:\>python inner.py
Name= Charles
Dob= 10/5/1988
```

It is not compulsory to create inner class object inside outer class. That means, we need not write the following statement in the Person class constructor:

```
self.db = self.Dob()
```

If we do not write this, then there is no relation between the outer class object and inner class object. Then how to refer to inner class members is the question. In this case, we have to create outer class object and then using dot operator, we should mention the inner class object as:

```
x = Person().Dob()    # create inner class object
x.display()    # call inner class method
print(x.yy)    # refer to inner class instance variable
```

This concept is shown in Program 14.

Program

Program 14: A Python program to create another version of Dob class within Person class.

```
# inner class example - v2.0
class Person:
    def __init__(self):
        self.name = 'Charles'

    def display(self):
        print('Name= ', self.name)

    # this is inner class
    class Dob:
        def __init__(self):
            self.dd = 10
            self.mm = 5
            self.yy = 1988

        def display(self):
            print('Dob= {}/{}/{}'.format(self.dd, self.mm, self.yy))

# creating Person class object
p = Person()
p.display()
# create Dob class object as sub object to Person class object
x = Person().Dob()
x.display()
print(x.yy)
```

Output:

```
C:\>python inner.py
Name= Charles
Dob= 10/5/1988
1988
```

Points to Remember

- A class is a model or plan to create objects. The objects of a class are also called instances.
- A class contains attributes which are nothing but variables.
- A class can contain methods which are useful to process variables.
- A method is a function that is written inside a class.
- The object class is the base class from where all other classes are derived.
- To use a class, generally we should create an instance. To create an instance of a class, we can write:

  instancename = Classname()
- A constructor is a special method that is useful to declare and initialize the instance variables. The general format of the constructor is:

  def __init__(self, parameters):

- A constructor is called only once at the time of creating an instance or object.
- 'self' is a variable that contains by default the memory address of the instance. We need not pass anything to this variable.
- The 'self' variable becomes the first parameter for constructor and instance methods.
- Instance variables are the variables whose separate copy is created in every instance (or object). Instance variables are referenced as instancename.var.
- Class variables are the variables whose single copy is available to all the instances of the class. Class variables are also called static variables. Class variables are referenced as classname.var.
- A namespace represents a memory block where names are mapped (or linked) to objects. A class will have class namespace and an instance will have its own namespace called instance namespace.
- The variables in the class namespace are referenced as classname.var. The variables in the instance namespace are referenced as instancename.var.
- Instance methods are the methods which act upon the instance variables of the class. Instance methods are bound to instances (or objects) and hence called as: instancename.method().
- Instance methods use 'self' as first default parameter.
- Instance methods are again classified as accessor methods and mutator methods. Accessor methods access or read the instance variables; whereas, mutator methods not only read the instance variables but also modify them.
- Generally, accessor methods are written in the form of getXXX() and hence they are also called getter methods. Mutator methods are written in the form of setXXX() and hence are called setter methods.
- Class methods are the methods which act on the class variables or static variables. These methods are written using @classmethod decorator above them. These methods are generally called using the classname.method().
- Class methods are written using 'cls' as their first parameter.
- Static methods are used when some processing is related to the class but does not need the class or its instances to perform any work. Static methods are written with a decorator @staticmethod above them. Static methods are called in the form of classname.method().
- It is possible to create inner classes within a class. To refer to the inner class members, we can create inner class object as:

  innerobj = Outerclass().Innerclass()

  innerobj = outerobj.innerobj

CHAPTER

14

INHERITANCE AND POLYMORPHISM

Software development is a team effort. Several programmers will work as a team to develop software. When a programmer develops a class, he will use its features by creating an instance to it. When another programmer wants to create another class which is similar to the class already created, then he need not create the class from the scratch. He can simply use the features of the existing class in creating his own class. Let's take an example to understand this.

A programmer in the software development is creating Teacher class with setter() and getter() methods as shown in Program 1. Then he saved this code in a file 'teacher.py'.

Program

Program 1: A Python program to create Teacher class and store it into teacher.py module.

```
# this is Teacher class. save this code in teacher.py file
class Teacher:
    def setid(self, id):
        self.id = id

    def getid(self):
        return self.id

    def setname(self, name):
        self.name = name

    def getname(self):
        return self.name

    def setaddress(self, address):
        self.address = address

    def getaddress(self):
        return self.address
```

```
    def setsalary(self, salary):
        self.salary = salary

    def getsalary(self):
        return self.salary
```

When the programmer wants to use this Teacher class that is available in teacher.py file, he can simply import this class into his program and use it as shown here:

Program

Program 2: A Python program to use the Teacher class.

```
# save this code as inh.py file
# using Teacher class
from teacher import Teacher
# create instance
t = Teacher()

# store data into the instance
t.setid(10)
t.setname('Prakash')
t.setaddress('HNO-10, Rajouri gardens, Delhi')
t.setsalary(25000.50)

# retrieve data from instance and display
print('id= ', t.getid())
print('name= ', t.getname())
print('address= ', t.getaddress())
print('salary= ', t.getsalary())
```

Output:

```
C:\>python inh.py
id= 10
name= Prakash
address= HNO-10, Rajouri gardens, Delhi
salary= 25000.5
```

So, the program is working well. There is no problem. Once the Teacher class is completed, the programmer stored teacher.py program in a central database that is available to all the members of the team. So, Teacher class is made available through the module teacher.py, as shown in Figure 14.1:

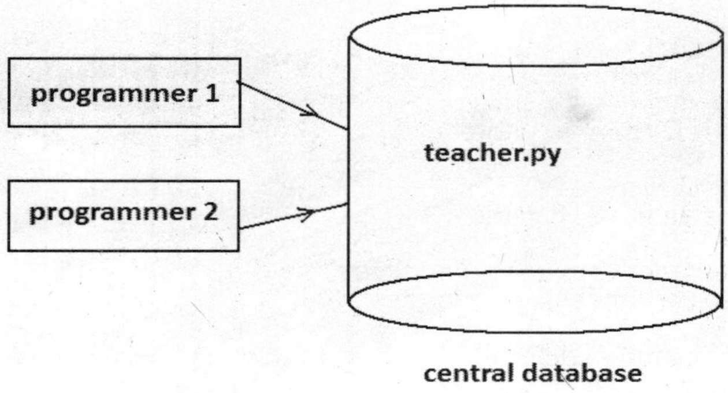

Figure 14.1: The teacher.py module is created and available in the project database

Now, another programmer in the same team wants to create a Student class. He is planning the Student class without considering the Teacher class as shown in Program 3.

Program

Program 3: A Python program to create Student class and store it into student.py module.

```
# this is Student class -v1.0. save it as student.py
class Student:
    def setid(self, id):
        self.id = id

    def getid(self):
        return self.id

    def setname(self, name):
        self.name = name

    def getname(self):
        return self.name

    def setaddress(self, address):
        self.address = address

    def getaddress(self):
        return self.address

    def setmarks(self, marks):
        self.marks = marks

    def getmarks(self):
        return self.marks
```

Now, the second programmer who created this Student class and saved it as student.py can use it whenever he needs. Using the Student class is shown in Program 4.

Program

Program 4: A Python program to use the Student class which is already available in student.py

```
# save this code as inh.py
# using Student class
from student import Student
# create instance
s = Student()

# store data into the instance
s.setid(100)
s.setname('Rakesh')
s.setaddress('HNO-22, Ameerpet, Hyderabad')
s.setmarks(970)
```

```
# retrieve data from instance and display
print('id= ', s.getid())
print('name= ', s.getname())
print('address= ', s.getaddress())
print('marks= ', s.getmarks())
```

Output:

```
C:\>python inh.py
id= 100
name= Rakesh
address= HNO-22, Ameerpet, Hyderabad
marks= 970
```

So far, so nice! If we compare the Teacher class and the Student classes, we can understand that 75% of the code is same in both the classes. That means most of the code being planned by the second programmer in his Student class is already available in the Teacher class. Then why doesn't he use it for his advantage? Our idea is this: instead of creating a new class altogether, he can reuse the code which is already available. This is shown in Program 5.

Program

Program 5:A Python program to create Student class by deriving it from the Teacher class.

```
# Student class - v2.0.save it as student.py
from teacher import Teacher
class Student(Teacher):
    def setmarks(self, marks):
        self.marks = marks

    def getmarks(self):
        return self.marks
```

The preceding code will be same as the first version of the Student class. Observe this code. In the first statement we are importing Teacher class from teacher module so that the Teacher class is now available to this program. Then we are creating Student class as:

```
class Student(Teacher):
```

This means the Student class is derived from Teacher class. Once we write like this, all the members of Teacher class are available to the Student class. Hence we can use them without rewriting them in the Student class. In addition, the following two methods are needed by the Student class but not available in the Teacher class:

```
def setmarks(self, marks):
def getmarks(self):
```

Hence, we wrote only these two methods in the Student class. Now, we can use the Student class as we did earlier. Creating the instance to the Student class and calling the methods as:

```
# create instance
s = Student()
# store data into the instance
s.setid(100)
s.setname('Rakesh')
s.setaddress('HNO-22, Ameerpet, Hyderabad')
s.setmarks(970)

# retrieve data from instance and display
print('id= ', s.getid())
print('name= ', s.getname())
print('address= ', s.getaddress())
print('marks= ', s.getmarks())
```

In other words, we can say that we have created Student class from the Teacher class. This is called inheritance. The original class, i.e. Teacher class is called base class or super class and the newly created class, i.e. the Student class is called the sub class or derived class. So, how can we define inheritance? Deriving new classes from the existing classes such that the new classes inherit all the members of the existing classes, is called inheritance. The syntax for inheritance is:

```
class Subclass(Baseclass):
```

The next question is why the base class members are automatically available to sub class? When an object to Student class is created, it contains a copy of Teacher class within it. This means there is a relation between the Teacher class and Student class objects. This is the reason Teacher class members are available to Student class. Note that we do not create Teacher class object, but still a copy of it is available to Student class object. Please see the object diagram of Student class in Figure 14.2. We can understand that all the members (i.e., variables and methods) of Teacher class as well as Student class are available in the Student class object.

Then, what is the advantage of inheritance? Please look at Student class version 1 and Student class version 2. Clearly, second version is smaller and easier to develop. By using inheritance, a programmer can develop the classes very easily. Hence programmer's productivity is increased. Productivity is a term that refers to the code developed by the programmer in a given span of time. If the programmer used inheritance, he will be able to develop more code in less time. So, his productivity is increased. This will increase the overall productivity of the organization, which means more profits for the organization and better growth for the programmer.

In inheritance, we always create only the sub class object. Generally, we do not create super class object. The reason is clear. Since all the members of the super class are available to sub class, when we create an object, we can access the members of both the super and sub classes. But if we create an object to super class, we can access only the super class members and not the sub class members.

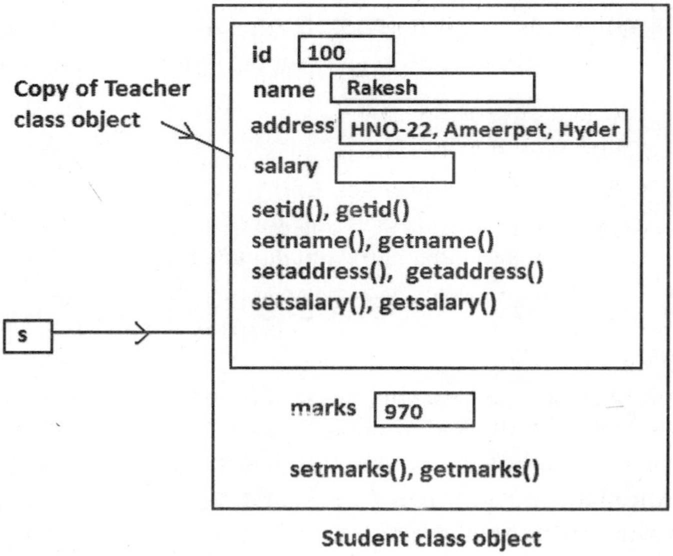

Figure 14.2: Student class object contains a copy of Teacher class object

Constructors in Inheritance

In the previous programs, we have inherited the Student class from the Teacher class. All the methods and the variables in those methods of the Teacher class (base class) are accessible to the Student class (sub class). Are the constructors of the base class accessible to the sub class or not – is the next question we will answer. In Program 6, we are taking a super class by the name 'Father' and derived a sub class 'Son' from it. The Father class has a constructor where a variable 'property' is declared and initialized with 800000.00. When Son is created from Father, this constructor is by default available to Son class. When we call the method of the super class using sub class object, it will display the value of the 'property' variable.

Program

Program 6: A Python program to access the base class constructor from sub class.

```
# base class constructor is available to sub class
class Father:
    def __init__(self):
        self.property = 800000.00

    def display_property(self):
        print('Father\'s property= ', self.property)

class Son(Father):
    pass   # we do not want to write anything in the sub class
```

```
# create sub class instance and display father's property
s = Son()
s.display_property()
```

Output:

```
C:\>python inh.py
Father's property= 800000.0
```

The conclusion is this: like the variables and methods, the constructors in the super class are also available to the sub class object by default.

Overriding Super Class Constructors and Methods

When the programmer writes a constructor in the sub class, the super class constructor is not available to the sub class. In this case, only the sub class constructor is accessible from the sub class object. That means the sub class constructor is replacing the super class constructor. This is called *constructor overriding.* Similarly in the sub class, if we write a method with exactly same name as that of super class method, it will override the super class method. This is called *method overriding.* Consider Program 7.

Program

Program 7: A Python program to override super class constructor and method in sub class.

```
# overriding the base class constructor and method in sub class
class Father:
    def __init__(self):
        self.property = 800000.00

    def display_property(self):
        print('Father\'s property= ', self.property)

class Son(Father):
    def __init__(self):
        self.property = 200000.00

    def display_property(self):
        print('Child\'s property= ', self.property)

# create sub class instance and display father's property
s = Son()
s.display_property()
```

Output:

```
C:\>python inh.py
Child's property= 200000.00
```

In Program 7, in the sub class, we created a constructor and a method with exactly same names as those of super class. When we refer to them, only the sub class constructor and method are executed. The base class constructor and method are not available to the sub class object. That means they are overridden. Overriding should be done when the programmer wants to modify the existing behavior of a constructor or method in his sub class.

In this case, how to call the super class constructor so that we can access the father's property from the Son class? For this purpose, we should call the constructor of the super class from the constructor of the sub class using the super() method.

The super() Method

super() is a built-in method which is useful to call the super class constructor or methods from the sub class. Any constructor written in the super class is not available to the sub class if the sub class has a constructor. Then how can we initialize the super class instance variables and use them in the sub class? This is done by calling the super class constructor using the super() method from inside the sub class constructor. super() is a built-in method in Python that contains the history of super class methods. Hence, we can use super() to refer to super class constructor and methods from a sub class. So super() can be used as:

```
super().__init__()       # call super class constructor
super().__init__(arguments)# call super class constructor and pass
                            # arguments
super().method()    # call super class method
```

When there is a constructor with parameters in the super class, we have to create another constructor with parameters in the sub class and call the super class constructor using super() from the sub class constructor. In the following example, we are calling the super class constructor and passing 'property' value to it from the sub class constructor.

```
# this is sub class constructor
def __init__(self, property1=0, property=0):
    super().__init__(property)  # send property value to superclass
                                # constructor
    self.property1= property1   # store property1 value into subclass
                                # variable
```

As shown in the preceding code, the sub class constructor has 2 parameters. They are 'property1' and 'property'. So, when we create an object (or instance) to sub class, we should pass two values, as:

```
s = Son(200000.00, 800000.00)
```

Now, the first value 200000 is stored into 'property1' and the second value 800000.00 is stored into 'property'. Afterwards, this 'property' value is sent to super class constructor in the first statement of the sub class constructor. This is shown in Program 8.

Program

Program 8: A Python program to call the super class constructor in the sub class using super().

```
# accessing base class constructor in sub class
class Father:
```

```
        def __init__(self, property=0):
            self.property = property

        def display_property(self):
            print('Father\'s property= ', self.property)

    class Son(Father):
        def __init__(self, property1=0, property=0):
            super().__init__(property)
            self.property1= property1

        def display_property(self):
            print('Total property of child= ', self.property1 + self.property)

    # create sub class instance and display father's property
    s = Son(200000.00, 800000.00)
    s.display_property()
```

Output:

```
C:\>python inh.py
Total property of child= 1000000.0
```

To understand the use of super() in a better way, let's write another Python program where we want to calculate areas of a square and a rectangle. Here, we are writing a Square class with one instance variable 'x' since to calculate the area of square, we need one value. Another class Rectangle is derived from Square. So, the value of 'x' is inherited by Rectangle class from Square class. To calculate area of rectangle we need two values. So, we take a constructor with two parameters 'x' and 'y' in the sub class. In this program, we are calling the super class constructor and passing 'x' value as:

```
super().__init__(x)
```

We are also calling super class area() method as:

```
super().area()
```

In this way, super() can be used to refer to the constructors and methods of super class.

Program

Program 9: A Python program to access base class constructor and method in the sub class using super().

```
# Accessing base class constructor and method in the sub class
class Square:
    def __init__(self, x):
        self.x = x

    def area(self):
        print('Area of square= ', self.x*self.x)

class Rectangle(Square):
    def __init__(self, x, y):
        super().__init__(x)
        self.y = y
```

```
        def area(self):
            super().area()
            print('Area of rectangle= ', self.x*self.y)

    # find areas of square and rectangle
    a, b = [float(x) for x in input("Enter two measurements: ").split()]
    r = Rectangle(a,b)
    r.area()
```

Output:

```
C:\>python inh.py
Enter two measurements: 10  5.5
Area of square= 100.0
Area of rectangle= 55.0
```

Types of Inheritance

As we have seen so far, the main advantage of inheritance is code reusability. The members of the super class are reusable in the sub classes. Let's remember that all classes in Python are built from a single super class called 'object'. If a programmer creates his own classes, by default object class will become super class for them internally. This is the reason, sometimes while creating any new class, we mention the object class name in parentheses as:

```
class Myclass(object):
```

Here, we are indicating that object is the super class for Myclass. Of course, writing object class name is not mandatory and hence the preceding code is equivalent to writing:

```
class Myclass:
```

Now, coming to the types of inheritance, there are mainly 2 types of inheritance available. They are:

- Single inheritance
- Multiple inheritance

Single Inheritance

Deriving one or more sub classes from a single base class is called 'single inheritance'. In single inheritance, we always have only one base class, but there can be n number of sub classes derived from it. For example, 'Bank' is a single base class from where we derive 'AndhraBank' and 'StateBank' as sub classes. This is called single inheritance. Consider Figure 14.3. It is convention that we should use the arrow head towards the base class (i.e. super class) in the inheritance diagrams.

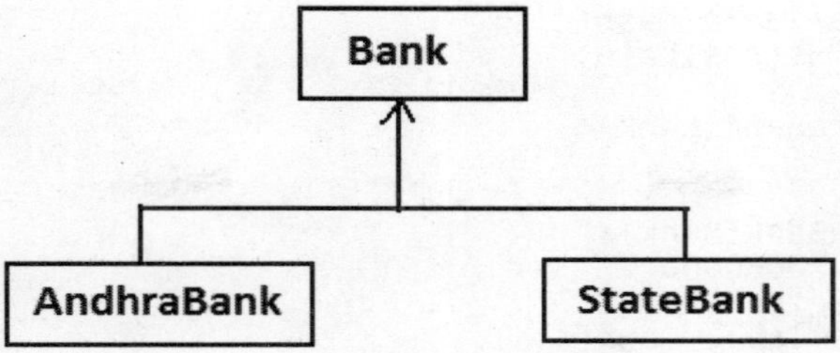

Figure 14.3: Single Inheritance Example

In Program 10, we are deriving two sub classes AndhraBank and StateBank from the single base class, i.e. Bank. All the members (i.e. variables and methods) of Bank class will be available to the sub classes. In the Bank class, we have some 'cash' variable and a method to display that, as:

```
class Bank(object):
    cash = 100000000
    @classmethod
    def available_cash(cls):
        print(cls.cash)
```

Here, the class variable 'cash' is declared in the class and initialized to 10 crores. The available_cash() is a class method that is accessing this variable as 'cls.cash'. When we derive AndhraBank class from Bank class as:

```
class AndhraBank(Bank):
```

The 'cash' variable and available_cash() methods are accessible to AndhraBank class and we can use them inside this sub class. Similarly, we can derive another sub class by the name StateBank from Bank class as:

```
class StateBank(Bank):
    cash = 20000000    # class variable in the present sub class
    @classmethod
    def available_cash(cls):
        print(cls.cash + Bank.cash)
```

Here, StateBank has its own class variable 'cash' that contains 2 crores. So, the total cash available to StateBank is 10 crores + 2 crores = 12 crores. Please observe the last line in the preceding code:

```
print(cls.cash + Bank.cash)
```

Here, 'cls.cash' represents the current class's 'cash' variable and 'Bank.cash' represents the Bank base class 'cash' variable.

Program

Program 10: A Python program showing single inheritance in which two sub classes are derived from a single base class.

```
# single inheritance
class Bank(object):
cash = 100000000
    @classmethod
```

```
        def available_cash(cls):
            print(cls.cash)

class AndhraBank(Bank):
    pass

class StateBank(Bank):
    cash = 20000000
    @classmethod
    def available_cash(cls):
        print(cls.cash + Bank.cash)

a = AndhraBank()
a.available_cash()

s = StateBank()
s.available_cash()
```

Output:

```
C:\>python inh.py
100000000
120000000
```

Multiple Inheritance

Deriving sub classes from multiple (or more than one) base classes is called 'multiple inheritance'. In this type of inheritance, there will be more than one super class and there may be one or more sub classes. All the members of the super classes are by default available to sub classes and the sub classes in turn can have their own members. The syntax for multiple inheritance is shown in the following statement:

```
class Subclass(Baseclass1, Baseclass2, … ):
```

The best example for multiple inheritance is that parents producing the children and the children inheriting the qualities of the parents. Consider Figure 14.4. Suppose, Father and Mother are two base classes and Child is the sub class derived from these two base classes. Now, whatever the members are found in the base classes are available to the sub class. For example, the Father class has a method that displays his height as 6.0 foot and the Mother class has a method that displays her color as brown. To make the Child class acquire both these qualities, we have to make it a sub class for both the Father and Mother class. This is shown in Program 11.

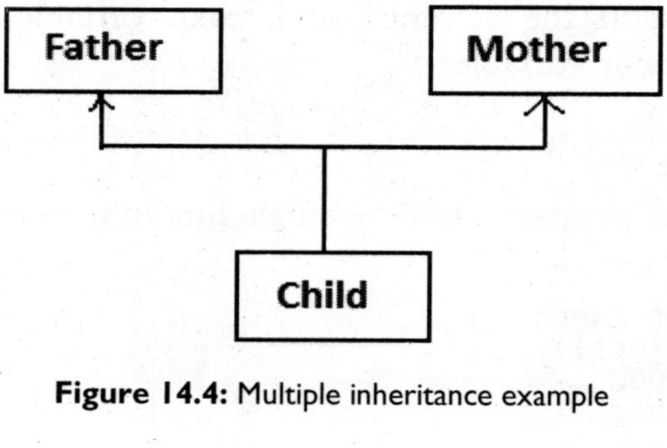

Figure 14.4: Multiple inheritance example

Program

Program 11: A Python program to implement multiple inheritance using two base classes.

```
# multiple inheritance
class Father:
    def height(self):
        print('Height is 6.0 foot')

class Mother:
    def color(self):
        print('Color is brown')

class Child(Father, Mother):
    pass

c = Child()
print('Child\'s inherited qualities: ')
c.height()
c.color()
```

Output:

```
C:\>python inh.py
Child's inherited qualities:
Height is 6.0 foot
Color is brown
```

Problems in Multiple Inheritance

If the sub class has a constructor, it overrides the super class constructor and hence the super class constructor is not available to the sub class. But writing constructor is very common to initialize the instance variables. In multiple inheritance, let's assume that a sub class 'C' is derived from two super classes 'A' and 'B' having their own constructors. Even the sub class 'C' also has its constructor. To derive C from A and B, we write:

```
class C(A, B):
```

Also, in class C's constructor, we call the super class super class constructor using super().__init__(). Now, if we create an object of class C, first the class C constructor is called. Then super().__init__() will call the class A's constructor. Consider Program 12.

Program

Program 12: A Python program to prove that only one class constructor is available to sub class in multiple inheritance.

```
# when super classes have constructors
class A(object):
    def __init__(self):
        self.a = 'a'
        print(self.a)
```

```
    class B(object):
        def __init__(self):
            self.b = 'b'
            print(self.b)

    class C(A, B):
        def __init__(self):
            self.c = 'c'
            print(self.c)
            super().__init__()

    # access the super class instance vars from C
    o = C()   # o is object of class C
```

Output:

```
C:\>python inh.py
c
a
```

The output of the program indicates that when class C object is created the C's constructor is called. In class C, we used the statement: super().__init__() that calls the class A's constructor only. Hence, we can access only class A's instance variables and not that of class B. In Program 12, we created sub class C, as:

```
class C(A, B):
```

This means class C is derived from A and B as shown in the Figure 14.5. Since all classes are sub classes of object class internally, we can take classes A and B are sub classes of object class.

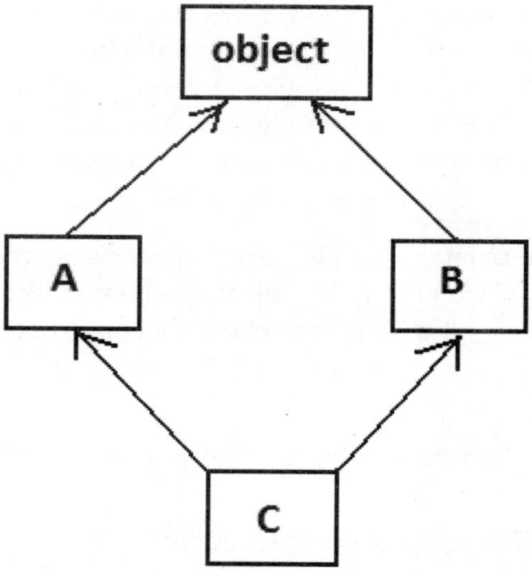

Figure 14.5: The effect of class C(A, B)

In the above figure, class A is at the left side and class B is at the right side for the class C. The searching of any attribute or method will start from the sub class C. Hence, C's constructor is accessed first. As a result, it will display 'c'. Observe the code in C's constructor:

```
    def __init__(self):
        self.c = 'c'
        print(self.c)
        super().__init__()
```

The last line in the preceding code, i.e. super().__init__() will call the constructor of the class which is at the left side. So, class A's constructor is executed and 'a' is displayed. If class A does not have a constructor, then it will call the constructor of the right hand side class, i.e. B. But since class A has a constructor, the search stopped here.

If the class C is derived as:

```
class C(B, A):
```

Then the output will be:

```
c
b
```

The problem we should understand is that the class C is unable to access constructors of both the super classes. It means C cannot access all the instance variables of both of its super classes. If C wants to access instance variables of both of its super classes, then the solution is to use super().__init__() in every class. This is shown in Program 13.

Program

Program 13: A Python program to access all the instance variables of both the base classes in multiple inheritance.

```
# when super classes have constructors - v2.0
class A(object):
    def __init__(self):
        self.a = 'a'
        print(self.a)
        super().__init__()

class B(object):
    def __init__(self):
        self.b = 'b'
        print(self.b)
        super().__init__()

class C(A, B):
    def __init__(self):
        self.c = 'c'
        print(self.c)
        super().__init__()

# access the super class instance vars from C
o = C()    # o is object of class C
```

Output:

```
C:\>python inh.py
c
a
b
```

We will apply the diagram given in Figure 14.5 to Program 13. The search will start from C. As the object of C is created, the constructor of C is called and 'c' is displayed. Then super().__init__() will call the constructor of left side class, i.e. of A. So, the constructor of A is called and 'a' is displayed. But inside the constructor of A, we again called its super class constructor using super().__init__(). Since 'object' is the super class for A, an attempt to execute object class constructor will be done. But object class does not have any constructor. So, the search will continue down to right hand side class of object class. That is class B. Hence B's constructor is executed and 'b' is displayed. After that the statement super().__init__() will attempt to execute constructor of B's super class. That is nothing but 'object' class. Since object class is already visited, the search stops here. As a result the output will be 'c', 'a', 'b'. Searching in this manner for constructors or methods is called *Method Resolution Order(MRO).*

Method Resolution Order (MRO)

In the multiple inheritance scenario, any specified attribute or method is searched first in the current class. If not found, the search continues into parent classes in depth-first, left to right fashion without searching the same class twice. Searching in this way is called Method Resolution Order (MRO). There are three principles followed by MRO.

- The first principle is to search for the sub class before going for its base classes. Thus if class B is inherited from A, it will search B first and then goes to A.
- The second principle is that when a class is inherited from several classes, it searches in the order from left to right in the base classes. For example, if class C is inherited from A and B as class C(A,B), then first it will search in A and then in B.
- The third principle is that it will not visit any class more than once. That means a class in the inheritance hierarchy is traversed only once exactly.

Understanding MRO gives us clear idea regarding which classes are executed and in which sequence. We can easily estimate the output when several base classes are involved. To know the MRO, we can use mro() method as:

```
Classname.mro()
```

This returns the sequence of execution of the classes, starting from the class with which the method is called. As depicted in Figure 14.6, we are going to create inheritance hierarchy with several classes. The sub class for all these classes is P. This is shown in Program 14.

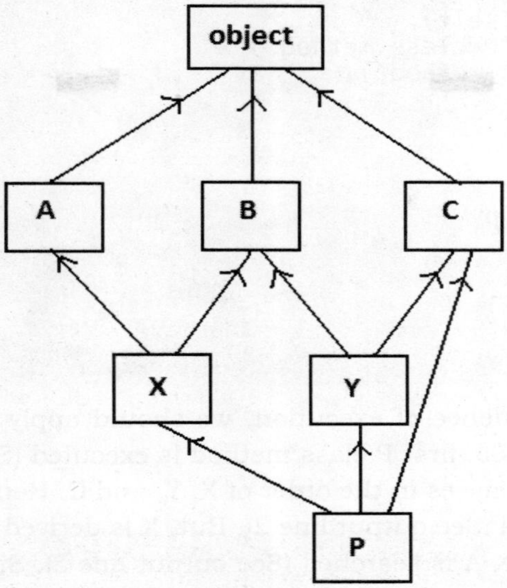

Figure 14.6: Inheritance hierarchy with several classes

Program

Program 14: A Python program to understand the order of execution of methods in several base classes according to MRO.

```
# multiple inheritance with several classes
class A(object):
    def method(self):
        print('A class method')
        super().method()

class B(object):
    def method(self):
        print('B class method')
        super().method()

class C(object):
    def method(self):
        print('C class method')

class X(A, B):
    def method(self):
        print('X class method')
        super().method()

class Y(B, C):
    def method(self):
        print('Y class method')
        super().method()
```

```
    class P(X,Y,C):
        def method(self):
            print('P class method')
            super().method()
    p = P()
    p.method()
```

Output:

```
    C:\>python inh.py
    P class method
    X class method
    A class method
    Y class method
    B class method
    C class method
```

To understand the sequence of execution, we should apply MRO. The sub class at the bottom-most level is P. So, first P class method is executed (See output line 1). This class is derived from 3 base classes in the order of X, Y, and C. Hence from left to right, P's first base class X is searched (See output line 2). But, X is derived from 2 more base classes in the order of A, B. Hence, A is searched (See output line 3). Since A does not have a user-defined super class, then it comes down to the class P's second base class, i.e. Y (See output line 4). But Y is derived from two more base classes in the order B, C. Hence from left to right, it searches in B first (See output line 5). Since class B does not have a user-defined super class, the search comes back to the 3rd base class of class P, i.e. class C (output line 6).

If we use mro() method on class P as:

```
    print(P.mro())
```

It will display the following output which can be matched with our program output:

```
    [<class '__main__.P'>, <class '__main__.X'>, <class '__main__.A'>,
<class '__main__.Y'>, <class '__main__.B'>, <class '__main__.C'>, <class
'object'>]
```

Polymorphism

Polymorphism is a word that came from two Greek words, *poly* means many and *morphos* means forms. If something exhibits various forms, it is called polymorphism. Let's take a simple example in our daily life. Assume that we have wheat flour. Using this wheat flour, we can make burgers, rotis, or loaves of bread. It means same wheat flour is taking different edible forms and hence we can say wheat flour is exhibiting polymorphism. Consider Figure 14.7:

Figure 14.7: Polymorphism where wheat flour takes different edible forms

In programming, a variable, object or a method will also exhibit the same nature as that of the wheat flour. A variable may store different types of data, an object may exhibit different behaviors in different contexts or a method may perform various tasks in Python. This type of behavior is called polymorphism. So, how can we define polymorphism? If a variable, object or method exhibits different behavior in different contexts, it is called polymorphism. Python has built-in polymorphism. The following topics are examples for polymorphism in Python:

- Duck typing philosophy of Python
- Operator overloading
- Method overloading
- Method overriding

Duck Typing Philosophy of Python

We know that in Python, the data type of the variables is not explicitly declared. This does not mean that Python variables do not have a type. Every variable or object in Python has a type and the type is implicitly assigned depending on the purpose for which the variable is used. In the following examples, 'x' is a variable. If we store integer into that variable, its type is taken as 'int' and if we store a string into that variable, its type is taken as 'str'. To check the type of a variable or object, we can use type() function.

```
x = 5    # store integer into x
print(type(x))    # display type of x
<class 'int'>

x = 'Hello'    # store string into x
print(type(x))    # display type of x
<class 'str'>
```

Python variables are names or tags that point to memory locations where data is stored. They are not worried about which data we are going to store. So, if 'x' is a variable, we can make it refer to an integer or a string as shown in the previous examples. We can conclude two points from this discussion:

1. Python's type system is 'strong' because every variable or object has a type that we can check with the type() function.
2. Python's type system is 'dynamic' since the type of a variable is not explicitly declared, but it changes with the content being stored.

Similarly, if we want to call a method on an object, we do not need to check the type of the object and we do not need to check whether that method really belongs to that object or not. For example, take a method call_talk() that accepts an object (or instance) .

```
def call_talk(obj):
    obj.talk()
```

The call_talk() method is receiving an object 'obj' from outside and using this object, it is invoking (or calling) talk() method. It is not required to mention the type of the object 'obj' or to check whether the talk() method belongs to that object or not. If the object passed to this method belongs to Duck class, then talk() method of Duck class is called. If the object belongs to Human class, then the talk() method of Human class is called. This is how Python understands. This is shown in Program 15.

Program

Program 15: A Python program to invoke a method on an object without knowing the type (or class) of the object.

```
# duck typing example
# Duck class contains talk() method
class Duck:
    def talk(self):
        print('Quack, quack!')

# Human class contains talk() method
class Human:
    def talk(self):
        print('Hello, hi!')

# this method accepts an object and calls talk() method
def call_talk(obj):
    obj.talk()

# call call_talk() method and pass an object
# depending on type of object, talk() method is executed
x = Duck()
```

```
call_talk(x)
x = Human()
call_talk(x)
```

Output:

```
C:\>python duck.py
Quack, quack!
Hello, hi!
```

The idea presented in Program 15 is that we do not need a type in order to invoke an existing method on an object. If the method is defined on the object, then it can be called. Thus, when we passed Duck object to call_talk(), it has called the talk() method of Duck type (i.e. Duck class). When we passed Human object to call_talk(), it has called talk() method of Human type.

During runtime, if it is found that the method does not belong to that object, there will be an error called 'AttributeError'. This is shown in Program 16.

Program

Program 16: A Python program to call a method that does not appear in the object passed to the method.

```
# duck typing example - v2.0
# Dog class contains bark() method
class Dog:
    def bark(self):
        print('Bow, wow!')

# Duck class contains talk() method
class Duck:
    def talk(self):
        print('Quack, quack!')

# Human class contains talk() method
class Human:
    def talk(self):
        print('Hello, hi!')

# this method accepts an object and calls talk() method
def call_talk(obj):
    obj.talk()

# call call_talk() method and pass an object
# depending on type of object, talk() method is executed
x = Duck()
call_talk(x)
x = Human()
call_talk(x)
x = Dog()
call_talk(x)   # ERROR occurs in this call
```

Output:

```
C:\>python duck1.py
Quack, quack!
Hello, hi!
Traceback (most recent call alst):
    File "duck1.py", line 27, in <module>
        call_talk(x)
    File "duck1.py", line 18, in call_talk
        obj.talk()
AttributeError: 'Dog' object has no attribute 'talk'
```

In Program 16, we are passing Dog class object to call_talk() method in the last statement. Using this object, call_talk() method called the talk() method as: obj.talk(). Since the object type is Dog, this call to talk() method tries to execute talk() method of Dog class which was not found. Hence there was an error.

In the preceding program, let's observe the call_talk() method that accepts an object 'obj' and calls talk() method on the object.

```
def call_talk(obj):
    obj.talk()   # call talk() method of object
```

This method is calling talk() method of the object 'obj'. It is not bothered about which class object it is. We can pass any class object as long as that object contains the talk() method. That means we can pass Duck object or Human object since they contain the talk() method. But when we pass the Dog object, there would be an error since it does not contain talk() method.

So in Python, we never worry about the type (class) of objects. The object type is distinguished only at runtime. If 'it walks like a duck and talks like a duck, it must be a duck' – this is the principle we follow. This is called *duck typing*. From the previous example, we can understand that the behavior of the talk() method is changing depending on the object type. This is an example for polymorphism of methods.

We can rewrite Program 16 where we can check whether the object passed to the call_talk() method has the method that is being invoked or not. This is done by rewriting the method as:

```
def call_talk(obj):
    if hasattr(obj, 'talk'):   # if obj has talk() method then
        obj.talk()             # call it on the object
    elif hasattr(obj, 'bark'): # if obj has bark() method then
        obj.bark()   # call it
```

In the preceding code, we are checking whether the object has a method or not with the help of hasattr() function. This function is written in the form of:

```
hasattr(object, attribute)
```

Here, 'attribute' may be a method or variable. If it is found in the object (i.e. in the class to which the object belongs) then this method returns True, else False. Checking the object type (or class) in this manner is called 'strong typing'. Please understand that this is not duck typing.

Program

Program 17: A Python program to check the object type to know whether the method exists in the object or not.

```
# strong typing example
# Dog class contains bark() method
class Dog:
    def bark(self):
        print('Bow, wow!')

# Duck class contains talk() method
class Duck:
    def talk(self):
        print('Quack, quack!')

# Human class contains talk() method
class Human:
    def talk(self):
        print('Hello, hi!')

# this method accepts an object and calls talk() method
def call_talk(obj):
    if hasattr(obj, 'talk'):
        obj.talk()
    elif hasattr(obj, 'bark'):
        obj.bark()
    else:
        print('Wrong object passed...')

# call call_talk() method and pass an object
# depending on type of object, talk() method is executed
x = Duck()
call_talk(x)
x = Human()
call_talk(x)
x = Dog()
call_talk(x)
```

Output:

```
C:\>python strong.py
Quack, quack!
Hello, hi!
Bow, wow!
```

Operator Overloading

We know that an operator is a symbol that performs some action. For example, '+' is an operator that performs addition operation when used on numbers. When an operator can perform different actions, it is said to exhibit polymorphism.

Program

Program 18: A Python program to use addition operator to act on different types of objects.

```
# overloading the + operator
# using + on integers to add them
print(10+15)

# using + on strings to concatenate them
s1 = "Red"
s2 = "Fort"
print(s1+s2)

# using + on lists to make a single list
a = [10, 20, 30]
b = [5, 15, -10]
print(a+b)
```

Output:

```
C:\>python op.py
25
RedFort
[10, 20, 30, 5, 15, -10]
```

In Program 18, the '+' operator is first adding two integer numbers. Then the same operator is concatenating two strings. Finally, the same operator is combining two lists of elements and making a single list. In this way, if any operator performs additional actions other than what it is meant for, it is called *operator overloading*. Operator overloading is an example for polymorphism.

Normally, addition operator '+' adds two numbers. For example, we can write 10+15. But we cannot use the addition operator to add two objects, as: obj1+obj2. Our intention of writing like this is to use the addition operator to add the data of these two objects. This is not possible. See the example program 19. In this program, we have two classes 'BookX' and 'BookY'. Each book has a number of pages which is given at the time of creating the objects as:

```
b1 = BookX(100)
b2 = BookY(150)
```

Now, if we write b1+b2, the addition operator cannot add the number of pages which are available in the objects since this operator cannot act on the objects.

Program

Program 19: A Python program to use addition operator to add the contents of two objects.

```
# Using + operator on objects
class BookX:
    def __init__(self, pages):
        self.pages = pages

class BookY:
```

```
    def __init__(self, pages):
        self.pages = pages

b1 = BookX(100)
b2 = BookY(150)
print('Total pages= ', b1+b2)
```

Output:

```
C:\>python op.py
Traceback (most recent call last):
  File "op.py", line 12, in <module>
    print('Total pages= ', b1+b2)
TypeError: unsupported operand type(s) for +: 'BookX' and 'BookY'
```

We can overload the '+' operator to act upon the two objects and perform addition operation on the contents of the objects. That means we are giving additional task to the '+' operator. This comes under operator overloading.

Let's go a bit into internal details. The '+' operator is in fact internally written as a special method, i.e. __add__(). So, if we add two numbers by writing a+b, the internal method is called as: a.__add__(b). By overriding this method to act upon objects, we can make the '+' operator to successfully act on the objects also. Since we want to override, we have to write the method with same name but with objects as:

```
def __add__(self, other):
    return self.a+other.b
```

Here, self.a represents the numeric content of first class and other.b represents the numeric content of second class. The preceding method should be written in the first class. To add the pages of BookX and BookY objects, we have to write this method as:

```
def __add__(self, other):
    return self.pages+other.pages
```

Program

Program 20: A Python program to overload the addition operator (+) to make it act on class objects.

```
# overloading + operator to act on objects
class BookX:
    def __init__(self, pages):
        self.pages = pages

    def __add__(self, other):
        return self.pages+other.pages
class BookY:
    def __init__(self, pages):
        self.pages = pages

b1 = BookX(100)
b2 = BookY(150)
print('Total pages= ', b1+b2)
```

Output:

```
C:\>python op1.py
Total pages= 250
```

Table 14.1 summarizes important operators and their corresponding internal methods that can be overridden to act on objects. These methods are called *magic methods*.

Table 14.1: Operators and Corresponding Magic Methods

Operator	Magic method
+	object.__add__(self, other)
-	object.__sub__(self, other)
*	object.__mul__(self, other)
/	object.__div__(self, other)
//	object.__floordiv__(self, other)
%	object.__mod__(self, other)
**	object.__pow__(self, other[, modulo])
+=	object.__iadd__(self, other)
-=	object.__isub__(self, other)
*=	object.__imul__(self, other)
/=	object.__idiv__(self, other)
//=	object.__ifloordiv__(self, other)
%=	object.__imod__(self, other[, modulo])
**=	object.__ipow__(self, other)
<	object.__lt__(self, other)
<=	object.__le__(self, other)
>	object.__gt__(self, other)
>=	object.__ge__(self, other)
==	object.__eq__(self, other)
!=	object.__ne__(self, other)

We will plan another program where we want to overload the greater than (>) operator. This operator is normally used on numbers to compare them. It returns True of False depending on the result. But if want to use it on objects, we have to overload it. For this purpose the magic method __gt__() should be overridden. For example, to compare the pages of two books, we can write this method as:

```
def __gt__(self, other):
    return self.pages>other.pages
```

The preceding method returns True if the pages in first object is greater than those of second object, otherwise False.

Program

Program 21: A Python program to overload greater than (>) operator to make it act on class objects.

```
# overloading > operator
class Ramayan:
    def __init__(self, pages):
        self.pages = pages

    def __gt__(self, other):
        return self.pages>other.pages

class Mahabharat:
    def __init__(self, pages):
        self.pages = pages

b1 = Ramayan(1000)
b2 = Mahabharat(1500)
if(b1>b2):
    print('Ramayan has more pages')
else:
    print('Mahabharat has more pages')
```

Output:

```
C:\>python op2.py
Mahabharat has more pages
```

Another example is where we have an Employee class that contains the name and daily salary of the employee. Another class Attendance contains the employee name and his number of working days. To get the total salary of the employee we have to multiply the daily salary with the number of days worked. That means we have to multiply the Employee object data with Attendance object data. For this purpose, we should overload the multiplication operator.

Since multiplication operator is internally represented by the magic method __mul__(), we have to rewrite or override this method to make it act on the objects as:

```
def __mul__(self, other):
    return self.salary*other.days
```

When * operator is used on the objects, this method is called and the required result is obtained.

Program

Program 22: A Python program to overload the multiplication (*) operator to make it act on objects.

```
# overloading the * operator
class Employee:
    def __init__(self, name, salary):
        self.name = name
        self.salary = salary

    def __mul__(self, other):
        return self.salary*other.days

class Attendance:
    def __init__(self, name, days):
        self.name = name
        self.days = days

x1 = Employee('Srinu', 500.00)
x2 = Attendance('Srinu', 25)
print('This month salary= ', x1*x2)
```

Output:

```
C:\>python op3.py
This month salary= 12500.0
```

Method Overloading

If a method is written such that it can perform more than one task, it is called *method overloading*. We see method overloading in the languages like Java. For example, we call a method as:

```
sum(10, 15)
sum(10, 15, 20)
```

In the first call, we are passing two arguments and in the second call, we are passing three arguments. It means, the sum() method is performing two distinct operations: finding sum of two numbers or sum of three numbers. This is called method overloading. In Java, to achieve this, we write two sum() methods with different number of parameters as:

```
sum(int a, int b) {}
sum(int a, int b, int c) {}
```

Since same name is given for these two methods, the user feels that the same method is performing the two operations. This is how the method overloading is done in Java.

Method overloading is not available in Python. Writing more than one method with the same name is not possible in Python. So, we can achieve method overloading by writing same method with several parameters. The method performs the operation depending on the number of arguments passed in the method call. For example, we can write a sum() method with default value 'None' for the arguments as:

```
    def sum(self, a=None, b=None, c=None):
        if a!=None and b!=None and c!=None:
            print('Sum of three= ', a+b+c)
        elif a!=None and b!=None:
            print('Sum of two= ', a+b)
```

Here, sum() has three arguments 'a','b','c' whose values by default are 'None'. This 'None' indicates nothing or no value and similar to 'null' in languages like Java. While calling this method, if the user enters three values, then the arguments: 'a',' b' and 'c' will not be 'None'. They get the values entered by the user. If the user enters only two values, then the first two arguments 'a' and 'b' only will take those values and the third argument 'c' will become 'None'. In this way, it is possible to find sum of either two numbers or three numbers.

Program

Program 23: A Python program to show method overloading to find sum of two or three numbers.

```
# method overloading
class Myclass:
    def sum(self, a=None, b=None, c=None):
        if a!=None and b!=None and c!=None:
            print('Sum of three= ', a+b+c)
        elif a!=None and b!=None:
            print('Sum of two= ', a+b)
        else:
            print('Please enter two or three arguments')

# call sum() using object
m = Myclass()
m.sum(10, 15, 20)
m.sum(10.5, 25.55)
m.sum(100)
```

Output:

```
C:\>python over.py
Sum of three= 45
Sum of two= 36.05
Please enter two or three arguments
```

In Program 23, the sum() method is calculating sum of two or three numbers and hence it is performing more than one task. Hence it is an overloaded method. In this way, overloaded methods achieve polymorphism.

Method Overriding

We already discussed constructor overriding and method overriding under inheritance section. When there is a method in the super class, writing the same method in the sub class so that it replaces the super class method is called 'method overriding'. The programmer overrides the super class methods when he does not want to use them in sub class. Instead, he wants a new functionality to the same method in the sub class.

In inheritance, if we create super class object (or instance), we can access all the members of the super class but not the members of the sub class. But if we create sub class object, then both the super class and sub class members are available since the sub class object contains a copy of the super class. Hence, in inheritance we always create sub class object.

In Program 24, we created Square class with the area() method that calculates the area of the square. Circle class is a sub class to Square class that contains the area() method rewritten with code to calculate area of circle. When we create sub class object as:

```
c = Circle()   # create sub class object
c.area(15)    # call area() method
```

Then the area() method of Circle class is called but not the area() method of Square class. The reason is that the area() method of sub class has overridden the area() method of the super class.

Program

Program 24: A Python program to override the super class method in sub class.

```
# method overriding
import math
class Square:
    def area(self, x):
        print('Square area= %.4f}'% x*x)

class Circle(Square):
    def area(self, x):
        print('Circle area= %.4f'% (math.pi*x*x))

# call area() using sub class object
c = Circle()
c.area(15)
```

Output:

```
C:\>python over.py
Circle area= 706.8583
```

Calling the area() method using Circle class object will execute Circle class area() method. But in case, the programmer wants to calculate the area of the square, he can call the same area() method using the Square class object. So, same area() method is performing two different tasks depending on the object type. This is an example for polymorphism.

Polymorphism is a powerful feature in all object oriented programming languages. We will observe polymorphism in case of abstract classes and interfaces in the next chapter.

Points to Remember

- The concept of deriving new classes from the existing classes such that the new classes inherit all the members of the existing classes is called inheritance.

- The already existing class is called super class or base class and the newly created class is called sub class or derived class.
- The syntax for inheritance is:

  class Subclass(Baseclass):
- The main advantage of inheritance is code reusability. This will increase the productivity of the organization.
- Since the sub class contains a copy of super class, all the members of the super class are available to the sub class.
- The variables, methods and also constructors of the super class are available to the sub class.
- Writing a constructor in the sub class will override the constructor of the super class. In that case, the super class constructor will not be available.
- Writing a method in the sub class with the same name as that of the super class method is called method overriding. In this case, the super class method is not available. Only the sub class method is executed always.
- super() is a method that is useful to refer to all members of the super class from a sub class. For example,

  super().__init__()   # call super class constructor

  super().__init__(arguments)   # call super class constructor and pass arguments

  super().method()   # call super class method
- Python supports single inheritance and multiple inheritance and all other forms of inheritance which may rise from combining these two types of inheritances.
- Deriving one or more sub classes from a single base class is called 'single inheritance'.
- Deriving sub classes from multiple (or more than one) base classes is called 'multiple inheritance'.
- Starting from the current class, searching in parent classes in depth-first, left to right fashion without searching the same class twice is called Method Resolution Order (MRO).
- If a variable, object or method exhibits different behavior in different contexts, it is called polymorphism.
- Python follows duck typing where the type of the object is not checked while invoking the method on the object. Any object is accepted as long as that method is found in the object.

- If any operator performs additional actions other than what it is meant for, it is called operator overloading. Operator overloading is an example for polymorphism.
- Magic methods are the methods which are internal representations of operator symbols.
- If a method is written such that it can perform more than one task, it is called method overloading. Method overloading is an example for polymorphism.
- When there is a method in the super class, writing the same method in the sub class so that it replaces the super class method is called method overriding. Method overriding is an example of polymorphism.

CHAPTER 15

ABSTRACT CLASSES AND INTERFACES

We know that a class is a model for creating objects (or instances). A class contains attributes and actions. Attributes are nothing but variables and actions are represented by methods. When objects are created to a class, the objects also get the variables and actions mentioned in the class. The rule is that anything that is written in the class is applicable to all of its objects. If a method is written in the class, it is available to all the class objects. For example, take a class Myclass that contains a method calculate() that calculates square value of a given number. If we create three objects to this class, all the three objects get the copy of this method and hence, from any object, we can call and use this method. Consider Program 1.

Program

Program 1: A Python program to understand that Myclass method is shared by all of its objects.

```
# A class with a method
class Myclass:
    def calculate(self, x):
        print('Square value= ', x*x)

# all objects share same calculate() method
obj1 = Myclass()
obj1.calculate(2)

obj2 = Myclass()
obj2.calculate(3)

obj3 = Myclass()
obj3.calculate(4)
```

Output:

```
C:\>python ex.py
Square value= 4
Square value= 9
Square value= 16
```

Of course, in the preceding program, the requirement of all the objects is same, i.e., to calculate square value. Then this program is alright. But, sometimes the requirement of the objects will be different and entirely dependent on the specific object only. For example, in the preceding program, if the first object wants to calculate square value, the second object wants the square root value and the third object wants cube value. In such a case, how to write the calculate() method in Myclass?

Since, the calculate() method has to perform three different tasks depending on the object, we cannot write the code to calculate square value in the body of calculate() method. On the other hand, if we write three different methods like calculate_square(), calculate_sqrt(), and calculate_cube() in Myclass, then all the three methods are available to all the three objects which is not advisable. When each object wants one method, providing all the three does not look reasonable. To serve each object with the one and only required method, we can follow the steps:

1. First, let's write a calculate() method in Myclass. This means every object wants to calculate something.
2. If we write body for calculate() method, it is commonly available to all the objects. So let's not write body for calculate() method. Such a method is called abstract method. Since, we write abstract method in Myclass, it is called abstract class.
3. Now derive a sub class Sub1 from Myclass, so that the calculate() method is available to the sub class. Provide body for calculate() method in Sub1 such that it calculates square value. Similarly, we create another sub class Sub2 where we write the calculate() method with body to calculate square root value. We create the third sub class Sub3 where we write the calculate() method to calculate cube value. This hierarchy is shown in Figure 15.1.
4. It is possible to create objects for the sub classes. Using these objects, the respective methods can be called and used. Thus, every object will have its requirement fulfilled.

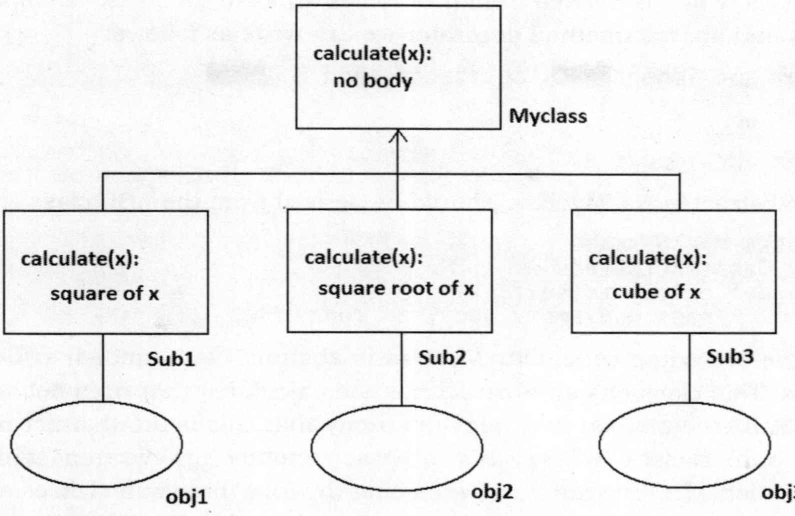

Figure 15.1: Defining a Method in Sub Classes to Suit the Objects

Abstract Method and Abstract Class

An abstract method is a method whose action is redefined in the sub classes as per the requirement of the objects. Generally abstract methods are written without body since their body will be defined in the sub classes anyhow. But it is possible to write an abstract method with body also. To mark a method as abstract, we should use the decorator @abstractmethod. On the other hand, a concrete method is a method with body.

An abstract class is a class that generally contains some abstract methods. Since, abstract class contains abstract methods whose implementation (or body) is later defined in the sub classes, it is not possible to estimate the total memory required to create the object for the abstract class. So, PVM cannot create objects to an abstract class.

Once an abstract class is written, we should create sub classes and all the abstract methods should be implemented (body should be written) in the sub classes. Then, it is possible to create objects to the sub classes.

In Program 2, we create Myclass as an abstract super class with an abstract method calculate(). This method does not have any body within it. The way to create an abstract class is to derive it from a meta class ABC that belongs to *abc* (abstract base class) module as:

```
class Abstractclass(ABC):
```

Since all abstract classes should be derived from the meta class ABC which belongs to *abc* (abstract base class) module, we should import this module into our program. A meta class is a class that defines the behavior of other classes. The meta class ABC defines that the class which is derived from it becomes an abstract class. To import abc module's ABC class and abstractmethod decorator we can write as follows:

```
from abc import ABC, abstractmethod
```

or

```
from abc import *
```

Now, our abstract class 'Myclass' should be derived from the ABC class as:

```
classs Myclass(ABC):
    @abstractmethod
    def calculate(self, x):
        pass   # empty body, no code
```

Observe the preceding code. Our Myclass is abstract class since it is derived from ABC meta class. This class has an abstract method calculate() that does not contain any code. We used @abstractmethod decorator to specify that this is an abstract method. We have to write sub classes where this abstract method is written with its body (or implementation). In Program 2, we are going to write three sub classes: Sub1, Sub2 and Sub3 where this abstract method is implemented as per the requirement of the objects. Since, the same abstract method is implemented differently for different objects, they can perform different tasks.

Program

Program 2: A Python program to create abstract class and sub classes which implement the abstract method of the abstract class.

```
# abstract class example
from abc import ABC, abstractmethod
class Myclass(ABC):
    @abstractmethod
    def calculate(self, x):
        pass   # empty body, no code

# this is sub class of Myclass
class Sub1(Myclass):
    def calculate(self, x):
        print('Square value= ', x*x)

# this is another sub class for Myclass
import math
class Sub2(Myclass):
    def calculate(self, x):
        print('Square root= ', math.sqrt(x))

# third sub class for Myclass
class Sub3(Myclass):
    def calculate(self, x):
        print('Cube value= ', x**3)

# create Sub1 class object and call calculate() method
obj1 = Sub1()
obj1.calculate(16)

# create Sub2 class object and call calculate() method
```

```
    obj2 = Sub2()
    obj2.calculate(16)
    # create Sub3 class object and call calculate() method
    obj3 = Sub3()
    obj3.calculate(16)
```

Output:

```
    C:\>python abs.py
    Square value= 256
    Square root= 4.0
    Cube value= 4096
```

In the preceding program, the same calculate() method written in the abstract class is implemented differently in the three sub classes and it is able to perform different tasks. Since the same method is performing various tasks, it is coming under polymorphism.

Let's take another example to understand the abstract class concept in a better way. We see many cars on the road. These cars are all objects of Car class. For example, Maruti, Santro, Benz are all objects of Car class. Suppose, we plan to write Car class, it contains all the attributes (variables) and actions (methods) of any car object in the world. For example, we can write the following members in Car class:

- **Registration number:** Every car will have a registration number and hence we write this as an instance variable in Car class. All cars whether it is Maruti or Santro should have a registration number. It means registration number is a common feature to all the objects. So, it can be written as an instance variable in the Car class.

- **Fuel tank:** Every car will have a fuel tank, opening and filling the tank is an action. To represent this action, we can write a method like: openTank()

  How do we open and fill the tank? Take the key, open the tank and fill fuel. Let's assume that all cars have same mechanism of opening the tank and filling fuel. So, the code representing the opening mechanism can be written in openTank() method's body. So it becomes a concrete method. A concrete method is a method with body.

- **Steering:** Every car will have a steering wheel and steering the car is an action. For this, we write a method as: steering()

  How do we steer the car? All the cars do not have same mechanism for steering. Maruti cars have manual steering. Santro cars have power steering. So, it is not possible to write a particular mechanism in steering() method. So, this method should be written without body in Car class. Thus, it becomes an abstract method.

- **Brakes:** Every car will have brakes. Applying brakes is an action and hence it can be represented as a method, as: braking()

  How do we apply brakes? All cars do not have same mechanism for brakes. Maruti cars have hydraulic brakes. Santro cars have gas brakes. So, we cannot write a particular braking mechanism in this method. This method, hence, will not have a body in Car class, and hence becomes abstract. See Figure 15.2:

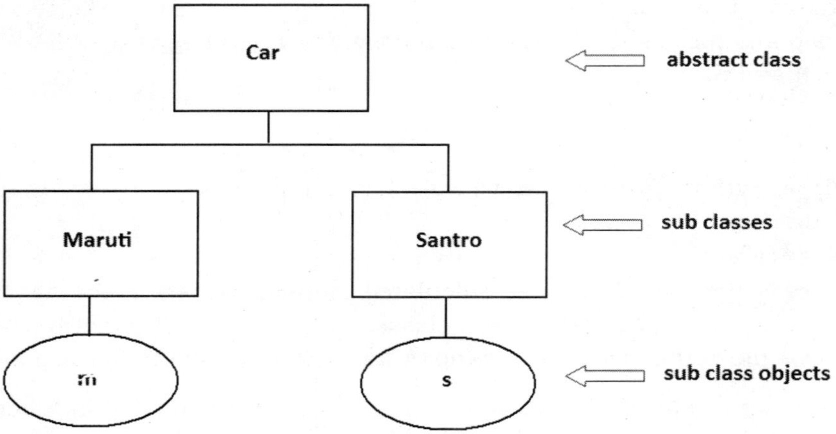

Figure 15.2: Abstract Car Class and its Sub Classes

So, the Car class has an instance variable, one concrete method and two abstract methods. Hence, Car class will become abstract class. See this class in Program 3 given here.

Program

Program 3: A Python program to create a Car abstract class that contains an instance variable, a concrete method and two abstract methods.

```
# This is an abstract class. Save this code as abs.py
from abc import *
class Car(ABC):
    def __init__(self, regno):
        self.regno = regno

    def openTank(self):
        print('Fill the fuel into the tank')
        print('for the car with regno ', self.regno)

    @abstractmethod
    def steering(self):
        pass

    @abstractmethod
    def braking(self):
        pass
```

Output:

```
C:\>python abs.py
C:\>
```

Now that we have written the abstract class, the next step is to derive sub classes from the Car class. In the sub classes, we should take the abstract methods of the Car class and implement (writing body in) them. The reason why we implement the abstract methods in the sub classes is that the implementation of these methods is dependent on the sub classes. In our program, let's write Maruti and Santro as the two sub classes where the two abstract methods will be implemented accordingly. See these sub classes in Programs 4 and 5.

Program

Program 4: A Python program in which Maruti sub class implements the abstract methods of the super class, Car.

```
# this is a sub class for abstract Car class
from abs import Car
class Maruti(Car):
    def steering(self):
        print('Maruti uses manual steering')
        print('Drive the car')
    def braking(self):
        print('Maruti uses hydraulic brakes')
        print('Apply brakes and stop it')
# create object to Maruti and use its features
m = Maruti(1001)
m.openTank()
m.steering()
m.braking()
```

Output:

```
C:\>python maruti.py
Fill the fuel into the tank
for the car with regno  1001
Maruti uses manual steering
Drive the car
Maruti uses hydraulic brakes
Apply brakes and stop it
```

Program

Program 5: A Python program in which Santro sub class implements the abstract methods of the super class, Car.

```
# this is a sub class for abstract Car class
from abs import Car
class Santro(Car):

    def steering(self):
        print('Santro uses power steering')
        print('Drive the car')

    def braking(self):
        print('Santro uses gas brakes')
        print('Apply brakes and stop it')

# create object to Santro and use its features
s = Santro(7878)
s.openTank()
s.steering()
s.braking()
```

Output:

```
C:\>python santro.py
Fill the fuel into the tank
for the car with regno  7878
Santro uses power steering
Drive the car
Santro uses gas brakes
Apply brakes and stop it
```

An ordinary class can be called rigid class since it can look after the common needs of the objects. There is no scope for catering the individual requirements of objects. Abstract classes are more flexible and useful than ordinary classes since they cater the common needs of the objects as well as their individual needs also.

Interfaces in Python

We learned that an abstract class is a class which contains some abstract methods as well as concrete methods also. Imagine there is a class that contains only abstract methods and there are no concrete methods. It becomes an interface. This means an interface is an abstract class but it contains only abstract methods. None of the methods in the interface will have body. Only method headers will be written in the interface. So an interface can be defined as a specification of method headers. Since, we write only abstract methods in the interface, there is possibility for providing different implementations (body) for those abstract methods depending on the requirements of objects. In the languages like Java, an interface is created using the key word 'interface' but in Python an interface is created as an abstract class only. The interface concept is not explicitly available in Python. We have to use abstract classes as interfaces in Python.

Since an interface contains methods without body, it is not possible to create objects to an interface. In this case, we can create sub classes where we can implement all the methods of the interface. Since the sub classes will have all the methods with body, it is possible to create objects to the sub classes. The flexibility lies in the fact that every sub class can provide its own implementation for the abstract methods of the interface.

Since, none of the methods have body in the interface, we may tend to think that writing an interface is mere waste. This is not correct. In fact, an interface is more useful when compared to the class owing to its flexibility of providing necessary implementation needed by the objects. Let's elucidate this point further with an example. We have some rupees in our hands. We can spend in rupees only by going to a shop where billing is done in rupees. Suppose we have gone to a shop where only dollars are accepted, we cannot use our rupees there. This money is like a 'class'. A class satisfies the only requirement intended for it. It is not useful to handle a different situation.

Suppose we have an international credit card. Now, we can pay by using our credit card in rupees in a shop. If we go to another shop where they expect us to pay in dollars, we can pay in dollars. The same credit card can be used to pay in pounds also. Here, the credit card is like an interface which performs several tasks. In fact, the credit card is a plastic card and does not hold any money physically. It contains just our name, our bank name and perhaps some number. But how the shop keepers are able to draw the money from the credit card? Behind the credit card, we got our bank account which holds the money from where it is transferred to the shop keepers. This bank account can be taken as a sub class which actually performs the task. See Figure 15.3:

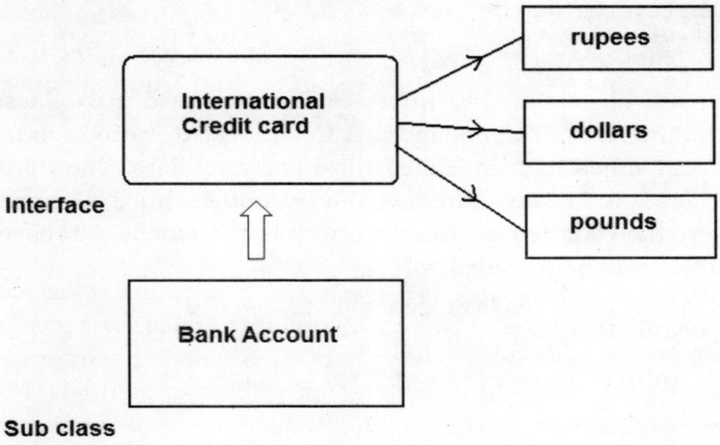

Figure 15.3: Interface and Sub Classes

Let's see how the interface concept is advantageous in software development. A programmer is asked to write a Python program to connect to a database and retrieve the data, process the data and display the results in the form of some reports. For this purpose, the programmer has written a class to connect to Oracle database, something like this:

```
# this class works with Oracle database only
class Oracle:
    def connect(self):
        print('Connecting to Oracle database...')

    def disconnect(self):
        print('Disconnected from Oracle.')
```

This class has a limitation. It can connect only to Oracle database. If a client (user) using any other database (for example, Sybase database) uses this code to connect to his database, this code will not work. So, the programmer is asked to design his code in such a way that it is used to connect to any database in the world. How is it possible?

One way is to write several classes, each to connect to a particular database. Thus, considering all the databases available in the world, the programmer has to write a lot of classes. This takes a lot of time and effort. Even though the programmer spends a lot of time and writes all the classes, by the time the software is released into the market, all the versions of the databases will change and the programmer is supposed to rewrite the classes again to suit the latest versions of databases. This is very cumbersome.

Interface helps to solve this problem. The programmer writes an interface 'Myclass' with abstract methods as shown here:

```
# an interface to connect to any database
class Myclass(ABC):
    @abstractmethod
    def connect(self):
        pass
    @abstractmethod
    def disconnect(self):
        pass
```

We cannot create objects to the interface. So, we need sub classes where all these methods of the interface are implemented to connect to various databases. This task is left for other companies that are called third party vendors. The third party vendors will provide sub classes to Myclass interface. For example, Oracle Corp people may provide a sub class where the code related to connecting to the Oracle database and disconnecting from the database will be provided as:

```
# this is a sub class to connect to Oracle
class Oracle(Myclass):
    def connect(self):
        print('Connecting to Oracle database...')

    def disconnect(self):
        print('Disconnected from Oracle.')
```

Note that 'Oracle' is a sub class of Myclass interface. Similarly, the Sybase company people may provide another implementation class 'Sybase', where code related to connecting to Sybase database and disconnecting from Sybase will be provided as:

```
# this is another sub class to connect to Sybase
class Sybase(Myclass):
    def connect(self):
        print('Connecting to Sybase database...')

    def disconnect(self):
        print('Disconnected from Sybase.')
```

Now, it is possible to create objects to the sub classes and call the connect() method and disconnect() methods from a main program. This main program is also written by the same programmer who develops the interface. Let's understand that the programmer who develops the interface does not know the names of the sub classes as they will be developed in future by the other companies. In the main program, the programmer is supposed to create objects to the sub classes without knowing their names. This is done using globals() function.

First, the programmer should accept the database name from the user. It may be 'Oracle' or 'Sybase'. This name should be taken in a string, say 'str'. The next step is to convert this string into a class name using the built-in function globals(). The globals() function returns a dictionary containing current global names and globals()[str] returns the name of the class that is in 'str'. Hence, we can get the class name as:

```
classname = globals()[str]
```

Now, create an object to this class and call the methods as:

```
x = classname()   # x is object of the class
x.connect()
x.disconnect()
```

The connect() method establishes connection with the particular database and disconnect() method disconnects from the database. The complete program is shown in Program 6.

Program

Program 6: A Python program to develop an interface that connects to any database.

```
# abstract class works like an interface
from abc import *
class Myclass(ABC):
    @abstractmethod
    def connect(self):
        pass
    @abstractmethod
    def disconnect(self):
        pass

# this is a sub class
class Oracle(Myclass):
    def connect(self):
        print('Connecting to Oracle database...')

    def disconnect(self):
        print('Disconnected from Oracle.')

# this is another sub class
class Sybase(Myclass):
    def connect(self):
        print('Connecting to Sybase database...')

    def disconnect(self):
        print('Disconnected from Sybase.')

class Database:
    # accept database name as a string
    str = input('Enter database name: ')

    # convert the string into classname
    classname = globals()[str]

    # create an object to that class
    x = classname()

    # call the connect() and disconnect() methods
    x.connect()
    x.disconnect()
```

Output:

```
C:\>python inter.py
Enter database name: Oracle
Connecting to Oracle database...
Disconnected from Oracle.
```

```
C:\>python inter.py
Enter database name: Sybase
Connecting to Sybase database...
Disconnected from Sybase.
```

When an interface is created, it is not necessary for the programmer to provide the sub classes for the interface. Any third party vendors can do that. The client or user purchases and uses the interface and the sub class depending on his requirements. If he wants to connect to Oracle, he will purchase Oracle sub class. If he wants to connect to Sybase, he will purchase Sybase sub class.

The question is how the third party vendors know which methods they should write in the sub classes? In this case, API documentation will help them. An API (Application Programming Interface) documentation file is a text file or html file that contains description of all the features of software, language or a product. After developing the software, the programmer creates API documentation file that contains description of all the classes, methods and attributes. This file is referred by the third party vendors to know about the interface and its methods. Then they write the same methods in the sub classes. This entire discussion is represented in Figure 15.4:

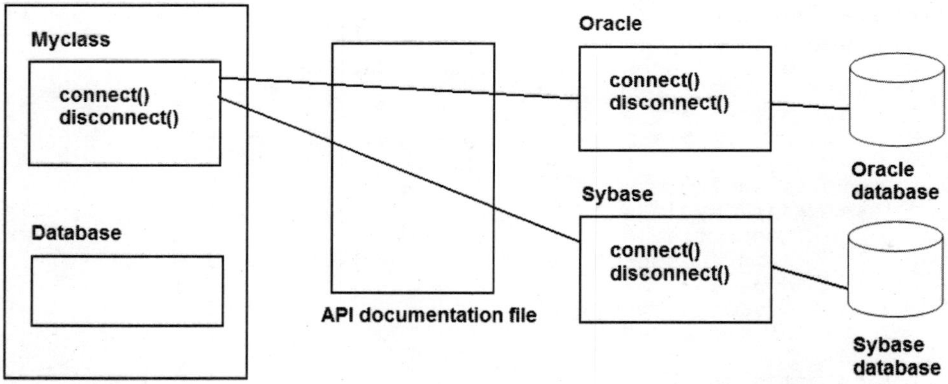

Figure 15.4: Interface Communicating with Different Databases

Let's take another example where interface is used. We want to write Printer interface which is used to send data to different printers. This interface has a method printit() that sends text to the printer and another method disconnect() that disconnects the printer after printing is done. Of course, this program is a model how the printer interface can be used. It does not send the text to a real printer. On the other hand, it displays the text on the screen.

Printer interface is implemented by IBM people such that it sends text to IBM printer. Similarly, Epson people provide a different implementation to the Printer interface such that it sends text to Epson printer. These sub classes are written as IBM and Epson classes.

To use a printer, first of all we should know which printer is used by the client. We assume that the printer name is generally stored in the config.txt file at the time of installing the printer driver software. So, open notepad (or any text editor) and create a file with the name config.txt and store a single line that represents the printer driver name as:

```
Epson
```

And then save the file. Alternately, we can store the name IBM in the config.txt file. The name of the printer available in the config.txt file can be read from the file using readline() method as:

```
with open("config.txt", "r") as f:
    str = f.readline()    # read printer name from f and store into str
```

This reads one line from the file containing the string 'Epson' which was already stored by us in the config.txt file. This 'Epson' would appear in 'str' as a string. Retrieving the class name from this 'str' is done using globals() method. Then we create an object to that class and use it.

Program

Program 7: A Python program which contains a Printer interface and its sub classes to send text to any printer.

```
# An interface to send text to any printer
from abc import *
# create an interface
class Printer(ABC):
    @abstractmethod
    def printit(self, text):
        pass
    @abstractmethod
    def disconnect(self):
        pass

# this is sub class for IBM printer
class IBM(Printer):
    def printit(self, text):
        print(text)

    def disconnect(self):
        print('Printing completed on IBM printer.')

# this is sub class for Epson printer
class Epson(Printer):
    def printit(self, text):
        print(text)

    def disconnect(self):
        print('Printing completed on Epson printer.')

class UsePrinter:
    # accept printer name as a string from configuration file
    with open("config.txt", "r") as f:
        str = f.readline()
```

```
        # convert the string into classname
        classname = globals()[str]

        # create an object to that class
        x = classname()

        # call the printit() and disconnect() methods
        x.printit('Hello, this is sent to printer')
        x.disconnect()
```

Output:

```
C:\>python inter1.py
Hello, this is sent to printer
Printing completed on Epson printer.
```

Please remember that we should run this program after creating the config.txt file. If we created the config.txt file with the string 'IBM', then the output of the preceding program would be:

```
Hello, this is sent to printer
Printing completed on IBM printer.
```

We can observe that the same printit() and disconnect() methods when called are performing different tasks in different contexts. They are sending text to Epson printer or IBM printer depending upon the user requirement. This is an example for polymorphism. Let's understand that the abstract classes and interfaces are examples for polymorphic behavior.

Abstract Classes vs. Interfaces

Python does not provide interface concept explicitly. It provides abstract classes which can be used as either abstract classes or interfaces. It is the discretion of the programmer to decide when to use an abstract class and when to go for an interface. Generally, abstract class is written when there are some common features shared by all the objects as they are. For example, take a class WholeSaler which represents a whole sale shop with text books and stationery like pens, papers and note books as:

```
# an abstract class
class WholeSaler(ABC):
    @abstractmethod
    def text_books(self):
        pass
    @abstractmethod
    def stationery(self):
        pass
```

Let's take Retailer1, a class which represents a retail shop. Retailer1 wants text books of X class and some pens. Similarly, Retailer2 also wants text books of X class and some papers. In this case, we can understand that the text_books() is the common feature shared by both the retailers. But the stationery asked by the retailers is different. This means, the stationery has different implementations for different retailers but there is a common feature, i.e., the text books. So in this case, the programmer designs the WholeSaler class as an abstract class. Retailer1 and Retailer2 are sub classes.

On the other hand, the programmer uses an interface if all the features need to be implemented differently for different objects. Suppose, Retailer1 asks for VII class text books and Retailer2 asks for X class text books, then even the text_books() method of WholeSaler class needs different implementations depending on the retailer. It means, the text_books() method and also stationery() methods should be implemented differently depending on the retailer. So, in this case, the programmer designs the WholeSaler as an interface and Retailer1 and Retailer2 become sub classes.

There is a responsibility for the programmer to provide the sub classes whenever he writes an abstract class. This means the same development team should provide the sub classes for the abstract class. But if an interface is written, any third party vendor will take the responsibility of providing sub classes. This means, the programmer prefers to write an interface when he wants to leave the implementation part to the third party vendors.

In case of an interface, every time a method is called, PVM should search for the method in the implementation classes which are installed elsewhere in the system and then execute the method. This takes more time. But when an abstract class is written, since the common methods are defined within the abstract class and the sub classes are generally in the same place along with the software, PVM will not have that much overhead to execute a method. Hence, interfaces are slow when compared to abstract classes.

Points to Remember

- An abstract method is a method whose action is redefined in the sub classes as per the requirement of the objects.
- Generally, an abstract method is written without any body. But it is possible to write an abstract method with body also.
- A method with body is called concrete method.
- An abstract class is a class that contains some abstract methods. An abstract class can also contain concrete methods.
- Abstract methods are written with a decorator @abstractmethod above them.
- It is not possible to create an object (or instance) to an abstract class.
- Every abstract class should derive from ABC class that is available in abc (abstract base class) module.
- All the abstract methods of the abstract class should be rewritten with body in the sub classes. That means the abstract methods should be overridden in the sub classes.
- We can create objects (or instances) to sub classes.

- If a sub class does not implement all the methods of the abstract super class, then that sub class should also be declared as abstract class and an object to that sub class cannot be created.
- An abstract class can perform various tasks through various implementations of its methods in the sub classes.
- An abstract class will become an interface when it contains only abstract methods and there are no concrete methods.
- It is not possible to create objects (or instances) to interfaces.
- All the methods of the interface should be implemented in its sub classes.
- The built-in function globals()[str] converts the string 'str' into a classname and returns the classname.
- All the features (or methods) of the interface should be described in a separate file called 'API documentation file'.
- An abstract class is written when there are some common features shared by all the objects.
- An interface is written when all the features are implemented differently for different objects.
- When an interface is written, any third party vendor can provide sub classes.
- Both the abstract classes and interfaces are examples for polymorphism.

CHAPTER 16

EXCEPTIONS

As human beings, we commit several errors. A software developer is also a human being and hence prone to commit errors either in the design of the software or in writing the code. The errors in the software are called 'bugs' and the process of removing them is called 'debugging'. Let's learn about different types of errors that can occur in a program.

Errors in a Python Program

In general, we can classify errors in a program into one of these three types:

- Compile-time errors
- Runtime errors
- Logical errors

Compile-Time Errors

These are syntactical errors found in the code, due to which a program fails to compile. For example, forgetting a colon in the statements like if, while, for, def, etc. will result in compile-time error. Such errors are detected by Python compiler and the line number along with error description is displayed by the Python compiler. Let's see Program 1 to understand this better. In this program, we have forgotten to write colon in the if statement, after the condition. This will raise SyntaxError.

Program

Program 1: A Python program to understand the compile-time error.

```
# example for compile-time error
x = 1
```

```
if x == 1
    print('Where is colon?')
```

Output:

```
C:\>python ex.py
  File "ex.py", line 3
    if x == 1
            ^
SyntaxError: invalid syntax
```

We know that Python statements are written in blocks using proper indentation. The default number of spaces used for indentation is 4. All the statements belonging to the same block should use same number of spaces before them. If there is any deviation in the spaces, then we can see IndentationError raised by Python compiler. Consider Program 2 where we are using unequal number of spaces for the print statements inside the if statement.

Program

Program 2: A Python program to demonstrate compile-time error.

```
# another compile-time error
x = 10
if x%2==0:
    print(x,' is divisible by 2')
        print(x,' is even number')
```

Output:

```
C:\>python ex.py
  File "ex.py", line 5
    print(x,' is even number')
    ^
IndentationError: unexpected indent
```

The Python compiler displays error message and the line number in case of compile-time errors. By checking the program source code and rewriting the statements properly, we can eliminate the compile-time errors.

Runtime Errors

When PVM cannot execute the byte code, it flags runtime error. For example, insufficient memory to store something or inability of the PVM to execute some statement come under runtime errors. Runtime errors are not detected by the Python compiler. They are detected by the PVM, only at runtime. The following program explains this further:

Program

Program 3: A Python program to understand runtime errors.

```
# example for runtime error
def concat(a, b):
    print(a+b)

# callconcat() and pass arguments
concat('Hai', 25)
```

Output:

```
C:\>python ex.py
Traceback (most recent call last):
  File "ex.py", line 6, in <module>
    concat('Hai', 25)
  File "ex.py", line 3, in concat
    print(a+b)
TypeError: Can't convert 'int' object to str implicitly.
```

In Program 3, we have written a function by the name 'concat' that accepts 2 arguments 'a' and 'b'. It adds them using '+' operator and displays the result. At the time of calling this function, if we pass two strings, they will be concatenated or joined. In this case, '+' acts like concatenation operator. On the other hand, if we pass 2 numbers, then they are added and result is displayed. In this case, '+' acts as addition operator. But, in the above example, we are passing one string and one number. Since the datatypes are not same, PVM shows 'TypeError'. In Python, compiler will not check the datatypes. Type checking is done by PVM during runtime.

Program 4 is also an example for runtime error. In this program, we are creating a list with 4 elements. The indexes (or position numbers) of these elements will be from 0 to 3. When we refer to the index 4 which is not in the list, there will be IndexError during runtime.

Program

Program 4: A Python program to demonstrate runtime error.

```
# another runtime error
animal = ['Dog', 'Cat', 'Horse', 'Donkey']
print(animal[4])
```

Output:

```
C:\>python ex.py
Traceback (most recent call last:
  File "ex.py", line 3, in <module>
    print(animal[4])
IndexError: list index out of range
```

In case of runtime error, the PVM displays the line number and the type of error. Most of the runtime errors can be eliminated by following the message given by PVM. For example, in the previous program, restricting the list index below 4 is the solution to eliminate the runtime error. But some runtime errors cannot be eliminated. In that case, we should handle those errors using 'exception handling mechanism' of Python.

Logical Errors

These errors depict flaws in the logic of the program. The programmer might be using a wrong formula or the design of the program itself is wrong. Logical errors are not detected either by Python compiler or PVM. The programmer is solely responsible for them. In the following program, the programmer wants to calculate incremented salary of an employee, but he gets wrong output, since he uses wrong formula.

Program

Program 5: A Python program to increment the salary of an employee by 15%.

```
# logical error
def increment(sal):
    sal = sal * 15/100
    return sal

# call increment() and pass salary
sal = increment(5000.00)
print('Incremented salary= %.2f' %sal)
```

Output:

```
C:\>python ex.py
Incremented salary= 750.00
```

By comparing the output of a program with manually calculated results, a programmer can guess the presence of a logical error. In Program 5, we are using the following formula to calculate the incremented salary:

```
sal = sal * 15/100
```

This is wrong since this formula calculates only the increment but it is not adding it to the original salary. So, the correct formula would be:

```
sal = sal + sal * 15/100
```

Compile time errors and logical errors can be eliminated by the programmer by modifying the program source code. In case of runtime errors, when the programmer knows which type of error occurs, he has to handle them using exception handling mechanism. The runtime errors which can be handled by the programmer are called *exceptions*. Before discussing exception handling mechanism, we will first understand what type of harm an exception can cause. Program 6 will help us in this regard.

Program

Program 6: A Python program to understand the effect of an exception.

```
# an exception example
# open a file
f = open("myfile", "w")

# do some processing on the file
# accept a, b values, store the result of a/b into the file
a, b = [int(x) for x in input("Enter two numbers: ").split()]
c = a/b
f.write("writing %d into myfile" %c)

# close the file
f.close()
print('File closed')
```

Output:

```
C:\>python ex.py
Enter two numbers: 10  2
File closed
```

When we execute Program 6, it opens a file by the name "myfile" using open() method, and then writes the result of a/b into that file using write() method. Finally, the file is closed using close() method. This program runs well if we give 'a' and 'b' values from the keyboard as: 10 and 2. Since a/b value is 5, this value (i.e. 5) is stored into the file. After that, the file is closed.

What happens if we enter 10 and 0 as values for 'a' and 'b' in the previous program. Let's see:

```
C:\>python ex.py
Enter two numbers: 10  0
Traceback (most recent call last):
  File "ex.py", line 8, in <module>
    c = a/b
ZeroDivisionError: division by zero
```

Since a/b represents 10/0 that gives infinity which is a huge quantity that cannot be stored into any variable, we are getting an error 'ZeroDivisionError'. When this error occurred, PVM is simply displaying the error message and immediately terminating the program in line number 8. Due to this abnormal termination, the subsequent statements in the program are not executed. Hence, f.close() is not executed and the file which is opened in the beginning of the program is not closed. This leads to loss of entire data that is already present in the file. A file that is opened in any mode should be closed properly. This ensures safety for the data present in the file.

So, when there is an error in a program, due to its sudden termination, the following things can be suspected:

- The important data in the files or databases used in the program may be lost.
- The software may be corrupted.
- The program abruptly terminates giving error message to the user making the user losing trust in the software.

Hence, it is the duty of the programmer to handle the errors. Please understand that we cannot handle all errors. We can handle only some types of errors which are called exceptions.

Exceptions

An exception is a runtime error which can be handled by the programmer. That means if the programmer can guess an error in the program and he can do something to eliminate the harm caused by that error, then it is called an 'exception'. If the programmer cannot do anything in case of an error, then it is called an 'error' and not an exception.

All exceptions are represented as classes in Python. The exceptions which are already available in Python are called 'built-in' exceptions. The base class for all built-in exceptions is 'BaseException' class. From BaseException class, the sub class 'Exception' is derived. From Exception class, the sub classes 'StandardError' and 'Warning' are derived.

All errors (or exceptions) are defined as sub classes of StandardError. An error should be compulsorily handled otherwise the program will not execute. Similarly, all warnings are derived as sub classes from 'Warning' class. A warning represents a caution and even though it is not handled, the program will execute. So, warnings can be neglected but errors cannot be neglected.

Just like the exceptions which are already available in Python language, a programmer can also create his own exceptions, called 'user-defined' exceptions. When the programmer wants to create his own exception class, he should derive his class from Exception class and not from 'BaseException' class. In Figure 16.1, we are showing important classes available in Exception hierarchy:

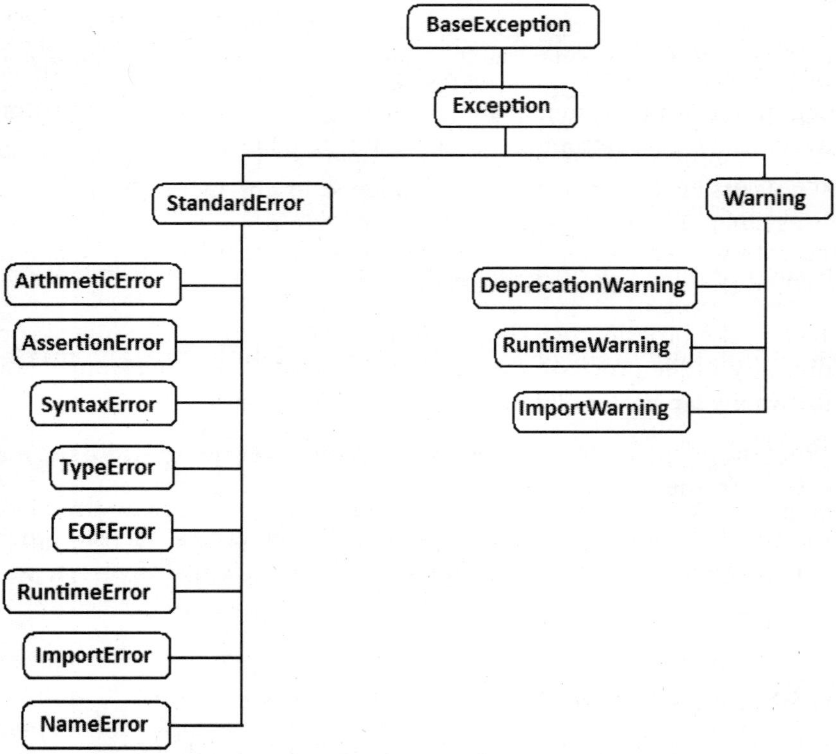

Figure 16.1: Important Exception Classes in Python

Exception Handling

The purpose of handling errors is to make the program *robust*. The word 'robust' means 'strong'. A robust program does not terminate in the middle. Also, when there is an error in the program, it will display an appropriate message to the user and continue execution. Designing such programs is needed in any software development. For this purpose, the programmer should handle the errors. When the errors can be handled, they are called exceptions.

To handle exceptions, the programmer should perform the following three steps:

Step 1: The programmer should observe the statements in his program where there may be a possibility of exceptions. Such statements should be written inside a 'try' block. A try block looks like as follows:

```
try:
    statements
```

The greatness of try block is that even if some exception arises inside it, the program will not be terminated. When PVM understands that there is an exception, it jumps into an 'except' block.

Step 2: The programmer should write the 'except' block where he should display the exception details to the user. This helps the user to understand that there is some error in the program. The programmer should also display a message regarding what can be done to avoid this error. Except block looks like as follows:

```
except exceptionname:
    statements   # these statements form handler
```

The statements written inside an except block are called 'handlers' since they handle the situation when the exception occurs.

Step 3: Lastly, the programmer should perform clean up actions like closing the files and terminating any other processes which are running. The programmer should write this code in the finally block. Finally block looks like as follows:

```
finally:
    statements
```

The specialty of finally block is that the statements inside the finally block are executed irrespective of whether there is an exception or not. This ensures that all the opened files are properly closed and all the running processes are properly terminated. So, the data in the files will not be corrupted and the user is at the safe-side.

Performing the above 3 tasks is called 'exception handling'. Remember, in exception handling, the programmer is not preventing the exception, as in many cases it is not possible. But the programmer is avoiding any damage that may happen to data and software. Let's rewrite program 6 to handle the ZeroDivisionError exception using try, except and finally blocks.

Program

Program 7: A Python program to handle the ZeroDivisionError exception.

```
# an exception handling example
try:
    f = open("myfile", "w")
    a, b = [int(x) for x in input("Enter two numbers: ").split()]
```

```
        c = a/b
        f.write("writing %d into myfile" %c)

    except ZeroDivisionError:
        print('Division by zero happened')
        print('Please do not enter 0 in input')

    finally:
        f.close()
        print('File closed')
```

Output:

```
C:\>python ex.py
Enter two numbers: 10  2
File closed

C:\>python ex.py
Enter two number: 10  0
Division by zero happened
Please do not enter 0 in input
File closed
```

From the preceding output, we can understand that the 'finally' block is executed and the file is closed in both the cases, i.e. when there is no exception and when the exception occurred. In the previous discussion, we used try-catch-finally to handle the exception. However, the complete exception handling syntax will be in the following format:

```
try:
    statements
except Exception1:
    handler1
except Exception2:
    handler2
else:
    statements
finally:
    statements
```

The 'try' block contains the statements where there may be one or more exceptions. The subsequent 'except' blocks handle these exceptions. When 'Exception1' occurs, 'handler1' statements are executed. When 'Exception2' occurs, 'hanlder2' statements are executed and so forth. If no exception is raised, the statements inside the 'else' block are executed. Even if the exception occurs or does not occur, the code inside 'finally' block is always executed. The following points are noteworthy:

- A single try block can be followed by several except blocks.
- Multiple except blocks can be used to handle multiple exceptions.
- We cannot write except blocks without a try block.
- We can write a try block without any except blocks.
- Else block and finally blocks are not compulsory.
- When there is no exception, else block is executed after try block.
- Finally block is always executed.

Types of Exceptions

There are several exceptions available as part of Python language that are called *built-in* exceptions. In the same way, the programmer can also create his own exceptions called *user-defined* exceptions. Table 16.1 summarizes some important built-in exceptions in Python. Most of the exception class names end with the word 'Error'.

Table 16.1: Some Important Built-in Exceptions

Exception Class Name	Description
Exception	Represents any type of exception. All exceptions are sub classes of this class.
ArithmeticError	Represents the base class for arithmetic errors iike OverflowError, ZeroDivisionError, FloatingPointError.
AssertionError	Raised when an assert statement gives error.
AttributeError	Raised when an attribute reference or assignment fails.
EOFError	Raised when input() function reaches end of file condition without reading any data.
FloatingPointError	Raised when a floating point operation fails.
GeneratorExit	Raised when generator's close() method is called.
IOError	Raised when an input or output operation failed. It raises when the file opened is not found or when writing data disk is full.
ImportError	Raised when an import statement fails to find the module being imported.
IndexError	Raised when a sequence index or subscript is out of range.
KeyError	Raised when a mapping (dictionary) key is not found in the set of existing keys.
KeyboardInterrupt	Raised when the user hits the interrupt key (normally Control-C or Delete).
NameError	Raised when an identifier is not found locally or globally.
NotImplementedError	Derived from 'RuntimeError'. In user defined base classes, abstract methods should raise this exception when they require derived classes to override the method.
OverflowError	Raised when the result of an arithmetic operation is too large to be represented. This cannot occur for long integers (which would rather raise 'MemoryError')
RuntimeError	Raised when an error is detected that doesn't fall in any of the other categories.
StopIteration	Raised by an iterator's next() method to signal that there are no more elements.

Exception Class Name	Description
SyntaxError	Raised when the compiler encounters a syntax error. Import or exec statements and input() and eval() functions may raise this exception.
IndentationError	Raised when indentation is not specified properly.
SystemExit	Raised by the sys.exit() function. When it is not handled, the Python interpreter exits.
TypeError	Raised when an operation or function is applied to an object of inappropriate datatype.
UnboundLocalError	Raised when a reference is made to a local variable in a function or method, but no value has been bound to that variable.
ValueError	Raised when a built-in operation or function receives an argument that has right datatype but wrong value.
ZeroDivisionError	Raised when the denominator is zero in a division or modulus operation.

We will now see how to work with built-in exceptions. In Program 8, we are trying to handle SyntaxError that is raised by eval() function. The eval() function accepts input in the form of a list, tuple or dictionary and evaluates the input properly. In this program, we are entering date in the form of year, month and date separating them by commas, e.g. 2016, 10, 3. When a group of values are entered separating them by commas, they are understood as a tuple by eval() function. While entering these values any letter is by mistake typed along with the value, there will be SyntaxError raised by the eval() function. This error is caught in except block and a message 'Invalid date entered' is displayed.

Program

Program 8: A Python program to handle syntax error given by eval() function.

```
# example for syntax error
try:
    date = eval(input("Enter date: "))
except SyntaxError:
    print('Invalid date entered')
else:
    print('You entered: ', date)
```

Output:

```
C:\>python ex.py
Enter date: 2016, 10, 3
You entered: (2016, 10, 4)
Enter date: 2016, 10b, 3
Invalid date entered
```

In the next program, we will accept a file name from the keyboard and then open it using open() function. If the file is not found, then IOError is raised. Then 'except' block will display a message: 'File not found'. If file is found, then all the lines of the file are read using readlines() method as:

```
n = len(f.readlines())
```

Here, f.readLines() will read the lines available in the file. Then len() function will return their number. This is stored into 'n'.

Program

Program 9: A Python program to handle IOError produced by open() function.

```
# example for IOError
# accept a filename
try:
    name = input('Enter filename: ')
    f = open(name, 'r')
except IOError:
    print('File not found: ', name)
else:
    n = len(f.readlines())
    print(name, 'has', n, 'lines')
    f.close()
```

Output:

```
C:\>python ex.py
Enter filename: ex.py
ex.py has 11 lines
C:\>python ex.py
Enter filename: abcd
File not found: abcd
```

In Program 10, we are defining a function avg() to find total and average of list of numbers. It returns total and average as:

```
return tot, avg
```

We can call this function and get these values into two variables 't' and 'a' as:

```
t,a = avg([1,2,3,4,5])    # call avg() and pass list of 5 elements.
```

In this case, the output will be:

```
Total= 15, Average= 3.0
```

But, a list can contain different types of elements. What happens if we give a list that contains some strings as:

```
t,a = avg([1,2,3,4,5, 'a'])   # call avg() and pass list of 6
                              #elements.
```

Since the last element is 'a' that cannot be added to other elements, avg() function cannot find total and average. It raises an exception by the name 'TypeError'. On the other hand, if we pass an empty list, then the number of elements becomes zero and while calculating average as total / n, there will be 'ZeroDivisionError'. We can handle these two exceptions using two except blocks as shown in the program.

Program

Program 10: A Python program to handle multiple exceptions.

```
# example for two exceptions
# a function to find total and average of list elements
def avg(list):
    tot=0
    for x in list:
        tot+=x
    avg = tot/len(list)
    return tot, avg

# call the avg() and pass a list
try:
    t,a = avg([1,2,3,4,5,'a'])   # here, give empty list and try.
    print('Total= {}, Average= {}'.format(t,a))
except TypeError:
    print('Type Error, please provide numbers. ')
except ZeroDivisionError:
    print('ZeroDivisionError, please do not give empty list. ')
```

Output:

```
C:\>python ex.py
Type Error, please provide numbers.
```

In the previous program, if we call avg() function and pass empty list as:

```
t,a = avg([1,2,3,4,5,'a'])
```

Then the following will be the output:

```
ZeroDivisionError, please do not give empty list.
```

The Except Block

The 'except' block is useful to catch an exception that is raised in the try block. When there is an exception in the try block, then only the except block is executed. It is written in various formats.

1. To catch the exception which is raised in the try block, we can write except block with the Exceptionclass name as:

```
except Exceptionclass:
```

2. We can catch the exception as an object that contains some description about the exception.

```
except Exceptionclass as obj:
```

3. To catch multiple exceptions, we can write multiple catch blocks. The other way is to use a single except block and write all the exceptions as a tuple inside parentheses as:

```
except (Exceptionclass1, Exceptionclass2, … ):
```

4. To catch any type of exception where we are not bothered about which type of exception it is, we can write except block without mentioning any Exceptionclass name as:

```
except:
```

In the previous Program 10, we are catching two exceptions using two except blocks. The same can be written using a single except block as:

```
except (TypeError, ZeroDivisionError):
    print('Either TypeError or ZeroDivisionError occurred. ')
```

The other way is not writing any exception name in except block. This will catch any type of exception, but the programmer cannot determine specifically which exception has occurred. For example,

```
except:
    print('Some exception occurred. ')
```

In Program 11, we are finding inverse of a given number. In this program, we are using try block without except block. When we want to use try block alone, we need to follow it with a finally block. Since we are not using except block, it is not possible to catch the exception.

Program

Program 11: A Python program to understand the usage of try with finally blocks.

```
# try without except block
try:
    x = int(input('Enter a number: '))
    y = 1 / x
finally:
    print("We are not catching the exception.")
print("The inverse is: ", y)
```

Output:

```
C:\>python ex.py
Enter a number: 5
We are not catching the exception.
The inverse is: 0.2
```

The assert Statement

The assert statement is useful to ensure that a given condition is True. If it is not true, it raises AssertionError. The syntax is as follows:

```
assert condition, message
```

If the condition is False, then the exception by the name AssertionError is raised along with the 'message' written in the assert statement. If 'message' is not given in the assert statement, and the condition is False, then also AssertionError is raised without message. In Program 12, we are using assert statement without a message. If the condition mentioned in the assert statement is False, thenAssertionError is raised.

Program

Program 12: A Python program using the assert statement and catching AssertionError.

```
# handling AssertionError
try:
    x = int(input('Enter a number between 5 and 10: '))
    assert x>=5 and x<=10
    print('The number entered: ', x)
except AssertionError:
    print('The condition is not fulfilled')
```

Output:

```
C:\>python ex.py
Enter a number between 5 and 10: 12
The condition is not fulfilled
```

The same program can be rewritten using a message after the condition in the assert statement. When the condition is False, the message is passed to AssertionError object 'obj' that can be displayed in the except block as shown in Program 13.

Program

Program 13: A Python program to use the assert statement with a message.

```
# handling AssertionError - v 2.0
try:
    x = int(input('Enter a number between 5 and 10: '))
    assert x>=5 and x<=10, "Your input is not correct"
    print('The number entered: ', x)
except AssertionError as obj:
    print(obj)
```

Output:

```
C:\>python ex.py
Enter a number between 5 and 10: 12
Your input is not correct
```

User-Defined Exceptions

Like the built-in exceptions of Python, the programmer can also create his own exceptions which are called 'User- defined exceptions' or 'Custom exceptions'. We know Python offers many exceptions which will raise in different contexts. For example, when a number is divided by zero, the ZeroDivisionError is raised. Similarly, when the datatype is not correct, TypeErroris raised.

But, there may be some situations where none of the exceptions in Python are useful for the programmer. In that case, the programmer has to create his own exception and raise it. For example, let's take a bank where customers have accounts. Each account is characterized by customer name and balance amount. The rule of the bank is that every customer should keep minimum Rs. 2000.00 as balance amount in his account. The programmer now is given a task to check the accounts to know every customer is maintaining minimum balance of Rs. 2000.00 or not. If the balance amount is below Rs. 2000.00, then the programmer wants to raise an exception saying 'Balance amount is less in the account of so and so person'. This will be helpful to the bank authorities to find out the customer.

So, the programmer wants an exception that is raised when the balance amount in an account is less than Rs 2000.00. Since there is no such exception available in Python, the programmer has to create his own exception. For this purpose, he has to follow these steps:

1. Since all exceptions are classes, the programmer is supposed to create his own exception as a class. Also, he should make his class as a sub class to the in-built 'Exception' class.

```
class MyException(Exception):
    def __init__(self, arg):
        self.msg = arg
```

   Here, 'MyException' class is the sub class for 'Exception' class. This class has a constructor where a variable 'msg' is defined. This 'msg' receives a message passed from outside through 'arg'.

2. The programmer can write his code; maybe it represents a group of statements or a function. When the programmer suspects the possibility of exception, he should raise his own exception using 'raise' statement as:

```
raise MyException('message')
```

   Here, raise statement is raising MyException class object that contains the given 'message'.

3. The programmer can insert the code inside a 'try' block and catch the exception using 'except' block as:

```
try:
    code
except MyException as me:
    print(me)
```

Here, the object 'me' contains the message given in the raise statement. All these steps are shown in Program 14. In this program, we are passing a dictionary with names and balances to the check() function. As dictionary elements, name is the key and balance is the value. The check() function displays these details and checks whether the balance is less than 2000.00. If it is so, then it raises MyException with a message: 'Balance amount is less in the account of so and so person'. This message is passed to 'except' block where it is displayed.

Program

Program 14: A Python program to create our own exception and raise it when needed.

```
# create our own class as sub class to Exception class
class MyException(Exception):
    def __init__(self, arg):
        self.msg = arg
```

```
    # write code where exception may raise
    # to raise the exception, use raise statement
    def check(dict):
        for k,v in dict.items():
            print('Name= {:15s} Balance= {:10.2f}'.format(k,v))
            if(v<2000.00):
                raise MyException('Balance amount is less in the account of
'+k)

    # our own exception is handled using try and except blocks
    bank = {'Raj':5000.00, 'Vani':8900.50, 'Ajay':1990.00,
'Naresh':3000.00}
    try:
        check(bank)
    except MyException as me:
        print(me)
```

Output:

```
    C:\>python ex.py
    Name=Raj                   Balance=5000.00
    Name= Vani                 Balance=8900.50
    Name= Ajay                 Balance=1990.00
    Balance amount is less in the account of Ajay
```

Logging the Exceptions

It is a good idea to store all the error messages raised by a program into a file. The file which stores the messages, especially of errors or exceptions is called a 'log' file and this technique is called 'logging'. When we store the messages into a log file, we can open the file and read it or take a print out of the file later. This helps the programmers to understand how many errors are there, the names of those errors and where they are occurring in the program. This information will enable them to pin point the errors and also rectify them easily. So, logging helps in debugging the programs.

Python provides a module 'logging' that is useful to create a log file that can store all error messages that may occur while executing a program.

There may be different levels of error messages. For example, an error that crashes the system should be given more importance than an error that merely displays a warning message. So, depending on the seriousness of the error, they are classified into 6 levels in 'logging' module, as shown in Table 16.2:

Table 16.2: Logging Error Level and their Predefined Numeric Values

Level	Numeric value	Description
CRITICAL	50	Represents a very serious error that needs high attention.
ERROR	40	Represents a serious error.
WARNING	30	Represents a warning message, some caution is

Level	Numeric value	Description
		needed.
INFO	20	Represents a message with some important information.
DEBUG	10	Represents a message with debugging information.
NOTSET	0	Represents that the level is not set.

As we know, by default, the error messages that occur at the time of executing a program are displayed on the user's monitor. Only the messages which are equal to or above the level of a WARNING are displayed. That means WARNINGS, ERRORS and CRITICAL ERRORS are displayed. It is possible that we can set this default behavior as we need.

To understand different levels of logging messages, we are going to write a Python program. In this program, first we have to create a file for logging (storing) the messages. This is done using basicConfig() method of logging module as:

```
logging.basicConfig(filename='mylog.txt', level=logging.ERROR)
```

Here, the log file name is given as 'mylog.txt'. The level is set to ERROR. Hence the messages whose level will be at ERROR or above, (i.e. ERROR or CRITICAL) will only be stored into the log file. Once, this is done, we can add the messages to the 'mylog.txt' file as:

```
logging.methodname('message')
```

The methodnames can be critical(), error(), warning(), info() and debug(). For example, we want to add a critical message, we should use critical() method as:

```
logging.critical('System crash - Immediate attention required')
```

Now, this error message is stored into the log file, i.e. 'mylog.txt'. Observe Program 15.

Program

Program 15: A Python program that creates a log file with errors and critical messages.

```
# understanding logging of error messages.
import logging

# store messages into mylog.txt file.
# store only the messages with level equal to or more than that of ERROR
logging.basicConfig(filename='mylog.txt', level=logging.ERROR)

# these messages are stored into the file.
logging.error("There is an error in the program.")
logging.critical("There is a problem in the design.")

# but these are not stored.
logging.warning("The project is going slow.")
logging.info("You are a junior programmer.")
logging.debug("Line no. 10 contains syntax error.")
```

Output:

```
C:\>python ex.py
C:\>
```

When the above program is executed, we can see a file created by the name 'mylog.txt' in our current directory. Open the file to see the following messages:

```
ERROR:root:There is an error in the program.
CRITICAL:root:There is a problem in the design.
```

In Program 15, we imported logging module as:

```
import logging
```

Since only the module is imported, we have to refer to its methods using this module name, as: logging.basicConfig(), logging.error(), etc. To avoid writing the module name before the methods, we can change the import statement as:

```
from logging import *
```

Here, we are importing all methods (* means all) from the logging module. That means, instead of importing the logging module, we are importing its methods. Hence, we can refer to the methods directly, without using the module name. We can refer to them simply as: basicConfig(), error(), etc.

Logging can be used to store all the exception messages which occur in a program. For this purpose, we should use exception() method to send messages to the log file. But this exception() method should be always used inside 'except' block only. For example, to store the exception message which is in 'e' into the log file, we can write the 'except' block as:

```
except Exception as e:   # exception message will be in the object 'e'
    logging.exception(e)   # store that message into log file
```

In Program 16, we are accepting two numbers 'a' and 'b' from the user and then finding the result of their division. When an exception occurs inside 'try' block, the 'except' block will catch it and the exception message will be stored into the object 'e'. This message is then written into the log file 'log.txt'.

Program

Program 16: A Python program to store the messages released by any exception into a log file.

```
# logging all messages from a program
import logging

# store logging messages into log.txt file
logging.basicConfig(filename='log.txt', level=logging.ERROR)
try:
    a = int(input('Enter a number: '))
    b = int(input('Enter another number: '))
    c = a/b

except Exception as e:
    logging.exception(e)
```

```
    else:
        print('The result of division: ', c)
```

Output:

```
C:\>python ex.py
Enter a number: 10
Enter another number: 20
The result of division:  0.5

C:\>python ex.py
Enter a number: 10
Enter another number: 0

C:\>python ex.py
Enter a number: 10
Enter another number: ab
```

Please observe that the program is executed 3 times with different inputs. First time, the values supplied are 10 and 20. With these values, the program executed well and there are no exceptions. Second time, the values supplied are 10 and 0. In this case, there is possibility for ZeroDivisionError. The message related to this exception will be stored into our log file. In the third time execution, the values entered are 10 and 'ab'. In this case, there is possibility for ValueError. The message of this exception will also be added to our log file. Now, we can open the log file 'log.txt' and see the following messages:

```
ERROR:root:division by zero
Traceback (most recent call last):
  File "ex.py", line 9, in <module>
    c = a/b
ZeroDivisionError: division by zero
ERROR:root:invalid literal for int() with base 10: 'ab'
Traceback (most recent call last):
  File "ex.py", line 8, in <module>
    b = int(input('Enter another number: '))
ValueError: invalid literal for int() with base 10: 'ab'
```

Points to Remember

- An exception is an error that can be handled by a programmer. If the programmer cannot handle it, then it will not be an exception, it will become an error.
- All exceptions occur only at runtime.
- The errors that occur at compilation time are not called exceptions. Also logical errors cannot come into exceptions category.
- When an exception occurs, the program terminates abruptly. Due to this, the important data in the files or databases may be lost or the program may be corrupted.
- All exceptions in Python are represented as classes.
- All exceptions are sub classes of 'BaseException' class.
- All errors (exceptions) are defined as sub classes of 'StandardError' class.

- All warnings are derived as sub classes from 'Warning' class.
- All user-defined exceptions should be derived from 'Exception' class.
- All exceptions in a Python program should be handled to make it robust.
- Exception handling is done using try-except-finally-else blocks.
- Try block contains the statements where there is a possibility for exceptions.
- Except block handles the exceptions that are raised in the try block.
- Finally block is always executed irrespective of whether there is an exception or not.
- When there is an exception in the try block, PVM jumps into relevant except block where the exception is handled.
- When there is no exception, then PVM does not execute except block, rather it will execute else block.
- To handle multiple exceptions, we can use multiple except blocks.
- To handle multiple exceptions, we can use single except block with all exception class names in a tuple.
- The 'assert' statement is useful to ensure that a given condition is True, otherwise to raise AssertionError.
- The exceptions which are already available in Python are called built-in exceptions. Similar to these exceptions, the programmer can also build his own exceptions, called user – defined exceptions.
- The 'raise' statement is useful to raise user-defined exceptions.
- The 'logging' module is useful to store exception or error messages into a log file. Logging is useful to debug the programs.

CHAPTER

FILES IN PYTHON 17

We use different files in our daily life. For example, we may keep all our school certificates in a file and call it 'certificates file'. This file contains several certificates or pages and each page contains some data. From this example, we can simply say that a file is a place for storing data. Similarly, when we go to an office, we can see a book that contains the attendance of the employees. This book is called 'attendance file' since it contains attendance data of employees. Let's understand that if the data is stored in a place, it is called a *file*.

Files

Data is very important. Every organization depends on its data for continuing its business operations. If the data is lost, the organization has to be closed. This is the reason computers are primarily created for handling data, especially for storing and retrieving data. In later days, programs are developed to process the data that is stored in the computer.

To store data in a computer, we need files. For example, we can store employee data like employee number, name and salary in a file in the computer and later use it whenever we want. Similarly, we can store student data like student roll number, name and marks in the computer. In computers' view, a file is nothing but collection of data that is available to a program. Once we store data in a computer file, we can retrieve it and use it depending on our requirements. Figure 17.1 shows the file in our daily life and the file stored in the computer:

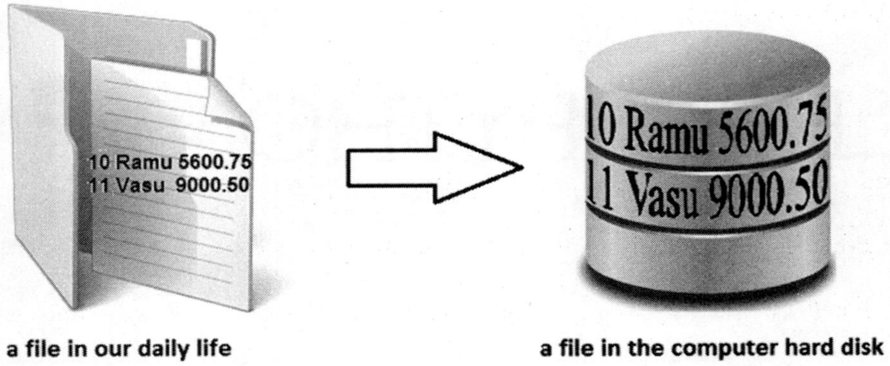

Figure 17.1: A file in our daily life is similar to a file in the computer

There are four important advantages of storing data in a file:

- When the data is stored in a file, it is stored permanently. This means that even though the computer is switched off, the data is not removed from the memory since the file is stored on hard disk or CD. This file data can be utilized later, whenever required.
- It is possible to update the file data. For example, we can add new data to the existing file, delete unnecessary data from the file and modify the available data of the file. This makes the file more useful.
- Once the data is stored in a file, the same data can be shared by various programs. For example, once employee data is stored in a file, it can be used in a program to calculate employees' net salaries or in another program to calculate income tax payable by the employees.
- Files are highly useful to store huge amount of data. For example, voters' list or census data.

Types of Files in Python

In Python, there are two types of files. They are:

- Text files
- Binary files

Text files store the data in the form of characters. For example, if we store employee name "Ganesh", it will be stored as 6 characters and the employee salary 8900.75 is stored as 7 characters. Normally, text files are used to store characters or strings.

Binary files store entire data in the form of bytes, i.e. a group of 8 bits each. For example, a character is stored as a byte and an integer is stored in the form of 8 bytes (on a 64 bit machine). When the data is retrieved from the binary file, the programmer can retrieve the data as bytes. Binary files can be used to store text, images, audio and video.

Image files are generally available in .jpg, .gif or .png formats. We cannot use text files to store images as the images do not contain characters. On the other hand, images contain pixels which are minute dots with which the picture is composed of. Each pixel can be represented by a bit, i.e. either 1 or 0. Since these bits can be handled by binary files, we can say that they are highly suitable to store images.

It is very important to know how to create files, store data in the files and retrieve the data from the files in Python. To do any operation on files, first of all we should open the files.

Opening a File

We should use open() function to open a file. This function accepts 'filename' and 'open mode' in which to open the file.

```
file handler = open("file name", "open mode", "buffering")
```

Here, the 'file name' represents a name on which the data is stored. We can use any name to reflect the actual data. For example, we can use 'empdata' as file name to represent the employee data. The file 'open mode' represents the purpose of opening the file. Table 17.1 specifies the file open modes and their meanings:

Table 17.1: The File Opening Modes

File open mode	Description
w	To write data into file. If any data is already present in the file, it would be deleted and the present data will be stored.
r	To read data from the file. The file pointer is positioned at the beginning of the file.
a	To append data to the file. Appending means adding at the end of existing data. The file pointer is placed at the end of the file. If the file does not exist, it will create a new file for writing data.
w+	To write and read data of a file. The previous data in the file will be deleted.
r+	To read and write data into a file. The previous data in the file will not be deleted. The file pointer is placed at the beginning of the file.
a+	To append and read data of a file. The file pointer will be at the end of the file if the file exists. If the file does not exist, it creates a new file for reading and writing.

File open mode	Description
x	To open the file in exclusive creation mode. The file creation fails if the file already exists.

Table 17.1 represents file open modes for text files. If we attach 'b' for them, they represent modes for binary files. For example, wb, rb, ab, w+b, r+b, a+b are the modes for binary files.

A buffer represents a temporary block of memory. 'buffering' is an optional integer used to set the size of the buffer for the file. In the binary mode, we can pass 0 as buffering integer to inform not to use any buffering. In text mode, we can use 1 for buffering to retrieve data from the file one line at a time. Apart from these, we can use any positive integer for buffering. Suppose, we use 500, then a buffer of 500 bytes size is used via which the data is read or written. If we do not mention any buffering integer, then the default buffer size used is 4096 or 8192 bytes.

When the open() function is used to open a file, it returns a pointer to the beginning of the file. This is called 'file handler' or 'file object'. As an example, to open a file for storing data into it, we can written the open() function as:

```
f = open("myfile.txt", "w")
```

Here, 'f' represents the file handler or file object. It refers to the file with the name "myfile.txt" that is opened in "w" mode. This means, we can write data into the file but we cannot read data from this file. If this file exists already, then its contents are deleted and the present data is stored into the file.

Closing a File

A file which is opened should be closed using the close() method. Once a file is opened but not closed, then the data of the file may be corrupted or deleted in some cases. Also, if the file is not closed, the memory utilized by the file is not freed, leading to problems like insufficient memory. This happens when we are working with several files simultaneously. Hence it is mandatory to close the file.

```
f.close()
```

Here, the file represented by the file object 'f' is closed. It means 'f' is deleted from the memory. Once the file object is lost, the file data will become inaccessible. If we want to do any work with the file again, we should once again open the file using the open() function.

In Program 1, we are creating a file where we want to store some characters. We know that a group of characters represent a string. After entering a string from the keyboard using input() function, we store the string into the file using write() method as:

```
f.write(str)
```

In this way, write() can be used to store a character or a group of characters (string) into a file represented by the file object 'f'.

Program

Program 1: A Python program to create a text file to store individual characters.

```
# creating a file to store characters
# open the file for writing data
f = open('myfile.txt', 'w')

# enter characters from keyboard
str = input('Enter text: ')

# write the string into file
f.write(str)

# closing the file
f.close()
```

Output:

```
C:\>python create.py
Enter text: This is my first line.
```

In Program 1, characters typed by us are stored into the file 'myfile.txt'. This file can be checked in the current directory where the program is executed. If we run this program again, the already entered data in the file is lost and the file will be created as a fresh file without any data. In this way, new data entered by us will only be stored into the file and the previous data is lost. If we want to retain the previous data and want to add the new data at the end of the file, then we have to open the file in append mode as:

```
f = open('myfile.txt', 'a')
```

The next step is to read the data from 'myfile.txt' and display it on the monitor. To read data from a text file, we can use read() method as:

```
str = f.read()
```

This will read all characters from the file 'f' and returns them into the string 'str'. We can also use the read() method to read only a specified number of bytes from the file as:

```
str = f.read(n)
```

where 'n' represents the number of bytes to be read from the beginning of the file.

Program

Program 2: A Python program to read characters from a text file.

```
# reading characters from file
# open the file for reading data
f = open('myfile.txt', 'r')

# read all characters from file
str = f.read()

# display them on the screen
```

```
print(str)

# closing the file
f.close()
```

Output:

```
C:\>python read.py
This is my first line.
```

If in Program 2, we use the read() method as:

```
str = f.read(4)
```

Then it will read only the first 4 bytes of the file and hence the output will be:

```
This
```

Working with Text Files Containing Strings

To store a group of strings into a text file, we have to use the write() method inside a loop. For example, to store strings into the file as long as the user does not type '@' symbol, we can write while loop as:

```
while str != '@':
    # write the string into file
    if(str != '@'):
        f.write(str+"\n")
```

Please observe the "\n" at the end of the string inside write() method. The write() method writes all the strings sequentially in a single line. To write the strings in different lines, we are supposed to add "\n" character at the end of each string.

Program

Program 3: A Python program to store a group of strings into a text file.

```
# creating a file with strings
# open the file for writing data
f = open('myfile.txt', 'w')

# enter strings from keyboard
print('Enter text (@ at end): ')
while str != '@':
    str = input()   # accept string into str
    # write the string into file
    if(str != '@'):
        f.write(str+"\n")

# closing the file
f.close()
```

Output:

```
C:\>python create1.py
This is my file line one.
This is line two.
@
```

Now, to read the strings from the "myfile.txt", we can use the read() method in the following way:

```
f.read()
```

This method reads all the lines of the text file and displays them line by line as they were stored in the "myfile.txt". Consider the following output:

```
This is my file line one.
This is line two.
```

There is another method by the name readlines() that reads all the lines into a list. This can be used as:

```
f.readlines()
```

This method displays all the strings as elements in a list. The "\n" character is visible at the end of each string, as:

```
['This is my file line one.\n', 'This is line two.\n']
```

If we want to suppress the "\n" characters, then we can use read() method with splitlines() method as:

```
f.read().splitlines()
```

In this case the output will be:

```
['This is my file line one.', 'This is line two.']
```

Program

Program 4: A Python program to read all the strings from the text file and display them.

```
# reading strings from a file
# open the file for reading data
f = open('myfile.txt', 'r')

# read strings from the file
print('The file contents are: ')
str = f.read()
print(str)

# closing the file
f.close()
```

Output:

```
C:\>python read1.py
The file contents are:
This is my file line one.
This is line two.
```

We will plan another program to append data to the existing "myfile.txt" and then to display the data. For this purpose, we should open the file in 'append and read' mode as:

```
f = open('myfile.txt', 'a+')
```

Once the file is opened in 'a+' mode, as usual we can use write() method to append the strings to the file. After writing the data, without closing the file, we can read strings from the file. But first of all, we should place the file handler to the beginning of the file using seek() method as:

```
f.seek(offset, fromwhere)
```

Here, 'offset' represents how many bytes to move. 'fromwhere' represents from which position to move. For example, 'fromwhere' is 0 represents from beginning of file, 1 represents from the current position in the file and 2 represents from the ending of file.

```
f.seek(10, 0)
```

This will position the file handler at 10th byte from the beginning of the file. So, any reading operation will read data from 10th byte onwards.

```
f.seek(0, 0)
```

This will position the file handler at the 0th byte from the beginning of the file. It means any reading operation will read the data quite from the beginning of the file.

Program

Program 5: A Python program to append data to an existing file and then displaying the entire file.

```
# appending and then reading strings
# open the file for reading data
f = open('myfile.txt', 'a+')

print('Enter text to append(@ at end): ')
while str != '@':
    str = input()    # accept string into str

    # write the string into file
    if(str != '@'):
        f.write(str+"\n")

# put the file pointer to the beginning of file
f.seek(0,0)

# read strings from the file
print('The file contents are: ')
str = f.read()
print(str)

# closing the file
f.close()
```

Output:

```
C:\>python append.py
Enter text to append(@ at end):
This line is added.
@
The file contents are:
This is my file line one.
This is line two.
This line is added.
```

Knowing Whether a File Exists or Not

The operating system (os) module has a sub module by the name 'path' that contains a method isfile(). This method can be used to know whether a file that we are opening really exists or not. For example, os.path.isfile(fname) gives True if the file exists otherwise False. We can use it as:

```
If os.path.isfile(fname):    # if file exists,
    f = open(fname, 'r')     # open it
else:
    print(fname+' does not exist')
    sys.exit()   # terminate the program
```

In Program 6, we are accepting the name of a file from the keyboard, checking whether the file exists or not. If the file exists, then we display the contents of the file; otherwise, we display a message that the file does not exist and then terminate the program.

Program

Program 6: A Python program to know whether a file exists or not.

```
# checking if file exists and then reading data
import os, sys

# open the file for reading data
fname = input('Enter filename: ')

if os.path.isfile(fname):
    f = open(fname, 'r')
else:
    print(fname+' does not exist')
    sys.exit()

# read strings from the file
print('The file contents are: ')
str = f.read()
print(str)

# closing the file
f.close()
```

Output:

```
C:\>python check.py
Enter filename: myfile.txt
The file contents are:
This is my file line one.
This is line two.
This line is added.

C:\>python check.py
Enter filename: yourfile.txt
yourfile.txt does not exist
```

Please observe that while running Program 6, we can enter the same program name 'check.py' to display the source code of the above program.

We can write another program to count the number of lines, words and characters in a text file. The logic is simple. We can use a for loop to read line by line from the file as:

```
for line in f:    # repeat the loop for all lines
    print(line)   # display one line at a time
```

Each line may contain some words. To find out the words, we have to split the line wherever there are spaces. This is done using line.split() method. But this method returns a list with the words.

```
for line in f:
    print(line)
    words = line.split()    # words is a list that contains all words in
                            # a line
    print(words)   # display the list
```

Now, to find out the number of words in a line, we can simply use len() function on 'words' list as len(words). Similarly, to find the number of characters in a line, we can use len(line). So, the total logic will be:

```
for line in f:
    print(line)
    words = line.split()
    print(words)
    cl +=1              # for each line add 1 to cl
    cw += len(words) # in each line add number of words to cw
    cc += len(line)  # in each line, add number of chars to cc
```

Program

Program 7: A Python program to count number of lines, words and characters in a text file.

```
# counting number of lines, words and characters in a file
import os, sys

# open the file for reading data
fname = input('Enter filename: ')

if os.path.isfile(fname):
    f = open(fname, 'r')
else:
    print(fname+' does not exist')
    sys.exit()

# initialize the counters to 0
cl= cw= cc = 0

# read line by line from the file
for line in f:
    words = line.split()
    cl +=1
    cw += len(words)
    cc += len(line)

print('No. of lines: ', cl)
print('No. of words: ', cw)
print('No. of characters: ', cc)
```

```
# close the file
f.close()
```

Output:

```
C:\>python count.py
Enter filename: myfile.txt
No. of lines:  3
No. of words:  13
No. of characters:  61
```

Working with Binary Files

Binary files handle data in the form of bytes. Hence, they can be used to read or write text, images or audio and video files. To open a binary file for reading purpose, we can use 'rb' mode. Here, 'b' is attached to 'r' to represent that it is a binary file. Similarly to write bytes into a binary file, we can use 'wb' mode. To read bytes from a binary file, we can use the read() method and to write bytes into a binary file, we can use the write() methods.

Let's write a program where we want to open an image file like .jpg, .gif or .png file and read bytes from that file. These bytes are then written into a new binary file. It means we are copying an image file as another file. This is shown in Program 8.

Program

Program 8: A Python program to copy an image file into another file.

```
# copying an image into a file
# open the files in binary mode
f1 = open('cat.jpg', 'rb')
f2 = open('new.jpg', 'wb')

# read bytes from f1 and write into f2
bytes = f1.read()
f2.write(bytes)

# close the files
f1.close()
f2.close()
```

Output:

```
C:\>python copy.py
C:\>
```

When the above program is run, it will copy the image file 'cat.jpg' into another file 'new.jpg'. In this program, our assumption is that the file 'cat.jpg' is already available in the current directory. Current directory is the directory where our program is running. Suppose, if the cat.jpg is not available in the current directory, but it is in another directory, then we have to supply the path of that directory to open() function, as:

```
f1 = open('c:\\rnr\\cat.jpg', 'rb')
```

The preceding statement tells that the cat.jpg file is available in 'rnr' sub directory in 'c:' drive. Please remember, the double backslashes in the path above are interpreted as single backslashes only.

The with Statement

The 'with' statement can be used while opening a file. The advantage of with statement is that it will take care of closing a file which is opened by it. Hence, we need not close the file explicitly. In case of an exception also, 'with' statement will close the file before the exception is handled. The format of using 'with' is:

```
with open("filename", "openmode") as fileobject:
```

Program

Program 9: A Python program to use 'with' to open a file and write some strings into the file.

```
# with statement to open a file
with open('sample.txt', 'w') as f:
    f.write('I am a learner\n')
    f.write('Python is attractive\n')
```

Output:

```
C:\>python with1.py
C:\>
```

In Program 9, we opened the file 'sample.txt' and stored two lines of text. This file is again opened using 'with' statement in Program 10 and the contents are displayed.

Program

Program 10: A Python program to use 'with' to open a file and read data from it.

```
# using with statement to open a file
with open('sample.txt', 'r') as f:
    for line in f:
        print(line)
```

Output:

```
C:\>python with2.py
I am a learner
Python is attractive
```

Pickle in Python

So far, we wrote some programs where we stored only text into the files and retrieved same text from the files. These text files are useful when we do not want to perform any calculations on the data. What happens if we want to store some structured data in the files? For example, we want to store some employee details like employee identification number (int type), name (string type) and salary (float type) in a file. This data is well structured and got different types. To store such data, we need to create a class Employee with the instance variables id, name and sal as shown here:

```
class Emp:
    def __init__(self, id, name, sal):
        self.id = id
        self.name = name
        self.sal = sal
    def display(self):
        print("{:5d} {:20s} {:10.2f}".format(self.id, self.name, 
self.sal))
```

Then we create an object to this class and store actual data into that object. Later, this object should be stored into a binary file in the form of bytes. This is called *pickle* or *serialization*. So, let's understand that pickle is a process of converting a class object into a byte stream so that it can be stored into a file. This is also called object serialization. Pickling is done using the dump() method of 'pickle' module as:

```
pickle.dump(object, file)
```

The preceding statement stores the 'object' into the binary 'file'. Once the objects are stored into a file, we can read them from the file at any time. *Unpickle* is a process whereby a byte stream is converted back into a class object. It means, unpickling represents reading the class objects from the file. Unpickling is also called *de-searialization*. Unpickling is done using the load() method of 'pickle' module as:

```
object = pickle.load(file)
```

Here, the load() method reads an object from a binary 'file' and returns it into 'object'. Let's remember that pickling and unpickling should be done using binary files since they support byte streams. The word *stream* represents data flow. So, byte stream represents flow of bytes.

We will understand pickling and unpickling more clearly with the help of an example. First of all let's create Emp class that contains employee identification number, name and salary. This is shown in Program 11.

Program

Program 11: A Python program to create an Emp class with employee details as instance variables.

```
# Emp class - Save this as Emp.py
class Emp:
    def __init__(self, id, name, sal):
        self.id = id
        self.name = name
        self.sal = sal

    def display(self):
        print("{:5d} {:20s} {:10.2f}".format(self.id, self.name, 
self.sal))
```

Output:

```
C:\>python Emp.py
C:\>
```

Our intention is to pickle Emp class objects. For this purpose, we have to import Emp.py file as a module since Emp class is available in that file.

```
import Emp
```

Now, an object to Emp class can be created as:

```
e = Emp.Emp(id, name, sal)
```

Please observe that 'e' is the object of Emp class. Since Emp class belongs to Emp module, we referred to it as Emp.Emp(). This object 'e' should be written to the file 'f' using dump() method of pickle module, as:

```
pickle.dump(e, f)
```

This logic is shown in Figure 17.2 and expressed in Program 12.

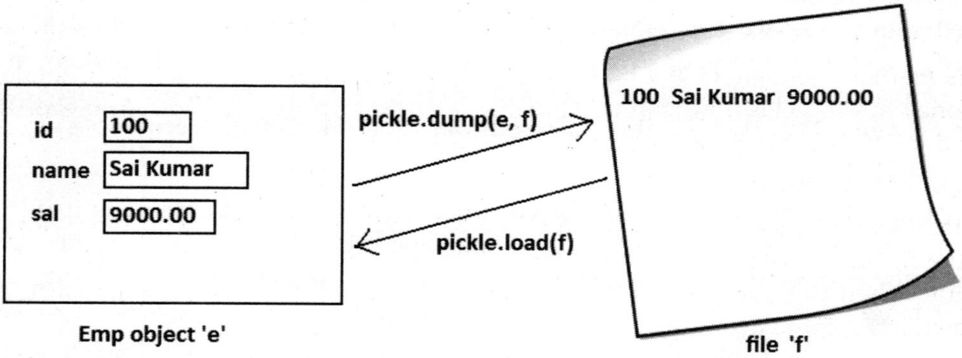

Figure 17.2: Pickling and unpickling a class object

Program

Program 12: A Python program to pickle Emp class objects.

```
# pickle - store Emp class objects into emp.dat file
import Emp, pickle

# open emp.dat file as a binary file for writing
f = open('emp.dat', 'wb')
n = int(input('How many employees? '))

for i in range(n):
    id = int(input('Enter id: '))
    name = input('Enter name: ')
    sal = float(input('Enter salary: '))

    # create Emp class object
    e = Emp.Emp(id, name, sal)

    # store the object e into the file f
```

```
        pickle.dump(e, f)

    # close the file
    f.close()
```

Output:

```
C:\>python pick.py
How many employees? 3
Enter id: 100
Enter name: Sai Kumar
Enter salary: 9000.00
Enter id: 101
Enter name: Ravi Teja
Enter salary: 8900.50
Enter id: 102
Enter name: Harsh Deep
Enter salary: 12000.75
```

In the previous program, we stored 3 Emp class objects into emp.dat file. If we want to get back those objects from the file, we have to unpickle them. To unpickle, we should use load() method of pickle module as:

```
obj = pickle.load(f)
```

This method reads an object from the file 'f' and returns it into 'obj'. Since this object 'obj' belongs to Emp class, we can use the display() method by using the Emp class to display the data of the object as:

```
obj.display()
```

In this way, using a loop, we can read objects from the emp.dat file. When we reach end of the file and could not find any more objects to read, then the exception 'EOFError' will occur. When this exception occurs, we should break the loop and come out of it. This is shown in Program 13.

Program

Program 13: A Python program to unpickel Emp class objects.

```
# unpickle or object de-serialization
import Emp, pickle

# open the file to read objects
f = open('emp.dat', 'rb')

print('Employees details: ')
while True:
    try:
        # read object from file f
        obj = pickle.load(f)
        # display the contents of employee obj
        obj.display()

    except EOFError:
        print('End of file reached...')
        break
```

```
    # close the file
    f.close()
```

Output:

```
C:\>python unpick.py
Employees details:
  100  Sai Kumar                  9000.00
  101  Ravi Teja                  8900.50
  102  Harsh Deep                12000.75
End of file reached...
```

The seek() and tell() Methods

We know that data in the binary files is stored in the form of bytes. When we conduct reading or writing operations on a binary file, a file pointer moves inside the file depending on how many bytes are written or read from the file. For example, if we read 10 bytes of data from a file, the file pointer will be positioned at the 10th byte so that it is possible to continue reading from the 11th byte onwards. To know the position of the file pointer, we can use the tell() method. It returns the current position of the file pointer from the beginning of the file. It is used in the form:

```
n = f.tell()
```

Here, 'f' represents file handler or file object. 'n' is an integer that represents the byte position where the file pointer is positioned.

In case, we want to move the file pointer to another position, we can use the seek() method. This method takes two arguments:

```
f.seek(offset, fromwhere)
```

Here, 'offset' represents how many bytes to move. 'fromwhere' represents from which position to move. For example, 'fromwhere' can be 0, 1 or 2. Here, 0 represents from the beginning of the file, 1 represents from the current position and 2 represents from the ending of the file. The default value of 'fromwhere' is 0, i.e. beginning of the file.

```
f.seek(10)    # same as f.seek(10, 0)
```

This will move the file pointer to the 11th byte (i.e. 10+1) from the beginning of the file (0 represents beginning of the file). So, any reading operation will read data from 11th byte onwards.

```
f.seek(-10, 2)
```

This will move the file pointer to the 9th byte (-10+1) from the ending of the file (2 represents ending of the file). The negative sign before 10 represents moving back in the file.

We will take an example to understand how these methods work in case of a binary file. Observe the following code snippet where we open a binary file 'line.txt' in 'r+b' mode so that it is possible to write data into the file and read data from the file.

```
with open('line.txt', 'r+b') as f:
    f.write(b'Amazing Python')
```

The file object is 'f'. The write() method is storing a string 'Amazing Python' into the file. Observe 'b' prefixed with this string to consider it as a binary string. Now, the string is stored in the file as shown in the Figure 17.3:

A	m	a	z	i	n	g		P	y	t	h	o	n	
1	2	3	4	5	6	7	8	9	10	11	12	13	14	**bytes**

Figure 17.3: The string's characters and their byte positions in the file.

First, we will move the file pointer to the 4th byte using seek() as:

```
f.seek(3)
```

The preceding method will put the file pointer at 3+1 = 4th position. So, file pointer will be at 'z'. If we print 2 bytes using read() method as:

```
print(f.read(2))
```

This will display 'zi'. Now, to know the position of the file pointer we can use tell() method as:

```
print(f.tell())
```

This will display 5. Now, to move the file pointer to 5th position from the ending of the file, we can use seek() method as:

```
f.seek(-6, 2)
```

This will move the file pointer to -6+1 = 5th position. It means it will be positioned at the character 'y'. We can display this character using read() method as:

```
print(f.read(1))
```

This will display 'y'. Now, we can find the position of the file pointer using the tell() method as:

```
print(f.tell())
```

This will display 10 as the character 'y' is at 10th position from the beginning of the file. Please remember the tell() method always gives the positions from the beginning of the file.

Random Accessing of Binary Files

Data in the binary files is stored in the form of continuous bytes. Let's take a binary file having 1000 bytes of data. If we want to access the last 10 bytes of data, it is not needed to search the file byte by byte from the beginning. It is possible to directly go to 991st byte using the seek() method as:

```
f.seek(900)
```

Then read the last 10 bytes using the read() method as:

```
f.read(10)
```

In this way, directly going to any byte in the binary file is called *random accessing.* This is possible by moving the file pointer to any location in the file and then performing reading or writing operations on the file as required.

A problem with binary files is that they accept data in the form of bytes or in binary format. For example, if we store a string into a binary file, as shown in the following statement, we will end up with an error.

```
str = 'Dear'
with open('data.bin', 'wb') as f:
    f.write(str)   # store str
    f.write('Hello')   # store 'Hello'
```

The preceding code will display the following error:

```
TypeError: 'str' does not support the buffer interface.
```

The reason behind this error is that we are trying to store strings into a binary file without converting them into binary format. So, the solution is to convert the ordinary strings into binary format before they are stored into the binary file. Now consider the following code:

```
str = 'Dear'
with open('data.bin', 'wb') as f:
    f.write(str.encode())
    f.write(b'Hello')
```

Converting a string literal into binary format can be done by prefixing the character 'b' before the string, as: b'Hello'. On the other hand, to convert a string variable into binary format, we have to use encode() method, as: str.encode().

The encode() method represents the string in byte format so that it can be stored into the binary file. Similarly, when we read a string from a binary file, it is advisable to convert it into ordinary text format using decode() method, as: str.decode().

In the following program, we are creating a binary file and storing a group of strings. One way to view the data of a binary file is as a group of records with fixed length. For example, we want to take 20 bytes (or characters) as one record and store several such records into the file. Program 14 demonstrates how to store names of cities as a group of records into cities.bin file. In this program, each record length is taken as 20. So, if the city name entered by the user is less than 20 characters length, then the remaining characters in the record will be filled with spaces. For example, if the user stores the city name 'Delhi', since 'Delhi' has only 5 characters, another 15 spaces will be attached at the end of this name and then it is stored into the file. In this way, each record is maintained with fixed length. Consider the following code:

```
ln = len(city)   # find length of city name. suppose it is 5
city = city + (20-ln)*' '   # add 15 spaces at the end of city name
```

Program

Program 14: A Python program to create a binary file and store a few records.

```
# create cities.bin file with cities names
# take the record size as 20 bytes
reclen = 20

# open the file in wb mode as binary file
with open("cities.bin", "wb") as f:
    # write data into the file
    n = int(input('How many entries? '))

    for i in range(n):
        city = input('Enter city name: ')
        # find the length of city
        ln = len(city)
        # increase the city name to 20 chars
        # by adding remaining spaces
        city = city + (reclen-ln)*' '
        # convert city name into byte string
        city = city.encode()
        # write the city name into the file
        f.write(city)
```

Output:

```
C:\>python create.py
How many entries? 4
Enter city name: Delhi
Enter city name: Hyderabad
Enter city name: Pune
Enter city name: Ahmedabad
```

Now, cities.bin file is created with 4 records. In each record, we stored the name of a city. The next step is to display a specific record from the file. This is shown in Program 15. In this program, we accept the record number and display that record. Suppose, we want to display 3rd record, first we should put the file pointer at the end of 2nd record. This is done by seek() method, as:

```
reclen = 20   # this is record length
f.seek(reclen * 2)
```

Once this is done, we can read the next 20 bytes using read() method that gives the 3rd record.

Program

Program 15: A Python program to randomly access a record from a binary file.

```
# reading city name based on record number
# take record length as 20 characters
reclen = 20

# open the file in binary mode for reading
with open('cities.bin', 'rb') as f:
    n = int(input('Enter record number: '))
    # move file pointer to the end of n-1 th record
    f.seek(reclen * (n-1))
```

```
        # get the n th record with 20 chars
        str = f.read(reclen)
        # convert the byte string into ordinary string
        print(str.decode())
```

Output:

```
C:\>python read.py
Enter record number: 3
Pune
```

The next question is how to search for a particular record in the binary file. Suppose, we want to know whether a particular city name is existing in the file or not, we should search record by record using the seek() method.

```
position = 0
f.seek(position)    # initially place the file pointer at 0th byte
position+=20    # every time increase it by 20 bytes
```

The preceding code should be written in a for loop that looks like this:

```
for i in range(n):
```

Here, 'i' indicates record number that changes from 0 to n-1 where n is the total number of records. Then, how to find the number of records in the file? For this purpose, first we should find the file size in bytes. This is given by getsize() method of 'path' sub module of 'os' module.

```
size = os.path.getsize('cities.bin')
```

By dividing the size of the file by the record length, we can get the number of records in the file as:

```
n = int(size/reclen)    # reclen is 20.
```

Program

Program 16: A Python program to search for city name in the file and display the record number that contains the city name.

```
# searching the city name in the file
import os

# take record length as 20 characters
reclen = 20

# find size of the file
size = os.path.getsize('cities.bin')
print('Size of file = {} bytes'.format(size))

# find number of records in the file
n = int(size/reclen)
print('No. of records = {}'. format(n))

# open the file in binary mode for reading
with open('cities.bin', 'rb') as f:
    name = input('Enter city name: ')
    # convert name into binary string
    name = name.encode()
```

```
    # position represents the position of file pointer
    position = 0

    # found becomes True if city is found in the file
    found = False

# repeat for n records in the file
for i in range(n):
        # place the file pointer at position
        f.seek(position)
        # read 20 characters
        str = f.read(20)
        # if found
        if name in str:
            print('Found at record no: ', (i+1))
            found=True
        # go to the next record
        position+=reclen

if not found :
    print('City not found')
```

Output:

```
C:\>python read1.py
Size of file = 80 bytes
No. of records = 4
Enter city name: Hyderabad
Found at record no: 2
```

To update the city name to a new name, first we should know the record number where the city name is found. This logic is presented already in Program 16. Suppose, the city name is found in record number 2 and after reading that record, the file pointer will be at the end of the record. Hence, we should get the file pointer back to the beginning of the record as:

```
f.seek(-20, 1)   # go back 20 bytes from current position
```

Then write the new city name in that place as:

```
f.write(newname)
```

Program

Program 17: A Python program to update or modify a record in a binary file.

```
# updating the city name in the file
import os

# take record length as 20 characters
reclen = 20

# find size of the file
size = os.path.getsize('cities.bin')
print('Size of file = {} bytes'.format(size))

# find number of records in the file
n = int(size/reclen)
print('No. of records = {}'. format(n))
```

```
# open the file in binary mode for reading
with open('cities.bin', 'r+b') as f:
    name = input('Enter city name: ')
    # convert name into binary string
    name = name.encode()

    newname = input('Enter new name: ')
    # find length of newname
    ln = len(newname)
    # add spaces to make its length to be 20
    newname = newname+ (20-ln)*' '
    # convert newname into binary string
    newname = newname.encode()

    # position represents the position of file pointer
    position = 0

    # found becomes True if city is found in the file
    found = False

    # repeat for n records in the file
    for i in range(n):
        # place the file pointer at position
        f.seek(position)
        # read 20 characters
        str = f.read(20)
        # if found
        if name in str:
            print('Updated record no: ', (i+1))
            found=True
            # go back 20 bytes from current position
            f.seek(-20, 1)
            # update the record
            f.write(newname)

        # go to the next record
        position+=reclen

    if not found :
        print('City not found')
```

Output:

```
C:\>python update.py
Size of file = 80 bytes
No. of records = 4
Enter city name: Hyderabad
Enter new name: Bangalore
Updated record no: 2
```

The next step is to develop logic to delete a record from the binary file. There is no way to delete some part of the data from a binary file. The only way to do this is to follow the steps shown here:

1. Suppose we want to delete a record that contains city name 'Bangalore' from cities.bin file. Copy all the records of this file into a temporary file, say file2.bin except the record which matches the city name 'Bangalore'. Now file2.bin contains all the records except the 'Bangalore' record.

2. The next step is to delete the original cities.bin file. This is done by using the remove() method of 'os' module as: os.remove("filename")
3. Rename the file2.bin file as cities.bin file. This is done by using the rename() method of 'os' module as: os.rename("oldfile", "newfile"). Now, this new cities.bin file contains all the records except the one which we deleted.

This logic is presented in Program 18.

Program

Program 18: A Python program to delete a specific record from the binary file.

```
# deleting a record from the file
import os

# take record length as 20 characters
reclen = 20

# find size of the file
size = os.path.getsize('cities.bin')

# find number of records in the file
n = int(size/reclen)

# open the cities.bin for reading
f1 = open('cities.bin', 'rb')

# open file2.bin for writing
f2 = open('file2.bin', 'wb')

# accept city name from keyboard
city = input('Enter city name to delete: ')

# add spaces so that it will have 20 characters length
ln = len(city)
city = city+(reclen-ln)*' '

# convert city name to binary string
city = city.encode()

# repeat for all the n records
for i in range(n):
    # read one record from f1 file
    str = f1.read(reclen)
    # if it is not the city name, store into f2 file
    if(str != city):
        f2.write(str)

print('Record deleted...')

# close the files
f1.close()
f2.close()
```

```
# delete the cities.bin file
os.remove("cities.bin")

# rename file2.bin as cities.bin
os.rename("file2.bin", "cities.bin")
```

Output:

```
C:\>python del.py
Enter city name to delete: Bangalore
Record deleted...
```

Random Accessing of Binary Files using mmap

mmap – 'memory mapped file' is a module in Python that is useful to map or link to a binary file and manipulate the data of the file as we do with the strings. It means, once a binary file is created with some data, that data is viewed as strings and can be manipulated using mmap module. The first step to use the mmap module is to map the file using the mmap() method as:

```
mm = mmap.mmap(f.fileno(), 0)
```

This will map the currently opened file (i.e. 'f') with the file object 'mm'. Please observe the arguments of mmap() method. The first argument is 'f.fileno()' .This indicates that fileno() is a handle to the file object 'f'. This 'f' represents the actual binary file that is being mapped. The second argument is zero(0) represents the total size of the file should be considered for mapping. So, the entire file represented by the file object 'f' is mapped in memory to the object 'mm'. This means, 'mm' will now onwards behave like the file 'f'.

Now, we can read the data from the file using read() or readline() methods as:

```
print(mm.read())     # displays entire file data
print(mm.readline())   # displays the first line of the file
```

Also, we can retrieve data from the file using slicing operator as:

```
print(mm[5:])   # display from 5th byte till the end
print(mm[5:10])   # display from 5th to 9th bytes
```

It is also possible to modify or replace the data of the file using slicing as:

```
mm[5:10] = str   # replace from 5th to 9th characters by string 'str'
```

We can also use find() method that returns the first position of a string in the file as:

```
n = mm.find(name)   # return the position of name in the file
```

We can also use seek() method to position the file pointer to any position we want as:

```
mm.seek(10, 0)   # position the file pointer to 10th byte from
# beginning of file
```

Let's remember that the memory mapping is done only for the binary files and not for the text files. So, first of all let's create a binary file where we want to store some strings. Suppose we want to store name and phone number into the file, we can use write() method as:

```
f.write(name+phone)
```

This will store name and phone number as one concatenated string into the file object 'f'. But we are supposed to convert these strings into binary (bytes) format before they are stored into the file. For this purpose, we should use encode() method as:

```
name = name.encode()   # convert name from string to binary string
```

The encode() method converts the strings into bytes so that they can be written into the file. Similarly, while reading the data from the file, we get only binary strings from the file. This binary string can be converted into ordinary string using decode() method as:

```
ph = ph.decode()   # convert bytes into a string
```

Now, let's write a program to create a phone book that contains names of persons and phone numbers in the form of a binary file.

Program

Program 19: A Python program to create phone book with names and phone numbers.

```
# create phonebook.dat file
# open the file in wb mode as binary file
with open("phonebook.dat", "wb") as f:
    # write data into the file
    n = int(input('How many entries? '))

    for i in range(n):
        name = input('Enter name: ')
        phone = input('Enter phone no: ')
        # convert name and phone from strings to bytes
        name = name.encode()
        phone = phone.encode()
        # write the data into the file
        f.write(name+phone)
```

Output:

```
C:\>python demo.py
How many entries? 3
Enter name: Viswajith
Enter phone no: 988012556
Enter name: Manoj
Enter phone no: 7700177001
Enter name: Dheerendra
Enter phone no: 8989189891
```

In Program 19, we have created the phonebook.dat file with 3 persons' names and phone numbers. We can go to the current directory and view the file contents in Notepad and it will look something like this:

```
Viswajith9880125567Manoj7700177001Dheerendra8989189891
```

The next step is to perform some operations like displaying all the entries of the file, display required information from the file or modify the contents of the file. This is done in Program 20.

Program

Program 20: A Python program to use mmap and performing various operations on a binary file.

```
# using mmap on a binary file.
import mmap, sys

# display a menu
print('1 to display all the entries')
print('2 to display phone number')
print('3 to modify an entry')
print('4 exit')
ch = input('Your choice: ')
if ch=='4':
    sys.exit()

with open("phonebook.dat", "r+b") as f:

    # memory-map the file, size 0 means whole file
    mm = mmap.mmap(f.fileno(), 0)

    # display the entire file
    if(ch == '1'):
        print(mm.read().decode())

    # display phone number
    if(ch == '2'):
        name = input('Enter name: ')
        # find position of name
        n = mm.find(name.encode())
        # go to end of name
        n1 = n+len(name)
        # display the next 10 bytes
        ph = mm[n1: n1+10]
        print('Phone no: ', ph.decode())

    # modify phone number
    if(ch == '3'):
        name = input('Enter name: ')
        # find position of name
        n = mm.find(name.encode())
        # go to end of name
        n1 = n+len(name)
        # enter new phone number
        ph1 = input('Enter new phone number: ')
        # the old phone number is 10 bytes after n1
        mm[n1: n1+10] = ph1.encode()

    # close the map
    mm.close()
```

Output:

```
C:\>python demo1.py
1 to display all the entries
2 to display phone number
3 to modify an entry
4 exit
Your choice: 2
```

```
Enter name: Manoj
Phone no: 7700177001
C:\> python demo1.py
1 to display all the entries
2 to display phone number
3 to modify an entry
4 exit
Your choice: 3
Enter name: Dheerendra
Enter new phone number: 9999911111
```

Zipping and Unzipping Files

We know that some softwares like 'winzip' provide zipping and unzipping of file data. In zipping the file contents, following two things could happen:

- The file contents are compressed and hence the size will be reduced.
- The format of data will be changed making it unreadable.

While zipping a file content, a zipping algorithm (logic) is used in such a way that the algorithm first finds out which bit pattern is most often repeated in the original file and replaces that bit pattern with a 0. Then the algorithm searches for the next bit pattern which is most often repeated in the input file. In its place, a 1 is substituted. The third repeated bit pattern will be replaced by 10, the fourth by 11, the fifth by 100, and so on. In this way, the original bit patterns are replaced by lesser number of bits. This file with lesser number of bits is called 'zipped file' or 'compressed file'.

To get back the original data from the zipped file, we can follow a reverse algorithm, which substitutes the original bit pattern wherever particular bits are found. This is shown in Figure 17.4:

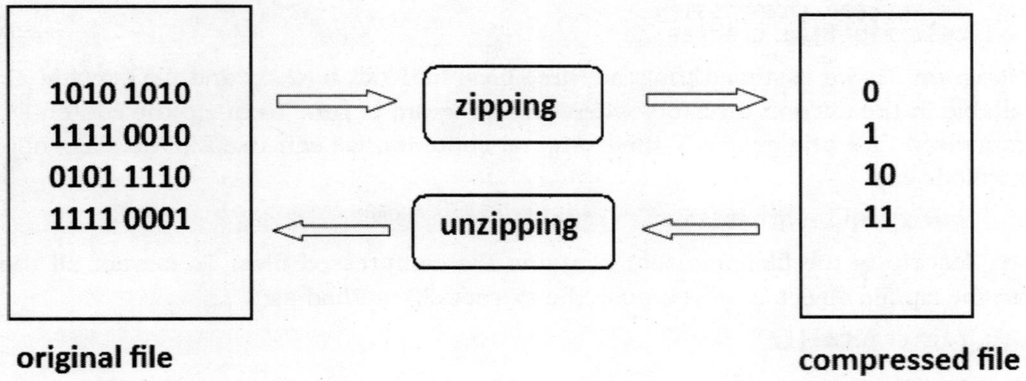

Figure 17.4: Zipping and unzipping a file

In Python, the module *zipfile* contains ZipFile class that helps us to zip or unzip a file contents. For example, to zip the files, we should first pass the zip file name in write mode with an attribute ZIP_DEFLATED to the ZipFile class object as:

```
f = ZipFile('test.zip', 'w', ZIP_DEFLATED)
```

Here, 'f' is the ZipFile class object to which test.zip file name is passed. This is the zip file that is created finally. The next step is to add the filenames that are to be zipped, using write() method as:

```
f.write('file1.txt')
f.write('file2.txt')
```

Here, we are writing two files: file1.txt and file2.txt into the object 'f'. Hence, these two files are compressed and stored into test.zip file. This is shown in Program 21.

Program

Program 21: A Python program to compress the contents of files.

```
# zipping the contents of files
from zipfile import *

# create zip file
f = ZipFile('test.zip', 'w', ZIP_DEFLATED)

# add some files. these are zipped
f.write('file1.txt')
f.write('file2.txt')
f.write('file3.txt')

# close the zip file
print('test.zip file created...')
f.close()
```

Output:

```
C:\>python compress.py
test.zip file created...
```

In Program 21, we assumed that the three files: file1.txt, file2.txt and file3.txt are already available in the current directory where this program is run. To unzip the contents of the compressed files and get back their original contents, we can use ZipFile class object in read mode as:

```
z = ZipFile('test.zip', 'r')
```

Here, test.zip is the filename that contains the compressed files. To extract all the files from the zip file object 'z', we can use the extractall() method as:

```
z.extractall()
```

This will extract all the files in uncompressed format into the current directory. If we want to extract them to another directory, we can mention the directory path in the extractall() method as:

```
z.extractall('f:\\python\core\sub')
```

Program

Program 22: A Python program to unzip the contents of the files that are available in a zip file.

```
# to view contents of zipped files
from zipfile import *

# Open the zip file
z = ZipFile('test.zip', 'r')

# extract all the file names which are in the zip file
z.extractall()
```

Output:

```
C:\>python uncompress.py
Contents of file1.txt
..............................
..............................
Contents of file2.txt
..............................
..............................
Contents of file3.txt
..............................
..............................
```

Working with Directories

The *os* (operating system) module represents operating system dependent functionality. This module is useful to perform some simple operations on directories. Let's assume we are working with the following directory path:

```
F:\py\enum
```

And we are currently in the directory F:\py where we are running our programs. If we want to know the currently working directory, we can use getcwd() method of 'os' module as shown in Program 23.

Program

Program 23: A Python program to know the currently working directory.

```
import os
# get current working directory
current = os.getcwd()
print('Current directory= ', current)
```

Output:

```
F:\py>python os.py
Current directory= F:\py
```

If we want to create our own directory in the present directory, we can use the mkdir() method. This method can be used as:

```
os.mkdir('mysub')
```

This will create mysub in the present directory. Suppose, we write the following statement:

```
os.mkdir('mysub/mysub2')
```

This will create mysub2 in the mysub directory. Consider Program 24.

Program

Program 24: A Python program to create a sub directory and then sub-sub directory in the current directory.

```
import os
# create a sub directory by the name mysub
os.mkdir('mysub')

# create a sub-sub directory by the name mysub2
os.mkdir('mysub/mysub2')
```

Output:

```
F:\py>python os.py
```

After executing Program 24, we can observe mysub directory in our current directory (F:\py) and inside the mysub directory, there would be another directory by the name mysub2. This can be verified by visiting the directory structure in our computer. The problem with mkdir() method is that it cannot create a sub directory unless the parent directory exists. For example in Program 24, since mysub is existing, it is able to create mysub2 inside that. If mysub does not exist, then it cannot create mysub2. In this case, makedirs() is a useful method. This method recursively creates the sub directories. For example, consider the following statement:

```
os.makedirs('newsub/newsub2')
```

This creates first newsub directory if it does not exist, and then it will create newsub2 inside it. Consider Program 25.

Program

Program 25: A Python program to use the makedirs() function to create sub and sub-sub directories.

```
import os
# create sub and sub-sub directories
os.makedirs('newsub/newsub2')
```

Output:

```
F:\py>python os.py
```

We can change our current working directory to another existing directory. For this purpose, we can use chdir() method. For example, if we want to change our directory to newsub2 which is in newsub, we can use chdir() method as:

```
goto = os.chdir(‘newsub/newsub2’)
```

Here, our assumption is that newsub is in the current directory and newsub contains newsub2. After executing the preceding statement, our current working directory will be newsub2. This is shown in Program 26.

Program

Program 26: A Python program to change to another directory.

```
import os
# change to newsub2 directory
goto = os.chdir('newsub/newsub2')

# get current working directory
current = os.getcwd()
print('Current directory= ', current)
```

Output:

```
F:\py>python os.py
Current directory= F:\py\newsub\newsub2
```

To remove a directory, we can use rmdir() method of ‘os’ module. Let’s suppose, our current directory is F:\py. In this, we have newsub directory and inside newsub, we have newsub2 directory. To remove newsub directory, we can write:

```
os.rmdir('newsub')
```

The rmdir() method will remove newsub since it is found in the current directory. Suppose, we write the following statement:

```
os.rmdir('newsub2')
```

This cannot remove newsub2 as it is not in the current directory (i.e. F:\py). newsub2 is inside newsub that is in the current directory. In this case, path should be given properly as:

```
os.rmdir('newsub/newsub2')
```

This will remove the newsub2 directory. Consider Program 27.

Program

Program 27: A Python program to remove a sub directory that is inside another directory.

```
import os
# to remove newsub2 directory
os.rmdir('newsub/newsub2')
```

Output:

```
F:\py>python os.py
```

There is another method removedirs() that recursively removes all the directories. For example, we write the following statement:

```
os.removedirs('mysub/mysub2/mysub3')
```

This will remove mysub3 first, then mysub2 and then mysub. In this way it can remove several sub-sub directories in a single stretch. In Program 28, our assumption is that we have mysub directory inside the current directory (i.e. F:\py). Also, mysub contains another sub directory mysub2 that again contains mysub3. We want to remove all the three sub directories using the removedirs() method.

Program

Program 28: A Python program to remove a group of directories in the path.

```
import os
# to remove mysub3, mysub2 and then mysub.
os.removedirs('mysub/mysub2/mysub3')
```

Output:

```
F:\py>python os.py
```

To give a new name to an existing directory, we can use rename() method in the following format:

```
os.rename('oldname', 'newname')
```

Here, 'oldname' of the directory is changed as 'newname'. In Program 29, we are renaming 'enum' as 'newenum'. The directory 'enum' is available in the current directory.

Program

Progarm 29: A Python program to rename a directory.

```
import os
# to rename enum as newenum
os.rename('enum', 'newenum')
```

Output:

```
F:\py>python os.py
```

We can go to our F:\py directory and check that the enum directory became newenum.

Sometimes, we want to know the contents of a directory. A directory may contain other directories or files. To display all the contents of a directory, we are equipped with walk() method in 'os' module. This method is used in the following format:

```
os.walk(path, topdown=True, onerror=None, followlinks=False)
```

This method returns an iterator object whose contents can be displayed using a for loop. This iterator object contains directory path, directory names and filenames found in a given directory path.

'path' represents the directory name. For current directory, we can use dot (.). Giving path is enough for walk() method.

If 'topdown' is True, the directory and its sub directories are traversed in top-down manner. If it is False, then the traversal will be in bottom-up manner.

'onerror' represents what to do when an error is detected. With 'onerror', we can specify a function to be executed if an error is encountered.

By default, walk() will not walk down into symbolic links that resolve to directories. We should set 'followlinks' to True to visit directories pointed to by symbolic links, on systems that support them.

In Program 30, we are going to display the contents of the current directory with the help of walk() method. Our assumption is that our current directory is F:\py that contains mysub directory and several files. mysub has another sub directory by the name mysub1 and a file. mysub1 has only one file. These directories and files can be identified from the output of this program.

Program

Program 30: A Python program to display all contents of the current directory.

```
import os
for dirpath, dirnames, filenames in os.walk('.'):
    print('Current path: ', dirpath)
    print('Directories: ', dirnames)
    print('Files: ', filenames)
    print()
```

Output:

```
F:\py>python os.py
Current path:  .
Directories:  ['mysub']
Files:  ['demo.py', 'demo1.py', 'emp.dat', 'Emp.py', 'files.py',
'new.jpg', 'os.py', 'os1.txt', 'output.txt', 'phonebook.dat', 'random.py',
'test.py', 'update.py']
```

```
Current path:  .\mysub
Directories:  ['mysub1']
Files:  ['myfile.txt']

Current path:  .\mysub\mysub1
Directories:  []
Files:  ['myfile1.txt']
```

In Program 30, we used os.walk('.') to display the contents of the current directory. If we want to display the contents of only the mysub directory which is in current directory, we can use walk() method as:

```
os.walk('mysub')
```

Running Other Programs from Python Program

The 'os' module has the system() method that is useful to run an executable program from our Python program. This method is similar to system() function of C language. It is used as system('string') where 'string' represents any command or executable file name. See the following examples:

```
os.system('dir')   # display directory contents on DOS operating system
os.system('python demo.py')   # run demo.py program
```

In Program 31, we are going to display the file names in the current directory that have .py extension. That means we are not displaying all files in the directory but filtering out only python program files. This can be done using DOS operating system command: dir *.py. We should remember that '*' is called wild card character that represents 'all'. So, *.py indicates all files that have .py extension name.

Program

Program 31: A Python program to display Python program files available in the current directory.

```
import os
# execute dir command of DOS operating system
os.system('dir *.py')
```

Output:

```
F:\py>python os.py
Volume in drive F is New Volume
 Volume Serial Number is 8683-5D92
 Directory of F:\py
04/09/2016  09:09 PM               483 demo.py
04/09/2016  09:52 PM             1,203 demo1.py
04/08/2016  11:20 PM               260 Emp.py
04/14/2016  09:31 PM               482 files.py
04/14/2016  11:27 PM                85 os.py
```

```
04/10/2016  07:17 PM               556 random.py
04/10/2016  08:26 PM                82 test.py
04/10/2016  09:02 PM             1,513 update.py
               8 File(s)          4,664 bytes
               0 Dir(s)  136,625,213,440 bytes free
```

Points to Remember

- The data stored on a secondary storage media like hard disk or CD is called a file.
- Once the data is stored in a file, the same data can be shared by several programs.
- There are two types of files supported by Python: text files and binary files.
- Text files store data in the form of text or characters. Binary files store data in the form of bytes.
- The open() method opens a file for some operation like writing, reading or appending. The close() method closes the file.
- The read() method reads the file content while write() method stores data into file.
- For binary files, we have to add 'b' at the end of file open mode. For example, 'wb' represents write mode for a binary file.
- Binary files are useful to handle text files, image files or audio or video files.
- We need not close the file if we open the file using with statement.
- Pickle or serialization is the concept of storing objects into a binary file. Unpickle or de-serialization is the concept of retrieving objects from a binary file.
- In pickling, we use dump() method and in unpickling we use load() method.
- In a binary file, to move the file pointer to any position, we can use seek() method.
- In a binary file, to know the position of the file pointer, we can use tell() method.
- The encode() method converts the string into bytes so that it can be written into a binary file.
- A binary string can be converted into ordinary string using decode() method.
- Accessing the contents of a file randomly by moving the file pointer to any byte in the file is called random accessing. seek() and tell() methods are used in random accessing of a file.
- Random accessing is also possible using mmap (memory mapped file) module.
- Zipping and unzipping of files can be done using ZipFile class of zipfile module.

- The os (operating system) module is useful to perform several operations on directories like finding the currently working directory, changing to a particular directory, renaming or deleting directories and listing the contents of a directory.
- The system() method of os module is useful to run commands or executable programs from our Python program.

CHAPTER 18

REGULAR EXPRESSIONS IN PYTHON

Many a times, we are needed to extract required information from given data. For example, we want to know the number of people who contacted us in the last month through Gmail or we want to know the phone numbers of employees in a company whose names start with 'A' or we want to retrieve the date of births of the patients in a hospital who joined for treatment for hypertension, etc. To get such information, we have to conduct the searching operation on the data. Once we get the required information, we have to extract that data for further use. Regular expressions are useful to perform such operations on data. Let's learn more about regular expressions.

Regular Expressions

A regular expression is a string that contains special symbols and characters to find and extract the information needed by us from the given data. A regular expression helps us to search information, match, find and split information as per our requirements. A regular expression is also called simply *regex*. Regular expressions are available not only in Python but also in many languages like Java, Perl, AWK, etc.

Python provides *re* module that stands for regular expressions. This module contains methods like compile(), search(), match(), findall(), split(), etc. which are used in finding the information in the available data. So, when we write a regular expression, we should import re module as:

```
import re
```

Regular expressions are nothing but strings containing characters and special symbols. A simple regular expression may look like this:

```
reg = r'm\w\w'
```

In the preceding line, the string is prefixed with 'r' to represent that it is a raw string. Generally, we write regular expressions as raw strings. Let's understand why this is so. When we write a normal string as:

```
str = 'This is normal\nstring'
```

Now, print(str) will display the preceding string in two lines as:

```
This is normal
string
```

Thus the '\n' character is interpreted as new line in the normal string by the Python interpreter and hence the string is broken there and shown in the new line. In regular expressions when '\n' is used, it does not mean to throw the string into new line. There '\n' has a different meaning and it should not be interpreted as new line. For this purpose, we should take this as a 'raw' string. This is done by prefixing 'r' before the string.

```
str = r'This is raw\nstring'
```

When we display this string using print(str), the output will be:

```
This is raw\nstring
```

So, the normal meaning of '\n' is escaped and it is no more an escape character in the preceding example. Since '\n' is not an escape character, it is interpreted as a character with different meaning in the regular expression by the Python interpreter. Similarly, the characters like '\t', '\w', '\c', etc. should be interpreted as special characters in the regular expressions and hence the expressions should be written as raw strings. If we do not want to write the regular expressions as raw strings, then the alternative is to use another backslash before such characters. For example, we can write:

```
reg = r'm\w\w'   # as raw string
reg = 'm\\w\\w'   # as normal string
```

But using backslashes like this may be confusing for the programmer. Now, let's go back to our first regular expression:

```
reg = r'm\w\w'
```

This expression is written in single quotes to represent that it is a string. The first character 'm' represents that the words starting with 'm' should be matched. The next character '\w' represents any one character in A to Z, a to z and 0 to 9. Since we used two '\w' characters, they represent any two characters after 'm'. So, this regular expression represents words or strings having three characters and with 'm' as first character. The next two characters can be any alphanumeric.

Yes, we developed our first regular expression! The next step is to compile this expression using compile() method of 're' module as:

```
prog = re.compile(r'm\w\w')
```

Now, prog represents an object that contains the regular expression. The next step is to run this expression on a string 'str' using the search() method or match() method as:

```
str = 'cat mat bat rat'   # this is the string on which regular
# expression will act
result = prog.search(str)   # searching for regular expression in str
```

The result is stored in 'result' object and we can display it by calling the group() method on the object as:

```
print(result.group())
mat
```

This is how a regular expression is created and used. We write all the steps at one place to have better idea:

```
import re
prog = re.compile(r'm\w\w')
str = 'cat mat bat rat'
result = prog.search(str)
print(result.group())
mat
```

In the preceding code, the regular expression after compilation is available in prog object. So, we need not compile the expression again and again when we want to use the same expression on other strings. This will improve the speed of execution. For example, let's use the same regular expression on a different string as:

```
str1 = 'Operating system format'
result = prog.search(str1)
print(result.group())
mat
```

Figure 18.1 shows how to execute the regular expressions in the Python IDLE window:

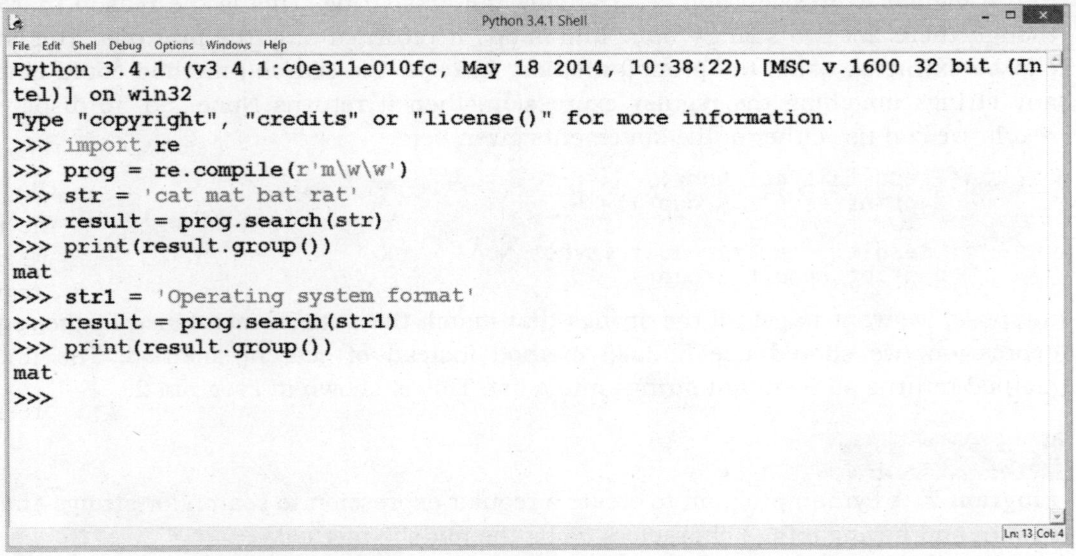

Figure 18.1: Executing regular expressions in Python IDLE

Instead of compiling the first regular expression and then running the next one, we can use a single step to compile and run all the regular expression as:

```
result = re.search(r'm\w\w', str)
```

The preceding code is equivalent to:

```
prog = re.compile(r'm\w\w')
result = prog.search(str)
```

So, the general form of writing regular expressions is as follows:

```
result = re.search('expression', 'string')
```

In the following program, the same regular expression is used on a different string. Consider Program 1.

Program

Program 1: A Python program to create a regular expression to search for strings starting with m and having total 3 characters using the search() method.

```
import re

str = 'man sun mop run'
result = re.search(r'm\w\w', str)
if result:    # if result is not None
    print(result.group())
```

Output:

```
C:\>python reg.py
man
```

Observe the output of Program 1. The search() method searches for the strings according to the regular expression and returns only the first string. This is the reason that even though there are two strings 'man' and 'mop', it returned only the first one. This string can be extracted using the group() method. In case, the search() method could not find any strings matching the regular expression, then it returns None. So, to display the result, we can use either of the statements given here:

```
if result is not None:
    print(result.group())

if result:    # if result is not None
    print(result.group())
```

Suppose, we want to get all the strings that match the pattern mentioned in the regular expression, we should use findall() method instead of search() method. The findall() method returns all resultant strings into a list. This is shown in Program 2.

Program

Program 2: A Python program to create a regular expression to search for strings starting with m and having total 3 characters using the findall() method.

```
import re
str = 'man sun mop run'
```

```
result = re.findall(r'm\w\w', str)
print(result)
```

Output:

```
C:\>python reg.py
['man', 'mop']
```

In Program 2, the findall() method returned the result as a list. The elements of the list can be displayed using a for loop as:

```
for s in result:
    print(s)
```

There is another method by the name match() that returns the resultant string only if it is found in the beginning of the string. The match() method will give None if the string is not in the beginning. Let's consider Program 3 and Program 4.

Program

Program 3: A Python program to create a regular expression using the match() method to search for strings starting with m and having total 3 characters.

```
import re
str = 'man sun mop run'
result = re.match(r'm\w\w', str)
print(result.group())
```

Output:

```
C:\>python reg.py
man
```

Program

Program 4: A Python program to create a regular expression using the match() method to search for strings starting with m and having total 3 characters.

```
import re
str = 'sun man mop run'
result = re.match(r'm\w\w', str)
print(result)
```

Output:

```
C:\>python reg.py
None
```

There is a method split() that splits the given string into pieces according to the regular expression and returns the pieces as elements of a list. Suppose we write a regular expression as:

```
re.split(r'\W+', str)
```

Observe the regular expression '\W'. This is capital 'W' which is reverse to the small 'w' so far used. 'w' represents any one alpha numeric character, i.e. A-Z, a-z, 0-9. But 'W' represents any character that is not alpha numeric. So, the work of this regular expression is to split the string 'str' at the places where there is no alpha numeric character. The '+' after W represents to match 1 or more occurrences indicated by W. The result is that the string will be split into pieces where 1 or more non alpha numeric characters are found. Consider Program 5.

Program

Program 5: A Python program to create a regular expression to split a string into pieces where one or more non alpha numeric characters are found.

```
import re
str = 'This; is the: "Core" Python\'s book'
result = re.split(r'\W+', str)
print(result)
```

Output:

```
C:\>python reg.py
['This', 'is', 'the', 'Core', 'Python', 's', 'book']
```

Sometimes, regular expressions can also be used to find a string and then replace it with a new string. For this purpose, we should use the sub() method of 're' module. The format of this method is:

```
sub(regular expression, new string, string)
```

For example, sub('Ahmedabad', 'Allahabad', str) will replace 'Ahmedabad' with 'Allahabad' in the string 'str'. Consider Program 6.

Program

Program 6: A Python program to create a regular expression to replace a string with a new string.

```
import re
str = 'Kumbhmela will be conducted at Ahmedabad in India.'
res = re.sub(r'Ahmedabad', 'Allahabad', str)
print(res)
```

Output:

```
C:\>python reg.py
Kumbhmela will be conducted at Allahabad in India.
```

So, regular expressions are used to perform the following important operations:

- Matching strings
- Searching for strings
- Finding all strings
- Splitting a string into pieces
- Replacing strings

The following methods belong to the 're' module that are used in the regular expressions:

- The match() method searches in the beginning of the string and if the matching string is found, it returns an object that contains the resultant string, otherwise it returns None. We can access the string from the returned object using group() method.
- The search() method searches the string from beginning till the end and returns the first occurrence of the matching string, otherwise it returns None. We can use group() method to retrieve the string from the object returned by this method.
- The findall() method searches the string from beginning till the end and returns all occurrences of the matching string in the form of a list object. If the matching strings are not found, then it returns an empty list. We can retrieve the resultant strings from the list using a for loop.
- The split() method splits the string according to the regular expression and the resultant pieces are returned as a list. If there are no string pieces, then it returns an empty list. We can retrieve the resultant string pieces from the list using a for loop.
- The sub() method substitutes (or replaces) new strings in the place of existing strings. After substitution, the main string is returned by this method.

Sequence Characters in Regular Expressions

Sequence characters match only one character in the string. Let's list out the sequence characters which are used in regular expressions along with their meanings in Table 18.1:

Table 18.1: Special Sequence Characters in Regular Expressions

Character	Its description
\d	Represents any digit (0 to 9)
\D	Represents any non-digit
\s	Represents white space. Ex: \t\n\r\f\v
\S	Represents non-white space character
\w	Represents any alphanumeric (A to Z, a to z, 0 to 9)
\W	Represents non-alphanumeric
\b	Represents a space around words

Character	Its description
\A	Matches only at start of the string
\Z	Matches only at end of the string

Each of these sequence characters represents a single character matched in the string. For example, '\w' indicates any one alphanumeric character. Suppose we write it as [\w]*. Here '*' represents 0 or more repetitions. Hence [\w]* represents 0 or more alphanumeric characters.

Let's write a regular expression to retrieve all words starting with 'a'. This can be written as:

```
r'a[\w]*'
```

Here, 'a' represents the word should start with 'a'. Then [\w]* represents repetition of any alphanumeric characters. Consider Program 7.

Program

Program 7: A Python program to create a regular expression to retrieve all words starting with a in a given string.

```
import re
str = 'an apple a day keeps the doctor away'
result = re.findall(r'a[\w]*', str)

# findall() returns a list, retrieve the elements from list
for word in result:
    print(word)
```

Output:

```
C:\>python reg.py
an
apple
a
ay
away
```

Please observe the output. It contains 'ay' which is not a word. This 'ay' is part of the word 'away'. So, it is displaying both 'ay' and 'away' as they are starting with 'a'. We do not want like this. We want only the words starting with 'a'. Since a word will have a space in the beginning or ending, we can use '\b' before and after the words in the regular expression. So, the regular expression will become:

```
result = re.findall(r'\ba[\w]*\b', str)
```

This will retrieve only the word and not the part of the words. So, the output will be:

```
an
apple
a
away
```

Program 8 is an attempt to retrieve all the words starting with a numeric digit like 0, 1, 2 or 9. The numeric digit is represented by '\d' and hence, the expression will be: r'\d[\w]*'.

Program

Program 8: A Python program to create a regular expression to retrieve all words starting with a numeric digit.

```
import re
str = 'The meeting will be conducted on 1st and 21st of every month'
result = re.findall(r'\d[\w]*', str)
for word in result:
    print(word)
```

Output:

```
C:\>python reg.py
1st
21st
```

In Program 9, we are trying to retrieve all words having 5 characters length. The expression can be written something like this: r'\b\w{5}\b'. The character '\b' represents a space. We used this character in the beginning and ending of the expression so that we get the words surrounded by spaces. \w{5} represents a word containing any alphanumeric characters repeated for 5 times. A character in curly braces, e.g. {m} represents repetition for m times.

Program

Program 9: A Python program to create a regular expression to retrieve all words having 5 characters length.

```
import re
str = 'one two three four five six seven 8 9 10'
result = re.findall(r'\b\w{5}\b', str)
print(result)
```

Output:

```
C:\>python reg.py
['three', 'seven']
```

In Program 9, instead of using the findall() method, if we use the search() method, it will return the first occurrence of the result only.

Program

Program 10: A Python program to create a regular expression to retrieve all words having 5 characters length using search().

```
# search() will give the first matching word only.
import re
str = 'one two three four five six seven 8 9 10'
```

```
result = re.search(r'\b\w{5}\b', str)
# to retrieve the word from result object, use group()
print(result.group())
```

Output:

```
C:\>python reg.py
three
```

We will improve our search a little bit further. Now, we want to find all words which are at least 4 characters long. That means words with 4, 5 or any number of characters will be retrieved. For this purpose, we can write the regular expression as: r'\b\w{4,}\b'. Observe the number 4 and a comma in curly braces. This represents 4 or above number of characters.

Program

Program 11: A Python program to create a regular expression to retrieve all the words that are having the length of at least 4 characters.

```
import re
str = 'one two three four five six seven 8 9 10'
result = re.findall(r'\b\w{4,}\b', str)
print(result)
```

Output:

```
C:\>python reg.py
['three', 'four', 'five', 'seven']
```

Similarly, the program 12 helps us to retrieve all words with 3 to 5 characters length. Observe the curly braces with 3, 5 as: {3,5} that indicate 3 to 5 number of characters.

Program

Program 12: A Python program to create a regular expression to retrieve all words with 3 or 4 or 5 characters length.

```
import re
str = 'one two three four five six seven 8 9 10'
result = re.findall(r'\b\w{3,5}\b', str)
print(result)
```

Output:

```
C:\>python reg.py
['one', 'two', 'three', 'four', 'five', 'six', 'seven']
```

We know '\d' represents a numeric digit (0 to 9). So, if we use it as: r'\b\d\b', it represents single digits in the string amidst of spaces.

Program

Program 13: A Python program to create a regular expression to retrieve only single digits from a string.

```
import re
str = 'one two three four five six seven 8 9 10'
```

```
result = re.findall(r'\b\d\b', str)
print(result)
```

Output:

```
C:\>python reg.py
['8', '9']
```

Suppose in the preceding program, we write the regular expression as: r'\b\d\d\b', it retrieves double digits (like 10, 02, 89 etc.) from the string.

'\A' is useful to match the words at the beginning of a string. Similarly, '\Z' is useful to match the words at the end of a string. For example, we want to find whether a string contains at its end a word starting with 't' or not. We can write an expression as: r't[\w]*\Z'. Here, 't' represents that the word should start with 't'. [\w]* represents any characters after 't'. The last '\Z' represents searching should be done at the ending of the string. Consider Program 14.

Program

Program 14: A Python program to create a regular expression to retrieve the last word of a string, if it starts with t.

```
import re
str = 'one two three one two three'
result = re.findall(r't[\w]*\Z', str)
print(result)
```

Output:

```
C:\>python reg.py
['three']
```

Quantifiers in Regular Expressions

In regular expressions, some characters represent more than one character to be matched in the string. Such characters are called 'quantifiers'. For example, if we write '+' it represents 1 or more repetitions of the preceding character. Hence, if we write an expression as: r'\d+', this indicates that all numeric digits which occur for 1 or more times should be extracted. Table 18.2 shows quantifiers available in Python:

Table 18.2: Quantifiers Used in Regular Expressions

Character	Its description
+	1 or more repetitions of the preceding regexp
*	0 or more repetitions of the preceding regexp
?	0 or 1 repetitions of the preceding regexp
{m}	Exactly m occurrences

Character	Its description
{m, n}	From m to n. m defaults to 0. n to infinity

In the next program, we are going to retrieve the phone number of a person from a string using the regular expression: r'\d+'.

Program

Program 15: A Python program to create a regular expression to retrieve the phone number of a person.

```
import re
str = 'Nageswara Rao: 9706612345'
res = re.search(r'\d+', str)
print(res.group())
```

Output:

```
C:\>python reg.py
9706612345
```

In Program 15, suppose we are asked to retrieve the person's name and not his phone number. Now, how to do that? Very simple. Instead of writing '\d', we use '\D' in the regular expression as '\D' represents all characters except numeric characters. [See Table 18.1]

Program

Program 16: A Python program to create a regular expression to extract only name but not number from a string.

```
import re
str = 'Nageswara Rao: 9706612345'
res = re.search(r'\D+', str)
print(res.group())
```

Output:

```
C:\>python reg.py
Nageswara Rao:
```

The special character '+' represents 1 or more repetitions. Similarly, '*' represents 0 or more repetitions. Suppose, we want to write a regular expression that finds all words staring with either 'an' or 'ak', then we can use: r'a[nk][\w]*'. Here, observe a[nk]. This represents either 'n' or 'k' or both after 'a'.

Program

Program 17: A Python program to create a regular expression to find all words starting with 'an' or 'ak'.

```
import re
str = 'anil akhil anant arun arati arundhati abhijit ankur'
res = re.findall(r'a[nk][\w]*', str)
print(res)
```

Output:

```
C:\>python reg.py
['anil', 'akhil', 'anant', 'ankur']
```

We know that {m,n} indicates m to n occurrences. Suppose we take '\d{1,3}', it represents 1 to 3 occurrences of '\d'. Let's see how to use this. We have a string that contains names, id numbers and date of births as:

```
str = 'Vijay 20 1-5-2001, Rohit 21 22-10-1990, Sita 22 15-09-2000'
```

Now, we want to retrieve only date of births of the candidates. We can write a regular expression as: r'\d{2}-\d{2}-\d{4}'. This retrieves only numeric digits in the format of 2digits-2digits-4digits. Hence this can be used to retrieve the date of births as shown in Program 18.

Program

Program 18: A Python program to create a regular expression to retrieve date of births from a string.

```
import re
str = 'Vijay 20 1-5-2001, Rohit 21 22-10-1990, Sita 22 15-09-2000'
res = re.findall(r'\d{2}-\d{2}-\d{4}', str)
print(res)
```

Output:

```
C:\>python reg.py
['22-10-1990', '15-09-2000']
```

Please observe that the date of birth of Vijay, i.e. 1-5-2001 is not retrieved. The reason is the date and month here have only one digit. But our regular expression retrieves only if there are 2 digits. So, how to solve this problem? We can modify the regular expression such that it retrieves either 1 or 2 digits in the date or month as:

```
res = re.findall(r'\d{1,2}-\d{1,2}-\d{4}', str)
print(res)
['1-5-2001', '22-10-1990', '15-09-2000']
```

Special Characters in Regular Expressions

Characters with special significance shown in Table 18.3 can be used in regular expressions. These characters will make our searching easy.

Table 18.3: Special Characters in Regular Expressions

Character	Its description
\	Escape special character nature
.	Matches any character except new line
^	Matches beginning of a string

Character	Its description
$	Matches ending of a string
[...]	Denotes a set of possible characters. Ex: [6b-d] matches any characters ‘6’, ‘b’, ’c’ or ‘d’
[^...]	Matches every character except the ones inside brackets. Ex: [^a-c6] matches any character except ‘a’, ‘b’, ‘c’ or ‘6’
(...)	Matches the regular expression inside the parentheses and the result can be captured.
R | S	Matches either regex R or regex S

The carat (^) symbol is useful to check if a string is starting with a sub string or not. For example, to know a string is starting with ‘He’ or not, we can write the expression: r"^He". This is shown in Program 19.

Program

Program 19: A Python program to create a regular expression to search whether a given string is starting with ‘He’ or not.

```
import re
str = "Hello World"
res = re.search(r"^He", str)
if res:
    print ("String starts with 'He'")
else:
    print("String does not start with 'He'")
```

Output:

```
C:\>python reg.py
String starts with 'He'
```

Similarly, to know whether a string is ending with a word, we can use dollar ($) symbol. Suppose we write an expression as r"World$". This indicates a search for World in the ending of the main string, as shown in Program 20.

Program

Program 20: A Python program to create a regular expression to search for a word at the ending of a string.

```
import re
str = "Hello World"
res = re.search(r"World$", str)
if res:
    print ("String ends with 'World'")
else:
    print("String does not end with 'World'")
```

Output:

```
C:\>python reg.py
String ends with 'World'
```

Regular expressions conduct a case sensitive searching for the strings. Hence, in Program 20, if we use the expression with a small 'w' as: r"world$", then we will end up with wrong output as:

```
String does not end with 'World'
```

We can specify a case insensitive matching of strings with the help of IGNORECASE constant of 're' module. This is shown in Program 21.

Program

Program 21: A Python program to create a regular expression to search at the ending of a string by ignoring the case.

```
import re
str = "Hello World"
res = re.search(r"world$", str, re.IGNORECASE)
if res:
    print ("String ends with 'World'")
else:
    print("String does not end with 'World'")
```

Output:

```
C:\>python reg.py
String ends with 'World'
```

The square brackets [] in regular expressions represent a set of characters. For example, if we write [ABC], it represents any one character A or B or C. A hyphen (-) represents a range of characters. For example, [A-Z] represents any single character from the range of capital letters A to Z. Similarly, [a-z] represents any single lowercase letter. This is useful to retrieve names from a string. For example, a name like 'Rahul' starts with a capital letter and remaining are lowercase letters. To search such strings, we can use a regular expression as: '[A-Z][a-z]*'. This means the first letter should be any capital letter (from A to Z). Then the next letter should be a small letter. Observe the '*', it represents 0 or more repetitions of small letters should be considered.

Program

Program 22: A Python program to create a regular expression to retrieve marks and names from a given string.

```
# displaying marks and names
import re;
str = 'Rahul got 75 marks, Vijay got 55 marks, whereas Subbu got 98
marks.'

# extract only marks having 2 digits
marks = re.findall('\d{2}', str)
print(marks)
```

```
# extract names starting with a capital letter
# and remaining alphabetic characters
names = re.findall('[A-Z][a-z]*', str)
print(names)
```

Output:

```
C:\>python reg.py
['75', '55', '98']
['Rahul', 'Vijay', 'Subbu']
```

The pipe symbol (|) represents 'or'. For example, if we write 'am|pm', it finds the strings which are either 'am' or 'pm'.

Program

Program 23: A Python program to create a regular expression to retrieve the timings either 'am' or 'pm'.

```
import re
str = 'The meeting may be at 8am or 9am or 4pm or 5pm.'
res = re.findall(r'\dam|\dpm', str)
print(res)
```

Output:

```
C:\>python reg.py
['8am', '9am', '4pm', '5pm']
```

Using Regular Expressions on Files

We can use regular expressions not only on individual strings, but also on files where huge data is available. As we know, a file contains a lot of strings. We can open the file and conduct searching or matching etc. operations on the strings of the file using regular expressions. For this purpose, first we should open the file as:

```
f = open('filename', 'r')   # open the file for reading
```

Now, the data of the file is referenced by the file object or file handle 'f'. We can read line by line from the file object using a for loop as:

```
for line in f:
    res = re.findall(regexpression, line)
```

Here, the regexpression will act on each line (or string) of the file and the result will be added to res object. Since, the findall() method returns a list with resultant strings, the 'res' object shows a list. Hence, we can check if the list contains any elements by checking its size as:

```
if len(res)>0:   # if more than 0 elements are found, then display
    print(res)
```

Let's assume that a file by the name 'mails.txt' contains some information about a project where mail- ids of team members are mentioned. We can create this file by opening the Notepad and type some data as shown in Figure 18.2:

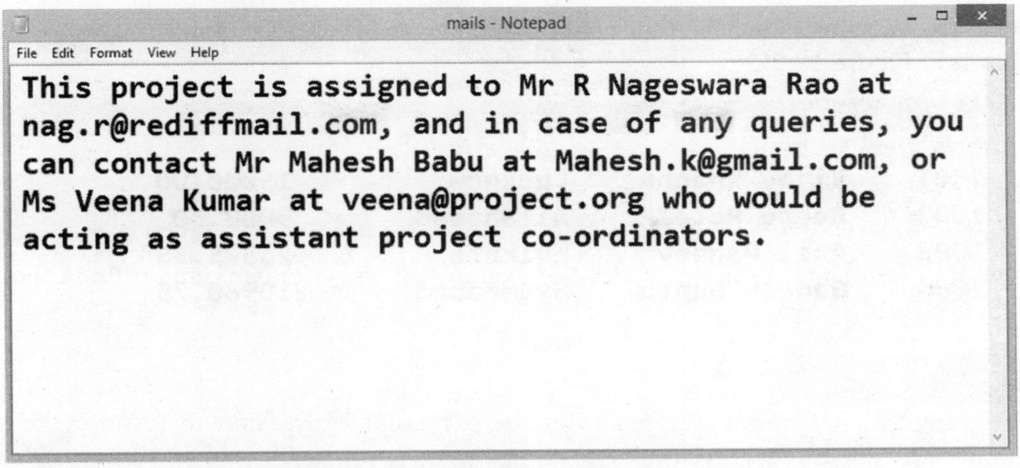

Figure 18.2: A text file that contains some data

Please observe that the file 'mails.txt' contains mail-ids of 3 people who are involved in the project and we want to retrieve these mail-ids using a regular expression. A simple regular expression for this may be in the form of: r'\S+@\S+'. From Table 18.1, we know that \S represents non-whitespace character. \S+ represents several characters. A mail id will have some characters before '@' symbol and after that also. For example, nag.r@rediffmail.com. In this mail-id, we can represent 'nag.r' with \S+ and then @ and after that we can represent 'rediffmail.com' with another \S+ character. Now observe Program 24 where we are opening the 'mails.txt' file and reading only the mail-ids.

Program

Program 24: A Python program to create a regular expression that reads email-ids from a text file.

```
import re
# open the file for reading
f = open('mails.txt', 'r')

# repeat for each line of the file
for line in f:
    res = re.findall(r'\S+@\S+', line)

# display if there are some elements in result
if len(res)>0:
    print(res)

# close the file
f.close()
```

Output:

```
C:\>python reg.py
['nag.r@redifmail.com,', 'Mahesh.k@gmail.com,', 'veena@project.org']
```

Let's take a 'salaries.txt' file that contains employee id number, name, city and salary as shown in Figure 18.3:

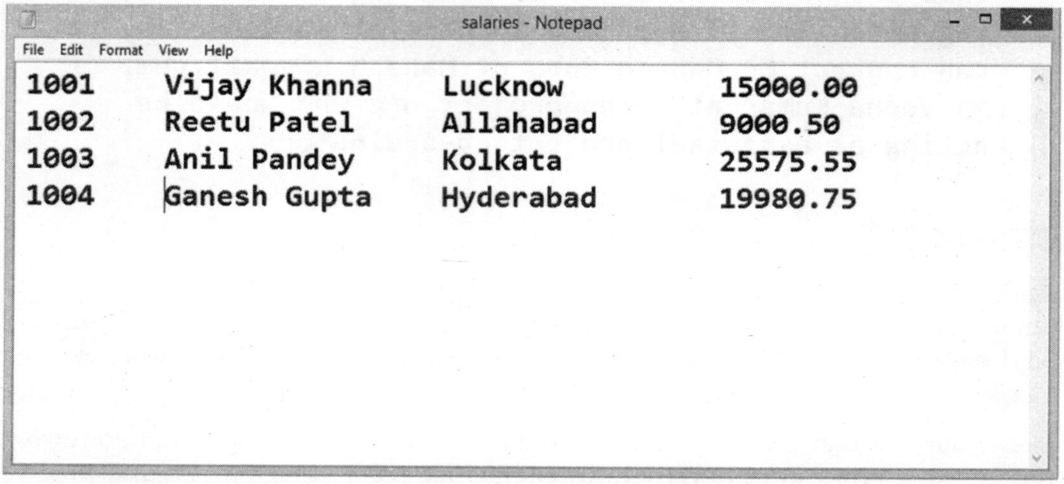

1001	Vijay Khanna	Lucknow	15000.00
1002	Reetu Patel	Allahabad	9000.50
1003	Anil Pandey	Kolkata	25575.55
1004	Ganesh Gupta	Hyderabad	19980.75

Figure 18.3: A file that contains employee salary details

We want to retrieve employee id numbers and their salaries only from the 'salaries.txt' file and write that information into another file, say 'newfile.txt'. The other information is not needed by us. Since employee id numbers are of 4 digits each, we can use a regular expression like: r'\d{4}' to retrieve the id numbers. Similarly, salaries are having 4 or more digits and a decimal point and then 2 digits. So, to retrieve the salaries, we can use regular expression: r'\d{4,}.\d{2}'. Once the id numbers and salaries are retrieved using the search() method, we can store them into the 'newfile.txt'. This is shown in Program 25.

Program

Program 25: A Python program to retrieve data from a file using regular expressions and then write that data into a file.

```
import re
# open the files
f1 = open('salaries.txt', 'r')
f2 = open('newfile.txt', 'w')

# repeat for each line of the file f1
for line in f1:
    res1 = re.search(r'\d{4}', line)   # extract id no from f1
    res2 = re.search(r'\d{4,}.\d{2}', line)   # extract salary from f1
    print(res1.group(), res2.group())   # display them
    f2.write(res1.group()+"\t")   # write id no into f2
    f2.write(res2.group()+"\n")   # write salary into f2

# close the files
f1.close()
f2.close()
```

Output:

```
C:\>python reg.py
1001  15000.00
1002  9000.50
1003  25575.55
1004  19980.75
```

We can open the 'newfile.txt' file by double clicking it and see the same data written into that file.

Retrieving Information from a HTML File

Let's see how to apply regular expressions on a HTML file and retrieve the necessary information. As an example, let's take a HTML file that contains some items for breakfast and their prices in the form of a table, as shown here:

```
<! breakfast.html>
<html>
<table border=2>
<tr align="center"><td>1</td> <td>Roti</td> <td>50.00</td></tr>
<tr align="center"><td>2</td> <td>Chapatti</td> <td>55.75</td></tr>
<tr align="center"><td>3</td> <td>Dosa</td> <td>48.00</td></tr>
<tr align="center"><td>4</td> <td>Idly</td> <td>25.00</td></tr>
<tr align="center"><td>5</td> <td>Vada</td> <td>38.90</td></tr>
<tr align="center"><td>6</td> <td>Coffee</td> <td>20.00</td></tr>
<tr align="center"><td>7</td> <td>Tea</td> <td>15.00</td></tr>
</table>
</html>
```

When we open this file, we can see the table in the browser (See Figure 18.4) where the values of item number, item name and price are displayed.

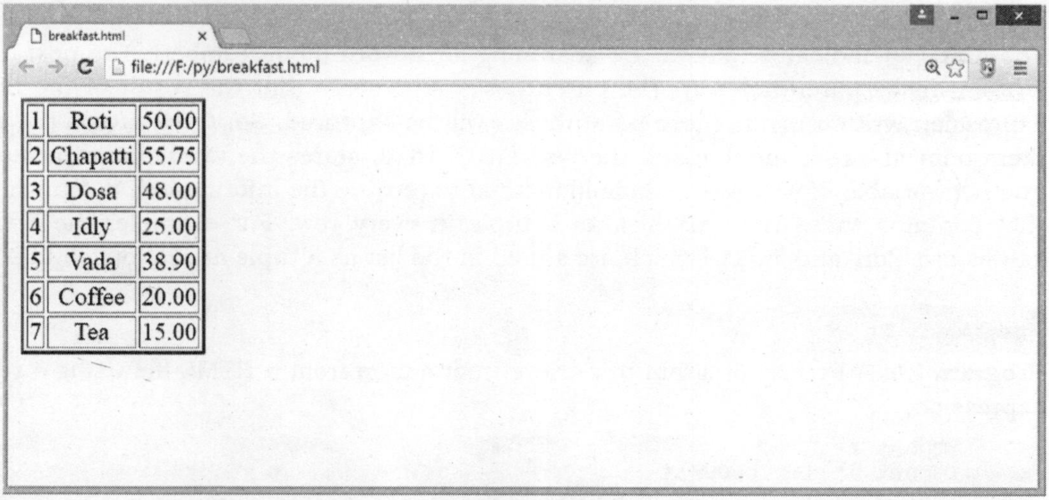

Figure 18.4: A HTML file that displays a table

Let's assume that this file is available in our computer in the directory as: F:\py\breakfast.html. To open this file, we have to use urlopen() method of urllib.request module in Python. So, we have to use the following code:

```
import urllib.request
f = urllib.request.urlopen(r'file:///f|py\breakfast.html')
```

Observe the raw string passed to urlopen() method. It contains the path of the .html file as:

```
file:///f|py\breakfast.html
```

The first word 'file:///' indicates file URL scheme that is used to refer to files in the local computer system. The next word 'f|py' indicates the drive name 'f' and the sub directory 'py'. In this, we have the file breakfast.html. Once this file is open, we can read the data using read() method as:

```
text = f.read()
```

But the data in the HTML files would be stored in the form of byte strings. Hence, we have to decode them into normal strings using the decode() method as:

```
str = text.decode()
```

Now, we have the string 'str'. We have to retrieve the required information from this string using a regular expression. Suppose we want to retrieve only item name and price, we can write:

```
r'<td>\w+</td>\s<td>(\w+)</td>\s<td>(\d\d.\d\d)</td>'
```

Please observe that the preceding expression contains three special characters: the first one is a \w+, the second one is (\w+) and the third one is (\d\d.\d\d). They are embedded in the tags <td> and </td>. So, the information which is in between the tags is searched.

The first \w+ indicates that we are searching for a word (item number). The next \w+ is written inside parentheses (). The parentheses represents that the result of the regular expression written inside these parentheses will be captured. So, (\w+) stores the words (item names) into a variable and the next (\d\d.\d\d) stores the words (item prices) into another variable. If we use the findall() method to retrieve the information, it returns a list that contains these two variables as a tuple in every row. For example, the first two values are 'Roti' and '50.00' which are stored in the list as a tuple as: [('Roti', '50.00')].

Program

Program 26: A Python program to retrieve information from a HTML file using a regular expression.

```
import re
import urllib.request

# open the html file using urlopen() method
f = urllib.request.urlopen(r'file:///f|py\breakfast.html')

# read data from the file object into text string
```

```
    text = f.read()

    # convert the byte string into normal string
    str = text.decode()

    # apply regular expression on the string
    result = re.findall(r'<td>\w+</td>\s<td>(\w+)</td>\s<td>(\d\d.\d\d)
    </td>', str)

    # display result
    print(result)

    # display the items of the result
    for item, price in result:
        print('Item= %-15s Price= %-10s' %(item, price))

    # close the file
    f.close()
```

Output:

```
    C:\>python reg.py
    [('Roti', '50.00'), ('Chapatti', '55.75'), ('Dosa', '48.00'), ('Idly',
'25.00'), ('Vada', '38.90'), ('Coffee', '20.00'), ('Tea', '15.00')]
    Item= Roti           Price= 50.00
    Item= Chapatti              Price= 55.75
    Item= Dosa                  Price= 48.00
    Item= Idly                  Price= 25.00
    Item= Vada                  Price= 38.90
    Item= Coffee                Price= 20.00
    Item= Tea                   Price= 15.00
```

Points to Remember

- A regular expression is a string that contains special symbols and characters to find and extract the information needed by us from the given data.
- Generally, we should use raw strings that start with 'r' in creation of regular expressions. We can also use normal strings but they are not advisable as they retain the meaning of escape characters.
- The match() method searches in the beginning of the string and returns result in an object.
- The search() method searches the string from beginning till the end and returns the first occurrence of the matching string in an object.
- The findall() method searches the string from beginning till the end and returns all occurrences of the matching string in the form of a list object.
- The split() method splits the string according to the regular expression and the resultant pieces are returned as a list.
- The sub() method substitutes new strings in the place of existing strings in the main string.

- \d represents any numeric digit from 0 to 9.
- \D represents any non-numeric digit.
- \s represents white space like \t, \n, \r, \f or \v.
- \S represents a character that is not white space.
- \w represents any alphanumeric character, i.e. A to Z, a to z, 0 to 9.
- \W represents any non-alphanumeric character.
- \A matches only at start of the string.
- \Z matches only at end of the string.
- + indicates 1 or more repetitions.
- * indicates 0 or more repetitions.
- ? indicates 0 or 1 repetitions of the preceding expression.
- {m} indicates exactly m occurrences.
- {m,n} indicates from m to n.
- . matches any character except new line.
- ^ matches beginning of a string.
- $ matches ending of a string.
- [...] denotes a set of possible characters.
- [^...] matches every character except the ones inside brackets.
- (...) matches the regular expression inside the parentheses and the result can be captured.
- R | S matches either R or S.
- It is possible to use regular expressions on files including HTML files.

CHAPTER 19

DATA STRUCTURES IN PYTHON

Handling one or two values is very easy in a program. For example, to store two values like 10 and 'Raj', we can take two variables and store these values into those variables. But this task will be difficult when there are several values. For example, let's take a small company having more than 100 employees whose details should be stored in memory and processed. In such cases, Python provides data structures like arrays, lists, tuples, sets and dictionaries. These data structures store elements in various models. Basically, a data structure represents arrangement of elements in memory in a particular model. Data structures are also known as abstract data types (ADTs).

Arrays and lists are similar. They can store a lot of elements (or values). There is no fixed size for arrays or lists. They can grow dynamically depending on the number of elements. The main difference between arrays and lists is that arrays can store only one type of element; whereas, lists can store different types of elements.

In the languages like C, C++ and Java, we talk about data structures where a structure (or container) is used to store a group of elements. The structure provides methods to handle the elements. For example, linked list, stack and queues are examples for fundamental data structures. In this chapter, we will have an idea regarding how these data structures can be created and used.

Lists are versatile data structures in Python since they can store any type of elements and it is possible to store different types of elements also. Internally, lists are implemented as arrays in Python. A list is created as an array having references to elements or objects. The problem in using arrays as lists is that all the operations may not be done in the same amount of time. Inserting and deleting elements at the end of the list would be faster than doing the same operations in the beginning or middle, since the entire list (i.e. array) elements need to shift towards right. However, except this minor inconvenience, lists can be used in our programs to create linked lists, stacks or queues.

When data is important, we should use file concept. For example employees' data like employee id number, name, address, department name, etc. should be stored permanently in a file so that it can be retrieved and utilized at any time. Sometimes, logic will be more important than data. We may want to store data in memory and apply some logic to get the results instantly. Here, we should use data structures. For example, let's take customers queue at the billing counter in a shopping mall. In this case, the information of the items purchased by the customers should be entered into computer and calculate the total bill amount immediately. In such cases, we need to use queue data structure since the customers should be cleared in 'first in first out' basis from the queue.

Now, we proceed further to discuss how to implement various fundamental data structures with the help of lists in Python.

Linked Lists

A linked list contains a group of elements in the form of nodes. Each node will have three fields:

1. The data field that contains data.
2. A link field that contains reference to the previous node.
3. Another link field that contains reference to the next node.

Link fields store references, i.e., memory locations. These link fields are useful to move from one node to another node in the linked list so that any operation can be done in a minimum amount of time. See Figure 19.1.

Linked list is very convenient to store data. The operations like inserting elements, removing elements, searching for an element etc. are done very quickly and almost in the same amount of time. Linked list is one of the fastest data structure. Hence, linked list is used where time critical operations are to be performed.

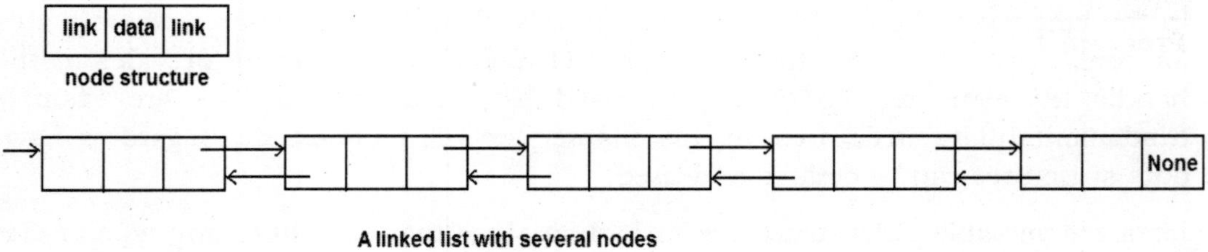

Figure 19.1: Node Structure and a Linked List with Nodes

Python provides list data type that can be used to implement linked lists. The following are the operations that are generally performed on linked lists:

- **Traversing the linked list:** This means visiting every node and displaying the data of the node. Thus all the elements of the node should be displayed. This can be done using a for loop on the list elements as:

```
for element in list:
    print(element)
```

- **Appending elements to the linked list:** This means adding elements at the end of the existing list. This can be done using the append() method of the list as: append(element)

- **Inserting elements into the linked list:** This means adding elements in a particular position in the existing list. This can be done using insert() method of the list in the following format:

```
insert(position, element)
```

- **Removing elements from the linked list:** This is done using remove() method of the list as remove(element). If the element being removed is not found, then this method raises ValueError.

- **Replacing elements in the linked list:** Replacing means deleting an element in a particular position and inserting a new element in the same position. There is no method available in lists in Python to handle this operation. But this can be achieved by first using remove() method and then insert() method.

- **Searching for an element location in the linked list:** This can be done using index() method available in lists. index(element) returns the position number of the element if exists in the list. If the element does not exist, then it raises ValueError.

- **Size of the linked list:** Finding the number of elements in the linked list is possible through len() method. len(list) returns an integer that gives the size of the list.

Program 1 shows how to create a linked list with string type elements. After creating a linked list, we are going to perform some operations on the list through a menu. A menu represents a group of items or options for the user so that the user can select any option. Depending on the user selection, we are supposed to perform the required operation.

Program

Program 1: A Python program to create a linked list and perform operations on the list.

```
# a linked list that stores a group of strings
# create an empty linked list
ll = []

# add some string type elements to ll
ll.append("America")
ll.append("Japan")
ll.append("India")

# display the list
print("The existing list= ", ll)

# display menu
choice=0
while choice<5:
    print('LINKED LIST OPERATIONS')
    print('1 Add element')
```

```
        print('2 Remove element')
        print('3 Replace element')
        print('4 Search for element')
        print('5 Exit')
        choice = int(input('Your choice: '))

        # perform a task depending on user choice
        if choice==1:
            element = input('Enter element: ')
            pos = int(input('At what position? '))
            ll.insert(pos, element)

        elif choice==2:
            try:
                element = input('Enter element: ')
                ll.remove(element)
            except ValueError:
                print('Element not found')

        elif choice==3:
            element = input('Enter new element: ')
            pos = int(input('At what position? '))
            ll.pop(pos)
            ll.insert(pos, element)

        elif choice==4:
            element = input('Enter element: ')
            try:
                pos = ll.index(element)
                print('Element found at position: ', pos)
            except ValueError:
                print('Element not found')
        else:
            break

        # display the list elements
        print('List = ', ll)
```

Output:

```
C:\>python list.py
The existing list= ['America', 'Japan', 'India']
LINKED LIST OPERATIONS
1 Add element
2 Remove element
3 Replace element
4 Search for element
5 Exit
Your choice: 1
Enter element: Russia
At what position? 1
List = ['America', 'Russia', 'Japan', 'India']
LINKED LIST OPERATIONS
1 Add element
2 Remove element
3 Replace element
4 Search for element
5 Exit
Your choice: 3
Enter new element: China
At what position? 2
```

```
List = ['America', 'Russia', 'China', 'India']
LINKED LIST OPERATIONS
1 Add element
2 Remove element
3 Replace element
4 Search for element
5 Exit
Your choice: 5
```

Stacks

A stack represents a group of elements stored in LIFO (Last In First Out) order. This means that the element which is stored as a last element into the stack will be the first element to be removed from the stack. Inserting elements (objects) into stack is called 'push operation' and removing elements from stack is called 'pop operation'. Searching for an element and returning it without removing it from the stack is called 'peep operation'. Insertion and deletion of elements take place only from one side of the stack, called 'top' of the stack, as shown in Figure 19.2. The other side of the stack is called 'bottom' of the stack which is closed and thus does not allow any operations.

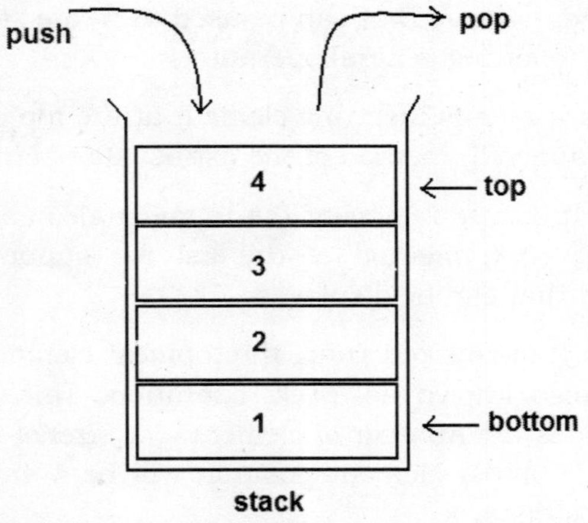

Figure 19.2: A Stack with some Elements

Stacks must strictly follow LIFO order where the last element pushed on to the top of the stack should be popped first. Let's take a hotel where a pile of plates are made available to the customers in a counter. These plates are accessible in such a way that the last washed plate will be available to the first customer. If the customer takes the top plate (the 3rd plate) from the pile, the weight on the spring will be lessened and the next plate (2nd one) will come up. See Figure 19.3(a). If the elements are stored in memory in this model, then it is called a stack.

Similarly, a Compact Disk holder where the CDs are arranged such that the last CD is available first is also an example of a stack. See Figure 19.3(b). If the elements are arranged in memory as CDs are in the holder, it is called a stack.

(a) a pile of plates (b) a group of CDs

Figure 19.3: Examples for Stacks

A stack is internally used by the operating system to save the program execution environment. It means that when the program is running, the state of the variables and information about the execution status are stored in a stack. Another use of stack is in expression evaluation. While evaluating expressions like ax +by * 5, they are converted into postfix or prefix notations using a stack and stored into the stack. Later, they are retrieved from the stack and evaluated according to certain rules.

Python provides list data types that can be used to create stacks. We should first create a Stack class with the following general operations:

- **Push operation:** It means inserting element at the top of the stack. This can be done with the help of append() method of the list as: st.append(element) where 'st' is a list.
- **Pop operation:** It means removing the topmost element from the stack. This can be performed using pop() method of the list as: st.pop(). This method returns the removed element that can be displayed.
- **Peep operation:** It means returning the topmost element without deleting it from the stack. Peep is also known as 'peek' operation. This is done by returning st[n-1] element where 'n' is the number of elements (or size) of the stack. So, if the stack has 5 elements, the topmost element position will be 4 since the elements are referred from 0th to 4th positions.
- **Searching operation:** It means knowing the position of an element in the stack from the top of the stack. For this purpose, the list's index() method can be used as: st.index(element) which returns the position number 'n' of the element from the beginning (or bottom) of the stack. Once this is known, we can get its position from the top of the stack as: size of the stack – n.
- **Empty stack or not:** This can be judged by simply testing whether the list 'st' is empty or not. We can use an expression as: 'return st == []' that returns True if 'st' is empty else False.

Now, let's develop Stack class with methods to perform previously mentioned operations.

Program

Program 2: A Python program to create a Stack class that can perform some important operations.

```
# Stack class - save this as stack.py
class Stack:
    def __init__(self):
        self.st = []

    def isempty(self):
        return self.st == []

    def push(self, element):
        self.st.append(element)

    def pop(self):
        if self.isempty():
            return -1
        else:
            return self.st.pop()

    def peep(self):
        n = len(self.st)
        return self.st[n-1]

    def search(self, element):
        if self.isempty():
            return -1
        else:
            try:
                n = self.st.index(element)
                return len(self.st)-n
            except ValueError:
                return -2

    def display(self):
        return self.st
```

Output:

```
C:\>python stack.py
C:\>
```

The next step is to use this Stack class in any of our programs. We are using Stack class and performing various operations on the stack with the help of a menu in Program 3. Since we want to use the Stack class of stack.py program, we have to import Stack class from stack.py module as:

```
from stack import Stack
```

Program

Program 3: A Python program to perform various operations on a stack using Stack class.

```
# using the Stack class of stack.py program
from stack import Stack
# create empty stack object
```

```
s = Stack()

# display menu
choice=0
while choice<5:
    print('STACK OPERATIONS')
    print('1 Push element')
    print('2 Pop element')
    print('3 Peep element')
    print('4 Search for element')
    print('5 Exit')
    choice = int(input('Your choice: '))

    # perform a task depending on user choice
    if choice==1:
        element = int(input('Enter element: '))
        s.push(element)

    elif choice==2:
        element = s.pop()
        if element == -1:
            print('The stack is empty')
        else:
            print('Popped element= ', element)

    elif choice==3:
        element = s.peep()
        print('Topmost element= ', element)

    elif choice==4:
        element = int(input('Enter element: '))
        pos = s.search(element)
        if pos == -1:
            print('The stack is empty')
        elif pos == -2:
            print('Element not found in the stack')
        else:
            print('Element found at position: ', pos)

    else:
        break

    # display the contents of stack object
    print('Stack= ', s.display())
```

Output:

```
C:\>python st.py
STACK OPERATIONS
1 Push element
2 Pop element
3 Peep element
4 Search for element
5 Exit
Your choice: 1
Enter element: 10
:
:
Stack= [10, 20, 30, 40, 50]
STACK OPERATIONS
1 Push element
```

```
2 Pop element
3 Peep element
4 Search for element
5 Exit
Your choice: 2
Popped element= 50
Stack= [10, 20, 30, 40]
STACK OPERATIONS
1 Push element
2 Pop element
3 Peep element
4 Search for element
5 Exit
Your choice: 3
Topmost element= 40
Stack= [10, 20, 30, 40]
STACK OPERATIONS
1 Push element
2 Pop element
3 Peep element
4 Search for element
5 Exit
Your choice: 4
Enter element: 30
Element found at position: 2
Stack= [10, 20, 30, 40]
```

Queues

We see many queues in our daily life. We see people standing in queues at railway counters, bank ATM counters, super market bill counters, cinema ticket counters, etc. In any queue, the person who is in the first place will get the service first and then comes out of the queue. Any new person will add at the end of the queue. Let's understand that the element that first entered the queue will be deleted first from the queue. This is called FIFO (First In First Out) order. Figure 19.4 shows a queue of people standing at a bank ATM machine:

Figure 19.4: A Queue at a Bank ATM Machine

In the same way, if we can arrange the elements in memory in such a way that the first element will come out first, then that arrangement is called a queue. The rule is that in case of a queue, deletion of elements should be done from the front of the queue and insertion of elements should be done only at its end. It is not possible to do any operations in the middle of the queue. See Figure 19.5:

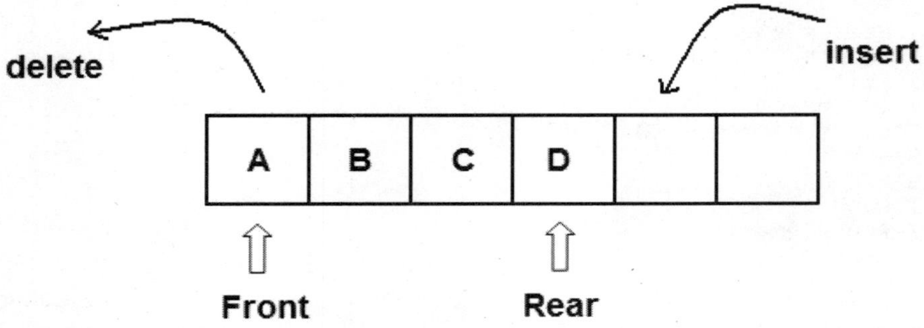

Figure 19.5: A Queue with some Elements

Python provides list data type that can be used to create queues. We should first create a Queue class that can perform the following general operations:

- **Adding a new element:** It means inserting element at the rear (or back) end of the queue. This can be done using append() method of list as: append(element).
- **Deleting an element:** It represents removing the element from the front of the queue. We can use list's pop() method to remove the 0th element, as: pop(0).
- **Searching the position of an element:** This is possible using index() method available for lists. Index(element) returns the position number from the front of the list. If the element is found at 1st position, the index() method returns 0th position. Hence we may have to add 1 to the position number returned by the index() method.

Now, we are going to develop Queue class in the following program and save the program as que1.py. Please see Program 4.

Program

Program 4: A Python program to create a Queue class using list methods.

```
# Queue class - Save this as que1.py
class Queue:
    def __init__(self):
        self.qu = []

    def isempty(self):
        return self.qu == []

    def add(self, element):
        self.qu.append(element)
```

```
    def delete(self):
        if self.isempty():
            return -1
        else:
            return self.qu.pop(0)

    def search(self, element):
        if self.isempty():
            return -1
        else:
            try:
                n = self.qu.index(element)
                return n+1
            except ValueError:
                return -2

    def display(self):
        return self.qu
```

It is possible to use this Queue class of que1.py module in any Python program. In Program 5, we create a queue with float values and then perform some important operations on the queue through a menu.

Program

Program 5: A Python program to perform some operations on a queue.

```
# using the Queue class of que1.py program
from que1 import Queue

# create empty queue object
q = Queue()

# display menu
choice=0
while choice<4:
    print('QUEUE OPERATIONS')
    print('1 Add element')
    print('2 Delete element')
    print('3 Search for element')
    print('4 Exit')
    choice = int(input('Your choice: '))

    # perform a task depending on user choice
    if choice==1:
        element = float(input('Enter element: '))
        q.add(element)

    elif choice==2:
        element = q.delete()
        if element == -1:
            print('The queue is empty')
        else:
            print('Removed element= ', element)

    elif choice==3:
        element = float(input('Enter element: '))
        pos = q.search(element)
        if pos == -1:
```

```
            print('The queue is empty')
        elif pos == -2:
            print('Element not found in the queue')
        else:
            print('Element found at position: ', pos)

    else:
        break

    # display the contents of queue object
    print('Queue= ', q.display())
```

Output:

```
C:\>python myqueue.py
QUEUE OPERATIONS
1 Add element
2 Delete element
3 Search for element
4 Exit
Your choice: 1
Enter element: 10.5
:
:
Queue= [10.5, 22.5, 30.0, 45.0, 50.75]
QUEUE OPERATIONS
1 Add element
2 Delete element
3 Search for element
4 Exit
Your choice: 3
Enter element: 22.5
Element found at position: 2
Queue= [10.5, 22.5, 30.0, 45.0, 50.75]
QUEUE OPERATIONS
1 Add element
2 Delete element
3 Search for element
4 Exit
Your choice: 2
Removed element= 10.5
Queue= [22.5, 30.0, 45.0, 50.75]
QUEUE OPERATIONS
1 Add element
2 Delete element
3 Search for element
4 Exit
Your choice: 4
```

Deques

Every time when we store an element at the end of a queue, internally the size of the queue should be increased. Similarly, when we delete an element at the front, all the elements should be shifted towards front (i.e. left), otherwise there will be empty memory blocks created at the beginning of the queue that may not be reusable. Such troubles can be eliminated if we can allow the insertions and deletions at both ends of the queue. This type of queue is called double-ended queue or simply 'deque'. See Figure 19.6:

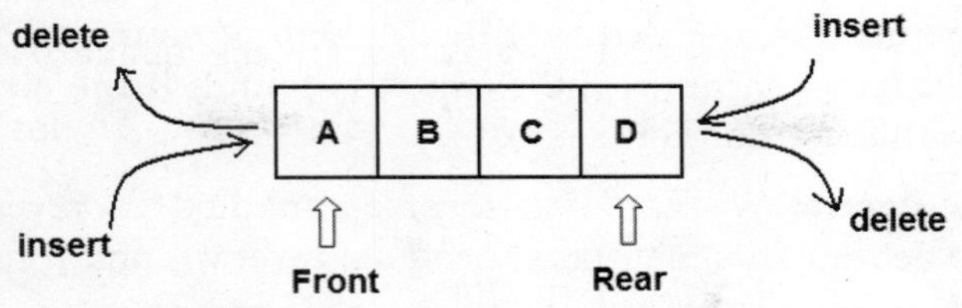

Figure 19.6: The Deque Data Structure

In deque, we can add elements at the front and at the end as well. Similarly, we can remove the elements from the front and from the rear side (end) also. So, deques are more flexible and can be imagined as generalized form of queues and stacks that we discussed in the previous sections. For example, if we insert the delete the elements only from one end of the deque, then it becomes a stack. If we insert the elements from one end and delete the elements from the other end, then it becomes a queue.

In Python, a class by the name 'deque' is provided in 'collections' module to work with deques. Python people used arrays internally in implementing lists which form the basis for creating queues. But in case of deques, they used doubly linked lists to implement the deques. Hence, deques are faster than the normal queues. To create a deque, we should simply create an object to deque class as:

```
d = deque()
```

In this case, the deque can accommodate arbitrary number of elements. We can restrict the size of the deque by specifying 'maxlen' attribute as:

```
d = deque(maxlen= 100)
```

In the preceding statemnet, we are creating a deque which can accommodate a maximum of 100 elements only. The following are the operations provided in deque class in Python:

- **Adding element at the front:** Assuming that the front will be at the left side of the deque, we can add an element at the front using appendleft() method, as: appendleft(element).
- **Deleting element at the front:** This can be done using popleft() method, as: element = popleft(). This method returns a copy of the element that is deleted.
- **Adding element at the rear:** This can be done using append() method that adds the element at the right side of the deque, i.e. at the rear. The way we can use the append() method is: append(element).
- **Deleting element at the rear:** This can be achieved by calling pop() method on the deque. This method when called without any argument will remove the element at the rear of the deque.
- **Deleting element at any place:** This can be done using remove() method. If we use remove(element), it will remove the element from the rear part of the deque. This method raises ValueError if the element being removed is not found.

- **Searching for an element in the deque:** We can find out how many times an element has occurred in the deque with the help of count() method. count(element) will return the number of times the element is found. If the element is not found in the deque, then this method returns 0.
- **Reversing the deque:** We can use reverse() method to reverse the order of the elements in the deque. This method is used as: reverse() and it returns None.

In Program 6, we are creating a deque that can store characters or strings. Also, we are using a menu to perform some important operations on the deque.

Program

Program 6: A Python program to create and use deque.

```
# deque operations
from collections import deque

# create an emtpy deque
d = deque()

choice=0
while choice<7:
    print('DEQUE OPERATIONS')
    print('1 Add element at front')
    print('2 Remove element at front')
    print('3 Add element at rear')
    print('4 Remove element at rear')
    print('5 Remove element in the middle')
    print('6 Search for element')
    print('7 Exit')
    choice = int(input('Your choice: '))

    # perform a task depending on user choice
    if choice==1:
        element = input('Enter element: ')
        d.appendleft(element)

    elif choice==2:
        if len(d) == 0:
            print('Deque is empty')
        else:
            d.popleft()

    elif choice==3:
        element = input('Enter element: ')
        d.append(element)

    elif choice==4:
        if len(d) == 0:
            print('Deque is empty')
        else:
            d.pop()

    elif choice==5:
        element = input('Enter element: ')
        try:
            d.remove(element)
```

```
        except ValueError:
            print('Element not found')

    elif choice==6:
        element = input('Enter element: ')
        c = d.count(element)
        print('No of times the element found: ', c)
    else:
        break

    # display the deque elements using for loop
    print('Deque= ', end='')
    for i in d:
        print(i, ' ', end='')
    print()    # move cursor to next line
```

Output:

```
C:\>python deque.py
DEQUE OPERATIONS
1 Add element at front
2 Remove element at front
3 Add element at rear
4 Remove element at rear
5 Remove element in the middle
6 Search for element
7 Exit
Your choice: 1
Enter element: A
Deque= A
DEQUE OPERATIONS
1 Add element at front
2 Remove element at front
3 Add element at rear
4 Remove element at rear
5 Remove element in the middle
6 Search for element
7 Exit
Your choice: 1
Enter element: B
Deque= B  A
DEQUE OPERATIONS
1 Add element at front
2 Remove element at front
3 Add element at rear
4 Remove element at rear
5 Remove element in the middle
6 Search for element
7 Exit
Your choice: 3
Enter element: C
:
:
Deque= B  A  C  D  E  F
DEQUE OPERATIONS
1 Add element at front
2 Remove element at front
3 Add element at rear
4 Remove element at rear
5 Remove element in the middle
6 Search for element
```

```
7 Exit
Your choice: 2
Deque= A   C  D  E  F
DEQUE OPERATIONS
1 Add element at front
2 Remove element at front
3 Add element at rear
4 Remove element at rear
5 Remove element in the middle
6 Search for element
7 Exit
Your choice: 6
Enter element: E
No of times the element found: 1
Deque= A   C  D  E  F
```

Points to Remember

- A data structure represents logical arrangement of elements in memory in a particular model. Data structures are also known as abstract data types (ADTs).
- Stacks, linked lists and queues are important data structures which are most used in software.
- To create stacks, linked lists and queues, we can use lists available in Python.
- A linked list is a set of nodes such that each node contains a data field to store data and two link fields to refer to the previous node and next node.
- Insertion, deletion and replacing the elements are important operations in case of a linked list.
- A stack represents a group of elements arranged in memory in LIFO (Last In First Order) manner.
- Push, pop and peep (or peek) operations are important in case of stacks.
- A queue is a data structure where the first element which entered the queue will come out first. This is called FIFO (First In First Out) order.
- In a queue, the elements are added only at the rear (or back) side of the queue and they are removed from the front of the queue.
- Adding the elements and removing the elements are the two important operations on queues.
- A double-ended queue (or deque) is a queue where elements can be inserted or deleted from both ends.
- Deques are more efficient than the normal queues in terms of memory usage and speed.
- Adding elements at the front and at the rear, deleting the elements at the front and rear are the two important operations that one can perform on a deque.

CHAPTER

DATE AND TIME 20

In the lives of human beings, dates and times are very important. For example, an employee's experience is counted depending on the joining date and time. His age is calculated on the basis of his birthday. Bank people pay interest amounts on the deposits depending on the days elapsed. Most often, project releasing dates will disturb the sleep of software developers. Dates and times will impact our lives either directly or indirectly. Hence, it is important to know how to work with dates and times in Python. Python provides three modules: *datetime, time* and *calendar* that help us to deal with dates, times, durations and calendars. The recent module is the 'datetime' module that deals with dates along with times. The 'datetime' module contains four important classes by the names 'datetime', 'date', 'time' and 'timedelta'.

- The datetime class handles a combination of date and time. It contains attributes: year, month, day, hour, minute, second, microsecond, and tzinfo.
- The date class handles dates of Gregorian calendar, without taking time zone into consideration. It has the attributes: year, month, and day.
- The time class handles time assuming that every day has exactly 24 X 60 X 60 seconds. Its attributes: hour, minute, second, microsecond, and tzinfo.
- The timedelta class is useful to handle the durations. The duration may be the difference between two date, time, or datetime instances.

The epoch

The 'epoch' is the point where the time starts. This point is taken as the 0.0 hours of January 1st of the current year. For Unix, the epoch is 0.0 hours of January 1st of 1970. It is possible to measure the time in seconds since the epoch using time() function of 'time' module. Consider Program 1.

Program

Program 1: A Python program to measure the time in seconds since the epoch.

```
# knowing the time since the epoch
import time
epoch = time.time()   # call time() function of time module
print(epoch)
```

Output:

```
C:\>python ep.py
1462077746.917558
```

Please observe the output of the previous program. This indicates how many seconds are gone since the epoch, i.e. since the beginning of the current year. This number is not that much useful unless we see it in the form of date and time. To convert these seconds into date and time, we can use localtime() function of 'time' module as:

```
dt = time.localtime(seconds-since-epoch)
```

This function returns an object similar to C language structure by the name 'struct_time'. From this object, it is possible to access the attributes either using an index or using a name. For example, to access the year number, we can use the index value 0 or the name: tm_year. Consider Table 20.1:

Table 20.1: The 'struct_time' Indexes and Related Attributes

Index	Attribute	Values
0	tm_year	4 digit year number like 2016.
1	tm_mon	range [1, 12]
2	tm_mday	range [1, 31]
3	tm_hour	range [0, 23]
4	tm_min	range [0, 59]
5	tm_sec	range [0, 61], including leap seconds
6	tm_wday	range [0, 6], Monday is 0
7	tm_yday	range [1, 366]
8	tm_isdst	[0, 1 or -1], 0 = no DST, 1 = DST is in effect, -1 = not known
	tm_zone	timezone name

Program

Program 2: A Python program to get date and time from the epoch time.

```
# converting the epoch time into date and time
import time

# localtime() converts the epoch time into time_struct object t
t = time.localtime(1462077746.917558)

# retrieve the date from the structure t
d = t.tm_mday
m = t.tm_mon
y = t.tm_year
print('Current date is: %d - %d - %d' %(d, m, y))

# retrieve the time from the structure t
h = t.tm_hour
m = t.tm_min
s = t.tm_sec
print('Current time is: %d : %d : %d' %(h,m,s))
```

Output:

```
C:\>python ep.py
Current date is: 1 - 5 - 2016
Current time is: 10 : 12 : 26
```

Another way to convert the epoch time into date and time is by using ctime() function of 'time' module. This function takes epoch time in seconds and returns corresponding date and time in string format. This is shown in Program 3.

Program

Program 3: A Python program to convert epoch time into corresponding date and time.

```
# convert epoch time into date and time using ctime()
import time
t = time.ctime(1462077746.917558)    # ctime() with epoch seconds
print(t)
```

Output:

```
C:\>python ep2.py
Sun May  1 10:12:26 2016
```

Date and Time Now

The current date and time as shown in our computer system can be known using the following:

- ctime() function of 'time' module
- now() method of 'datetime' class of 'datetime' module
- today() method of 'datetime' class of 'datetime' module

When ctime() is used without passing any epoch time, it returns the current date and time in string format. This is shown in Program 4.

Program

Program 4: A Python program to know the current date and time using ctime() function.

```
# finding current date and time using ctime()
import time
t = time.ctime()     # ctime() without epoch time
print(t)
```

Output:

```
C:\>python ep3.py
```

Tue May 3 20:31:00 2016To know the current date and time, we can also take the help of now() method of 'datetime' class that belongs to 'datetime' module. This method returns an object that contains date and time information in any timezone. The time zone information should be provided to this method. If the time zone is not provided, then it takes the local time zone. For example, when we use this method in India, it gives the date and time according to IST (India Standard Time) that is 5.30 hours ahead of Greenwich Mean Time. This is called local time zone of India.

The now() method returns 'datetime' class object. We can access the day, month and year information from this object using the attributes day, month and year. Similarly, to access the time information, we can use the attributes hour, minute and second.

Program

Program 5: A Python program to know the local date and time.

```
# finding current date and time
from datetime import *
now = datetime.now()
print(now)

print('Date now: {}/{}/{}'.format(now.day, now.month, now.year))
print('Time now: {}:{}:{}'.format(now.hour, now.minute, now.second))
```

Output:

```
C:\>python date.py
2016-05-01 11:12:34.706623
Date now: 1/5/2016
Time now: 11:12:34
```

The 'datetime' module contains a class by the name 'datetime' that contains today() method. This method returns the date and time information. The same module contains another class by the name 'date'. This class also contains today() method that returns only date as shown in Program 6.

Program

Program 6: A Python program to know today's date and time.

```
# finding today's date and time
from datetime import *

# today() of datetime class gives date and time
tdm = datetime.today()
print("Today's date and time= ",tdm)

# today() of date class gives the date only
td = date.today()
print("Today's date= ", td)
```

Output:

```
C:\>python dates.py
Today's date and time=  2016-05-01 11:33:14.725549
Today's date=  2016-05-01
```

Combining Date and Time

We can create 'datetime' class object by combining date class object and time class objects using combine() method. Please remember that the date and time classes belong to 'datetime' module. For example, we can create a date class object with some date as:

```
d = date(2016, 4, 29)
```

Similarly, we can create time class object and store some time as:

```
t = datetime.time(15, 30)
```

Now, the combine() method is a class method in the class 'datetime' that can combine the previously created objects as:

```
dt = datetime.combine(d, t)
```

Program

Program 7: A Python program to create datetime object by combining date and time objects.

```
# combining date and time
from datetime import *
d = date(2016, 4, 29)
t = time(15, 30)
dt = datetime.combine(d, t)
print(dt)
```

Output:

```
C:\>python dates.py
2016-04-29 15:30:00
```

The 'datetime' class object is created in 3 different ways. The first way is to create the object using now() method as:

```
dt1 = datetime.now()
```

The second way of creating 'datetime' object is by using combine() method as:

```
dt2 = datetime.combine(d, t)
```

The third way of creating 'datetime' object is by directly creating the object and passing the date and time values as:

```
dt3 = datetime(year=2016, month=6, day=24)
dt4 = datetime(2016, 6, 24, 18, 30)
dt5 = datetime(year=2016, month=6, day=24, hour=15, minute=30)
```

We can change the content of the 'datetime' object by calling replace() method on the object as:

```
dt6 = dt5.replace(year=2017, month=10)
```

In the preceding statement, the year and month values which are already available in dt5 object are changed to 2017 and 10, respectively and the new object holding these new values will be dt6.

Program

Program 8: A Python program to create a datetime object and then change its contents.

```
# creating datetime object and change its contents
from datetime import *

# create a datetime object
dt1 = datetime(year=2016, month=6, day=24, hour=15, minute=30,
      second=15)
print(dt1)

# change its year, month and hour values
dt2 = dt1.replace(year=2017, hour=20, month=10)
print(dt2)
```

Output:

```
C:\>python dates.py
2016-06-24 15:30:15
2017-10-24 20:30:15
```

Formatting Dates and Times

The contents of the 'datetime',' date' and 'time' classes objects can be formatted using strftime() method. 'strftime' represents 'string format of time'. This method converts the objects into a specified format and returns the formatted string. To understand this, let's call the today() method on date class as:

```
td = datetime.date.today()
print(td)
```

The preceding statements may display the current date as:

```
2016-05-01
```

But, we want to display this date in a different format as:

```
01, May, 2016
```

This is possible using strftime() method on the 'td' object as:

```
td.strftime("%d, %B, %Y")
```

Here, '%d' indicates the day of the month in two digit format as 01. '%B' indicates the month's full name as May and '%Y' indicates the four digit year number as 2016. These are called 'format codes' for strftime() method. In Program 9, we are formatting the current date using strftime() method as discussed so far.

Program

Program 9: A Python program to convert a date into a required string format.

```
# formating the date
from datetime import *

# get current date into td object
td = date.today()
print(td)

# format the td and convert into string str
str = td.strftime("%d, %B, %Y")
print(str)
```

Output:

```
C:\>python dates.py
2016-05-01
01, May, 2016
```

The format codes are mentioned in Table 20.2:

Table 20.2: Format Codes Used in strftime() Method

Format Code	Meaning	Example
%a	Weekday as an abbreviated name.	Sun, Mon, ... Sat
%A	Weekday as full name.	Sunday, Monday, ... Saturday
%w	Weekday as a decimal number, where 0 is Sunday and 6 is Saturday.	0, 1, ... 6
%d	Day of the month as a zero-padded decimal number.	01, 02, ... 31
%b	Month as an abbreviated name.	Jan, Feb, ... Dec
%B	Month as full name.	January, February, ... December
%m	Month as zero-padded decimal number.	01, 02, ... 12

Format Code	Meaning	Example
%y	Year without century as a zero-padded decimal number.	00, 01, ... 99
%Y	Year with century as decimal number.	0001, 0002, ... 2016, ... 9999
%H	Hour (24-hour clock) as zero-padded decimal number.	00, 01, ... 23
%I	Hour (12-hour clock) as a zero-padded decimal number.	01, 02, ... 12
%p	Either AM or PM.	AM, PM
%M	Minute as a zero-padded decimal number.	00, 01, ... 59
%S	Second as a zero-padded decimal number.	00, 01, ... 59
%f	Microsecond as a decimal number, zero-padded on the left.	000000, 000001, ... 999999
%Z	Time zone name.	(empty), UTC, EST, CST
%j	Day of the year as a zero-padded decimal number.	001, 002, ... 366
%U	Week number of the year (Sunday as the first day of the week) as a zero padded decimal number. All days in a new year preceding the first Sunday are considered to be in week 0.	00, 01, ... 53
%W	Week number of the year (Monday as the first day of the week) as a decimal number. All days in a new year preceding the first Monday are considered to be in week 0.	00, 01, ... 53
%c	Appropriate date and time representation.	Tue Aug 16 21:30:00 1988
%x	Appropriate date representation.	08/16/88 (None); 08/16/1988 (en_US)

Format Code	Meaning	Example
%X	Appropriate time representation.	21:30:00 (en_US)
%%	A single % character.	%

From Table 20.2, we can understand that the format code '%j' is useful to display the day number in the year. So, we can find the day of the year as:

```
td.strftime("%j")
```

This returns a string that contains the day number in the year. We can also find the week day name with the help of '%A' as:

```
td.strftime("%A")
```

This may display 'Sunday', 'Monday', ... etc. These things are shown in Program 10.

Program

Program 10: A Python program to find the day of the year and the week day name.

```
# finding the day of the year
from datetime import *

# get today's date
td = date.today()
print(td)   # display content of td object

# %j returns day of the year as: 001,002,...366.
s1 = td.strftime("%j")
print('Today is ', s1, 'th day of the current year')

# find the week day name
s2 = td.strftime("%A")
print('It is ', s2)
```

Output:

```
C:\>python dates.py
2016-05-01
Today is  122 th day of the current year
It is  Sunday
```

Let's create another Program 11, in which the datetime object 'dt' contains the date and time. We want to show only the time in the format as: Hours: Minutes: Seconds. This can be done using strftime() method.

Program

Program 11: A Python program to format the time using strftime() method.

```
# formatting the current time
from datetime import *

# create datetime object with current date and time
dt = datetime.now()
```

```
print(dt)    # display content of dt object

# display only time
print('Current time: ', dt.strftime("%H:%M:%S"))
```

Output:

```
C:\>python dates.py
2016-05-01 14:55:18.118699
Current time:  14:55:18
```

In Program 12, we enter a date from the keyboard and display the day of the week. To enter the date from the keyboard, we can use input() function in the following format:

```
d, m, y = [int(x) for x in input("Enter a date: ").split('/')]
```

The preceding statement receives a string with three values separated by a '/'. This string is split into three values by the split() method, where a '/' is found. Each of these three values are converted into integers by int(x) function and returned into the variables: d, m, y. Once we got the d, m, y, we can create date class object dt using date class as:

```
dt = date(y, m, d)
```

Now, the date is available in 'dt' object. We can display this date in which ever format we want using strftime() method. The format code '%w' represents day number and '%A' represents the name of the week day.

Program

Program 12: A Python program to accept a date from the keyboard and display the day of the week.

```
# finding day of the week.
from datetime import *

# accept date, month and year from the keyboard
d, m, y = [int(x) for x in input("Enter a date: ").split('/')]

# store them in date class object 'dt'
dt = date(y, m, d)

# %w - day number and %A full name of the week day
print(dt.strftime('Day %w of the week. This is %A'))
```

Output:

```
C:\>python dates.py
Enter a date: 29/6/1966
Day 3 of the week. This is Wednesday
```

In Program 13, we create two date class objects with the dates given by the user from the keyboard. Let the date, month and year be d1, m1 and y1. The date class object will be created as:

```
dt1 = date(y1, m1, d1)
```

Here, 'dt1' represents the date class object that stores the year, month and date in that order. In the same way, we can create another date object 'dt2' that stores another date. Now, we can subtract them, as:

```
dt = dt1 - dt2
```

Here, the difference in the days between these two dates is returned into 'dt'. Please remember when we find the difference between two date class objects, the resultant object belongs to 'timedelta' class. So, 'dt' is an object of 'timedelta' class.

The 'timedelta' class has three attributes: days, seconds and microseconds. Hence, we can get the days from the 'dt' object by writing: dt.days. The next step is to find the difference number of weeks between the two given dates. For this purpose, we can simply divide the days by 7 and take only the quotient. This can be done by divmod() function. divmod() is a built-in function that returns the pair of quotient and remainder of division a/b as:

```
quotient, remainder = divmod(a, b)   # quotient= a//b and remainder=
# a%b
```

So, to get the weeks, we have to divide the days by 7 using divmod() function as:

```
weeks, days = divmod(dt.days, 7)
```

Here, 'weeks' represents the number of weeks and remaining days are given by 'days'. Similarly, to find the difference number of months, we have to divide the days by 30 and take quotient as:

```
months, days = divmod(dt.days, 30)
```

Program

Program 13: A Python program to find the difference in number of days, weeks and months between two given dates.

```
# difference days, weeks and months between two dates
from datetime import *

# enter the two dates from the keyboard
d1, m1, y1 = [int(x) for x in input("Enter first date: ").split('/')]
d2, m2, y2 = [int(x) for x in input("Enter second date: ").split('/')]

# create date class objects with the input
dt1 = date(y1, m1, d1)
dt2 = date(y2, m2, d2)

# find days difference between these two dates
dt = dt1 - dt2
print('Days difference= ', dt)

# find difference in weeks
weeks, days = divmod(dt.days, 7)
print('Weeks difference= ', weeks)

# find difference in months
months, days = divmod(dt.days, 30)
print('Months difference= ', months)
```

Output:

```
C:\>python diff.py
Enter first date: 12/2/1970
Enter second date: 11/5/1968
Days difference= 642 days, 0:00:00
Weeks difference= 91
Months difference= 21
```

It is possible to find the difference between dates and times also. Since both the date and time are involved, we should use datetime class for this purpose.

```
d1 = datetime(2000, 6, 25, 8, 00, 25)
d2 = datetime(2016, 5, 20, 7, 55, 15)
```

The difference between these two datetime class objects will give us another object 'diff' as:

```
diff = d2-d1
```

In fact, this 'diff' object is an object of 'timedelta' class. Any 'timedelta' class object contains three attributes: days, seconds and microseconds. Hence, we can refer to them as:

```
diff.days
diff.seconds
diff.microseconds
```

Since we can access days and seconds, the other values like hours and minutes can be obtained from these values. See Program 14.

Program

Program 14: A Python program to find difference between two dates along with times.

```
# difference between two dates along with times.
from datetime import *

# create two datetime objects that store date and time
d1 = datetime(2000, 6, 25, 8, 00, 25)
d2 = datetime(2016, 5, 20, 7, 55, 15)

# find the difference in days and time
diff = d2-d1
print(diff)

# divide days by 7 to get weeks and remaining days
weeks, days = divmod(diff.days, 7)

# divide seconds by 3600 to get hours and remaining seconds
hrs, secs = divmod(diff.seconds, 3600)

# divide remaining seconds by 60 to get minutes
mins = secs//60   # get minutes

# take remaining seconds from the remainder of division
secs = secs % 60   # get remaining seconds

print('Difference is %d weeks, %d days, %d hours, %d minutes and %d
     seconds' % (weeks, days, hrs, mins, secs))
```

Output:

```
C:\>python diff.py
5807 days, 23:54:50
Difference is 829 weeks, 4 days, 23 hours, 54 minutes and 50 seconds
```

Finding Durations using 'timedelta'

The 'timedelta' class of 'datetime' module is useful to find the durations like difference between two dates or finding the date after adding a period to an existing date. It is possible to know the future dates or previous dates using 'timedelta'. The 'timedelta' class object is available in the following format:

```
timedelta(days=0, seconds=0, microseconds=0, milliseconds=0, minutes=0,
    hours=0, weeks=0)
```

All arguments passed to the 'timedelta' object are optional and default to 0. Arguments may be integers or floats, and may be positive or negative.

Only days, seconds and microseconds are stored internally in the 'timedelta' object. Arguments are converted to those units as:

- A millisecond is converted to 1000 microseconds.
- A minute is converted to 60 seconds.
- An hour is converted to 3600 seconds.
- A week is converted to 7 days.

Suppose, we have some date and time in 'datetime' class object, as:

```
d1 = datetime(2016, 4, 29, 16, 45, 0)   # 29th Apr, 2016 and 16.45
    # hours
```

We want to know the future date by adding 10 days, 12 hours, 20 minutes and 10 seconds time duration to the date 'd1'. This is possible by creating a 'timedelta' object using these arguments as:

```
period1 = timedelta(days=10, seconds=10, minutes=20, hours=12)
```

This duration, which is represented as 'period1', should be added to the date and time value in 'd1' as: d1+ period1. This will give us the future date and time.

Program

Program 15: A Python program to find future date and time from an existing date and time.

```
# finding future date and time
from datetime import *

# store the date and time in datetime object: d1
d1 = datetime(2016, 4, 29, 16, 45, 0)

# define the duration using timedelta object: period1
period1 = timedelta(days=10, seconds=10, minutes=20, hours=12)
```

```
# add the duration to d1 and display
print('The new date and time is: ', d1+period1)
```

Output:

```
C:\>python dates.py
The new date and time is: 2016-05-10  05:05:10
```

In Program 16, we are using 'timedelta' to display the next 10 dates starting from a given date or from the present date. Suppose the present date is 'd', then we have to add 'timedelta' object as:

```
nextdate = d + timedelta(days=x)
```

Here, by changing 'x' values from 1 to 9, we can display the next 10 dates.

Program

Program 16: A Python program to display the next 10 dates continuously.

```
# displaying a range of continuous dates
from datetime import *

# start with today.
d = date.today()
print(d)

# or any other date
# d = date(1966, 6, 29)

# add 1 to 9 days and get future dates.
for x in range(1, 10):
    nextdate = d + timedelta(days=x)
    print(nextdate)
```

Output:

```
C:\python dates.py
2016-04-30
2016-05-01
2016-05-02
2016-05-03
2016-05-04
2016-05-05
2016-05-06
2016-05-07
2016-05-08
2016-05-09
```

Comparing Two Dates

It is possible to compare two 'date' class objects just like comparing two numbers. For example, d1 and d2 are to be compared, we can write:

d1 == d2

d1> d2

d1<d2

These expressions return either True or False. Similarly it is possible to compare the 'datetime' class objects also. In Program 17, we are accepting date of births of two persons and determining who is older. This is done by first storing the date of births in two separate date class objects b1 and b2 and then comparing them using the if statement.

Program

Program 17: A Python program to accept date of births of two persons and determining the older person.

```
# to know who is older
from datetime import *

# enter birth dates and store into date class objects
d1, m1, y1 = [int(x) for x in input("Enter first person's birth date (DD/MM/YYYY): ").split('/')]
b1 = date(y1, m1, d1)

d2, m2, y2 = [int(x) for x in input("Enter second person's birth date (DD/MM/YYYY): ").split('/')]
b2 = date(y2, m2, d2)

# compare the birth dates
if b1 == b2:
    print('Both persons are of equal age')
elif b1 > b2:
    print('The second person is older')
else:
    print('The first person is older')
```

Output:

```
C:\>python dates.py
Enter first person's birth date (DD/MM/YYYY): 10/1/1990
Enter second person's birth date (DD/MM/YYYY): 10/2/1989
The second person is older
```

Sorting Dates

One of the best ways to sort a group of dates is to store them into a list and then apply list's sort() method. This will sort all the dates which are available in the list. We can store the date class objects into the list using append() method as:

```
list.append(d)
```

Here, 'd' represents the date class object that is being appended to the list 'list'.

Program

Program 18: A Python program to sort a group of given dates in ascending order.

```
# sorting dates
from datetime import *

# take an empty list
```

```
group = []

# add today's date to list, i.e. 2016-04-30
group.append(date.today())

# create some more dates and add them to list
d = date(2015, 6, 29)
group.append(d)
d = date(2014, 6, 30)
group.append(d)

# add 25 days to the date and add to list
group.append(d+timedelta(days=25))

# sort the list
group.sort()

# display sorted dates
for d in group:
    print(d)
```

Output:

```
C:\python dates.py
2014-06-30
2014-07-25
2015-06-29
2016-04-30
```

Stopping Execution Temporarily

To stop execution of a program temporarily for a given amount of time, we can use sleep() function of 'time' module. This function is used in the format:

```
sleep(seconds)
```

Here, the time 'seconds' can be given as 3 to represent the sleeping effect for 3 seconds. It can be given as 3.5 or 4.2 etc. also. When this function is called, the PVM suspends execution of the program for those many seconds.

In Program 19, we want to generate random numbers in the range from 100 to 200. A random number is a number that cannot be guessed by any one. We cannot imagine which number we are going to get. To generate a range of random numbers, we can use randrange() function of 'random' module.

```
num = randrange(100, 200, 5)
```

The preceding randrange() function generates a random number 'num' in the range from 100 to 200 in steps of 5.

Program

Program 19: A Python program to generate random numbers in a range with some time delay between each number.

```
# to generate random numbers between 100 and 200 every 3.5 secs
import time, random
```

```
# generate 10 random numbers
for i in range(10):
    # generate in the range 100 to 200
    num=random.randrange(100, 200, 5)
    print(num)
    # suspend execution for 3.5 seconds
    time.sleep(3.5)
```

Output:

```
C:\>python rand.py
195
160
105
175
185
195
185
100
115
165
```

Knowing the Time taken by a Program

Python provides two functions: perf_counter() and process_time() of 'time' module to measure the time difference between two points in a program. Hence, these functions can be used to measure the time taken for execution of a Python program.

- **perf_counter():** This function returns the time duration in fractional seconds. It measures the time taken by the program to execute a group of statements. It includes the time elapsed during sleep of the processor.
- **process_time():** This function returns the time duration in fractional seconds. It measures the total time taken by the program and CPU in executing a group of statements. But it will not count the time elapsed during sleep of the processor.

Simply speaking, the perf_counter() function is useful to correctly measure the time taken by a program. If we want to measure the time taken by the program + CPU's time in executing the program statements, then only we should use process_time(). Since CPU's time may differ from processor to processor, this is generally not taken into consideration while calculating the time taken by the program. So, the performance of a program is obtained through perf_couner() function.

When we call the perf_counter() function in a statement as:

```
t1 = perf_counter()
```

The preceding statement will start counting the time in seconds including fraction of seconds. When we want to count the time at the end of a program (or group of statements), we should call this function, again as:

```
t2 = perf_counter()
```

Now, the difference t2-t1 gives us the time spent between the two points 't1' and 't2' in the program. In Program 20, we are calculating the time taken by the program including the time that is spent in sleeping by the processor.

Program

Program 20: A Python program to find the execution time of a program.

```
# to measure the time taken by the program
from time import *

# note the starting time of the program
t1 = perf_counter()

# do some processing
i, sum = 0, 0
while(i<1000000):
    sum+=i
    i+=1

# make the processor or PVM sleep for 3 seconds
# this is also measured by the perf_counter()
sleep(3)

# note the ending time of the program
t2 = perf_counter()

# find time for the program in seconds
print('Execution time = %f seconds' %(t2- t1))
```

Output:

```
C:\>python time.py
Execution time = 3.289487 seconds
```

In Program 20, the perf_counter() function counts the sleep time of 3 seconds that is given in the program using sleep(3) function. In this program, if we replace the perf_counter() function with process_time() function, the result may be as follows:

```
Execution time = 0.312500 seconds
```

This is showing less execution time, since process_time() did not take the effect of sleep(3) function in the program. But this function adds some fractional seconds that are used by CPU while executing this code.

Working with Calendar Module

The 'calendar' module is useful to create calendar for any month or year. This module is also useful to know whether a given year is leap year or not. The isleap() function of calendar module is useful for this purpose.

Program

Program 21: A Python program to enter a year number and display whether it is leap or not.

```
# to test whether leap year or not
from calendar import *
y = int(input('Enter year: '))

if(isleap(y)):
    print(y, ' is leap year')
else:
    print(y, ' is not leap')
```

Output:

```
C:\>python leap.py
Enter year: 2016
2016 is leap year
```

The 'calendar' module has 'month' function that is useful to display calendar for a specific month. For example, to display a calendar for the May month of year 2016, we can use this function as:

```
str = month(2016, 5)    # return calendar for May 2016
```

The string 'str' returned by this month() function contains the calendar which can be displayed using print() function. This is shown in Program 22.

Program

Program 22: A Python program to display the calendar for a given month and year.

```
# to display calendar of given month of the year
from calendar import *

# ask for month and year
yy = int(input("Enter year: "))
mm = int(input("Enter month: "))

# display the calendar for that month
str = month(yy,mm)
print(str)
```

Output:

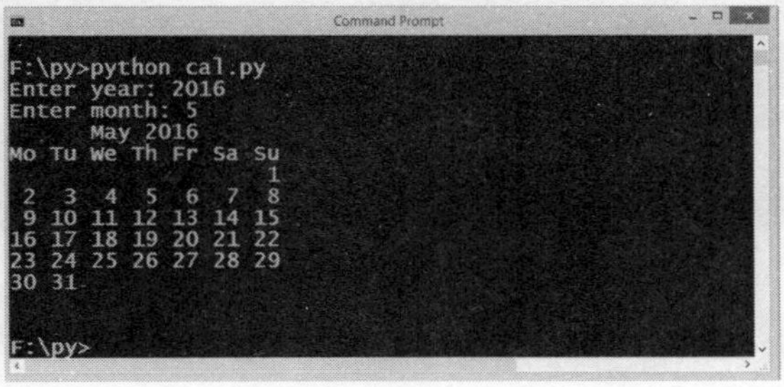

Figure 20.1: The Output of the Program 22

If we want to display a calendar for all the months of an entire year, we can use calendar() function of 'calendar' module. This function returns the calendar as a string with several lines and is used in the following format:

```
calendar(year, w=2, l=1, c=6, m=3)
```

Here, 'year' represents the year number for which the calendar is needed. 'w' represents the width between two columns. Its default value is 2. 'l' represents the blank lines between two rows. Its default value is 1. 'c' represents column-wise space between two months. Its default value is 6. 'm' represents the number of months to be displayed in a row. Its default value is 3. Of course, the values of 'w', 'l', 'c' and 'm' are not compulsory.

Program

Program 23: A Python program to display the calendar for all months of a given year.

```
# to display calendar for entire year
from calendar import *
year = int(input('Enter year: '))
print(calendar(year, 2, 1, 8, 3))
```

Output:

```
Command Prompt
F:\py>python cal.py
Enter year: 2016
                                  2016

       January                         February                         March
Mo Tu We Th Fr Sa Su            Mo Tu We Th Fr Sa Su            Mo Tu We Th Fr Sa Su
             1  2  3             1  2  3  4  5  6  7                1  2  3  4  5  6
 4  5  6  7  8  9 10             8  9 10 11 12 13 14             7  8  9 10 11 12 13
11 12 13 14 15 16 17            15 16 17 18 19 20 21            14 15 16 17 18 19 20
18 19 20 21 22 23 24            22 23 24 25 26 27 28            21 22 23 24 25 26 27
25 26 27 28 29 30 31            29                              28 29 30 31

        April                           May                             June
Mo Tu We Th Fr Sa Su            Mo Tu We Th Fr Sa Su            Mo Tu We Th Fr Sa Su
             1  2  3                               1                   1  2  3  4  5
 4  5  6  7  8  9 10             2  3  4  5  6  7  8             6  7  8  9 10 11 12
11 12 13 14 15 16 17             9 10 11 12 13 14 15            13 14 15 16 17 18 19
18 19 20 21 22 23 24            16 17 18 19 20 21 22            20 21 22 23 24 25 26
25 26 27 28 29 30               23 24 25 26 27 28 29            27 28 29 30
                                30 31

        July                           August                        September
Mo Tu We Th Fr Sa Su            Mo Tu We Th Fr Sa Su            Mo Tu We Th Fr Sa Su
             1  2  3             1  2  3  4  5  6  7                      1  2  3  4
 4  5  6  7  8  9 10             8  9 10 11 12 13 14             5  6  7  8  9 10 11
11 12 13 14 15 16 17            15 16 17 18 19 20 21            12 13 14 15 16 17 18
18 19 20 21 22 23 24            22 23 24 25 26 27 28            19 20 21 22 23 24 25
25 26 27 28 29 30 31            29 30 31                        26 27 28 29 30

       October                         November                        December
Mo Tu We Th Fr Sa Su            Mo Tu We Th Fr Sa Su            Mo Tu We Th Fr Sa Su
                1  2                1  2  3  4  5  6                      1  2  3  4
 3  4  5  6  7  8  9             7  8  9 10 11 12 13             5  6  7  8  9 10 11
10 11 12 13 14 15 16            14 15 16 17 18 19 20            12 13 14 15 16 17 18
```

Figure 20.2: The Output of Program 23

Points to Remember

- The datetime class handles a combination of date and time.
- The date class handles dates of Gregorian calendar, without taking time zone into consideration.
- The time class handles time assuming that every day has exactly 24 X 60 X 60 seconds.
- The timedelta class is useful to handle the durations. The duration may be the difference between two date, time, or datetime instances.
- The number of seconds elapsed since the epoch can be determined using time() function of 'time' module.
- To get date and time from the epoch seconds, we can use localtime() and ctime() functions of 'time' module.
- To know the current date and time, we can use ctime() function of 'time' module.
- To know the current date and time, we can take the help of now() method of 'datetime' class that belongs to 'datetime' module.
- The today() method of datetime class returns the current date and time. Similarly today() method of date class returns only the current date.
- The combine() method is useful to combine date and time and returns datetime class object.
- The replace() method is useful to change the contents of datetime class object.
- The contents of the datetime, date and time classes objects can be formatted using strftime() method. This method contains several format codes to format the date and time values.
- The divmod() method returns the quotient and remainder of division. It is used as:

  quotient, remainder = divmod(a, b)   # quotient= a//b and remainder= a%b
- The timedelta class of 'datetime' module is useful to find the durations like difference between two dates or finding the date after adding a period to an existing date.
- To stop execution of a program temporarily for a given amount of time, we can use sleep() function of 'time' module.
- To generate a range of random numbers, we can use randrange() function of 'random' module.
- Python provides two functions: perf_counter() and process_time() of 'time' module to measure the time difference between two points in a program.

- The perf_counter() function is useful to return the time taken by the program to execute a group of statements including the sleeping time of the process.
- The process_time() function measures the total time taken by the program and CPU in executing a group of statements excluding the sleeping time of the process.
- The isleap() function of 'calendar' module is useful for testing whether a year is leap or not.
- The month(y, m) function of 'calendar' module is useful to display a month's calendar.
- The calendar(year) function of 'calendar' module is useful to display a year's calendar.

CHAPTER 21

THREADS

A thread represents a separate path of execution of a group of statements. In a Python program, if we write a group of statements, then these statements are executed by Python Virtual Machine (PVM) one by one. This execution is called a thread, because PVM uses a thread to execute these statements. This means that in every Python program, there is always a thread running internally which is appointed by the PVM to execute the program statements. What is this thread? Let's write a program to see what a thread is.

Program

Program 1: A Python program to find the currently running thread in a Python program.

```
# every Python program is run by main thread
import threading
print('Let us find the current thread')

# find the name of the present thread
print('Currently running thread:',threading.current_thread().getName())

# check if it is main thread or not
if threading.current_thread() == threading.main_thread():
    print('The current thread is the main thread')
else:
    print('The current thread is not main thread')
```

Output:

```
C:\>python th.py
Let us find the current thread
Currently running thread: MainThread
The current thread is the main thread
```

In the preceding program, we have imported 'threading' module which is needed while dealing with threads. This module contains a method 'current_thread()' that returns an object containing the information about the presently running thread in the program. We can access its name using the getName() method as:

```
name = current_thread().getName()# return the name of the current
                                 # thread
```

This is shown as 'MainThread' which is the name of an internal class in Python. We can also access the main thread's information by calling 'main_thread()' method. Hence it is possible to compare whether the current thread is the main thread or not using:

```
if threading.current_thread() == threading.main_thread():
    print('The current thread is the main thread')
```

This statement has displayed the output: The current thread is the main thread. So, from Program 1, we can understand that in every Python program, there is always a default thread called 'Main thread' that executes the program statements.

A thread represents execution of statements. The way the statements are executed is of two types:

- Single tasking
- Multitasking

Single Tasking

A task means doing some calculation, processing, etc. Generally, a task involves execution of a group of statements, for example executing a program. In 'single tasking' environment, only one task is given to the processor at a time. Consider Figure 21.1. Here, let's take an example of a student who goes to the lab to write some programs. He types his first program. It may be taking some 10 minutes. When he is typing his program, the microprocessor is sitting idle, without any work. After typing is completed, he submits the program to the processor. The processor executes it within a millisecond. Since nowadays, processors can execute millions of instructions per second, even if the student has written a program of 100 lines, the processor will not take more than a fraction of a second to complete its execution. After verifying the results, the student has started typing the second program. It may take another 10 or 15 minutes. Within this time, the processor sits idle, waiting for the job. When the student submits the second program, then it works for a fraction of a second on the program. Then again it goes into idle state. From this discussion, we can understand that the processor is sitting idle without any work for most of the time.

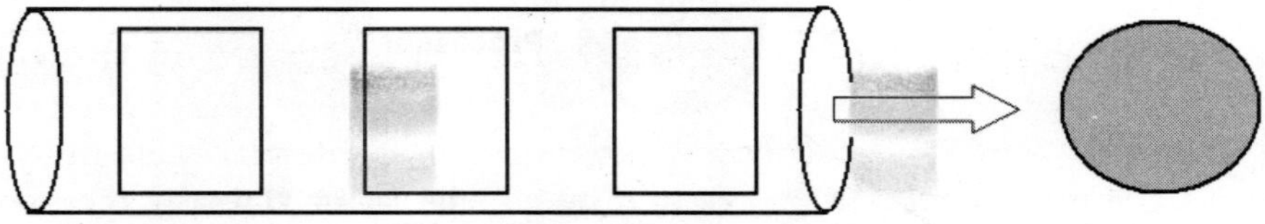

Figure 21.1: Single Tasking

In single tasking, only one task is given to the processor at a time. This means we are wasting a lot of processor time and the microprocessor has to sit idle without any job for a long time. This is the drawback in single tasking. But, in some cases where the tasks should be executed one by one without any time gap, single tasking would be preferable. For example, printing the marks sheets of students on the printer.

Multitasking

To use the processor's time in an optimum way, we can give it several jobs at a time. This is called multitasking. But how can we give several jobs at a time? Suppose there are 4 tasks that we want to execute. We load them into the memory, as shown in Figure 21.2. The memory is divided into 4 parts and the jobs are loaded there. Now, the microprocessor has to execute them all at a time. So the processor will take small time duration, like a millisecond and divide this time between the number of jobs. Here, there are 4 jobs. So we get ¼ millisecond time for each job. This small part of the processor time is called 'time slice'. It will allot exactly ¼ millisecond time for executing each of the jobs. Within this time slice, it will try to execute each job. Suppose, the processor started at first job, it will spend exactly ¼ millisecond time executing the first job. Within this time duration, if it could not complete the first job, then what it does? In that case, it stores the intermediate results till then it obtained in a temporary memory, and then it goes to the second task. It then spends exactly ¼ millisecond time executing the second task. Within this time, if it can complete this task, no problem. Suppose it could not complete this task, then it goes to the third task, storing the results in a temporary memory. Similarly, it will spend exactly ¼ millisecond for the third task, and another ¼ millisecond for the fourth task. After executing the fourth task, it will come back to the first task, in a circular manner. This is called 'round robin' method. In short, executing tasks in a circular manner such that coming back to the first task after completing the last task is called as round robin method.

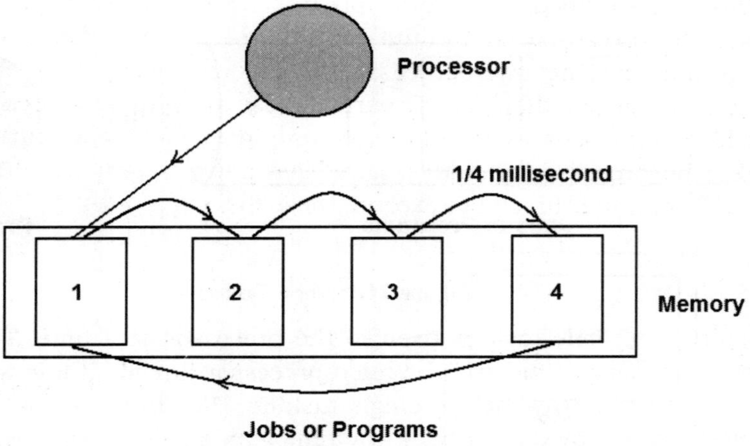

Figure 21.2: Process-based multitasking

The processor, after returning to the first task, again starts execution from the point, where it has left that task earlier. It will execute the first task exactly for ¼ millisecond this time, and proceeds to the second task and then third and fourth before coming back to the first task in a round robin way. So if you have submitted the first job, you can understand that the processor is executing your job for ¼ millisecond and then keeping you waiting for another ¾ millisecond, while it is going and executing the other tasks. After ¾ millisecond, it is again coming back to your job and executing it for another ¼ millisecond time. But you will not be aware that you are kept waiting for ¾ millisecond time, as this time is very small. You will feel that the processor is spending its time executing your job only. Similarly, the second person who submitted the second job will also feel that only his job is being executed by the processor. The third and fourth persons will also feel the same way. It is something like all the 4 jobs are executed by the processor simultaneously. This is called multitasking.

Generally, we have only one processor in our computer system. One processor has to execute several tasks means that it has to execute them in a round robin method. Strictly speaking, this is not multitasking. Since the processor is quickly executing the tasks one by one, we feel all the jobs are executed by the processor at a time. Multitasking cannot be a real phenomenon with single processor systems. If we want to really achieve multitasking, we need computers with multiple processors.

The main advantage of multitasking is to use the processor time in a better way. We are engaging most of the processor time and it is not sitting idle. In this way, we can complete several tasks at a time, and thus achieve good performance.

Multitasking is of two types: a) Process-based multitasking b) Thread-based multitasking. So far, we discussed the first type, i.e. Process-based multitasking. Now let's think about thread-based multitasking.

In process-based multitasking, several programs are executed at a time by the microprocessor. In thread-based multitasking, several parts of the same program is executed at a time by the microprocessor. Consider Figure 21.3. Here, we have a program. In this program, there are 2 parts. These parts may represent two separate blocks of code or two separate methods containing code. Each part may perform a separate task. The processor should execute two parts (tasks) simultaneously. So the processor uses 2 separate threads to execute these two parts.

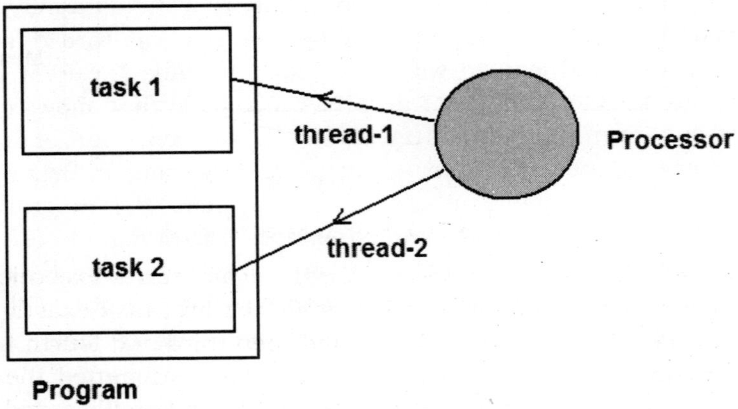

Figure 21.3: Thread-based multitasking

Each thread can be imagined as an individual process that can execute a separate set of statements. We can imagine these threads as hands of the microprocessor. We have 2 hands, so we can do 2 things at a time. Similarly, if a processor has 2 threads, it can do 2 tasks at a time. This is called thread-based multitasking.

Differences between a Process and a Thread

A process represents a group of statements which are executed by the PVM using a main thread. We can take a running program as an example for a process. Each process will have its own memory, a program counter that keeps track of the instruction being executed and a stack that holds the data. The data of one process is generally isolated from another process. It means the data or result of a process is generally not available to another process unless both the processes communicate explicitly.

A thread also represents a group of statements within a program. When we want to use threads, we have to create them separately which are in turn run by the main thread. Threads will not have their own memory and program counter. The data of one thread is shared easily by another thread. So, it is possible that a thread can easily modify the data of another thread.

Any program utilizes resources like memory and processor time. Hence it is called heavy weight process. But a thread is a small part of the program that takes very less memory and processor time. Hence threads are called light weight processes.

Concurrent Programming and GIL

In Python, it is possible to create multiple processes and set them to work simultaneously. In the same way, it is possible to create multiple threads and set them to execute different parts of the program simultaneously. Executing the tasks or parts of a program simultaneously is called 'concurrent programming'.

When more than one thread is running at a time, the data of one thread is available to another thread. In such cases, there is a possibility that the data may undergo unwanted manipulations. This happens especially when more than one thread is acting on the data simultaneously. This will lead to wrong results. It means the PVM is not thread safe. Hence, PVM uses an internal global interpreter lock (GIL) that allows only a single thread to execute at any given moment. GIL does not allow more than one thread to run at a time. This becomes an obstacle to write concurrent programs in Python. Even when there are many processors available in a computer system, the programmer can use the capability of only one processor at a time due to the restriction imposed by GIL. However, GIL will not impose this restriction of using only one thread at a time, in case of normal Python programs that take some input and provide output. GIL will impose this restriction on applications that involve heavy amounts of CPU processing or those involving multiple processors.

Uses of Threads

Threads are highly useful when we want to perform more than one task simultaneously. This is also known as 'concurrent programming'. This makes the threads to be used in the following situations:

- Threads are mainly used in server-side programs to serve the needs of multiple clients on a network or Internet. On Internet, a server machine has to cater to the needs of thousands of clients at a time. For this purpose, if we use threads in the server, they can do various jobs at a time, thus they can handle several clients.
- Threads are also used to create games and animation. Animation means moving objects from one place to another. In many games, generally we have to perform more than one task simultaneously. There, threads will be of invaluable help. For example, in a game, a flight may be moving from left to right. A machine gun should shoot it, releasing the bullets at the flight. These two tasks should happen simultaneously. For this purpose, we can use 2 threads, one thread will move the flight and the other one will move the bullet, simultaneously towards the flight.

Creating Threads in Python

Python provides 'Thread' class of *threading* module that is useful to create threads. To create our own thread, we are supposed to create an object of Thread class. The following are the different ways of creating our own threads in Python:

- Creating a thread without using a class
- Creating a thread by creating a sub class to Thread class
- Creating a thread without creating sub class to Thread class

Creating a Thread without using a Class

The purpose of a thread is to execute a group of statements like a function. So, we can create a thread by creating an object of Thread class and pass the function name as target for the thread as:

```
t = Thread(target=functionname, [args=(arg1, arg2, ...)])
```

Here, we are creating the Thread class object 't' that represents our thread. The 'target' represents the function on which the thread will act. 'args' represents a tuple of arguments which are passed to the function. Once the thread is created like this, it should be started by calling the start() method as:

```
t.start()
```

Then the thread 't' will jump into the target function and executes the code inside that function. This is shown in Program 2.

Program

Program 2: A Python program to create a thread and use it to run a function.

```
# creating a thread without using a class
from threading import *

# create a function
def display():
    print('Hello I am running')

# create a thread and run the function for 5 times
for i in range(5):
    # create the thread and specify the function as its target
    t = Thread(target=display)
    # run the thread
    t.start()
```

Output:

```
C:\>python th.py
Hello I am running
Hello I am running
Hello I am running
Hello I am running
Hello I am running
```

We can slightly improve the previous program such that we can pass arguments or data to the display() function. This is done in Program 3. In this program, we are passing a string to the display() function at the time of creating the thread as:

```
t = Thread(target=display, args=('Hello', ))
```

Please observe the comma (,) after the argument 'Hello' mentioned in the tuple. We should remember that when a single element is specified in a tuple, a comma is needed after that element.

Program

Program 3: A Python program to pass arguments to a function and execute it using a thread.

```
# creating a thread without using a class - v2.0
from threading import *

# create a function
def display(str):
    print(str)

# create a thread and run the function for 5 times
for i in range(5):
    t = Thread(target=display, args=('Hello', ))
    t.start()
```

Output:

```
C:\>python th.py
Hello
Hello
Hello
Hello
Hello
```

Creating a Thread by Creating a Sub Class to Thread Class

Since the 'Thread' class is already created by the Python people in threading module, we can make our class as a sub class to Thread class so that we can inherit the functionality of the Thread class. This can be done by writing the following statement:

```
class MyThread(Thread):
```

Here, 'MyThread' represents the sub class of 'Thread' class. Now, any methods of Thread class are also available to our sub class. The 'Thread' class has the run() method which is also available to our sub class, i.e. to 'MyThread' class. The specialty of the run() method is that every thread will run this method when it is started. So, by overriding the run() method, we can make the threads run our own run() method. Overriding a method – means writing our own method with the same name as the run() method of the super class.

The next step is to create the object of the 'MyThread' class which contains a copy of the super class, i.e. the 'Thread' class.

```
t1 = MyThread()
```

Here, 't1' is the object of 'MyThread' class which represents our thread. Now, we can run this thread by calling the start() method as: t1.start(). Now the thread will jump into the run() method of 'MyThread' class and executes the code available inside it.

Many times, it is better to wait for the completion of the thread by calling the join() method on the thread as:

```
t1.join()
```

This will wait till the thread completely executes the run() method. A thread will terminate automatically when it comes out of the run() method.

Program

Program 4: A Python program to create a thread by making our class as sub class to Thread class.

```
# creating our own thread
from threading import Thread

# create a class as sub class to Thread class
class MyThread(Thread):

    # override the run() method of Thread class
    def run(self):
        for i in range(1, 6):
            print(i)

# create an instance of MyThread class
t1 = MyThread()

# start running the thread t1
t1.start()

# wait till the thread completes execution
t1.join()
```

Output:

```
C:\>python th.py
1
2
3
4
5
```

Sometimes, threads may want to act on the data available in the class. It means, if the class has instance variables, the threads can act on them. For this purpose, we have to write a constructor inside our class as:

```
def __init__(self, str):
    self.str = str
```

This constructor accepts a string 'str' and initializes an instance variable 'self.str' with that string. But there is a restriction here. When we write a constructor, it will override the constructor of the super class, i.e. of 'Thread' class. So, to retain the functionality of the 'Thread' class, we have to call its constructor from our sub class constructor as:

```
def __init__(self, str):
    Thread.__init__(self)# call Thread class constructor
    self.str = str
```

Program

Program 5: A Python program to create a thread that accesses the instance variables of a class.

```
# a thread that accesses the instance variables
from threading import *

# create a class as sub class to Thread class
class MyThread(Thread):

    # constructor that calls Thread class constructor
    def __init__(self, str):
        Thread.__init__(self)
        self.str = str

    # override the run() method of Thread class
    def run(self):
        print(self.str)

# create an instance of MyThread class and pass the string
t1 = MyThread('Hello')

# start running the thread t1
t1.start()

# wait till the thread completes execution
t1.join()
```

Output:

```
C:\>python th.py
Hello
```

Creating a Thread without Creating Sub Class to Thread Class

We can create an independent class say 'MyThread' that does not inherit from 'Thread' class. Then we can create an object 'obj' to 'MyThread' class as:

```
obj = MyThread('Hello')
```

The next step is to create a thread by creating an object to 'Thread' class and specifying the method of the 'MyThread' class as its target as:

```
t1 = Thread(target=obj.display, args=(1, 2))
```

Here, 't1' is our thread which is created as an object of 'Thread' class. 'target' represents the display() method of 'MyThread' object 'obj'. 'args' represents a tuple of values passed to the method. When the thread 't1' is started, it will execute the display() method of 'MyThread' class. This is shown in Program 6.

Program

Program 6: A Python program to create a thread that acts on the object of a class that is not derived from the Thread class.

```
# creating a thread without making sub class to Thread class
from threading import *
# create our own class
class MyThread:

    # a constructor
    def __init__(self, str):
        self.str = str

    # a method
    def display(self, x, y):
        print(self.str)
        print('The args are: ', x, y)

# create an instance to our class and store 'Hello' string
obj = MyThread('Hello')

# create a thread to run display method of obj
t1 = Thread(target=obj.display, args=(1, 2))

# run the thread
t1.start()
```

Output:

```
C:\>python th.py
Hello
The args are: 1, 2
```

Thread Class Methods

Before proceeding further about the uses of threads and other intricacies, let's first have a look at the methods and properties available in Thread class and their description. These are given in Table 21.1,where 't' represents the Thread class object:

Table 21.1: Thread class Methods and Properties

Method or property	Description
t.start()	Starts the thread. It must be called at most once per thread object. It arranges for the object's run() method to be invoked in a separate thread of control.
t.join([timeout])	Waits until the thread terminates or a timeout occurs. 'timeout' is a floating point number specifying a timeout for the operation in seconds (or fraction of seconds).
t.is_alive()	Returns True if the thread is alive in memory and False otherwise. A thread is alive from the moment the start() method returns until its run() method terminates.

Method or property	Description
t.setName(name)	Gives a name to the thread.
t.getName()	Returns name of the thread.
t.name	This is a property that represents the thread's name.
t.setDaemon(flag)	Makes a thread a daemon thread if the flag is True.
t.isDaemon()	Returns True if the thread is a daemon thread, otherwise False.
t.daemon	This is a property that takes either True or False to set the thread as daemon or not.

Single Tasking using a Thread

A thread can be employed to execute one task at a time. Suppose there are 3 tasks and these are executed by a thread one by one, then it is called single tasking. Let's plan a program for preparation of tea in three steps as:

1. Boil milk and tea powder for 5 minutes. This is task1.
2. Add sugar and boil for 3 minutes. This is task2.
3. Filter it and serve. This is task3.

These 3 tasks can be represented as separate methods: task1(), task2() and task3(). These three methods should be called from a main method of the class as:

```
def prepareTea(self):# this is main method
    self.task1()
    self.task2()
    self.task3()
```

Here, the main method is prepareTea() from where the other methods are called. When we create the thread, we have to make this main method as target for the thread. Then the thread will jump into this main method and execute all the other 3 methods one by one. This is shown in Program 7. In this program, we are showing the time with the help of sleep() function of *time* module as:

```
sleep(seconds)
```

This function temporarily suspends execution of the running thread for the specified time given in seconds.

Program

Program 7: A Python program to show single tasking using a thread that prepares tea.

```
# single tasking using a single thread
from threading import *
from time import *

# create our own class
class MyThread:
```

```
    # a method that performs 3 tasks one by one
    def prepareTea(self):
        self.task1()
        self.task2()
        self.task3()

    def task1(self):
        print('Boil milk and tea powder for 5 minutes...', end='')
        sleep(5)
        print('Done')

    def task2(self):
        print('Add sugar and boil for 3 minutes...', end='')
        sleep(3)
        print('Done')

    def task3(self):
        print('Filter it and serve...', end='')
        print('Done')

# create an instance to our class
obj = MyThread()

# create a thread and run prepareTea method of obj
t = Thread(target=obj.prepareTea)
t.start()
```

Output:

```
C:\>python single.py
Boil milk and tea powder for 5 minutes...Done
Add sugar and boil for 3 minutes...Done
Filter it and serve...Done
```

The time taken by a thread in performing some activity can be shown as time delay using the sleep() function. Please observe that in task1() method, while boiling milk and tea powder for 5 minutes, we used sleep(5). Thus, the time is actually delayed for 5 seconds to represent the 5 minutes boiling activity.

Multitasking using Multiple Threads

In multitasking, several tasks are executed at a time. For this purpose, we need more than one thread. For example, to perform 2 tasks, we can take 2 threads and attach them to the 2 tasks. Then those tasks are simultaneously executed by the two threads. Using more than one thread is called 'multi threading' and multi threading is used in multitasking.

When we go to a movie theatre, generally a person is there at the door—checking and cutting the tickets. When we enter the hall, there is another person who shows the chairs to us. Suppose there is only one person (1 thread) doing these two tasks. He has to first cut the ticket and then come along with the first person to show the chair. Then he goes back to the door to cut the second ticket and then again walk with the second person to show the chair. Like this, if he does the things one by one, it takes a lot of time, and even though the show is over, there will be still people left outside the door waiting to enter the hall! This is pretty well known to the theatre management. So what they do? They employ two persons (2 threads) for this purpose. The first person will cut the ticket, and the second one will show the chair. When the second person is showing the chair, the first person cuts the second ticket. Like this, both the persons can act simultaneously and hence there will be no wastage of time. This is shown in Program 8.

Program

Program 8: A Python program that performs two tasks using two threads simultaneously.

```
# multitasking using two threads
from threading import *
from time import *

class Theatre:
    # constructor that accepts a string
    def __init__(self, str):
        self.str = str

    # a method that repeats for 5 tickets
    def movieshow(self):
        for i in range(1, 6):
            print(self.str," : ", i)
            sleep(0.1)

# create two instances to Theatre class
obj1 = Theatre('Cut ticket')
obj2 = Theatre('Show chair')

# create two threads to run movieshow()
t1 = Thread(target=obj1.movieshow)
t2 = Thread(target=obj2.movieshow)

# run the threads
t1.start()
t2.start()
```

Output:

```
C:\>python multi.py
Cut ticket:1
Show chair:1
Cut ticket:2
Show chair:2
Show chair:3
Cut ticket:3
Show chair:4
Cut ticket:4
Show chair:5
Cut ticket:5
```

Please run the Program 8 several times and you can see the results are varying and sometimes they are absurd. For example, in the preceding output, showing the chair for ticket number 3 is done before cutting the ticket. This is because we expected that the thread 't1' should act first and then the thread 't2' should act. Contrary to this, the thread 't2' responded prior to the thread 't1'. This is called 'race condition'. Race condition is a situation that occurs when threads are not acting in an expected sequence, thus leading to unreliable output. Race condition can be eliminated using 'thread synchronization'.

Let's take the case of railway reservation. Every day several people want reservation of a berth for them. Let's think that only one berth is available in a train, and two passengers (threads) are asking for that berth. Let's assume that in reservation counter no.1, the clerk has sent a request to the server to allot that berth to his passenger. In counter no.2, the second clerk has also sent a request to the server to allot that berth to his passenger. It means two passengers are competing for the same berth. Let's see to whom that berth is allotted.

Program

Program 9: A program where two threads are acting on the same method to allot a berth for the passenger.

```
# multitasking using two threads
from threading import *
from time import *
class Railway:

    # constructor that accepts no. of available berths
    def __init__(self, available):
        self.available = available

    # a method that reserves berth
    def reserve(self, wanted):
        # display no. of available berths
        print('Available no. of berths= ', self.available)

        # if available >= wanted, allot the berth
        if(self.available>= wanted):
            # find the thread name
            name = current_thread().getName()
            # display berth is allotted for the person
            print('%d berths allotted for %s' %(wanted, name))
            # make time delay so that the ticket is printed
            sleep(1.5)
            # decrease the no. of available berths
            self.available-= wanted
        else:
            # if available < wanted, then say sorry
            print('Sorry, no berths to allot')

# create instance to Railway class
# specify only one berth is available
obj = Railway(1)

# create two threads and specify 1 berth is needed
t1 = Thread(target=obj.reserve, args=(1,))
t2 = Thread(target=obj.reserve, args=(1,))

# give names to the threads
t1.setName('First Person')
t2.setName('Second Person')
```

```
# run the threads
t1.start()
t2.start()
```

Output:

```
C:\>python multi.py
Available no. of berths=1
1 berths allotted for First Person
Available no. of berths=1
1 berths allotted for Second Person
```

The output of the preceding program is not correct. The threads 't1' and 't2' are running on the reserve() method of Railway class. Since we have taken the available number of berths as 1, when thread 't1' enters the reserve() method, it sees available number of berths as 1 and hence, it allots it to First Person and displays:

```
1 berths allotted for First Person
```

Then it will sleep for 1.5 seconds. In this time, the ticket will be printed on the printer. When the first thread is sleeping, thread 't2' also enters the reserve() method, and it also sees that there is 1 berth remaining. The reason for this is that the available number of berths is not yet updated by the first thread. So the second thread also sees 1 berth as available, and it allots the same berth to the Second Person. Then the thread 't2' will also go into sleep state. Thread 't1' wakes up first, and then it updates the available number of berths as:

```
self.available-= wanted
```

Now available number of berths will become 0. But by this time, the second thread has already allotted the same berth to the Second Person also. Since both the threads are acting on the same object simultaneously, the result is unreliable.

What is the solution for this problem? You may think to update the number of berths first and then let the thread go for sleep. So, you want to write the following sequence of statements:

```
self.available-= wanted
sleep(1.5)
```

If you write in this way also, there is no guarantee that we will get correct output. It may display something like this:

```
Available no. of berths=1
1 berths allotted for First Person
Available no. of berths=1
Sorry, no berths to allot
```

So, we cannot rely on this program. The problem occurs here because 2 threads are simultaneously acting on the same method (or same object). This problem can be solved by allowing only one thread to access the reserve() method at any given moment of time. Suppose thread 't1' enters the method first, then any other thread should not be allowed to act on the same method till 't1' completes execution and comes out. This is called thread synchronization or thread safe.

Thread Synchronization

When a thread is already acting on an object, preventing any other thread from acting on the same object is called 'thread synchronization' or 'thread safe'. The object on which the threads are synchronized is called 'synchronized object' or 'mutex'(mutually exclusive lock). Thread synchronization is recommended when multiple threads are acting on the same object simultaneously. Thread synchronization is done using the following techniques:

- Using locks
- Using semaphores

Locks

Locks can be used to lock the object on which the thread is acting. When a thread enters the object, it locks the object and after the execution is completed, it will unlock the object and comes out of it. It is like a room with only one door. A person has entered the room and locked it from behind. The second person who wants to enter the room should wait till the first person comes out. In this way, a thread also locks the object after entering it. Then the next thread cannot enter it till the first thread comes out. This means the object is locked mutually on threads. So, this locked object is called 'mutex' (mutually exclusive lock). Consider Figure 21.4:

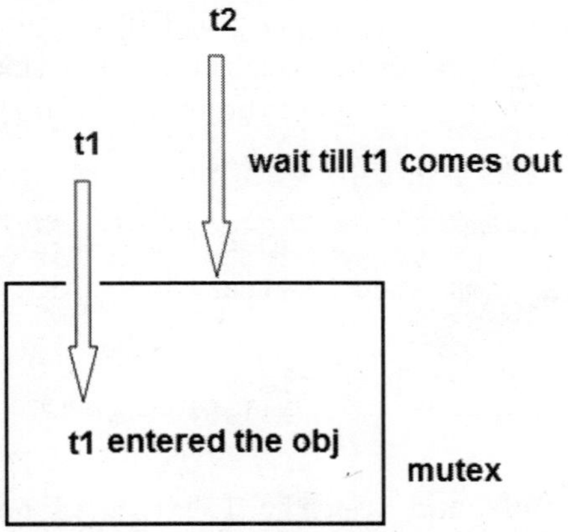

Figure 21.4: Thread Synchronization

We can create a lock by creating an object of Lock class as:

```
l = Lock()
```

To lock the current object, we should use acquire() method as:

```
l.acquire()
```

To unlock or release the object, we can use release() method as:

```
l.release()
```

In Program 10, we are using locks to lock the Railway class object so that we can achieve thread synchronization and thus get correct output.

Program

Program 10: A Python program achieving thread synchronization using locks.

```
# Thread synchronization using locks
from threading import *
from time import *

class Railway:
    # constructor that accepts no. of available berths
    def __init__(self, available):
        self.available = available
        # create a lock object
        self.l = Lock()

    # a method that reserves berth
    def reserve(self, wanted):
        # lock the current object
        self.l.acquire()
        # display no. of available berths
        print('Available no. of berths= ', self.available)

        # if available >= wanted, allot the berth
        if(self.available>= wanted):
            # find the thread name
            name = current_thread().getName()
            # display berth is allotted for the person
            print('%d berths allotted for %s' %(wanted, name))
            # make time delay so that the ticket is printed
            sleep(1.5)
            # decrease the no. of available berths
            self.available-= wanted
        else:
            # if available < wanted, then say sorry
            print('Sorry, no berths to allot')
        # task is completed, release the lock
        self.l.release()

# create instance to Railway class
# specify only one berth is available
obj = Railway(1)

# create two threads and specify 1 berth is needed
t1 = Thread(target=obj.reserve, args=(1,))
t2 = Thread(target=obj.reserve, args=(1,))

# give names to the threads
t1.setName('First Person')
t2.setName('Second Person')

# run the threads
t1.start()
t2.start()
```

Output:

```
C:\>python multi.py
Available no. of berths=1
1 berths allotted for First Person
Available no. of berths=0
Sorry, no berths to allot
```

Semaphore

A semaphore is an object that provides synchronization based on a counter. A semaphore is created as an object of Semaphore class as:

```
l = Semaphore(countervalue)# here the counter value by default is 1
```

If the 'counter value' is not given, the default value of the counter will be 1. When the acquire() method is called, the counter gets decremented by 1 and when release() method is called, it is incremented by 1. These methods are used in the following format:

```
l.acquire()# make counter 0 and then lock
# code that is locked by semaphore
l.release()# counter is 0 so unlock and make counter 1
```

In Program 10, to use the semaphore way of locking, replace the following statement

```
self.l = Lock()
```

in the constructor of the Railway class with the following statement that uses Semaphore object:

```
self.l = Semaphore()
```

Deadlock of Threads

Even if we synchronize the threads, there is possibility of other problems like 'deadlock'. Let's understand this with an example.

Daily, thousands of people book tickets in trains and cancel tickets also. If a programmer is to develop code for this, he may visualize that booking tickets and cancelling them are reverse procedures. Hence, he will write these 2 tasks as separate and opposite tasks, and assign 2 different threads to do these tasks simultaneously. Booking tickets and cancelling tickets involve train and compartments which we consider as two objects.

To book a ticket, the 'bookticket' thread first enters the train object to verify the tickets are available or not. Then it enters the compartment object and reserves the ticket in a particular compartment. It may change the status of the ticket as 'reserved'.

Similarly, if a passenger wants to cancel a ticket, the 'cancelticket' thread first enters the compartment object and updates the status of the ticket as 'available'. Then it enters the train object and updates the available number of tickets.

Since two threads are acting on the train and compartment objects simultaneously, the results may not be reliable and hence we have to lock these two objects. For this purpose, we have to use two locks each for train and compartment. There is possibility that the two locks are used by each thread in the following format:

```
# bookticket thread
lock-1:
lock on train
    lock-2:
    lock on compartment

# cancelticket thread
lock-2:
lock on compartment
    lock-1:
    lock on train
```

First 'bookticket' thread locks on train. At the same time, 'cancelticket' thread locks on compartment. When 'bookticket' thread wants to lock on compartment, it will find that the compartment object is already locked by 'cancelticket'. Hence it will wait for the 'cancelticket' thread to release the lock. Similarly, the 'cancelticket' thread wants to lock the train object but finds that it was already locked by 'bookticket' thread. So, 'cancelticket' thread waits for the 'bookticket' thread to release the lock on train. In this way, both the threads will continue forever in waiting state for each other to release the objects. This is called 'deadlock' of threads which is depicted in Figure 21.5. The deadlock state of threads is shown in Program 11.

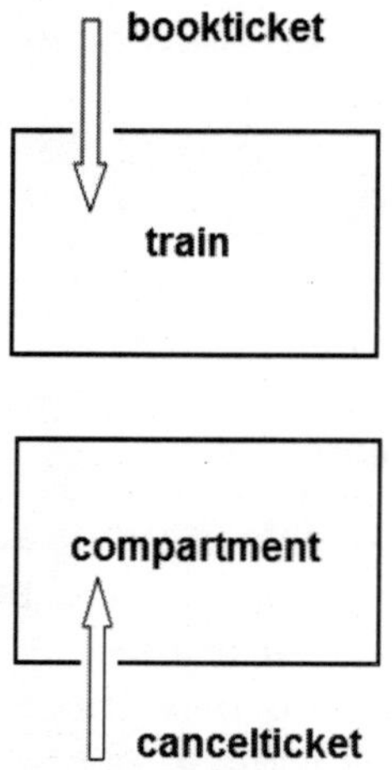

Figure 21.5: Deadlock of Threads

Program

Program 11: A Python program to show dead lock of threads due to locks on objects.

```
# dead lock of threads
from threading import *

# take two locks
l1 = Lock()
l2 = Lock()
```

```
# create a function for booking a ticket
def bookticket():
     l1.acquire()
     print('Bookticket locked train')
     print('Bookticket wants to lock on compartment')
     l2.acquire()
     print('Bookticket locked compartment')
     l2.release()
     l1.release()
     print('Booking ticket done...')

# create a function for cancelling a ticket
def cancelticket():
     l2.acquire()
     print('Cancelticket locked compartment')
     print('Cancelticket wants to lock on train')
     l1.acquire()
     print('Cancelticket locked train')
     l1.release()
     l2.release()
     print('Cancellation of ticket is done...')

# create two threads and run them
t1 = Thread(target=bookticket)
t2 = Thread(target=cancelticket)
t1.start()
t2.start()
```

Output:

```
C:\>python deadlock.py
Bookticket locked train
Bookticket wants to lock on compartment
Cancelticket locked compartment
Cancelticket wants to lock on train
```

From the output of Program 11, we can understand that the further execution of the program is halted and the booking and cancellation are not done. This is called 'deadlock' of threads.

When a thread has locked an object and waiting for another object to be released by another thread, and the other thread is also waiting for the first thread to release the first object, both the threads will continue waiting forever. This is called thread 'deadlock'.

When Thread deadlock occurs, any further execution is stopped and the program will come to a halt. Thread deadlock is a drawback in a program. The programmer should take care to avoid any such deadlocks in his programs.

Avoiding Deadlocks in a Program

There is no specific solution for the problem of deadlocks. It depends on the logic used by the programmer. The programmer should design his program in such a way, that it does not form any deadlock. For example, in the preceding program, if the programmer used the locks in the following format, he could have avoided the deadlock situation:

```
# bookticket thread
lock-1:
lock on train
    lock-2:
    lock on compartment
# cancelticket thread
lock-1:
lock on compartment
    lock-2:
    lock on train
```

This logic is implemented in Program 12 that shows how to avoid deadlock of bookticket and cancelticket threads. This time the program will not halt and execute completely.

Program

Program 12: A Python program with good logic to avoid deadlocks.

```
# solution for dead lock of threads
from threading import *

# take two locks
l1 = Lock()
l2 = Lock()

# create a function for booking a ticket
def bookticket():
    l1.acquire()
    print('Bookticket locked train')
    print('Bookticket wants to lock on compartment')
    l2.acquire()
    print('Bookticket locked compartment')
    l2.release()
    l1.release()
    print('Booking ticket done...')

# create a function for cancelling a ticket
def cancelticket():
    l1.acquire()
    print('Cancelticket locked compartment')
    print('Cancelticket wants to lock on train')
    l2.acquire()
    print('Cancelticket locked train')
    l2.release()
    l1.release()
    print('Cancellation of ticket is done...')

# create two threads and run them
t1 = Thread(target=bookticket)
t2 = Thread(target=cancelticket)
t1.start()
t2.start()
```

Output:

```
C:\>python deadlock.py
```

```
Bookticket locked train
Bookticket wants to lock on compartment
Bookticket locked compartment
Booking ticket done...
Cancelticket locked compartment
Cancelticket wants to lock on train
Cancelticket locked train
Cancellation of ticket is done...
```

Communication between Threads

In some cases, two or more threads should communicate with each other. For example, a Consumer thread is waiting for a Producer to produce the data (or some goods). When the Producer thread completes production of data, then the Consumer thread should take that data and use it. The Consumer thread does not know how much time it takes for the Producer to complete the production. Let's first plan the Producer class.At the producer side, we will take a list 'lst' to which the items will be added. The Producer produces 10 items and each time an item is produced, we can display a message 'Item produced...'

```
for i in range(1, 11):# repeat from 1 to 10
    lst.append(i)# add item to list
    sleep(1)# every item may take some time
    print('Item produced...')
```

In the Producer class, we take another boolean type variable 'dataprodover' and initialize it to False. The idea is to make the 'dataprodover' variableTrue when the production of all the 10 items is completed.

```
dataprodover=True
```

This will inform the Consumer that the production is over and hence you can utilize the data available in the list 'lst'. When the Producer is busy producing the data, now and then the Consumer will check if 'dataprodover' is True or not. If 'dataprodover' is True, then Consumer takes the data from the list and uses it. If the 'dataprodover' shows False, then Consumer will sleep for some time (say 100 milliseconds) and then again checks the 'dataprodover' to know whether it is True or not. The way to implement this logic at Consumer side is:

```
# sleep for 100 ms as long as dataprodover is False
# prod represents Producer instance that contains dataprodover
while prod.dataprodover==False:
    sleep(0.1)
```

In this way, the Producer and Consumer can communicate with each other. But this is not an efficient way of communication. Why? Consumer checks the 'dataprodover' at some point of time, and finds it False. So it goes into sleep for the next 100 milliseconds. Meanwhile, the data production may be over. But Consumer comes out of sleep after 100 milliseconds and then only it can find 'dataprodover' is True. This means that there may be a time delay of 1 to 99 milliseconds to receive the data after its actual production is completed. Consider Figure 21.6:

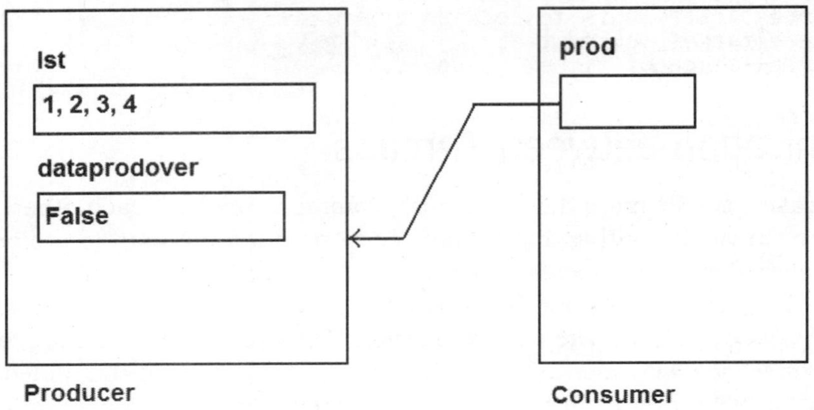

Figure 21.6: Communication between Producer and Consumer threads

Program

Program 13: A Python program where Producer and Consumer threads communicate with each other through a boolean type variable.

```
# thread communication
from threading import *
from time import *

# create Producer class
class Producer:
    def __init__(self):
        self.lst = []
        self.dataprodover=False

    def produce(self):
        # create 1 to 10 items and add to the list
        for i in range(1, 11):
            self.lst.append(i)
            sleep(1)
            print('Item produced...')

        # inform the consumer that the data production is completed
        self.dataprodover=True

# create Consumer class
class Consumer:
    def __init__(self, prod):
        self.prod = prod

    def consume(self):
        # sleep for 100 ms as long as dataprodover is False
        while self.prod.dataprodover==False:
            sleep(0.1)
```

```
            # display the content of list when data production is over
            print(self.prod.lst)

    # create Producer object
    p = Producer()

    # create Consumer object and pass Producer object
    c = Consumer(p)

    # create producer and consumer threads
    t1 = Thread(target=p.produce)
    t2 = Thread(target=c.consume)

    # run the threads
    t1.start()
    t2.start()
```

Output:

```
C:\>python commu1.py
Item produced...
Item produced...
Item produced...
Item produced...
Item produced...
Item produced...
Item produced...
Item produced...
Item produced...
Item produced...
[1, 2, 3, 4, 5, 6, 7, 8, 9, 10]
```

Please understand that the first 10 lines in the output are displayed by the Producer thread to indicate that the items are being produced. After all the 10 items are produced, the Consumer thread takes the list and displays the contents of the list in the last line.

How can we improve the efficiency of communication between threads? Python provides two important ways for this. They are:

- Using notify() and wait() methods.
- Using a queue

Thread Communication using nofity() and wait() Methods

The Condition class of *threading* module is useful to improve the speed of communication between the threads. The Condition class object is called condition variable and is created as:

```
cv = Condition()
```

This class contains methods which are used in thread communication. For example, the notify() method is useful to immediately inform the Consumer thread that the data production is completed. The notify_all() method is useful to inform all waiting Consumer threads at once that the production is over. These methods are used by the Producer thread.

The Consumer thread need not check if the data production is over or not through a boolean type variable like 'dataprodover'. The Consumer can simply wait till it gets the notification from the notify() or notify_all() methods. Consumer can wait using the wait() method which terminates when Producer invokes notify() or notify_all() methods. The wait() method is written in the form as follows:

```
cv.wait(timeout=0)
```

This will wait till the notification is received. But once the notification is received, there will not be any delay (timeout is 0 seconds) in receiving the product. So, this form of the wait() method will not waste even a single millisecond to receive the data after the actual production is completed. Thus, the notify(), notify_all() and wait() methods provide efficient means of communication between threads. A point we should remember is that these methods should be used in between the acquire() and release() methods which are useful to lock and unlock the Condition variable.

Program

Program 14: A Python program where thread communication is done through notify() and wait() methods of Condition object.

```
# thread communication using Condition object
from threading import *
from time import *

# create Producer class
class Producer:
    def __init__(self):
        self.lst = []
        self.cv = Condition()

    def produce(self):
        # lock the condition object
        self.cv.acquire()

        # create 1 to 10 items and add to the list
        for i in range(1, 11):
            self.lst.append(i)
            sleep(1)
            print('Item produced...')

        # inform the consumer that production is completed
        self.cv.notify()

        # release the lock
        self.cv.release()

# create Consumer class
class Consumer:
    def __init__(self, prod):
        self.prod = prod

    def consume(self):
        # get lock on condition object
        self.prod.cv.acquire()
```

```
        # wait only for 0 seconds after the production
        self.prod.cv.wait(timeout=0)

        # release the lock
        self.prod.cv.release()

        # display the contents of list
        print(self.prod.lst)

# create Producer object
p = Producer()

# create Consumer object and pass Producer object
c = Consumer(p)

# create producer and consumer threads
t1 = Thread(target=p.produce)
t2 = Thread(target=c.consume)

# run the threads
t1.start()
t2.start()
```

Output:

```
C:\>python commu2.py
Item produced...
Item produced...
Item produced...
Item produced...
Item produced...
Item produced...
Item produced...
Item produced...
Item produced...
Item produced...
[1, 2, 3, 4, 5, 6, 7, 8, 9, 10]
```

Thread Communication using a Queue

The Queue class of *queue* module is useful to create a queue that holds the data produced by the Producer. The data can be taken from the queue and utilized by the Consumer. A queue is a FIFO (First In First Out) structure where the data is stored from one side and deleted from the other side. Queues are useful when several Producers want to communicate with several Consumers. Another advantage is that while using queues, we need not use locks since queues are thread safe.

To create a Queue object, we can simply write:

```
q = Queue()
```

Suppose, we want to insert an item 'i' into the queue 'q', we can use the put() method, as:

```
q.put(i)
```

The put() method is used by Producer to insert items into the queue. The Consumer uses the get() method to retrieve the items from the queue as:

```
# prod is the instance of Producer class that contains the queue 'q'
x = prod.q.get(i)
```

The q.empty() method returns True if the queue is empty, otherwise it returns False. Similarly, the q.full() method returns True if the queue is full, else False.

In Program 15, we create a queue 'q' at Producer side. The Producer places each item 'i' into the queue using q.put(i) method. The Consumer receives the item immediately from the queue using prod.q.get(i) method. Here, 'prod' is a reference to the Producer object from the Consumer object. Producer places 10 items into the queue and all the items are received one by one by the Consumer. Consider Figure 21.7:

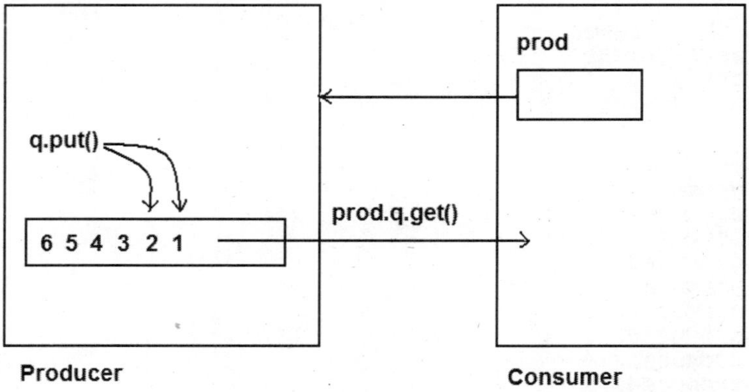

Figure 21.7: Producer-Consumer communication using a queue

Program

Program 15: A Python program that uses a queue in thread communication.

```
# thread communication using a queue
from threading import *
from time import *
from queue import *

# create Producer class
class Producer:
    def __init__(self):
        self.q = Queue()

    def produce(self):
        # create 1 to 10 items and add to the queue
        for i in range(1, 11):
            print('Producing item: ', i)
            self.q.put(i)
            sleep(1)
```

```
# create Consumer class
class Consumer:
    def __init__(self, prod):
        self.prod = prod

    def consume(self):
        # receive 1 to 10 items from the queue
        for i in range(1, 11):
            print('Receiving item: ', self.prod.q.get(i))

# create Producer object
p = Producer()

# create Consumer object and pass Producer object
c = Consumer(p)

# create producer and consumer threads
t1 = Thread(target=p.produce)
t2 = Thread(target=c.consume)

# run the threads
t1.start()
t2.start()
```

Output:

```
C:\>python commu3.py
Producing item:1
Receiving item:1
Producing item:2
Receiving item:2
Producing item:3
Receiving item:3
Producing item:4
Receiving item:4
Producing item:5
Receiving item:5
Producing item:6
Receiving item:6
Producing item:7
Receiving item:7
Producing item:8
Receiving item:8
Producing item:9
Receiving item:9
Producing item:10
Receiving item:10
```

Daemon Threads

Sometimes, we need threads to run continuously in memory. For example, let's take an Internet server that runs continuously and caters to the needs of the clients. Another example is garbage collector that runs continuously and deletes the unused variables and objects while a Python program is being executed. Such threads which run continuously are called 'daemon' threads. Generally daemon threads are used to perform some background tasks. For example, a daemon thread may send data to the printer in the background while the user is working with other applications.

To make a thread a daemon thread, we can use the setDaemon(True) method or assign True to daemon property.

In Program 16, we are creating a function display() that displays a number once in a second, starting from 1 to 5. This function is executed by normal thread 't'. Then we create another function display_time() that displays system date and time once in every 2 seconds. This function is executed by another thread 'd' which we make daemon by writing:

```
d.daemon = True
```

When both the threads are started, the results are shown in the output at the end of the program.

Program

Program 16: A Python program to understand the creation of daemon thread.

```
# creating a daemon thread
from threading import *
from time import *

# to display numbers from 1 to 5 every second
def display():
    for i in range(5):
        print('Normal thread: ', end='')
        print(i+1)
        sleep(1)

# to display date and time once in every 2 seconds
def display_time():
    while True:
        print('Daemon thread: ', end='')
        print(ctime())
        sleep(2)

# create a normal thread and attach it to display() and run it
t = Thread(target=display)
t.start()

# create another thread and attach it to display_time()
d = Thread(target=display_time)

# make the thread daemon
d.daemon = True

# run the daemon thread
d.start()
```

Output:

```
C:\>python daemon.py
Normal thread: 1
Daemon thread: Fri May 20 18:52:06 2016
Normal thread: 2
Daemon thread: Fri May 20 18:52:08 2016
Normal thread: 3
Normal thread: 4
```

```
Daemon thread: Fri May 20 18:52:10 2016
Normal thread: 5
```

The Program 16 terminates when the normal thread 't' after displaying the number '5' is terminated. The reason is that when the normal threads are terminated, the main thread will also terminate and thus the program is also terminated. So, the daemon thread is also terminated in this program. To make the daemon thread not to terminate, we have to ask the PVM to wait till the daemon thread completely executes. This is done by using the join() method as:

```
d.join()# wait till d completes
```

Add the preceding code as last line in Program 16 and you will see that the daemon thread continues forever. The daemon thread continuously executes even after the main thread is terminated in the program. The output in this case will be as follows:

```
Normal thread: 1
Daemon thread: Fri May 20 19:04:27 2016
Normal thread: 2
Daemon thread: Fri May 20 19:04:29 2016
Normal thread: 3
Normal thread: 4
Daemon thread: Fri May 20 19:04:31 2016
Normal thread: 5
Daemon thread: Fri May 20 19:04:33 2016
Daemon thread: Fri May 20 19:04:35 2016
Daemon thread: Fri May 20 19:04:37 2016
Daemon thread: Fri May 20 19:04:39 2016
Daemon thread: Fri May 20 19:04:41 2016
:
:
:
```

Points to Remember

- A thread represents a separate path of execution of a group of statements. A thread can be imagined as a light weight process that executes a group of statements.
- The statements of every Python program are executed by a default thread called 'Main thread'.
- The current_thread().getName() method returns the name of the currently running thread.
- Executing the tasks only one at a time is called single tasking. Single tasking cannot use the processor time in efficient manner.
- Executing more than one task at a time is called multitasking. Multitasking utilizes the process time in an optimum manner.
- Multitasking is of two types: a) Process-based multitasking and b) thread-based multitasking.
- A running program is an example for a process.

- PVM uses an internal global interpreter lock (GIL) that allows only a single thread to execute at any given moment. Thus GIL is thread-safe.
- We can create a thread by creating an object to Thread class, as:

  t = Thread(target=functionname, [args=(arg1, arg2, ...)])
- We can create a thread as an instance of sub class to Thread class. In this case, we have to override the run() method of Thread class in the sub class.
- Race condition is a situation that occurs when threads are not acting in an expected sequence, thus leading to unreliable output. Race condition can be eliminated using 'thread synchronization'.
- When a thread is already acting on an object, preventing any other thread from acting on the same object is called 'thread synchronization' or 'thread safe'.
- The object on which the threads are synchronized is called 'synchronized object' or 'mutex'(mutually exclusive lock).
- Lock and Semaphore classes are useful to synchronize the threads.
- When a thread has locked an object and waiting for another object to be released by another thread, and the other thread is also waiting for the first thread to release the first object, both the threads will continue waiting forever. This is called thread 'deadlock'.
- The notify() and wait() methods of Condition class are useful to implement efficient communication between threads.
- A queue can also be used to achieve efficient thread communication.
- Queues are useful in communication between multiple Producers and multiple Consumers. Moreover, they are thread safe.
- A daemon thread is a thread that runs continuously. Generally daemon threads are used for background processing.

GRAPHICAL USER INTERFACE

CHAPTER 22

A person who interacts with a software or application is called a 'user'. There are two ways for a user to interact with any application. The first way is where the user gives some commands to perform the work. For example, if he wants to print a file's contents, he can type PRINT command. Here the user should know the syntax and correct usage of PRINT command. Only then he can interact with the application. This type of environment where the user uses commands or characters to interact with the application is called CUI (Character User Interface).One example for CUI is MS-DOS operating system. The disadvantage of CUI is that the user has to remember several commands and their usage with correct syntax. A person who does not know anything in computers will find CUI very difficult.

The second way to interact with an application is through graphics, pictures or images. Here the user need not remember any commands. He can perform the task just by clicking on relevant images. For example, to send data to printer, the user will simply click on the Printer image (or picture). Then he has to tell how many copies he wants and the printing will continue. This environment where the user can interact with an application through graphics or images is called GUI (Graphical User Interface). One example for GUI is Windows operating system. GUI offers the following advantages:

- It is user-friendly. The user need not worry about any commands. Even a layman will be able to work with the application developed using GUI.
- It adds attraction and beauty to any application by adding pictures, colors, menus, animation, etc. For example, all websites on Internet are developed using GUI to lure their visitors and improve their business.
- It is possible to simulate the real life objects using GUI. For example, a calculator program may actually display a real calculator on the screen. The user feels that he is interacting with a real calculator and he would be able to use it without any difficulty or special training. So, GUI eliminates the need of user training.

- GUI helps to create graphical components like push buttons, radio buttons, check buttons, menus, etc. and use them effectively.

GUI in Python

Python offers *tkinter* module to create graphics programs. The *tkinter* represents 'toolkit interface' for GUI. This is an interface for Python programmers that enable them to use the classes of TK module of TCL/TK language. Let's see what this TCL/TK is. The TCL (Tool Command Language) is a powerful dynamic programming language, suitable for web and desktop applications, networking, administration, testing and many more. It is open source and hence can be used by any one freely. TCL language uses TK (Tool Kit) language to generate graphics. TK provides standard GUI not only for TCL but also for many other dynamic programming languages like Python. Hence, this TK is used by Python programmers in developing GUI applications through Python's *tkinter* module.

The following are the general steps involved in basic GUI programs:

1. First of all, we should create the root window. The root window is the top level window that provides rectangular space on the screen where we can display text, colors, images, components, etc.
2. In the root window, we have to allocate space for our use. This is done by creating a canvas or frame. So, canvas and frame are child windows in the root window.
3. Generally, we use canvas for displaying drawings like lines, arcs, circles, shapes, etc. We use frame for the purpose of displaying components like push buttons, check buttons, menus, etc. These components are also called 'widgets'.
4. When the user clicks on a widget like push button, we have to handle that event. It means we have to respond to the events by performing the desired tasks.

Now, let's proceed further with the top level window or root window and learn to create it.

The Root Window

To display the graphical output, we need space on the screen. This space that is initially allocated to every GUI program is called 'top level window' or 'root window'. We can say that the root window is the highest level GUI component in any tkinter application. We can reach this root window by creating an object to Tk class. This is shown in Program 1. The root window will have a title bar that contains minimize, resize and close options. When you click on close 'X' option, the window will be destroyed.

Program

Program 1: A Python program to create root window or top level window.

```
# import all components from tkinter
from tkinter import *
```

```
# create the root window
root = Tk()

# wait and watch for any events that may take place
# in the root window
root.mainloop()
```

Output:

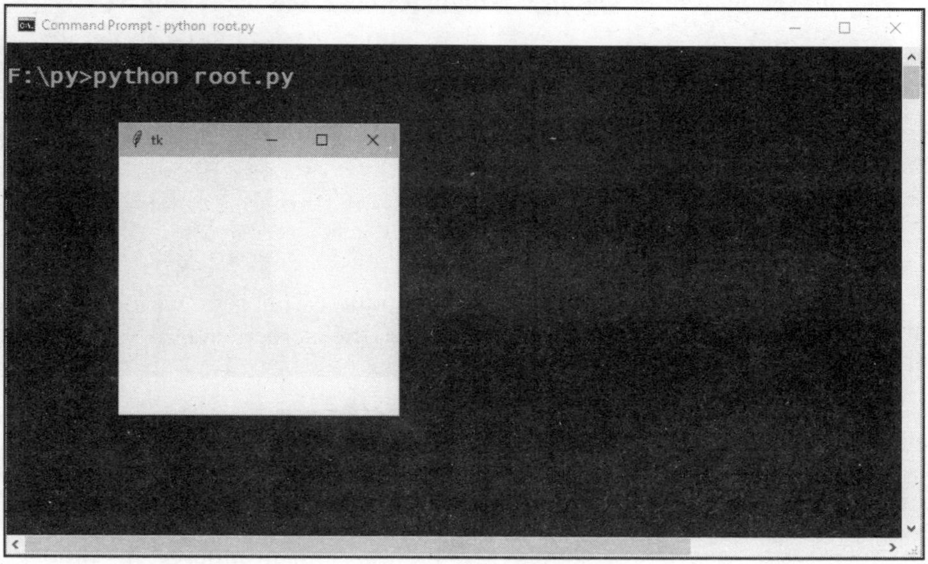

Figure 22.1: Output of Program 1

Program 1 can be improved to display our own title in the root window's title bar. We can also set the size of the window to something like 400 pixels X 300 pixels. It is also possible to replace the TK's leaf image with an icon of our choice. For this, we need to use the .ico file that contains an image. These improvements are shown in Program 2.

Program

Program 2: A Python program to create root window with some options.

```
from tkinter import *

# create top level window
root = Tk()

# set window title
root.title("My window")

# set window size
root.geometry("400x300")

# set window icon
root.wm_iconbitmap('image.ico')
# display window and wait for any events
root.mainloop()
```

Output:

Figure 22.2: Output of Program 2

Fonts and Colors

A font represents a type of displaying letters and numbers. In tkinter, fonts are mentioned using a tuple that contains font family name, size and font style as:

```
fnt =('Times', -40, 'bold italic underline overstrike')
```

Here, the font family name is 'Times' and font size is 40 pixels. If the size is a positive number, it indicates size in points. If the size is a negative number, it indicates size in pixels. The style of the font can be 'bold', 'italic', 'underline', 'overstrike'. We can mention any one or more styles as a string. The following program is useful to know the available font families in your system. All fonts are available in tkinter.font module inside tkinter module.

Program

Program 3: A Python program to know the available font families.

```
from tkinter import *
from tkinter import font

# create root window
root = Tk()

# get all the supported font families
list_fonts = list(font.families())

# display them
print(list_fonts)
```

Output:

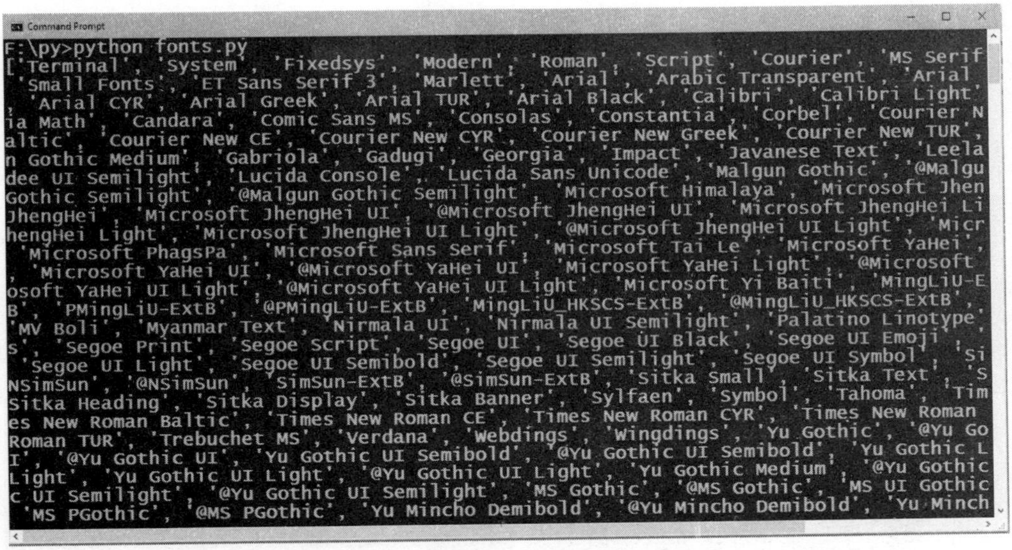

Figure 22.3: Output of Program 3

Colors in tkinter can be displayed directly by mentioning their names as: blue, lightblue, darkblue, red, lightred, darkred, black, white, yellow, magenta, cyan, etc. We can also specify colors using the hexadecimal numbers in the format:

```
#rrggbb# 8 bits per color
#rrrgggbbb# 12 bits per color
```

For example, #000000 represents black and #ff0000 represents red. In the same way, #000fff000 represents puregreenand#00ffffis c yan(greenplusblue). Table 22.1 gives some standard color names:

Table 22.1: Colors to be used in tkinter

AliceBlue	DeepPink1 *to* DeepPink4	LemonChiffon1 *to* LemonChiffon4	RoyalBlue
AntiqueWhite	DeepSkyBlue	magenta	RoyalBlue1 *to* RoyalBlue4
AntiqueWhite1 *to* AntiqueWhite4	DeepSkyBlue1 *to* DeepSkyBlue4	magenta1 *to*magenta4	salmon
aquamarine	DodgerBlue	maroon	salmon1 *to* salmon4

aquamarine1 *to* aquamarine4	DodgerBlue1 *to* DodgerBlue4	maroon1 *to* maroon4	SeaGreen
azure	firebrick	MistyRose	SeaGreen1 *to* SeaGreen4
azure1 *to* azure4	firebrick1 *to* firebrick4	MistyRose1 *to* MistyRose4	tan
beige	gold	NavajoWhite	tan1 *to* tan4
bisque	gold1 *to* gold4	NavajoWhite1 *to* NavajoWhite4	thistle
bisque1 to bisque4	goldenrod	OliveDrab	thistle1 *to* thistle4
BlanchedAlmond	goldenrod1 *to* goldenrod4	OliveDrab1 *to* OliveDrab4	tomato
blue	gray / grey	orange	tomato1 *to* tomato4
BlueViolet	gray0 *to* gray100 / grey0 *to* grey100	orange1 *to* orange4	turquoise
blue1 *to* blue4	green	OrangeRed	turquoise1 *to* turquoise4
brown	green1 *to* green4	OrangeRed1 *to* OrangeRed4	VioletRed
brown1 *to* brown4	GreenYellow	orchid	VioletRed1 *to* VioletRed4
burlywood	honeydew	orchid1 *to* orchid4	wheat

burlywood1 *to* burlywood4	honeydew1 *to* honeydew4	PeachPuff	wheat1 *to* wheat4
CadetBlue	HotPink	PeachPuff1 *to* PeachPuff4	white
CadetBlue1 *to* CadetBlue4	HotPink1 *to* HotPink4	pink	yellow
chocolate	IndianRed	pink1 *to* pink4	yellow1 *to* yellow4
chocolate1 *to* chocolate4	IndianRed1 *to* IndianRed4	plum	YellowGreen light/dark blue
coral	ivory	plum1 *to* plum4	light/dark cyan
coral1 *to* coral4	ivory1 *to* ivory4	purple	light/dark goldenrod
cornsilk	khaki	purple1 *to* purple4	light/dark gray
cornsilk1 *to* cornsilk4	khaki1 *to* khaki4	red	light/dark green
cyan	LavenderBlush	red1 *to* red4	light/dark grey
cyan1 *to* cyan4	LavenderBlush1 *to* LavenderBlush4	RosyBrown	light/dark salmon
DeepPink	LemonChiffon	RosyBrown1 *to* RosyBrown4	light/dark sea green

Working with Containers

A container is a component that is used as a place where drawings or widgets can be displayed. In short, a container is a space that displays the output to the user. There are two important containers:

- **Canvas:** This is a container that is generally used to draw shapes like lines, curves, arcs and circles.
- **Frame:** This is a container that is generally used to display widgets like buttons, check buttons or menus.

After creating the root window, we have to create space, i.e. the container in the root window so that we can use this space for displaying any drawings or widgets.

Canvas

A canvas is a rectangular area which can be used for drawing pictures like lines, circles, polygons, arcs, etc. To create a canvas, we should create an object to Canvas class as:

```
c = Canvas(root, bg="blue", height=500, width=600, cursor='pencil')
```

Here, 'c' is the Canvas class object. 'root' is the name of the parent window. 'bg' represents background color, 'height' and 'width' represent the height and width of the canvas in pixels. A pixel (picture element) is a minute dot with which all the text and pictures on the monitor are composed. When the monitor screen resolution is 1360 X 768, it indicates that the screen can accommodate 1360 pixels width-wise and 768 pixels height-wise. Consider Figure 22.4 to understand the pixels and screen coordinates in pixels. The top left corner of the screen will be at (0, 0) pixels as x and y coordinates. When we move from left to right, the x coordinate increases and when we move from top to bottom, the y coordinate increases. Thus the top right corner will be at (1360, 0). The bottom left corner will be at (0, 768) and the bottom right corner will be at (1360, 768).

The option 'cursor' represents the shape of the cursor in the canvas. Important cursor shapes are: arrow, box_spiral, center_ptr, circle, clock, coffee_mug, cross, cross_reverse, crosshair, diamond_cross, dot, double_arrow, exchange, hand1, hand2, heart, left_ptr, mouse, pencil, plus, question_arrow, right_ptr, star, tcross, top_side, umbrella, watch, xterm, X_cursor.

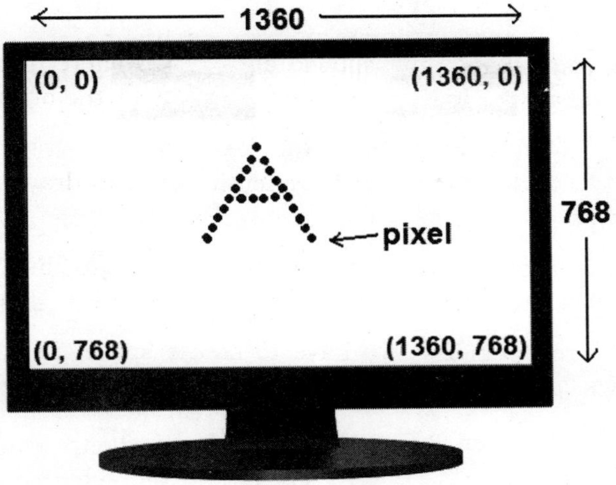

Figure 22.4: The pixels and screen coordinates

Colors in the canvas can be displayed directly by mentioning their names as: blue, lightblue, darkblue, red, lightred, darkred, black, white, yellow, magenta, cyan, etc. We can also specify colors using hexadecimal numbers in the format:

```
#rrggbb# 8 bits per color
#rrrgggbbb# 12 bits per color
```

For example, #000000 represents black and #ff0000 represents red. In the same way, #000fff000 represents puregreenand#00ffffis cyan(greenplusblue).

Once the canvas is created, it should be added to the root window. Then only it will be visible. This is done using the pack() method, as follows:

```
c.pack()
```

After the canvas is created, we can draw any shapes on the canvas. For example, to create a line, we can use create_line() method, as:

```
id = c.create_line(50, 50, 200, 50, 200, 150, width=4, fill="white")
```

This creates a line with the connecting points (50, 50), (200, 50) and (200, 150). 'width' specifies the width of the line. The default width is 1 pixel. 'fill' specifies the color of the line. The create_line() method returns an identification number.

To create an oval, we can use the create_oval() method. An oval is also called ellipse.

```
id = c.create_oval(100, 100, 400, 300, width=5, fill="yellow",
          outline="red", activefill="green")
```

This creates an oval in the rectangular area defined by the top left coordinates (100,100) and bottom lower coordinates (400, 300). If the rectangle has same width and height, then the oval will become a circle. 'width' represents the width of the oval in pixels. 'fill' represents the color to fill and 'outline' represents the color to be used for the border. The option 'activefill' represents the color to be filled when the mouse is placed on the oval.

A polygon represents several points connected by either straight lines or smooth lines. To create a polygon, we can use the create_polygon() method as:

```
id = c.create_polygon(10, 10, 200, 200, 300, 200, width=3,
     fill="green", outline="red", smooth=1, activefill="lightblue")
```

Here, the polygon is created using the points (10, 10), (200, 200), (300, 200) and then the last point is again connected to the first point, i.e. (10, 10). The option 'smooth' can become 0 or 1. If 0, it indicates a polygon with sharp edges and 1 indicates a polygon with smooth edges.

Similarly, to create a rectangle or square shaped box, we can use the create_rectangle() method as:

```
id = c.create_rectangle(500, 200, 700, 600, width=2, fill="gray",
     outline="black", activefill="yellow")
```

Here, the rectangle will be formed with the top left coordinate at (500, 200) pixels and the lower bottom coordinate at (700, 600). The color of the rectangle will change from gray to yellow when the mouse is placed on the rectangle.

It is also possible to display some text in the canvas. For this purpose, we should use the create_text() method as:

```
id = c.create_text(500, 100, text="My canvas", font= fnt,
     fill="yellow", activefill="green")
```

Here, the 'font' option is showing 'fnt' object that can be created as:

```
fnt =('Times', 40, 'bold')
fnt =('Times', -40, 'bold italic underline')
```

The first option 'Times' represents the font family name. This can be 'Times', 'Helvetica', 'Courier', etc. The second option represents a number (40) that indicates the size of the font in points. If we want to mention the size of the font in pixels, we should use minus sign before the size (-40). The third option indicates the style of the font. There are 3 styles: bold, italic and underline. We can mention any one or all the styles. If do not want any style, we need not mention this option.

Whatever we discussed so far can be shown in Program4.

Program

Program 4: A GUI program that demonstrates the creation of various shapes in canvas.

```
from tkinter import *

# create root window
root = Tk()

# create Canvas as a child to root window
c = Canvas(root, bg="blue", height=700, width=1200, cursor='pencil')

# create a line in the canvas
id = c.create_line(50, 50, 200, 50, 200, 150, width=4, fill="white")

# create an oval in the canvas
```

```
id = c.create_oval(100, 100, 400, 300, width=5, fill="yellow",
     outline="red", activefill="green")

# create a polygon in the canvas
id = c.create_polygon(10, 10, 200, 200, 300, 200, width=3,
     fill="green", outline="red", smooth=1, activefill="lightblue")

# create a rectangle in the canvas
id = c.create_rectangle(500, 200, 700, 600, width=2, fill="gray",
     outline="black", activefill="yellow")

# create some text in the canvas
fnt =('Times', 40, 'bold italic underline')
id = c.create_text(500, 100, text="My canvas", font= fnt,
     fill="yellow", activefill="green")

# add canvas to the root window
c.pack()

# wait for any events
root.mainloop()
```

Output:

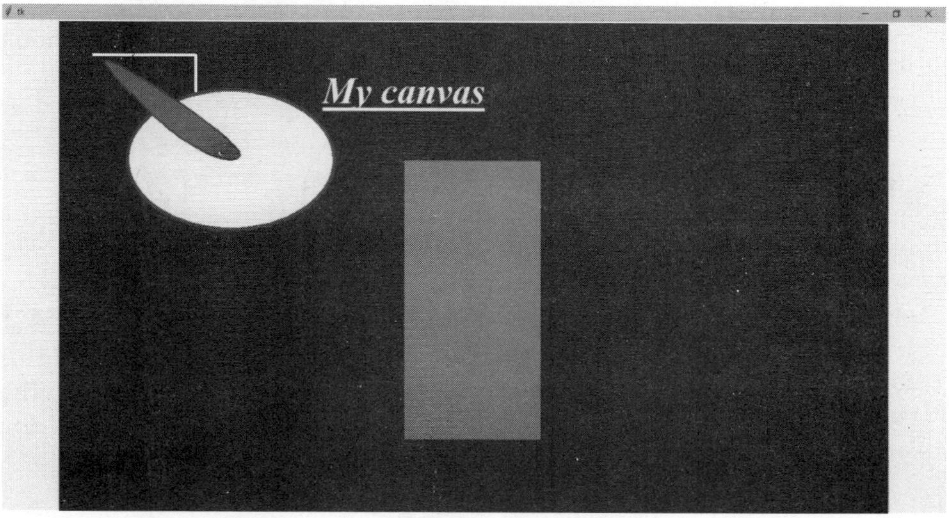

Figure 22.5: Output of Program 4

Another important shape that we can draw in the canvas is an arc. An arc represents a part of an ellipse or circle. Arcs can be created using the create_arc() method as:

```
id = c.create_arc(100, 100, 400, 300, width=3, start=270, extent=180,
     outline="red", style="arc")
```

Here, the arc is created in the rectangular space defined by the coordinates (100, 100) and (400, 300). The width of the arc will be 3 pixels. The arc will start at an angle 270 degrees and extend for another 180 degrees (i.e. up to 450 degrees means 450 – 360 = 90 degrees). The outline of the arc will be in red color. 'style' option can be "arc" for drawing arcs. 'style' can be "pie slice" and"chord". Arcs drawn with these styles are shown in Figure 22.6:

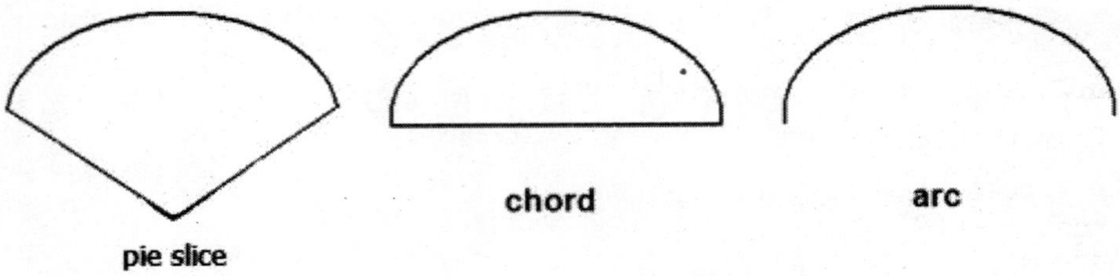

Figure 22.6: Different Styles of Arc

As mentioned, the option 'start' represents an angle of the arc where it has to start and 'extent' represents the angle further which the arc should extend. These angles should be taken in counter clock-wise direction, taking the 3 O' clock position as 0 degrees. Thus, the 12 O' clock position will show 90 degrees, the 9 O' clock will be 180 and the 6 O' clock will represent 270 degrees. Consider Figure 22.7:

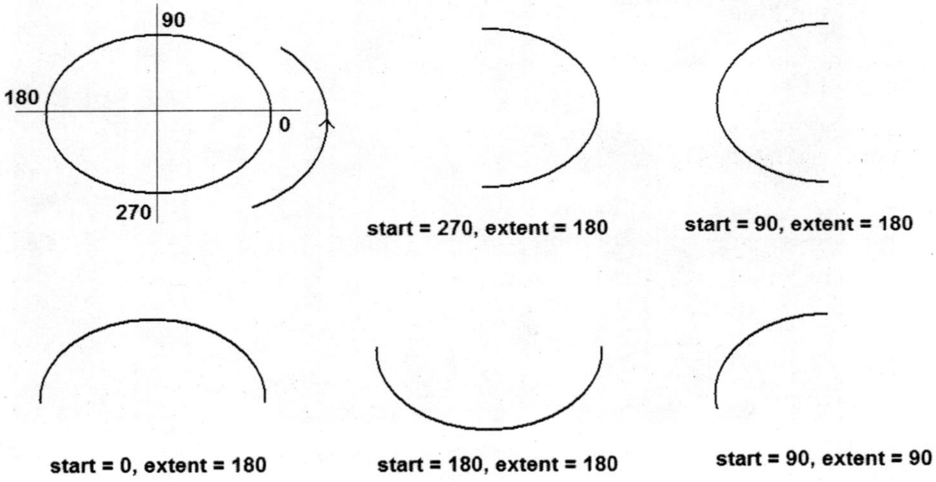

Figure 22.7: Understanding Start and Extent of Arcs

The value of the extent should be added to the starting angle so that we can understand where the arc will stop. For example,

```
id = c.create_arc(500, 100, 800, 300, width=3, start=90, extent=180,
outline="red", style="arc")
```

Here, the arc is created in the rectangular space defined by the coordinates (500, 100) and (800, 300). The arc starts at 90 degrees and extends by 180 degrees. So, the arc's ending position will be at 90+180 = 270 degrees.

Program

Program 5: A Python program to create arcs in different shapes.

```
from tkinter import *

# create root window
root = Tk()

# create Canvas as a child to root window
c = Canvas(root, bg="white", height=700, width=1200)

# create arcs in the canvas
id = c.create_arc(100, 100, 400, 300, width=3, start=270, extent=180,
    outline="red", style="arc")
id = c.create_arc(500, 100, 800, 300, width=3, start=90, extent=180,
    outline="red", style="arc")
id = c.create_arc(100, 400, 400, 600, width=3, start=0, extent=180,
    outline="blue", style="arc")
id = c.create_arc(500, 400, 800, 600, width=3, start=180, extent=180,
    outline="blue", style="arc")
id = c.create_arc(900, 400, 1200, 600, width=3, start=90, extent=90,
    outline="black", style="arc")

# add canvas to the root
c.pack()

# wait for any events
root.mainloop()
```

Output:

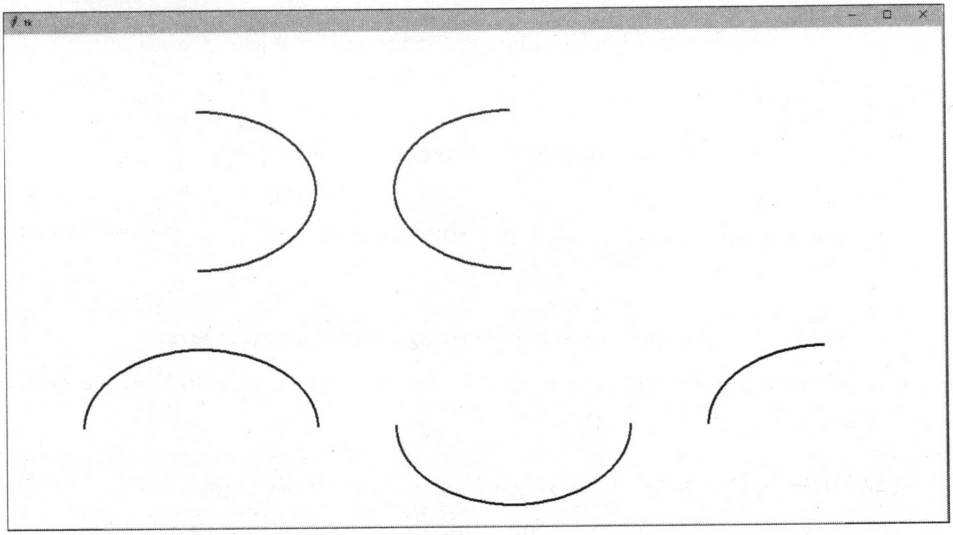

Figure 22.8: Output of Program 5

We can display an image in the canvas with the help of create_image() method. Using this method, we can display the images with the formats .gif,.pgm,or.ppm. We should first load the image into a file using PhotoImage class as:

```
file1 = PhotoImage(file="cat.gif")# load cat.gif into file1
```

Now, the image is available in 'file1'. This image can be displayed in the canvas using create_image() method as:

```
id = c.create_image(500, 200, anchor=NE, image=file1,
     activeimage=file2)
```

Here, the image is displayed relative to the point represented by the coordinates (500, 200). The image can be placed in any direction from this point indicated by 'anchor' option. The directions are represented by actual 8 directions on the earth: NW, N, NE, E, SE, S, SW, W and CENTER. The positions of the directions are shown in Figure 22.9.'image' represents the image file name that should be displayed in the canvas. 'activeimage' represents the image file name that should be displayed when the mouse is placed on the image. Program 5 shows these concepts.

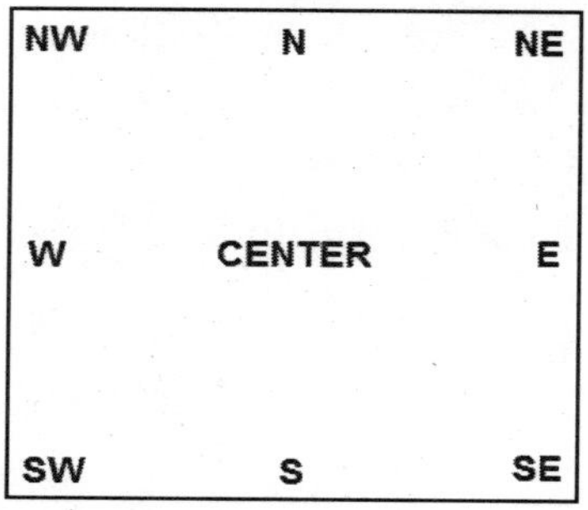

Figure 22.9: Directions that can be used in Anchor Option

Program

Program 6: A Python program to display images in the canvas.

```
from tkinter import *

# create root window
root = Tk()

# create Canvas as a child to root window
c = Canvas(root, bg="white", height=700, width=1200)

# copy images into files
file1 = PhotoImage(file="cat.gif")
file2 = PhotoImage(file="puppy.gif")

# display the image in the canvas in NE direction
# when mouse is placed on cat image, we can see puppy image
id = c.create_image(500, 200, anchor=NE, image=file1,
     activeimage=file2)
```

```
# display some text below the image
id = c.create_text(500, 500, text="This is a thrilling photo", font=
     ('Helvetica', 30, 'bold'), fill="blue")

# add canvas to the root
c.pack()

# wait for any events
root.mainloop()
```

Output:

Figure 22.10: Output of Program 6

In Program 7, we use polygon and rectangle to create a house. Then we create green bushes using arcs at left and right sides of the house. A Moon image (.gif file) is shown at the top left corner and text is displayed below the house.

Program

Program 7: A Python program to display drawing in the canvas.

```
from tkinter import *

# create root window
root = Tk()

# create Canvas as a child to root window. Background color is dark
# blue.
c = Canvas(root, bg="#091e42", height=700, width=1200)

# create the house
c.create_polygon(600,250,700,200,800,250,800,400,600,400, width=2,
     fill="yellow", outline="red")
c.create_line(600,250,800,250, width=2, fill="red")
c.create_rectangle(650,275,750,375, fill="red")

# create 3 bushes at left side of house
```

```
    x1,y1=0,350
    x2,y2=200,450
    for i in range(3):
        c.create_arc(x1,y1,x2,y2, start=0, extent=180, fill="green")
        x1+=200
        x2+=200

    # create 2 bushes at right side of house
    c.create_arc(800,350,1000,450, start=0, extent=180, fill="green")
    c.create_arc(1000,350,1200,450, start=0, extent=180, fill="green")

    # display Moon image
    file1 = PhotoImage(file="moon.gif")
    c.create_image(10, 100, anchor=NW, image=file1)

    # display some text below the image
    id = c.create_text(600, 600, text="My Happy Home!", font= ('Helvetica',
        30, 'bold'), fill="magenta")

    # add canvas to the root
    c.pack()

    # wait for any events
    root.mainloop()
```

Output:

Figure 22.11: Output of Program 7

Frame

A frame is similar to canvas that represents a rectangular area where some text or widgets can be displayed. Our root window is in fact a frame. To create a frame, we can create an object of Frame class as:

```
    f= Frame(root, height=400, width=500, bg="yellow", cursor="cross")
```

Here, 'f' is the object of Frame class. The frame is created as a child of 'root' window. The options 'height' and 'width' represent the height and width of the frame in pixels. 'bg' represents the back ground color to be displayed and 'cursor' indicates the type of the cursor to be displayed in the frame.

Once the frame is created, it should be added to the root window using the pack() method as follows:

```
f.pack()
```

Program

Program 8: A GUI program to display a frame in the root window.

```
from tkinter import *

# create root window
root = Tk()

# give a title for root window
root.title("My Frame")

# create a frame as child to root window
f= Frame(root, height=400, width=500, bg="yellow", cursor="cross")

# attach the frame to root window
f.pack()

# let the root window wait for any events
root.mainloop()
```

Output:

Figure 22.12: Output of Program 8

Widgets

A widget is a GUI component that is displayed on the screen and can perform a task as desired by the user. We create widgets as objects. For example, a push button is a widget that is nothing but an object of Button class. Similarly, label is a widget that is an object of Label class. Once a widget is created, it should be added to canvas or frame. The following are important widgets in Python:

- Button
- Label
- Message
- Text
- Scrollbar
- Checkbutton
- Radiobutton
- Entry
- Spinbox
- Listbox
- Menu

In general, working with widgets takes the following four steps:

1. Create the widgets that are needed in the program. A widget is a GUI component that is represented as an object of a class. For example, a push button is a widget that is represented as Button class object.

   As an example, suppose we want to create a push button, we can create an object to Button class as:

```
b = Button(f, text='My Button')
```

   Here, 'f' is Frame object to which the button is added. 'My Button' is the text that is displayed on the button.

2. When the user interacts with a widget, he will generate an event. For example, clicking on a push button is an event. Such events should be handled by writing functions or routines. These functions are called in response to the events. Hence they are called 'callback handlers' or 'event handlers'. Other examples for events are pressing the Enter button, right clicking the mouse button, etc.

   As an example, let's write a function that may be called in response to button click.

```
def buttonClick(self):
    print('You have clicked me')
```

3. When the user clicks on the push button, that 'clicking' event should be linked with the 'callback handler' function.Then only the button widget will appear as if it is performing some task.

   As an example, let's bind the button click with the function as:

```
b.bind('<Button-1>', buttonClick)
```

Here, 'b' represents the push button. <Button-1> indicates the left mouse button. When the user presses the left mouse button, the 'buttonClick' function is called as these are linked by bind() method in the preceding code.

4. The preceding 3 steps make the widgets ready for the user. Now, the user has to interact with the widgets. This is done by entering text from the keyboard or pressing mouse button. These are called events. These events are continuously monitored by our program with the help of a loop, called 'event loop'.

   As an example, we can use the mainloop() method that waits and processes the events as:

```
root.mainloop()
```

Here, 'root' is the object of root window in Python GUI. The events in root window are continuously observed by the mainloop() method. It means clicking the mouse or pressing a button on the keyboard are accepted by mainloop() and then the mainloop() calls the corresponding even handler function.

The preceding steps will become clearer once we get into the actual programming. Hence, let's proceed further to create a push button widget and handle the event generated by the user when the button is clicked.

Button Widget

A push button is a component that performs some action when clicked. These buttons are created as objects of Button class as:

```
b = Button(f, text='My Button', width=15, height=2, bg='yellow',
    fg='blue', activebackground='green', activeforeground='red')
```

Here, 'b' is the object of Button class. 'f' represents the frame for which the button is created as a child. It means the button is shown in the frame. The 'text' option represents the text to be displayed on the button. 'width' represents the width of the button in characters. If an image is displayed on the button instead of text, then 'width' represents the width in pixels. 'height' represents the height of the button in textual lines. If an image is displayed on the button, then 'height' represents the height of the button in pixels. 'bg' represents the foreground color and 'fg' represents the back ground color of the button. 'activebackground' represents the background color when the button is clicked. Similarly, 'activeforeground' represents the foreground color when the button is clicked.

We can also display an image on the button as:

```
# first load the image into file1
file1 = PhotoImage(file="cat.gif")

# create a push button with image
b = Button(f, image=file1, width=150, height=100, bg='yellow',
    fg='blue', activebackground='green', activeforeground='red')
```

In the preceding statement, observe that the width and height of the button are mentioned in pixels.

In Program 9, we create a frame first and then create a push button with some options and add the button to the frame. Then we link the mouse left button with the buttonClick() method using bind() method as:

```
b.bind('<Button-1>', buttonClick)
```

Here, <Button-1> represents the mouse left button that is linked withbuttonClick() method. It means when the mouse left button is clicked, the buttonClick() method is called. This method is called event handler.

In the place of <Button-1>, we can also use <Button-2>. In this case, mouse middle button is linked with the event handler method. The middle button is not found in most of the mouses now-a-days. <Button-3> represents the mouse right button. Similarly, <Enter> represents that the event handler method should be executed when the mouse pointer is placed on the push button.

Program

Program 9: A Python program to create a push button and bind it with an event handler function.

```
from tkinter import *

# method to be called when the button is clicked
def buttonClick(self):
    print('You have clicked me')

# create root window
root = Tk()

# create frame as child to root window
f = Frame(root, height=200, width=300)

# let the frame will not shrink
f.propagate(0)

# attach the frame to root window
f.pack()

# create a push button as child to frame
b = Button(f, text='My Button', width=15, height=2, bg='yellow',
     fg='blue', activebackground='green', activeforeground='red')

# attach button to the frame
b.pack()
# bind the left mouse button with the method to be called
b.bind("<Button-1>", buttonClick)

# the root window handles the mouse click event
root.mainloop()
```

Output:

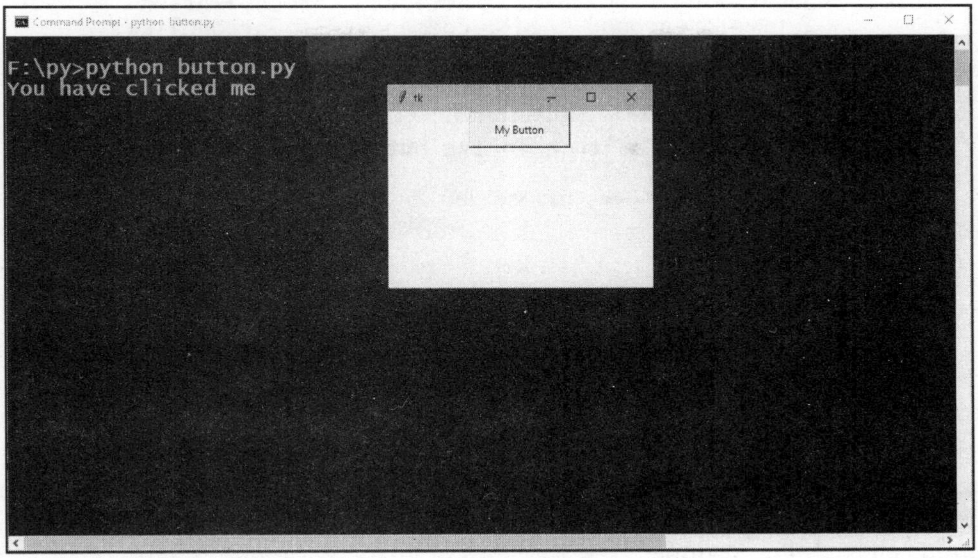

Figure 22.13: Output of Program 9

In the preceding program, we want to make 2 modifications. First, we will eliminate bind() method and we will use 'command' option to link the push button with event handler function as:

```
b = Button(f, text='My Button', width=15, height=2, bg='yellow',
    fg='blue', activebackground='green', activeforeground='red',
    command=buttonClick)
```

Secondly, we will rewrite the same program using class concept where the entire code will be written inside a class. This is shown in Program 10 which gives same output as Program 9.

Program

Program 10: A Python program to create a push button and bind it with an event handler function using command option.

```
from tkinter import *
class MyButton:

    # constructor
    def __init__(self, root):
        # create a frame as child to root window
        self.f = Frame(root, height=200, width=300)
        # let the frame will not shrink
        self.f.propagate(0)

        # attach the frame to root window
        self.f.pack()

        # create a push button as child to frame and bind it to
```

```
            #buttonClickmethod
            self.b = Button(self.f, text='My Button', width=15, height=2,
            bg='yellow', fg='blue', activebackground='green',
            activeforeground='red', command=self.buttonClick)

            # attach button to the frame
            self.b.pack()

        # method to be called when the button is clicked
        def buttonClick(self):
            print('You have clicked me')

    # create root window
    root = Tk()

    # create an object to MyButton class
    mb = MyButton(root)

    # the root window handles the mouse click event
    root.mainloop()
```

When we create several buttons, we need to know which button is clicked by the user. This will help us to perform the task depending on the button clicked. In this case, we have to call the event handler function by passing some argument that represents which button is clicked. For example,

```
b1 = Button(f, text='Red', width=15, height=2, command=lambda:
     buttonClick(1))
```

Here, we are creating a push button 'b1'. Please observe the 'command' option. Here, we are using the 'lambda' expression to pass the argument 1 to the buttonClick() method, in the following format:

```
command=lambda: buttonClick(arg1, arg2, ... )
```

Usually, 'command' option allows us to mention the method name only and it is not possible to pass arguments to the method. Suppose we want to pass arguments, then we need to use lambda expression as shown in the previous statement.

In Program 11, we are creating 3 push buttons by the names 'Red', 'Green' and 'Blue'. When the user clicks a button we will change the back ground color of the frame according to the button clicked. This is possible by passing an integer 1, 2 or 3 to the event handler method to indicate which button is clicked. This integer is stored in a variable 'num' at the method.

When the button is clicked, we are changing the background color of the frame as:

```
def buttonClick(self, num):
    if num==1:
        self.f["bg"]= 'red'
    if num==2:
        self.f["bg"]= 'green'
```

Here, observe that the 'bg' is the option of the frame 'f'. To set the back ground color of the frame, we can write:

```
self.f["bg"]= 'red'# set new color for bg
```

In the same way, we can set other options for the frame as:

```
self.f["height"]= 500# set new height
self.f["width"]= 600# set new width
```

You can follow the same procedure to set new values for the options of any widget.

Program

Program 11: A Python program to create three push buttons and change the background of the frame according to the button clicked by the user.

```
from tkinter import *

class MyButton:
    # constructor
    def __init__(self, root):
        # create a frame as child to root window
        self.f = Frame(root, height=400, width=500)

        # let the frame will not shrink
        self.f.propagate(0)

        # attach the frame to root window
        self.f.pack()

    # create 3 push buttons and bind them to buttonClick method and
# pass a number
        self.b1 = Button(self.f, text='Red', width=15, height=2,
                         command=lambda: self.buttonClick(1))
        self.b2 = Button(self.f, text='Green', width=15, height=2,
                         command=lambda: self.buttonClick(2))
        self.b3 = Button(self.f, text='Blue', width=15, height=2,
                         command=lambda: self.buttonClick(3))

        # attach buttons to the frame
        self.b1.pack()
        self.b2.pack()
        self.b3.pack()

    # method to be called when the button is clicked
    def buttonClick(self, num):
        # set the background color of frame depending on the button
        # clicked
        if num==1:
        self.f["bg"]= 'red'
        if num==2:
        self.f["bg"]= 'green'
        if num==3:
        self.f["bg"]= 'blue'

    # create root window
    root = Tk()
    # create an object to MyButton class
    mb = MyButton(root)

    # the root window handles the mouse click event
    root.mainloop()
```

Output:

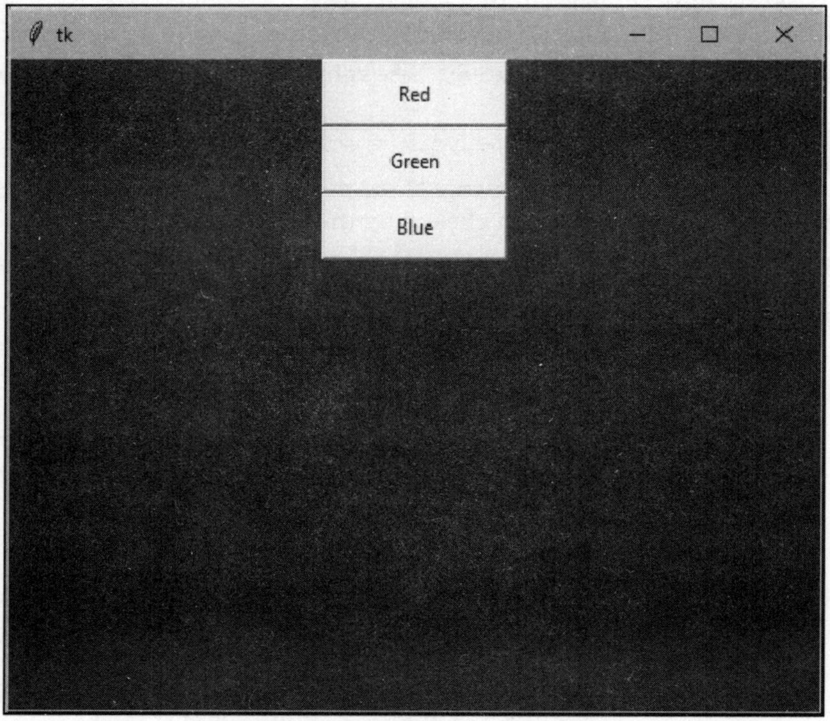

Figure 22.14: Output of Program 11

Arranging Widgets in the Frame

Once we create widgets or components, we can arrange them in the frame in a particular manner. Arranging the widgets in the frame is called 'layout management'. There are three types of layout managers.

- Pack layout manager
- Grid layout manager
- Place layout manager

We will discuss about these layout managers one by one. Pack layout manager uses pack() method. This method is useful to associate a widget with its parent component. While using the pack() method, we can mention the position of the widget using 'fill' or 'side' options.

```
    b.pack(fill=X)
    b.pack(fill=Y)
```

The 'fill' option can take the values: X, Y, BOTH, NONE. The value X represents that the widget should occupy the frame horizontally and the value Y represents that the widget should occupy vertically. BOTH represents that the widget should occupy in both the directions. NONE represents that the widget should be displayed as it is. The default value is NONE. Along with 'fill' option, we can use 'padx' and 'pady' options that represent how much space should be left around the component horizontally and vertically. For example,

```
b1.pack(fill=Y, padx=10, pady=15)# occupy vertically. Space on x-axis
# 10 px, on y-axis 15 px.
b2.pack(fill=X, padx=10, pady=15)# occupy horizontally. Space on x-
# axis 10 px, on y-axis 15 px.
b3.pack(fill=X)# occupy horizontally. No space outside the widget
b4.pack(fill=X)# occupy horizontally. No space outside the widget
```

The output in this case is shown in Figure 22.15:

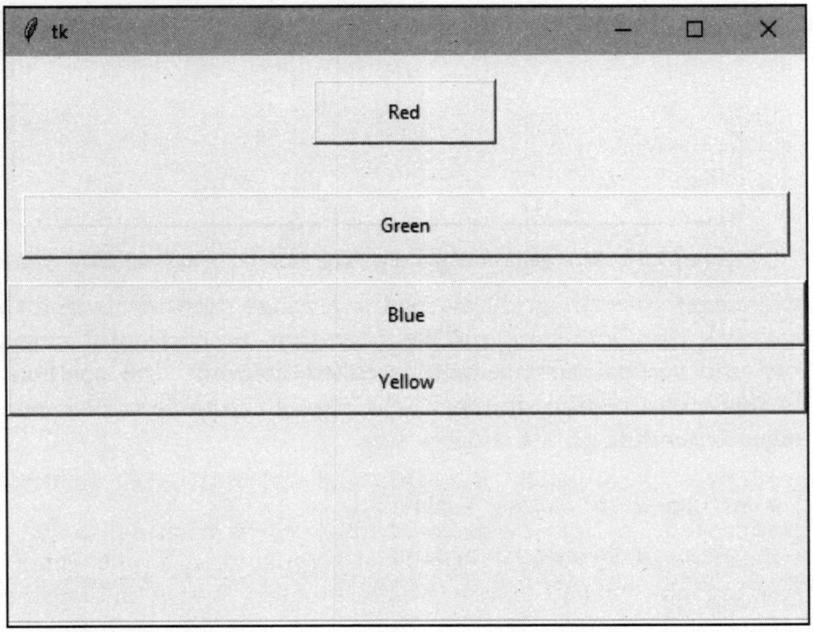

Figure 22.15: Arrangement of buttons using pack() method with 'fill' option

The pack() method can take another option 'side' which is used to place the widgets side by side. 'side' can take the values LEFT, RIGHT, TOP or BOTTOM. The default value is TOP. For example,

```
b1.pack(side=LEFT, padx=10, pady=15)# align towards left with 10 px
    # and 15 px spaces
b2.pack(side=LEFT, padx=10, pady=15)# align towards left with 10px and
    # 15 px spaces
b3.pack(side=RIGHT)# align towards right with 0 px space around the
    # widget
b4.pack()# align towards top with 0 px space around the widget
```

The preceding statements will produce the following output, as shown in Figure 22.16:

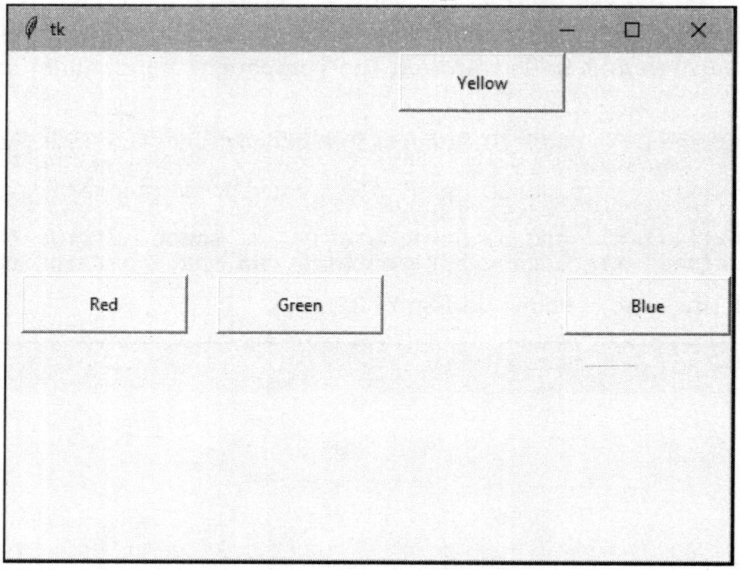

Figure 22.16: Arrangement of buttons using pack() method with 'side' option

Grid layout manager uses the grid() method to arrange the widgets in a two dimensional table that contains rows and columns. We know that the horizontal arrangement of data is called 'row' and vertical arrangement is called 'column'. The position of a widget is defined by a row and a column number. The size of the table is determined by the grid layout manager depending on the widgets size.

```
b1.grid(row=0, column=0, padx=10, pady=15)# display in 0th row, 0th
    # column with spaces around
b2.grid(row=0, column=1, padx=10, pady=15)# display in 0th row, 1st
    # column with spaces around
b3.grid(row=0, column=2)# display in 0th row, 2nd column without spaces
    # around
b4.grid(row=1, column=3)# display in 1st row, 3rd column without spaces
    # around
```

The preceding statements will produce the following output, as shown in Figure 22.17:

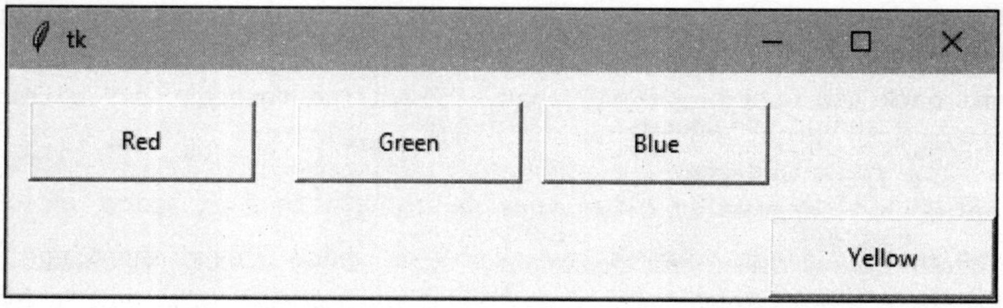

Figure 22.17: Arrangement of buttons using grid() method

Place layout manager uses the place() method to arrange the widgets. The place() method takes x and y coordinates of the widget along with width and height of the window where the widget has to be displayed. For example,

```
b1.place(x=20, y=30, width=100, height=50)# display at (20, 30)
     # coordinates in the window 100 pxwidth and 50 pxheight
b2.place(x=20, y=100, width=100, height=50)# display at (20, 100)
b3.place(x=200, y=100, width=100, height=50)# display at (200, 100)
b4.place(x=200, y=200, width=100, height=50)# display at (200, 100)
```

The preceding statements will produce the following output, shown in Figure 22.18:

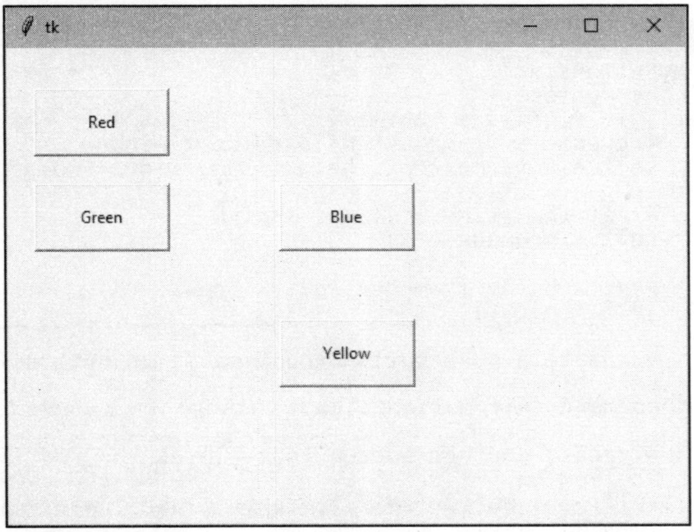

Figure 22.18: Arrangement of buttons using the place() method

Label Widget

A label represents constant text that is displayed in the frame or container. A label can display one or more lines of text that cannot be modified. A label is created as an object of Label class as:

```
lbl = Label(f, text="Welcome to Python", width=20, height=2,
     font=('Courier', -30, 'bold underline '), fg='blue', bg='yellow')
```

Here, 'f' represents the frame object to which the label is created as a child. 'text' represents the text to be displayed. 'width' represents the width of the label in number of characters and 'height' represents the height of the label in number of lines. 'font' represents a tuple that contains font name, size and style. 'fg' and 'bg' represents the foreground and background colors for the text.

In Program 12, we are creating two push buttons. We display 'Click Me' on the first button. When this button is clicked, we will display a label "Welcome to Python". This label is created in the event handler method buttonClick() that is bound to the first button. We display another button 'Close' that will close the root window upon clicking. The close button can be created as:

```
b2 = Button(f, text='Close', width=15, height=2, command=quit)
```

Please observe the 'command' option that is set to 'quit'. This represents closing of the root window.

Program

Program 12: A Python program to display a label upon clicking a push button.

```
from tkinter import *

class MyButtons:
    # constructor
    def __init__(self, root):
        # create a frame as child to root window
        self.f = Frame(root, height=350, width=500)

        # let the frame will not shrink
        self.f.propagate(0)

        # attach the frame to root window
        self.f.pack()

        # create a push button and bind it to buttonClick method
        self.b1 = Button(self.f, text='Click Me', width=15, height=2,
        command=self.buttonClick)

        # create another button that closes the root window upon
        # clicking
        self.b2 = Button(self.f, text='Close', width=15, height=2,
        command=quit)

        # attach buttons to the frame
        self.b1.grid(row=0, column=1)
        self.b2.grid(row=0, column=2)
        # the event handler method
        def buttonClick(self):
        # create a label with some text
        self.lbl = Label(self.f, text="Welcome to Python", width=20,
                   height=2, font=('Courier', -30, 'bold underline '),
                   fg='blue')

        # attach the label in the frame
        self.lbl.grid(row=2, column=0)

# create root window
root = Tk()

# create an object to MyButtons class
mb = MyButtons(root)

# the root window handles the mouse click event
root.mainloop()
```

Output:

Figure 22.19: Output of Program 12

Message Widget

A message is similar to a label. But messages are generally used to display multiple lines of text where as a label is used to display a single line of text. All the text in the message will be displayed using the same font. To create a message, we need to create an object of Message class as:

```
m = Message(f, text='This is a message that has more than one line of
     text.', width=200, font=('Roman', 20, 'bold italic'), fg='dark
     goldenrod')
```

Here, 'text' represents the text to be displayed in the message. The 'width' option specifies the message width in pixels. 'font' represents the font for the message. We can use options 'fg' for specifying foreground color and 'bg' for specifying background color for the message text.

Program

Program 13: A Python program to display a message in the frame.

```
from tkinter import *

class MyMessage:
    # constructor
    def __init__(self, root):
        # create a frame as child to root window
        self.f = Frame(root, height=350, width=500)

        # let the frame will not shrink
        self.f.propagate(0)

        # attach the frame to root window
        self.f.pack()

        # create a Message widget with some text
        self.m = Message(self.f, text='This is a message that has more
        than one line of text.', width=200, font=('Roman', 20, 'bold
            italic'), fg='dark goldenrod')

        # attach Message to the frame
        self.m.pack(side=LEFT)

# create root window
```

```
root = Tk()

# create an object to MyMessage class
mb = MyMessage(root)

# the root window handles the mouse click event
root.mainloop()
```

Output:

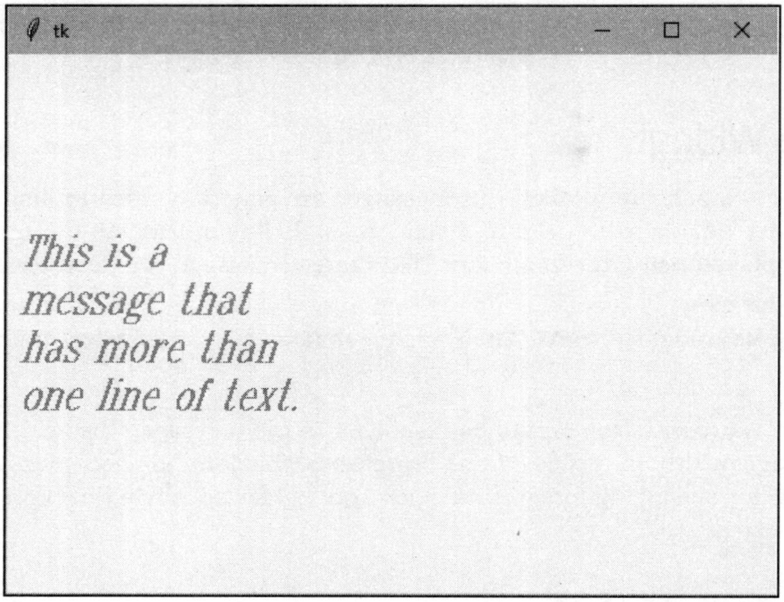

Figure 22.20: Output of Program 13

Text Widget

Text widget is same as a label or message. But Text widget has several options and can display multiple lines of text in different colors and fonts. It is possible to insert text into a Text widget, modify it or delete it. We can also display images in the Text widget. One can create a Text widget by creating an object to Text class as:

```
t = Text(root, width=20, height=10, font=('Verdana', 14, 'bold'),
    fg='blue', bg='yellow', wrap=WORD)
```

Here, 't' represents the object of Text class. 'root' represents an object of root window or frame. 'width' represents the width of the Text widget in characters. 'height' represents the height of the widget in lines. The option 'wrap' specifies where to cut the line. wrap=CHAR represents that any line that is too long will be broken at any character. wrap=WORD will break the line in the widget after the last word that fits in the line. wrap=NONE will not wrap the lines. In this case, it is better to provide a horizontal scroll bar to view the lines properly in the Text widget.

Once the Text widget is created, we can insert any text using the insert() method as:

```
t.insert(END, 'Text widget\nThis text is inserted into the Text
     widget.\n This is second line\n and this is third line\n')
```

Here, the first argument END represents that the text is added at the end of the previous text. We can also use CURRENT to represent that the text is added at the current cursor position.The second argument is the text that is added to the Text widget.

It is possible to display an image like a photo using the image_create() method as:

```
img = PhotoImage(file='moon.gif')# store moon.gif into img object
t.image_create(END, image=self.img)# append img to Text widget at the
# end
```

It is possible to mark some part of the text as a tag and provide different colors and font for that text. For this purpose, first we should specify the tag using the tag_add() method as:

```
t.tag_add('start', '1.0', '1.11')
```

Here, the tag name is 'start'. It contains characters (or text) from 1st row 0th character till 1st row 11th character.Now, we can apply colors and font to this tag text using the config() method as:

```
t.tag_config('start', background='red', foreground='white',
     font=('Lucida console', 20, 'bold italic'))
```

Here, we are applying 'red' background and 'white' foreground and 'Lucida console' font to the text that is already named as 'start' tag. In this way, we can have several tags in the Text widget.

In many cases, it is useful to add scroll bars to the Text widget. A scroll bar is a bar that is useful to scroll the text either horizontally or vertically. For example, we can create a vertical scroll bar by creating an object to Scrollbar class as:

```
s = Scrollbar(root, orient=VERTICAL, command= t.yview)
```

Here, 'orient' indicates whether it is a vertical scroll bar or horizontal scroll bar. The 'command' option specifies to which widget this scroll bar should be connected. 't.yview' represents that the scroll bar is connected to 't', i.e. Text widget and 'yview' is for vertical scrolling.

```
t.configure(yscrollcommand=s.set)
```

We should set the 'yscrollcommand' option of the Text widget 't' to 's.set' method. In this way, the scroll bar 's' is connected to Text widget 't'.

Program

Program 14: A Python program to create a Text widget with a vertical scroll bar attached to it. Also, highlight the first line of the text and display an image in the Text widget.

```
from tkinter import *

class MyText:
    # constructor
```

```
    def __init__(self, root):
        # create a Text widget with 20 chars width and 10 lines height
        self.t = Text(root, width=20, height=10, font=('Verdana', 14,
            'bold'), fg='blue', bg='yellow', wrap=WORD)

        # insert some text into the Text widget
        self.t.insert(END, 'Text widget\nThis text is inserted into the
        Text widget.\n This is second line\n and this is third line\n')

        # attach Text to the root
        self.t.pack(side=LEFT)

        # show image in the Text widget
        self.img = PhotoImage(file='moon.gif')
        self.t.image_create(END, image=self.img)

        # create a tag with the name 'start'
        self.t.tag_add('start', '1.0', '1.11')

        # apply colors to the tag
        self.t.tag_config('start', background='red',
        foreground='white',font=('Lucida console', 20, 'bold italic'))

        # create a Scrollbar widget to move the text vertically
        self.s = Scrollbar(root, orient=VERTICAL, command=
        self.t.yview)

        # attach the scroll bar to the Text widget
        self.t.configure(yscrollcommand=self.s.set)

        # attach the scroll bar to the root window
        self.s.pack(side=RIGHT, fill=Y)

# create root window
root = Tk()

# create an object to MyText class
mt = MyText(root)
# the root window handles the mouse click event
root.mainloop()
```

Output:

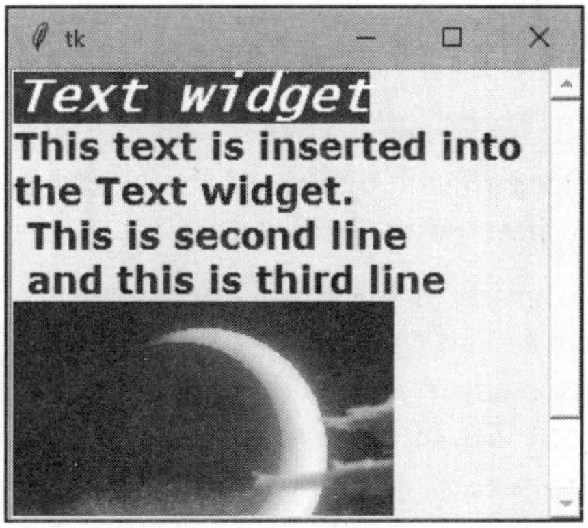

Figure 22.21: Output of Program 14

Scrollbar Widget

A scroll bar is a widget that is useful to scroll the text in another widget. For example, the text in the Text, Canvas, Frame or Listbox can be scrolled from top to bottom or left to right using scroll bars. There are two types of scroll bars. They are horizontal and vertical. The horizontal scroll bar is useful to view the text from left to right. The vertical scroll bar is useful to scroll the text from top to bottom. To create a scroll bar, we have to create Scrollbar class object as:

```
h = Scrollbar(root, orient=HORIZONTAL, bg='green', command=t.xview)
```

Here, 'h' represents the Scrollbar object which is created as a child to 'root' window. The option 'orient' indicates HORIZONTAL for horizontal scroll bars and VERTICAL indicates vertical scroll bars. 'bg' represents back ground color for the scroll bar. This option may not work in Windows since Window operating system may force some default back ground color for the scroll bar which will not be disturbed by the *tkinter*. The option 'command' represents the method that is to be executed. The method 'xview' is executed on the object 't'. Here, 't' may represent a widget like Text widget or Listbox.

Similarly, to create a vertical scroll bar 'v', we can write:

```
v = Scrollbar(root, orient=VERTICAL, bg='green', command=t.yview)
```

After creating the scroll bar, it should be attached to the widget like Text widget or Listbox as:

```
t.configure(xscrollcommand=h.set)
```

Here, 't' indicates Text widget. 'xscrollcommand' calls the set() method of horizontal scroll bar. In the same way, we can attach vertical scroll bar as:

```
t.configure(yscrollcommand=v.set)
```

Finally, the scroll bar should be attached to the root window using the pack() or grid() methods as:

```
h.pack(side=BOTTOM, fill=X)
```

Here, we are attaching the horizontal scroll bar at the bottom of the widget and it spreads across X - axis. Similarly, to attach vertical scroll bar, we can use the following statement:

```
v.pack(side=RIGHT, fill=Y)
```

Program

Program 15: A Python program to create a horizontal scroll bar and attach it to a Text widget to view the text from left to right.

```
from tkinter import *

class MyScrollbar:
    # constructor
    def __init__(self, root):
```

```
        # create a Text widget with 70 chars width and 15 lines height
        self.t = Text(root, width=70, height=15, wrap=NONE)

        # insert some text into the Text widget
        for i in range(50):
            self.t.insert(END, "This is some text ")

        # attach Text widget to root window at the top
        self.t.pack(side=TOP, fill=X)

        # create a horizontal scroll bar and attach it to Text widget
        self.h = Scrollbar(root, orient=HORIZONTAL,
        command=self.t.xview)

        # attach Text widget to the horizontal scroll bar
        self.t.configure(xscrollcommand=self.h.set)

        # attach Scrollbar to root window at the bottom
        self.h.pack(side=BOTTOM, fill=X)

# create root window
root = Tk()

# create an object to MyScrollbar class
ms = MyScrollbar(root)
# the root window handles the mouse click event
root.mainloop()
```

Output:

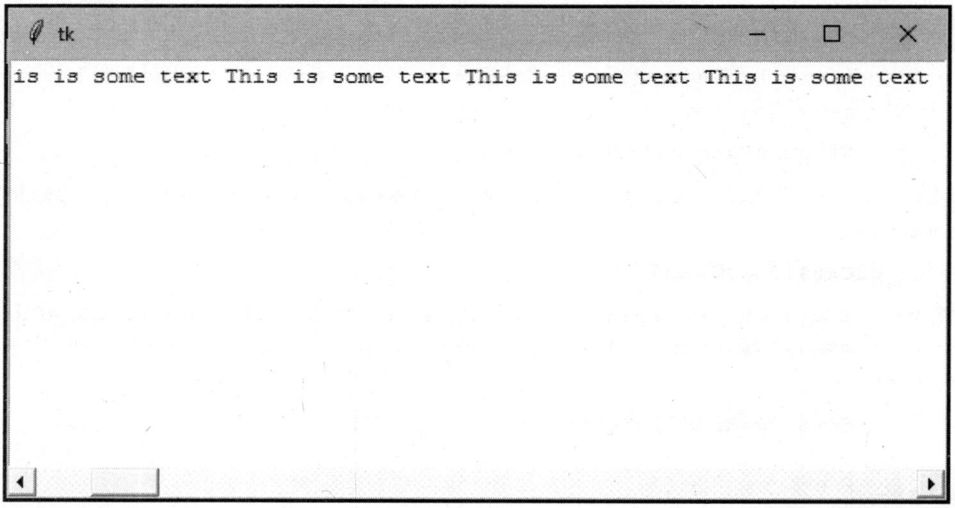

Figure 22.22: Output of Program 15

Checkbutton Widget

Check buttons, also known as check boxes are useful for the user to select one or more options from available group of options. Check buttons are displayed in the form of square shaped boxes. When a check button is selected, a tick mark is displayed on the button. We can create check buttons using the Checkbutton class as:

```
c1 = Checkbutton(f, bg='yellow', fg= 'green', font=('Georgia', 20,
     'underline'), text='Java', variable= var1, command=display)
```

Here, 'c1' is the object of Checkbutton class that represents a check button. 'f' indicates frame for which the check button becomes a child. 'bg' and 'fg' represent the back ground and fore ground colors used for check button. 'font' represents the font name, size and style. 'text' represents the text to be displayed after the check button. The option 'variable' represents an object of IntVar() class. 'command' represents the method to be called when the user clicks the check button.

The class 'IntVar' is useful to know the state of the check button, whether it is clicked or not. The IntVar class object can be created as:

```
var1 = IntVar()
```

When the check button is clicked or selected, the value of 'var1' will be 1, otherwise its value will be 0. To retrieve the value from 'var1', we should use the get() method, as:

```
x = var1.get()# x value can be 1 or 0
```

Program

Program 16: A Python program to create 3 check buttons and know which options are selected by the user.

```
from tkinter import *

class Mycheck:
    # constructor
    def __init__(self, root):
        # create a frame as child to root window
        self.f = Frame(root, height=350, width=500)

    # let the frame will not shrink
    self.f.propagate(0)

    # attach the frame to root window
    self.f.pack()

    # create IntVar class variables
    self.var1 = IntVar()
    self.var2 = IntVar()
    self.var3 = IntVar()

    # create check boxs and bind them to display method
    self.c1 = Checkbutton(self.f, bg='yellow', fg= 'green',
            font=('Georgia', 20, 'underline'), text='Java',
            variable= self.var1, command=self.display)
    self.c2 = Checkbutton(self.f, text='Python', variable=
             self.var2,command=self.display)
    self.c3 = Checkbutton(self.f, text='.NET', variable= self.var3,
            command=self.display)

    # attach check boxes to the frame
    self.c1.place(x=50, y=100)
```

```
        self.c2.place(x=200, y=100)
        self.c3.place(x=350, y=100)

    def display(self):
        # retrieve the control variable values
        x = self.var1.get()
        y = self.var2.get()
        z = self.var3.get()

        # string is empty initially
        str = ''

        # catch user choice
        if x==1:
            str += 'Java '
        if y==1:
            str+= 'Python '
        if z==1:
            str+= '.NET '

        # display the user selection as a label
        lbl = Label(text=str, fg='blue').place(x=50, y=150, width=200,
                  height=20)
# create root window
root = Tk()

# create an object to MyButtons class
mb = Mycheck(root)

# the root window handles the mouse click event
root.mainloop()
```

Output:

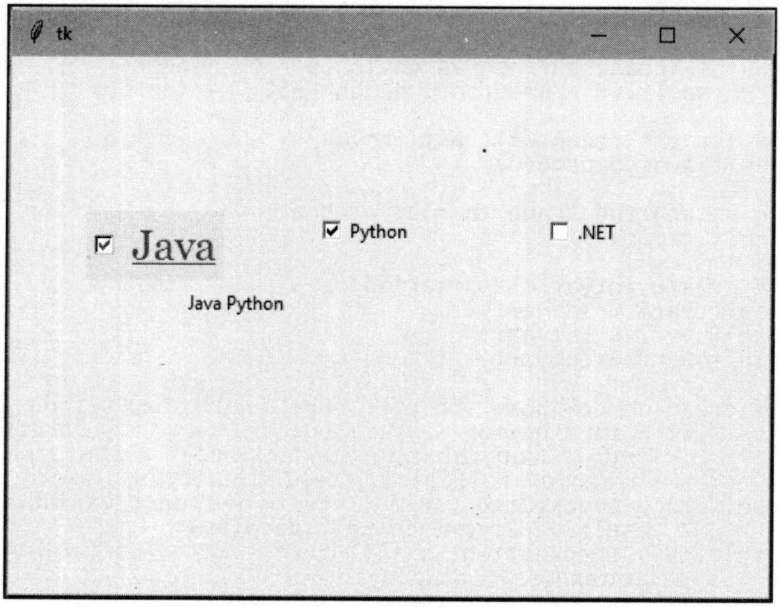

Figure 22.23: Output of Program 16

Radiobutton Widget

A radio button is similar to a check button, but it is useful to select only one option from a group of available options. A radio button is displayed in the form of round shaped button. The user cannot select more than one option in case of radio buttons. When a radio button is selected, there appears a dot in the radio button. We can create a radio button as an object of the Radiobutton class as:

```
r1 = Radiobutton(f, bg='yellow', fg= 'green', font=('Georgia', 20,
     'underline'), text='Male', variable= var, value=1,
     command=display)
```

The option 'text' represents the string to be displayed after the radio button. 'variable' represents the object of IntVar class. 'value' represents a value that is set to this object when the radio button is clicked. The object of IntVar class can be created as:

```
var = IntVar()
```

When the user clicks the radio button, the value of this 'var' is set to the value given in 'value' option, i.e. 1. It means 'var' will become 1 if the radio button 'r1' is clicked by the user. In this way, it is possible to know which button is clicked by the user.

Program

Program 17: A Python program to create radio buttons and know which button is selected by the user.

```
from tkinter import *

class Myradio:
    # constructor
    def __init__(self, root):
        # create a frame as child to root window
        self.f = Frame(root, height=350, width=500)

        # let the frame will not shrink
        self.f.propagate(0)

        # attach the frame to root window
        self.f.pack()

        # create IntVar class variable
        self.var = IntVar()

        # create radio buttons and bind them to display method
        self.r1 = Radiobutton(self.f, bg='yellow', fg= 'green',
            font=('Georgia', 20, 'underline'), text='Male',
            variable= self.var, value=1, command=self.display)
        self.r2 = Radiobutton(self.f, text='Female', variable=
        self.var,value=2, command=self.display)

        # attach radio buttons to the frame
        self.r1.place(x=50, y=100)
        self.r2.place(x=200, y=100)

    def display(self):
        # retrieve the control variable value
```

```
        x = self.var.get()

        # string is empty initially
        str = ''

        # catch user choice
        if x==1:
            str += 'You selected: Male '
        if x==2:
            str+= 'You selected: Female '

        # display the user selection as a label
        lbl = Label(text=str, fg='blue').place(x=50, y=150, width=200,
              height=20)
# create root window
root = Tk()

# create an object to MyButtons class
mb = Myradio(root)
# the root window handles the mouse click event
root.mainloop()
```

Output:

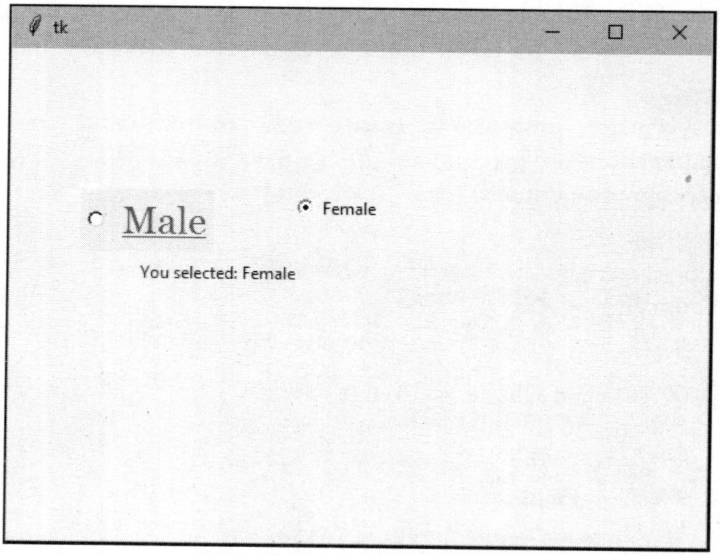

Figure 22.24: Output of Program 17

Entry Widget

Entry widget is useful to create a rectangular box that can be used to enter or display one line of text. For example, we can display names, passwords or credit card numbers using Entry widgets.An Entry widget can be created as an object of Entry class as:

```
e1 = Entry(f, width=25, fg='blue', bg='yellow', font=('Arial', 14),
     show='*')
```

Here, 'e1' is the Entry class object. 'f' indicates the frame which is the parent component for the Entry widget. 'width' represents the size of the widget in number of characters. 'fg' indicates the fore ground color in which the text in the widget is displayed. 'bg' represents the back ground color in the widget. 'font' represents a tuple that contains font family name, size and style. 'show' represents a character that replaces the originally typed characters in the Entry widget. For example, show='*' is useful when the user wants to hide his password by displaying stars in the place of characters.

After typing text in the Entry widget, the user presses the Enter button. Such an event should be linked with the Entry widget using bind() method as:

```
e1.bind("<Return>", self.display)
```

When the user presses Enter (or Return) button, the event is passed to display() method. Hence, we are supposed to catch the event in the display method, using the following statement:

```
def display(self, event):
```

As seen in the preceding code, we are catching the event through an argument 'event' in the display() method. This argument is never used inside the method. The method consists of the code that is to be executed when the user pressed Enter button.

Program

Program 18: A Python program to create Entry widgets for entering user name and password and display the entered text.

```
from tkinter import *

class MyEntry:
    # constructor
    def __init__(self, root):
        # create a frame as child to root window
        self.f = Frame(root, height=350, width=500)

        # let the frame will not shrink
        self.f.propagate(0)

        # attach the frame to root window
        self.f.pack()

        # labels
        self.l1 = Label(text='Enter User name: ')
        self.l2 = Label(text='Enter Password: ')

        # create Entry widget for user name
        self.e1 = Entry(self.f, width=25, fg='blue', bg='yellow',
                        font=('Arial', 14))

        # create Entry widget for pass word. the text in the widget is
            # replaced by stars (*)
        self.e2 = Entry(self.f, width=25, fg='blue', bg='yellow',
                        show='*')

        # when user presses Enter, bind that event to display method
```

```
        self.e2.bind("<Return>", self.display)

        # place labels and entry widgets in the frame
        self.l1.place(x=50, y=100)
        self.e1.place(x=200, y=100)
        self.l2.place(x=50, y=150)
        self.e2.place(x=200, y=150)
    def display(self, event):
        # retrieve the values from the entry widgets
        str1 = self.e1.get()
        str2 = self.e2.get()

        # display the values using labels
        lbl1 = Label(text='Your name is: '+str1).place(x=50, y=200)
        lbl2 = Label(text='Your password is: '+str2).place(x=50, y=220)
# create root window
root = Tk()

# create an object to MyButtons class
mb = MyEntry(root)

# the root window handles the mouse click event
root.mainloop()
```

Output:

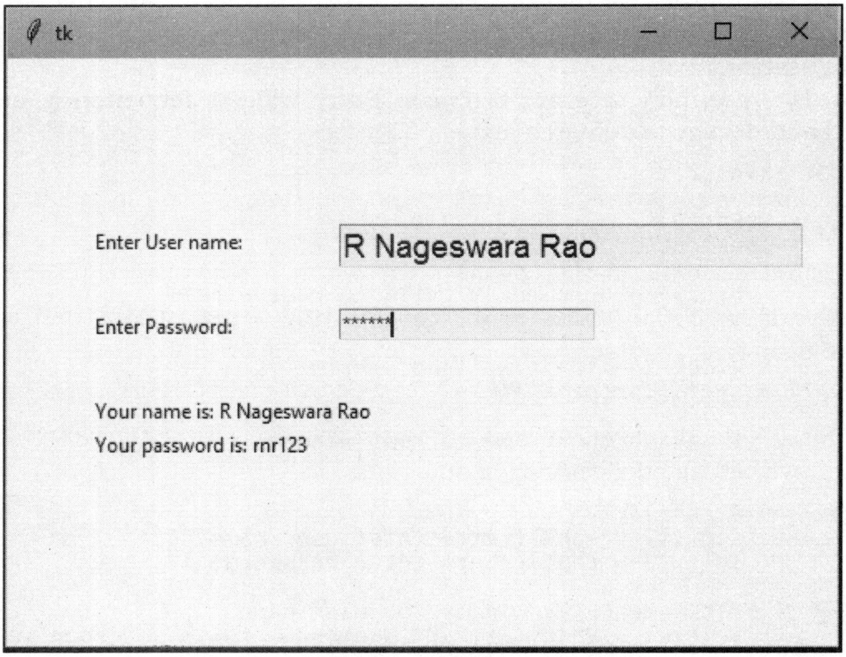

Figure 22.25: Output of Program 18

Spinbox Widget

A Spinbox widget allows the user to select values from a given set of values. The values may be a range of numbers or a fixed set of strings.

The spin box appears as a long rectangle attached with arrowheads pointing towards up and down. The user can click on the arrowheads to see the next value or previous value. The user can also edit the value being displayed in the spin box just like he can do in case of an Entry widget.

A spin box is created as an object of Spinbox class. To create a spin box with numbers ranging from 5 to 15, we can write the following statement:

```
s1 = Spinbox(f, from_= 5, to=15, textvariable=val1, width=15,
     fg='blue', bg='yellow', font=('Arial', 14, 'bold'))
```

Here, 'f' represents the parent widget. 'from_' indicates the starting value and 'to' indicates the ending value in the spin box. 'textvariable' shows the control variable, i.e. val1 that is created as an object of the IntVar class, as follows:

```
val1 = IntVar()
```

'val1' is a control variable that receives the displayed value in the spin box. Similarly, we can create a spin box with strings by specifying the strings as a tuple as shown in the following statement:

```
s2 = Spinbox(f, values=('Hyderabad', 'Delhi', 'Kolkata', 'Bangalore'),
     textvariable=val2, width=15, fg='black', bg='green',
     font=('Arial', 14, 'bold italic'))
```

Here, the fixed strings that are displayed in the spin box are mentioned in the 'values' option as a tuple as shown in the following statement:

```
values=('Hyderabad', 'Delhi', 'Kolkata', 'Bangalore')
```

The 'textvariable' option indicates the control variable value 'val2' that is created as an object of StringVar class as shown in the following statement:

```
val2 = StringVar()
```

'val2' contains the displayed string in the spin box. To retrieve the values from the control variables, we can use the get() method as:

```
a = val1.get()# get the number from val1
s = val2.get()# get the string from val2
```

Program

Program 19:A Python program to create two spin boxes and retrieve the values displayed in the spin boxes when the user clicks on a push button.

```
from tkinter import *

class MySpinbox:
    # constructor
    def __init__(self, root):
```

```
        # create a frame as child to root window
        self.f = Frame(root, height=350, width=500)

        # let the frame will not shrink
        self.f.propagate(0)

        # attach the frame to root window
        self.f.pack()

        # these are control variables for Spinboxes
        self.val1 = IntVar()
        self.val2 = StringVar()

        # create Spinbox with numbers from 5 to 15
        self.s1 = Spinbox(self.f, from_= 5, to=15,
                  textvariable=self.val1,width=15, fg='blue',
                  bg='yellow', font=('Arial', 14, 'bold'))

        # create Spinbox with a tuple of strings
        self.s2 = Spinbox(self.f, values=('Hyderabad', 'Delhi',
                  'Kolkata','Bangalore'), textvariable=self.val2,
                  width=15, fg='black',bg='LightGreen', font=('Arial',
                  14, 'bold italic'))

        # create a Button and bind it with display() method
        self.b = Button(self.f, text='Get values from spinboxes',
           command=self.display)

        # place Spinboxes and button widgets in the frame
        self.s1.place(x=50, y=50)
        self.s2.place(x=50, y=100)
        self.b.place(x=50, y=150)

    def display(self):
        # retrieve the values from the Spinbox widgets
        a = self.val1.get()
        s = self.val2.get()

        # display the values using labels
        lbl1 = Label(text='Selected value is: '+str(a)).place(x=50,
              y=200)
        lbl2 = Label(text='Selected city is: '+s).place(x=50, y=220)

# create root window
root = Tk()

# create an object to MySpinbox class
mb = MySpinbox(root)

# the root window handles the mouse click event
root.mainloop()
```

Output:

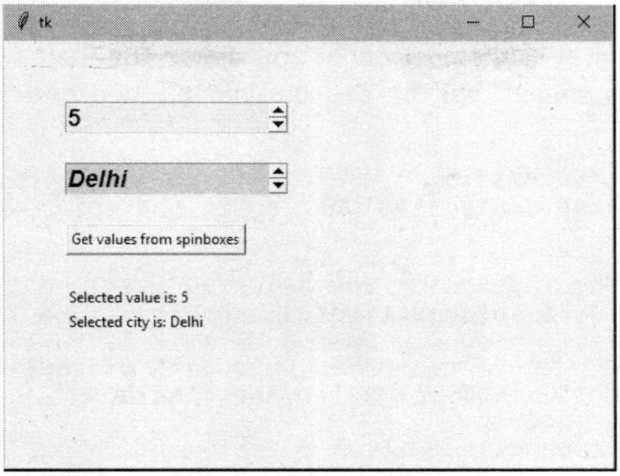

Figure 22.26: Output of Program 19

Listbox Widget

A list box is useful to display a list of items in a box so that the user can select 1 or more items. To create a list box, we have to create an object of Listbox class, as:

```
lb = Listbox(f, font="Arial 12 bold", fg='blue', bg='yellow', height=8,
        width=24, activestyle='underline', selectmode=MULTIPLE)
```

Here, 'lb' is the list box object. The option 'height' represents the number of lines shown in the list box. 'width' represents the width of the list box in terms of number of characters and the default is 20 characters. The option 'activestyle' indicates the appearance of the selected item. It may be 'underline', 'dotbox' or 'none'. The default value is 'underline'. The option 'selectmode' may take any of the following values:

- **BROWSE:** Normally, we can select one item (or line) out of a list box. If we click on an item and then drag to a different item, the selection will follow the mouse. This is the default value of 'selectmode' option.
- **SINGLE:** This represents that we can select only one item(or line) from all available list of items.
- **MULTIPLE:** We can select 1 or more number of items at once by clicking on the items. If an item is already selected, clicking second time on the item will un-select it.
- **EXTENDED:** We can select any adjacent group of items at once by clicking on the first item and dragging to the last item.

Once the list box is created, we should insert items into the list box using insert() method as:

```
lb.insert(0, 'Standford University')
lb.insert(1, ' Oxford University')
```

To bind the ListboxSelect event with a method, we can use the bind() method as:

```
lb.bind('<<ListboxSelect>>', on_select)
```

The meaning of the previous statement is that when the user selects any items in the list box, the method on_select() will be called. This method can be written something like this:

```
def on_select(event):
    # create an empty list box
    lst = []

    # know the indexes of the selected items
    indexes = lb.curselection()

    # retrieve the items names depending on indexes
    # append the items names to the list box
    for i in indexes:
        lst.append(lb.get(i))
```

Observe the on_select() method. It has a parameter 'event' that is useful to catch the ListboxSelect event. We need not do anything with this event inside the method. To retrieve the indexes or position numbers of the selected items, we can use curselection() method of Listbox class. Suppose, we want to know the names of the items based on the indexes, we can use get() method of the Listbox class. In the on_select() method, we are appending the names of the selected items to a list box. Later the contents of this list box can be displayed in a Text box.

Program

Program 20: A Python program to create a list box with Universities names and display the selected Universities names in a text box.

```
from tkinter import *
class ListboxDemo:
    def __init__(self, root):
        self.f = Frame(root, width=700, height=400)
        # let the frame will not shrink
        self.f.propagate(0)

        # attach the frame to root window
        self.f.pack()

        # create a label
        self.lbl = Label(self.f, text="Click one or more of the
                   Universities below:", font="Calibri 14")
        self.lbl.place(x=50, y=50)

        # create list box with Universities names
        self.lb = Listbox(self.f, font="Arial 12 bold", fg='blue',
                  bg='yellow', height=8, selectmode=MULTIPLE)
        self.lb.place(x=50, y=100)

        # using for loop, insert items into list box
        for i in ["Standford University", "Oxford University", "Texas
        A&MUniversity", "Cambridge University", "University of
        California"]:
```

```
            self.lb.insert(END, i)

        # bind the ListboxSelect event to on_select() method
        self.lb.bind('<<ListboxSelect>>', self.on_select)

        # create text box to display selected items
        self.t = Text(self.f, width=40, height=6, wrap=WORD)
        self.t.place(x=300, y=100)

    def on_select(self, event):
        # create an empty list box
        self.lst = []

        # know the indexes of the selected items
        indexes = self.lb.curselection()

        # retrieve the items names depending on indexes
        # append the items names to the list box
        for i in indexes:
            self.lst.append(self.lb.get(i))

        # delete the previous content of the text box
        self.t.delete(0.0, END)
        # insert the new contents into the text box
        self.t.insert(0.0, self.lst)

# create root window
root = Tk()

# title for the root window
root.title("List box demonstration.")

# create object to our class
obj = ListboxDemo(root)

# handle any events
root.mainloop()
```

Output:

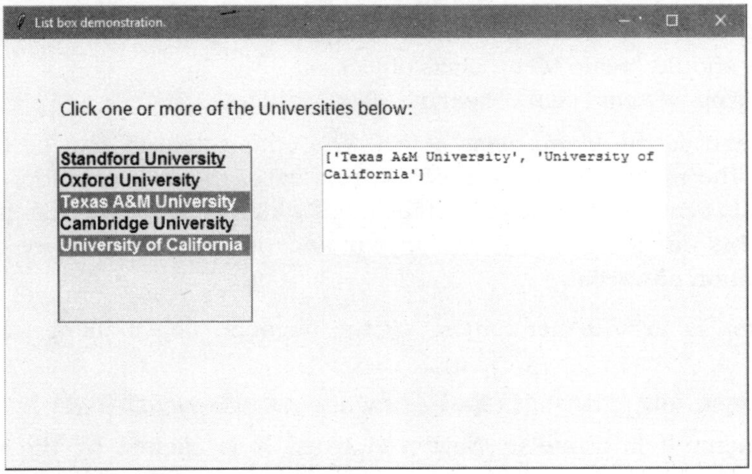

Figure 22.27: Output of Program 20

Menu Widget

A menu represents a group of items or options for the user to select from. For example, when we click on 'File' menu, it may display options like 'New', 'Open', 'Save', etc. We can select any option depending on our requirements. 'New', 'Open', 'Save' – these options are called menu items. Thus, a menu is composed of several menu items. Similarly, 'Edit' is a menu with menu items like 'Cut', 'Copy', 'Paste', etc. Generally, we see menus displayed in a bar, called menu bar. Consider Figure 22.28 to understand the terms menu bar, menu and menu item:

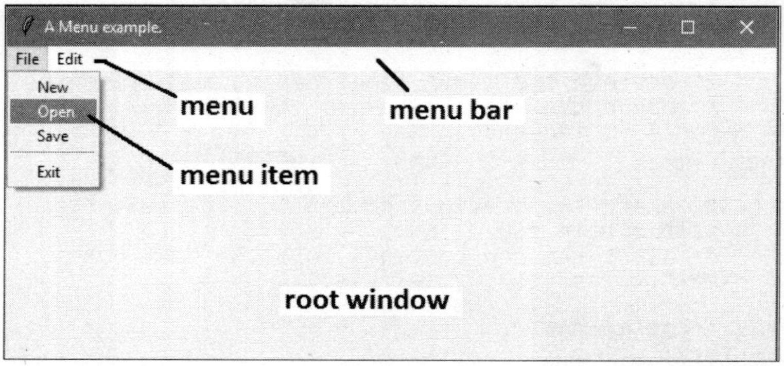

Figure 22.28: A menu bar with menus and menu items displayed in the root window

To create a menu, we should use the following steps:

1. First of all, we should create a menu bar as a child to root window. This is done using Menu class as:

```
menubar = Menu(root)
```

2. This menu bar should be attached to the root window using config() method as:

```
root.config(menu=menubar)
```

3. The next step is to create a menu with a group of menu items. For this purpose, first of all we should create Menu class object as:

```
filemenu = Menu(root, tearoff=0)
```

Here, 'filemenu' is the Menu class object. The option 'tearoff' can be 0 or 1. When this option is 1, the menu can be torn off. In this case, the first position (position 0) in the menu items is occupied by the tear-off element which is a dashed line. If this option value is 0, then this dashed line will not appear and the menu items are displayed starting from 0th position onwards.

The next step is to add menu items to the filemenu object using the add_command() method as:

```
filemenu.add_command(label="New", command=donothing)
```

Here, the menu item name is 'New' and when it is clicked by the user, the method donothing() will be called. In this way, we can add any number of menu items to filemenu object. When we want to display a horizontal line that separates a group of menu items from another group of menu items, we can use the add_separator() method, as given in the following statement:

```
filemenu.add_separator()
```

After adding all menu items to filemenu object, we should give it a name and add it to menu bar using add_cascade() method as:

```
menubar.add_cascade(label="File", menu=filemenu)
```

The 'menu' option tells that the 'File' menu is composed of all menu items that are added already to filemenu object.

Program

Program 21: A Python program to create a menu bar and adding File and Edit menus with some menu items.

```
# to display a menubar with File and Edit menus
from tkinter import *

class MyMenuDemo:
    def __init__(self, root):
        # create a menubar
        self.menubar = Menu(root)

        # attach the menubar to the root window
        root.config(menu=self.menubar)

        # create file menu
        self.filemenu = Menu(root, tearoff=0)

        # create menu items in file menu
        self.filemenu.add_command(label="New", command=self.donothing)
        self.filemenu.add_command(label="Open", command=self.donothing)
        self.filemenu.add_command(label="Save", command=self.donothing)

        # add a horizontal line as separator
        self.filemenu.add_separator()

        # create another menu item below the separator
        self.filemenu.add_command(label="Exit", command=root.destroy)

        # add the file menu with a name 'File' to the menubar
        self.menubar.add_cascade(label="File", menu=self.filemenu)

        # create edit menu
        self.editmenu = Menu(root, tearoff=0)

        # create menu items in edit menu
        self.editmenu.add_command(label="Cut", command=self.donothing)
        self.editmenu.add_command(label="Copy", command=self.donothing)
        self.editmenu.add_command(label="Paste",command=self.donothing)

        # add the edit menu with a name 'Edit' to the menubar
        self.menubar.add_cascade(label="Edit", menu=self.editmenu)
```

```
    def donothing(self):
        pass
# create root window
root = Tk()

# title for the root window
root.title("A Menu example.")

# create object to our class
obj = MyMenuDemo(root)

# define the size of the root window
root.geometry('600x350')

# handle any events
root.mainloop()
```

The output of this program will be exactly as shown in Figure 22.9. The output shows 2 menus attached to the menu bar. The first one is 'File' menu with 4 menu items: New, Open, Save and Exit. Observe the horizontal line below the 'Save' option and above the 'Exit' option. This horizontal line is called 'separator'. The second menu attached to the menu bar is the 'Edit' menu which has 3 menu items: Cut, Copy and Paste. But none of these menu items will work, except the 'Exit' menu item. When the user clicks on File → Exit item, the destroy() method is called that destroys the root window and hence the root window will be closed. When the other items like File → Open is clicked, the donothing() method is called that does nothing.

Can't we make the other menu items workable? Our intention is that when the user clicks on File → Open item, we want to display a file open dialog box where the user can select a file. Then we read data from the file and display it in a Text widget. This can be done by writing a method open_file(). In this method, first we should open a file dialog box for the user to select a file to open as:

```
filename = filedialog.askopenfilename(parent=root, title='Select a
file', filetypes=(("Python files", "*.py"),("All files",
"*.*")))
```

The 'filedialog' is a sub module in tkinter and hence it should be imported separately. In this module, we have askopenfilename() method where we are supposed to specify which type of files to open using 'filetypes' option in the following format:

```
filetypes=(("name", "extension"), ("name", "extension"))
```

Once the user selects a file in the dialog box, the filename is available to us in 'filename' object. Now, we can open this file and read its contents and display them in a Text box.

Similarly, we can make the File → Save item workable by writing a method save_file(). In this method, we should first open a file dialog box for the user and ask him the filename on which to save the data. This is done using asksaveasfilename() method of filedialog module as:

```
filename = filedialog.asksaveasfilename(parent=root,
defaultextension=".txt")
```

Here, the 'defaultextension' option specifies the default extension of files when we do not mention any. Our assumption here is that the user already has a file typed in the text box. When the user specifies the file name the typed data in the text box will be stored into the file with the name specified by the user.

Program 22 is a refinement for the Program 21. In Program 22, we are showing how to work with File → Open option and File → Save options by writing the methods: open_file() and save_file().

Program

Program 22: A GUI Program to display a menu and also to open a file and save it through the file dialog box.

```
from tkinter import *
from tkinter import filedialog

class MyMenuDemo:
    def __init__(self, root):
        # create a menubar
        self.menubar = Menu(root)

        # attach the menubar to the root window
        root.config(menu=self.menubar)

        # create file menu
        self.filemenu = Menu(root, tearoff=0)

        # create menu items in file menu
        self.filemenu.add_command(label="New", command=self.donothing)
        self.filemenu.add_command(label="Open", command=self.open_file)
        self.filemenu.add_command(label="Save", command=self.save_file)

        # add a horizontal line as separator
        self.filemenu.add_separator()

        # create another menu item below the separator
        self.filemenu.add_command(label="Exit", command=root.destroy)

        # add the file menu with a name 'File' to the menubar
        self.menubar.add_cascade(label="File", menu=self.filemenu)

        # create edit menu
        self.editmenu = Menu(root, tearoff=0)

        # create menu items in edit menu
        self.editmenu.add_command(label="Cut", command=self.donothing)
        self.editmenu.add_command(label="Copy", command=self.donothing)
        self.editmenu.add_command(label="Paste",command=self.donothing)

        # add the edit menu with a name 'Edit' to the menubar
        self.menubar.add_cascade(label="Edit", menu=self.editmenu)
    def donothing(self):
        pass

    # method for opening a file and display its contents in a text box
```

```
    def open_file(self):
        # open a file dialog box and accept the file name
        self.filename =filedialog.askopenfilename(parent=root,title=
                        'Select afile',filetypes=(("Python files",
                        *.py"),("All files","*.*")))

        # if cancel button is not clicked in the dialog box
        if self.filename != None:
            # open the file in read mode
            f = open(self.filename, 'r')
            # read the contents of the file
            contents = f.read()
            # create a Text box and add it to root window
            self.t = Text(root, width=80, height=20, wrap=WORD)
            self.t.pack()
            # insert the file contents in the Text box
            self.t.insert(1.0,contents)
            # close the file
            f.close()

    # method to save a file that is already in the text box
    def save_file(self):
        # open a file dialog box and type a file name
        self.filename = filedialog.asksaveasfilename(parent=root,
            defaultextension=".txt")
        # if cancel button is not clicked in the dialog box
        if self.filename != None:
            # open the file in read mode
            f = open(self.filename, 'w')
            # get the contents of the text box
            contents = str(self.t.get(1.0, END))
            # store the file contents into the file
            f.write(contents)
            # close the file
            f.close()

# create root window
root = Tk()

# title for the root window
root.title("A Menu example.")

# create object to our class
obj = MyMenuDemo(root)

# define the size of the root window
root.geometry('600x350')

# handle any events
root.mainloop()
```

Output:

The execution of Program 22 shows a menu. When you select the File→Open option, you will get the Select a file dialog box, as shown in Figure 22.29:

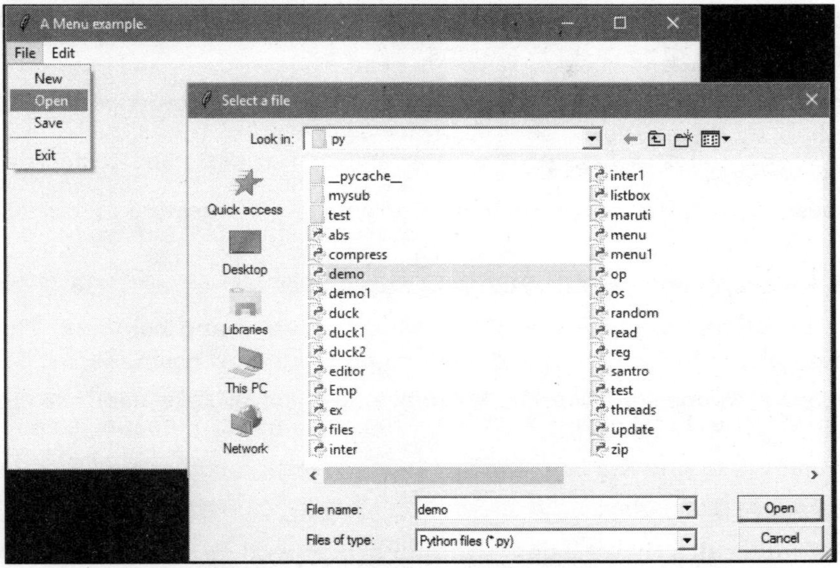

Figure 22.29: Displaying Select a file Dialog Box

If you select the File→Save option, you will get the Save As dialog box, as shown in Figure 22.30:

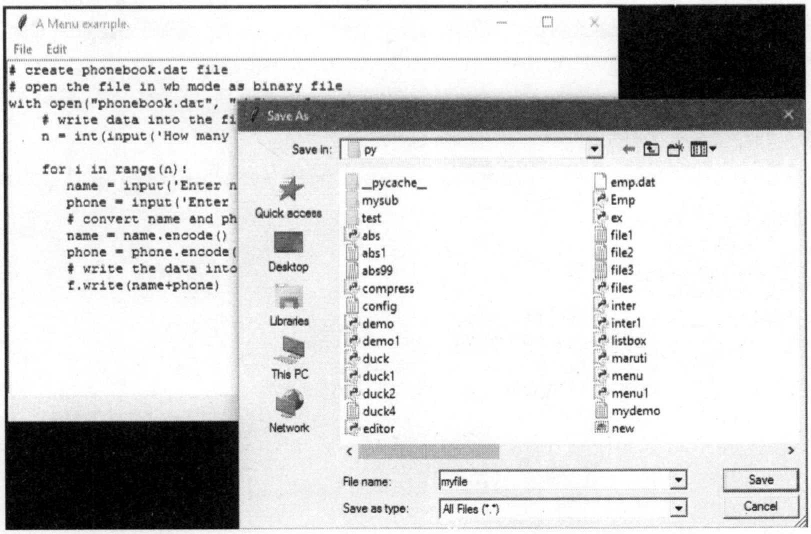

Figure 22.30: Displaying Save As Dialog Box

Creating Tables

A table is useful to display data in the form of rows and columns. Unfortunately, Python does not provide a Table widget to create a table. But we can create a table using alternate methods. For example, we can make a table by repeatedly displaying Entry widgets in the form of rows and columns.

To create a table with 5 rows and 4 columns, we can use 2 for loops as:

```
for i in range(5):
    for j in range(4):
```

Inside these loops, we have to create an Entry widget by creating an object of Entry class, as:

```
e = Entry(root, width=20, fg='blue', font=('Arial', 16, 'bold'))
```

Now, we need logic to place this Entry widget in rows and columns. This can be done using grid() method to which we can pass row and column positions, as:

```
e.grid(row=i, column=j)  # here i and j indicate row and column
positions
```

We can insert data into the Entry widget using insert() method, as:

```
e.insert(END, data)
```

Here, 'END' indicates that the data continues to append at the end of the previous data in the Entry widget.

This logic is used in Program 23, to create a table using the data that is coming from a list. We have taken a list containing 5 tuples and each tuple contains 4 values which indicate employee id number, name, city and salary. Hence we will have a table with 5 rows and 4 columns in each row. This program can be applied on the data coming from a database to display the entire data in the form of a table.

Program 23: A GUI Program to display a table with several rows and columns.

```
# table creation

from tkinter import *
class MyTable:
    def __init__(self, root):
        # code for creating the table
        for i in range(total_rows):
            for j in range(total_cols):
                self.e = Entry(root, width=20, fg='blue',
                         font=('Arial', 16, 'bold'))
                self.e.grid(row=i, column=j)
                self.e.insert(END, lst[i][j])


# take the data
lst = [(1001, 'Geeta Kumari', 'Chandigarh', 12078.88),
(1002, 'Vinod Teja', 'Hyderabad', 20000.50),
```

```
        (1003, 'Ravi Shankar', 'Bangalore', 14500.75),
        (1004, 'Lakshmi Prasanna', 'New Delhi', 9500.00),
        (1005, 'Nageswara Pillai', 'Chennai', 21786.40)]

# find the no. of rows and cols in the list
total_rows = len(lst)
total_cols = len(lst[0])

# create root window
root = Tk()
mt = MyTable(root)
root.mainloop()
```

Output:

1001	Geeta Kumari	Chandigarh	12078.88
1002	Vinod Teja	Hyderabad	20000.5
1003	Ravi Shankar	Bangalore	14500.75
1004	Lakshmi Prasanna	New Delhi	9500.0
1005	Nageswara Pillai	Chennai	21786.4

Points to Remember

- GUI (Graphical User Interface) is a method of user interaction with an application through images, pictures and menus.
- GUI is user-friendly and also useful to create attractive applications.
- The space that is initially allocated to every GUI program is called 'top level window' or 'root window'. We can reach to this window by creating an object to Tk() class.
- A Canvas is a container that is generally used to draw shapes like lines, curves, arcs and circles.
- A Frame is a container that is generally used to display widgets like buttons, check buttons or menus.
- Button, Label, Message, Text, Scrollbar, Checkbutton, Radiobutton, Entry, Spinbox, Listbox and Menu are important widgets in Python's tkinter.
- Generally, it is possible to specify the widgets height, width, font, foreground color and background color using options when the widget is created. The active foreground and active background options represent the foreground color and background color when the mouse is placed over the widget.
- An event represents user interaction with a widget. For example, clicking the mouse button or pressing a key on the keyboard is known as event.
- A callback handler or event handler is a function that is called when an event is generated by the user.

- The bind() method is used to bind an event with an even handler function.
- Pack, Grid and Place layout managers are used to arrange widgets in the frame in a particular manner.
- A button widget represents a push button which performs an action when the user clicks on it.
- A label represents constant text that may span one or more lines. The text in the label is only for the purpose of viewing and not for modifying.
- A message displays multiple lines of text that cannot be modified.
- A text widget is the same as message widget that can display multiple lines of text with more options to insert, delete or modify text.
- A scroll bar is a widget that is generally attached to another widget for scrolling the text.
- Check buttons, also known as check boxes, are square-shaped buttons that are useful to select one or more options from the available groups of options.
- Radio buttons are round-shaped buttons and are useful to select only one option from a group of available options.
- Entry widget is useful to create a rectangular box that can be used to display or enter one line of text.
- A spin box is a long rectangle that allows the user to select values from a given set of values. The values may be a range of numbers or a fixed set of strings.
- A list box is useful to display a list of items in a box so that the user can select 1 or more items.
- A menu represents a group of items or options for the user to select from.
- Menu and menu items are created as Menu class objects. The menu is added to menu bar using add_cascade() method and menu items are added to menu using add_command() methods.

CHAPTER 23

NETWORKING IN PYTHON

Interconnection of computers is called a network. A simple network can be formed by connecting two computers using a cable. Thus, a network can have two computers or two thousand computers. For example, Internet is the largest network on the earth where millions of computers are connected.

The main advantage of a network is sharing the resources. The data and files available in a computer can be shared with other computers in the network. For example, the bank customers' information can be shared among all branches of the bank existing in a country. It is also possible to share the hardware in the network. For example, the CPU of a computer in the network can be used by other computers to process and return the results. Similarly, there is no need of having individual printer for each computer in the network. All computers can share a single printer in such a way that the user can sit on any computer and give 'print' command to the printer.

In a network, some computers receive data or services from other computers. The computers that receive services are called 'client' machines. Other computers which provide their services in the network are called 'server' machines. For example, a computer requesting a file from another computer in the network is called a 'client' and the other computer sending the file is called a 'server'. Let's understand that both the 'client' and 'server' machines need software to receive or send the data. It means we need a program at client side and another program at server side whose role is to establish communication between those computers. It is also possible that a client sometimes acts as a server and a server acts as a client.

There are three requirements to establish a network:

- **Hardware:** Includes the computers, cables, modems, routers, hubs, etc.
- **Software:** Includes programs to communicate between servers and clients.
- **Protocol:** Represents a way to establish connection and helps in sending and receiving data in a standard format.

Let's now discuss Protocol in some detail.

Protocol

A protocol represents a set of rules to be followed by every computer on the network. Protocol is useful to physically move data from one place to another place on a network. While sending data or receiving data, the computers in the network should follow some rules. For example, if a computer wants to send a file on a network, it is not possible to send the entire file in a single step. The file should be broken into small pieces and then only they can be sent to other computer. The following are the two types of protocol models based on which other protocols are developed.

- TCP/IP Protocol
- UDP

TCP/IP Protocol

TCP (Transmission Control Protocol) / IP (Internet Protocol) is the standard protocol model used on any network, including Internet.

TCP/IP model has got the following five layers:

- Application layer
- TCP
- IP
- Data link layer
- Physical layer

Application layer is the topmost layer of the TCP/IP model that directly interacts with an application (or data). This layer receives data from the application and formats the data. Then it sends that data to the next layer called TCP in the form of continuous stream of bytes. The TCP, upon receiving the data from the Application layer, will divide it into small segments called 'packets'. A packet contains a group of bytes of data. These packets are then sent to the next IP layer. IP layer inserts the packets into envelopes called 'frames'. Each frame contains a packet, the IP address of destination computer, the IP address of source computer, and some additional bits useful in error detection and correction. These frames are then sent to Data link layer which dispatches them to correct destination computer on the network. The last layer, which is called the Physical layer, is used to physically transmit data on the network using the appropriate hardware. Consider Figure 23.1:

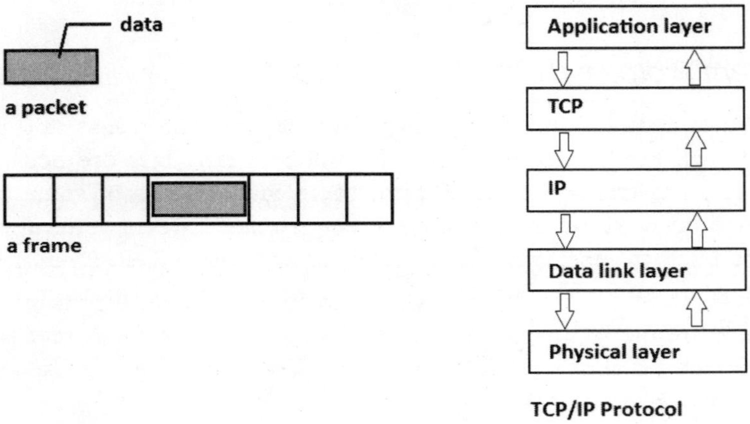

Figure 23.1: Packet, Frame and TCP/IP Protocol Layers

Of course, to send data from one place to another, first of all the computers should be correctly identified on the network. This is done with the help of IP addresses. An IP address is a unique identification number given to every computer on the network. It contains four integer numbers in the range of 0 to 255 and separated by a dot as:

```
216.58.194.197
```

This IP address may represent, for example a website on a server machine on Internet as:

```
www.gmail.com
```

Therefore, to open 'gmail.com' site, we can type the site address as 'www.gmail.com' or its IP address as '216.58.194.197'. But when we type the IP address in numeric form, that number is mapped to the website automatically. This mapping service is available on Internet, which is called 'DNS' (Domain Naming service or system). So, Domain Naming System (DNS) is a service on Internet that maps the IP addresses with corresponding website names. On Internet, IP addresses of 4 bytes are used and this version is called IP address version 4. The next new version of IP address is version 6, which uses 16 bytes to identify a computer.

TCP/IP takes care of number of bits sent and whether all the bits are received duly by the destination computer. So it is called 'connection oriented reliable protocol'. Every transmitted bit is accountable in this protocol. Hence, this protocol is highly suitable for transporting data reliably on a network. Almost all the protocols on Internet use TCP/IP model internally.

HTTP (Hyper Text Transfer Protocol) is the most widely used protocol on Internet, which is used to transfer web pages (.html files) from one computer to another computer on Internet. FTP (File Transfer Protocol) is useful to download or upload files from and to the server. SMTP (Simple Mail Transfer Protocol) is useful to send mails on network. POP (Post Office Protocol) is useful to receive mails into the mail boxes. NNTP (Network News Transfer Protocol) is used to transfer news articles on Internet.

User Datagram Protocol (UDP)

UDP is another protocol that transfers data in a connection less and unreliable manner. It will not check how many bits are sent or how many bits are actually received at the other side. During transmission of data, there may be loss of some bits. Also, the data sent may not be received in the same order. Hence UDP is generally not used to send text. UDP is used to send images, audio files, and video files. Even if some bits are lost, still the image or audio file can be composed with a slight variation that will not disturb the original image or audio.

Sockets

It is possible to establish a logical connecting point between a server and a client so that communication can be done through that point. This point is called 'socket'. Each socket is given an identification number, which is called 'port number'. Port number takes 2 bytes and can be from 0 to 65,535. Establishing communication between a server and a client using sockets is called 'socket programming'.

We should use a new port number for each new socket. Similarly, we should allot a new port number depending on the service provided on a socket. Every new service on the net should be assigned a new port number. Please have a look at some already allotted port numbers for the services shown in Table 23.1. The port numbers from 0 to 1023 are used by our computer system for various applications (or services) and hence we should avoid using these port numbers in our networking programs.

Table 23.1: Some Reserved Port Numbers and Associated Services

Port Number	Application or Service
13	Date and time services
21	FTP which transfers files
23	Telnet, which provides remote login
25	SMTP, which delivers mails
67	BOOTP, which provides configuration at boot time
80	HTTP, which transfers web pages

Port Number	Application or Service
109	POP2, which is a mailing service
110	POP3, which is a mailing service
119	NNTP, which is for transferring news articles
443	HTTPS, which transfers web pages securely

The point of the story is that a server on a network uses socket to connect to a client. When the server wants to communicate with several clients simultaneously, several sockets are needed. Every socket will have a different port number, as shown in Figure 23.2:

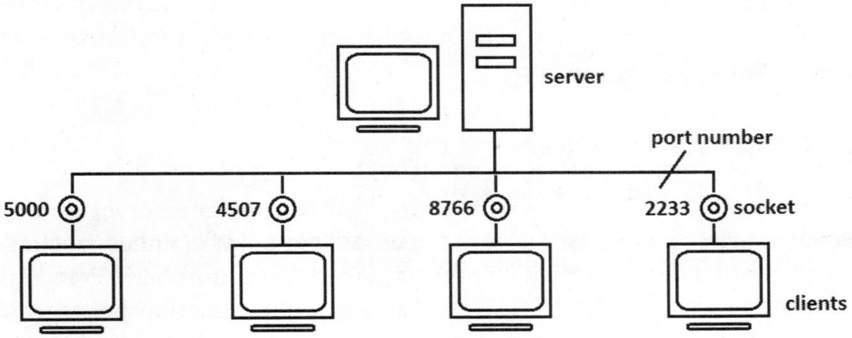

Figure 23.2: A Server Connected with Clients through Sockets

To create a socket, Python provides *socket* module. The socket() function of socket module is useful to create a socket object as:

```
s = socket.socket(address_family, type)
```

Here, the first argument 'address_family' indicates which version of the IP address should be used, whether IP address version 4 or version 6. This argument can take either of the following two values:

```
socket.AF_INET     # Internet protocol (IPv4) - this is default
socket.AF_INET6     # Internet protocol (IPv6)
```

The second argument is 'type' which represents the type of the protocol to be used, whether TCP/IP or UDP. This can assume one of the following two values:

```
socket.SOCK_STREAM    # for TCP - this is default
socket.SOCK_DGRAM    # for UDP
```

Knowing IP Address

To know the IP Address of a website on Internet, we can use gethostbyname() function available in socket module. This function takes the website name and returns its IP Address. For example,

```
addr = socket.gethostbyname('www.google.co.in')
```

will return the IP Address of google.co.in website into 'addr' variable. If there is no such website on Internet, then it returns 'gaierror' (Get Address Information Error).

Program

Program 1: A Python program to find the IP address of a website.

```
# knowing IP address of a website
import socket

# take the server name
host = 'www.google.co.in'

try:
    # know the ip address of the website
    addr = socket.gethostbyname(host)
    print('IP Address= '+ addr)

except socket.gaierror:    # if get address info error occurs
    print('The website does not exist')
```

Output:

```
C:\>python ip.py
IP Address= 216.58.221.35
```

URL

URL (Uniform Resource Locator) represents the address that is specified to access some information or resource on Internet. Look at the example URL:

http://www.dreamtechpress.com:80/index.html

The URL contains four parts:

- The protocol to use (http://).
- The server name or IP address of the server (www.dreamtechpress.com).
- The third part represents port number, which is optional (:80).
- The last part is the file that is referred. This would be generally index.html or home.html file (/index.html).

When a URL is given, we can parse the URL and find out all the parts of the URL with the help of urlparse() function of *urllib.parse* module in Python. We can pass the URL to urlparse() function, it returns a tuple containing the parts of the URL.

```
tpl = urllib.parse.urlparse('urlstring')
```

We can retrieve the individual parts of the URL from the tuple 'tpl' using the following attributes:

- scheme = this gives the protocol name used in the URL.
- netloc = gives the website name on the net with port number if present.
- path = gives the path of the web page.
- port = gives the port number.

We can also get the total URL from the tuple by calling geturl() function. These details are shown in Program 2.

Program

Program 2: A Python program to retrieve different parts of the URL and display them.

```
# to find different parts of a URL
import urllib.parse
# take any url
url = 'http://www.dreamtechpress.com:80/engineering/computer-science.html'

# get a tuple with parts of the url
tpl = urllib.parse.urlparse(url)

# display the contents of the tuple
print(tpl)

# display different parts of the url
print('Scheme= ',tpl.scheme)
print('Net location= ',tpl.netloc)
print('Path= ', tpl.path)
print('Parameters= ',tpl.params)
print('Port number= ',tpl.port)
print('Total url= ',tpl.geturl())
```

Output:

```
C:\>python urlparse.py
ParseResult(scheme='http', netloc='www.dreamtechpress.com:80',
     path='/engineering/computer-science.html', params='', query='',
     fragment='')
Scheme= http
Net location= www.dreamtechpress.com:80
Path= /engineering/computer-science.html
Parameters=
Port number= 80
Total url=http://www.dreamtechpress.com:80/engineering/computer-science.html
```

Reading the Source Code of a Web Page

If we know the URL of a Web page, it is possible to get the source code of the web page with the help of urlopen() function. This function belongs to *urllib.request* module. When we provide the URL of the web page, this function stores its source code into a file-like object and returns it as:

```
file = urllib.request.urlopen("https://www.python.org/")
```

Now, using read() method on 'file' object, we can read the data of that object. This is shown in Program 3. Please remember that while executing this program, we should have Internet connection switched on in our computer.

Program

Program 3: A Python program that reads the source code of a Web page.

```
# reading source code of a website page from Internet
import urllib.request

# store the url of the page into file object
file = urllib.request.urlopen("https://www.python.org/")

# read data from file and display
print(file.read())
```

Output:

```
C:\>python pageread.py
b'<!doctype html>\n<!--[if lt IE 7]><html class="no-js ie6 lt-ie7 lt-
ie8 lt-ie9"><![endif]-->\n<!--[if IE 7]><html class="no-js ie7 lt-ie8 lt-
ie9"><![endif]-->\n<!--[if IE 8]><html class="no-js ie8 lt-ie9"><![endif]--
>\n<!--[if gt IE 8]><!--><html class="no-js" lang="en" dir="ltr"><!--
<![endif]-->\n\n<head>\n    <meta charset="utf-8">\n    <meta http-equiv="X-
UA-Compatible" content="IE=edge">\n\n    <link rel="prefetch"
href="//ajax.googleapis.com/ajax/libs/jquery/1.8.2/jquery.min.js">\n\n
<meta name="application-name" content="Python.org">\n    <meta
name="msapplication-tooltip" content="The official home of the Python
Programming Language">\n    <meta name="apple-mobile-web-app-title"
content="Python.org">\n    <meta name="apple-mobile-web-app-capable"
content="yes">\n    <meta name="apple-mobile-web-app-status-bar-style"
content="black">\n\n    <meta name="viewport" content="width=device-width,
initial-scale=1.0">\n    <meta name="HandheldFriendly" content="True">\n
<meta name="format-detection" content="telephone=no">\n    <meta http-
equiv="cleartype" content="on">\n    <meta http-equiv="imagetoolbar"
content="false">\n\n    <script
src="/static/js/libs/modernizr.js"></script>\n\n    <link
href="/static/stylesheets/style.css" rel="stylesheet" type="text/css"
title="default" />\n    <link href="/static/stylesheets/mq.css"
rel="stylesheet" type="text/css" media="not print, braille, embossed, speech,
tty" />\n    \n\n    <!--[if (lte IE 8)&(!IEMobile)]>\n    <link
href="/static/stylesheets/no-mq.css" rel="stylesheet" type="text/css"
media="screen" />\n    \n    \n    <![endif]-->\n\n    \n    <link rel="icon"
type="image/x-icon" href="/static/favicon.ico">\n    <link rel="apple-touch-
icon-precomposed" sizes="144x144" href="/static/apple-touch-icon-144x144-
precomposed.png">\n    <link rel="apple-touch-icon-precomposed"
sizes="114x114" href="/static/apple-touch-icon-114x114-precomposed.png">\n
<link rel="apple-touch-icon-precomposed" sizes="72x72" href="/static/apple-
```

```
touch-icon-72x72-precomposed.png">\n    <link rel="apple-touch-icon-
precomposed" href="/static/apple-touch-icon-precomposed.png">\n    <link
rel="apple-touch-icon" href="/static/apple-touch-icon-precomposed.png">\n\n
\n    <meta name="msapplication-TileImage" content="/static/metro-icon-
144x144-precomposed.png"><!-- white shape -->\n    <meta name="msapplication-
TileColor" content="#3673a5"><!-- python blue -->\n    <meta
name="msapplication-navbutton-color" content="#3673a5">\n\n    <title>Welcome
to Python.org</title>\n\n
      :
      :
```

Downloading a Web Page from Internet

It is also possible to download the entire web page from Internet and save it into our computer system. Of course, the images of the web page may not be downloaded. To download the web page, we should have Internet connection switched on in our computer.

First we should open the web page using the urlopen() function. This function returns the content of the web page into a file like object. Now, we can read from this object using read() method as:

```
file = urllib.request.urlopen("https://www.python.org/")
content = file.read()
```

The urlopen() function can raise 'urllib.error.HTTPError' if the web page is not found. The next step is to open a file and write the 'content' data into that file. Since web pages contain binary data, to store the web pages, we have to open the file in binary write mode as:

```
f = open('myfile.html', 'wb')  # we want to write data into myfile.html
f.write(content)   # write it
```

Program

Program 4: A Python program to download a Web page from Internet and save it into our computer.

```
# reading a website page from Internet and saving it in our system
import urllib.request

try:
    # store the url of the page into file object
    file = urllib.request.urlopen("https://www.python.org/")

    # read data from file and store into content object
    content = file.read()

except urllib.error.HTTPError:
    print('The web page does not exist')
    exit()
```

```
# open a file for writing
f = open('myfile.html', 'wb')

# write content into the file
f.write(content)

# close the file
f.close()
```

Output:

```
C:\>python pageread1.py
```

The previous command will generate the myfile.html in your current directory. Now, go to the current directory to see myfile.html file that appears as shown in Figure 23.3:

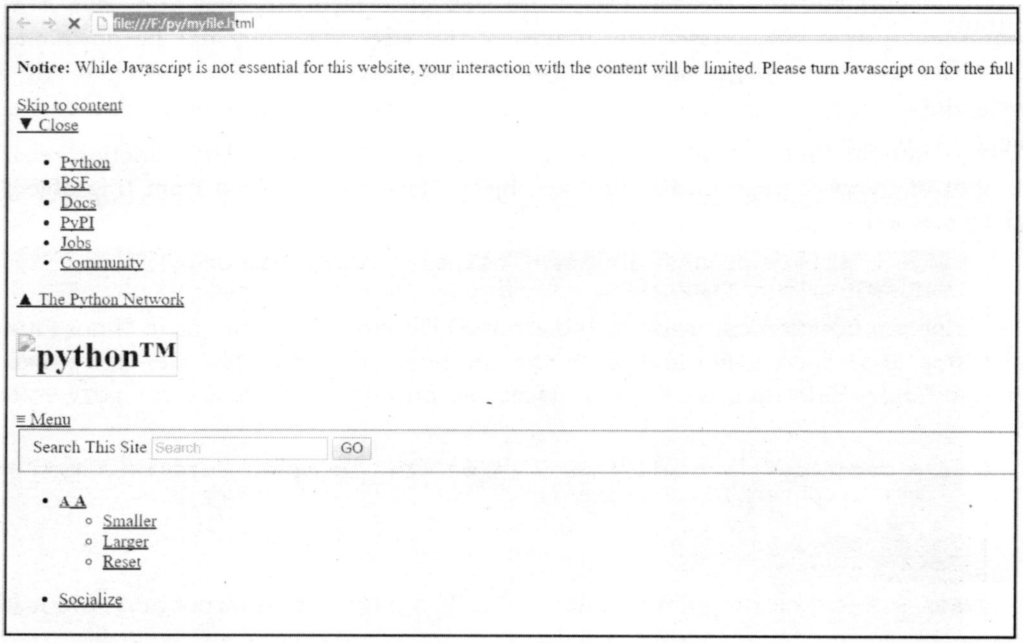

Figure 23.3: Output of Program 4

Downloading an Image from Internet

We can connect our computer to Internet and download images like .jpg, .gif or .png files from Internet into our computer system by writing a simple Python program. For this purpose, we can use urlretrieve() function of *urllib.request* module. This function takes the URL of the image file and our own image file name as arguments.

```
download = urllib.request.urlretrieve(url, "myimage.jpg")
```

Here, 'download' is a tuple object. 'url' represents the URL string of the image location on Internet. "myimage.jpg" is the name of the file on which the image will be downloaded.

Program

Program 5: A Python program to download an image from the Internet into our computer system.

```
# downloading an image from Internet
import urllib.request

# copy the image url
url = "http://stuffpoint.com/nature/image/43322-nature-sandy-
    wallpaper.jpg"

# download the image as myimage.jpg in current directory
download = urllib.request.urlretrieve(url, "myimage.jpg")
```

Output:

```
C:\>python imageread.py
```

Go to the current directory to find myimage.jpg file and if you open it, you can see the image as shown in Figure 23.4:

Figure 23.4: Output of Program 5

A TCP/IP Server

A server is a program that provides services to other computers on the network or Internet. Similarly a client is a program that receives services from the servers. When a server wants to communicate with a client, there is a need of a socket. A socket is a point of connection between the server and client. The following are the general steps to be used at server side:

1. Create a TCP/IP socket at server side using socket() function.

```
s = socket.socket(socket.AF_INET, socket.SOCK_STREAM)
```

   Here, socket.AF_INET represents IP Address version 4 and socket.SOCK_STREAM indicates that we are using TCP/IP protocol for communication with client. Anyhow, a socket uses IP address version 4 and TCP/IP protocol by default. Hence, we can create a socket without giving protocol version and type of the protocol as:

```
s = socket.socket()    # this uses TCP/IP protocol by default
```

2. Bind the socket with host name and port number using bind() method. Here, host name can be an IP Address or a web site name. If we want to run this program in an individual computer that is not connected in any network, then we can take hose name as 'localhost'. This represents that the server is running in the local system and not on any network. The IP Address of the 'localhost' is 127.0.0.1. As an alternative to 'localhost', we can also mention this IP Address. bind() method is used in the following format:

```
s.bind((host, port))    # here, (host, port) is a tuple.
```

3. We can specify maximum number of connections using listen() method as:

```
s.listen(5);    # maximum connections allowed are 5
```

4. The server should wait till a client accepts connection. This is done using accept() method as:

```
c, addr = s.accept()    # this method returns c and addr
```

   Here, 'c' is connection object that can be used to send messages to the client. 'addr' is the address of the client that has accepted the connection.

5. Finally, using send() method, we can send message strings to client. The message strings should be sent in the form of byte streams as they are used by the TCP/IP protocol.

```
c.send(b"message string")
```

   Observe the 'b' prefixed before the message string. This indicates that the string is a binary string. The other way to convert a string into binary format is using encode() method, as:

```
string.encode()
```

6. After sending the messages to the client, the server can be disconnected by closing the connection object as:

```
c.close()
```

Program

Program 6: A Python program to create a TCP/IP server program that sends messages to a client.

```
# a TCP/IP server that sends messages to client
import socket

# take the server name and port number
host = 'localhost'
port = 5000

# create a socket at server side using TCP/IP protocol
s = socket.socket(socket.AF_INET, socket.SOCK_STREAM)

# bind the socket with server and port number
s.bind((host, port))

# allow maximum 1 connection to the socket
s.listen(1)

# wait till a client accepts connection
c, addr = s.accept()

# display client address
print("Connection from: ", str(addr))

# send messages to the client after encoding into binary string
c.send(b"Hello client, how are U")
msg = "Bye!"
c.send(msg.encode())

# disconnect the server
c.close()
```

Save this program as Server1.py. Let's not run this server program now. We will run it after developing the client program since the server needs a client that receives data.

A TCP/IP Client

A client is a program that receives the data or services from the server. We use the following general steps in the client program:

1. At the client side, we should first create the socket object that uses TCP/IP protocol to receive data. This is done as:

```
s = socket.socket(socket.AF_INET, socket.SOCK_STREAM)
```

2. Connect the socket to the server and port number using connect() method.

```
s.connect((host, port))
```

3. To receive the messages from the server, we can use recv() method as:

```
msg = s.recv(1024)
```

Here, 1024 indicates the buffer size. This is the memory used while receiving the data. It means, at a time, 1024 bytes of data can be received from the server. We can change this limit in multiples of 1024. For example, we can use 2048 or 3072 etc. The received strings will be in binary format. Hence they can be converted into normal strings using decode() method.

4. Finally, we should disconnect the client by calling close() method on the socket object as:

```
s.close()
```

Program

Program 7: A Python program to create TCP/IP client program that receives messages from the server.

```
# a TCP/IP client that receives messages from server
import socket

# take the server name and port number
host = 'localhost'
port = 5000

# create a client side socket using TCP/IP protocol
s = socket.socket(socket.AF_INET, socket.SOCK_STREAM)

# connect it to server and port number
s.connect((host, port))

# receive message string from server, at a time 1024 B
msg = s.recv(1024)

# repeat as long as message strings are not empty
while msg:
    print('Received: '+ msg.decode())
    msg = s.recv(1024)

# disconnect the client
s.close()
```

Save the above program as Client1.py. The Programs 6 and 7 should be opened in two separate DOS windows and then executed. First we run the Server1.py program in the left side DOS window and then we run the Client1.py program in the right side DOS window. We can see the client's IPAddress and the port number being displayed at the server side window. The messages sent by the server are displayed at the client side window, as shown in the output.

Output:

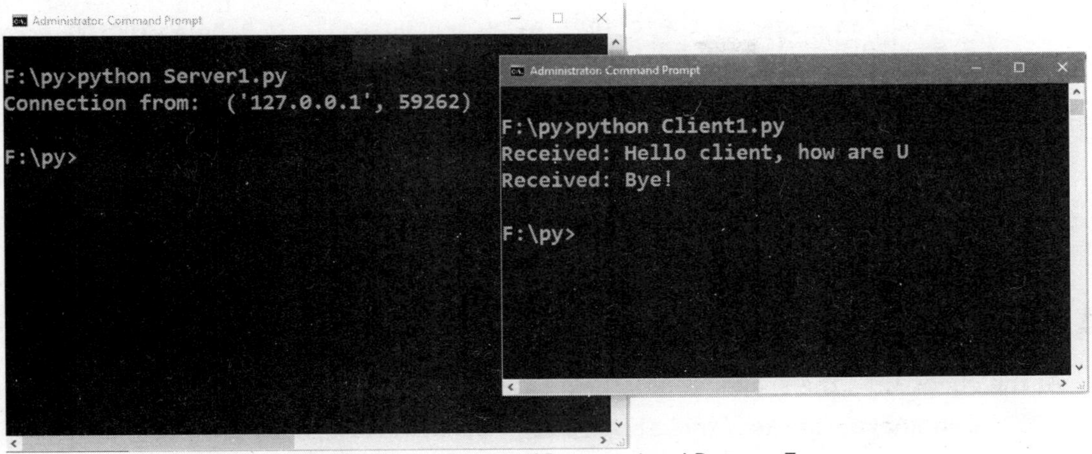

Figure 23.5: Output of Program 6 and Program 7

A UDP Server

If we want to create a server that uses UDP protocol to send messages, we have to specify socket.SOCK_DGRAM while creating the socket object, as:

```
s = socket.socket(socket.AF_INET, socket.SOCK_DGRAM)
```

It means the server will send data in the form of packets called 'datagrams'. Now, using sendto() function, the server can send data to the client. Since UDP is a connection-less protocol, server does not know where the data should be sent. Hence we have to specify the client address in sendto() function, as:

```
s.sendto("message string", (host,port))
```

Here, the "message string" is the binary string to be sent. The tuple (host, port) represents the host name and port number of the client.

In Program 8, we are creating a server to send data to the client. The server will wait for 5 seconds after running it, and then it sends two messages to the client.

Program

Program 8: A Python program to create a UDP server that sends messages to the client.

```
# a UDP server that sends messages to client
import socket
import time

# take the server name and port number
host = 'localhost'
port = 5000

# create a socket at server side to use UDP protocol
s = socket.socket(socket.AF_INET, socket.SOCK_DGRAM)
```

```
# let the server waits for 5 seconds
time.sleep(5)

# send messages to the client after encoding into binary string
s.sendto(b"Hello client, how are U", (host, port))
msg = "Bye!"
s.sendto(msg.encode(), (host,port))

# disconnect the server
s.close()
```

Save this program as Server2.py. We will run this program only after the client program is also ready.

A UDP Client

At the client side, the socket should be created to use UDP protocol as:

```
s = socket.socket(socket.AF_INET, socket.SOCK_DGRAM)
```

The socket should be bound to the server using bind() method as:

```
s.bind((host, port))
```

Now, the client can receive messages with the help of recvfrom() method as:

```
msg, addr = s.recvfrom(1024)
```

This method receives 1024 bytes at a time from the server which is called buffer size. This method returns the received message into 'msg' and the address of the server into 'addr'. Since the client does not know how many messages (i.e. strings) the server sends, we can use recvfrom() method inside a while loop and receive all the messages as:

```
while msg:
    print('Received: '+ msg.decode())
    msg, addr = s.recvfrom(1024)
```

But the problem here is that the client will hang when the server disconnects. To rectify this problem, we have to set some time for the socket so that the client will automatically disconnect after that time elapses. This is done using settimeout() method.

```
s.settimeout(5)
```

This method instructs the socket to block when 5 seconds time is elapsed. Hence if the server disconnects, the client will wait for another 5 seconds time and disconnects. The settimeout() method can raise socket.timeout exception.

Program

Program 9: A Python program to create a UDP client that receives messages from the server.

```
# a UDP client that receives messages from server
import socket

# take the server name and port number
host = 'localhost'
port = 5000
```

```
# create a client side socket that uses UDP protocol
s = socket.socket(socket.AF_INET, socket.SOCK_DGRAM)

# connect it to server with host name and port number
s.bind((host, port))

# receive message string from server, at a time 1024 B
msg, addr = s.recvfrom(1024)

try:
    # let the socket blocks after 5 seconds if the server disconnects
    s.settimeout(5)

    # repeat as long as message strings are not empty
    while msg:
        print('Received: '+ msg.decode())
        msg, addr = s.recvfrom(1024)

except socket.timeout:
    print('Time is over and hence terminating...')

# disconnect the client
s.close()
```

Save this program as Client2.py. Now, run the Client2.py program in a DOS window and the Server2.py program in another DOS window. It is better to run the Client2.py program first so that it will wait for the server. Then run the Server2.py program. This program will send two strings to the client after 5 seconds from the time of its execution. The client receives them. Once the server is disconnected, the client will wait for another 5 seconds and then terminates, as shown in the output.

Output:

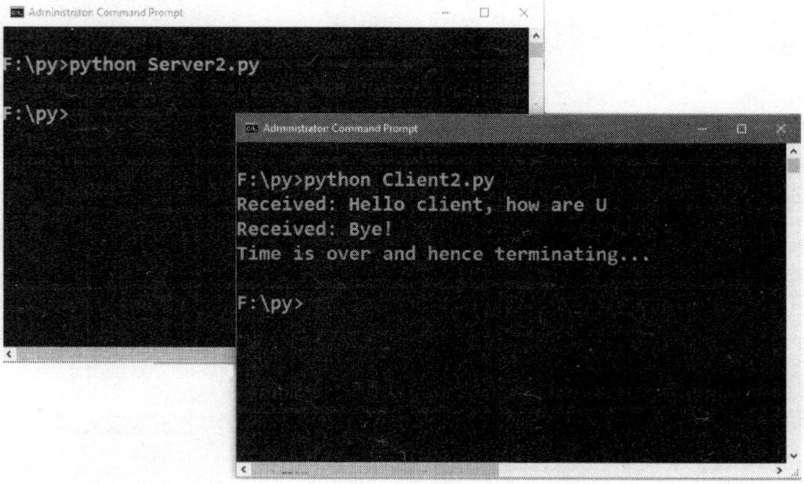

Figure 23.6: Output of Program 8 and Program 9

Remove the settimeout() method from Client2.py program and re-run both the client and server. You can observe that the client hangs and it will never terminate.

File Server

A file server is a server program that accepts a file name from a client, searches for the file on the hard disk and sends the content of the file to the client. When the requested file is not found at server side, the server sends a message to the client saying 'File does not exist'. We can create a file server using TCP/IP type of socket connection.

Program

Program 10: A Python program to create a file server that receives a file name from a client and sends the contents of the file.

```
# a server that sends file contents to client
import socket

# take server name and port number
host = 'localhost'
port = 6767
# create a TCP socket
s = socket.socket()

# bind socket to host and port number
s.bind((host, port))

# maximum 1 connection is accepted
s.listen(1)

# wait till client accepts a connection
c, addr = s.accept()
print('A client accepted connection')

# accept file name from client
fname = c.recv(1024)

# convert file name into a normal string
fname = str(fname.decode())
print("File name received from client: "+fname)
try:
    # open the file at server side
    f = open(fname, 'rb')

    # read content of the file
    content = f.read()

    # send file content to client
    c.send(content)
    print('File content sent to client')

    # close the file
    f.close()
```

```
except FileNotFoundError:
    c.send(b'File does not exist')

# disconnect server
c.close()
```

Save this program as Fileserver.py and wait till we develop the client program also.

File Client

A file client is a client side program that sends a request to the server to search for a file and send the file contents. We have to type the file name from the key board at the file client. This file name is sent to the file server and the file contents are received by the client in turn. We can create a file client program using TCP/IP type of socket connection.

Program

Program 11: A Python program to create a file client program that sends a file name to the server and receives the file contents.

```
# a client that sends and receives data
import socket

# take server name and port number
host = 'localhost'
port = 6767

# create a TCP socket
s = socket.socket()

# connect to server
s.connect((host, port))

# type file name from the keyboard
filename = input("Enter filename: ")

# send the file name to the server
s.send(filename.encode())

# receive file content from server
content = s.recv(1024)
print(content.decode())

# disconnect the client
s.close()
```

Save this program as Fileclient.py. Now run the Fileserver.py and Fileclient.py programs in separate DOS windows. Enter file name in the Fileclient.py program and you can see the file contents displayed at the client, as shown in the output.

Output:

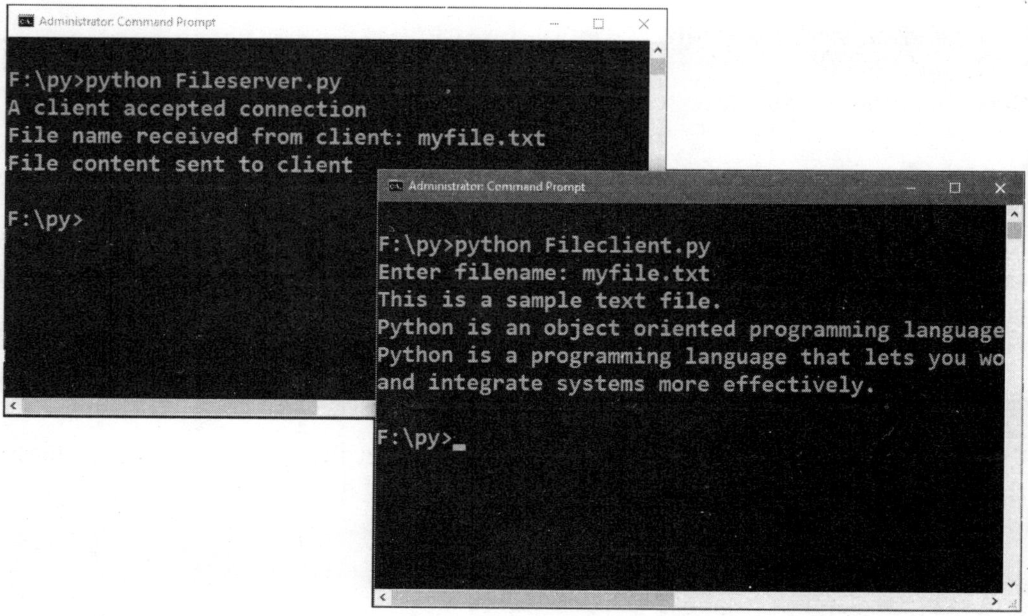

Figure 23.7: Output of Program 10 and Program 11

Two-Way Communication between Server and Client

It is possible to send data from client to the server and make the server respond to the client's request. After receiving the response from server, the client can again ask for some information from the server. In this way both the server and client can establish two-way communication with each other. It means sending and receiving data will be done by both the server and client. The following programs will give you an idea of how to achieve this type of communication. These programs are at very fundamental level and need refinement. When refined, we can get programs for server and client which can take part in real chatting.

Program

Program 12: A Python program to create a basic chat server program in Python.

```
# a server that receives and sends messages - save this as chatserver.py
import socket
host = '127.0.0.1'
port = 9000

# create server side socket
s = socket.socket()
s.bind((host, port))
```

```
# let maximum number of connections are 1 only
s.listen(1)

# wait till a client connects
c, addr = s.accept()
print("A client connected")

# server runs continuously
while True:
    # receive data from client
    data = c.recv(1024)

    # if client sends empty string, come out
    if not data:
        break
    print("From client: "+str(data.decode()))

    # enter response data from server
    data1 = input("Enter response: ")

    # send that data to client
    c.send(data1.encode())

# close connection
c.close()
```

Program

Program 13: Creating a basic chat client program in Python.

```
# a client that sends and receives messages - save this code as
# chatclient.py
import socket
host = '127.0.0.1'
port = 9000

# create client side socket
s = socket.socket()
s.connect((host, port))

# enter data at client
str = input("Enter data: ")

# continue as long as exit not entered by user
while str != 'exit':
    # send data from client to server
    s.send(str.encode())

    # receive the response data from server
    data = s.recv(1024)
    data = data.decode()
    print("From server: "+data)

    # enter data
    str = input("Enter data: ")

# close connection
s.close()
```

Now run the chatserver.py and chatclient.py programs in separate DOS windows. Start entering data first in the chatclient. This data is received by the chatserver. Then enter response at the chatserver which will be sent to chatclient as shown in the output.

Output:

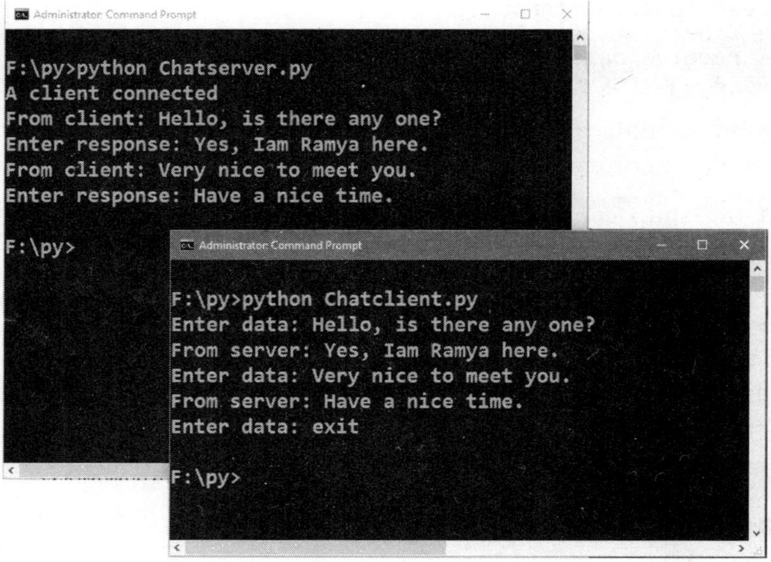

Figure 23.8: Output of Program 12 and Program 13

Sending a Simple Mail

It is possible to develop a Python program that can send a mail to any email address from any email address. For this purpose, we need SMTP class of *smtplib* module. When we create an object of SMTP class, we actually connect to smtp (simple mail transfer protocol) server that is useful to send the mail. For example to connect to gmail.com server we can write:

```
server = smtplib.SMTP('smtp.gmail.com', 587)
```

Here, we want to connect to gmail.com website using its port number 587. If we want to connect to any other mail server, we are supposed to provide that server name along with its port number. Once we connect to mail server, we can send the mail using send_message() method as:

```
server.send_message(msg)
```

Here, 'msg' represents the total message string including the address to which the mail should be sent, address from where the mail is sent, subject of the mail and body of the mail. This 'msg' is represented as an object of MIMEText class which belongs to *email.mime.text* module. The word 'MIME' (Multi-Purpose Internet Mail Extensions) indicates an extension of the original Internet e-mail protocol that lets people use the protocol to exchange different kinds of data on the Internet. Now, let's see how to create the 'msg' object:

```
msg = MIMEText(body)   # here, body indicates mail body text
```

Once the 'msg' is created, we can fill in the details like from address, to address and subject as:

```
msg['From'] = fromaddr
msg['To'] = toaddr
msg['Subject'] = "SUBJECT LINE OF OUR MESSAGE"
```

Of course, before sending the email, we have to log into the server with a valid password. This is done in two steps as shown below:

1. First put the smtp connection into TLS (Transport Layer Security) mode. This will start the process of verifying authenticity of the sender.

```
server.starttls()
```

2. Next, we have to login to the server with our mail address and pass word. This is done using login() method as:

```
server.login(fromaddr, "password")
```

All these steps are shown in Program 14 in a proper sequence. Just follow each step one by one and you will be able to send the mail easily.

Program

Program 14: A Python program to create a Python program to send email to any mail address.

```
# sending email using a Python program
import smtplib
from email.mime.text import MIMEText

# first type the body text for our mail
body = '''This is my text mail. This is sent to you from my Python
      program. I think you appreciated me.'''

# create MIMEText class object with body text
msg = MIMEText(body)

# from which address the mail is sent
fromaddr = "nagesh.faculty@gmail.com"

# to which address the mail is sent
toaddr = "nageswara.r@rediffmail.com"

# store the addresses into msg object
msg['From'] = fromaddr
msg['To'] = toaddr
msg['Subject'] = "HAI FRIEND"

# connect to gmail.com server using 587 port number
server = smtplib.SMTP('smtp.gmail.com', 587)

# put the smtp connection in TLS mode.
server.starttls()
```

```
    # login to the server with your correct password
    server.login(fromaddr, "mypassword")

    # send the message to the server
    server.send_message(msg)
    print('Mail sent...')

    # close connection with server
    server.quit()
```

Output:

```
C:\>python mail.py
Mail sent...
```

While running this program, our computer should have been connected to the Internet. This program is sending the mail through gmail.com server. Now-a-days, the gmail.com server people are using more security levels and hence this program may show an error like 'SMTPAuthenticationError' which means that the gmail.com server does not allow this program to communicate. In that case, we have to inform the gmail.com server to allow "less secure apps" also. You can do this by logging into your Gmail account and then visiting the following page:

```
https://www.google.com/settings/security/lesssecureapps
```

In this page, we should click on 'Turn on' option against 'Access for less secure apps'. Then the less secure applications like our Program 14 are allowed by gmail.com server. Then we can run this program successfully. A caution is to 'Turn off' the 'Access for less secure apps' option after execution of this program is over. You can verify in the rediffmail.com's inbox that the mail sent by our program reached nageswara.r@rediffmail.com:

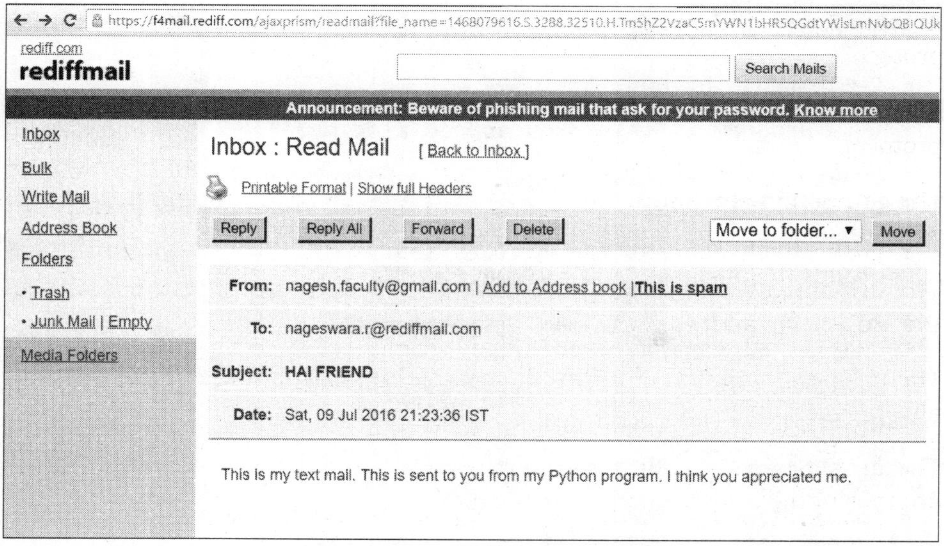

Figure 23.9: Output of Program 14

Points to Remember

- Interconnection of computers is called a network.
- The main advantage of a network is sharing the resources like data, files, software and hardware.
- The computers which receive data from a network are called clients and the computers which provide services are called servers.
- A protocol represents a set of rules to be followed by every computer on the network. The two protocol models are TCP/IP and UDP. All other protocols are developed based on these two protocols.
- TCP/IP is a connection oriented protocol that transmits data reliably.
- UDP is a connection less protocol and may not transmit data reliably.
- An IP address is a unique identification number given to every computer on the network. It contains four integer numbers in the range of 0 to 255 and separated by a dot.
- A socket is a logical point of connection between a server and a client. Data is transmitted through sockets only.
- Every socket is identified with a unique number, called port number.
- Port number is a 2 byte number and ranges from 0 to 65535.
- A socket with the constant socket.SOCK_STREAM is created to work with TCP/IP protocol.
- A socket with the constant socket.SOCK_DGRAMis created to transmit data on UDP protocol.
- The gethostbyname() function of socket module is useful to find the IP Address of any website.
- The urlparse() function of urllib.parse module is useful to retrieve different parts of the URL.
- The urlopen() function of urllib.request module is useful to retrieve the source code of a web page.
- The urlretrieve() function of urllib.request module is useful to copy an image file with another name into our computer system.

- The messages are transmitted between the server and client in the form of binary strings.

- The encode() method converts a normal string into binary string and decode() method converts a byte stream into a normal string.

- SMTP class of smtplib module and MIMEText class of email.mime.text module are provided in Python to send emails on Internet.

PYTHON'S DATABASE CONNECTIVITY

CHAPTER 24

Data is very important for any organization to continue its operations. The data may be related to employees in the organization or the operational data like product information, raw material prices, sales information, profits and losses. Without data, no organization will survive. Hence, data is very important and it should never be lost.

DBMS

To store data, we can use a file or a database. A file stores data in the secondary storage device, like hard disk, either in text format or binary format.

A database represents collection of data. Just like a file, we can store data into a database. Once the data is stored in a database, we need to perform some operations on data, for example, modifying the existing data, deleting the unwanted data, or retrieving the data from the database, etc. To perform such operations, a database comes with a software. This is called a database management system (DBMS). Hence, we can say:

```
DBMS = database + software to manage the data
```

Examples for DBMS are MySQL, Oracle, Sybase, SQL Server, etc. The question that arises in our mind may be this: when we have files to handle data, why we need a DBMS? The following section throws light on the benefits of using a DBMS.

Advantages of a DBMS over Files

- If we go for files, we have to write a lot of programming. For example, to store data into a file, we have to write a program; to retrieve data, we need another program; and to modify data, we should write yet another program. A lot of programmer's time is consumed in developing these programs. If we use DBMS, we can achieve all these tasks without writing any programs. We can store data, retrieve it, modify or delete it by giving simple commands. These commands are written in a language called SQL (Structured Query Language). Thus, a programmer's duty is simplified.

- Generally, each file contains data that is not related to another file's data. When there is no relationship between the files, it would be difficult to fulfill the information needs of the user. The user may wish to see the information that has some relationship and that is stored in various files. Accessing such data is difficult for the programmers. In DBMS, various pieces of data can be related and retrieved easily using keys concept.
- Files are not so efficient in handling large volumes of data. It would be a difficult task to enter large data into a file or retrieving it from the file. But, DBMS can handle large volumes of data efficiently and easily.
- When multiple users are accessing the data concurrently from the same file, there are chances of wrong results or inconsistent changes to the existing data. DBMS will take care of such problems.
- Once the changes are made to the file, we cannot roll them back. In case of DBMS, we can restore the previous state of data by rolling back the changes.
- Files offer very weak security for data; whereas, DBMS offers very good protection for the data.

Types of Databases Used with Python

When data is stored in a database like MySQL or Oracle, we can retrieve the data using a Python program and process it in order to display the desired reports. It means our Python programs can connect to various databases. Some of the important databases which can be connected through Python are MySQL, Oracle, Microsoft SQL Server, Sybase, Informix, Firebird (and Interbase), IBM DB2, Ingres, PostgreSQL, SAP DB (also known as MaxDB) and Microsoft Access.

To work with any database, please remember that we should have that database already installed in our computer system. To connect to that database, we need a driver or connector program that connects the database with Python programs. Then only we can develop Python programs to connect to the database.

In this chapter, we will focus on two most important databases: MySQL and Oracle, and how to work with these databases in Python. First, we will see how to install MySQL database software, its corresponding connector and then how to work with MySQL through Python.

Installation of MySQL Database Software

MySQL is an open source database software that is used by many top development companies to store and retrieve data. MySQL can manage several databases at a time. The data in a database is stored in the form of tables. A table contains several rows and columns of data. For example, we can store employee data like employee identification number, employee name, gender, salary, etc. details in the form of a table. Once the data is stored in MySQL, it is possible to retrieve that data, process it and display the reports using Python programs.

Since we want to work with MySQL database in Python language, first of all we should have MySQL software installed on our computer system. The following steps will be helpful to you to install a copy of MySQL if you do not have one in your computer.

1. Open the mysql.com website using the following URL: https://dev.mysql.com/downloads/windows/installer/

   This is shown in Figure 24.1:

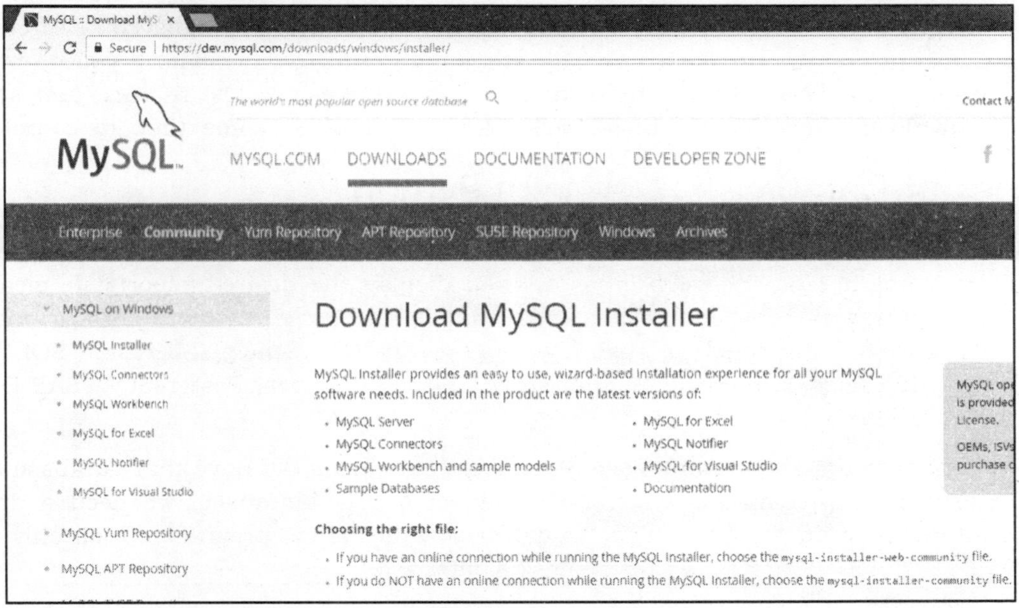

Figure 24.1: Downloading MySQL Database Software

2. Scroll the Web page till the end. At the bottom of the page, we can see 'Windows (x86, 32-bit), MSI Installer' (mysql-installer-community-5.7.20.0.msi) option, which is approximately 380 MB file. At the right hand side, we can see the 'Download' button (Figure 24.2).

3. Click the Download button, as shown in Figure 24.2:

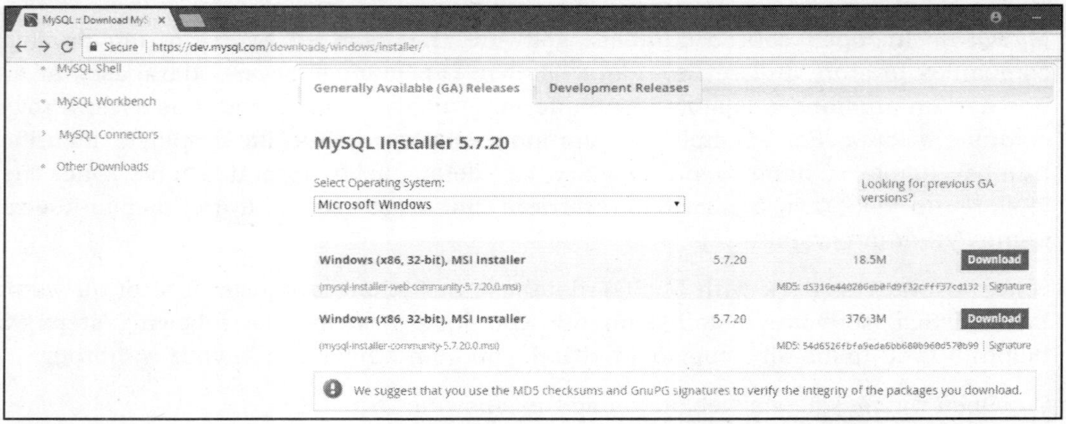

Figure 24.2: Downloading Windows MSI Installer

4. After clicking the 'Download' button, we can see another page with a heading:

   'Begin Your Download - mysql-installer-community-5.7.20.0.msi'. You can create an account or you can use an already existing account to download. If you do not want to create a new account, then we can click on the link: 'No thanks, just start my download'. Now the download will start and it takes some time to complete the download.

5. Double click the downloaded file to see the dialog box, as shown in Figure 24.3:

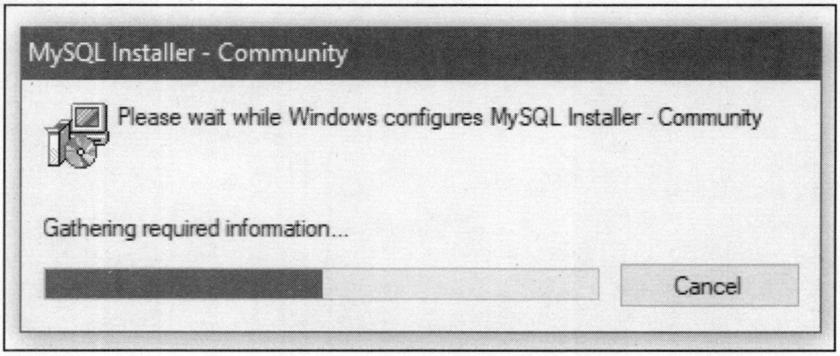

Figure 24.3: Running the MySQL Installer File

It will display MySQL installer dialog box (Figure 24.4).

6. Accept the license terms and click the 'Next' button, as shown in Figure 24.4:

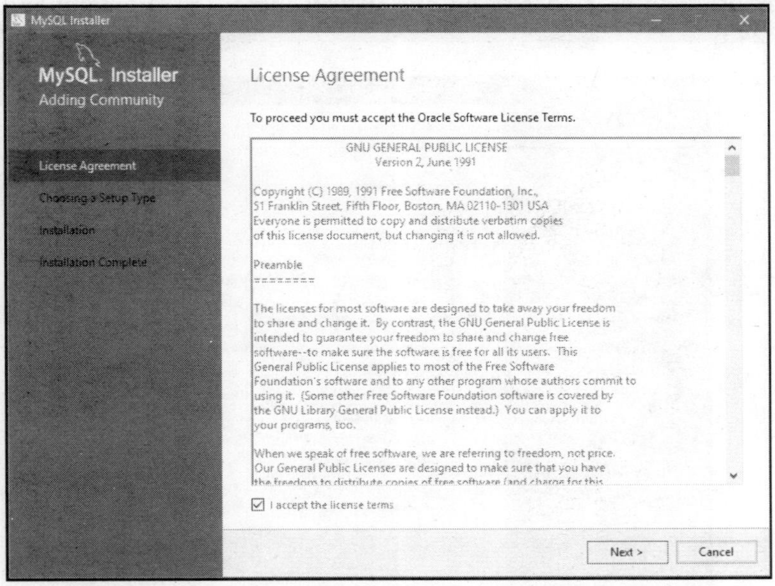

Figure 24.4: The MySQL Installer License Agreement Screen

The Choosing a Setup Type appears (Figure 24.5).

7. Select the 'Developer Default' radio button and then click the 'Next' button, as shown in Figure 24.5:

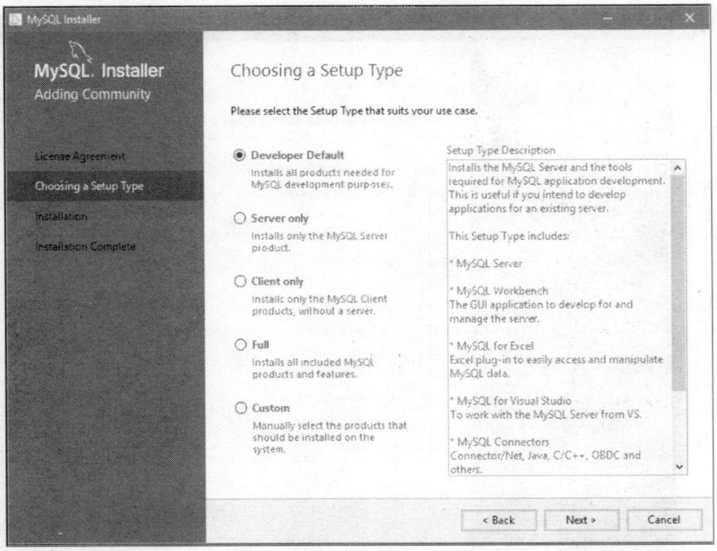

Figure 24.5: Selecting the Setup Type for MySQL Installation

The Installation screen appears (Figure 24.6).

8. Click the 'Execute' button in the 'Installation' dialog box. The installation of components gets started one by one. It will install all the components, as shown in Figure 24.6:

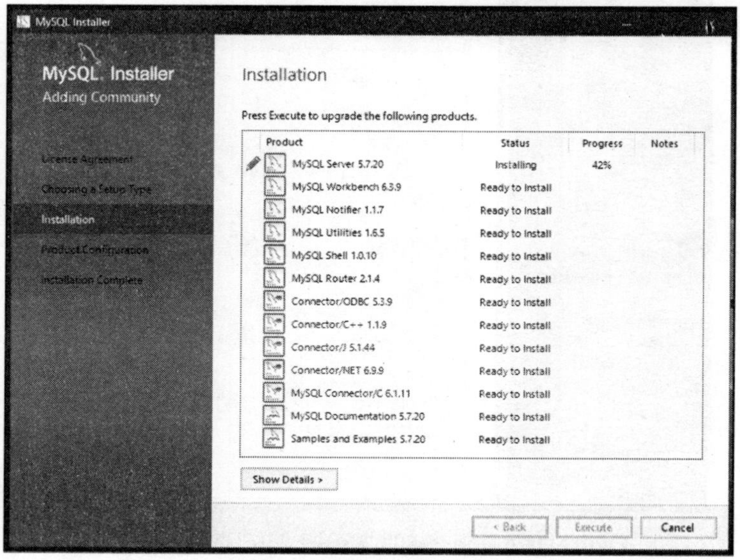

Figure 24.6: Installing All the Components

When the installation of the software is completed, we see the screen (Figure 24.7).

9. Click the 'Next' button, as shown in Figure 24.7:

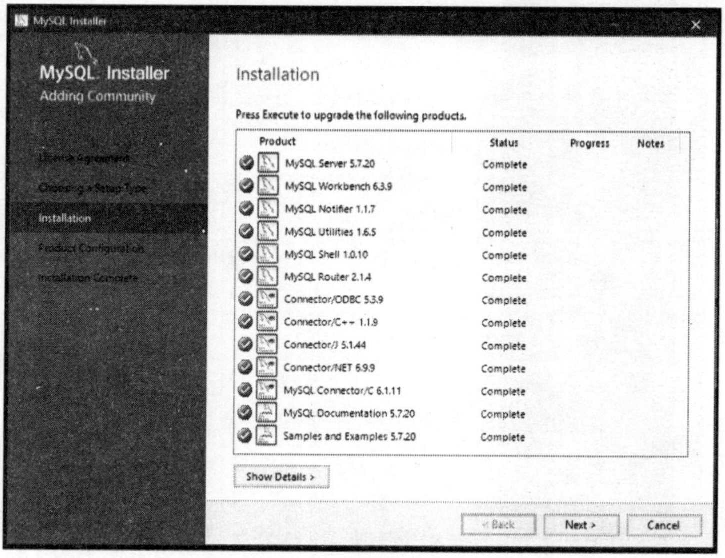

Figure 24.7: The Installation Completion Page

Now the 'Product Configuration' page appears.

10. Click the 'Next' button, as shown in Figure 24.8:

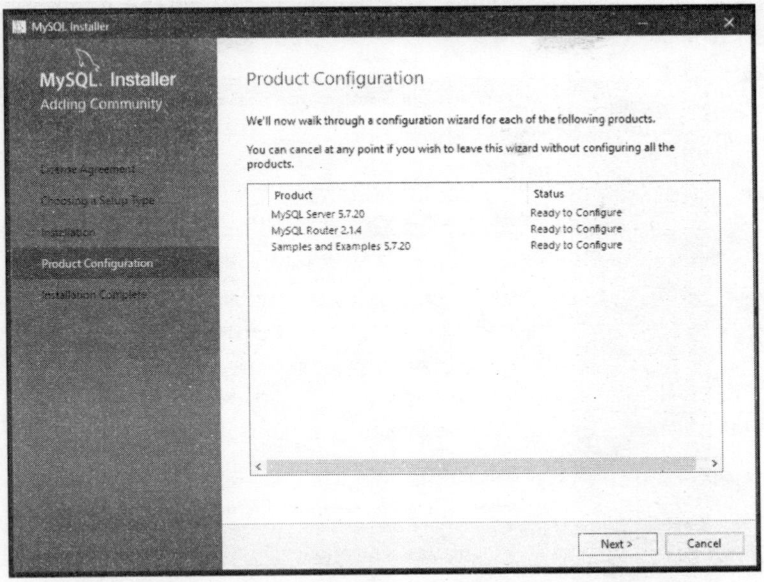

Figure 24.8: The Product Configuration Page

The 'Type and Networking' page appears (Figure 24.9).

11. Click the 'Next' button, as shown in Figure 24.9:

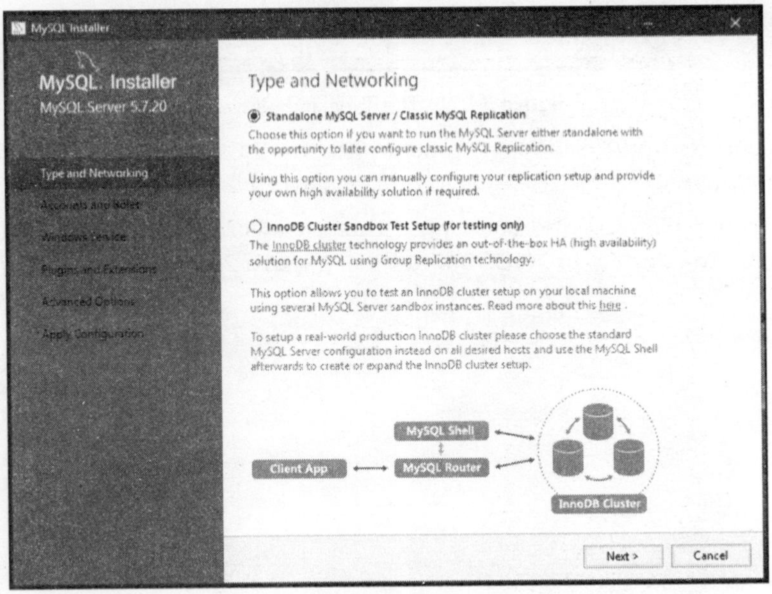

Figure 24.9: The Type and Networking Page

In the next page, we will find the server configuration.

12. Click the 'Next' button in the 'Type and Networking' page, as shown in Figure 24.10:

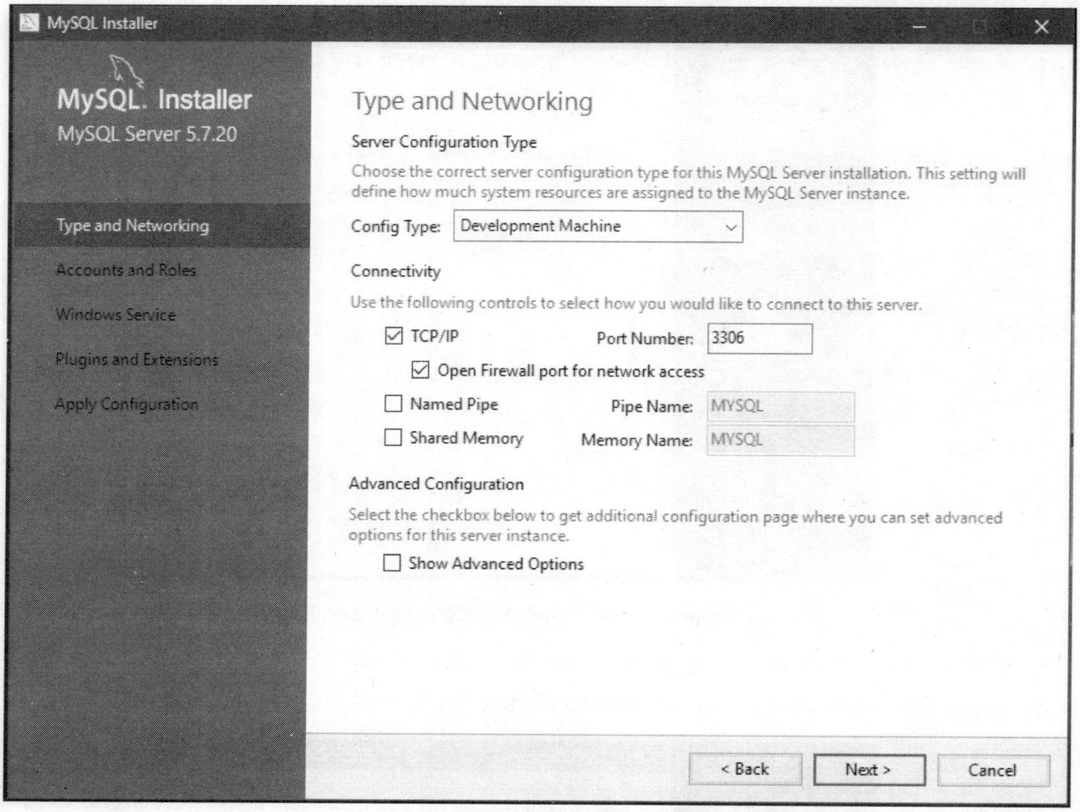

Figure 24.10: The Type and Networking Page

The 'Accounts and Roles' page appears (Figure 24.11). In the 'Accounts and Roles' page, we have to enter the MySQL root password 2 times.

13. Enter your password and remember this password as we have to use this password every time to connect to MySQL database (Figure 24.11).

14. Click the Next button, as shown in Figure 24.11:

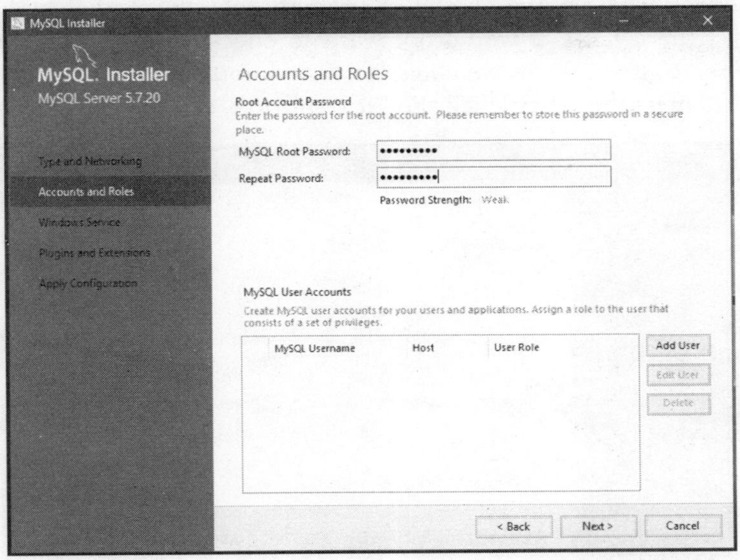

Figure 24.11: Entering Root Password in the Accounts and Roles Page

15. Click the 'Next' button in the subsequent pages. The last page with the name 'Apply Configuration' appears (Figure 24.12).
16. Click the 'Execute' button, as shown in Figure 24.12:

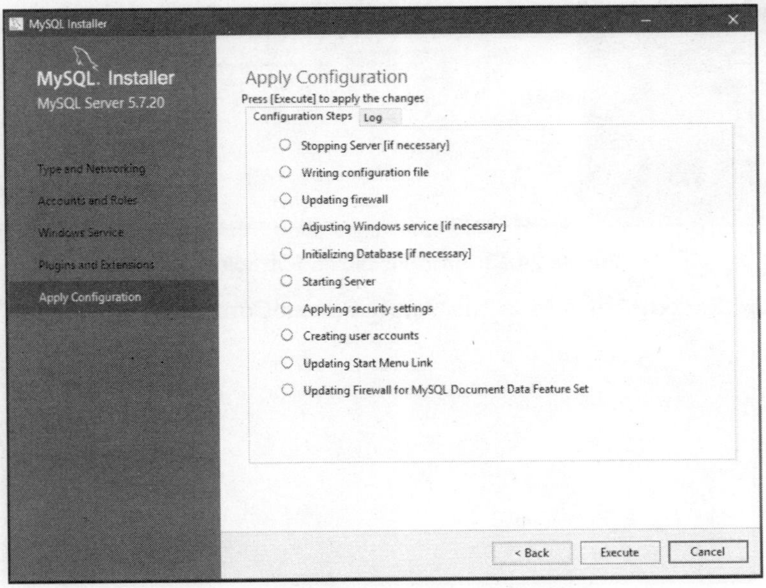

Figure 24.12: The Apply Configuration Page

This will complete our installation of MySQL database server.

17. In the next page, click the 'Next' button. It will display 'Connect to Server' page where we can check whether the MySQL is properly installed or not by clicking the 'Check' button (Figure 24.13). If we do not want to check the software, we can simply click the 'Cancel' button. When we click the 'Check' button, it will display the 'Connection successful' message. Then click the 'Next' button, as shown in Figure 24.13:

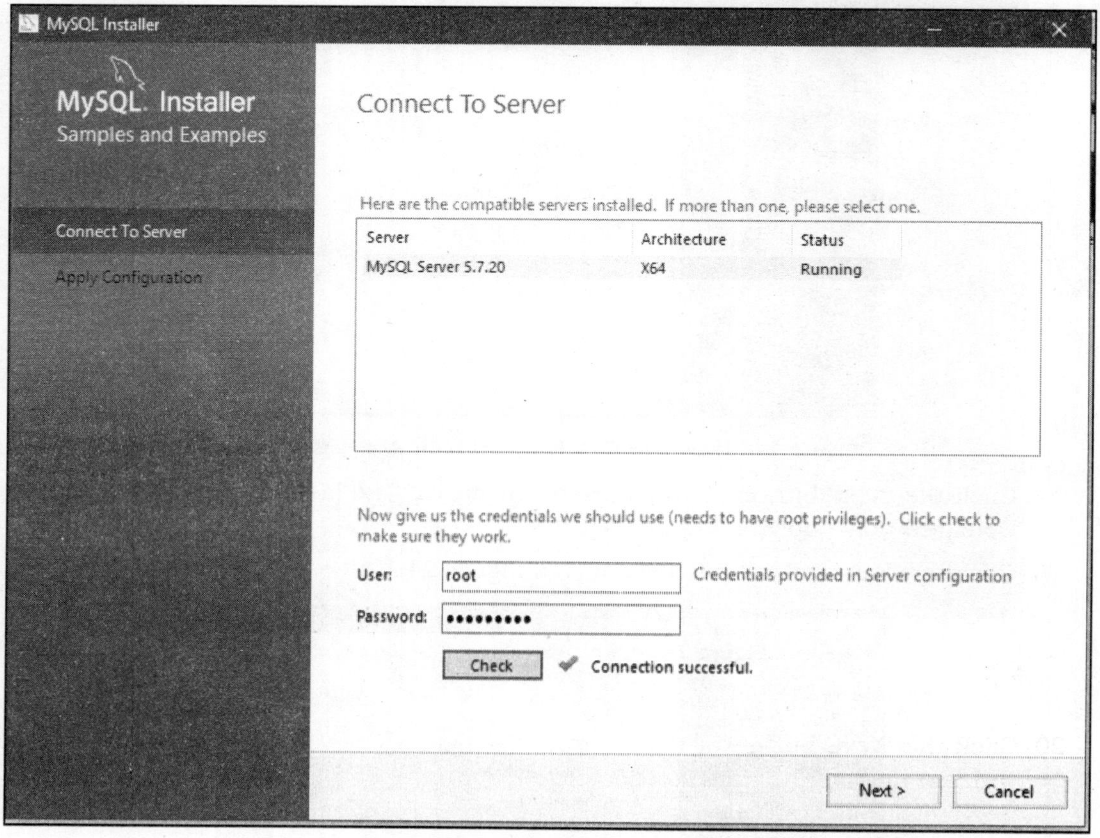

Figure 24.13: Checking the MySQL Software Installation

18. Click the 'Execute' button in the 'Apply Server Configuration' page (Figure 24.14).

19. Click the 'Finish' button. Consider Figure 24.14:

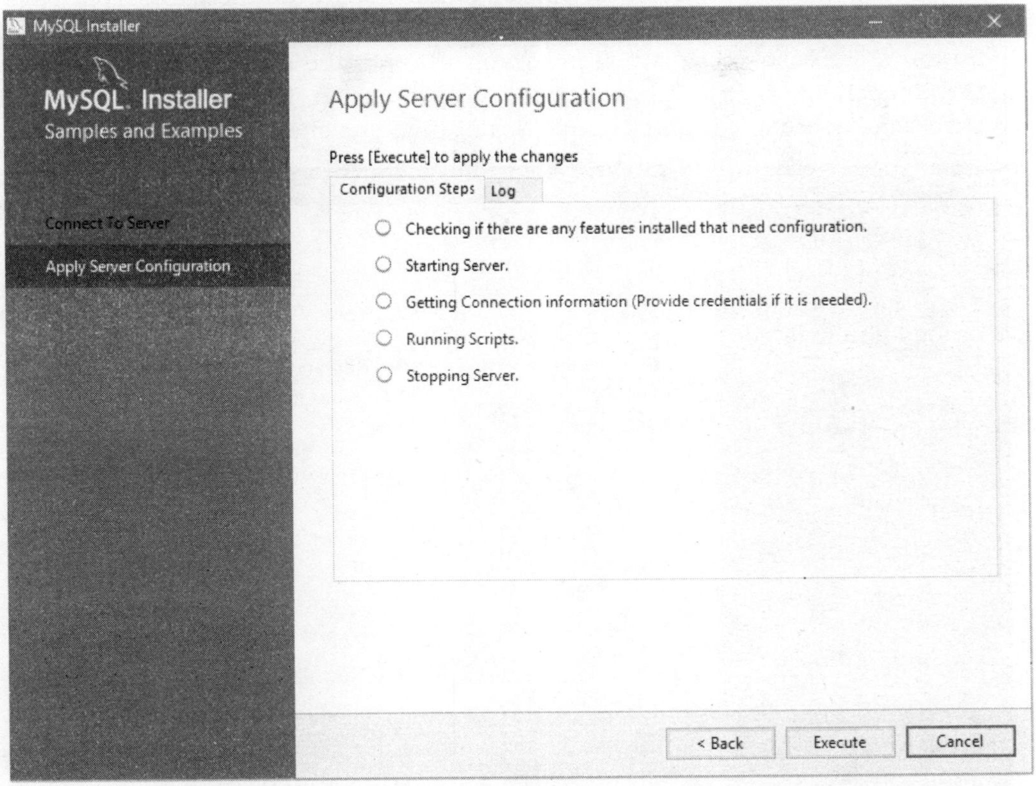

Figure 24.14: The Apply Server Configuration Page

20. Click the 'Next' button in the 'Product Configuration' page. It will display final page with the message 'Installation complete' (Figure 24.15)

21. Click the 'Finish' button to complete the installation, as shown in Figure 24.15:

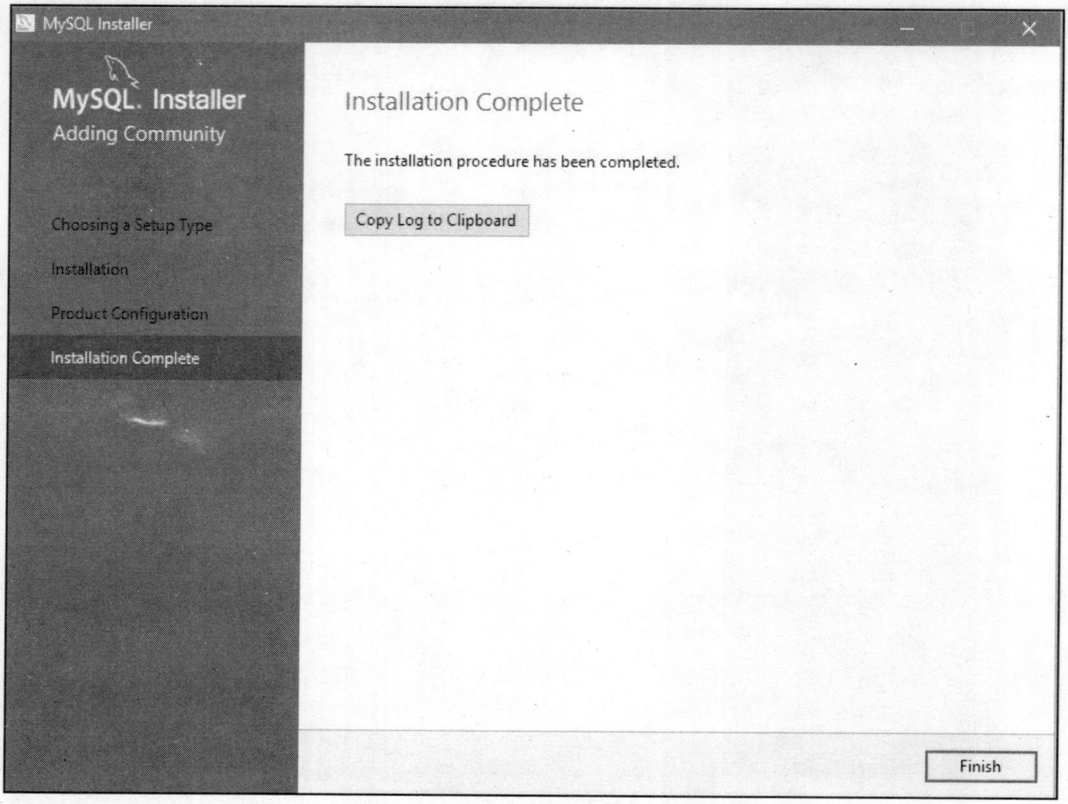

Figure 24.15: The MySQL Installation Complete Page

Verifying MySQL in the Windows Operating System

We can verify that the MySQL database software has been properly installed in our computer system by clicking on 'Start' button at the lower left corner on the desktop. In Windows 10, click on Start→All apps. Then select 'M' to see all applications starting with the letter 'M'. The 'MySQL' option appears, as shown in Figure 24.16:

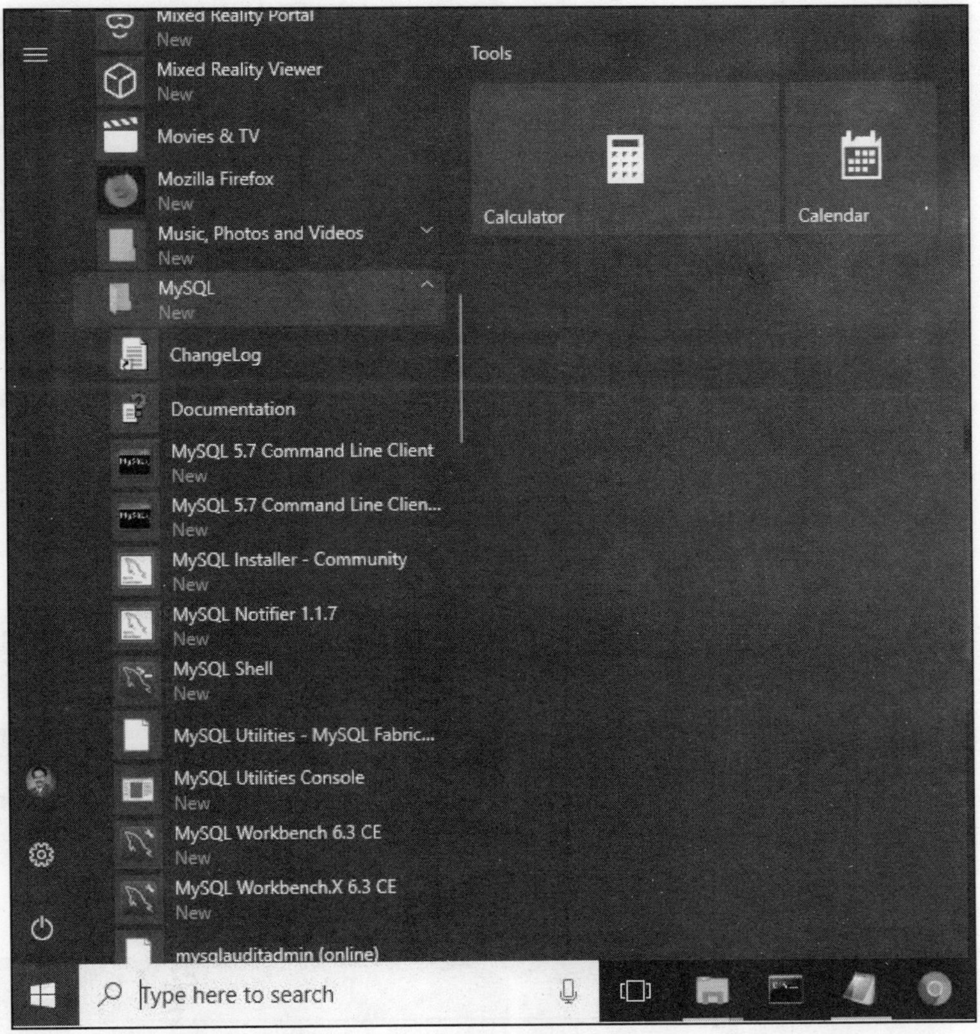

Figure 24.16: Verifying the Presence of MySQL in Windows 10

Installing MySQLdb Module

To communicate with MySQL database from Python, we need a program that becomes an interface to the MySQL database server. 'MySQLdb' is an interface between the MySQL server and Python programs. Unless we install this interface, our Python programs cannot communicate with MySQL database. The following steps represent how to install the MySQLdb interface:

1. Visit the following web page as shown in Figure 24.17:

   https://pypi.python.org/pypi/mysqlclient

In this page, we can find a file by the name 'mysqlclient-1.3.12-cp36-cp36m-win_amd64.whl (md5)'. This is the file used with Python 3.6 version of 64-bit installation. Download this file into your system.

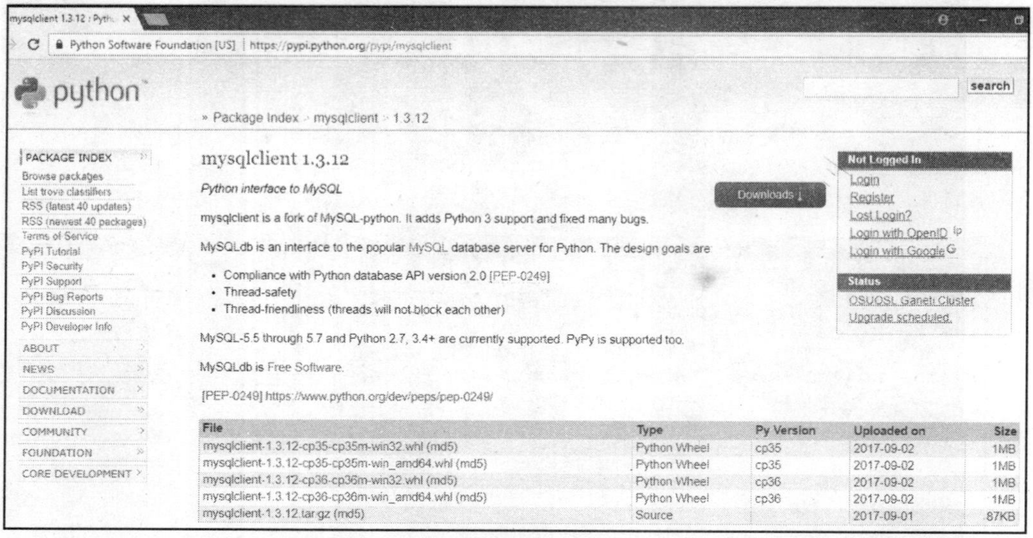

Figure 24.17: Downloading the MySQLdb Interface for Python

2. The downloaded file name will be: mysqlclient-1.3.12-cp36-cp36m-win_amd64.whl, which is a .whl file. Such files cannot be executed by double clicking. We can execute such files using 'pip' program supplied with Python. Hence, go to that directory where this .whl file is available and type there pip command at System prompt as:

   C:\> pip install mysqlclient-1.3.12-cp36-cp36m-win_amd64.whl

   Now the installation will take place as shown in Figure 24.18:

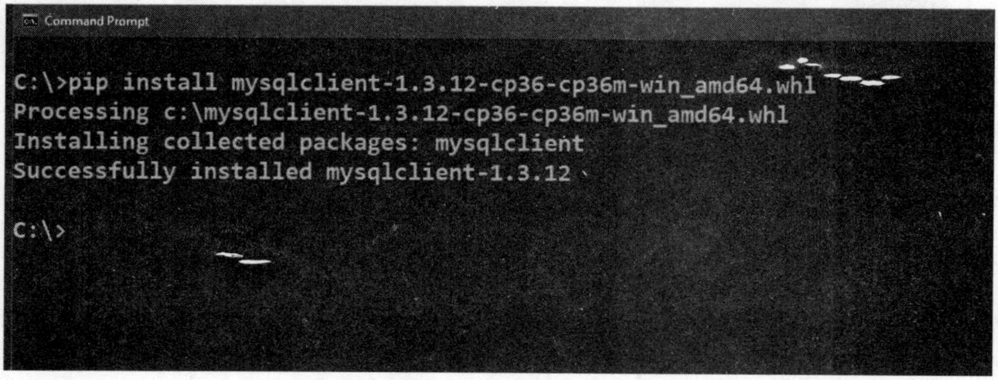

Figure 24.18: Installing the MySQLdb Interface for Python

Verifying the MySQLdb Interface Installation

If the MySQLdb interface for Python has been installed successfully, we can see a new module by the name 'MySQLdb' is added to the existing modules in Python library. Go to Python IDLE shell window and type the following at Python prompt:

```
>>> help('modules')
```

As a result, it will display all the available modules of Python. We should be able to locate 'MySQLdb' module (in the beginning of the list) among them. This represents that the MySQLdb interface for Python has been successfully installed, as shown in Figure 24.19:

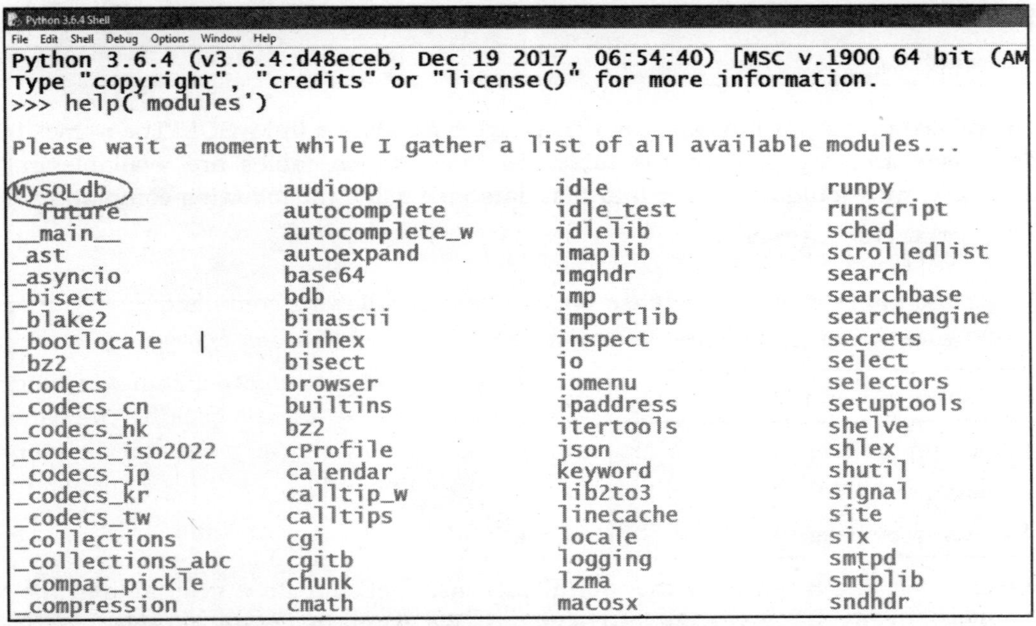

Figure 24.19: The Installed MySQLdb Module in Python

Working with MySQL Database

We will first understand how to enter into MySQL database and issue some SQL commands to store and retrieve data. In Windows 10, to open MySQL, we can use the following steps from Start button on the desktop:

Start → MySQL →MySQL 5.7 Command Line Client

It will ask for password and we have to provide the same password that we have already typed at the time of installation of MySQL.

```
Enter password:  nag123
```

Now, we can see mysql prompt where we can enter SQL commands. For example, to see which databases are existing in MySQL, we can give the following command:

```
mysql>  show databases;
```

Database
information_schema
mysql
performance_schema
sakila
sys
world

The preceding output indicates that there are 6 databases in MySQL. The names of these databases are displayed in the table. To know which tables are available in 'world' database, we should first enter into that database using the following command:

```
mysql>  use world;
Database changed
```

To see the tables of world database, we can use the following command:

```
mysql>  show tables;
```

Tables_in_world
city
country
countrylanguage

Hence, there are 3 tables in the 'world' database. Let's create a new table in the 'world' database by using 'create table' command. We want to create a table by the name 'emptab' with columns employee number (eno), employee name (ename) and salary (sal).

```
mysql>  create table emptab(enoint, ename char(20), sal float);
Query OK, 0 rows affected (0.65 sec)
```

Let's see the description of 'emptab' by giving desc command.

```
mysql>desc emptab;
```

Field	Type	Null	Key	Default	Extra
eno	int(11)	YES		NULL	
ename	char(20)	YES		NULL	
sal	float	YES		NULL	

3 rows in set (0.33 sec)

We did not store any data into 'emptab'. Now let's store some rows into this table.

```
mysql>  insert into emptab values(1001, "Nagesh", 7800);
Query OK, 1 row affected (0.11 sec)
mysql>  insert into emptab values(1002, "Ganesh", 8900.50);
Query OK, 1 row affected (0.10 sec)
```

In this way, we can store some rows into 'emptab'. To see all the rows of the table, we can use 'select statement' as:

```
mysql>  select * from emptab;
```

eno	ename	sal
1001	Nagesh	7800
1002	Ganesh	8900.5
1003	Vijaya	9099.99
1004	Reethu	6799.0

2 rows in set (0.00 sec)

Suppose, we want to update the salary of an employee, whose employee number is 1003,

```
mysql>update emptab set sal = sal+1000 where eno = 1003
Query OK, 1 row affected (0.09 sec)
Rows matched: 1  Changed: 1  Warnings: 0
```

If we want to delete the row of an employee whose name is "Ganesh",

```
mysql>  delete from emptab where ename="Ganesh";
Query OK, 1 row affected (0.10 sec)
```

Finally, to close MySQL, we can give 'quit' command. This will lead us to system prompt.

```
mysql>  quit;
Bye
```

Using MySQL from Python

To work with MySQL in a Python program, we have to use *MySQLdb* module. We can import this module as:

```
import MySQLdb
```

To establish connection with MySQL database, we use the connect() method of *MySQLdb* module as:

```
conn = MySQLdb.connect(host='localhost', database='world',
user='root', password='nag123')
```

The connect() method returns MySQLConnection class object 'conn'. This method takes the following parameters:

```
host= In the network, server' ip address should be given as host. If we
     use individual computer, then the string 'localhost' can be
     supplied.
database= This is the database name to connect to.
user= this represents the user name. Generally this is 'root'.
password= This indicates the root password.
```

The next step is to create cursor class object by calling the cursor() method on 'conn' object as:

```
cursor = conn.cursor()
```

The 'cursor' object is useful to execute SQL commands on the database. For this purpose, we can use the execute() method of 'cursor' object as:

```
cursor.execute("select * from emptab")
```

The resultant rows retrieved from the table are stored in the 'cursor' object. We can get them from the 'cursor' object using the fetchone() or fetchall() methods.

```
row = cursor.fetchone()     # get 1 row
rows = cursor.fetchall()    # get all rows
```

Finally, we can close the connection with MySQL by closing the cursor and connection objects as:

```
cursor.close()
conn.close()
```

Retrieving All Rows from a Table

After establishing connection with MySQL database using connect() method, we have to create 'cursor' object. Then we have to call the execute() method which executes our SQL command as:

```
cursor.execute("select * from emptab")
```

Our assumption in this case is that we have 'emptab' table already available in the 'world' database in MySQL. The rows of the 'emptab' will be available in the 'cursor' object. We can retrieve them by using the fetchone() method as shown below:

```
row = cursor.fetchone()         # retrieve the first row
while row is not None:          # if that row exists then
    print(row)                  # display it
    row = cursor.fetchone()     # get the next row
```

This logic is shown in the Program 1 where we are retrieving all the rows of the 'emptab' from MySQL database software.

Program

Program 1: A Python program to retrieve and display all rows from the employee table.

```
# displaying all rows of emptab
```

```
import MySQLdb

# connect to MySQL database
conn = MySQLdb.connect(host='localhost', database='world', user=
'root', password='nag123')

# prepare a cursor object using cursor() method
cursor = conn.cursor()

# execute a SQL query using execute() method
cursor.execute("select * from emptab")

# get only one row
row = cursor.fetchone()

# if the row exists
while row is not None:
    print(row)   # display it
    row = cursor.fetchone()   # get the next row

# close connection
cursor.close()
conn.close()
```

Output:

```
C:\>python db.py
Connected to MySQL database
(1001, 'Nagesh', 7800.0)
(1002, 'Ganesh', 8900.5)
(1003, 'Vijaya', 9099.99)
(1004, 'Reethu', 6799.0)
```

We can also use the fetchall() method that retrieves all rows from the 'emptab' table and stores them in an iterator, as:

```
rows = cursor.fetchall()
```

Now, we can retrieve the rows one by one from 'rows' iterator using a for loop as:

```
for row in rows:
    print(row)   # display each row
```

Program

Program 2: A Python program to retrieve and display all rows from the employee table.

```
# displaying all rows of emptab - v2.0
import MySQLdb

# connect to MySQL database
conn = MySQLdb.connect(host='localhost', database='world',
user='root', password='nag123')

# prepare a cursor object using cursor() method
cursor = conn.cursor()

# execute a SQL query using execute() method
cursor.execute("select * from emptab")

# get all rows
```

```
rows = cursor.fetchall()

# display the number of rows
print('Total number of rows= ', cursor.rowcount)

# display the rows from rows object
for row in rows:
    print(row)   # display each row

# close connection
cursor.close()
conn.close()
```

Output:

```
C:\>python db.py
Connected to MySQL database
Total number of rows= 4
(1001, 'Nagesh', 7800.0)
(1002, 'Ganesh', 8900.5)
(1003, 'Vijaya', 9099.99)
(1004, 'Reethu', 6799.0)
```

Please observe the output of the previous programs. The output is displayed in the form of tuples. We can format the output and display the rows in better manner. Since we know that the rows are available in the 'rows' iterator, we can use a for loop and retrieve eno, ename and sal values which are the columns in the table as:

```
for row in rows:
eno = row[0]   # first column value
ename = row[1]   # second column value
sal = row[2]   # third column value
print('%-6d %-15s %10.2f'% (eno, ename, sal))
```

This is shown in Program 3 which is a slight improvement of Program 2.

Program

Program 3: A Python program to retrieve all rows from employee table and display the column values in tabular form.

```
# displaying all rows of emptab - v3.0
import MySQLdb

# connect to MySQL database
conn = MySQLdb.connect(host='localhost', database='world',
user='root', password='nag123')

# prepare a cursor object using cursor() method
cursor = conn.cursor()

# execute a SQL query using execute() method
cursor.execute("select * from emptab")

# get all rows
rows = cursor.fetchall()

# display the number of rows
print('Total number of rows= ', cursor.rowcount)
```

```
# display the rows from rows object
for row in rows:
    eno = row[0]
    ename = row[1]
    sal = row[2]
    print('%-6d %-15s %10.2f'% (eno, ename, sal))

# close connection
cursor.close()
conn.close()
```

Output:

```
C:\>python db.py
Connected to MySQL database
Total number of rows=  4
1001  Nagesh         7800.00
1002  Ganesh         8900.50
1003  Vijaya         9099.99
1002  Reethu         6799.00
```

Inserting Rows into a Table

To insert a row into a table, we can use SQL insert command as:

```
str = "insert into emptab(eno, ename, sal) values(9999, 'Srinivas',
     9999.99)"
```

Here, we are inserting values for eno, ename and sal columns into 'emptab' table. The total command is taken as a string 'str'. Now we can execute this command by passing it to execute() method as:

```
cursor.execute(str)   # SQL insert statement in the str is executed
```

After inserting a row into the table, we can save it by calling the commit() method as:

```
conn.commit()
```

In case there is an error, we can un-save the row by calling the rollback() method as:

```
conn.rollback()
```

Program

Program 4: A Python program to insert a row into a table in MySQL.

```
# inserting a row into emptab
import MySQLdb

# connect to MySQL database
conn = MySQLdb.connect(host='localhost', database='world',
user='root', password='nag123')

# prepare a cursor object using cursor() method
cursor = conn.cursor()

# prepare SQL query string to insert a row
str = "insert into emptab(eno, ename, sal) values(9999, 'Srinivas',
     9999.99)"
```

```
    try:
        # execute the SQL query using execute() method
        cursor.execute(str)

        # save the changes to the database
        conn.commit()
        print('1 row inserted...')

    except:
        # rollback if there is any error
        conn.rollback()

    # close connection
    cursor.close()
    conn.close()
```

Output:

```
C:\>python db.py
Connected to MySQL database
1 row inserted...
```

We can improve this program so that it is possible to insert several rows into 'emptab' from the keyboard. For this purpose, we can write an insert_rows() function as:

```
def insert_rows(eno, ename, sal):
```

When this function is called, we have to pass values for the arguments eno, ename and sal. These values can be stored in a tuple as:

```
args = (eno, ename, sal)
```

Now, our SQL command for inserting a row can be:

```
str = "insert into emptab(eno, ename, sal) values('%d', '%s', '%f')"
```

Here, we are just mentioning the '%d', '%s' and '%f' as format strings for values. These format strings assume the values from 'args' supplied to the function. Now, we can call the execute() method as:

```
cursor.execute(str % args)
```

Please observe the '%' symbol between the SQL command string 'str' and the 'args' tuple. This is a better way of using execute() method. The string 'str' will be executed by substituting the argument values in the place of format strings. If we pass 10, 'Venu' and 7777.77 as values for the arguments, the string will become:

```
insert into emptab(eno, ename, sal) values(10, 'Venu', 7777.77)
```

To understand this simple substitution, consider Figure 24.20:

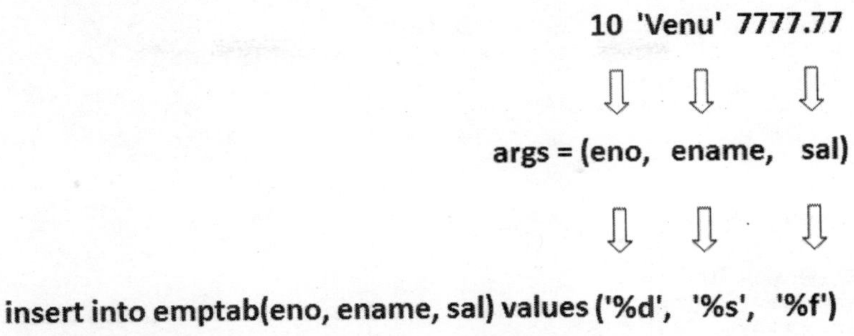

Figure 24.20: Argument Values are Passed to SQL Command

Program 5: A Python program to insert several rows into a table from the keyboard.

```
# inserting several rows from keyboard into emptab
import MySQLdb

# function to store row into the emptab table
def insert_rows(eno, ename, sal):

    # connect to MySQL database
    conn = MySQLdb.connect(host='localhost', database='world',
user='root', password='nag123')

    # prepare a cursor object using cursor() method
    cursor = conn.cursor()

    # prepare SQL query string to insert a row
    str = "insert into emptab(eno, ename, sal) values('%d', '%s',
'%f')"

    # define the arguments
    args = (eno, ename, sal)

    try:
        # execute the SQL query using execute() method
        cursor.execute(str % args)

        # save the changes to the database
        conn.commit()
        print('1 row inserted...')

    except:
        # rollback if there is any error
        conn.rollback()

    finally:
        # close connection
        cursor.close()
        conn.close()

# enter rows from keyboard
n = int(input('How many rows? '))
```

```
    for i in range(n):
        x = int(input('Enter eno: '))
        y = input('Enter name: ')
        z = float(input('Enter salary: '))
        # pass eno, name and salary to insert_rows() function
        insert_rows(x, y, z)
        print('-----------------------')
```

Output:

```
C:\>python db.py
How many rows? 2
Enter eno: 10
Enter name: Venu
Enter salary: 7777.77
1 row inserted...
-----------------------------
Enter eno: 11
Enter name: Teja
Enter salary: 7878.78
1 row inserted...
-----------------------------
```

Deleting Rows from a Table

We can accept the employee number from the keyboard and delete the corresponding row in the employee table. For this purpose, we can use the SQL command as:

```
delete from emptab where eno = '%d'
```

Here, '%d' represents the integer number supplied to the command as argument. This is nothing but the employee number, i.e., eno.

Program

Program 6: A Python program to delete a row from emptab by accepting the employee number.

```
# deleting a row from emptab depending on eno
import MySQLdb

# function to delete row from the emptab table
def delete_rows(eno):

    # connect to MySQL database
    conn = MySQLdb.connect(host='localhost', database='world',
     user='root', password='nag123')

    # prepare a cursor object using cursor() method
    cursor = conn.cursor()

    # prepare SQL query string to delete a row
    str = "delete from emptab where eno = '%d'"

    # define the arguments
    args = (eno)
    try:
```

```
        # execute the SQL query using execute() method
        cursor.execute(str % args)

        # save the changes to the database
        conn.commit()
        print('1 row deleted...')

    except:
        # rollback if there is any error
        conn.rollback()

    finally:
        # close connection
        cursor.close()
        conn.close()

# enter employee number whose row is to be deleted
x = int(input('Enter eno: '))

# pass eno to delete_rows() function
delete_rows(x)
```

Output:

```
C:\>python db.py
Enter eno: 1002
1 row deleted...
```

Updating Rows in a Table

To modify the values in a row, we can use update command. For example, to increase the salary of an employee by 1000, we can write:

```
Update emptab set sal = sal+1000 where eno = '%d'
```

Here, '%d' represents the argument value, i.e. the employee number. This can be passed from the keyboard.

Program

Program 7: A Python program to increase the salary of an employee by accepting the employee number from keyboard.

```
# updating the salary in emptab depending on eno
import MySQLdb

# function to update row from the emptab table
def update_rows(eno):

    # connect to MySQL database
    conn = MySQLdb.connect(host='localhost', database='world',
user='root', password='nag123')

    # prepare a cursor object using cursor() method
    cursor = conn.cursor()

    # prepare SQL query string to update the salary in a row
    str = "update emptab set sal = sal+1000 where eno = '%d'"
```

```
        # define the arguments
        args = (eno)
        try:
            # execute the SQL query using execute() method
            cursor.execute(str % args)

            # save the changes to the database
            conn.commit()
            print('1 row updated...')

        except:
            # rollback if there is any error
            conn.rollback()

        finally:
            # close connection
            cursor.close()
            conn.close()

    # enter employee number whose row is to be updated
    x = int(input('Enter eno: '))

    # pass eno to update_rows() function
    update_rows(x)
```

Output:

```
C:\>python db.py
Enter eno: 1003
1 row updated...
```

Creating Database Tables through Python

So far, we used 'emptab' table that was already created in the MySQL database. It is also possible to create any table in the MySQL database using a Python program. Once the table is created, we can insert the rows through a Python program. Suppose we want to create emptab table with the columns: eno, ename, sex and salary, we can write a SQL command as follows:

```
create table emptab(enoint, ename char(20), sex char(1), salary float)
```

We can understand that eno is integer type, ename is declared as 20 characters sixe, sex as 1 character size and salary as a float type column.

Before the emptab is created, we can check if any table already exists by that name in the database and we can delete that table using drop table command as:

```
drop table if exists emptab
```

The above command should be first executed and after that, we can create the new emptab table.

Program

Program 8: A Python program to create emptab in MySQL database.

```
    # creating a table by the name emptab in MySQL database
    import MySQLdb

    # connect to MySQL database
    conn = MySQLdb.connect(host='localhost', database='world',
  user='root', password='nag123')

    # prepare a cursor object using cursor() method
    cursor = conn.cursor()

    # delete table if already exists
    cursor.execute("drop table if exists emptab")

    # prepare sql string to create a new table
    str = "create table emptab(enoint, ename char(20), sex char(1), salary
  float)"

    # execute the query to create the table
    cursor.execute(str)
    print('Table created...')
    # close connection
    cursor.close()
    conn.close()
```

Output:

```
    C:\>python db.py
    Connected to MySQL database
    Table created...
```

To check if the emptab is properly created, we can go to MySQL prompt and give the following command:

```
    mysql>desc emptab;
```

Field	Type	Null	Key	Default	Extra
eno	int(11)	YES		NULL	
ename	char(20)	YES		NULL	
sex	char(1)	YES		NULL	
sal	float	YES		NULL	

4 rows in set (0.00 sec)

It would be better if we can use GUI environment to connect and communicate with a database. In the following program, we are displaying an Entry box where the user enters employee number and retrieves the corresponding employee row from the 'emptab' table. The row is again displayed using a label in the Frame.

Program

Program 9: A Python program using GUI to retrieve a row from a MySQL database table.

```
# retrieving rows from a table in MySQL database - a GUI application
import MySQLdb
from tkinter import *

# create root window
root = Tk()

# a function that takes employee number and displays the row
def retrieve_rows(eno):

    # connect to MySQL database
    conn = MySQLdb.connect(host='localhost', database='world',
user='root', password='nag123')

    # prepare a cursor object using cursor() method
    cursor = conn.cursor()

    # prepare SQL query string to retreive a row
    str = "select * from emptab where eno = '%d'"

    # define the arguments
    args = (eno)

    # execute the SQL query using execute() method
    cursor.execute(str % args)
    # get only one row
    row = cursor.fetchone()

    # if the row exists display it using a label
    if row is not None:
        lbl = Label(text= row, font=('Arial', 14)).place(x=50, y=200)

    # close connection
    cursor.close()
    conn.close()

# a function that takes input from Entry widget
def display(self):

    # retrieve the value from the entry widget
    str = e1.get()

    # display the values using label
    lbl = Label(text='You entered: '+str, font=('Arial',
     14)).place(x=50, y=150)

    # call the function that retrieves the row
    retrieve_rows(int(str))

# create a frame as child to root window
f = Frame(root, height=350, width=600)
```

```
    # let the frame will not shrink
    f.propagate(0)

    # attach the frame to root window
    f.pack()

    # label
    l1 = Label(text='Enter employee number: ', font=('Arial', 14))

    # create Entry widget for accepting employee number
    e1 = Entry(f, width=15, fg='blue', bg='yellow', font=('Arial', 14))

    # when user presses Enter, bind that event to display method
    e1.bind("<Return>", display)

    # place label and entry widgets in the frame
    l1.place(x=50, y=100)
    e1.place(x=300, y=100)

    # handle the events
    root.mainloop()
```

Output:

```
    C:\>python guiretrieve.py
```

The preceding program displays the output, as shown in Figure 24.21:

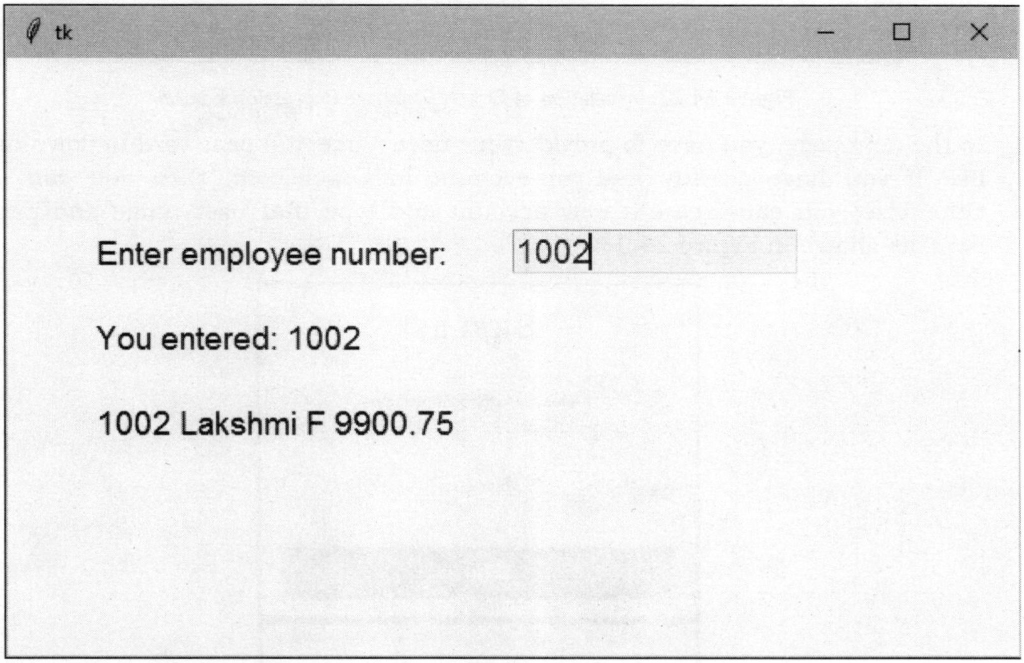

Figure 24.21: Output of Program 9

So far we worked with MySQL database. Now, we will see how to install Oracle database software, its corresponding connector and finally how to work with Oracle through Python.

Installation of Oracle 11g

Let's first install Oracle 11g express edition by going to oracle.com website at the following link:

```
http://www.oracle.com/technetwork/database/database-technologies/express-edition/downloads/index.html
```

1. In this page, first click the 'Accept License Agreement' radio button and then click the file with the name Oracle Database Express Edition 11g Release 2 for Windows x64, as shown in Figure 24.22:

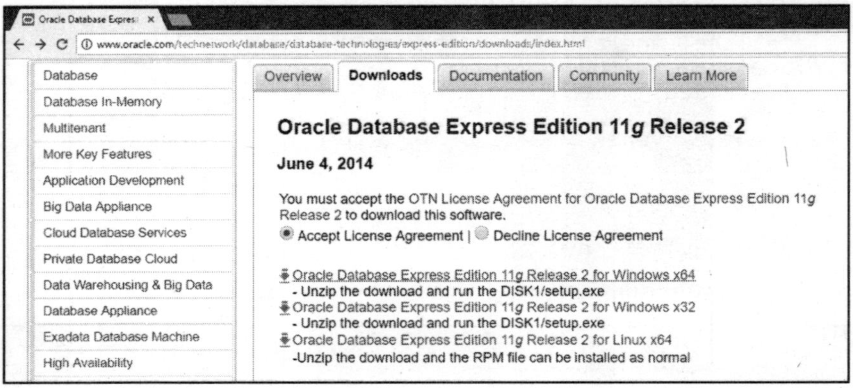

Figure 24.22: Installation of Oracle Database Expression Edition

2. In the next page, you have to provide your user name and password to download this file. If you have already had an account in Oracle.com, then you can use it. Otherwise, you can create a new account and type that user name and password here, as shown in Figure 24.23:

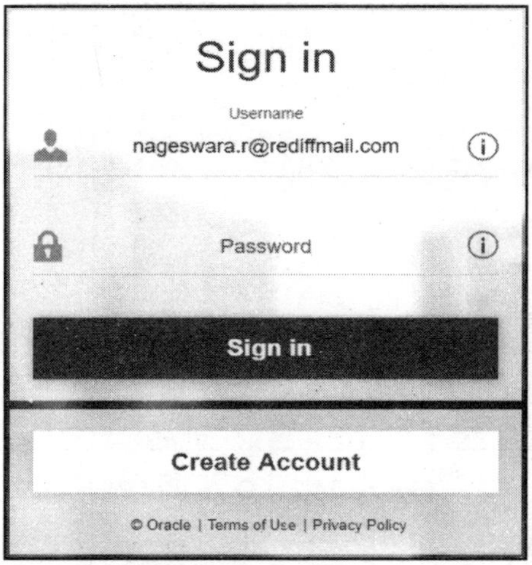

Figure 24.23: Using Oracle Account Details to Download the File

3. The downloaded file is a zip file with the name OracleXE112_Win64. Right click and select 'extract here'. This would extract all files into a separate directory by the name: OracleXE112_Win64/DISK1.
4. Open the DISK1 directory and we see 'setup' icon. Double click on 'setup' and then the InstallShield wizard will be initiated, as shown in Figure 24.24:

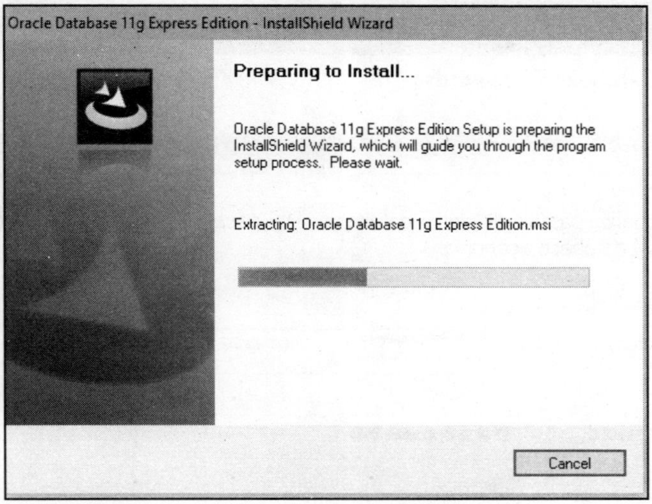

Figure 24.24: Starting the Installation

The InstallShield wizard will be ready to install Oracle database software.

5. Click the 'Next' button, as shown in Figure 24.25:

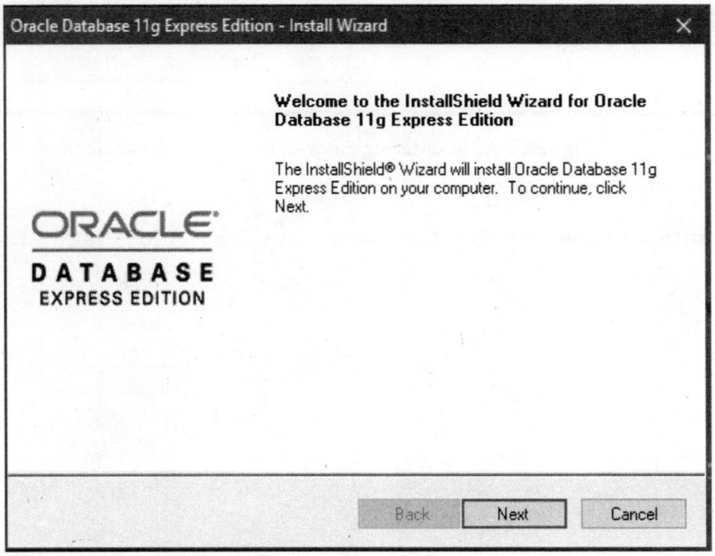

Figure 24.25: InstallShield Wizard is Ready to Install Oracle Database

It will ask for a password which is used with root user name SYSTEM. Enter the password for 2 times. We should remember the password since we will use this password in our Python programs in future. In this window, we entered 'Nagesh123' as password.

6. Click the 'Next' button to proceed, as shown in Figure 24.26:

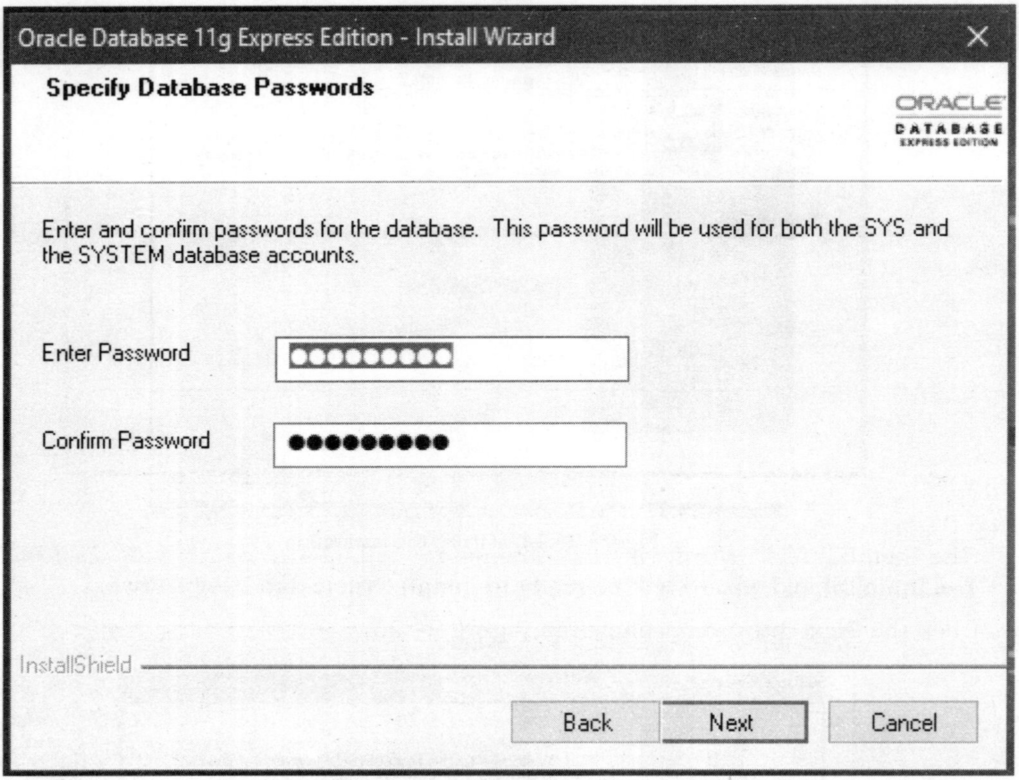

Figure 24.26: Entering Password for Oracle Installation

It will create a directory by the name oraclexe and install the software in this directory.

7. Click the 'Install' button to proceed, as shown in Figure 24.27:

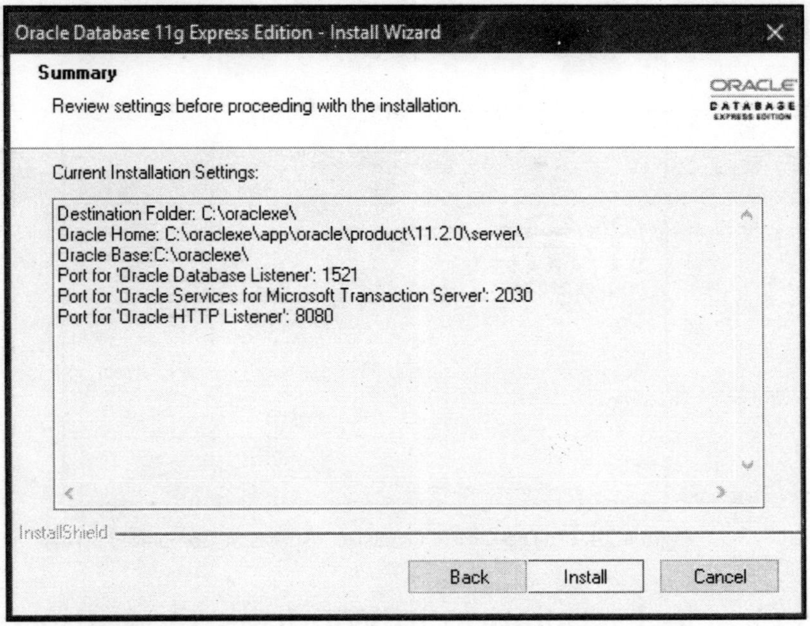

Figure 24.27: The Destination Directory for Oracle Installation

The InstallShield wizard will start the installation of Oracle database. This will take a few minutes, as shown in Figure 24.28:

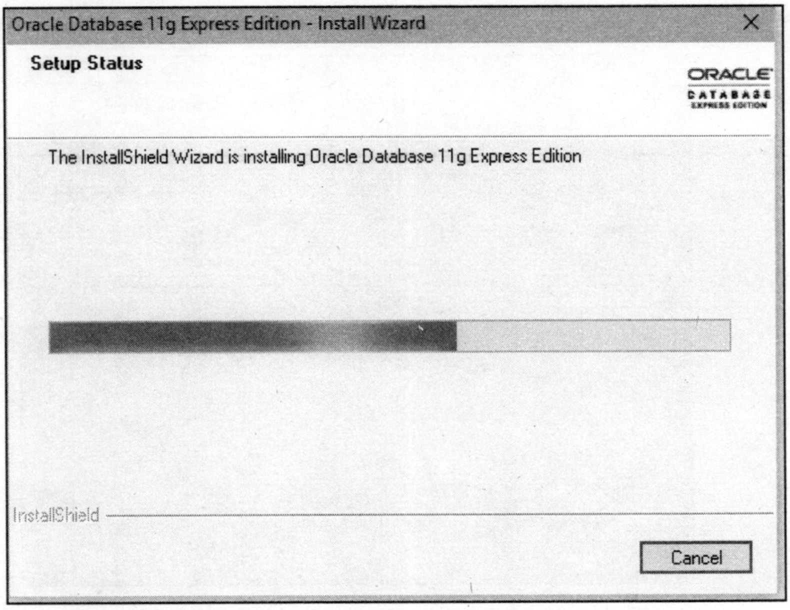

Figure 24.28: The Oracle Database Software is being Installed

8. Once the database software installation is completed, click the 'Finish' button, as shown in Figure 24.29:

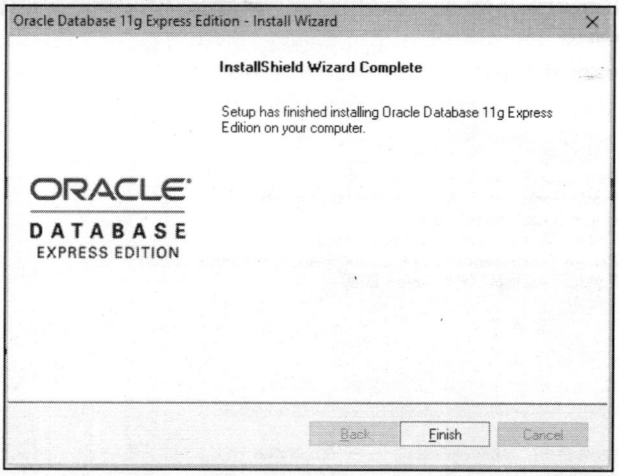

Figure 24.29: The Oracle Database Installation Completed Screen

Verifying Oracle Installation in Windows Operating System

We can verify that the Oracle database software has been properly installed in our Computer system by clicking on 'Start' button at the lower left corner on the desktop. In Windows 10, click the 'Start' button and then, select 'O' to see all applications starting with the letter 'O'. We can see 'Oracle Database 11g Express Edition' in Figure 24.30:

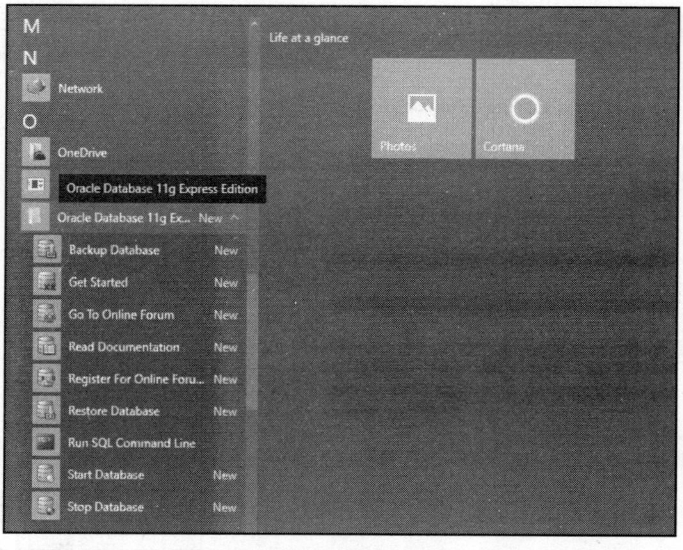

Figure 24.30: Verifying Oracle Installation in Windows 10

Installing Oracle Database Driver

We have to install a driver or connector software that connects the Oracle database with our Python programs. The name of the driver needed is 'cx_Oracle' and it can be installed using the 'pip' command that comes with Python by default. We should go to the system prompt and type the command as shown below:

```
C:\> pip install cx_Oracle
```

This will search for the latest version of the driver and install it into our system, as shown in Figure 24.31:

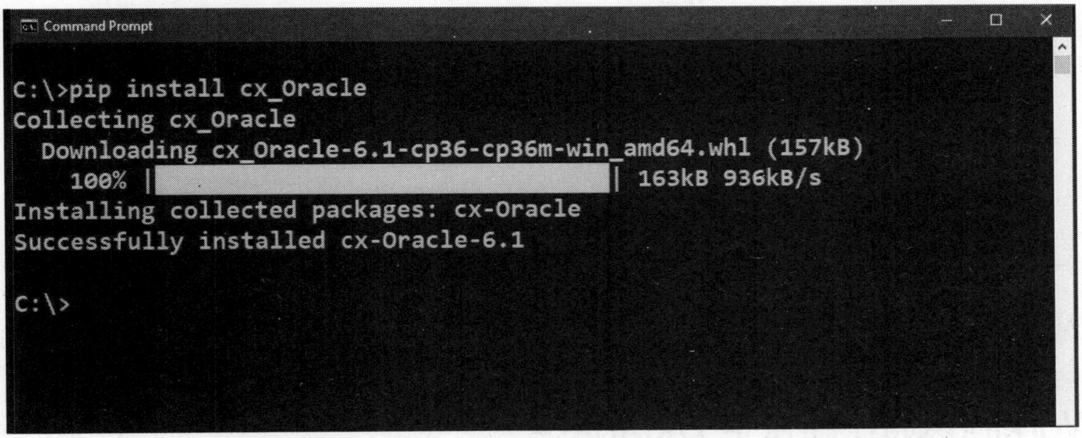

Figure 24.31: Downloading the Oracle Driver for Python 3.6.4

Verifying the Driver Installation

If the Oracle driver (or connector) for Python has been installed successfully, we can see a new module by the name 'cx_Oracle' added to the existing modules in Python library. Open the Python IDLE shell window and type the following at Python prompt:

```
>>> help('modules')
```

As a result, it will display all the available modules of Python. We should be able to locate 'cx_Oracle' module among them. This represents that the Oracle driver for Python has been successfully installed, as shown in Figure 24.32:

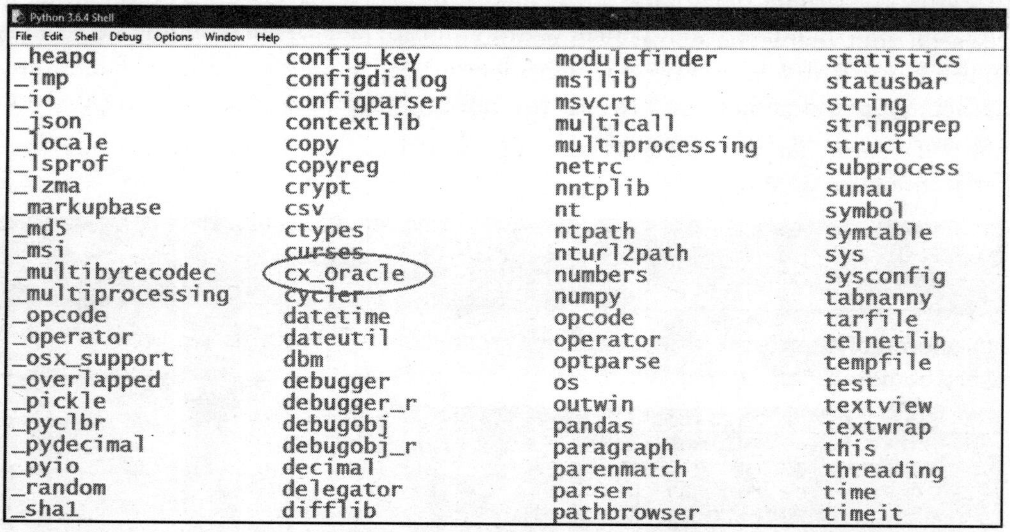

Figure 24.32: Verifying the Newly Added Module cx_oracle

Working with Oracle Database

We will first understand how to enter Oracle database and issue some SQL commands to store and retrieve data in the form of tables. To open Oracle, we can use the following steps from Start button on the Windows 10 taskbar:

Start → Oracle Database 11g Express Edition → Run SQL Command Line

It will display SQL prompt as shown below:

```
SQL>
```

Now, we should connect to Oracle database by typing 'connect' command. Then it will ask for user name and password.

```
SQL> connect
Enter user-name: SYSTEM
Enter password: Nagesh123
Connected.
SQL>
```

To see the available tables in the Oracle databases, we can give the following SQL command:

```
SQL> select * from tab;
```

It will display around 174 tables or more, which are already present in the database.

Suppose, we want to create a table with the name 'emptab' with 3 columns: eno (int type), ename (String type) and sal (float type), we can type SQL command as:

```
SQL> create table emptab(eno int, ename varchar2(20), sal float);
Table created.
```

It is seen that using the above SQL command, we have created a table by the name of 'emptab', in which varchar2(20) represents that we can store a maximum of 20 characters in ename column. To see the information about the table created by us, we can use description command as:

```
SQL>desc emptab;
Name        Null?          Type
-----------------------------------------------------
ENO                        NUMBER(38);
ENAME                      VARCHAR2(20);
SAL                        FLOAT(126);
```

Let's store rows into the table 'emptab' created by us. For this purpose, we should use 'insert' command as:

```
SQL> insert into emptab values(&eno, '&ename', &sal);
Enter value for eno: 1001
Enter value for ename: Vijaya
Enter value for sal: 8900.95
old 1: insert into emptab values(&eno, '&ename', &sal)
new 1: insert into emptab values(1001, 'Vijaya', 8900.95)
1 row created.
```

In this way, we inserted a row into oracle database. To enter another row, the above command can be repeated by typing '/' at SQL prompt as:

```
SQL>/
Enter value for eno: 1002
Enter value for ename: Gopal
Enter value for sal: 5600.55
```

To save all entered rows into the table, we can use 'commit' command as:

```
SQL> commit;
```

To see all the rows of our emptab, we should use 'select' command in the following way:

```
SQL> select * from emptab;
ENO          ENAME                SAL
------------------------------------------------------------
1001         Vijaya               8900.95
1002         Gopal                5600.55
1003         Sekhar               9988
1004         Vimala               7870.5
```

In the above command, '*' represents all the columns of the rows. If we want only eno and ename columns, we can give select command as:

```
SQL> select eno, ename from emptab;
ENO          ENAME
-----------------------------------
1001         Vijaya
1002         Gopal
1003         Sekhar
1004         Vimala
```

In case we want to retrieve the names of employees whose salary is more than Rs. 6000.00, we can give the following command:

```
SQL> select ename from emptab where sal>6000;
ENAME
-------------
Vijaya
Sekhar
Vimala
```

Let's now update the salary of an employee in emptab. Let's increase the salary by Rs. 1000 to the employee whose eno is 1002.

```
SQL> update emptab set sal= sal+1000 where eno=1002;
1 row updated.
```

If we want to delete an employee row whose eno is 1001, we give:

```
SQL> delete from emptab where eno= 1001;
1 row deleted.
```

Now, we want to insert one row related to a new employee 'Mahendra' as:

```
SQL> insert into emptab values(9999, 'Mahendra', 13000);
1 row created.
```

To save all the changes into the database, we can use 'commit' command. Similarly, to unsave the changes, 'rollback' can be used.

```
SQL> rollback;
Rollback completed.
```

Now we will close the SQL window giving 'exit' command as:

```
SQL> exit;
```

Using Oracle Database from Python

To work with Oracle database in a Python program, we have to use *cx_Oracle* module. This module can be imported as:

```
import cx_Oracle;
```

To establish connection with Oracle database, we use connect() method of *cx_Oracle* module as:

```
conn = cx_Oracle.connect('SYSTEM/Nagesh123@localhost')
```

The connect() method returns cx_Oracle.Connection class object 'conn'. This method takes the following parameters:

```
SYSTEM: this is the user name for Oracle database.
Nagesh123: this is the pass word given at the time of Oracle database
      installation.
localhost: this indicates the IP Address of the Oracle server machine.
     When we are not in the network and we are running this program in
     an individual computer, we can mention 'localhost' to represent
     that the server is also found in the local system.
```

The next step is to create cursor class object by calling the cursor() method on 'conn' object as:

```
cursor = conn.cursor()
```

The 'cursor' object is useful to execute SQL commands on the database. For this purpose, we can use the execute() method of 'cursor' object as:

```
cursor.execute("select * from emptab")
```

The resultant rows retrieved from the table are stored in the 'cursor' object. We can get them from the 'cursor' object using the fetchone() or fetchall() methods.

```
row = cursor.fetchone()    # get 1 row
rows = cursor.fetchall()    # get all rows
```

Finally, we can close the connection with MySQL by closing the cursor and connection objects as:

```
cursor.close()
conn.close()
```

Program

Program 10: A Python program to connect to Oracle database and retrieve rows from emptab table.

```
# to retrieve all rows of emptab from Oracle database
import cx_Oracle

# connect to Oracle database
conn = cx_Oracle.connect('SYSTEM/Nagesh123@localhost')

# prepare a cursor object using cursor() method
cursor = conn.cursor()
# execute a SQL query using execute() method
cursor.execute("select * from emptab")

# get only one row
row = cursor.fetchone()

# if the row exists
while row is not None:
    print(row)   # display it
    row = cursor.fetchone()   # get the next row

# close connection
cursor.close()
conn.close()
```

Output:

```
C:\>python ora.py
(1001, 'Vijaya', 8900.95)
(1002, 'Gopal', 6600.55)
(1003, 'Sekhar', 9988.0)
(1004, 'Vimala', 7870.5)
```

We can observe that this program is similar to the one we have used to retrieve rows from MySQL database. All programs which are given earlier in this chapter with MySQL are also valid with Oracle database. The only difference is that we have to import cx_Oracle instead of importing the MySQLdb module. Also, while establishing the connection with database, the format of the string that contains username and password will change. To let you understand this, we are giving another program that increases the salary of an employee by accepting employee number from the keyboard. Program 11 will do this work.

Program

Program 11: A Python program to increase the salary of an employee by accepting the employee number from keyboard.

```
# updating the salary in emptab depending on eno
import cx_Oracle

# function to update row from the emptab table
def update_rows(eno):
    # connect to Oracle database
    conn = cx_Oracle.connect('SYSTEM/Nagesh123@localhost')

    # prepare a cursor object using cursor() method
    cursor = conn.cursor()

    # prepare SQL query string to update the salary in a row
    str = "update emptab set sal = sal+1000 where eno = '%d'"

    # define the arguments
    args = (eno)
    try:
        # execute the SQL query using execute() method
        cursor.execute(str % args)
        # save the changes to the database
        conn.commit()
        print('1 row updated...')

    except:
        # rollback if there is any error
        conn.rollback()

    finally:
        # close connection
        cursor.close()
        conn.close()

# enter employee number whose row is to be updated
x = int(input('Enter eno: '))

# pass eno to update_rows() function
update_rows(x)
```

Output:

```
C:\>python db.py
Enter eno: 1003
1 row updated...
```

Stored Procedures

A stored procedure is a set of statements written using PL/SQL (Procedural Language/ Structured Query Language). To perform some calculations on the tables of a database, we can use stored procedures. Stored procedures are written and stored at database server. When a client contacts the server, the stored procedure is executed, and the results are sent to the client. Let's have more clarity on which one is client and which one is server. In Oracle, the client is SQL command line application that displays SQL> prompt. The server is the database server that runs in the system. This server takes the SQL commands from the client, executes them and returns the results to the client. In this way, every database will have a client and database server.

Stored procedures are compiled once and stored in executable form at server side. The memory for stored procedures is not allocated every time they are called. Stored procedures are stored in cache memory at server side and they are immediately available to clients. This makes speedy retrieval of data and information from the database. This is the main advantage of stored procedures. Stored procedures can be developed in all most all databases like Oracle or MySQL.

To understand the stored procedure concept, let's write a stored procedure in Oracle by the name 'myproc.sql' to increase the salary by Rs. 1000 of an employee whose eno is given by the user. Here we are assuming that the table emptab already exists in the database. First connect to the Oracle database and then type the following stored procedure at the SQL> prompt:

```
-- myproc.sql
-- to increase the salary of employee whose eno is given
create or replace procedure myproc(no in int, isal out float) as
salary float;
begin
    select sal into salary from emptab where eno=no;
    isal := salary+1000;
end;
/
```

In the last line, '/' indicates to execute the procedure at server side. In the above code, we use create or replace keyword to create the procedure. The procedure name is 'myproc'. It has two parameters: 'no' which is called in parameter and 'isal' which is called out parameter. When a client calls this procedure, it supplies the value for in parameter. The result is calculated and stored in out parameter, which is sent back to the client. Figure 24.33 shows how to type the stored procedure:

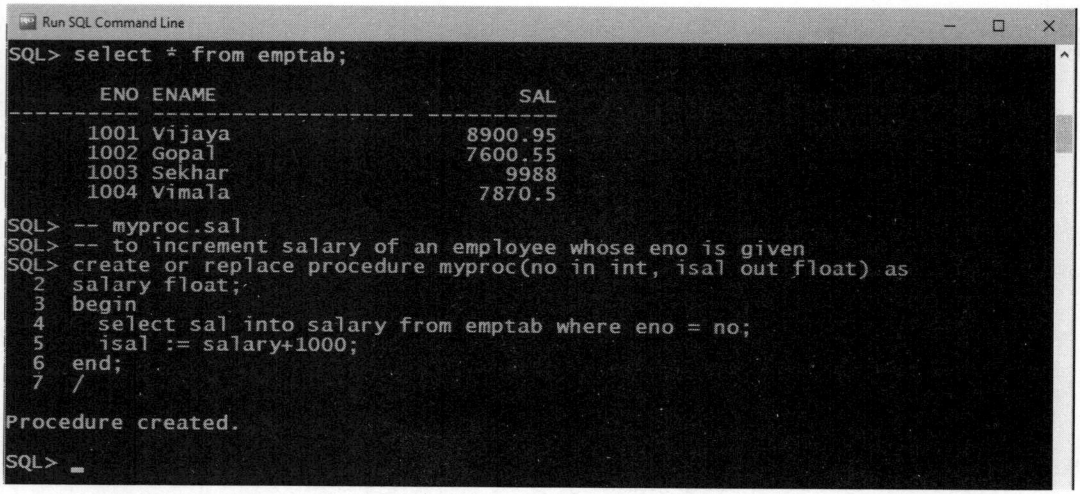

Figure 24.33: Running the Stored Procedure at Server Side

When the value of 'no' is sent by the client, the corresponding row is retrieved by the following statement:

```
select sal into salary from emptab where eno=no;
```

This will store the salary of the employee into 'salary' variable. This salary is then incremented by Rs.1000 and then stored into the out parameter 'isal'. The value in 'isal' is then available to the client.

The next step is calling this stored procedure from our Python program. To do so, we need the callproce() method of cursor object. For example, we can write:

```
result = cursor.callproc('myproc' , args)
```

In the above statement, callproc() is used to call the stored procedure: 'myproc'. After procedure's name, we got 'args' that represents a list of arguments to be passed to the procedure. Since our stored procedure contains one 'in' parameter and one 'out' parameter, we have to pass two arguments as:

```
args = [eno, isal] #pass eno as in parameter and isal as out parameter
```

To retrieve the data from the out parameter, first we should declare the data type of the parameter as:

```
isal = cursor.var(cx_Oracle.NUMBER)
```

Here, the out parameter is declared as NUMBER type. All types are defined in cx_Oracle module as constants shown below:

```
cx_Oracle.NUMBER
cx_Oracle.STRING
cx_Oracle.BOOLEAN
cx_Oracle.DATETIME
```

Once the 2nd parameter (i.e., out parameter) is registered, the callproc() will execute the procedure and the result is returned into result variable. The result contains a list where result[0] indicates the in parameter and result[1] indicates the out parameter. It means result[1] contains the incremented salary.

Program

Program 12: A Python program to execute a stored procedure and get the results from Oracle database.

```
# updating the salary in emptab depending on eno by calling a stored
# procedure
import cx_Oracle

# function to update row from the emptab table
def update_rows(eno):
    # connect to Oracle database
    conn = cx_Oracle.connect('SYSTEM/Nagesh123@localhost')

    # prepare a cursor object using cursor() method
    cursor = conn.cursor()

    # declare isal variable as NUMBER datatype
    isal = cursor.var(cx_Oracle.NUMBER)

    # define args as a list. eno is in parameter and isal is out
    # parameter
    args = [eno, isal]

    # call stored procedure using callproc() method and pass in and out
    # parameters
    result = cursor.callproc('myproc' , args)

    # result[0] indicates the eno value and result[1] indicates isal
    # value
    print('The incremented salary for emp id %d is %.2f' % (result[0],
          result[1]))

    # close connection
    cursor.close()
    conn.close()
# enter employee number whose row is to be updated
x = int(input('Enter eno: '))
# pass eno to update_rows() function
update_rows(x)
```

Output:

```
C:\>python proc.py
Enter eno: 1002
The incremented salary for emp id 1002 is 8600.55
```

Points to Remember

- A database management system (DBMS) represents software that stores and manages data.
- DBMS has several advantages over files for storing data.

- We can work with any database like MySQL or Oracle using Python programs. It means we can create tables and perform operations like insertion, deletion or updation on the tables using Python programs.
- To work with MySQL database from Python, we need two things: MySQL database software and the MySQL client interface software. These two should have been installed in our computer system.
- After installing the MySQL interface, we can see a new module by the name 'MySQLdb' in the Python library.
- To work with Oracle database from Python, we need two things: Oracle database software and the driver software. These two should have been installed in our computer system.
- After installing the Oracle driver, we can see a new module by the name 'cx_Oracle' in the Python library.
- The connect() method is useful to connect to the database. We have to pass username and password along with server name (or IP Address) to this method.
- The connect() method returns connection object. When we call cursor() method with connection object, we get cursor object. This object is useful to execute any SQL command or query. For example, cursor.execute('sqlcommandstring') is the format for executing an SQL command.
- The fetchone() method retrieves only one row from the table. On the other hand, the fetchall() method retrieves all rows depending on the SQL command.
- The SQL commands are almost same for all databases like MySQL or Oracle.

CHAPTER 25

DATA SCIENCE USING PYTHON

Data plays an important role in our lives. For example, a chain of hospitals contain data related to medical reports and prescriptions of their patients. A bank contains thousands of customers' transaction details. Share market data represents minute-to-minute changes in the values of the shares. In this way, the entire world is roaming around huge data.

Every piece of data is precious as it may affect the business organization which is using that data. So, we need some mechanism to store that data. Moreover, data may come from various sources. For example, in a business organization, we may get data from Sales department, Purchase department, Production department, etc. Such data is stored in a system called 'data warehouse'. We can imagine data warehouse as a central repository of integrated data from different sources.

Once the data is stored, we should be able to retrieve it based on some pre-requisites. A business company wants to know about how much amount they had spent in the last 6 months on purchasing the raw material or how many items had been found defective in their production unit. Such data cannot be easily retrieved from the huge data available in the data warehouse. We have to retrieve the data as per the needs of the business organization. This is called data analysis or data analytics where the data that is retrieved will be analyzed to answer the questions raised by the management of the organization. A person who does data analysis is called 'data analyst'. Please see Figure 25.1:

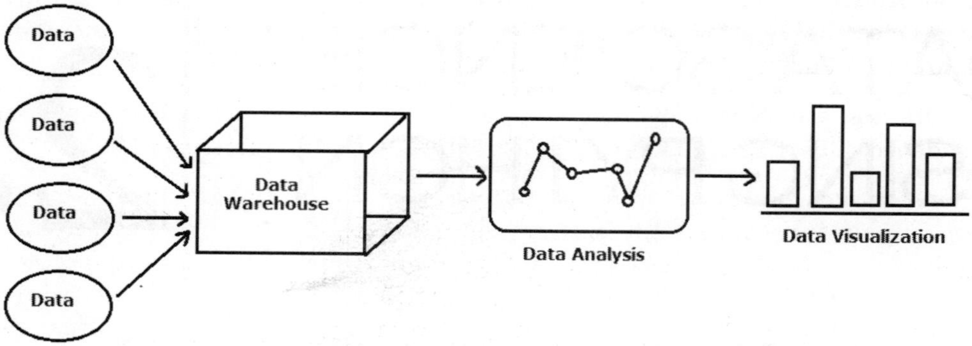

Figure 25.1: Data analysis and data visualization

Once the data is analyzed, it is the duty of the IT professional to present the results in the form of pictures or graphs so that the management will be able to understand it easily. Such graphs will also help them forecast the future of their company. This is called data visualization. The primary goal of data visualization is to communicate information clearly and efficiently using statistical graphs, plots and diagrams.

Data science is a term used for techniques to extract information from the data warehouse, analyze them and present the necessary data to the business organization in order to arrive at important conclusions and decisions. A person who is involved in this work is called 'data scientist'. We can find important differences between the roles of data scientist and data analyst as shown in Table 25.1:

Table 25.1: Differences Between Data Scientist and Data Analyst

Data Scientist	Data Analyst
Data scientist formulates the questions that will help a business organization and then proceed in solving them.	Data analyst receives questions from the business team and provides answers to them.
Data scientist will have strong data visualization skills and the ability to convert data into a business story.	Data analyst simply analyzes the data and provides information requested by the team.
Perfection in mathematics, statistics and programming languages like Python and R are needed for a data scientist.	Perfection in data warehousing, big data concepts, SQL and business intelligence is needed for a data analyst.
Data scientist estimates the unknown information from the known data.	Data analyst looks at the known data from a new perspective.

Data Frame

Data frame is an object that is useful in representing data in the form of rows and columns. For example, the data may come from a file or an Excel spreadsheet or from a

Python sequence like a list or tuple. We can represent that data in the form of a data frame. Once the data is stored into the data frame, we can perform various operations that are useful in analyzing and understanding the data.

Data frames are generally created from .csv (comma separated values) files, Excel spreadsheet files, Python dictionaries, list of tuples or list of dictionaries.

Python contains *pandas* which is a package useful for data analysis and manipulation. Also, *xlrd* is a package that is useful to retrieve data from Excel files. We should download these packages separately as they are developed by third-party people. You can see Chapter 2 to know how to download and install these packages. DataFrame is the main object in pandas package. We will first discuss various ways of creating data frame objects.

Creating Data Frame from an Excel Spreadsheet

Let us assume that we have a large volume of data present in an Excel spreadsheet file by the name 'empdata.xlsx', as shown in Figure 25.2:

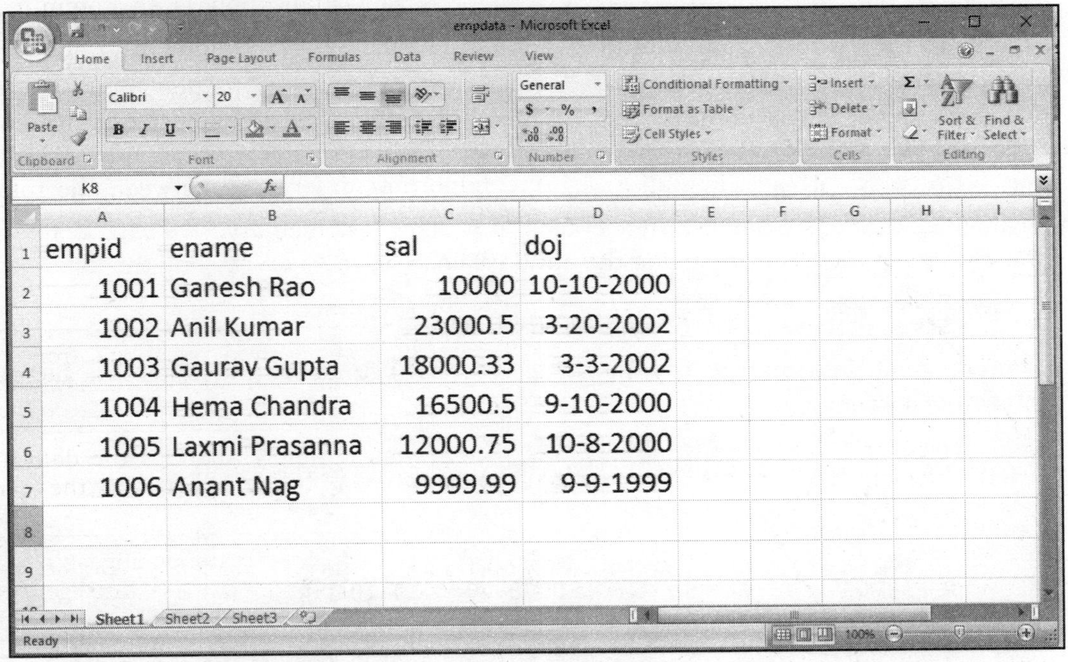

Figure 25.2: An excel file that contains employee data

This file contains data related to employee id number, name, salary and date of joining the company. Alternately, we can create this file on our own by opening Microsoft Office Excel and type in the data. When we save the data with the file name 'empdata', it will be saved with an extension '.xlsx'.

To create the data frames, we should first import the pandas package. We may need *xlrd* package also that is useful in extracting data from Excel files. To read the data from Excel file, we should use read_excel() function of pandas package in the following format:

```
read_excel('file path', 'sheet number')
```

If our Excel file is available in 'F:' drive and 'python\PANDAS' subdirectory, open the Python IDLE window and type the commands as shown below:

```
>>> import pandas as pd
>>> import xlrd
>>> df = pd.read_excel("f:\\python\PANDAS\empdata.xlsx", "Sheet1")

>>> df

   empid            ename       sal        doj
0   1001       Ganesh Rao  10000.00 2000-10-10
1   1002       Anil Kumar  23000.50 2002-03-20
2   1003     Gaurav Gupta  18000.33 2002-03-03
3   1004     Hema Chandra  16500.50 2000-09-10
4   1005  Laxmi Prasanna  12000.75 2000-10-08
5   1006        Anant Nag   9999.99 1999-09-09
```

Thus, we created the data frame by the name 'df'. Please observe the first column having numbers from 0 to 5. This additional column is called 'index column' and added by the data frame.

Creating Data Frame from .csv Files

In many cases, the data will be in the form of .csv files. A .csv file is a comma-separated values file that is similar to an Excel file but it takes less memory. We can create the .csv file by saving the Excel file using the option: File -> Save As and typing the following:

```
File name: empdata
Save as type: CSV (Comma delimited)
```

We can read data from a .csv file using read_csv() function that takes the file path as shown below:

```
>>> import pandas as pd
>>> df = pd.read_csv("f:\\python\PANDAS\empdata.csv")

>>> df

   empid            ename       sal        doj
0   1001       Ganesh Rao  10000.00   10-10-00
1   1002       Anil Kumar  23000.50  3-20-2002
2   1003     Gaurav Gupta  18000.33   03-03-02
3   1004     Hema Chandra  16500.50   10-09-00
4   1005  Laxmi Prasanna  12000.75   08-10-00
5   1006        Anant Nag   9999.99   09-09-99
```

Creating Data Frame from a Python Dictionary

It is possible to create a Python dictionary that contains employee data. Let us remember that a dictionary stores data in the form of key-value pairs. In this case, we take 'empid', 'ename', 'sal', 'doj' as keys and corresponding lists as values. Let us first create a dictionary by the name 'empdata' as shown below:

```
>>> empdata = {"empid": [1001, 1002, 1003, 1004, 1005, 1006],
    "ename": ["Ganesh Rao", "Anil Kumar", "Gaurav Gupta", "Hema Chandra",
"Laxmi Prasanna", "Anant Nag"],
    "sal": [10000, 23000.50, 18000.33, 16500.50, 12000.75, 9999.99],
    "doj": ["10-10-2000", "3-20-2002", "3-3-2002", "9-10-2000", "10-8-
2000", "9-9-1999"]}
```

Now, let us convert this empdata dictionary into a data frame by passing this dictionary to DataFrame class object as:

```
>>> df = pd.DataFrame(empdata)

>>> df
          doj  empid           ename       sal
0  10-10-2000   1001      Ganesh Rao  10000.00
1   3-20-2002   1002      Anil Kumar  23000.50
2    3-3-2002   1003    Gaurav Gupta  18000.33
3   9-10-2000   1004    Hema Chandra  16500.50
4   10-8-2000   1005  Laxmi Prasanna  12000.75
5    9-9-1999   1006       Anant Nag   9999.99
```

Creating Data Frame from Python List of Tuples

It is possible to create a list of tuples that contains employee data. A tuple can be treated as a row of data. Suppose, if we want to store the data of 6 employees, we have to create 6 tuples. Let us first create a list of 6 tuples by the name 'empdata' as shown below:

```
>>> empdata = [(1001, 'Ganesh Rao', 10000.00, '10-10-2000'),
(1002, 'Anil Kumar', 23000.50, '3-20-2002'),
(1003, 'Gaurav Gupta', 18000.33, '03-03-2002'),
(1004, 'Hema Chandra', 16500.50, '10-09-2000'),
(1005, 'Laxmi Prasanna', 12000.75, '08-10-2000'),
(1006, 'Anant Nag', 9999.99, '09-09-1999')]
```

Now, let us convert this list of tuples into a data frame by passing this dictionary to DataFrame class object as:

```
>>> df = pd.DataFrame(empdata, columns=["eno", "ename", "sal", "doj"])
```

Since the original list of tuples does not have column names, we have to include the column names while creating the data frame as shown in the preceding statement. Now let us display the data frame as:

```
>>> df

    eno           ename       sal         doj
0  1001      Ganesh Rao  10000.00  10-10-2000
1  1002      Anil Kumar  23000.50   3-20-2002
2  1003    Gaurav Gupta  18000.33  03-03-2002
3  1004    Hema Chandra  16500.50  10-09-2000
4  1005  Laxmi Prasanna  12000.75  08-10-2000
5  1006       Anant Nag   9999.99  09-09-1999
```

Operations on Data Frames

Once we create a data frame, we can do various operations on it. These operations help us in analyzing the data or manipulating the data. The reader is advised to refer to the list of all operations available in pandas at the following link:

```
    https://pandas.pydata.org/pandas-
docs/stable/generated/pandas.Series.html
```

First we will create a data frame from a .csv file using read_csv() function as shown below. This data frame will be the basis for our operations.

```
>>> df = pd.read_csv("f:\\python\PANDAS\empdata.csv")

>>> df

   empid           ename       sal         doj
0   1001      Ganesh Rao  10000.00    10-10-00
1   1002      Anil Kumar  23000.50   3-20-2002
2   1003    Gaurav Gupta  18000.33    03-03-02
3   1004    Hema Chandra  16500.50    10-09-00
4   1005  Laxmi Prasanna  12000.75    08-10-00
5   1006       Anant Nag   9999.99    09-09-99
```

Knowing Number of Rows and Columns

To know the number of rows and columns available in the data frame, we can use shape attribute. It returns a tuple that contains number of rows and columns as:

```
>>> df.shape
(6, 4)
```

Suppose, we want to retrieve only rows or columns, we can read that number from the tuple as:

```
>>> r, c = df.shape
>>> print(r)    # display only no of rows
6
```

Retrieving Rows from Data Frame

The method head() gives the first 5 rows and the method tail() returns the last 5 rows, as shown below:

```
>>> df.head()

   empid           ename       sal         doj
0   1001      Ganesh Rao  10000.00  10-10-2000
1   1002      Anil Kumar  23000.50    3-3-2002
2   1003    Gaurav Gupta  18000.33    3-3-2002
3   1004    Hema Chandra  16500.50    3-3-2002
4   1005  Laxmi Prasanna  12000.75   10-8-2000

>>> df.tail()

   empid           ename       sal         doj
1   1002      Anil Kumar  23000.50    3-3-2002
2   1003    Gaurav Gupta  18000.33    3-3-2002
3   1004    Hema Chandra  16500.50    3-3-2002
```

```
4    1005  Laxmi Prasanna  12000.75  10-8-2000
5    1006       Anant Nag   9999.99   9-9-1999
```

To display only the first 2 rows, we can use head() method by passing 2 to it as:

```
>>> df.head(2)

   empid        ename      sal         doj
0   1001  Ganesh Rao   10000.0  10-10-2000
1   1002  Anil Kumar   23000.5    3-3-2002
```

Similarly, to display the last 2 rows, we can use tail(2) as shown below:

```
>>> df.tail(2)

   empid           ename       sal        doj
4   1005  Laxmi Prasanna  12000.75  10-8-2000
5   1006       Anant Nag   9999.99   9-9-1999
```

Retrieving a Range of Rows

We can treat the data frame as an object and retrieve the rows from it using slicing. For example, if we write df[2:5], we can get 2nd row to 4th row (excludes 5th row).

```
>>> df[2:5]

   empid           ename       sal        doj
2   1003    Gaurav Gupta  18000.33   3-3-2002
3   1004    Hema Chandra  16500.50   3-3-2002
4   1005  Laxmi Prasanna  12000.75  10-8-2000
```

Similarly, to display alternate rows, we can use df[0::2] or df[::2] as shown below:

```
>>> df[0::2]

   empid           ename       sal         doj
0   1001      Ganesh Rao  10000.00  10-10-2000
2   1003    Gaurav Gupta  18000.33    3-3-2002
4   1005  Laxmi Prasanna  12000.75   10-8-2000
```

To display the rows in reverse order, we can use negative step size in slicing as:

```
>>> df[5:0:-1]

   empid           ename       sal        doj
5   1006       Anant Nag   9999.99   9-9-1999
4   1005  Laxmi Prasanna  12000.75  10-8-2000
3   1004    Hema Chandra  16500.50   3-3-2002
2   1003    Gaurav Gupta  18000.33   3-3-2002
1   1002      Anil Kumar  23000.50   3-3-2002
```

To Retrieve Column Names

To retrieve the column names from the data frame, we can use columns attribute as:

```
>>> df.columns

Index(['empid', 'ename', 'sal', 'doj'], dtype='object')
```

To Retrieve Column Data

To get the column data, we can mention the column name as subscript. For example, df.empid will display all employee id numbers. This can also be done using df['empid'] which is shown below:

```
>>> df.empid

0    1001
1    1002
2    1003
3    1004
4    1005
5    1006
Name: empid, dtype: int64

>>> df['empid']
0    1001
1    1002
2    1003
3    1004
4    1005
5    1006
Name: empid, dtype: int64
```

Similarly, to display employee names, we can use df.ename or df['ename'].

Retrieving Data from Multiple Columns

To retrieve multiple columns data, we can provide the list of column names as subscript to data frame object as df[[list of column names]]. For example, to display the employee ids and their names, we can write:

```
>>> df[['empid', 'ename']]

   empid           ename
0   1001      Ganesh Rao
1   1002      Anil Kumar
2   1003    Gaurav Gupta
3   1004    Hema Chandra
4   1005  Laxmi Prasanna
5   1006       Anant Nag
```

Finding Maximum and Minimum Values

It is possible to find the highest value using max() method and the least value using min() method. These methods are applied to columns containing numerical data. For example, to know the highest salary and the least salary, we can use as:

```
>>> df['sal'].max()

23000.5

>>> df['sal'].min()

9999.9899999999998
```

Displaying Statistical Information

We have describe() method that displays very important information like number of values, average, standard deviation, minimum, maximum, 25%, 50% and 75% of the total value. This information is highly useful for statistical analysis.

```
>>> df.describe()

              empid           sal
count      6.000000      6.000000
mean    1003.500000  14917.011667
std        1.870829   5181.037711
min     1001.000000   9999.990000
25%     1002.250000  10500.187500
50%     1003.500000  14250.625000
75%     1004.750000  17625.372500
max     1006.000000  23000.500000
```

Performing Queries on Data

We can retrieve rows based on a query. The query should be given as subscript in the data frame object. For example, to retrieve all the rows where salary is greater than Rs. 10000, we can write:

```
>>> df[df.sal>10000]

   empid            ename       sal        doj
1   1002       Anil Kumar  23000.50  3-20-2002
2   1003     Gaurav Gupta  18000.33   03-03-02
3   1004     Hema Chandra  16500.50   10-09-00
4   1005  Laxmi Prasanna   12000.75   08-10-00
```

To retrieve the row where salary is maximum, we can write:

```
>>> df[df.sal == df.sal.max()]

   empid       ename      sal        doj
1   1002  Anil Kumar  23000.5  3-20-2002
```

Suppose, we want to show data from some columns based on a query, we can mention the list of columns and then the query as: df[[column names]][query]. For example, to display only id numbers and names where the salary is greater than Rs. 10000, we can write:

```
>>> df[['empid', 'ename']][df.sal>10000]

   empid            ename
1   1002       Anil Kumar
2   1003     Gaurav Gupta
3   1004     Hema Chandra
4   1005  Laxmi Prasanna
```

Knowing the Index Range

The first column is called index column and it is generated in the data frame automatically. We can retrieve the index information using index attribute as:

```
>>> df.index

RangeIndex(start=0, stop=6, step=1)
```

Setting a column as Index

We know the index column is automatically generated. If we do not want this column and we want to set a column from our data as index column, that is possible using set_index() method. The column with unique values can be set as index column. For example, to make 'empid' column as index column for our data frame, we can write:

```
>>> df1 = df.set_index('empid')
```

The above statement creates another data frame 'df1' that uses 'empid' as index column. We can verify this by displaying df1 as:

```
>>> df1

                 ename       sal        doj
empid
1001        Ganesh Rao  10000.00  10-10-2000
1002        Anil Kumar  23000.50    3-3-2002
1003      Gaurav Gupta  18000.33    3-3-2002
1004      Hema Chandra  16500.50    3-3-2002
1005   Laxmi Prasanna   12000.75   10-8-2000
1006         Anant Nag   9999.99    9-9-1999
```

We can find the empid being used as index column in the new data frame 'df1' as above. However, the original data frame 'df' in this case is not modified and it still uses automatically generated index column. If we want to modify the original 'df' and set empid as index column, we should add 'inplace=True' as shown below:

```
>>> df.set_index('empid', inplace=True)

>>> df
                 ename       sal        doj
empid
1001        Ganesh Rao  10000.00    10-10-00
1002        Anil Kumar  23000.50   3-20-2002
1003      Gaurav Gupta  18000.33    03-03-02
1004      Hema Chandra  16500.50    10-09-00
1005    Laxmi Prasanna  12000.75    08-10-00
1006         Anant Nag   9999.99    09-09-99
```

Once we set 'empid' as index, it is possible to locate the data of any employee by passing employee id number to loc attribute as:

```
>>> df.loc[1004]

ename     Hema Chandra
sal            16500.5
doj           3-3-2002
Name: 1004, dtype: object
```

Resetting the Index

To reset the index value from 'empid' back to auto-generated index number, we can use reset_index() method with inplace=True option as:

```
>>> df.reset_index(inplace=True)

>>> df

   empid           ename       sal         doj
0   1001      Ganesh Rao  10000.00  10-10-2000
1   1002     Anil Kumar   23000.50    3-3-2002
2   1003    Gaurav Gupta  18000.33    3-3-2002
3   1004   Hema Chandra   16500.50    3-3-2002
4   1005 Laxmi Prasanna   12000.75   10-8-2000
5   1006       Anant Nag   9999.99    9-9-1999
```

Sorting the Data

To sort the data coming from a .csv file, first let us read the data from the file into a data frame using read_csv() function as:

```
>>> df = pd.read_csv("f:\\python\PANDAS\empdata2.csv",
parse_dates=['doj'])
```

Here, we are loading the data from empdata2.csv file and also informing to take 'doj' as date type field using parse_dates option. Now let us display the data frame as:

```
>>> print(df)

   empid           ename       sal        doj
0   1001      Ganesh Rao  10000.00 2000-10-10
1   1002      Anil Kumar  23000.50 2002-03-03
2   1003    Gaurav Gupta  18000.33 2002-03-03
3   1004    Hema Chandra  16500.50 2002-03-03
4   1005  Laxmi Prasanna  12000.75 2000-08-10
5   1006       Anant Nag   9999.99 1999-09-09
```

To sort the rows on 'doj' column into ascending order, we can use sort_values() method as:

```
>>> df1 = df.sort_values('doj')

>>> df1

   empid           ename       sal        doj
5   1006       Anant Nag   9999.99 1999-09-09
4   1005  Laxmi Prasanna  12000.75 2000-08-10
0   1001      Ganesh Rao  10000.00 2000-10-10
1   1002      Anil Kumar  23000.50 2002-03-03
2   1003    Gaurav Gupta  18000.33 2002-03-03
3   1004    Hema Chandra  16500.50 2002-03-03
```

To sort in descending order, we should use an additional option 'ascending = False' as:

```
>>> df1 = df.sort_values('doj', ascending=False)
```

Sorting on multiple columns is also possible. This can be done using an option 'by' in the sort_values() method. For example, we want to sort on 'doj' in descending order and in that 'sal' in ascending order. That means, when two employees have same 'doj', then their salaries will be sorted into ascending order.

```
>>> df1 = df.sort_values(by=['doj', 'sal'], ascending=[False, True])

>>> df1

   empid           ename       sal         doj
3   1004    Hema Chandra  16500.50  2002-03-03
2   1003    Gaurav Gupta  18000.33  2002-03-03
1   1002      Anil Kumar  23000.50  2002-03-03
0   1001     Ganesh Rao   10000.00  2000-10-10
4   1005  Laxmi Prasanna  12000.75  2000-08-10
5   1006       Anant Nag   9999.99  1999-09-09
```

Handling Missing Data

In many cases, the data that we receive from various sources may not be perfect. That means there may be some missing data. For example, 'empdata1.csv' file contains the following data where employee name is missing in one row and salary and date of joining are missing in another row. Please see Figure 25.3:

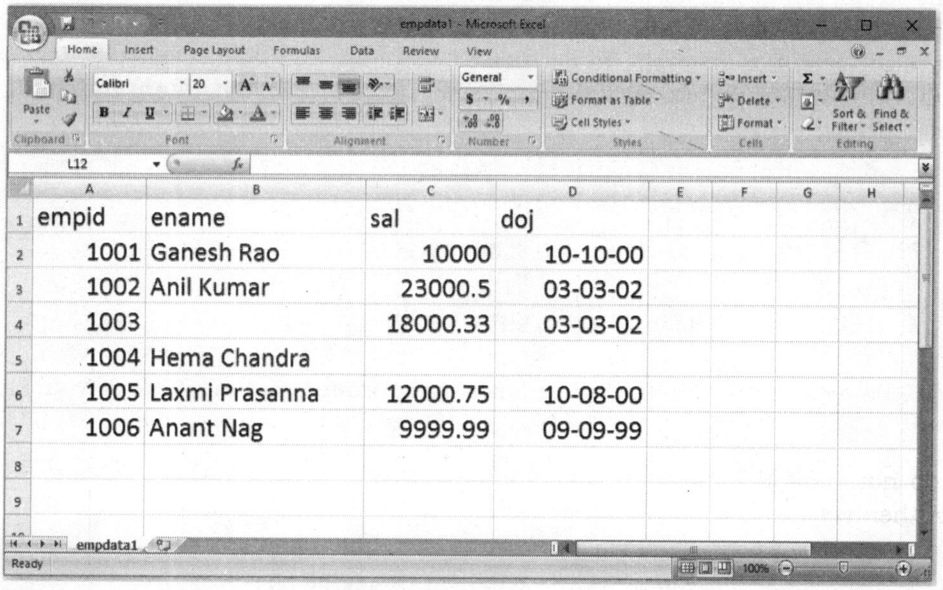

empid	ename	sal	doj
1001	Ganesh Rao	10000	10-10-00
1002	Anil Kumar	23000.5	03-03-02
1003		18000.33	03-03-02
1004	Hema Chandra		
1005	Laxmi Prasanna	12000.75	10-08-00
1006	Anant Nag	9999.99	09-09-99

Figure 25.3: A .csv file with missing data

When we convert the data into a data frame, the missing data is represented by NaN (Not a Number). NaN is a default marker for the missing value. Please observe the following data frame:

```
>>> import pandas as pd
>>> df = pd.read_csv("f:\\python\PANDAS\empdata1.csv")

>>> df
```

```
   empid          ename       sal       doj
0   1001     Ganesh Rao  10000.00  10-10-00
1   1002     Anil Kumar  23000.50  03-03-02
2   1003            NaN  18000.33  03-03-02
3   1004   Hema Chandra       NaN       NaN
4   1005 Laxmi Prasanna  12000.75  10-08-00
5   1006      Anant Nag   9999.99  09-09-99
```

We can use fillna() method to replace the Na or NaN values by a specified value. For example, to fill the NaN values by 0, we can use:

```
>>> df1 = df.fillna(0)

>>> df1

   empid          ename       sal       doj
0   1001     Ganesh Rao  10000.00  10-10-00
1   1002     Anil Kumar  23000.50  03-03-02
2   1003              0  18000.33  03-03-02
3   1004   Hema Chandra      0.00         0
4   1005 Laxmi Prasanna  12000.75  10-08-00
5   1006      Anant Nag   9999.99  09-09-99
```

But this is not so useful as it is filling any type of column with zero. We can fill each column with a different value by passing the column names and the value to be used to fill in the column. For example, to fill 'ename' column with 'Name missing', 'sal' with 0.0 and 'doj' with '00-00-00', we should supply these values as a dictionary to fillna() method as shown below:

```
>>> df1 = df.fillna({'ename': 'Name missing', 'sal': 0.0, 'doj':'00-00-
00'})

>>> df1

   empid          ename       sal       doj
0   1001     Ganesh Rao  10000.00  10-10-00
1   1002     Anil Kumar  23000.50  03-03-02
2   1003   Name missing  18000.33  03-03-02
3   1004   Hema Chandra      0.00  00-00-00
4   1005 Laxmi Prasanna  12000.75  10-08-00
5   1006      Anant Nag   9999.99  09-09-99
```

If we do not want the missing data and want to remove those rows having Na or NaN values, then we can use dropna() method as:

```
>>> df1 = df.dropna()

>>> df1

   empid          ename       sal       doj
0   1001     Ganesh Rao  10000.00  10-10-00
1   1002     Anil Kumar  23000.50  03-03-02
4   1005 Laxmi Prasanna  12000.75  10-08-00
5   1006      Anant Nag   9999.99  09-09-99
```

In this way, filling the necessary data or eliminating the missing data is called 'data cleansing'.

Data Visualization

When data is shown in the form of pictures, it becomes easy for the user to understand it. Representing the data in the form of pictures or graphs is called 'data visualization'. For this purpose, we can use pyplot submodule of the matplotlib module. Installation of matplotlib is already discussed in Chapter 2. For complete information about this module, you can refer to the page:

```
https://matplotlib.org/api/pyplot_summary.html
```

Bar Graph

A bar graph represents data in the form of vertical or horizontal bars. It is useful to compare the quantities. Now, let us see how to create a bar graph with employee id numbers on X-axis and their salaries on Y-axis. We will take this data from the data frame. First of all, we should import the packages as:

```
import matplotlib.pyplot as plt   # for drawing the graph
import pandas as pd   # for creating the data frame
```

Suppose the data frame is created from 'empdata' as:

```
df = pd.DataFrame(empdata)
```

This data frame 'df' contains various pieces of data like empid, ename, sal and doj. We want to take only the 'empid' and 'sal' for the purpose of drawing the graph. This is done as:

```
x = df['empid']
y = df['sal']
```

We can draw the bar graph by calling bar() function of pyplot module as:

```
plt.bar(x, y, label='Employee data', color='red')
```

We can display a label (or title) on X-axis and Y-axis using xlabel() and ylabel) functions as:

```
plt.xlabel('Employee ids')
plt.ylabel('Employee salaries')
```

We can provide company's title using title() function as:

```
plt.title('MICROSOFT INC')
```

We can also display legend that refers to colors and labels of data especially when different sets of data are plotted as:

```
plt.legend()
```

Finally, the graph can be displayed by calling the show() function as:

```
plt.show()
```

Program

Program 1: A Python program to display employee id numbers on X-axis and their salaries on Y-axis in the form a bar graph.

```
# bar graph with ids, salaries
import matplotlib.pyplot as plt
import pandas as pd

# take employee data as a dictionary
empdata = {"empid": [1001, 1002, 1003, 1004, 1005, 1006],
"ename": ["Ganesh Rao", "Anil Kumar", "Gaurav Gupta", "Hema Chandra",
"Laxmi Prasanna", "Anant Nag"],
"sal": [10000, 23000.50, 18000.33, 16500.50, 12000.75, 9999.99],
"doj": ["10-10-2000", "3-20-2002", "3-3-2002", "9-10-2000", "10-8-
2000", "9-9-1999"]}

# create a data frame
df = pd.DataFrame(empdata)

# extract empid and salary data into x and y vars
x = df['empid']
y = df['sal']

# create bar graph
plt.bar(x,y, label='Employee data', color='red')

# set x and y axis labels
plt.xlabel('Employee ids')
plt.ylabel('Employee salaries')

# set company title
plt.title('MICROSOFT INC')

# show legend
plt.legend()

# display the graph
plt.show()
```

Output:

```
C:\> python bar.py
```

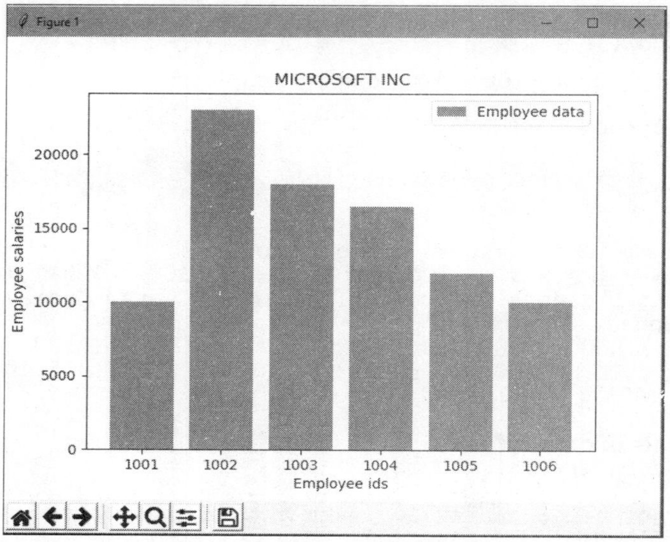

From the above output, we can infer that the employee with id number 1002 is drawing the highest salary and next to him the employee with id number 1003.

We can create bar graphs from more than one data set that are coming from multiple data frames. For example, we can plot the empid and salaries for 2 departments: Sales team and Production team. For this purpose, we can call the bar() function two times as:

```
plt.bar(x,y, label='Sales dept', color='red')
plt.bar(x1, y1, label='Production dept', color='green')
```

Program

Program 2: A program to display employee id numbers on X-axis and their salaries on Y-axis in the form of a bar graph for two departments of a company.

```
# bar graph with ids, salaries for two depts
import matplotlib.pyplot as plt

# take employee ids and salaries for Sales dept
x = [1001, 1003, 1006, 1007, 1009, 1011]
y = [10000, 23000.50, 18000.33, 16500.50, 12000.75, 9999.99]

# take employee ids and salaries for Production dept
x1 = [1002, 1004, 1010, 1008, 1014, 1015]
y1 = [5000, 6000, 4500.00, 12000, 9000, 10000]

# create bar graphs
plt.bar(x,y, label='Sales dept', color='red')
plt.bar(x1, y1, label='Production dept', color='green')

# set the labels and legend
plt.xlabel('emp id')
```

```
plt.ylabel('salaries')
plt.title('MICROSOFT INC')
plt.legend()

# display the bar graph
plt.show()
```

Output:

```
C:\> python bars.py
```

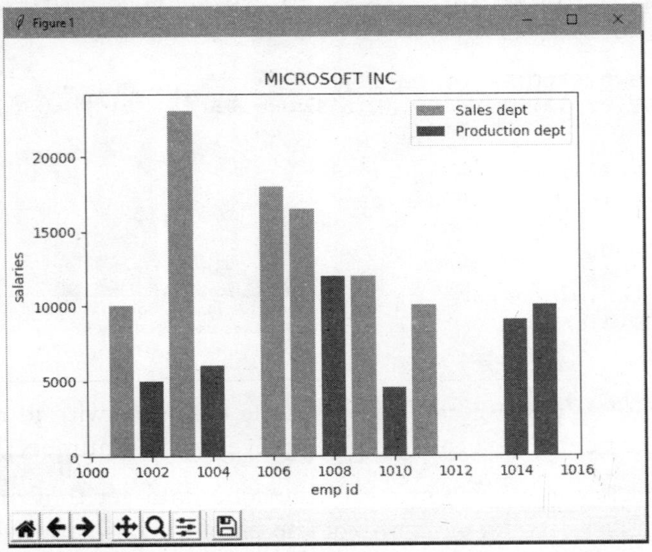

From the above output, we can understand that the Sales department people are drawing more salaries when compared to those of the Production department.

Histogram

Histogram shows distributions of values. Histogram is similar to bar graph but it is useful to show values grouped in bins or intervals. For example, we can collect the age of each employee in a company and show it in the form of a histogram to know how many employees are there in the range of 0-10 years, 10-20 years, etc. For this purpose, we should take the employee ages and bins (or intervals) as:

```
emp_ages = [22,45,30,59,58,56,57,45,43,43,50,40,34,33,25,19]
bins = [0,10,20,30,40,50,60]   # of 10 years' range
```

The bins list contains 0,10,20... This indicates the ranges from 0 to 9, 10 to 19, etc., excluding the outer limit. To draw the histogram, we should use hist() function as:

```
plt.hist(emp_ages, bins, histtype='bar', rwidth=0.8, color='cyan')
```

Here, histtype is 'bar' to show the histogram in the form of bars. The other types can be 'barstacked', 'step', 'stepfilled'. The option rwidth = 0.8 indicates that the bar's width is 80%. There will be a gap of 10% space before and after the bar. If this is decreased, then the bar's width will be narrowed.

Program

Program 3: A program to display a histogram showing the number of employees in specific age groups.

```
# histogram of employee ages
import matplotlib.pyplot as plt

# take individual employee ages and range of ages
emp_ages = [22,45,30,59,58,56,57,45,43,43,50,40,34,33,25,19]
bins = [0,10,20,30,40,50,60]

# create histogram of bar type
plt.hist(emp_ages, bins, histtype='bar', rwidth=0.8, color='cyan')

# set labels
plt.xlabel('employee ages')
plt.ylabel('no. of employees')
plt.title('ORACLE CORP')
plt.legend()

# draw the histogram
plt.show()
```

Output:

```
C:\> python histo.py
```

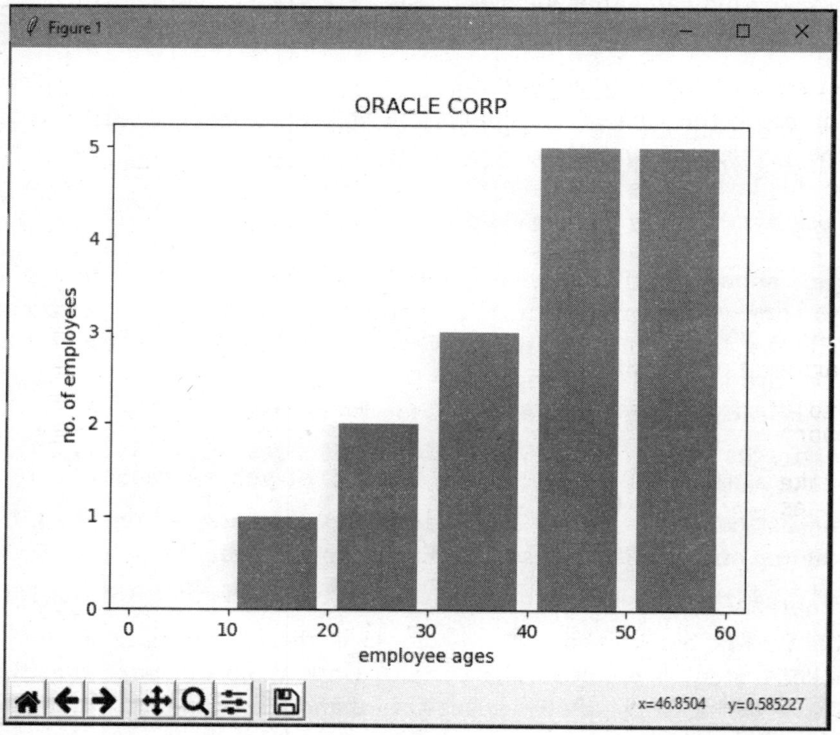

From the output, we can understand that this company has more employees in the age group of 40 to 59 years. It infers that most employees in the company are above the age of 40.

Creating a Pie Chart

A pie chart shows a circle that is divided into sectors and each sector represents a proportion of the whole. For example, we can take different departments in a company and their employees. Suppose, there are 4 departments and their employees are in the percentages of 50%, 20%, 15% and 15%. These can be represented as slices in a pie chart.

To create a pie chart, we can use pie() function as:

```
    plt.pie(slices, labels=depts, colors=cols, startangle=90, explode=(0,
0.2, 0, 0), shadow=True, autopct='%.1f%%' )
```

Here, labels=depts indicates a list of labels. colors=cols indicates a list of colors. startangle=90 indicates that the pie chart will start at 90 degrees (12 o'clock position). If this option is not mentioned, then it starts by default at 0 degrees (3 o'clock position).

The option explode=(0,0.2, 0,0) indicates whether the slices in the pie chart should stand out or not. Here, 0 indicates that the corresponding slide will not come out of the chart. But the next 0.2 indicates that the second slice should come out slightly. Its values 0.1 to 1 indicate how much it should come out of the chart.

The option shadow=True indicates that the pie chart should be displayed with a shadow. This will improve the look of the chart. The option autopct='%.1f%%' indicates how to display the percentages on the slices. Here, %.1 indicates that the percentage value should be displayed with 1 digit after decimal point. The next two % symbols indicate that only one symbol is to be displayed.

Program

Program 4: A program to display a pie chart showing the percentage of employees in each department of a company.

```
    # to display employees of different depts in pie chart
    import matplotlib.pyplot as plt

    # take the percentages of employees of 4 departments
    slices = [50, 20, 15, 15]

    # take the departments names
    depts = ['Sales', 'Production', 'HR', 'Finance']

    # take the colors for each department
    cols = ['magenta', 'cyan', 'brown', 'gold']

    # create a pie chart
    plt.pie(slices, labels=depts, colors=cols, startangle=90, explode=(0,
0.2, 0, 0), shadow=True, autopct='%.1f%%' )
```

```
# set titles and legend
plt.title('WIPRO')
plt.legend()

# show the pie chart
plt.show()
```

Output:

```
C:\> python pie.py
```

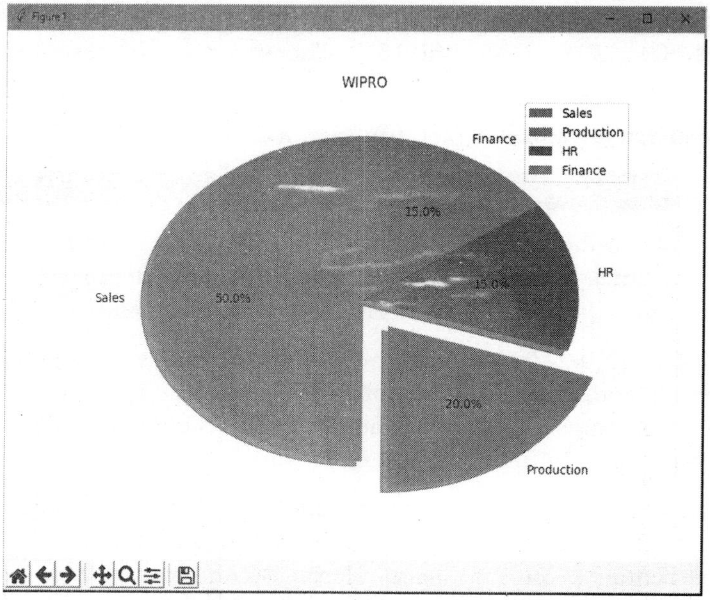

The graph clearly shows that 50% of the employees in the company are from the Sales department. Also, we want to grab the focus on Production department. Hence, that slice is dragged out.

Creating Line Graph

A line graph is a simple graph that shows the results in the form of lines. To create a line graph, we need x and y coordinates. For example,

```
plt.plot(x, y, 'colorname')
```

Here, the plot() function creates the line graph. x and y represent lists of coordinates for X- and Y-axes. 'colorname' indicates the color name to be used for the line.

Program

Program 5: A program to create a line graph to show the profits of a company in various years.

```
# to display profits of a company year-wise
import matplotlib.pyplot as plt
```

```
years = ['2012', '2013', '2014', '2015', '2016', '2017']
profits = [9, 10, 10.5, 8.8, 10.9, 9.75]

# create the line graph
plt.plot(years, profits, 'blue')

# set title and labels
plt.title('XYZ COMPANY')
plt.xlabel('Years')
plt.ylabel('Profits in Million Rs')

# show the line chart
plt.show()
```

Output

```
C:\> python line.py
```

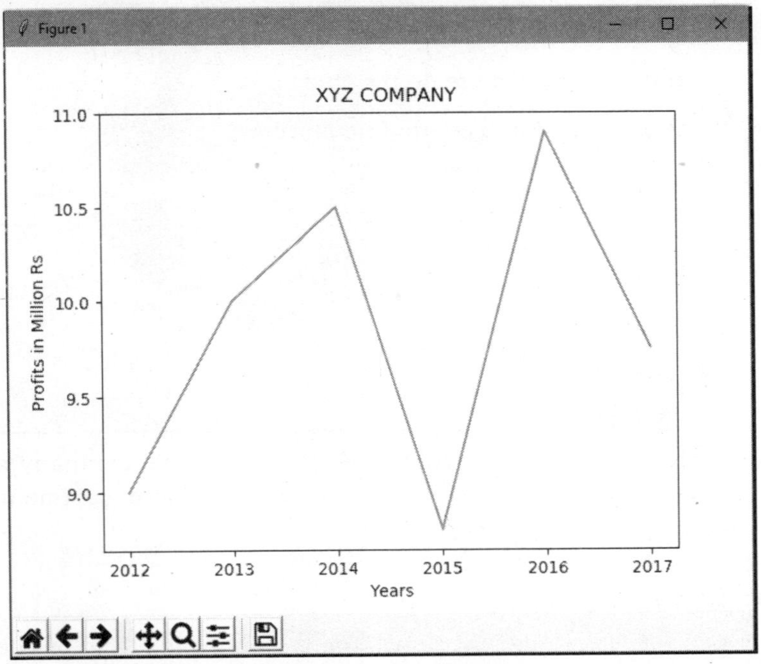

From the above output, we can understand that the profits of the company are the highest during the year 2016 and the least during the year 2015.

Points to Remember

- A data warehouse is a central repository of integrated data from different sources.
- Data analysis or data analytics involves the data to be analyzed to answer the questions raised by the management of the organization.
- Data visualization is to communicate information clearly and efficiently using statistical graphs, plots and diagrams.

- Data science is a term used for techniques to extract information from the data warehouse, analyze them and present the necessary data to the business.
- Data frame is an object in the pandas module that is useful to represent data in the form of rows and columns.
- Data frames are generally created from .csv (comma-separated values) files, Excel spreadsheet files, Python dictionaries, list of tuples or list of dictionaries.
- Once a data frame is created, we can retrieve data from the data frame and perform various operations on it.
- The matplotlib.pyplot package is the module used in data visualization.
- The bar() function is useful to create bar graphs.
- The hist() function is useful to create histograms.
- The pie() function is useful to create pie charts.
- The plot() function is useful to create line graphs.

PROGRAM INDEX